T0231051

BLOOD
SAFETY
and
SURVEILLANCE

BLOOD SAFETY and SURVEILLANCE

edited by

Jeanne V. Linden
Wadsworth Center
New York State Department of Health
Albany, New York

Celso Bianco
New York Blood Center
New York, New York

informa
healthcare

New York   London

First published in 2001 by Marcel Dekker, Inc.

This edition published in 2011 by Informa Healthcare, Telephone House, 69-77 Paul Street, London EC2A 4LQ, UK.

Simultaneously published in the USA by Informa Healthcare, 52 Vanderbilt Avenue, 7th Floor, New York, NY 10017, USA.

Informa Healthcare is a trading division of Informa UK Ltd. Registered Office: 37–41 Mortimer Street, London W1T 3JH, UK. Registered in England and Wales number 1072954.

A CIP record for this book is available from the British Library.

Library of Congress Cataloging-in-Publication Data available on application

ISBN-13: 9780824702632

Orders may be sent to: Informa Healthcare, Sheepen Place, Colchester, Essex CO3 3LP, UK
Telephone: +44 (0)20 7017 5540
Email: CSDhealthcarebooks@informa.com
Website: http://informahealthcarebooks.com/

For corporate sales please contact: CorporateBooksIHC@informa.com
For foreign rights please contact: RightsIHC@informa.com
For reprint permissions please contact: PermissionsIHC@informa.com

Foreword

The blood contains the soul . . .

Such was the claim of the Chinese in the year 1000 B.C.! Since that time, the importance of blood has largely moved from the spiritual to the medicinal arena. Over the centuries, belief in the therapeutic benefits of blood has evolved in a dramatic manner. At one time in the Roman empire, gladiators drank the blood of their fallen opponents to reinvigorate themselves. Elsewhere, others sought rebirth from being showered with the blood of a sacrificed bull.

The first blood transfusion is credited to Richard Lower, who transfused the blood of one dog into another in 1665 (1). In July 1667, Jean Dennis, a young French physician, performed the first known human transfusion using lamb blood, preceding Lower's similar attempts by only a few months:

> The project of causing the blood of an healthy animal to pass into the veins of one diseased, having been conceived *about ten years ago*, in the illustrious Society of *Virtuosi* which assembles at your houses and your goodness having received *M. Emmeriz* and my self, very favorably at such times as we have perform'd to entertain you either with discourse concerning it, or the sight of some not inconsiderable effects of it (2).

Needless to say, these experiments—however apparently successful in the short term—led unavoidably to the death of the recipients. Eventually, the French Faculty of Medicine, as well as the Royal Society in London, criminalized blood transfusion.

Although other blood transfusion experiments were done in the eighteenth and nineteenth centuries, the first true scientific breakthrough occurred in 1900 with the discovery by Karl Landsteiner of the A, B, and O blood groups (3). From then on, progress was fast and remarkable, aided by the exigencies of World Wars I and II as well as by the work of organizations such as the Red Cross. Scores of discoveries occurred during subsequent decades, leading to improvement of blood transfusion and to its complete clinical acceptance. Indeed, millions of persons have benefited from blood transfusions.

However, the question remains: Is blood transfusion free of risk? Of course, the issue is not the safety of the procedure itself, but that of the blood supply. Are there sometimes reactions to the blood that is transfused? Is the blood a vector to transmit diseases? Unfortunately, despite all the considerable advances in blood banking and blood safety, the answer to these questions is yes.

This volume, edited by Jeanne V. Linden and Celso Bianco, provides up-to-date information about the various risks of transfused blood, with a focus on immunological complications and on transmissible disease risks. But it does more, because it describes strategies of minimizing these risks. The editors have assembled a roster of contributors who are well-recognized experts in their fields.

As we enter a new millennium, patients all over the world will be the beneficiaries of a routine procedure—blood transfusion—and it should be as safe as possible. That is what this book is about. The health professionals involved in the practice of blood or blood product transfusions will benefit from this volume, but the patients will benefit even more if the strategies described are followed!

Claude Lenfant, M.D.
Bethesda, Maryland

REFERENCES

1. Lower R. The success of the experiment of transfusing the blood of one animal to another. Philos Trans Royal Soc London 1666; 1:352.
2. Dennis J. A letter concerning a new way of curing sundry diseases by transfusion of blood. Philos Trans Royal Soc London 1667; 2:489–504.
3. Landsteiner J. Uber agglutinationserscheinungen normallen menschlichen blutes. Wien Klin Wochenschr 1901; 14:1132–1134.

Preface

Human immunodeficiency virus (HIV) infection has become the most feared complication of blood transfusion. Fear of acquired immunodeficiency syndrome (AIDS) has triggered a series of radical changes in transfusion medicine. These changes have focused mostly on the transmission of viruses. Other infectious and noninfectious complications have been less well appreciated. One of the major goals of this book is to examine transfusion risks in a broader context, and to present some strategies to minimize these risks. A special effort was dedicated to areas that have received less attention in recent years, particularly errors and accidents, and the role of public health agencies as expressed by those in charge of monitoring and regulation. Between 1990 and 1999, as risks of transmission of HIV and hepatitis became relatively minuscule, there were 168 reports to FDA of fatal hemolytic reactions due to ABO-incompatible transfusion through error. This is an average of 17 cases a year, far exceeding deaths from transfusion-associated infectious agents. The book also attempts to provide physicians and other health care providers with the information necessary for appropriate counseling of patients who may need, or who have received, blood transfusions and for counseling of blood donors with abnormal screening test results.

The first chapter examines the contributions that blood donor screening procedures make to transfusion safety. The remainder of the book is organized in related sections to facilitate reference. Immunological complications discussed include hemolytic transfusion reactions, other types of reactions, alloimmunization, graft-versus-host disease, transfusion-related acute lung injury, and immunomodulation resulting from allogeneic transfusion. Also included is an overview of transfusion-related errors and methods to prevent errors that may lead to

v

transfusion of incompatible blood. The following section describes various infection-related complications resulting from infectious agents that 1) are present at least transiently in the circulation of donors, 2) survive the blood collection and storage conditions in at least one component, and 3) are infectious to human recipients when infused. Some agents pose risk mostly to immunocompromised patients, who constitute an increasing proportion of recipients of blood and blood products today because of HIV infection, transplants, and chemotherapy for malignancies.

Diseases that pose transfusion risks in various parts of the world are included because the book is intended for a worldwide audience, and also because some of these diseases could potentially become important in North America. An overview of infectious disease risks sets the stage for the remaining chapters in this section, including a description of current screening for transmissible disease markers, bacterial contamination, viruses transmissible by transfusion (hepatitis viruses, human T-lymphotropic virus, cytomegalovirus, and others), and other infectious agents, including parasites and prions.

The last section focuses on methods employed to reduce risks of transmission of disease by transfusion of blood and blood products. Contents include a summary of current surveillance efforts in the United States, alternatives to allogeneic blood transfusion, leukoreduction, viral inactivation, and red blood cell substitutes. They also review the contributions of quality programs, professional standards, and federal regulatory oversight to blood safety. A chapter presenting a cost-effectiveness analysis of various risk reduction strategies completes this section.

Efforts have been made to present the text in a user-friendly fashion for easy reference. Tables have been presented whenever possible. A comprehensive index facilitates the location of pertinent material. Reference lists are not intended to be comprehensive, but to present relevant, recent references, including review articles that could be consulted for further detail. A zero-risk blood supply is not possible. However, we hope that this book will provide information to put risks in perspective and encourage employment of risk reduction strategies.

We wish to thank all the authors for their efforts. They are a diverse group of experts in their fields. We believe their aggregate contributions have resulted in a well-rounded single resource for a multifaceted and highly complex subject.

Jeanne V. Linden
Celso Bianco

Contents

Contributors

Kenneth C. Anderson, M.D. Department of Adult Oncology, Dana-Farber Cancer Institute, Medical Director, Kraft Family Blood Donor Center, and Professor of Medicine, Harvard Medical School, Boston, Massachusetts

James P. AuBuchon, M.D. Professor of Pathology and Medicine, Dartmouth-Hitchcock Medical Center, Lebanon, New Hampshire

James B. Battles, Ph.D. Associate Professor, Office of Medical Education, University of Texas, Southwestern Medical Center, Dallas, Texas

Ehud Ben-Hur, Ph.D. Consultant in Photomedicine, New York, New York

Lucia M. Berte, M.A., MT(ASCP)SBB, DLM, CQA(ASQ),CQMgr. Quality Systems Consultant, Elmhurst, Illinois

Celso Bianco, M.D. Vice President, Medical Affairs, New York Blood Center, New York, New York*

Morris A. Blajchman, M.D., F.R.C.P.(C.) Professor, Department of Pathology and Medicine, McMaster University, and Hamilton Centre Canadian Red Cross Society, Hamilton, Ontario, Canada

---

Current affiliation: Executive Vice President, America's Blood Centers, Washington, D.C.

José O. Bordin, M.D., Ph.D. Associate Professor, Hematology and Transfusion Medicine Services, Escola Paulista de Medicina, São Paulo, Brazil

Mark E. Brecher, M.D. Director, Transfusion Medicine Service, and Professor, Pathology and Laboratory Medicine, University of North Carolina, Chapel Hill, North Carolina

Ritchard G. Cable, M.D. Medical Director, American Red Cross Blood Services—Connecticut Region, Farmington, Connecticut

Mary E. Chamberland, M.D., M.P.H. Assistant Director for Blood Safety, Division of Viral and Rickettsial Diseases, Centers for Disease Control and Prevention, Atlanta, Georgia

Roger Y. Dodd, Ph.D. Head, Transmissible Diseases Department, Holland Laboratory, American Red Cross, Rockville, Maryland

Walter H. Dzik, M.D. Director, Blood Bank and Tissue Typing Laboratory, Beth Israel Deaconess Hospital, and Harvard Medical School, Boston, Massachusetts

Jay S. Epstein, M.D. Director, Office of Blood Research and Review, Center for Biologics Evaluation and Research, U.S. Food and Drug Administration, Rockville, Maryland

Lawrence T. Goodnough, M.D. Professor of Medicine and Pathology, Departments of Pathology and Internal Medicine, Washington University School of Medicine, St. Louis, Missouri

Christopher J. Gresens, M.D. Associate Medical Director, Sacramento Medical Foundation Blood Centers, Sacramento, California

Mary Gustafson, M.S., MT(ASCP)SBB Director, Division of Blood Applications, Office of Blood Research and Review, Center for Biologics Evaluation and Research, U.S. Food and Drug Administration, Rockville, Maryland

Paul V. Holland, M.D. Medical Director and CEO, Sacramento Medical Foundation Blood Centers, Sacramento, California

Bernard Horowitz, Ph.D. VITEX (V.I. Technologies, Inc.), New York, New York

Harold S. Kaplan, M.D. Professor of Clinical Pathology and Director, Transfusion Medicine, New York-Presbyterian Hospital, New York, New York

Rima F. Khabbaz, M.D. Deputy Director, Division of Viral and Rickettsial Diseases, Centers for Disease Control and Prevention, Atlanta, Georgia

Elizabeth J. Kicklighter, M.D. Warren G. Magnuson Clinical Center, National Institutes of Health, Bethesda, Maryland

Harvey G. Klein, M.D. Chief, Department of Transfusion Medicine, Warren G. Magnuson Clinical Center, National Institutes of Health, Bethesda, Maryland

Steven Kleinman, M.D. Clinical Professor, Department of Pathology, University of British Columbia, Vancouver, British Columbia, Canada

Jeanne V. Linden, M.D., M.P.H. Director, Blood and Tissue Resources, New York State Department of Health, Wadsworth Center, Empire State Plaza, Albany, New York

Anne B. McDonald, M.D. Fellow, Transfusion Medicine, New England Deaconess Hospital, Boston, Massachusetts

Jay E. Menitove, M.D. Executive Director and Medical Director, Community Blood Center of Greater Kansas City, Kansas City, Missouri

David E. Nevalainen, Ph.D., MT(ASCP), CQA(ASQ) Quality Consultant, Health Care, Bailey's Harbor, Wisconsin

Mark A. Popovsky, M.D. Executive Director and Chief Medical Officer, American Red Cross Blood Services—New England Region; Associate Clinical Professor of Pathology, Harvard Medical School; and Beth Israel Hospital, Boston, Massachusetts

Alfred M. Prince, M.D. Member/Head, Laboratory of Virology, Lindsley F. Kimball Research Institute, New York Blood Center, New York, New York

Maria Rios, Ph.D. Manager and Research Scientist, Scientific and Technological Services Department, New York Blood Center, New York, New York

Hillary V. Schaeffler Director, Standards and International Affairs, American Association of Blood Banks, Bethesda, Maryland

Laura L. Spinelli, M.D.   Fellow in Hematopathology, Department of Pathology, University of North Carolina, Chapel Hill, North Carolina

Christopher P. Stowell, M.D., Ph.D.   Director, Blood Transfusion Service, Department of Pathology, Harvard Medical School and Massachusetts General Hospital, Boston, Massachusetts

Zbigniew M. Szczepiorkowski, M.D., Ph.D.   Associate Director, Blood Transfusion Service, Department of Pathology, Harvard Medical School and Massachusetts General Hospital, Boston, Massachusetts

Gary E. Tegtmeier, Ph.D.   Director, Viral Testing Laboratories, Community Blood Center of Greater Kansas City, Kansas City, Missouri

Jonathan Trouern-Trend   Epidemiology and Surveillance Program, American Red Cross ARCNET, Farmington, Connecticut

Jay E. Valinsky, Ph.D.   Vice President, Laboratory and Technical Services, New York Blood Center, New York, New York

Iain J. Webb, M.D.   Medical Director, Cell Manipulation and Gene Transfer Laboratories, Dana-Farber Cancer Institute, and Instructor in Medicine, Harvard Medical School, Boston, Massachusetts

Silvano Wendel, M.D.   Medical Director, Blood Bank, Hospital Sirio Libanes, São Paulo, Brazil

1
Impact of Blood Donor Screening Procedures on Transfusion Safety

Steven Kleinman
University of British Columbia, Vancouver, British Columbia, Canada

I. INTRODUCTION

A major goal of transfusion medicine practice in the last decade has been to reduce the risk of transfusion-transmitted infection to as low a level as possible. In order to approach the desired level of zero risk from transfused allogeneic blood, multiple layers of safety are needed. Methods utilized in attempting to maximize safety from donated allogeneic units include donor-selection criteria, donor-screening procedures, confidential unit exclusion (CUE) and telephone callback procedures, laboratory testing, and modification of the blood unit after collection, either by leukocyte removal or physicochemical procedures for pathogen inactivation.

This chapter will focus on donor selection and screening procedures, CUE and callback procedures, product recall, and recipient notification in the event that a potentially infectious unit has been transfused.

II. IMPLEMENTATION OF DONOR-SCREENING PROCEDURES

When it is first suspected that an infectious agent may be transmitted by transfusion, the initial response is to develop donor deferral policies using epidemiological data derived from high-risk populations (1). After this initial step, subsequent review and debate often leads to the nationwide implementation of a particular donor-screening procedure following recommendations of the Food and Drug Administration (FDA) and/or the American Association of Blood Banks (AABB) (2,3). Because of the current regulatory, political, and legal climate, a screening procedure is rarely rescinded even if there is no good evidence for its effectiveness. Since screening procedures tend to become permanent, it is important to carefully evaluate their expected utility by pilot studies in blood donor populations prior to widespread implementation. If this is not done adequately, the result will be the addition of procedures that do little or nothing to increase transfusion safety but will result in deferral of safe donors. In recent years, some procedures have been implemented without any pilot data, whereas in other cases evaluations of potential new donor interview questions have been performed (4,5).

For diseases for which there are no routine laboratory tests (e.g., Creutzfeldt-Jacob disease, Chagas' disease, babesiosis), donor-screening procedures are the only method available for increasing transfusion safety. In contrast, for those infectious diseases for which routine blood donor testing is performed, the importance of donor-screening procedures relates to their ability to identify some potentially infectious donors during the infectious seronegative window period (6).

While there are distinct advantages to eliminating donors with possible risks of disease transmission, there are also negative consequences of this approach. Because donor deferral criteria often have poor specificity, a large number of safe donors will be deferred (6,7). While this dilemma has been well recognized, there is no available algorithm to decide whether a given procedure or screening question should be implemented. In reality, such decisions attempt to balance the following factors: the extent of disease transmission, the severity of the consequences of such disease to the recipient, the expected sensitivity (effectiveness) of the procedure, and the number of donors lost by implementation of the procedure.

III. METHODOLOGICAL APPROACHES FOR EVALUATING EFFICACY

It would seem logical that better compliance with existing donor deferral criteria or the implementation of new donor-screening questions would improve the safety of the blood supply. However, this conclusion is based upon the often unproven assumption that a deferral criterion has been demonstrated to enhance transfusion safety. Most donor questions have been implemented without effective measurements of their yield. Therefore, if a deferral criterion is inappropriate or outdated, more effective application of this criterion will not enhance transfusion safety.

The ideal way to study the efficacy of a new donor-screening procedure would be to perform infectious disease screening on those donors deferred by the procedure comparing their rate of seropositivity to that of acceptable donors. To my knowledge, this approach has never been utilized for studying health history questions, almost certainly due to logistic considerations. These include obtaining an informed consent from the deferred donor for infectious disease testing and performing a separate phlebotomy to obtain a venous sample from individuals who are not eligible to donate a unit of blood.

A second approach for evaluating screening procedures is to measure the rate of donor deferral following the implementation of new or modified donor-screening procedures. In this approach, it is inferred that an increased number of deferred donors indicates the interdiction of an increased number of infectious donors. However, measured changes in the donor deferral rate may be misleading; even questions with high specificity will result in the identification of many more false-positive than true-positive donors due to very low prevalence of transfusion-transmitted infections (7). Therefore, an increased deferral rate may actually be a measure of the relative cost of the intervention to the blood donor collection system (i.e., deferral of otherwise acceptable donors), rather than an indication of increased safety.

A third approach has been used recently by investigators from the Retrovirus Epidemiology Donor Study (REDS) (8,9). They mailed an anonymous survey questionnaire to recent successful donors for the purpose of determining the percentage of such donors who would admit to behavioral infectious disease risk factors that they had previously denied at the time of their donation. While these data establish the rate of failure to obtain accurate answers to screening questions (see below), they do not provide information as to how many of these donors were infected and/or capable of transmitting infection through their donated unit.

IV. MECHANISMS FOR SELECTING SAFE DONORS AND SAFE UNITS FOR TRANSFUSION

Outlined in Table 1 are types of donor-screening and product-selection procedures, exclusive of laboratory testing, implemented to enhance transfusion safety. These procedures are discussed below with regard to theoretical rationale, as well as past, present, and future applications. When available, data to support the use of the procedures are given.

A. Selection by Donor Group or Donor Site

Because of the known spread of hepatitis between individuals inhabiting particular types of institutions, blood collection agencies do not collect blood at homes

Table 1 Blood Safety Procedures (Excluding Laboratory Testing)

Timing	Procedure
Predonation	1. Exclusion of donor groups/donor sites
	2. Elimination of donation incentives
	3. Donor education
At donation site prior to donation	4. Self-exclusion in response to written material
	5. Health history interview
	6. Donor deferral registry[a]
	7. Confidential unit exclusion (CUE)
Postdonation	8. Telephone call-back
	9. Product retrieval
	10. Recipient notification

[a]This mechanism can be used either to disqualify the donor at the collection site or to discard the collected unit prior to release from the blood center.

for the mentally retarded or prisons (10,11). In order to decrease the risk of human immunodeficiency virus (HIV) transmission, blood collection agencies do not collect from groups or institutions that are known to be comprised of male homosexuals (12). Initially, these policies were instituted as primary protective safety measures prior to the development of laboratory testing for the infectious agents of hepatitis and acquired immunodeficiency syndrome (AIDS). However, despite routine laboratory testing for these agents, these policies still remain prudent in order to eliminate donors from settings where there is a high risk of acute seronegative infection.

B. Impact of Donor Incentives

The primary example of a donor incentive associated with disease transmission is the payment of cash in exchange for blood donation. Because of this, FDA, in 1978, instituted regulations that required the labeling of a blood unit as either volunteer or paid (13), reading, in part, as follows: "A paid donor is a person who receives monetary payment for a blood donation. A volunteer donor is a person who does not receive monetary payment for a blood donation. Benefits, such as time off from work, membership in blood assurance programs, and cancellation of nonreplacement fees that are not readily convertible to cash, do not constitute monetary payment within the meaning of this paragraph." At about the same time that FDA established its regulation, several states passed legislation virtually prohibiting the use of commercial donor blood (13). The FDA regulations sparked extensive discussions about the appropriate definition of a volunteer blood donor, which are still unresolved 20 years later (14–16).

These regulatory and statutory requirements were instituted in response to data indicating that commercial blood donors were more likely than volunteer blood donors to transmit hepatitis to recipients. This conclusion was supported by several lines of evidence: higher rates of hepatitis B surface antigen (HBsAg) positivity in commercial donors, higher rates of hepatitis B and non-A, non-B hepatitis in recipients of paid versus volunteer donor blood, and, most definitively, documentation in a well-studied cohort of transfusion recipients that the elimination of commercial blood resulted in substantially fewer cases of posttransfusion hepatitis (17–20). An analysis of the transition from commercial donor to volunteer blood in New Mexico indicated that virtually 100% of the commercial donor population ceased donating with the removal of the cash incentive (21), indicating that this incentive was apparently the sole motivator for donation in this large group of commercial donors.

While paid blood doors are now very uncommon, the U.S. plasma industry still depends on commercial donors. It is of interest that seropositivity rates among this donor population for newly implemented blood screening tests [human T-cell lymphotrophic virus, type I (HTLV-I) and hepatitis C virus (HCV)] are markedly higher than among volunteer blood donors (22,23), mimicking the situation identified in the 1970s with regard to commercial blood donors and HBsAg testing. It thus appears that a significant percentage of commercial donors have relatively high rates of infection with multiple infectious disease agents, raising the possibility that rates for as-yet-undiscovered transmissible agents would also be higher.

Although the increased risk of blood contamination from commercial donors has been documented, it has also been recognized that it is not the actual act of payment that makes commercial donors unsafe; rather, it is due to the financial incentive attracting donors from a population (i.e., of a lower socio-economic class) with a higher rate of infectious disease (24,25). Two recent reports have indicated that populations of paid donors drawn from different segments of society than were the commercial donors of the 1960s and 1970s were no less safe than volunteer donors (26,27). In one study of carefully screened repeat-paid plateletpheresis donors in the Midwest, the infectious disease marker rate was equivalent to that of the same blood centers' volunteer blood donor population, suggesting that both groups have equivalent safety (27). However, extrapolating these results to other populations of paid donors is not appropriate given the use of special donor-selection criteria at the study blood center. These criteria required a previous whole blood donation, an orientation session, and an 8-week waiting period before donors were accepted into the paid plateletpheresis program (28).

An incentive would be expected to be detrimental to blood safety if it resulted in the recruitment of a population that has a higher risk of transmitting infectious disease than does the general blood donor population. If such an "unsafe" population of donors was to be recruited, the combined application of donor-screening procedures and laboratory testing would be unable to lower the risk to that of the general donor population for two reasons. First, a significant percentage of donors infected with HIV, human T-cell lymphotropic virus (HTLV), or hepatitis C virus (HCV) will not admit to a recognized risk factor even after careful postdonation interviews, thereby escaping detection by donor-screening procedures (29–33). The second factor relates to donors who would have admitted to risk factors at the donation interview in the absence of incentives but who would knowingly give untruthful answers to interview questions when motivated by the desire to obtain the offered donor incentive (34–36).

Currently there are limited data to assess whether the use of donor incentives other than direct payment of cash (e.g., time off from work, gifts, a monetary credit for blood nonreplacement fees, participation in a group assurance plan, or working towards recognition as a multigallon donor) have an influence on blood safety (37). REDS investigators conducted a small anonymous pilot mail survey, which asked donors if they had received any one of 10 different incentives at the time of their most recent donation and correlated these responses with behavioral risk factors for infectious disease (38). They found that donors who reported receiving a gift or extra time off from work had marginally higher levels of behavioral risk; however, these were no higher than risk levels associated with particular demographic characteristics such as 25- to 44-year age group, male gender, or first-time donor status. In postdonation interviews of donors identified as HIV seropositive, Centers for Disease Control and Prevention (CDC) investigators established that the incentive of extra time off from work was a major motivational factor for donation in 3.4% of such donors, and receipt of a gift was a major motivator in 2.5% (39). However, they also found that the desire to help the community was the primary motivation for donation for most of the HIV-seropositive donors. A recent case report of an HIV seroconverting donor from the Midwest established that this person continued to donate because of his employer's policy of granting 4–8 hours time off from work if a successful blood donation was completed (40). In aggregate, these recent data suggest that the use of donor incentives do not have a large impact on the safety of donated blood. Nevertheless, they also suggest that further study of the impact of extra time off and/or gifts on transfusion safety should be undertaken. Consequently, REDS has recently completed a new large-scale donor survey that included detailed questions about donor incentives.

Several studies have suggested that incentives are more effective in attracting blood donation by persons who have never previously donated than in influencing repeat donations in previous donors (37). If this proves to be the case, it has implications for how we think about the use of incentives. If an incentive attracts a large percentage of first-time donors from a different population group than the usual first-time donors, one might hypothesize that transfusion safety could be compromised. However, if a particular incentive is used to solicit more frequent donations from repeat donors (e.g., recognition of gallon donation status), it may be less likely to be detrimental to transfusion safety. It has also been suggested that an incentive might have a lesser impact on transfusion safety if it is provided to all persons who present at the donation site, whether or not they complete a successful donation (41).

The appropriateness of specific donor-recruitment techniques and the definition of acceptable donor incentives have been addressed in a recent policy statement by the American Association of Blood Banks (AABB). The AABB statement suggests criteria that individual blood centers can use to help determine whether a specific incentive might have an adverse impact on transfusion safety. The U.S. National Marrow Donor Registry and, internationally, the Council of Europe have also recently clarified their definitions of voluntary donation (42,43).

C. Impact of HIV Test Seeking

An additional mechanism of safeguarding the blood supply by removing a rather unique donor incentive for a particular high-risk population was the establishment of alternative testing sites for HIV antibody in 1985. In order to prevent donation for the purpose of obtaining HIV test results, federal and state governments established alternative test sites at which free and anonymous anti-HIV testing could be obtained (44). Data from such programs indicated that HIV-seropositive rates were significantly higher than those found at blood centers (45). Although it is uncertain how many alternative test site clients would have donated blood if there had been no other way to obtain HIV test results, at least two studies have indicated that some percentage would have done so (45,46).

The concern about HIV test seeking is still pertinent a decade after HIV donor screening was first begun. Postdonation interviews have indicated that the motivation for donation in 15–29% of HIV-seropositive donors was to obtain their HIV antibody test result (34–36,47). Furthermore, of donors who responded to the REDS anonymous mail survey in 1993, 6.0% indicated that they had donated blood some time in the past to obtain an HIV antibody test result; moreover, 3.2% stated that they had done so within the past 12 months (48). The implementation of HIV-1 p24 antigen testing in 1996 raised further concerns that this more sensitive HIV screening test might encourage an even greater amount of HIV test seeking in prospective donors (the so-called magnet effect) (49). However, an analysis of HIV seropositivity rates in donors following the first 6 months of HIV p24 antigen testing showed no significant change when compared to a 6-month interval prior to such testing, indicating that a magnet effect, if it occurred at all, was not observed to affect transfusion safety (50).

It is clear that some blood donors are donating to receive the perceived benefit of free and confidential HIV testing. Blood centers currently provide information to blood donors about the inappropriateness of HIV test seeking, and some centers specifically ask donors whether they are donating to get an HIV test. Nevertheless, it appears that more effective ways are needed to educate prospective donors that donating to obtain HIV antibody test results may endanger transfusion recipients.

D. Donor Education and Donor Self-Exclusion

In 1983, with the recognition that AIDS could be transmitted by blood transfusion, specific groups were identified as being at high risk of AIDS (e.g., male homosexuals with multiple partners and intravenous drug users who shared needles) (1,6,51). Through the use of the media and through discussion with gay community leaders, blood centers made extensive efforts to inform the public, prior to arriving at the donation site, that individuals with such risk factors should not donate blood. In some locations, this community education was augmented by distribution of written information concerning donor eligibility at the time of donor recruitment.

Blood donors were provided with written material at the collection site, which included a description of risk factors (or risk groups) for AIDS and for other transfusion-transmissible agents (52); donors were instructed that if they belonged to a risk group or had a risk factor, they should not proceed with the donation process.

The process of a donor evaluating his or her own eligibility has been termed self-exclusion. Data obtained from 1983 through 1985 indicate that self-exclusion was effective in decreasing the risk of AIDS transmission. A survey of gay men showed that many who had donated prior to the recognition of the AIDS epidemic subsequently ceased their donation behavior (53). Data from New York City, Los Angeles, and San Francisco indicated that there were decreased donations from the populations at highest risk for transmitting HIV (7,54–56).

Since 1983, educational materials have been modified periodically to reflect the latest knowledge of transfusion-transmissible disease and have been required reading for each prospective donor at the donation site.

E. Health History Interview

1. General Considerations

History-based donor screening was originally established to reduce the risk of transfusion-transmitted hepatitis. In 1983, with the recognition of the possible transmission of HIV by transfusion, the health history interview assumed new importance and became more complex and probing than it had previously been (1,51). The trend of adding medically sophisticated questions and/or socially sensitive behavioral questions to the donor interview has continued to the present day.

Health history interview questions designed to defer donors with increased risk of infectious disease transmission can be broadly classified into several categories. Table 2 indicates the diseases for which the various categories of questions have been applied based upon known epidemiological risk factors.

Several methods have been utilized to conduct health history interviews: these include the oral approach, the self-administered written approach, and the combined approach. In the oral approach, a donor interviewer asks the donor all health history questions and records the responses on the donor card. In the self-administered approach, the donor checks off yes or no answers on the donor card after reading each question. In the combined approach, the donor may self-administer some questions and orally respond to others, or the donor may self-administer all questions and then respond a second time to selected questions orally presented by the donor interviewer. Regardless of the approach utilized, if the donor gives answers that may potentially affect his or her eligibility, the donor interviewer needs to elicit further information and to document this on the donor history form.

Until recently, there was little standardization of donor questioning in different blood centers in the United States. In 1991, a consortium of California blood centers reported on their 3-year effort to design and implement a uniform medical donor history card (57). The process used to generate the card was one of consensus building among the medical directors of the various blood centers with the final questions being approved by the Center for Biologic Evaluation and Research (CBER) of the FDA. Limitations of this approach were an inability to pretest the questions in donor populations prior to their implementation and the reliance on medical directors rather than social scientists or communication

Table 2 Health History Interview Questions

Category	Disease prevented
Medical history of a specific disease	AIDS, hepatitis, malaria, Chagas' disease, babesiosis, CJD
Medical symptoms compatible with a specific disease	AIDS, bacteremia, viremia
Blood exposure by needlestick injury or blood transfusion	AIDS, hepatitis
Medical treatment	Creutzfeldt-Jakob disease
Sexual or drug use activities of donor or sexual partner(s)	AIDS, HTLV-I/II, hepatitis
Previous residence in or visit to endemic area	Malaria

experts to design questions. More recently, the AABB developed an FDA-approved uniform donor history card. This is preapproved by FDA for use by any blood collection center in the United States, provided that it is used without alteration of any of the existing questions (58). There are no data to evaluate whether the use of this uniform card has resulted in enhanced transfusion safety.

As donor interview questions have become more standardized, it has become apparent that uniformity is lacking in the standard operating procedures used when a donor answers a screening question with a response that requires further evaluation. Recently, two blood centers have reported that they have standardized their response to over 240 donor eligibility conditions (59). Since the ultimate decision as to whether to accept a particular donor rests on medical judgment, uniformity in evaluating a donor's medical history is inherently diffi-cult. In problematic situations, it is sometimes easier for staff to accept rather than reject a blood donor. Rejection may make the donor feel bad, may make the donor anxious about his or her infectious disease status, and, in the case of directed donors, may be perceived by the donor as a denial of a right to donate (60,61). Obviously, it is incumbent upon nursing and medical staff to make the proper safety decisions and not to be unduly influenced by these factors.

2.   Review of Data

In addition to asking the right questions during the donor interview, it is also necessary to obtain the right answers. Interviews with HIV- and HCV-seropositive donors conducted after these donors have been notified of their test results show that a high percentage of such donors will admit to a history of risky sexual behavior or past intravenous drug use that they had denied prior to donating (30,62). Recently, these data from seropositive donors have been complemented by observations in a large geographically diverse donor population (9). In 1993, REDS investigators mailed a 53-question optical scan format questionnaire to 50,162 allogeneic blood donors who successfully donated blood within the previous 1–2 months at one of five participating REDS blood centers. Donors were randomly sampled with the exception of oversampling of those younger than 26 and those in minority ethnic and racial groups to compensate for their lower proportional representation in the donor population. The questionnaire contained items related to demographics, donation history, comprehension of written donation literature, the use of CUE or callback procedures, sexual history, injection drug use history, other history related to HIV risk, HIV test seeking, donor's knowledge about AIDS, and donor's knowledge about donor eligibility criteria. Multipart questions were used to determine the time intervals (corre-sponding to intervals used in blood donor screening) in which events occurred: these included ever, since 1977, within the past 12 months, and within the past 3 months. Questions pertaining to sexual behavior and injection drug use were preceded by a short statement explaining their purpose and the need for truthful answers and giving the respondent permission to not answer any objectionable questions.

Of 50,162 donors sampled, 34,726 (69.2%) responded and 98.1% of the respondents answered all of the risk questions. The data were analyzed by using sampling weights to adjust for differential sampling and/or response rates among different demographic groups. A total of 1.9% of respondents reported at least one behavioral risk that should have resulted in donor deferral. In 0.4%, this risk occurred in the prior 3 months, a time frame compatible with acute seronegative window period infection. These data demonstrate a low level of behavioral risk that was not eliminated by donor questioning, laboratory testing, or CUE and callback procedures. Given the strong psychological denial donors may have about HIV risk behaviors or illicit activities, there is probably an inherent limitation to the sensitivity that can be achieved by behavioral questioning (34). Nevertheless, these data indicate that continued efforts to improve the sensitivity of behavioral screening appear to be warranted (63).

3. Practical Aspects

Table 3 lists some of the important parameters that can be examined to potentially increase the quality of the answers given in the donor health history interview.

Because the health history interview involves questions of a delicate nature, it is important to ensure that the interview is conducted in a private and confidential fashion. This can be difficult in the blood mobile setting. Two studies have documented that the majority of donors felt that privacy during the history interview was adequate (34,64). A study conducted by the American Red Cross with 4651 donors at a variety of blood drives found that 74% of donors perceived their privacy to be adequate at the health history station; this increased to 94% when mobile visual partitions (standing screens) were used (64). These privacy screens appeared to make a useful contribution to the donor's perception of privacy. Auditory privacy (the inability to hear another donor's health history interview) was considered as good to excellent by 92% of donors and increased slightly to 97% when a device was used to mask extraneous noise. The second

Table 3 Issues in Optimizing Donor Health History Screening

1. Privacy and confidentiality of health history
2. Donor's comprehension of written material
3. Adequacy of interpreters
4. Interviewer training and competency
5. Time constraints

study revealed that subsequent to donor notification, 31% of HIV-seropositive donors stated they had felt a lack of privacy during the health history interview, with 20% stating that they would have changed their answers to interview questions if they had been in a more private situation (34). While the data from these studies are somewhat encouraging, it is also disturbing that a small percentage of routine donors and a greater percentage of HIV-seropositive donors in these two studies stated that privacy was inadequate; such perceptions may affect donor responses to sensitive sexual or drug use behavior questions during the donor interview. Therefore, it remains important to continue to improve the perception of privacy at the health history station.

One approach to the health history interview that could address donors' privacy concerns and thereby might result in eliciting more truthful risk behavior information is the use of a computer interactive interview. In one study of this technique in 272 donors, the subjects stated that they had a feeling of increased privacy compared to the usual interview format (65). In addition, the rate of deferrals for HIV-related symptoms or risk behaviors was significantly increased when compared to the usual interview format. Unfortunately, these data must be interpreted cautiously because of inherent limitations in the study design. Because of FDA requirements, the group given the computer interview was also screened by standard health history screening techniques. In addition, unlike the health history interview, the computer interview was conducted anonymously, without the donor providing any identifying information that could link their responses to a permanent record.

Despite these preliminary data and initial enthusiasm for the computer interactive approach, additional studies of computerized screening have not been published (65a). This most likely reflects the difficulty in conducting such studies in an FDA-regulated environment.

A prospective donor's ability to understand predonation written materials can often pose a problem. In the past, this material has often been written at an educational level that required a high degree of reading comprehension. More recently, attempts have been made to rewrite such material at a lower grade level. A second solution to this problem has been to place less reliance on the use of written material. To this end, the AABB and FDA have recommended that in the case of HIV risk factors, a verbal discussion occur between the interviewer and the donor (66,67). In addition to presenting HIV risk factor information to donors with limited written comprehension skills, this verbal discussion also serves the purpose of emphasizing the significance and importance of this information to all donors.

Another potential problem occurs when the prospective donor does not speak English well or at all. In this setting, it is important to have the questionnaire administered in the donor's native language. Multilingual staff are useful in this regard; otherwise, an interpreter will be needed to assist in the interview.

The use of an interpreter poses problems if the interpreter is either a relative or a fellow employee. Since many HIV risk questions are of an extremely personal nature, this creates a situation in which the donor may not give a truthful history to the interpreter. Currently there is no consensus as to how to solve this problem; one possible solution is not to accept such donors unless an independent interpreter not known by the donor can be used (6).

Factors such as the adequacy of training for donor room personnel, the level of accreditation of such staff, and the level of staff competency have received increased attention in the last several years as a result of blood centers' need to comply with the FDA's Good Manufacturing Practices (cGMP) regulations. In the interview setting, a broad definition of competency would extend beyond the simple ability to follow SOP and would include the ability to build rapport with the donor so as to be able to effectively solicit information during the interview. It is plausible that the attitude of interviewers with regard to sexual behavior may have an impact on their ability to elicit truthful sexual behavior histories; however, there are no data in the blood donor setting to address this issue.

The goal of maximizing donor throughput at the collection site, which is important both for productivity and donor convenience, may also affect the quality of the donor interview. Despite the pressures to process donors quickly, it is important that the donor be given sufficient time to think carefully about answers to interview question, particularly since it may be necessary to recall behaviors from many years ago (68).

Some critics have charged that the donor interview should be renamed the donor interrogation and that the regulatory emphasis on cGMP has led to the focus on donors as suppliers of raw material rather than as human beings with a complex motivational structure (61,69). As the health history has continued to get longer and more obtrusive, concerns have been expressed that donors may not be capable of recalling all pertinent significant events (68). A related criticism has been that by asking donors questions about events in the remote past (since 1977), donors become less focused on recent risk behaviors, which are more relevant to the possibility of a donation occurring during the infectious seronegative window. Suggestions have been made that repeat donors not undergo the same broad-based health history interview that is required of first-time donors (61,69).

In summary, based upon current knowledge of logistical difficulties, each blood collection organization must carefully examine its own operations and devise procedures that maximize the ability to obtain correct answers from donors. In addition, there is a national need for educational materials and the health history questionnaire to be validated across all demographic strata of blood donors using scientifically proven methods (9,65a). Input from behavioral scientists will be needed to refine this validation approach and to design appropriate research protocols.

V. DONOR SCREENING FOR SPECIFIC TRANSMISSIBLE AGENTS OR CONDITIONS

A. Human Immunodeficiency Virus

1. Current Criteria

A full-scale revision of FDA recommendations for screening prospective donors for prevention of HIV transmission was issued in April 1992 (66). These recommendations state that prospective donors:

1. Must receive both oral and written information concerning HIV (AIDS) risk factors and the potential for HIV transmission through donated blood. This information should include informing the donor that in early HIV infection a donor may be infectious and capable of transmitting HIV despite a negative test for HIV antibody.
2. Should be given specific information as to how they can obtain an HIV antibody test at a site other than the donor center.
3. Should be told that all units of donated blood will be tested for HIV antibody, and, if positive, the donor will be notified of the test result and his or her name placed on a donor deferral registry.
4. Should be advised not to donate if symptoms that may be compatible with HIV infection are present. These symptoms include persistent fevers, night sweats, unexplained weight loss, persistent cough or shortness of breath, persistent diarrhea, swollen lymph nodes that persist for longer than one month, presence of whitish oral lesions, or presence of bluish purple spots on the skin or in the mouth.
5. Should be asked direct health history questions about behaviors that put them at risk for HIV. Preferably these questions should be asked orally.

The specific information to be obtained from donors during the donor interview includes answers to the following:

Have you ever had clinical or laboratory evidence of AIDS or HIV infection?
(For Men) Have you had sex with another man even once since 1977?
Have you ever injected intravenous drugs?
Have you engaged in sex in exchange for money or drugs since 1977?
Have you received clotting factor concentrates for hemophilia or other clotting disorders?

If a donor answers yes to any of the above questions, he or she is permanently deferred as a blood donor.

The donor should also be asked questions regarding behaviors during the previous 12-month interval. A yes answer to any of these questions will lead to a temporary deferral which is removed 12 months after the last potential exposure. These questions are:

> In the past 12 months, have you had sex with a person who has HIV infection or AIDS?
>
> In the past 12 months, have you had sex with a person who currently or previously used intravenous drugs?
>
> (For Women) In the past 12 months, have you had sex with a man who has had sex with another man (i.e., a man who is bisexual)?
>
> In the past 12 months, have you had sex with a prostitute?
>
> In the past 12 months, have you had sex with a person receiving clotting factor concentrates?
>
> In the past 12 months, have you had syphilis or gonorrhea?
>
> In the past 12 months, have you had a blood transfusion?
>
> In the past 12 months, have you had an accidental needlestick injury or a blood splash to a mucous membrane or to nonintact skin?

At the conclusion of the medical history, donors must sign a consent that specifically states that they understand that they should not donate blood if they are at risk for HIV infection.

Two additional changes to HIV screening procedures have been implemented since these comprehensive recommendations in 1992. In 1995, FDA recommended that individuals who are inmates of correctional institutions and individuals who have been incarcerated for more than 72 consecutive hours during the previous 12 months be deferred for 12 months from their last date of incarceration (70). FDA stated that this information could be provided to donors through the predonation written material and did not indicate that this question was required as part of the health history interview. In 1996, FDA recommended that three questions be added to the direct questions on high-risk behavior to exclude donors who are at increased risk for HIV-1 group O infection (71). One of these questions relates to birth in or residence in Cameroon or surrounding West African countries where HIV-1 group O infection has been identified. The others refer to blood transfusion or medical treatment received in those countries and to sexual contact with anyone who was born in or lived in those countries since 1977. These questions are similar in format to the type of geographic exclusion questions for HIV-2 exposure that were made obsolete by the introduction of HIV-2 antibody screening in 1992 (72).

2. Rationale for the Current Criteria

When donor-screening procedures for preventing AIDS were first implemented in the early to mid-1980s, most blood centers in the United States did not ask donors direct questions about sexual orientation or behavior (i.e., a question from the nurse to the donor such as "Have you ever had sex with another male?") (6). At the time there were no available data to indicate that more explicit questioning might result in deferral of an increased number of high-risk persons; indeed, one hypothesis was that direct questioning about a person's sexual orientation might lead to untruthful answers because of concerns about maintaining the confidentiality of information (6,12). A more direct approach also posed the possibility of embarrassing or offending potential blood donors.

In the late 1980s, the donor interview process was reevaluated based upon information obtained from interviews with HIV-seropositive donors and the recognition of a much more open societal attitude towards discussing issues of sexual orientation and sexual behavior. A retrospective study demonstrated that asking donors direct oral questions about sexual behavior resulted in a fivefold increase in HIV-related deferrals from 1.46 to 7.31 donors per month in one blood center (73). A second blood center conducted a survey concerning donors' attitudes toward being asked such explicit sexual behavior questions. Of 1204 regular blood donors who responded, over 90% endorsed the use of these questions, while only 1% felt that the questions might cause them to stop donating (73). Subsequently, a prospectively designed study was performed in two U.S. blood centers to address the effectiveness of donor-screening procedures, including revised donor information brochures, the use of an AIDS information video, and the use of a set of behavior-oriented direct questions asked orally by the health historian. This study strongly suggested that the use of direct, behavior-oriented oral questions led to a statistically significant increase in donors deferred for HIV risk behavior (63). A second study, performed by the American Red Cross, compared deferral rates in three groups, each of approximately 4000 donors, using direct behavior-oriented questions, indirect comprehension questions, and more generalized written interview questions; this study reached a similar conclusion with regard to the benefit of direct oral questioning (74). The current FDA and AABB recommendations suggest, but do not require, that direct questions be asked orally (66,67).

With the implementation of anti-HIV testing in 1985, anti-HIV-positive blood donors were identified, notified of their test results, and interviewed. These interviews revealed that although many HIV-seropositive donors were men who had sex with other men, they did not consider themselves to be at risk for HIV infection (75). It became apparent that a person might respond very differently if asked whether he were a member of a specific group (i.e., a homosexual man) as opposed to being asked if he had ever engaged in a specific behavior (i.e., having sex with another male). The FDA therefore recommended in September 1985 that "any male who has had sex with another male since 1977" should not donate blood (76). The recommendation emphasized that individuals who had had only a single homosexual experience should refrain from donating.

Three additional studies, summarized in Table 4, have examined the reasons why HIV-seropositive donors with known risk factors donated blood (34–36). The CDC Multicenter Study included 512 donors (304 of whom had HIV risk factors) from 20 blood centers; the American Red Cross (ARC) Multicenter Study included 80 donors with HIV risk factors from three geographic areas; and the National Institutes of Health (NIH) study included 98 donors with HIV risk factors from Washington, DC. These studies show a similar profile of motivations for donation by HIV seropositive donors. One major reason for donating was the donors' self-assessment that they were not at risk for HIV infection; CDC data indicated that many of these donors were in psychological denial about their HIV risk. A second motivation for donation was social or peer pressure to donate; in the CDC Study this pressure came from an employer or fellow employees, rather than from the blood center, in 75% of cases. Another group of donors was at least partially motivated to donate in order to obtain their HIV antibody test results. Some persons who donated indicated that they misunderstood the accuracy of the HIV antibody tests; some donors concluded that their donations were safe because they had previously tested HIV antibody-negative, while other donors felt they would not be jeopardizing recipients since, if they were infectious, the HIV antibody test would inevitably be positive and their blood would not be utilized. Data from these studies contributed to a revision of donor questioning to include more specific HIV risk questions; these changes are reflected in current FDA recommendations and in the AABB's uniform donor history card (58,66).

A preponderance of data has demonstrated that the theoretical possibility of long-term persistent HIV infection in the absence of detectable HIV antibody, HIV antigen, or clinical symptoms does not exist or is exceedingly rate (77–81).

Table 4 Motivations for Donation by HIV-1 Antibody–Positive Blood Donors

	Motivation (%)		
Reasons	CDC multicenter[a]	ARC multicenter	NIH
Denial of risk	NA	61	26
Social pressure	27	29	15
Wanted to get test results	15	29	26
Previous HIV-seronegative test	9	NA	NA
Positive test would stop blood from being transfused	10	NA	14
Misunderstood the pamphlet	7	NA	6
Other	32	NA	13

NA = Data not available in this format.
[a]Some donors gave more than one reason.

These data have demonstrated that seroconversion for HIV is highly likely to occur within 6 months of HIV exposure (81) and that HIV nucleic acid cannot be detected in HIV antibody-negative individuals from high-risk groups who are at risk for latent HIV infection. Thus, HIV risk behaviors that can be defined as ending at a specific point in time (i.e., sex with a particular person who demonstrated HIV risk behaviors, an accidental exposure to blood, a blood transfusion), should only defer a prospective donor until serological testing can definitively prove that the individual is free of HIV infection. In order to allow for outliers and to therefore be absolutely certain that the required time for seroconversion has elapsed, a 12-month deferral interval for these behaviors has been selected.

Other behaviors, such as past intravenous drug use or male-to-male sex even once since 1977, still require a lifetime deferral. The unproven rationale for a permanent deferral for a remote past history of male-to-male sex is that this behavior represents a lifestyle choice, which may not be limited to a defined time interval. To my knowledge, there are no data to support this contention and it seems scientifically inappropriate to have differing deferral intervals for potential homosexual and heterosexual exposure to HIV. With regard to intravenous drug users, a permanent deferral seems appropriate give the higher seroprevalence of most known infectious agents in this population and the concern that a past injection drug user is more likely to be a carrier of other unidentified transfusion transmissible agents.

As heterosexual transmission of HIV infection becomes more common in the United States (82), it is to be anticipated that such a shift will be reflected in the demographics of HIV-seropositive blood donors. Thus far, however, no dramatic changes have occurred. In a CDC study of HIV-seropositive donors from 20 blood centers, the number of seropositive donors who acquired their HIV infection by heterosexual exposure did not increase significantly when 1990–1991 data were compared to data from 1988–1989 (30). American Red Cross data indicate that the rate of HIV-seropositive female donors has remained constant from 1988 to 1992; however, a slightly decreasing rate of HIV-seropositive male donors has resulted in an increased percentage of females among all HIV-seropositive donors (83).

The risk of heterosexual spread of HIV has been addressed by several items in the 1992 FDA recommendations (66). Several potential heterosexual risk exposures are a cause for 12-month deferrals. These include sex with an intravenous drug user, sex with a prostitute, sex with a bisexual man, and sex with a person using clotting factor concentrates. In the early years of the AIDS epidemic, donors who had immigrated to the United States from a country (e.g., Haiti and sub-Saharan Africa countries) in which heterosexual activity played a major role in transmission of HIV infection were permanently deferred (1,6). Questions pertaining to geographic exclusion were continued until 1992 for sub-Saharan

Africa as a safeguard against transmitting HIV-2, an HIV strain more prevalent in this region. With the implementation of HIV-2 antibody testing, deferral policies based on geographic factors were no longer necessary and were discontinued until 1996 when similar concerns about the inability of HIV screening tests to detect HIV-1 group O infection prompted their reinstatement for Cameroon and adjoining countries (71,72,84). In 1992, FDA added a history of syphilis or gonorrhea to the list of 12-month deferrals (66). The rationale for this policy was the assumption that acquisition of either of these sexually transmitted diseases would indicate that a prospective donor had an increased risk of acquisition of HIV through heterosexual activity.

A recent study evaluated the impact of a proposed change in deferral criteria for heterosexual exposure to HIV (30). This study analyzed the responses of HIV-seropositive donors with regard to their number of sexual partners in the last year and during their lifetime; furthermore, similar response data were cited from surveys of noninfected donors. The authors concluded that the implementation of their proposed deferral criteria would be very nonspecific, leading to deferral of high percentages of noninfected donors while providing only a marginal increase in blood safety.

It is well established that HIV is not transmitted by casual contact; therefore, persons who have had close contact with individuals who are anti-HIV-positive or who have AIDS should not be deferred as blood donors (85). If a person admits to living in the same household as an HIV-infected person, the potential for sexual or body fluid contact with that individual should be determined; if such contact has not occurred, the donor should not be deferred.

3. Hearsay Evidence of HIV Risk

On occasion, donor interviewers may acquire information that is difficult to evaluate because it has been obtained from a third party, such as a spouse, a sex partner, or a fellow worker (hearsay evidence) (6). For example, a third party may assert that a particular donor is at risk for HIV even though the donor has responded that he is not at risk. In this situation, the blood center will need to decide whether to use the collected unit and whether to defer the donor from future donations. The AABB has recommended that blood centers have written procedures indicating how such information will be assessed for validity (86). In such a case, the blood center is faced with fulfilling two obligations: protecting the safety of a potential transfusion recipient and avoiding falsely placing a donor on a computerized deferral list based on a third-party accusation. One possible approach to this dilemma is for a blood center physician or a senior nursing staff member to reinterview the donor. It can be explained to the donor that additional information has prompted the need to reassess the donor's eligibility. The physician can emphasize the importance of truthful history in protecting recipient safety and can review HIV risk factor information with the donor. The physician can obtain answers to explicit HIV risk questions from the donor. If the donor admits to risk, he can be deferred. On the other hand, if the donor denies all HIV risk, the physician will need to make a decision as to whether to believe the donor or the third party. Unfortunately, there are no precise guidelines as to how such a decision should be made. My belief is that when the third-party evidence is not convincing and when the donor insists they have been truthful, the correct procedure is to advise the donor that he is eligible to make future donations. The donor will be reinterviewed and retested for HIV antibody on subsequent donations, thereby providing some degree of confirmation of their safety.

One blood center reported their one-year experience with a protocol for contacting the donor after third-party information was received (87). Eleven such reports were received, 10 donors were interviewed, and 7 donors were determined to be acceptable for future donation. The investigators stated that all contacted donors were open, cooperative, and understanding of the blood center's position. They concluded that the policy of confronting donors with third-party information was effective in resolving these difficult donor suitability decisions.

4. Surveillance and Monitoring

At least three areas of continued monitoring are necessary to ensure that HIV-related donor deferral criteria are optimally effective for preventing potentially HIV-infected persons from donating; these are continued observation of HIV-seropositive donor demographics, continued assessment of the risk factors and motivation for donation of HIV-infected donors, and evaluation of whether donor history questions are successful in eliminating persons with known HIV risk factors. The first two of these items are undergoing continued assessment by the multicenter CDC HIV Seropositive Donor Study. The third item, the effectiveness of donor history questions, is being addressed by another anonymous survey recently conducted by the NHLBI-sponsored Retrovirus Donor Epidemiology Study.

B. Hepatitis

Federal guidelines for preventing transfusion-transmitted hepatitis were established decades ago in the Code of Federal Regulations (CFR) (3). The current regulations require the following deferral policies: (a) donors with a history of viral hepatitis are permanently deferred; (b) donors with a history of close contact with someone who has viral hepatitis are deferred for 12 months following their last potential exposure; and (c) donors who have received a blood transfusion are deferred for 12 months. [Although the CFR indicates a 6-month deferral for these categories, subsequent FDA memos to blood establishments changed this deferral to 12 months (88). This change was based upon establishing consistency with HIV deferral time intervals as well as the observed lag period to HCV seroconversion following HCV exposure using first-generation HCV tests (89)]. In addition, a person testing positive for HBsAg or known to have previously tested positive for HBsAg is also permanently deferred as a blood donor.

Recently, FDA clarified that a history of viral hepatitis applies only to clinical disease and that deferral is not required when the donor's history is based solely on a positive serological test result (i.e., anti-HBc or anti-HBs) that indicates past exposure to HBV (90). Furthermore, the permanent deferral requirement for a history of viral hepatitis no longer applies to an episode of viral hepatitis occurring before the age of 10. (91). This recent change in FDA policy is based upon epidemiological evidence that viral hepatitis in childhood, occurring prior to the onset of sexual activity, is almost exclusively due to infection with the hepatitis A virus (HAV) (92). Since HAV infection does not induce a chronic carrier state, it is evident that persons who acquired HAV in the remote past do not pose a hazard to transfusion recipients (93). Such reasoning raises the issue of whether donors with a history of HAV at any age should be acceptable as blood donors (94,95). Although medical knowledge supports the safety of donations from these individuals, such a policy would be of limited value since it would be difficult to prove definitively that a particular past episode of viral hepatitis was due to HAV. Because of this problem in establishing accurate diagnosis, it is still required that donors who present with a stated history of HAV above age 10 be deferred.

In the past, blood collection agencies deferred all donors with a history of jaundice (96). Currently the policy at most blood centers is to question the donor concerning the etiology of the jaundice and to accept those donors whose history of jaundice is related to the neonatal period or to obstructive biliary tract disease.

Other donor deferral criteria for potential hepatitis risk are based on the known parenteral routes of spread of HBV and HCV. Persons who have ever injected intravenous drugs by needle have long been deferred as blood donors due to hepatitis risk; the importance of this criterion has been reemphasized with the advent of the HIV epidemic.

Donors with a history of tattoos are deferred for 12 months because of the possibility of hepatitis spread by contaminated needles (2). Donors who have had needle exposure through ear piercing, skin piercing, acupuncture, or electrolysis should also be considered for a possible 12-month deferral (2,6). In such cases it should be evaluated whether these procedures were performed utilizing disposable sterile needles as occurs in a professional setting; if so, deferral is not necessary. If it cannot be verified that sterile technique was followed, then consideration should be given to deferring such donors for 12 months.

Donors receiving hepatitis B immunoglobulin (HBIG) should be deferred for 12 months following such administration because of the underlying hepatitis

B exposure risk. On the other hand, donors receiving hepatitis B vaccine do not need to be deferred unless the vaccine was given for a recent exposure to HBV.

According to FDA regulations, donors who have had close contact with a patient with acute viral hepatitis should be deferred for 12 months (88). Clearly, sexual contact is included in this definition; it is less clear how to define nonsexual close contact. One commonly used definition is the sharing of household, kitchen, or toilet facilities, as would occur with living in the same household (6). In the case of HBV, this definition appears reasonable, in that it has been demonstrated that HBV can rarely be transmitted from an acutely infected patient to a household contact, probably through nonsexual contact with body fluids (97). Data for nonsexual household transmission of HCV are more equivocal, and it is unclear whether nonsexual contacts of such patients pose a risk to recipients (98). Nevertheless, FDA requires that such prospective donors must be deferred. On the other hand, persons who occasionally eat a meal or visit a patient who has viral hepatitis may have little hepatitis risk; medical judgment should be utilized to determine whether a particular donor with this type of history should be deferred.

FDA requirements do not formally apply to sexual or close contacts of asymptomatic or symptomatic chronic carriers of HBV and HCV. Given the high rates of sexual and body fluid transmission of HBV, the same 12-month deferral criterion should be applied to contacts of chronic HBV carriers. With regard to HCV, data suggest that sexual transmission occurs with a low enough frequency to make it safe to accept sexual partners of HCV carriers (99). Deferral policies for close, nonsexual contacts of HCV carriers are more problematic given the scarcity of reproducible clinical data; current data do not support the need to defer such contacts (98).

C. Parasitic Diseases

Transfusion-transmitted malaria is common in some parts of the world but is rare in the United States, occurring at an estimated rate of 0.25 cases per million donated units for 1972–1988 (100,101). Policies for preventing such transmissions rely on donor questioning during the health history interview.

The deferral criteria for malaria risk were revised by FDA in 1994 (102). Travelers to a malaria endemic area are deferred for one year after their return to the United States (provided they have not had malarial symptoms), whereas immigrants from or residents of malarial endemic countries are deferred for 3 years after their departure from the endemic country. Donors with a history of malaria are deferred for 3 years after becoming asymptomatic. Previous deferral criteria in place from 1974 to 1994 had required that travelers to a malaria endemic area be deferred for 3 years if they had received antimalarial prophylaxis and for 6 months if they had not, because it was believed that prophylaxis might extend the latency period (3,101). The revised deferral criteria no longer use the receipt of chemoprophylaxis as a determinant of the length of deferral.

Travelers to malarial endemic areas are deferred for one year because, if infected, nonimmune persons will develop symptoms within this time frame. The 3-year deferral period for immigrants from such areas is based on the premise that such individuals may have partial tolerance to malarial parasites, thereby resulting in the delay of malarial symptoms in an infected donor beyond one year (3,100,101). The 3-year deferral for persons with a history of malaria is based on the general consensus that *Plasmodium falciparum* organisms will be cleared within 2 years and that *P. vivax* or *P. ovale* will be cleared within 3 years of the resolution of symptoms in the vast majority of cases. This latter policy represents a compromise between prevention of transmission and acceptable levels of donor deferral, in that it is well known that a *P. malariae* chronic carrier state may persist for decades, resulting in transfusion transmission many years after the resolution of symptoms (103,104).

The CDC recently reported three cases of transfusion-transmitted malaria, two of which were fatal (104a). In these two cases, the donors did not accurately report their malaria risk information during the donor interview. These cases have prompted an FDA review of malarial donor interview questions.

Chagas' disease has been commonly transmitted by transfusion in Latin America, but has only rarely been transmitted in this fashion in the United States (105). Research studies conducted in the United States have attempted to identify risk factors that might be associated with previous exposure to the causative organism, *Trypanosoma cruzi*; these risk factors include birth in a country endemic for Chagas' disease, extended time spent in an endemic area, and lower socioeconomic level (106). One institution with a large Hispanic donor population has included Chagas risk questioning as part of its donor health history interview and has performed investigational testing for *T. cruzi* antibody on donors with affirmative answers prior to releasing blood for transfusion (5). However, because of the low risk of documented transfusion-transmitted *T. cruzi* infection in North America (four cases) and the low specificity of these proposed questions, AABB-required health history questioning is confined to asking donors whether they have ever had Chagas' disease (2).

Babesiosis is a rare, malaria-like illness caused by a protozoan parasite, *Babesia microti*, which invades human erythrocytes. Human transmission occurs as a result of tick bites, most commonly in the summer months in particular regions of the United States. Transfusion-transmitted babesiosis, although rare, has been reported as a consequence of blood donation by asymptomatic carriers (107,108). Strategies for eliminating transfusion risk by restricting donations from endemic areas in the summer months or by questioning donors as to a history of tick bites have been considered but have been judged to be largely ineffective, although some centers nonetheless do avoid blood collection in highly endemic areas during the summer (108,109). Currently, AABB-required health history questioning is confined to asking donors whether they have ever had babesiosis (110).

D. Creutzfeldt-Jacob Disease

Creutzfeldt-Jacob disease (CJD) is a rare, fatal, degenerative neurological disease with a long asymptomatic latent period (111). The etiological agent is thought by most experts to be a prion, although some favor a viral etiology (112). CJD has been transmitted from human to human by the transplantation of dura mater, the injection of pituitary-derived human growth hormone, and the reuse of EEG electrodes; a single case of transmission by a corneal transplant has also been reported (113). There are no reported cases of transmission by blood transfusion, and epidemiological studies have not provided any evidence for such transmission (114,115). Nevertheless, because of the long incubation phase of the disease (as demonstrated from growth hormone transmissions) and the inability of conventional sterilization methods to inactivate the organism, the theoretical risk of CJD transmission from asymptomatic donors to recipients of blood components or plasma derivatives cannot be ruled out (116). Policies designed to prevent this theoretical transfusion transmission of CJD have been adopted with regard to donor deferral, product recall, and, in some cases, recipient notification (117–120).

The initial concern for blood transfusion safety arose from the fact that some persons who received therapeutic injections of cadaver-derived pituitary human growth hormone developed CJD, thus raising the possibility that other recipients of this hormonal product may have become asymptomatic chronic carriers of the CJD agent (121,122). To eliminate possible risk to transfusion recipients, FDA issued a 1987 recommendation that all prospective donors be asked if they have ever received human growth hormone (117,118,122). If the growth hormone was pituitary derived (i.e., the injection was given before the availability of recombinant growth hormone in 1985), the donor was indefinitely deferred.

In 1995 and 1996, FDA issued additional recommendations to further lower the theoretical risk of transfusion-transmitted CJD by deferral of donors and recall of previously acceptable donations (119,120). These recommendations included the addition of questions about the receipt of a dura mater transplant and a family history of CJD in a blood relative. Donors who respond affirmatively are indefinitely deferred. A 9-month experience with CJD questioning at one large blood center demonstrated that approximately one in 10,000 donors were deferred for possible CJD risk, with 83% of the deferrals due to the donor having one blood relative with CJD (123).

Since 90% of CJD cases are sporadic rather than familial, it should be expected that a family history of one blood relative with CJD would be most likely due to the sporadic occurrence of the disease. Therefore, in 1996, FDA policy for product recall for CJD was revised to indicate that product recall of previously transfused single donor product and manufactured pooled plasma derivatives was not necessary if a donor gave a history of only one family member with CJD. Rather, the criteria for product recall would require two blood relatives with CJD or genetic testing that was diagnostic of the familial variant (120). In 1998, based on a review of international data, FDA amended its product recall guidance to exclude recall of plasma-derivative products for donors with a history of classical CJD or risk factors for classical CJD (120a).

E. New Variant Creutzfeldt-Jacob Disease

New variant Creutzfeldt-Jacob disease (nvCJD) is a fatal, degenerative neurological disease newly discovered in the United Kingdom in 1996 (120b). To date, approximately 12 cases occur annually in the United Kingdom and only two cases have been detected outside the United Kingdom (120c). The etiological agent of nvCJD is the same agent that causes bovine spongiform encephalopathy (BSE) (120d). The spread of the agent from cattle to humans and the detection of the nvCJD prion in lymphoid tissue has raised concerns that nvCJD could be transmitted by blood transfusion (120c–120e). No cases of transfusion-transmitted nvCJD have been reported, but the observation period has been too short to draw any firm conclusions. In 1998 and 1999, FDA advisory committees and public policy committees in Canada debated proposals to defer donors who had traveled to the United Kingdom as a means of reducing the theoretical risk of transmission of nvCJD through transfusion (120f). In June 1999, FDA announced a donor deferral policy calling for deferral of donors who had spent more than 6 months in the United Kingdom between 1981 and 1996.

F. Bacterial Disease

Another potential fatal complication of transfusion is bacterial infection (124). Bacteria can be introduced into the donor unit at the time of collection if the donor is bacteremic, if the skin site is not properly decontaminated, if there is an undetected abscess adjacent to the phelbotomy site, or through introduction of a small skin plug in the phlebotomy needle (124–126). Examination of the skin at the venipuncture site is conducted before phlebotomy, and strict requirements for assuring the sterility of the site are adhered to by the phlebotomist (2,127). Blood is not collected from persons who are febrile at the time of donation, who state that they do not feel well, or who are taking systemic antibiotics (2). In the past, blood centers have temporarily deferred donors with a history of dental procedures for up to 72 hours because of the high frequency of postprocedure bacteremia. These criteria have been liberalized with the recognition that many other types of trauma to mucous membranes not evaluated at the time of donation may also cause bacteremia (128). It has been recommended that donors need only be deferred for 24–72 hours after particular traumatic types of dental procedures, such as root canals and tooth extractions; some blood centers no longer inquire about recent dental procedures, and no such question is present on the AABB uniform donor history card (58,124).

Unlike other infectious diseases, the risk of bacterial infection applies also to candidates for autologous donation, as a result of the ability of gram-negative rods to multiply at refrigerator temperatures and secrete endotoxin into the blood bag (129). For this reason, autologous donors who are taking antibiotics or who give a history of recent or concurrent medical procedures are evaluated for the possibility of bacteremia and deferred accordingly.

G. Other Infectious Disease Considerations

Donors are asked whether they have had a previous history of syphilis or gonorrhea in the past 12 months as a means of decreasing the risk of HIV transmission. There is no requirement to ask donors about other types of venereal disease such as herpes simplex, genital warts, or chlamydia.

Donors who have received live, attenuated viral vaccines are deferred for 2 weeks (except for rubeola and varicella, which are 4-week deferrals). Donors receiving toxoid or killed viral vaccines should not be deferred (2).

Over the last decade, experience with transfusion-transmitted viruses such as HIV and HCV has clearly demonstrated that in the absence of laboratory testing, asymptomatic donors with chronic, latent viral infection may endanger recipients (1,6). Concern for this type of circumstance may lead to deferral of donors with unusual histories (i.e., chronic fatigue syndrome in quiescence, treated Dengue fever), despite the fact that there is no definitive evidence of their potential infectivity.

H. Donors with a History of Malignancy

Donors with a history of malignancy pose a theoretical risk to recipients; however, no cases of transfusion-transmitted malignancy have been reported. Since many transfusion recipients are immunosuppressed, it may be theoretically possible that malignant cells circulating in a donor's blood could engraft and multiply in a recipient, provided there was a sufficient degree of genetic matching. In order to decrease the possibility of this occurrence, donors are questioned about a history of cancer. In most blood centers, a donor with a history of a solid organ tumor will be deferred and will be eligible to donate only if he or she has been symptom-free and considered to be clinically cured for a defined time period, usually 5 or 10 years. Donors with a history of hematological malignancy are still permanently deferred. Donors with specific malignancies that have been fully excised are not deferred (e.g., basal cell cancer of skin, cervical carcinoma in situ), since the tumor is known to be low grade and not capable of hematogenous spread.

VI. ADDITIONAL MECHANISMS FOR SELECTING SAFE DONORS OR SAFE UNITS

A. Donor Deferral Registries

Donor deferral registries began as an effort to decrease the risk of transfusion-associated hepatitis at a time when other, more specific methods were not available. More recently their use has been extended to include donors who might transmit HIV and other infections (3,130,131).

These registries are computer, microfiche, or manual files of names and identifying information from donors who have been deferred for specified reasons. Individual blood centers have established inhouse (local) donor deferral registries to comply with a section of the Code of Federal Regulations that states that persons who have ever tested positive for HBsAg or anti-HIV should no longer be accepted as blood donors (3,131). The rationale of donor deferral registries is that individuals with a previous positive test result may revert to a negative test result at a later date despite the fact that they could still transmit disease. This situation could occur because of either a biological phenomenon or a testing error. Donor deferral registries also include the names of donors who have previously volunteered information (i.e., history of intravenous drug use, hepatitis, or high-risk AIDS activity) that should have permanently excluded them as blood donors. Donors who volunteer such information at one visit may be tempted to withhold the information at a subsequent visit, especially if their self-assessment is that the history ought not to have precluded them as blood donors.

The donor deferral registry can be used in one of two ways. In most blood centers in recent years, the donor's name is checked against the deferral registry prior to donation; no blood is collected if the donor is listed on the registry. This method is highly desirable in that it avoids the unnecessary phlebotomy of ineligible donors, and it prevents the potential for an error leading to the release of the ineligible donor unit. The alternate method of complying with the requirements for a donor deferral registry was to collect the unit from the donor and to subsequently, at a central location, check the donor deferral registry prior to placing the unit into inventory. The unit was quarantined and destroyed if the donor's name was found on the registry.

Since donors may not always donate to the same blood collection agency, some states have created statewide donor deferral registries that include the names of donors deferred at any blood collection agency within the state (130). The American Red Cross uses a national system in which donors who are entered into specific categories of the deferral registry at an individual Red Cross region also have their names included in a national registry (130,131). Because of donor confidentiality concerns, donor deferral registries that extend beyond an individual blood center do not list the reason for donor entry into the registry.

Over the past 10 years, the size and complexity of donor deferral registries have increased enormously. For example, the national component of the American Red Cross donor deferral registry contains over 20 separate deferral categories and over 300,000 donor names (130,131). It has been estimated that there may be up to 3 million entries in donor deferral registries throughout the United States (130). The problems associated with managing such expanded deferral registries have also increased dramatically, creating a major source of difficulty in adhering to FDA regulations. These regulations and blood center standard operating procedures require that if a donor is listed in certain permanent deferral categories on a donor deferral registry, additional donations from that individual should not be distributed for transfusion. Difficulties in complying with this requirement have resulted in numerous product recalls of subsequent units donated by individuals who should have been placed on donor deferral registries according to standard operating procedures. To my knowledge, there have been no documented instances of these subsequently transfused units (which tested infectious disease negative) causing adverse outcomes in recipients. These operational data suggest that donor deferral registries may not contribute significantly to the enhancement of transfusion safety, given the other layers of safety that are built into the system. A study to evaluate the usefulness of a regional donor deferral registry demonstrated that 0.41% of donors who donated to a hospital-based blood bank were later placed in that institution's donor deferral registry and yet also donated to a regional blood center in the same geographic location (132). These data can be interpreted to indicate that if donor deferral registries are believed to be of value, their extension to regional registries may offer some additional benefit.

Problems encountered in managing donor deferral registries include difficulty in obtaining accurate information to uniquely identify a donor, the existence of multiple records for the same donor due to conflicting information obtained on separate donations, the need to move donors from one category of the registry to another, and the fact that some information leads to permanent deferral while other data only result in deferral if the phenomenon [e.g., a positive anti-hepatitis B core (anti-HBc) test] occurs on two occasions (130).

Maintenance and continuous use of national or statewide donor deferral registries is time-consuming, logistically complex, and expensive. Unfortunately it has remained difficult to assess whether such massive efforts afford significant increases in safety to the blood transfusion recipient.

B. Confidential Unit Exclusion

The procedure known as confidential unit exclusion (CUE) was introduced at many blood centers following a 1986 FDA recommendation stating that at the time of donation donors should be offered a procedure by which they could designate confidentially whether or not their blood should be transfused to others (133). The rationale for CUE was to provide an opportunity for those donors who felt pressured to donate (from peers, fellow employees, employers, etc.) at a workplace or community blood drive to indicate that their blood should not be transfused. The CUE procedure works as follows: after the health history interview but prior to donation of the unit, each blood donor indicates whether his or her unit should or should not be used; if a donor neglects to make any indication, the unit will not be used.

Numerous small studies have attempted to evaluate the sensitivity, specificity, or predictive value of the CUE procedure (134–141). Assessments of the efficacy of CUE have focused primarily on the frequency of its use by HIV-seropositive donors; these data have been somewhat conflicting and have led to differing conclusions about the value of the CUE procedure. Furthermore, those studies in which follow-up interviews were performed with donors who chose the CUE option have consistently established that the majority of donors selecting this option did so either as a result of misunderstanding or error (138–142). These latter findings have prompted suggestions that the CUE procedure be modified to make it more understandable to blood donors, thereby improving its specificity (135,138). Several modifications to the CUE procedure have occurred since 1986. Many centers have switched from the use of a manual ballot separated from the donor history card to the use of a peel-off barricaded sticker that the donor affixes to the history card. There have also been simplifications in the wording of the CUE form, clearer written and oral instructions as to the purpose of CUE, and clearer instructions as to how to correctly complete the process.

In some blood centers, donors who have chosen CUE are placed on the donor deferral registry, whereas at other centers they are not. In some centers donors are recontacted and provided with a mechanism such as a donor interview to reestablish their ability to donate (143).

The rate of discard of blood as a result of the CUE procedure has decreased from 7 per thousand donations in the early years (134,144,145) to 2–4 per thousand in more contemporary reports (141,144,145). It is probable that some of this decrease has resulted from improvements in the CUE procedure. Other factors that may also have contributed are fewer persons with HIV risk presenting at the donation site or a greater number of deferrals of such individuals during the health history interview.

Recently, two large studies have attempted to reevaluate whether CUE is a useful procedure (144,145). In addition to looking at whether HIV-seropositive donors excluded their blood from transfusion, these two studies were able to analyze whether donors who were demonstrated to seroconvert for HIV (i.e., HIV-seronegative donation followed by HIV-seropositive donation) used the CUE option on their preseroconversion sample. This is the most relevant group for evaluation of CUE's effect on transfusion safety, since, unlike HIV-seropositive units, these units would otherwise be transfused to recipients if the CUE procedure were not in place (137,144). Investigators from the CDC compiled data on the use of CUE at the time of the preseroconversion donation of 322 HIV seroconverting donors at 40 blood centers from January 1987 through December 1990 (144). They found that 3.4% of such donations were excluded; however, 9 of the 11 exclusions came from one center (New York Blood Center), which has consistently shown results for the CUE procedure that differ from the remainder of the United States (54,135). If these data are eliminated, the data from the remaining 39 centers indicate that 2 of 246, or 0.8%, of HIV-seroconverting donors used this option. REDS analyzed the CUE process in 1.5 million donations made at five blood centers in 1991 and 1992. These investigators found that 8% of 169 HIV-seropositive donations were excluded and subsequently found that 6% (2 of 33) of HIV-seroconverting donors used this option on their pre-seroconversion unit (145,146). Given the very low rate of HIV transmission by transfusion and the low rate at which such seroconverting donors may choose the CUE option, it has been estimated that this procedure may interdict one additional HIV infectious unit per 7.14 million blood donations (146).

Despite its projected ineffectiveness in decreasing HIV risk from transfusion, many still advocate retaining CUE as part of the donation process based on other sources of data. Several studies have demonstrated that donors who use CUE have higher rates of seropositivity for many infectious disease markers (140,144,145,147) and that some individuals who use CUE admit to HIV risk factors (139,142). The previously described anonymous mailed REDS survey correlated the donor's stated use of CUE (or telephone callback) with admitted behavioral risk factors for infectious disease (9). This study found that all behavioral risks, with the exception of injection drug use and history of transfusion in the past year, were reported statistically significantly more frequently in donors who used CUE. In aggregate, the relative prevalence of any reported risk behavior in donors who used CUE was 7.6-fold greater than in those who did not and was 9.4-fold greater for risk behaviors in the prior 3 months. However, CUE was not used by the majority of donors who reported behavioral risk (low sensitivity) and was used more frequently in donors without behavioral risk (low specificity).

In 1992, FDA analyzed the then available data on CUE sensitivity and specificity and stated that the CUE procedure was no longer mandatory, and its use was left to the discretion of each individual blood center (66). Currently some blood centers who previously used the CUE procedure have discontinued it.

In summary, CUE has poor sensitivity and specificity but nevertheless may prevent the transfusion of a very small number of units that cause infection in recipients.

C. Telephone Callback and Postdonation Information Reports

A further safeguard intended to increase transfusion safety is the mechanism of telephone callback (1). At the time of blood donation, donors receive instructions that they may call the blood center sometime after the donation to report additional pertinent medical history information. Telephone callbacks fall into two prominent categories. Donors may call back to report the development of an acute illness, such as fever, upper respiratory tract infection, or a gastrointestinal disorder, occurring from several hours to several days postdonation. Donors may also call back to indicate risk factors for HIV or other infectious diseases that might not have been disclosed at the time of donation.

In a 2-year series (1993–1994) at one large American Red Cross center, 199 (40%) of 492 reports of postdonation information were obtained through the mechanism of telephone callback (148). Postdonation information reports occurred at a rate of approximately 0.033% of donations. Classification of the postdonation reports revealed that 30% were due to acute illness, 25% to possible hepatitis risk, and 29% to possible HIV risk.

A Canadian blood center evaluated the occurrence of bacteremia in blood units drawn from donors who called back to report diarrhea, vomiting, fever, severe pharyngitis, or diagnosed streptococcal pharyngitis within 7 days of donation (149). All 187 components (from 99 such donors) cultured for bacteria were negative. These negative data had 95% confidence intervals of 4% in red cells and plasma and 18% in platelet concentrates. These limited data indicate that the risks to recipients are small (if any) if such donated units are transfused prior to receiving call back information from the donor.

An 8-year experience with telephone callback and its potential impact on HIV transmission has been reported from San Francisco (150). The blood center averaged 24 donor-initiated callbacks per year in which donors revealed HIV-related risk factors that they had not disclosed at the time of donation. Despite these risk factors, all such donated units tested HIV seronegative. On follow-up investigation, however, it was found that two donors subsequently seroconverted for HIV. These data suggest that telephone callback may have had a beneficial effect on eliminating infectious HIV window period units; however, because of the small number of observations, it is not possible to evaluate the extent of this impact.

Blood centers must have established policies for managing postdonation telephone callback information. Usually this information will be received by nursing or other staff, who will complete required documentation. A useful additional step is for a medical director to subsequently review these data and to decide whether withdrawal of the product is necessary. One large blood center has reported its experience that 52% of such postdonation reports did not require product withdrawal (151). In general, if postdonation information caused the donor to be deferred, blood centers will quarantine and destroy any components that have not yet been shipped and will transmit such information, usually by letter, to the hospital transfusion services that have received components from the donation. The transfusion service will retrieve any such indate components and either return them to the blood center or destroy them.

Postdonation information reports that affect the eligibility evaluation of the donor must be reported by licensed blood establishments to the FDA (152). In FDA's summary of error and accident reports for fiscal year 1996, 5620 reports of postdonation information were received, 1137 (20%) of which resulted from telephone callbacks from the donor to the blood center (153). These postdonation reports accounted for 51% of the error and accident reports received by FDA from blood establishments.

D. Market Withdrawal, Product Retrieval, and Recipient Notification

Information obtained through telephone callback is usually received within days of a given donation. In contrast to telephone callback, there are other circumstances leading to market withdrawal (e.g., a request to remove a blood component from active inventory) in which information is not received by the blood center until weeks, months, or even years after the donation of the unit. These circumstances include a change in donor suitability requirements that retrospectively disqualify previous donations from a given donor or a record review leading to the discovery of improperly processed or released units.

Unfortunately, there are no clear-cut guidelines as to how the hospital transfusion service should handle the varied and complex situations that may arise following telephone callback–driven or other market withdrawals. In such cases, the hospital transfusion service medical director must decide whether to inform the recipient's physician that a recent blood transfusion has a higher than usual risk of transmitting infection. The hospital transfusion service medical director can use medical judgment to resolve each specific case but must follow a written standard operating procedure for evaluating and documenting market withdrawal information received from the blood supplier. The information provided by the blood center to the transfusion service physician is often insufficient to either adequately assess risk to the recipient or structure an informed notification message to the recipient's physician. In such instances, the transfusion service physician should consider telephoning the blood center to obtain additional pertinent donor information that may assist with the recipient notification decision or message. In some cases, it may be helpful to the transfusion center physician if donor center personnel are able to recall the donor in a timely manner and obtain further clarifying history or pertinent serological testing.

Consider the case of a unit transfused from a donor who later reports HIV risk factors. If such information is forwarded to a recipient, it would be expected to cause anxiety. Furthermore, since HIV antibody testing will not be able to definitively resolve the situation for several weeks to several months, this anxiety may not be easily alleviated. In my opinion, the best way to handle such a situation is for a blood center physician or designee to recontact the donor who volunteered the information and attempt to get a specific and accurate history and, if possible, a follow-up HIV test. This may allow the hospital transfusion service medical director to better estimate the likelihood of risk to the recipient. Using this information, the decision as to when and whether to notify the recipient's physician and/or the recipient and the details of the specific notification message can be determined.

The American Association of Blood Banks has issued an Association Bulletin to assist transfusion services in developing policies for physician and recipient notification in cases in which the transfused component was obtained from a donor who later revealed risk factors for or had a clinical diagnosis of Creutzfeldt-Jacob disease (154). The situation with regard to these recipients is problematic, since the possibility of transfusion transmission is only theoretical and there is no diagnostic testing available for the recipient subsequent to notification. The AABB states that the ultimate responsibility for deciding to withhold information from a recipient rests with the recipient's physician and not with the medical director of the transfusion service or with the institution. The AABB suggests that each hospital convene a committee, such as an Ethics Committee or an Institutional Review Board, that could develop criteria for informing or not informing patients of possible transfusion exposure to CJD. These criteria would allow physicians at the institution to individualize decisions for particular patients.

VII. RECIPIENT NOTIFICATION (LOOKBACK) PROGRAMS

Lookback is the term used for a program of notifying large groups of recipients of their risk of having been exposed to an infectious agent at the time of a previous transfusion (155). Targeted lookback is a program to identify recipients of prior units donated by specific donors who have subsequently been identified as infected with a specific agent (e.g., HIV). It involves tracing of previous donation and product shipment records by blood centers and tracing of transfusion records by hospital transfusion services in order to identify the individuals who received these specific blood components. These recipients, if still living and locatable, can then be notified of their potential risk, usually by their physician. Laboratory testing can be performed to determine whether infection occurred.

A generalized lookback program (also termed universal lookback) is a program in which all recipients transfused within a designated time frame are informed of their potential risk of infection from their transfusion. This program can be implemented either through a public education campaign using the media or communications to physicians or through direct mailings to recipients transfused during the given time frame. This latter approach requires identification of such recipients through hospital record searches.

The decision to perform targeted or generalized lookback programs for a specific transmissible agent must consider multiple factors. Traditional public health concerns, such as the yield and cost of the procedures, must be evaluated. Public health authorities also need to consider lookback programs in the context of more widespread screening programs to detect persons infected by routes other than transfusion. In addition, an effective lookback program should ensure the adequacy of diagnostic testing services, the adequacy of communication and counseling resources for identified recipients, and medical follow-up for these individuals. Another factor that may influence decisions concerning lookback programs is the ethical premise that an individual has the right to know information that might affect his or her future health. Additionally, liability concerns may also influence institutional decision making.

In conjunction with considering these public health, ethical, and legal issues, I believe that the answers to a critical set of medical questions are important when formulating policies with regard to lookback for any transmissible agent. These questions are:

1. Is there evidence that the agent is transmissible by a particular blood component?
2. Is there a diagnostic test to determine if infection has occurred in the recipient?
3. Are there known modes of secondary transmission which can be interrupted by the recipient having knowledge of his infection?
4. Are there medical means to monitor and assess the progression of the disease in the recipient?
5. Is there treatment available?

These can be more concisely summarized into two broad considerations: halting secondary spread of infection and the potential for intervening, or at least monitoring, the natural history of the disease.

Testing of donated blood for anti-HIV, anti-HTLV, and anti-HCV has given rise to the identification of blood donors who are HIV, HTLV, or HCV infected and who have given previous, transfusable donations prior to the implementation of blood screening. These donors may have been infectious at the time of their previous donation; therefore, recipients of these previous donations are at increased risk of acquiring these infections. Currently, FDA requires targeted lookback to be performed for donors identified as HIV antibody positive and has established a rule requiring the transfusing institution to assume ultimate responsibility for notification of the recipient or next of kin (66,156). A more limited time frame of lookback, i.e., units transfused in the prior 3 months, is required for donors identified as HIV p24 antigen positive (157). Although FDA does not require targeted lookback for HTLV infection, the AABB has established such a requirement (2,158). After several years of debate, FDA issued guidance requiring that a targeted lookback program be conducted for recipients of blood products from HCV antibody–positive donors. The specific requirements as to which recipients must be informed are complex because of the evolution of HCV screening and confirmatory tests (158). All transfusion recipients prior to 1992 are also part of a generalized lookback programs for HCV under the direction of the U.S. Public Health Service (159).

VIII. CONCLUSION

Optimal donor-screening procedures represent a balance between maximizing safety for both recipient and donor and minimizing the unnecessary deferral of safe blood donors. Given the importance of recipient safety, decisions about donor-screening policies tend to favor the use of less specific procedures in an effort to enhance transfusion safety. In some cases, such enhancement can be demonstrated, while in other cases it is inferred from indirect evidence and in still other cases data may be completely lacking. Donor-screening policies can be evaluated scientifically, providing that the inherent limitations of the methodology used in this type of operational research are recognized. Additional attention to quality assurance of donor-screening procedures is warranted due to the difficult logistical situations that exist in some blood collection settings. Decisions regarding product retrieval and recipient notification are complex and require consideration of multiple factors.

REFERENCES

1. Kleinman S. Donor screening procedures and their role in enhancing transfusion safety. In: Smith D, Dodd RY, eds. Transfusion-Transmitted Infections. Chicago: American Society of Clinical Pathologists, 1991:207.
2. Klein HG, ed. Standards for Blood Banks and Transfusion Services. 17th ed. Bethesda, MD: American Association of Blood Banks, 1996.
3. U.S. Department of Health and Human Services, Food and Drug Administration.

The Code of Federal Regulations. Washington, DC: U.S. Government Printing Office, 1996. (Revised annually.)

4. Grossman BJ, Kollins P, Lau PM, et al. Screening blood donors for gastrointestinal illness: a strategy to eliminate carriers of Yersinia enterocolitica. Transfusion 1991, 31:500.

5. Appleman MP, Shulman IA, Saxena S, Kirchhoff LV. Use of a questionnaire to identify potential blood donors at risk for infection with *Trypansoma cruzi*. Transfusion 1993; 33:61.

6. Kleinman S. Donor selection and screening procedures. In: Nance SJ, ed. Blood Safety, Current Challenges. Bethesda, MD: American Association of Blood Banks, 1992:169.

7. Kaplan HS, Kleinman SH. AIDS: blood donor studies and screening methods. In: Barker LF, Dodd RY, eds. Infection, Immunity and Blood Transfusion. New York: Alan R. Liss, 1985: 297.

8. Zuck TF, Thomson RA, Schreiber GB, Gilcher RO, Kleinman SH, et al. The Retrovirus Epidemiology Donor Study (REDS): rationale and methods. Transfusion 1995; 35:944.

9. Williams AE, Thomson RA, Schreiber GB, et al. Estimates of infectious disease risk factors in US blood donors. JAMA 1997; 277:967.

10. Schafer IA, Mosley JW. A study of viral hepatitis in a penal institution. Ann Intern Med 1958; 149:1162.

11. Krugman S, Friedman H, Latimer C. Hepatitis A and B: serologic survey of various population groups. Am J Med Sci 1978; 275:249.

12. American Association of Blood Banks, American Red Cross, Council of Community Blood Centers: Joint statement on acquired immune deficiency syndrome related to transfusion, January 13, 1983.

13. Barker LF. International forum: Which criteria must be fulfilled for a donation or a donor to be considered voluntary? Vox Sang 1978; 34:363.

14. Morris JP. International forum: Which criteria must be fulfilled for a donation or a door to be considered voluntary? Vox Sang 1978; 34:369.

15. Beal RW, van Aken VG. Gift or goods? Vox Sang 1992; 63:1.

16. American Association of Blood Banks: Donor Incentives. Association Bulletin 94-6, October 1994.

17. Cherubin CE, Prince AM. Serum hepatitis specific antigen (SH) in commercial and volunteer sources of blood. Transfusion 1971; 11:25.

18. Szmuness W, Prince AM, Brotman B, Hirsch RL. Hepatitis B antigen and antibody in blood donors: an epidemiologic study. J Infect Dis 1973; 127:17.

19. Allen JG, Dawson D, Saymore WA, et al. Blood transfusion and serum hepatitis: use of monochloroacetate as an antibacterial agent in plasma. Ann Surg 1959; 150:455.

20. Alter HJ, Holland PV, Purcell RH, et al. Post transfusion hepatitis after exclusion of commercial and hepatitis B antigen positive donors. Ann Intern Med 1972; 77:691.

21. Surgenor DM, Cerveny JF. A study of the conversion from paid to altruistic blood donors in New Mexico. Transfusion 1978; 18:54.

22. Canavaggio M, Leckie G, Allain JP, et al. The prevalence of antibody to HTLV-I/II

in United States plasma donors and in United States and French hemophiliacs. Transfusion 1990; 30:780.

23. Dawson GJ, Lesniewski RR, Stewart JL, et al. Detection of antibodies to hepatitis C virus in U.S. blood donors. J Clin Microbiol 1991; 29:551.

24. Mosley JW, Galambos JT. Viral hepatitis. In: Schiff L, ed. Disease of the Liver. Philadelphia: JB Lippincott, 1975:500.

25. Kahn RA. Donor screening to prevent posttransfusion hepatitis. In: Keating LJ, Silvergleid AJ, eds. Hepatitis. Washington, DC: American Association of Blood Banks, 1981:99.

26. Taswell HA. Directed, paid and self donors. In: Clark GM, ed. Competition in Blood Services. Arlington, VA: American Association of Blood Banks, 1987:137.

27. Strauss RG, Ludwig GA, Smith MV, et al. Concurrent comparison of the safety of paid cytapheresis and volunteer whole-blood donors. Transfusion 1994; 34:116.

28. Huestis DW, Taswell HF. Donors and dollars (editorial). Transfusion 1994; 34:96.

29. Petersen LR, Doll LS. Human immunodeficiency virus type 1-infected blood donors: epidemiologic, laboratory and donation characteristics. Transfusion 1991; 31:698.

30. Petersen LR, Doll LS, White CR, et al. Heterosexually acquired human immunodeficiency virus infection and the United States blood supply: considerations for screening of potential blood donors. Transfusion 1993; 33:552.

31. Operskalski EA, Schiff ER, Kleinman SH, et al. Epidemiologic background of blood donors with antibody to human T-cell lymphotropic virus. Transfusion 1989; 29:746.

32. Lee HH, Swanson P, Rosenblatt JD, et al. Relative prevalence and risk factors of HTLV-I and HTLV-II infection in US blood donors. Lancet 1991; 337:1435.

33. Kolho EK, Krusius T. Risk factors for hepatitis C virus antibody positivity in blood donors in a low-risk country. Vox Sang 1992; 63:192.

34. Doll LS, Petersen LR, White CR, et al. Human immunodeficiency virus type 1-infected blood donors: behavioral characteristics and reasons for donation. Transfusion 1991; 31:704.

35. Leitman SF, Klein HG, Melpolder JJ, et al. Clinical implications of positive tests for antibodies to human immunodeficiency virus type 1 in asymptomatic blood donors. N Engl J Med 1989; 321:917.

36. Williams A, Kleinman S, Lamberson H, et al. Assessment of the demographic and motivational characteristics of HIV seropositive blood donors. Paper presented at the III International Conference on AIDS, Washington, DC, June 1987.

37. Mayo DJ. Evaluating donor recruitment strategies. Transfusion 1992; 32:797.

38. Williams AE, Watanabe K, Hansma D, et al. Prevalence and risk relationships of blood donation incentives. Abstracts of FDA Workshop on incentives for volunteer (nonrenumerated) donors. Bethesda, MD, September 1996.

39. Kleinman S. Donor incentives and motivation for donation: data from the CDC sponsored multicenter study of HIV seropositive blood donors. Abstracts of FDA Workshop on incentives for volunteer (nonrenumerated) donors. Bethesda, MD, September 1996.

40. McFarland JG, Aster RH, Buggy BP. Paid time off for blood donation—an incentive to be less than truthful? Transfusion 1997; 37:447.

41. Kleinman SH, Shapiro A. The agreement to donate blood: Presenting information to blood donors and obtaining consent. In: Smith DM, Carlson KB, eds. Current Scientific/Ethical Dilemmas in Blood Banking. Arlington, VA: American Association of Blood Banks, 1987:29.

42. Director of Recruitment Development, National Marrow Donor Program. Policy regarding donor incentives at time of recruitment. Memorandum to donor center & recruitment group coordinators and donor center medical directors, November 22, 1993.

43. Council of Europe. Guide to the Preparation Use and Quality Assurance of Blood Components. Strasbourg: Council of Europe Press, 1992:12.

44. Mason JO. Alternative sites for screening blood for antibodies to AIDS virus. N Engl J Med 1985; 313:1157.

45. Forstein M, Page PL, Coburn TJ. Alternative sites for screening blood for antibodies to AIDS virus. N Engl J Med 1985; 313:1158.

46. Snyder AJ, Vergeront JM. Safeguarding the blood supply by providing opportunities for anonymous HIV testing. N Engl J Med 1988; 319:374.

47. Lackritz EM, Kennedy MB, Doll LS, et al. Risk behaviors and test seeking among HIV-1 positive blood donors. Transfusion 1995; 35(suppl):42S.

48. Williams AE, Thomson RA, Horton JA, Kleinman SH. Characterization of active blood donors who recently donated blood primarily to receive an HIV test. Transfusion 1995; 35(suppl):42S.

49. Korelitz JJ, Busch MP, Williams AE. Antigen testing for human immunodeficiency virus (HIV) and the magnet effect: Will the benefit of a new HIV test be offset by the numbers of higher-risk, test seeking donors attracted to blood centers? Transfusion 1996; 36:203.

50. Stramer SL, Salemi BL, Sievert WS, et al. Evaluation of US blood donations testing positive for HIV-1 p24 antigen. Transfusion 1996; 36(suppl):38S.

51. Dodd RY. Donor screening for HIV in the United States. In: Madhok R, Forbes CD, Evatt BL, eds. Blood, Blood Products and AIDS. London: Chapman & Hall, 1987:143.

52. Director, Office of Biologics Research and Review, Food and Drug Administration. Recommendations to decrease the risk of transmitting acquired immune deficiency syndrome (AIDS) from blood donors. Memorandum to all establishments collecting human blood for transfusion, March 24, 1983.

53. Seage III GR, Barry MA, Landers S, et al. Patterns of blood donations among individuals at risk for AIDS, 1984. Am J Public Health 1988; 78:576.

54. Pindyk J, Waldman A, Zang E, et al. Measures to decrease the risk of acquired immunodeficiency syndrome transmission by blood transfusion. Transfusion 1985; 25:3.

55. Perkins HA, Samson S, Busch MP. How well has self-exclusion worked? Transfusion 1988; 28:601.

56. Busch MP, Young MJ, Samson SM, et al. Risk of human immunodeficiency virus transmission by blood transfusions prior to the implementation of HIV antibody screening in the San Francisco Bay Area. Transfusion 1991; 31:4.

57. Kolins J, Silvergleid AJ. Creating a uniform donor medical history questionnaire. Transfusion 1991; 31:349.

58. American Association of Blood Banks. Uniform donor history questionnaire. Association Bulletin #95-5, Bethesda, MD, June 2, 1995.
59. Sutor LJ, Sussman H, McCraw L, Fortenberry D. Regional standardization of the blood donor medical history screening. Transfusion 1996; 36(suppl):88S.
60. Piliavan JA. Temporary deferral and donor return. Transfusion 1987; 27:199.
61. Sayers MH. Duties to donors. Transfusion 1992; 32:465.
62. Maclennan S, Barbara JA, Hewitt P, et al. Screening blood donations for HCV. Lancet 1992; 339:131.
63. Mayo DJ, Rose AM, Matchett SE, et al. Screening potential blood donors at risk for human immunodeficiency virus. Transfusion 1991; 31:466.
64. Kline L, Friedman LI, Dempesy D, et al. Assessment of blood donor privacy during health history interviews. Transfusion 1996; 36:456.
65. Locke SE, Kowaloff HB, Hoff RG, et al. Computer-based interview for screening blood donors for risk of HIV transmission. JAMA 1992; 268:1301.
65a. Kleinman S, Williams AE. Donor selection procedures: Is it possible to improve them. Trans Med Rev 1998, 12:288.
66. Director, Center for Biologics Evaluation and Research. Recommendations for the prevention of human immunodeficiency virus (HIV) transmission by blood and blood products. Memorandum to all registered blood establishments, April 23, 1992.
67. American Association of Blood Banks. Statement and recommendations of the American Association of Blood Banks regarding donor history questions. Memorandum to institutional members, July 29, 1989.
68. Mosley JW. Who should be our blood donors? Transfusion 1991; 31:684.
69. Westphal RG. Donors and the United States blood supply. Transfusion 1997; 37:237.
70. Director, Center for Biologics Evaluation and Research, Food and Drug Administration. Recommendations for the deferral of current and recent inmates of correctional institutions as donors of whole blood, blood components, source leukocytes, and source plasma. Memorandum to all registered blood establishments, June 8, 1995.
71. Director, Center for Biologics Evaluation and Research, Food and Drug Administration. Interim recommendations for deferral of donors at increased risk for HIV-1 group O infection. Memorandum to all registered blood and plasma establishments, December 11, 1996.
72. O'Brien RT, George JR, Holberg SD. Human immunodeficiency virus type 2 infection in the United States: epidemiology, diagnosis, and public health implications. JAMA 1992; 267:2775.
73. Silvergleid AJ, Leparc GF, Schmidt PJ. Impact of explicit questions about high-risk activities on donor attitudes and donor referral patterns-results in two community blood centers. Transfusion 1989; 29:362.
74. Gimble JG, Friedman LI. Effects of oral donor questioning about high-risk behaviors for human immunodeficiency virus infection. Transfusion 1992; 32:446.
75. Schorr JB, Berkowitz A, Cumming PD, et al. Prevalence of HTLV-III antibody in American blood donors. N Engl J Med 1985; 313:384.
76. Director, Office of Biologics Research and Review, Food and Drug Administration. Revised definition of high risk groups with respect to acquired immunodeficiency

syndrome (AIDS) transmission from blood and plasma donors. Memorandum to all registered blood establishments, September 3, 1985.

77. Sheppard HW, Dondero D, Arnon J, Winkelstein Jr W. An evaluation of the polymerase chain reaction in HIV-1 seronegative men. J AIDS 1991; 4:819.

78. Eble BE, Busch MP, Khayam-Bashi H, et al. Resolution of infection status of HIV-seroindeterminate and high-risk seronegative individuals using PCR and virus-culture: absence of persistent silent HIV-1 infection in a high-prevalence area. Transfusion 1992; 32:503.

79. Jackson JB. Human immunodeficiency virus (HIV) indeterminate Western blots and latent HIV infection. Transfusion 1992; 32:497.

80. Centers for Disease Control and Prevention. Persistent lack of detectable HIV-1 antibody in a person with HIV infection—Utah, 1995. MMWR 1996; 45:181.

81. Busch MP, Satten GA. Time course of viremia and antibody seroconversion following primary HIV infection: implications for management of exposed health care workers. Am J Med 1997; 102(suppl 5B):117.

82. Brookmeyer R. Reconstruction and future trends of the AIDS epidemic in the United States. Science 1991; 253:37.

83. U.S. Department of Health and Human Services, Public Health Service, Centers for Disease Control and Prevention. National HIV Serosurveillance Summary. Results Through 1992. Vol. 3, Atlanta, GA, 1993.

84. Schable C, Zekeng L, Pau CP, et al. Sensitivity of United States HIV antibody tests for detection of HIV-1 group O infections. Lancet 1994; 334:1333.

85. Friedland GH, Saltzman BR, Rogers MF, et al. Lack of transmission of HTLV-III/LAV infection to household contacts of patients with AIDS or AIDS related complex with oral candidiasis. N Engl J Med 1986; 314:344.

86. American Association of Blood Banks. Management of hearsay information about blood donors. Association Bulletin #93-4, Bethesda, MD, December 2, 1993.

87. Elliot D, Craig L, Price T. Resolving hearsay information received on a blood donor. Transfusion 1995; 35(suppl):71S.

88. Director, Center for Biologics Evaluation and Research, Food and Drug Administration. Revised recommendations for testing whole blood, blood components, source plasma and source leukocytes for antibody to hepatitis C virus encoded antigen (anti-HCV). Memorandum to all registered blood establishments, April 23, 1992.

89. Alter HJ, Purcell RH, Shih JW, et al. Detection of antibody to hepatitis C virus in prospective followed transfusion recipients with acute and chronic non-A, non-B hepatitis. N Engl J Med 1989; 321:1494.

90. Director, Center for Biologics Evaluation and Research, Food and Drug Administration. Donor suitability related to laboratory testing for viral hepatitis and a history of viral hepatitis. Memorandum to all registered blood establishments, December 22, 1993.

91. Director, Center for Biologics Evaluation and Research, Food and Drug Administration. Exemptions to permit persons with a history of viral hepatitis before the age of eleven years to serve as donors of whole blood and plasma: alternative procedures, 21 CFR 640.120. Memorandum to all registered blood establishments, April 23, 1992.

92. Trepo C. International forum: Should donors with a history of jaundice still be rejected? Vox Sang 1981; 41:110.

93. Sheretz RJ, Russell BA, Reuman PD. Transmission of hepatitis A by transfusion of blood products. Arch Intern Med 1984; 144:1579.

94. Alter HJ. Discussion: transfusion associated hepatitis. In: Polesky H, Walker RH, eds. Safety in Transfusion Practices. Skokie, IL: College of American Pathologists, 1980:32.

95. Polesky HF, Hanson M. Tests for viral hepatitis markers in blood donors. In: Polesky HF, Walker RH, eds. Safety in Transfusion Practices. Skokie, IL: College of American Pathologists, 1980:17.

96. Aach RD. International forum: Should donors with a history of jaundice still be rejected? Vox Sang 1981; 41:110.

97. Perillo RP, Gleb L, Campbell C, et al. Hepatitis B antigen, DNA polymerase activity, and infection of household contacts with hepatitis B virus. Gastroenterology 1979; 76:1319.

98. Alter MJ. The detection, transmission, and outcome of hepatitis C virus infection. Infect Agents Dis 1993; 2:155.

99. Seeff, LB, Alter HJ. Spousal transmission of the hepatitis C virus? Ann Intern Med 1994; 120:807.

100. Guerrero IC, Weniger BC, Schultz MG. Transfusion malaria in the United States, 1972–1981. Ann Intern Med 1983; 99:221.

101. Nahlen BL, Lobel HO, Cannon SE, Campbell CC. Reassessment of blood donor selection criteria for United States travelers to malarious areas. Transfusion 1991; 31:798.

102. Director, Center for Biologics Evaluation and Research, Food and Drug Administration. Recommendations for deferral of donors for malaria risk. Memorandum to all registered blood establishments, July 26, 1994.

103. Sazama K. Prevention of transfusion-transmitted malaria: Is it time to revisit the standards? Transfusion 1991; 31:786.

104. Bruce-Chwatt LJ. International Forum: Which are the appropriate modifications of existing regulations designed to prevent transmission of malaria by blood transfusion, in view of the increasing frequency of travel to endemic areas? Vox Sang 1987; 52:138.

104a. Centers for Disease Control and Prevention. Transfusion-transmitted malaria—Missouri and Pennsylvania MMWR 1999; 48:253.

105. Wendal S, Gonzaga AL. Chagas' disease and blood transfusion: a new world problem? Vox Sang 1993; 64:1.

106. Leiby DA, Yund J, Read EJ, et al. Risk factors for Trypanosoma cruzi infection in seropositive blood donors. Transfusion 1996; 36(suppl):57S.

107. Mintz ED, Anderson JF, Cable RG, et al. Transfusion-transmitted babesiosis: a case report from a new endemic area. Transfusion 1991; 31:365.

108. Gerber MA, Shapiro ED, Krause PJ, et al. The risk of acquiring Lyme disease or babesiosis from a blood transfusion. J Infect Dis 1994; 170:231.

109. Popovsky MA, Lindberg LE, Syrek AL, Page PL. Prevalence of babesia antibody in a selected blood donor population. Transfusion 1988; 28:59.

110. American Association of Blood Banks Bulletin. Recommendations regarding babe-

siosis and potential transmission of blood transfusion. American Association of Blood Banks, Arlington, VA, July 29, 1989.

111. Brown P, Gibbs CJ, et al. Human spongiform encephalopathy: the NIH series of 300 cases of experimentally transmitted disease. Ann Neurol 1994; 44:513.

112. DeArmond SJ, Pruisner SB. Etiology and pathogenesis of prion diseases. Am J Pathol 1995; 146:785.

113. Brown P, Preece MA, Will RG. Friendly fire in medicine: hormones, homografts, and Creutzfeldt-Jacob disease. Lancet 1992; 340:24.

114. Esmonde TFG, Will RG, Slattery JM, et al. CJD and blood transfusion. Lancet 1993; 341:205.

115. Heye N, Hensen S, Muller N. CJD and blood transfusion. Lancet 1994; 343:298.

116. Brown P. Can Creutzfeldt-Jacob disease be transmitted by transfusion. Curr Opin Hematol 1995; 2:472.

117. Director, Office of Biologics Research and Review, Food and Drug Administration; Deferral of donors who have received human pituitary derived growth hormone. Memorandum to all registered blood establishments, November 25, 1987.

118. Acting Director, Office of Blood Research and Review, Center for Biologics Evaluation and Research, Food and Drug Administration. Deferral of blood and plasma donors based on medications. Memorandum to all registered blood and plasma establishments, July 28, 1993.

119. Director, Center for Biologics Evaluation and Research, Food and Drug Administration. Precautionary measures to further reduce the possible risk of transmission of Creutzfeldt-Jacob disease by blood and blood products. Memorandum to all registered blood and plasma establishments, August 8, 1995.

120. Director, Center for Biologics Evaluation and Research, Food and Drug Administration. Revised precautionary measures to further reduce the possible risk of transmission of Creutzfeldt-Jacob disease by blood and blood products. Memorandum to all registered blood and plasma establishments and all establishments engaged in manufacturing plasma derivatives, December 11, 1996.

120a. Center for Biologics Evaluation and Research, Food and Drug Administration. Change to the Guidance entitled "Revised precautionary measures to further reduce the possible risk of transmission of Creutzfeldt-Jacob disease by blood and blood products." September 1998.

120b. Will RG, Ironside JW, Zeidler M, et al. A new variant of Creutzfeldt-Jacob disease in the UK. Lancet 1996; 347:921–925.

120c. Murphy MF. New variant Creutzfeldt-Jacob disease (nvCJD): the risk of transmission by blood transfusion and the potential benefit of leukocyte-reduction of blood components. Transfusion Med Rev 1999; 13:75–83.

120d. Hill AF, Debruslais M, Joiner S, et al. The same prion strain causes vCJD and BSE. Nature 1997; 389:448–450.

120e. Hill AF, Butterworth RJ, Joiner S, et al. Investigation of variant Creutzfeldt-Jacob disease and other human prion diseases with tonsil biopsy samples. Lancet 1999; 353:183–189.

120f. Hoey J, Giulivi A, Todkill AM. New variant Creutzfeldt-Jakob disease and the blood supply: Is it time to face the music? (editorial). Can Med Assoc J 1998; 159(6):669–670.

121. Fradkin JE, Schonberger LB, Mills JL, et al. CJD in pituitary growth hormone recipients in the United States. JAMA 1991; 265:880.

122. Holland PV. Why a new standard to prevent Creutzfeld-Jacob disease? Transfusion 1988; 28:293.

123. Kessler D, Bianco C. Donor deferrals related to Creutzfeldt-Jacob disease. Transfusion 1996; 36(suppl):57S.

124. Goldman M, Blajchman MA. Blood product-associated bacterial sepsis. Trans Med Rev 1991; 5:73.

125. Blajchman MA, Ali AM. Bacteria in the blood supply: an overlooked issue in transfusion medicine. In: Nance SJ, ed. Blood Safety: Current Challenges. Bethesda, MD: American Association of Blood Banks, 1992: 213.

126. Anderson KC, Lew MA, Gorgone BC, et al. Transfusion-related sepsis after prolonged platelet storage. Am J Med 1986; 81:405.

127. American Association of Blood Banks. Bacterial contamination of blood products. Association Bulletin #96-6, Bethesda, MD, August 7, 1996.

128. Ness PM, Perkins HA. Transient bacteremia after dental procedures and other minor manipulations. Transfusion 1980; 20:82.

129. Richards C, Kolins J, Trindade CD. Autologous transfusion-transmitted *Yersinia enterocolitica*. JAMA 1992; 268:1541.

130. Sherwood WC. Donor deferral registries. Transfusion Med Rev 1993; VII:121.

131. Grossman BJ, Springer KM. Blood donor deferral registries: highlights of a conference. Transfusion 1992; 32:868.

132. Grewal ID, Domen RE, Hirschler NV. The value of shared donor deferral registries. Transfusion 1995; 35(suppl):66S.

133. Department of Health and Human Services, Food and Drug Administration. Additional recommendations for reducing further the number of units of blood and plasma donated for transfusion or for further manufacture by persons at increased risk of HTLV-III/LAV infection. Memorandum to all registered blood establishments, October 30, 1986.

134. Ciavetta J, Nusbacher J, Wall A. Donor self-exclusion patterns and human immunodeficiency virus antibody test results over a twelve month period. Transfusion 1989; 29:81.

135. Loiacono BR, Carter GR, Carter CS, et al. Efficacy of various methods of confidential unit exclusion in identifying potentially infectious blood donations. Transfusion 1989; 29:823.

136. Busch MP, Perkins HA, Holland PV, et al. Questionable efficacy of confidential unit exclusion (letter). Transfusion 1990; 30:668.

137. Petersen LR, Busch MP. Confidential unit exclusion: How should it be evaluated? Transfusion 1991; 31:870.

138. Kean CA, Hsueh Y, Querin JJ, et al. A study of confidential unit exclusion. Transfusion 1990; 30:707.

139. Wolles S, Galel S. Value of confidential unit exclusion. Transfusion 1993; 33(suppl):80S.

140. Kessler D, Valinsky JE, Bianco C. Sensitivity and Specificity of confidential unit exclusion (CUE)-Does it work? Transfusion 1993; 33(suppl):35S.

141. Menitove JE, Lewandowski C, Ashworth LW, et al. Confidential unit exclusion

process continues to identify donors with an increased frequency of HIV seropositivity. Transfusion 1991; 31:69S.

142. Kleinman S, Crawley P. An assessment of HIV related donor screening procedures. Transfusion 1988; 28(suppl):42S.

143. Weitekamp LA, Meyer TL. Second chance for self deferring donors. Transfusion 1995; 35(suppl):72S.

144. Petersen LR, Lackritz E, Lewis WF, et al. The effectiveness of the confidential unit exclusion option. Transfusion 1994; 34:865.

145. Korelitz JJ, Williams AE, Busch MP, et al. Demographic characteristics and prevalence of serologic markers among donors who use the confidential unit exclusion process: The Retrovirus Epidemiology Donor Study. Transfusion 1994; 34:870.

146. Kleinman SH, Busch MP, Korelitz JJ, Schreiber GB. The incidence/window period model and its use to assess the risk of transfusion-transmitted HIV and HCV infection. Trans Med Rev 1997; 11:155.

147. Nusbacher J, Chiavetta J, Naiman R, et al. Evaluation of a confidential method of excluding blood donors exposed to human immunodeficiency virus: studies on hepatitis and cytomegalovirus markers. Transfusion 1987; 27:207.

148. Kimball P, Popovsky MA. Analysis of post-donation information: need for improved pre-donation education. Transfusion 1995; 35(suppl):34S.

149. Goldman M, Long A, Roy G, et al. Incidence of positive bacterial cultures after donor call-back (letter). Transfusion 1996; 36:1035.

150. Samson SA, Edmiston RK, Busch MP, Perkins HA: How well has donor call-back worked? Transfusion 1993; 33(suppl):35S.

151. Keelan LT, Grindon AJ. Units saved by investigation of post-donation information. Transfusion 1996; 36(suppl):16S.

152. Director, Center for Biologics Evaluation and Research, Food and Drug Administration. Guidance regarding post donation information reports. Memorandum to all registered blood and plasma establishments, December 10, 1993.

153. Center for Biologics Evaluation and Research, Division of Inspections and Surveillance. Error and Accident Reports-Summary for FY-96, April, 1997.

154. American Association of Blood Banks. Guidance on notifying recipients of blood components from a donor who subsequently was diagnosed as having CJD and/or CJD risk factors. Association Bulletin 96-4, May 3, 1996.

155. Busch MP. Let's look at human immunodeficiency virus lookback before leaping into hepatitis C virus lookback. Transfusion 1991; 31:655.

156. Department of Health and Human Services. Current good manufacturing practices for blood and blood components; notification of consignees receiving blood and blood components at increased risk for transmitting HIV. Fed Reg 1996; 61:47413.

157. Director, Center for Biologics Evaluation and Research, Food and Drug Administration. Recommendations for donor screening with a licensed test for HIV-1 antigen Memorandum to all registered blood and plasma establishments, August 8, 1995.

158. Center for Biologics Evaluation and Research. Food and Drug Administration. Current Good Manufacturing Practice for Blood and Blood Components: (1) Quarantine and disposition of prior collections from donors with repeatedly reactive screening tests for Hepatitis C virus (HCV); (2) Supplemental testing and the notification of consignees and transfusion recipients of donor test results for antibody to HCV (anti-HCV). Draft Guidance for industry, Rockville, MD, June 1999.

159. U.S. Public Health Service. Briefing document on public health service options for the identification of hepatitis C virus infection among prior transfusion recipients, Washington, D.C., March 28, 1996.

2
Hemolytic Transfusion Reactions

Elizabeth J. Kicklighter and Harvey G. Klein
National Institutes of Health, Bethesda, Maryland

I. HISTORICAL PERSPECTIVES

The concept of blood transfusion began with the description of the circulation of blood by William Harvey in 1628. By the late 1660s, Jean Denis in France and Richard Lowery in England were performing the first documented blood transfusions into humans. Both used animals as the source of blood (1). In view of what is now known about "antispecies" antibodies, it is not surprising that the first description of a hemolytic transfusion reaction (HTR) was recorded by Denis in 1668 after giving a second infusion of calf's blood to a patient. Some of the same symptoms described with this reaction—diaphoresis, back pain, tachycardia, dyspnea, gastrointestinal distress, and dark urine—remain classic findings for the severe HTRs seen today (2). Denis's patient died after a third transfusion attempt, and blood transfusions were subsequently banned by the French and British medical societies (3).

In 1818, James Blundell rekindled interest in blood transfusion for use primarily in the treatment of postpartum hemorrhage. He was the first to transfuse blood from one human to another and to discourage the use of animals as donors (1). The mortality rate of his patients was extremely high. However, because Blundell's patients were very ill, the role of incompatible blood and hemolytic reactions in their clinical course is difficult to evaluate. Nevertheless, indiscriminate use of blood transfusions by others during this period resulted in unacceptable rates of severe hemolytic reactions (4).

The modern era of blood transfusion began with Karl Landsteiner's discover of the ABO blood group system in 1900. Initially, few people understood the significance of Landsteiner's reports. In 1907, Richard Weil and Reuben Ottenburg were among the first to recognize that if red cells bearing "foreign" ABO antigens are infused into a recipient with the corresponding antibodies (isohemagglutinins), severe acute hemolysis could result. Ottenburg became the first to perform ABO typing of patient and donor prior to transfusion (5). Unfortunately, clinicians often refused to comply with requests for pretransfusion laboratory specimens, giving Ottenburg many opportunities to observe the extremes of immune-mediated hemolysis that occur as a result of ABO incompatibility. In 1921, Unger hastened the acceptance of pretransfusion testing by publishing a series of cases with serious acute HTRs that could have been avoided by honoring pretransfusion testing demonstrating ABO incompatibility (6). Because few red cell antigens outside of the ABO system can be directly agglutinated by human antibodies, no new blood group systems were found for more than 25 years.

In 1945, the development of the antiglobulin test by Coombs et al. revolutionized the field of immunohematology. The indirect and direct antiglobulin tests (IAT and DAT, respectively) are the primary means by which antibodies to red cell antigens are detected. The ability to detect antibody on red cells provided a critical tool for recognizing immune-mediated HTRs. Of the 254 classified red cell antigens and 23 established blood group systems (7), many were first detected by an antiglobulin test performed on patients with HTRs or accelerated destruction of transfused red cells.

A better understanding of the immune response to foreign red cell antigens and rigorous pretransfusion testing have made transfusion of blood remarkably safe. Still, 0.5–3% of all transfusions result in some adverse event (8) (Table 1). The majority of adverse effects are relatively innocuous. Of the life-threatening reactions, the general public tends to focus on transfusion-transmitted infections. Nevertheless, the risk of immune-mediated hemolysis often necessitates extensive serological testing to evaluate compatibility between donor and recipient and arguably may be the most important factor limiting the availability of blood. Acute HTRs remain the most common cause of immediate life-threatening complications associated with blood transfusion.

II. CLASSIFICATION OF TRANSFUSION-RELATED HEMOLYSIS

An HTR is defined as the immune destruction of red cells mediated by an antibody directed against the corresponding red cell antigen despite the best efforts to provide compatible cells (9). HTRs are categorized as being acute or delayed, as well as intravascular or extravascular. The manifestations, differential diagnosis, and management can vary significantly among these groups.

Table 1 Classification of Transfusion Reactions

Acute
  Immune Mediated
    Acute hemolytic transfusion reaction (AHTR)
    Transfusion-related acute lung injury
    Febrile nonhemolytic transfusion reaction
    Urticarial reaction
    Anaphylactic
  Non-Immune Mediated
    Nonimmune hemolysis
    Bacterial contamination
    Volume overload
    Metabolic
    Embolic
Delayed
  Immune Mediated
    Delayed hemolytic transfusion reaction
      (DHTR)
    Posttransfusion purpura
    Graft-versus-host disease
  Non–Immune Mediated
    Transfusion-transmitted infection
    Iron overload

However, not all incidents of transfusion-related hemolysis are HTRs, nor are they all mediated through immunological pathways. Several nonimmune mechanisms can result in transfusion-related hemolysis (2). In addition, not all hemolysis seen during or after blood transfusion results from the blood infusion itself. Hemolysis that is temporally related but not etiologically related to transfusion can be termed a "pseudo"-HTR. Therefore, the history, careful analysis of events, and laboratory evaluation of hemolysis during or after a transfusion all play critical roles in the immediate and subsequent management of suspected HTRs.

A. Immune-Mediated Versus Non–Immune-Mediated Hemolysis

An HTR occurs when a blood recipient has or subsequently develops antibodies directed against antigens found on transfused red cells, resulting in accelerated destruction of those cells. The recipient may mount an immune response if the antigens on the infused cells are recognized as foreign. Antigenic stimulation may occur as a result of blood transfusion, transplantation, or pregnancy. Pregnancy presents a much lower immunogenic challenge than does blood transfusion, probably because the number of foreign antigens is limited to those of the father and because the number of cells entering the mother's circulation is often too small to initiate a primary response (10). However, immune-mediated HTRs are almost three times more common in females than in males because of prior sensitization during pregnancy (9). The susceptibility to alloimmunization as a result of transfusion appears to be the same in males and females. The risk of forming an alloantibody to a (non-ABO) red cell antigen after the infusion of one unit of red cells has been estimated to be 1% (11). The increased frequency of HTRs reported with age appears simply to reflect the increased frequency of transfusion with age (9).

There is a wide spectrum of potential immune responses to allogeneic red cells. The range of outcomes includes immediate intravascular hemolysis; delayed extravascular hemolysis characterized by red cell alloantibodies, which promote phagocytosis by macrophages; seroconversion without obvious hemolysis; or, at the far end of the spectrum, no detectable immune response. Acute intravascular hemolysis usually results from preformed complement-fixing antibodies. The best known examples are the ABO "naturally occurring" isohemagglutinins, which occur in the absence of exposure to allogeneic red cells. Delayed hemolysis characteristically results from a secondary or anamnestic response to a previously encountered antigen. Seroconversion in this context is defined as the detection of red cell alloantibodies after antigenic stimulation. Seroconversion without evidence of clinical hemolysis is characteristic of a primary immune response. In some cases there may have been subclinical hemolysis that resulted in clearing of the sensitizing red cells. No detectable immune response is defined as an absence of red cell alloantibodies in individuals who have had repeated exposure to red cell alloantigens (3).

To complicate matters further, the clinical significance of red cell alloantibodies varies widely. Antibodies to some red cell antigens never result in hemolysis, but most antibodies vary significantly in their clinical activity and may result in severe hemolysis in one patient while resulting in delayed, subclinical, or no hemolysis in another patient. Anti-A and anti-B usually cause immediate, life-threatening hemolysis, but case reports document patients without symptoms, even after transfusion of an entire unit of ABO-incompatible blood. Antibodies to red cell antigens in the Rh, Kell, Kidd, or Duffy systems may cause extremely serious hemolysis in one patient but only shortened red cell survival with no significant clinical symptoms in another (6). The detection of a red cell antibody does not mean that hemolysis will occur. While in vitro hemolysis and a broad thermal amplitude often suggest a clinically significant antibody, no single laboratory test or combination of tests allows one to determine the specific in vivo activity of an alloantibody. As a rule of thumb, antibodies that react in vitro at temperatures of 30°C and above should be respected, whereas most antibodies that react only at colder temperatures, even when present in high titers, are clinically unimportant.

The immunogenicity of red cell antigens varies widely. Immune responses to the Rh(D) red cell antigen have been studied most carefully. The D antigen is among the most immunogenic and clinically significant of the red cell allo-antigens. Sixty to 80% of D-negative individuals will produce anti-D after repeated immunizations (12). Anti-D is capable of causing severe HTRs. The dose of D-positive cells required for primary immunization can vary from less than 1 mL to as much as 200 mL (12). The time of appearance of anti-D after primary immunization varies among individuals. Low levels of anti-D may first be detected at about 4 weeks (10), or anti-D may not be detected by standard serologic techniques for up to 5 months after exposure to the D antigen (13). There have been few systematic studies of immune responses to alloantigens other than D. In general, D-negative subjects who form anti-D are capable of forming other red cell alloantibodies, whereas those who do not form anti-D seldom form any red cell alloantibodies (10).

In contrast to active immunization, which results in the formation of red cell alloantibodies by the recipient, transfusion of plasma-containing components can result in passive transfer of donor antibodies to the recipient. If the passively acquired antibody is directed against an antigen on recipient red cells or other transfused red cells in the recipient, accelerated destruction of the antigen-positive cells could occur. Because donors are screened for the presence of antibodies to common red cell antigens, these reactions are unusual. Two situations that might result in passive hemolysis are (a) emergency transfusion of group O whole blood to non–group O patients, or (b) use of plasma from donors who have a red cell alloantibody that is directed toward a low-incidence antigen not present on routine screening cells.

While immune-mediated hemolysis is the most common mechanism re-sponsible for severe HTRs, non–immune-mediated destruction of red cells must always be considered in the differential diagnosis of hemolytic reactions (Table 2). Non–immune-mediated hemolysis typically occurs before or during the infusion process and is due to improper component preparation, storage, or infusion. Some hemolysis may also be seen with the infusion of aged cells.

Non–immune-mediated hemolysis can produce signs and symptoms that mimic those of immune-mediated hemolysis, such as hemoglobinuria and ab-sence of the expected increment in hemoglobin, but the most severe symptoms and complications associated with immune-mediated hemolysis are usually ab-sent (2). A notable exception is hemolysis resulting from bacterial contamination of the blood unit, which often presents with fever and rigors that lead to shock before the entire unit is transfused. Fortunately, with current donor screening,

Table 2 Mechanisms of Nonimmune Hemolysis of Donor Cells

Transfusion of aged cells
Thermal hemolysis (overheating, freezing)
Osmotic hemolysis (inadequate deglycerolization, administration with hypotonic
    solutions or drugs)
Mechanical hemolysis (improper infusion devices, catheters, or needles)
Bacterial/parasitic contamination
Hemolysis due to congenital defects (G6PD deficiency, sickle trait)

---

aseptic methods of collection and storage, and meticulous handling of blood, the frequency of such reactions appears to be low.

Other mechanisms of non–immune-mediated hemolysis include thermal, mechanical, osmotic, and toxic damage to red cells from improper storage or handling (2). Either overheating or freezing without an appropriate cryopreservative can result in significant hemolysis. Appropriate thermal monitoring should be performed at every stage of blood collection, transport, storage, and infusion. Blood should never be stored in an unmonitored refrigerator or warmed with a device that has not been certified for this purpose. Transfusion of previously frozen but inadequately deglycerolized red cells can result in osmotic hemolysis. Osmotic hemolysis can also result from a simultaneous infusion of red cells and a hypotonic solution. Mechanical trauma can lyse transfused red cells, especially during infusion. For this reason, only pumps and other equipment that have been properly validated for infusion of blood and blood components should be used.

Non–immune-mediated hemolysis may occur in vivo posttransfusion, from congenital defects of transfused red cells, such as glucose-6-phosphate dehydrogenase (G6PD) deficiency, or from contamination with malarial parasites. The latter is common in the developing world, but rare in donors screened in the United States. Non–immune-mediated hemolysis can occur with the infusion of both allogeneic and autologous blood products. Since there are no screening tests for non–immune-mediated hemolysis that might occur in red cell units during storage, visual inspection of each unit for hemolysis prior to issue and prior to infusion is essential.

B. Acute Versus Delayed Transfusion Reactions

Acute hemolytic transfusion reactions (AHTR) are due to the immune-mediated destruction of red cells that occurs during or within hours of the infusion of blood. An AHTR represents immune-mediated hemolysis due to an antibody present in the recipient at the time of the infusion that reacts with donor red cells. Depending on the nature of the antibody and its ability to bind complement, the reaction can result in intravascular or extravascular hemolysis.

Delayed hemolytic transfusion reactions (DHTR) are the result of immune-mediated hemolysis that occurs days to weeks after the transfusion but is a direct result of the transfusion. There is usually an anamnestic antibody response in which antibody titers rise to detectable levels after transfusion of red cells that bear an alloantigen to which the recipient has been previously sensitized. Most DHTRs result in extravascular hemolysis. However, DHTRs can be associated with intravascular hemolysis, leading to life-threatening complications.

C. Intravascular Versus Extravascular Hemolysis

Intravascular hemolysis is the lysis of red cell membranes within the lumen of the blood vessel, with release of hemoglobin into the plasma. Immune-mediated intravascular hemolysis can occur if the antibody is capable of activating the complete complement cascade. Intravascular hemolysis is frequently rapid, occurring with only a few milliliters of blood, and can lead to shock, acute renal failure, bleeding due to disseminated intravascular coagulation (DIC), and death (14).

Extravascular hemolysis occurs when red cells are phagocytized by macrophages at the reticuloendothelial system (RES). Immune-mediated extravascular hemolysis occurs with alloantibodies that do not bind complement or that activate only a portion of the complement pathway. Most red cell antibodies will promote the removal of red cells via the RES, unlike anti-A and anti-B, which are most efficient at causing intravascular hemolysis. Extravascular hemolysis is usually not clinically severe, as the rate of hemolysis is usually much slower. Often, hemolytic reactions are a combination of intravascular and extravascular hemolysis. The clinical manifestations and therapy depend on the mechanism that predominates (14).

D. "Pseudo"-Hemolytic Transfusion Reactions

Finally, things are not always as they seem. Hemolysis that occurs during or after a transfusion may not be related to the transfusion (Table 3). For example, medications administered in temporal proximity to a transfusion may cause hemolysis of the recipient's own blood by several immune mechanisms or through a nonimmune mechanism such as hypotonicity (15). A patient with underlying G6PD deficiency or sickle cell trait might develop hemolysis, especially in the operative setting, which could mimic a transfusion reaction. Hemolysis may also result from an underlying primary infection in the patient, such as malaria, clostridial infection, or infectious mononucleosis, which is unrelated to transfusion. Hemolysis of red cells can be due to mechanical trauma from

Table 3 Mechanisms of Hemolysis from Causes Other than Transfusion:
"Pseudo"-Hemolytic Transfusion Reactions

Immune Mediated
  Autoimmune hemolytic anemia
  Drug-induced anemia: various immune mechanisms
Nonimmune Mediated
  Osmotic damage (hypotonic solutions, drugs, bladder irrigation)
  Congenital red cell abnormalities in recipient (sickle cell disease, sickle trait,
    G6PD deficiency)
  Infection-induced hemolysis (infection in recipient unrelated to transfusion: malaria,
    clostridial infection, etc.)
  Microangiopathic hemolysis (disseminated intravascular coagulation, thrombotic
    thrombocytopenic purpura/hemolytic uremic syndrome)
  Mechanical hemolysis (valvular and arterial prostheses, extracorporeal circulation)
  Reabsorption of blood from internal hemorrhage

---

valvular or arterial protheses, DIC, or thrombotic thrombocytopenic purpura-
hemolytic uremic syndrome. In addition, the picture of hemolysis, especially
delayed hemolysis, can be mimicked by the reabsorption of blood after an internal
hemorrhage or with a large hematoma (9).

Two clinical situations merit particular attention: (a) distinguishing between
a sickle cell crisis from a DHTR, and (b) distinguishing alloimmune hemolysis
from autoimmune hemolytic anemia, where the hemolysis is related to the
underlying disease process. Both situations present a difficult, but important,
diagnostic and management problem. These examples emphasize the importance
of obtaining a meticulous clinical history, physical examination, and pertinent
laboratory data when an HTR is suspected.

III. THE ACUTE HEMOLYTIC TRANSFUSION REACTION

AHTRs almost invariably represent immune-mediated hemolysis occurring as the
result of circulating red cell antibody in the recipient that is directed toward a red
cell antigen carried on the transfused red cells. The antibody may be "naturally
occurring" or one to which the recipient has been previously sensitized, resulting
in the rapid onset of hemolysis. The symptoms occur during or within hours of
the infusion. The most serious reactions usually result from ABO incompatibility,
but incompatibility in the Rh, Kell, Duffy, and Kidd systems exceed ABO blood
type mismatch in frequency as the cause of acute hemolysis (9).

The frequency of AHTRs appears to be declining (16). However, estimates
of AHTR frequency vary depending on the level of awareness of transfusion-

related complications in the persons performing the transfusions, as well as on the presence of underlying conditions in recipients that might mask the signs and symptoms of a hemolytic reaction. The estimated frequency of AHTRs is approximately 1 of 25,000 red cell units (17), while fatal HTRs occur in approximately 1 of 600,000 red cell units transfused (18).

In 1975, the U.S. Food and Drug Administration mandated the reporting of deaths associated with blood collection and transfusion. In 1990, Sazama reviewed these data for a 10 year period (1976 1985). The most commonly reported cause of death was acute immune-mediated hemolysis, accounting for 158 of 355 deaths (51%). Acute non–immune-mediated hemolysis accounted for 6 deaths, while delayed immune-mediated hemolysis was responsible for 26 deaths during this same period. ABO incompatibility clearly caused 131 of the 158 fatalities (83%). Of the remaining 27 deaths due to AHTR, most were suspected to be ABO related, but appropriate documentation was lacking. Only 9 of the 158 deaths due to AHTR were definitely the result of incompatibilities in other red cell antigen systems (19).

Case reviews indicate that fatal AHTRs have occurred as a result of human error, most commonly an error in identification at the time of blood infusion (77/158 or 49%) (Table 4). These errors tend to be associated with inadequate training of the personnel administering the blood in the proper identification procedures (19). In a review in New York State, Linden et al. reported the risk of a transfusion error as 1 in 12,000 red cell units transfused, with a 1 in 33,000 risk of an ABO- incompatible transfusion, and a risk of 1 in 600,000 for a fatal transfusion error. Forty-three percent of these errors resulted from failure to properly identify the patient or the unit prior to transfusion, and 11% resulted from identification errors at the time of recipient sample collection. While the majority (58%) of these errors occurred outside of the blood bank, the blood bank alone was responsible for 25% of errors; combined errors of the blood bank and other hospital services contributed to 17% of errors (18). AHTRs tend to occur in urgent situations that require large amounts of blood, such as during surgery, in the emergency department, or in the intensive care unit. But they can occur in any setting if proper operating procedure for handling and identifying blood products is not followed.

Table 4 Most Common Errors Resulting in Death

Blood given to wrong patient
Errors in obtaining and labeling pretransfusion specimen from patient
Serological mistakes
Clerical errors in laboratory
Wrong blood issued from laboratory

A. Clinical Presentation and Differential Diagnosis

Because the earliest signs and symptoms of hemolysis are nonspecific, all personnel involved with ordering and administering blood products must maintain a high level of suspicion (Table 5). Prompt recognition and appropriate management of a transfusion reaction may prevent a death (16,20). No pathognomonic signs or symptoms clearly differentiate an AHTR from other acute transfusion reactions. The clinical presentation may vary widely because signs and symptoms depend on a number of different factors, including the antibody specificity, the quantity of antigen on the transfused cells, the quantity of incompatible cells infused, the immunoglobulin class and subclass of the antibody, the antibody titer, the thermal amplitude of the antibody, the ability of the antibody to activate complement, as well as the clinical condition of the patient (2). Almost every symptom experienced during or after the infusion of red cells, except for isolated urticaria and/or simple pruritis, should raise the possibility of hemolysis and should be properly evaluated.

Classically, fever, defined as an increase in body temperature of greater than one degree Celsius, is considered the most common initial manifestation of immune hemolysis, whether acute or delayed (9). In approximately 50% of the cases, fever will be accompanied by chills (21). A patient often experiences a vague uneasiness and pain or discomfort at the infusion site during the early stages of an AHTR. Generalized flushing, nausea and other gastrointestinal symptoms, dyspnea, chest pain, back pain, and headache or lightheadedness occur less commonly. The most severe transfusion reactions may begin with hypotension and rapidly progress to shock. Hemolysis may result in hemoglobinemia and hemoglobinuria. Evidence of renal dysfunction, including oliguria or anuria, may be part of the clinical presentation in more severe reactions. Rarely, a patient may develop generalized oozing or fulminant bleeding as a result of DIC.

Table 5   Signs and Symptoms of Acute Hemolytic Transfusion Reaction

Fever, chills
Flushing, diaphoresis
Localized pain (infusion site, chest, back)
Anxiety, agitation, feeling of impending doom
Dyspnea, tachycardia
Gastrointestinal symptoms (nausea, emesis, diarrhea, abdominal pain)
Hemoglobinemia, hemoglobinuria
Hypertension, hypotension, shock
Oliguria, anuria
Generalized bleeding
Cardiac arrest

If the patient is unconscious, as when under anesthesia, after trauma, or in shock, or if the patient is an infant or a very young child, the diagnosis can be particularly difficult. Early prodromal symptoms may be absent. Hypotension, hemoglobinuria, shock, or a bleeding diathesis may be the first and only indication of an HTR (2). It is generally accepted that hemolytic reactions are underrecognized and underreported in these settings. These patients may be given additional units of incompatible blood prior to the realization that an HTR has occurred (3).

The clinical spectrum of an AHTR can vary from immediately life threatening to subclinical hemolysis. The severity of a reaction cannot be predicted by early signs and symptoms. Rarely, a patient may hemolyze an entire unit of blood and yet show no adverse clinical manifestations. However, any patient transfused with a unit of blood that is found to be incompatible because of an antibody associated with severe intravascular hemolysis must be monitored as if life-threatening hemolysis is occurring.

B. Pathophysiology of Potential Complications

The most feared complications of acute immune-mediated intravascular HTRs are hypotension progressing to shock, DIC with diffuse bleeding, and renal failure leading to oliguria and anuria (3). The morbidity and mortality rates of AHTR appear to be directly related to the occurrence of renal failure or DIC (21). It is important to understand the pathophysiology of these most serious complications so that the most effective intervention can be provided. Activation of the coagulation cascade and alteration of the vasomotor tone are among the most damaging consequences of these reactions and, if not recognized early and treated effectively, can result in a downward spiral of clinical events culminating in death.

Activation of the complement system by antigen-antibody complexes leads to the production of anaphylatoxins (C3a and C5a), causing degranulation of mast cells with the release of histamine and serotonin. These vasoactive amines are thought to increase vascular permeability and cause bronchial and intestinal smooth muscle contraction as well as release of lysosomal enzymes from neutrophils. In addition, C5a can act directly on capillaries to induce vasodilation, further worsening hypotension (10). Immune-mediated activation of complement and Factor XII (Hageman factor) can result in activation of the coagulation cascade and, if unchecked, can result in DIC with uncontrolled bleeding. Thromboplastic substances from lysed red cells probably only potentiate the intravascular coagulation. Nonimmune causes of hemolysis are not usually associated with DIC (2).

Activation of Hageman factor can also lead to the production and activation of bradykinin. Bradykinin causes increased capillary permeability and dilation of arterioles, resulting in hypotension, flushing, and localized pain. Another important group of intracellular mediators, catecholamines, are released in response to hypotension and in response to immune mechanisms. Catecholamine activation contributes to localized pain and can cause tachycardia and gastrointestinal symptoms such as nausea and vomiting (22).

The combined effects of systemic hypotension, renal vasoconstriction, and clotting within the renal vasculature often lead to renal ischemia. Depending on the degree and duration of ischemia, the effect may be a transient decrease in renal function, temporary acute tubular necrosis, or permanent renal failure secondary to bilateral renal cortical necrosis (3). In animal studies, free hemoglobin is not directly toxic to the kidneys except in the presence of dehydration and, by itself, is not thought to have a significant role in renal dysfunction (2).

Recently, there has been increased interest in the potential role of the cellular immune system during transfusion reactions. A variety of cytokines [tumor necrosis factor, interleukin (IL)-1, IL-6, IL-8, and monocyte chemoattractant protein] have been implicated as mediators of many of the systemic effects produced by immune-mediated intravascular hemolysis (23). New research into cytokines as inflammatory mediators in sepsis may lead to new therapeutic approaches for HTRs, because many of the same pathways are involved during intravascular hemolysis.

C. Management and Appropriate Follow-Up

An AHTR is a medical emergency. The highest morbidity and greatest risk of fatal reactions are with ABO-incompatible transfusions. Severe reactions have been reported with the infusion of as little as 5–20 mL of ABO-incompatible blood (21). Fatal reactions have been reported with as little as 30 mL (19). For this reason, whenever an AHTR is suspected the blood transfusion must be stopped immediately (Table 6). The unit of blood as well as the administration tubing should be removed down to the needle hub, maintaining intravenous access, but assuring that the patient receives no more of the component, including the 10–20 mL that might be present in the tubing. Because the most common cause of fatal AHTR is an identification error, a thorough check of labels on the unit should be done and the patient's identification verified. Personnel adminis-

Table 6   Initial Management of Acute Hemolytic Transfusion Reaction

Stop transfusion at needle hub; maintain intravenous access
Notify primary care physician
Repeat identification of patient and unit
Initiate support therapy to maintain blood pressure and renal function
Notify the transfusion department; initiate a transfusion-reaction workup

tering the blood should notify the patient's primary physician immediately. Treatment should be initiated as required clinically. The transfusion service should be notified immediately and a transfusion reaction workup initiated.

Prompt blood bank evaluation can eliminate a potential second AHTR. If there has been an identification error that involves mislabeled test samples or misidentified blood components, a second patient could be in danger of receiving a transfusion of incompatible blood. A patient who receives a random unit of blood will have a one-in-three chance of a "major ABO incompatibility" (patient's serum contains an ABO antibody to an antigen on the donor's red cells) that may result in a life-threatening transfusion reaction (10), and of these, about a tenth are associated with a fatal outcome (24).

Fortunately, severe, acute life-threatening HTRs are rare. It has not been possible to determine the most effective modes of therapy by means of controlled studies. Therapy is supportive and must be directed towards correcting or minimizing the pathophysiological events just described. Close monitoring and aggressive support in an intensive care setting is indicated for all patients with significant hemolysis.

Hypotension must be treated aggressively. Since the renal failure that may accompany HTRs is thought to result from renal ischemia, therapy should be directed toward the prevention of systemic hypotension and the maintenance of renal cortical blood flow. If hypotension or shock can be adequately treated, renal perfusion can usually be maintained and renal failure prevented (20).

One of the worst prognostic signs for the patient with an acute immune-mediated HTR is the development of fulminant DIC. Fortunately, in most cases the initiating immune hemolysis is short-lived, and few patients progress to DIC (3). The optimal therapy for DIC precipitated by a transfusion reaction remains controversial. Factors to consider when treating DIC include the severity of the reaction, the antibody involved, the amount of incompatible blood infused, and the patient's clinical status. The infusion of fresh frozen plasma, cryoprecipitate, and platelets may be necessary to stop hemorrhage and correct the coagulopathy. The most severe HTRs—those that result in DIC—are associated with the infusion of greater than 200 mL of ABO-incompatible blood. In the treatment of severe AHTRs, Goldfinger has recommended the prophylactic use of heparin to prevent DIC (22). However the efficacy of heparin in this setting is unknown. Many of these patients may already have a source of active bleeding for which the initial blood transfusion was ordered.

The response to all therapy should be closely monitored with frequent laboratory and clinical assessment, and subsequent therapy should be guided by both. The most useful measurements for ongoing hemolysis include hemoglobin concentration, fractionated bilirubin, and lactic dehydrogenase (LDH); standard measurements of coagulation and renal function are also indicated. The blood bank can perform serological studies to determine whether an offending antibody is present, identify the specificity of the antibody, monitor the removal of antigen-positive transfused red cells, and provide antigen-negative blood should further transfusions be necessary.

IV. THE DELAYED HEMOLYTIC TRANSFUSION REACTION

The definition of a DHTR is accelerated immune-mediated destruction of transfused red cells after a period of time, during which there is production of an alloantibody in the recipient to an alloantigen carried on the transfused cells. The first case of a delayed hemolytic reaction as a result of blood incompatibility was described by Boorman et al. in 1946 (25). In 1957, Fudenberg and Allen reported a series of cases and clearly established that, in a previously sensitized patient, a hemolytic reaction can occur even if pretransfusion testing fails to identify an alloantibody or incompatibility with the donor red cells. Thus, DHTRs became recognized as a distinct clinical entity (26).

The true incidence of DHTRs remains unknown. A significant number of these reactions go undetected. The accurate detection of a DHTR is largely determined by two factors: (a) the level of clinical awareness of this potential complication among the medical staff caring for patients, and (b) the sensitivity of the laboratory tests used for diagnosis. From 1974 to 1977, 35% of the DHTRs at the Mayo Clinic were recognized in the laboratory but were not suspected clinically. Signs or symptoms indicative of an HTR had not been appreciated (27). In three successive series from the Mayo Clinic, the reported increased frequency of DHTRs [1964–73: 1/11,650 units (28); 1974–77:1/4,000 units (27); 1978–80:1/1,500 units (29)] was attributed to increased clinical awareness combined with more sensitive methods of antibody detection.

It is even more difficult to assess mortality data for DHTRs. Most of the literature still consists of only individual case reports. Twenty-six deaths directly attributed to a DHTR were reported to the FDA from 1976 to 1985. Nearly all reports of fatal DHTRs involved patients with multiple antibodies (19). The majority of patients who died were extremely ill prior to the DHTR, making it very difficult to know to what extent the transfusion reaction contributed to their death.

It is possible for red cell alloantibodies formed during a primary immune response to lyse the transfused cells that initiated the response and result in a DHTR. However, most DHTRs result from a secondary or anamnestic immune response in patients previously sensitized by transfusion or pregnancy; the patient typically has no detectable antibodies prior to transfusion, but rapidly develop high titers of antibody after transfusion. Antibodies most often implicated are directed against antigens of the MNS, Rh, Kell, Kidd, or Duffy blood group systems. Because some antibodies rapidly decline to undetectable levels, only to reappear rapidly with subsequent stimulation, knowledge of prior red cell alloimmunization is essential to preventing the DHTR.

A. Clinical Presentation and Differential Diagnosis

Unlike the dramatic clinical presentations of the classic AHTR, most DHTRs are completely asymptomatic or associated with very mild symptoms resulting from the gradual destruction of sensitized donor red cells. Many reactions are noticed only because of an unexplained failure to maintain the patient's posttransfusion hemoglobin level or because of low-grade fever and/or mild jaundice with an elevated unconjugated bilirubin. As with AHTR, fever is the most frequent symptom (Table 7). The triad of fever, anemia, and a history of a recent blood transfusion should alert one to the possibility of a DHTR (28). These patients often have other potential causes of fever and anemia, and in the days to weeks after a transfusion, medical staff may fail to connect the prior transfusion with the current symptoms. In addition, there may be no overt symptoms, or the symptoms may be very mild, occurring after discharge, and not even noticed or reported by patients.

Such reactions usually come to light when a subsequent request for transfusion reveals the presence of a new red cell alloantibody and/or a newly positive DAT. The maximal rate of red cell destruction seems to occur between the 4th and 13th days, although the signs and symptoms are most commonly encountered on about the 7th day (10). The insidious presentation is typical of extravascular hemolysis. Hemoglobinuria and hemoglobinemia are seldom present (21). Some DHTRs with extravascular hemolysis are accompanied by oliguria, but acute renal failure rarely develops in the absence of intravascular hemolysis (30). Very infrequently, DHTRs may result in intravascular hemolysis and present with the devastating complications usually associated with AHTRs, such as hypotension, renal failure, and DIC.

The consideration of a DHTR is particularly important in transfused patients with sickle cell anemia. A DHTR occurring after a red cell exchange

Table 7 Expected Onset of Clinical and Laboratory Manifestations of a Delayed Hemolytic Transfusion Reaction

Positive direct antiglobulin test: 2–3 days posttransfusion
Spherocytes: 3–4 days posttransfusion
Free antibody detectable by indirect antiglobulin test: 5–7 days posttransfusion
Anemia: 5–7 days posttransfusion
Jaundice: 5–7 days posttransfusion
Hemoglobinuria: 5–7 days posttransfusion

transfusion may be very difficult to distinguish from a sickle cell crisis. These patients may become acutely ill as a result of a DHTR, with symptoms including vaso-occlusive crisis, bone infarction, renal insufficiency, and profound anemia. Initially, both DAT and IAT may be negative as a result of the clearance of sensitized red cells. Elevated bilirubin lactate dehydrogenase (LDH), and urinary hemoglobin, as well as other indications of hemolysis, may be present in both conditions. If DHTR is not considered and the symptom complex is attributed to a sickle cell crisis, these patients could continue to be transfused with antigen-positive blood (31,32).

When fever without hemolysis occurs days to weeks after a transfusion, transmission of an infectious agent or transfusion-associated graft-versus-host disease should be considered (21). If delayed intravascular hemolysis of both donor and recipient red cells is occurring, transfusion-induced malaria or babesiosis should be considered (33). The non–immune-mediated hemolysis of transfused G6PD-deficient red cells can also present with mild transient hemolysis several days after their infusion, accompanied by mild jaundice and a two- to threefold increase in bilirubin and LDH (3).

B. Management and Appropriate Follow-Up

In cases of predominately extravascular hemolysis with a slowly decreasing hemoglobin concentration and no other sequelae, adequate hydration and cautious clinical observation with careful monitoring of the hemoglobin and renal function are usually sufficient (14). If additional transfusions become necessary, the patient will require antigen-negative blood. In patients with significant intravascular hemolysis and more severe symptoms, management is supportive and should parallel that for the patient with a severe acute immune-mediated hemolysis.

It is also imperative that the clinical staff and patient be instructed in red cell alloantibody status and understand the importance of honoring these antibodies for all future transfusions, even when they can no longer be detected by pretransfusion screening tests. The patient must always be notified in writing and given personal documentation indicating the presence and specificity of a clinically significant red cell alloantibody. Widespread accessibility of blood bank records between medical facilities will further reduce the risk of a subsequent DHTR.

V.   LABORATORY EVALUATION OF THE SUSPECTED HEMOLYTIC TRANSFUSION REACTION

When an AHTR is suspected, the initial evaluation to confirm the presence of hemolysis and determine its etiology and clinical significance is ordinarily performed by the blood bank. Specimens sent to the blood bank should include a coagulated and anticoagulated tube of blood, along with all suspected units, IV tubing, and infusion sets. The patient's blood samples must be drawn carefully to avoid artifactual hemolysis. Symptoms that occur several hours after a transfusion may be observed during the infusion of a subsequent unit in a patient receiving multiple transfusions. The blood bank will perform a serological evaluation on all suspected units.

The blood bank's initial evaluation will include three steps: a clerical check, an evaluation of hemolysis, and an evaluation for any evidence of serological incompatibility. The clerical check will confirm the identity of the patient's sample and of the blood product(s), ensuring that there was no misidentification that could have resulted in the patient's receiving an incompatible unit.

Posttransfusion plasma will be examined for evidence of hemolysis. Intravascular hemolysis of as little as 5 mL of blood usually raises the plasma hemoglobin concentration to >50 mg/dL. This level of free plasma hemoglobin should be rapidly and easily detectable by gross visual inspection of the plasma/serum layer of a centrifuged blood specimen (6). Free hemoglobin is usually cleared from the plasma in 5–12 hours. If the posttransfusion blood sample is taken several hours after the transfusion, when the plasma could possibly be cleared of hemoglobin, an assay for the presence of methemalbumin might be useful (10). A posttransfusion urine sample can also be evaluated for any evidence of hemoglobinuria. It is important that the urine is tested for free hemoglobin and distinguished from hematuria and myoglobinuria.

Pre- and posttransfusion DATs are performed to check for serological incompatibility (8). A positive posttransfusion DAT with a mixed-field appearance is indicative of alloantibody coating antigen-positive transfused red cells. Newly detected antibodies coating transfused cells in this setting are virtually diagnostic of an immune basis for the hemolysis. Antibody may be demonstrable in the patient's serum using the IAT. However, the DAT may be positive days before free antibody can be detected. It may be possible to identify the alloantibody by eluting it from the red cells.

When an AHTR is suspected after the three initial checks, additional laboratory tests to determine the cause of the reaction may include confirmation of ABO and Rh(D) types on pre- and posttransfusion samples as well as the unit(s), repeat crossmatch, and other serological testing to detect alloantibodies and/or incompatibility with donor units. If no clerical error has occurred, the plasma is not grossly hemolyzed, and the DAT is negative or unchanged, an acute HTR is extremely unlikely. However, if rapid hemolysis of all antibody-coated red cells has occurred with rapid clearance of the free hemoglobin from the plasma, or if antibody-coated red cells are removed rapidly from the circulation by the reticuloendothelial system, immune-mediated AHTR is possible with a negative DAT (21).

If initial test results are unclear, additional confirmatory tests may be useful to verify an AHTR. One should also determine whether a patient achieved the expected hemoglobin rise after the transfusion: in a 70 kg adult, the hemoglobin should increase by 1 g/dL per unit of red cells when measured 15 minutes after the transfusion (34).

Serum bilirubin and LDH increase in both intravascular and extravascular hemolysis. Rising unconjugated bilirubin may be detectable as early as one hour postreaction, with peak levels occurring in 4–6 hours and disappearing in 24 hours if bilirubin excretion is normal. A serum haptoglobin level may be helpful in suspected hemolysis, but a precipitous decrease in haptoglobin level tends to occur very early and is not as reliable as hemoglobinemia. Visible hemoglobinemia develops after haptoglobin depletion, therefore little is gained by measuring haptoglobin when hemolysis is already visible. The usefulness of a haptoglobin level is also limited by the wide range of its normal values. Non–immune-mediated hemolysis will also lower haptoglobin concentrations.

When an immune-mediated DHTR has occurred, spherocytes observed on the peripheral blood smear may be an early indication of red cell destruction (14). A blood bank evaluation should be initiated in any case of suspected DHTR. If the evaluation reveals that a positive DAT has developed, demonstrating the presence of complement and/or antibody-coated red cells or the presence of previously undetected red cell antibodies associated with a rapid disappearance of transfused donor cells, then the diagnosis of a DHTR is made (21).

Characteristically, the DAT becomes positive a few days after transfusion and remains positive until the incompatible red cells are eliminated. Typically, antibody becomes detectable 4–7 days after transfusion and reaches a peak value 10–15 days after transfusion (10). Antibody eluted from the red cells may help identify the alloantibody when the antibody titer is low and difficult to detect in the serum.

VI. PRETRANSFUSION COMPATIBILITY TESTING

The goal of pretransfusion compatibility testing is to allow the selection of red cells that will circulate for an acceptable period and that will have a low risk for adverse effects (Figure 1). First and foremost is accurate and reliable ABO and Rh(D) typing of recipient and donor (35). In addition, pretransfusion compatibility tests are designed to detect the presence of potentially hemolytic red cell alloantibodies by use of both an antibody screen (patient's serum against a known panel of red cells) and the major crossmatch (patient's serum with donor red cells). The antibody screen detects alloantibodies to common red cell antigens that could go undetected in a major crossmatch because of the expression of a limited number of red cell antigen sites, as with heterozygous genes, or weakened

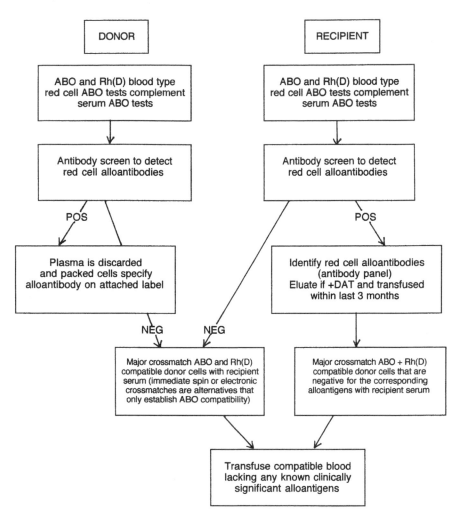

Figure 1   Pretransfusion compatibility testing.

expression of an antigen. On the other hand, the major crossmatch confers the ability to detect alloantibodies to uncommon antigens, which might not be present on the standard panel of screening cells but are present on the donor red cells that have been selected for the particular patient. The antibody screen and major cross match complement one another. The FDA requires that 18 red cell antigens representing the most clinically significant of the blood group systems be present on reagent red cells used for antibody screening. In addition, most other high-frequency antigens are present on reagent red cells (20). Only nine antibodies reactive to antigens not usually contained on commercial prepared red cell panel cells have been the reported cause of HTRs. A critical review of these reports reveals inadequate documentation in many instances (6). Under special conditions, an electronic or "computer" crossmatch may substitute for serological testing (36).

No in vitro test is capable of predicting the clinical significance of a red cell antibody. However, several serological characteristics of red cell alloantibodies correlate well with clinical consequences and form the basis for most of our clinical judgment. The two serological characteristics that have proved most helpful in predicting clinical significance are the antibody specificity, which is determined by demonstrating reactivity with the corresponding red cell antigen, and the antibody's in vitro reactivity at 30–37°C (37). Some antibodies are invariably associated with hemolytic events, while others have never been reported to cause untoward reactions in any patient. As previously discussed, the severity of the hemolysis caused by these antibodies varies dramatically. Experience gained from transfusing patients in life-threatening situations when compatible, antigen-negative blood supplies are unavailable or exhausted has illustrated that anticipated hemolysis may not occur or may be minimal (38). This situation is most likely to occur in the setting of a patient who has multiple red cell alloantibodies. Although every effort should be made to transfuse these patients with antigen-negative blood, in the emergency setting it may be necessary to transfuse blood that is positive for the antigen(s) thought to be the least clinically significant. In these situations, small aliquots should be infused slowly, with close clinical supervision and careful monitoring for any evidence of hemolysis. In less urgent situations where a negative crossmatch is difficult or impossible to obtain and the red cell antibodies are of questionable clinical significance, in vivo compatibility testing has been applied (15).

Just as the presence of an antibody does not necessarily mean that hemolysis will occur, the absence of an antibody does not guarantee safety. Although antibody screening and crossmatching with a recently obtained blood sample identify most red cell alloantibodies, state-of-the-art serological techniques do not identify all cases of incompatibility. Previously identified alloantibodies that may be clinically significant should always be honored. Many clinically significant antibodies become undetectable over time, only to reappear after transfusion of red cells bearing the corresponding antigen. In recent studies by Ramsey et al., 30–35% of clinically significant red cell alloantibodies become undetectable on follow-up screening within one year (with anti-Kidd undetectable in 59% of follow-up screens and anti-C undetectable in 45% of follow-up screens), and nearly 50% of all clinically significant alloantibodies became undetectable after 10 or more years (39).

Rarely, there will be cases where all evidence indicates immune-mediated accelerated destruction of red cells in the absence of demonstrable antibodies

(40). An HTR may occur, possibly repeatedly, without serological identification of an alloantibody by standard screening tests. This may become a serious clinical dilemma when additional transfusions are necessary. In such cases, more sensitive assays and more detailed testing may be required. It may be possible to confirm the identity of the incompatible antigen by radiolabeling a small aliquot of red cells expressing the suspect antigen and performing red cell survival studies in the patient (40). It is still assumed that the hemolysis in these cases is immune mediated even without detectable antibody, just as cases of autoimmune hemolytic anemia have been described in the absence of a positive DAT (many of these cases have been shown to have IgG on the red cell surface, which is undetectable by conventional techniques) (6).

VII. PREVENTIVE MEASURES

Numerous and sophisticated serological techniques can be applied to donor red cells and recipient serum in an effort to detect an incompatibility. However, the array of laboratory methods must be put in the proper perspective. Ironically, further perfecting the serological aspects of compatibility testing would prevent only a small number of the rarely fatal HTRs. Most deaths related to blood transfusion remain a consequence of giving incompatible blood to a patient as a result of human error, not of insufficiently sensitive laboratory screening techniques. Most of these erroneous blood administrations result from identification errors that occur outside of the blood bank.

Educating and training all involved personnel in the safe and correct handling of laboratory specimens and blood components remain the most critical steps in preventing death from blood transfusion. Errors are usually made during times of stress and are compounded by inadequate training.

Emergency transfusion of previously unhospitalized patients can be complicated by special problems in patient identification and accurate labeling of blood specimens. Even in extremely urgent clinical situations, a properly labeled patient sample must be drawn prior to any transfusions to allow appropriate testing for future transfusions and to serve as a pretransfusion reference in the event of a transfusion reaction. The blood bank cannot rely on old records or typing results from other institutions.

Clear and detailed standard operating procedure for handling laboratory specimens and blood components should be carefully developed and fully understood by well-trained clinical and laboratory personnel. The proper procedures should always be followed. Identification errors are most likely to occur when the blood is hung for transfusion, but they may occur at any point in the chain of sample collection, testing, blood preparation, storage, issue, and transfusion. It is important to remember that even with the use of autologous blood, the risk still exists of human error leading to transfusion of an incorrect unit of blood (16). Computer-assisted automation shows promise as a mechanism to reduce the chance of human error at several points in the transfusion process, including automated patient and donor identification, automated crossmatch, and automated release of blood. Interest is increasing in automated tracking systems that monitor identification from initial phlebotomy until the blood is transfused (41). Systems technology may prove to be the method of choice in preventing many of the so-called "clerical errors" that resist the most persistent training.

ACKNOWLEDGMENT

Much thanks to Ms. Jo Procter, M. Ed., MT, (ASCP) SBB, of the Transfusion Medicine Department for her careful reading and thoughtful assistance with the manuscript in draft.

REFERENCES

1. Wick MR. Blood transfusion. An historic and current perspective. Am J Clin Pathol 1989; 91(suppl):S2–S6.
2. Beauregard P, Blajchman MA. Hemolytic and pseudo-hemolytic transfusion reactions: an overview of the hemolytic transfusion reactions and the clinical conditions that mimic them. Transfusion Med Rev 1994; 8:184–199.
3. Brecher ME, Taswell HF. Hemolytic transfusion reactions. In: Rossi EC, Simon TL, Moss GS, eds. Principles of Transfusion Medicine. Baltimore: Williams and Wilkins, 1996:747–763.
4. Oberman HA. The history of transfusion medicine. In: Petz LD, Swisher SN, Kleinman S, et al., eds. Clinical Practice of Transfusion Medicine. New York: Churchill Livingstone, Inc., 1996:11–32.
5. Oberman HA. The crossmatch. A brief historical perspective. Transfusion 1981; 21:645–651.
6. Shulman IA, Petz LD. Red cell compatibility testing: clinical significance and laboratory methods. In: Petz LD, Swisher SN, Kleinman S, et al., eds. Clinical Practice of Transfusion Medicine. New York: Churchill Livingstone, 1996:199–244.
7. Daniels GL, Anstee DJ, Cartron JP, et al. Blood group terminology 1995. ISBT working party on terminology for red cell surface antigens. Vox Sang 1995; 69:265–279.
8. Jeter EK, Spivey MA. Noninfectious complications of blood transfusion. Hematol/Oncol Clin North Am 1995; 9:187–204.
9. Pineda AA, Brzica SM Jr, Taswell HP. Hemolytic transfusion reaction. Recent experience in a large blood bank. Mayo Clin Proc 1978; 53:387–390.
10. Mollison PL, Engelfriet CP, Contreras M. Blood Transfusion in Clinical Medicine. Oxford: Blackwell, 1993.

11. Lostumbro MM, Holland PV, Schmidt PJ. Isoimmunization after multiple transfusions. N Engl J Med 1966; 275:141–144.

12. Silberstein L, Spitalnik SL. Blood group antigens and antibodies. In: Rossi EC, Simon TL, Moss GS, eds. Principles of Transfusion Medicine. Baltimore: Williams and Wilkins, 1996:67–87.

13. Pollack W, Ascari WQ, Crispen JF, et al. Studies on Rh prophylaxis. Rh immune prophylaxis after transfusion with Rh-positive blood. Transfusion 1971; 11:340–344.

14. Baron B, Baron J. Blood products and plasmapheresis. In: Hall JB, Schmidt GA, Wood LDH, eds. Principles of Critical Care. New York: McGraw-Hill, 1992:

15. Silvergleid AJ, Wells RF, Hafleigh EB, et al. Compatibility test using 51-chromium-labeled red blood cells in crossmatch positive patients. Transfusion 1978; 18:8–14.

16. Linden JV, Kaplan HS. Transfusion errors: causes and effects. Transfusion Med Rev 1994; 8:169–183.

17. Walker RH. Special report: transfusion risks. Am J Clin Pathol 1987; 88:374–378.

18. Linden JV, Paul B, Dressier KP. A report of 104 transfusion errors in New York state. Transfusion 1992; 32:601–606.

19. Sazama K. Reports of 355 transfusion-associated deaths: 1976 through 1985. Transfusion 1990; 30:583–590.

20. Schulman IA. Safety in transfusion practices. Red cell compatibility testing issues. Clin Lab Med 1992; 12:685–699.

21. Jenner PW, Holland PV. Diagnosis and management of transfusion reactions. In: Petz LD, Swisher SN, Kleinman S, et al., eds. Clinical Practice of Transfusion Medicine. New York: Churchill Livingstone, 1996:905–927.

22. Goldfinger D. Acute hemolytic transfusion reactions: a fresh look at pathogenesis and considerations regarding therapy. Transfusion 1977; 17:985–987.

23. Davenport RD, Kunkel SL. Cytokine roles in hemolytic and nonhemolytic transfusion reactions. Transfusion Med Rev 1994; 8:157–168.

24. Murphy WG, McClelland DBL. Deceptively low morbidity from failure to practice safe blood transfusion: an analysis of serious blood transfusion errors. Vox Sang 1989; 57:59–62.

25. Boorman KE, Dodd BE, Loutit JF, et al. Some results of transfusion of blood to recipients with "cold" agglutinins. Br Med J 1946; 1:751.

26. Fudenberg H, Allen FH. Transfusion reactions in the absence of demonstrable incompatibility. N Engl J Med 1957; 256:1180–1184.

27. Moore BS, Taswell HF, Pineda AA, et al. Delayed hemolytic transfusion reactions. Evidence of the need for an improved pretransfusion compatibility test. Am J Clin Pathol 1980; 74:94–97.

28. Pineda AA, Taswell HF, Brzica SM Jr. Delayed hemolytic transfusion reaction. An immunologic hazard of blood transfusion. Transfusion 1978; 18:1–7.

29. Taswell HF, Pineda AA, Moore SB. Hemolytic transfusion reactions: frequency and clinical and laboratory aspects. In: Bell CA, ed. A Seminar on Immune-Mediated Red Cell Destruction. Washington, DC: American Association of Blood Banks, 1981:71–92.

30. Holland PV, Wallerstein RO. Delayed hemolytic transfusion reaction with acute renal failure. J Am Med Assoc 1968; 204:1007–1008.

31. Diamond WJ, Brown FL, Bitterman P, et al. Delayed hemolytic transfusion reaction presenting as sickle cell crisis. Ann Intern Med 1980; 93:231–233.

32. Milner PF, Squires JE, Larison PJ, et al. Posttransfusion crises in sickle cell anemia: role of delayed hemolytic reactions to transfusion. South Med J 1985; 78:1462–1468.

33. Smith RP, Evans AT, Popovsky M, et al. Transfusion-acquired babesiosis and failure of antibiotic treatment. J Am Med Assoc 1986; 256:2726–2727.

34. Wiesen AR, Hospenthal DR, Byrd JC, et al. Equilibrium of hemoglobin concentration after transfusion in medical inpatients not actively bleeding. Ann Intern Med 1994; 121:278–280.

35. Schulman IA. Controversies in red cell compatibility testing. In: Nance SJ, ed. Immune Destruction of Red Blood Cells. Arlington, VA: American Association of Blood Banks, 1989:171–199.

36. Butch SH, Judd WJ, Steiner EA, et al. Electronic verification of donor-recipient compatibility: the computer crossmatch. Transfusion 1994; 34:105–109.

37. Garratty G. Factors affecting the pathogenicity of red cell auto- and alloantibodies. In: Nance SJ, ed. Immune Destruction of Red Blood Cells. Arlington, VA: American Association of Blood Banks, 1989, pp 109–157.

38. Ramsey G, Cornell FW, Hahn L, et al. Red cell antibody problems in 1000 liver transplants. Transfusion 1987; 27:552.

39. Ramsey G, Smietana SJ. Long-term follow-up testing of red cell alloantibodies. Transfusion 1994; 34:122–124.

40. Harrison CR, Hayes TC, Trow LL, Benedetto AR. Intravascular hemolytic transfusion reaction without detectable antibodies: a case report and review of the literature. Vox Sang 1986; 51:96–101.

41. Jensen NJ, Crosson JT. An automated system for bedside verification of the match between patient identification and blood unit identification. Transfusion 1996; 36:216–221.

3

Other Reactions and Alloimmunization

Christopher J. Gresens and Paul V. Holland
Sacramento Medical Foundation Blood Centers, Sacramento, California

I. INTRODUCTION

Adverse reactions to transfusions are remarkably heterogeneous. Depending upon both the patient's condition and the blood component transfused, the patient may, on occasion, experience any of a variety of transfusion reactions. Some are precipitated by the reaction of endogenous factors (e.g., recipient antibodies) with corresponding antigens in the transfused components. Others may be caused by exogenous substances, such as cytokines, bacterial organisms (and/or their toxins), excess iron, donor antibodies, or even the citrate used as a blood anticoagulant. And, still, some untoward effects of transfusion are related to physiological processes as simple as volume overload.

It is our intent to familiarize the reader with some of the more common, but not usually life-threatening, transfusion reactions, delving into their (a) presentation; (b) etiology, pathophysiology, and important mediators; (c) frequency; (d) therapy; and (e) prevention. Special emphasis will be placed upon febrile, nonhemolytic reactions, allergic (both urticarial and anaphylactic) reactions, and transfusion-related alloimmunization. We will also briefly discuss transfusion-associated volume and iron overload, hypothermia and arrhythmias, citrate toxicity, air emboli, and isolated hypotensive platelet reactions. The generally more serious types of transfusion reactions, such as hemolytic transfusion reactions (HTRs), septic transfusions reactions (STRs), transfusion-related acute lung injury (TRALI), transfusion-associated graft-versus-host disease

(TA-GVHD), and posttransfusion purpura are discussed in detail elsewhere in this book and will therefore not be further covered in this chapter.

II. FEBRILE, NONHEMOLYTIC TRANSFUSION REACTIONS

By most definitions, any isolated temperature increase of greater than or equal to one degree Celsius in association with a transfusion, when there is no other reasonable explanation for the fever, is said to be a febrile, nonhemolytic transfusion reaction (FNHTR). The diagnosis is one of exclusion; therefore, other possible causes—both extraneous (e.g., neutropenic fevers) and related (e.g., an HTR or STR)—must first be ruled out. The temperature rise will generally begin anytime from early on in the transfusion to 1 or 2 hours after it has been completed. The FNHTR is one of the most common forms of acute transfusion reaction, occurring in association with approximately 1% of red blood cell (RBC) transfusions and anywhere from 5 to 30% of platelet transfusions (1,2).

Two major causes of FNHTRs have been recognized. The first, identified in the late 1950s (3), is the interaction between recipient antibodies (leuko-agglutinins) and donor leukocytes (4). The leukoagglutinins result from prior transfusions and/or pregnancies, and very often have human leukocyte antigen (HLA) specificity. It is widely accepted that RBC components, when leuko-reduced such that they contain fewer than 5×10^8 leukocytes, are associated with fewer FNHTRs than are their nonleukoreduced counterparts (5,6). Investigators have proposed that the leukoagglutinins interact with donor leukocytes and somehow cause the release of pyrogens (from patient macrophages and/or donor leukocytes), producing fever and chills (7).

While the antibody model accounts for many FNHTRs, there appears to be at least one more mechanism. This was demonstrated in the early 1990s, when it was shown that bedside leukoreduction had limited efficacy in the prevention of FNHTRs associated with platelet transfusions. Heddle et al. (2) and Muylle et al. (8) demonstrated that there appears to be a veritable "cytokine shower" (9), which can be linked to many of these febrile reactions. They showed that the age of the platelet component as well as the leukocyte count correlated with the probability that a febrile reaction will occur. After a nonleukoreduced platelet unit has been stored for 5 days at room temperature, the plasma contains significantly increased concentrations of interleukin-1 (IL-1), tumor necrosis factor-alpha (TNF-α), interleukin-6 (IL-6), and interleukin-8 (IL-8) (2,8,10,11). All these cytokines have been associated with febrile responses and can freely pass through filters (12). Corresponding levels of cytokines in prestorage leukoreduced platelet units remain at fairly constant levels throughout the storage period as a result of the reduction of the contained leukocytes (10). Not surprisingly, these units are associated with significantly reduced FNHTR rates. For example, Muylle et al.

observed that traditional platelet concentrates (PCs) were associated with a 9.3% incidence of "transfusion reactions" (primarily rigors and/or fevers), whereas PCs from which the buffy coats were removed prior to storage were associated with an incidence of only 2.7% ($p = 0.007$) (13).

Fortunately, FNHTRs are almost never serious, although they can, in some cases, be very uncomfortable to the patient. The fever usually responds to antipyretics, such as acetaminophen. As with other acute transfusion reactions, the transfusion should be discontinued and a work-up performed to rule out the more serious types of reactions for which fever may be the harbinger (e.g., acute HTRs, STRs, or TRALI). Most current literature states that the transfusion should not be restarted with the same unit (14). In certain situations, however, such as when the reaction is very mild, rapidly responds to antipyretics, and is definitively shown to be unrelated to the aforementioned serious causes, some believe that restarting the transfusion with the same unit may be acceptable (15).

The best means of preventing FNHTRs is to leukoreduce the cellular blood component that is to be transfused. As mentioned previously, leukoreduction of RBC units to levels of less than or equal to 5×10^8 leukocytes/unit eliminates most FNHTRs (16), regardless of whether the reduction is done before or after storage. Unfortunately, however, while poststorage leukoreduction (e.g., at the bedside or in the lab immediately prior to issue) is reasonably effective at preventing FNHTRs associated with RBC transfusions, it is less effective with those due to platelet transfusions. This is because the aforementioned pyrogens (IL-1, TNF-α, etc.) reach much higher levels in non–prestorage-leukoreduced platelet units than in similarly prepared RBC units, probably largely owing to the increased storage temperature for platelets. Prestorage leukoreduction has an obvious advantage here, in that it eliminates most of the leukocytes that would otherwise produce pyrogens in vitro.

These days, plateletpheresis units are often collected in a manner that automatically produces leukoreduced units and are therefore much less likely to cause FNHTRs. Some blood centers have utilized this approach to set up a virtually 100% leukoreduced plateletpheresis inventory, as the logistics needed to accomplish this are not overly complicated. Prestorage leukoreduction of RBC units and platelet concentrates, on the other hand, is a cumbersome process that can be difficult to perform on every unit, and often necessitates the establishment of a separate component inventory. For this reason, it has not usually been done (until recently) on a very large scale. However, as the U.S. healthcare system appears to be moving toward near-100% leukoreduced blood component inventories, more and more blood collection facilities are gearing up their prestorage leukoreduction processes for RBC and platelet concentrate units.

Generally, a patient will not receive leukoreduced cellular components expressly for the prevention of FNHTRs unless he or she has had two such documented reactions (assuming that the patient is not already receiving leukoreduced cellular components for another reason). This is because most patients who have one FNHTR will not have another one, despite receiving nonleukoreduced units (17). As a final note, one more means of reducing the risk of FNHTRs during platelet transfusions is to wash the product immediately prior to issue. Theoretically, this approach seems very appealing, as washing effectively removed donor plasma, as well as the cytokines contained within. In practical situations, however, washing should rarely be needed, except, perhaps, for the patient who is exquisitely sensitive to even the small levels of cytokines present in prestorage-leukoreduced platelet units.

III. ALLERGIC TRANSFUSION REACTIONS

A. Urticarial Reactions

The urticarial transfusion reactions generally manifest with some combination of localized erythema, hives, and pruritis and are unaccompanied by fever or other adverse findings. They are thought to result from the presence of soluble allergens in the donor plasma. The frequency of these reactions is said to be around 1% (17); however, this may be a falsely low value because of under-reporting. The accepted method of treatment is to interrupt the transfusion, administer an antihistamine (such as diphenhydramine), and wait for the symptoms to subside, at which point, if the reaction were a relatively mild one, the transfusion could be restarted. Conversely, if the symptoms were more severe (e.g., affecting a large portion of the patient's body surface area), the same unit should not be restarted.

Many allergic reactions can be prevented by the pretransfusion administration of an antihistamine. Rarely, the concomitant use of a corticosteroid (e.g., hydrocortisone) may be warranted. And in very unusual cases, such as when a patient has a history of repeated and/or severe urticarial reactions, it may be necessary to utilize only washed or deglycerolized red blood cells (18) and washed or resuspended platelets (19,20) for future transfusions.

B. Anaphylactic Transfusion Reactions

Anaphylaxis, fortunately a very rare reaction, may occur after the infusion of only a few milliliters of a blood component and can cause mortality or significant morbidity unless treated promptly (Table 1). Typically, some combination of coughing, bronchospasm, respiratory distress, vascular instability, nausea, abdominal cramps, vomiting, diarrhea, shock, and/or loss of consciousness will manifest. There is usually an absence of fever (helping to distinguish this reaction from acute HTRs, TRALI, and STRs). Also, several of the aforementioned findings will usually occur simultaneously, thereby allowing the differentiation of

Table 1 Some Proposed Causes of
Anaphylactic Transfusion Reactions

Donor IgA
Plasticizers/Sterilizing agents
Passively transferred donor IgE
Passively transferred donor allergens/drugs
HLA-incompatible platelet transfusions
Use of leukocyte reduction filters
Undefined plasma-soluble antigens

---

an anaphylactic reaction from the purported hypotensive platelet reaction (see Sec. X).

Many anaphylactic reactions are believed to occur as a result of the reaction of donor IgA with anti-IgA antibodies (class IgE) produced by IgA-deficient recipients. Approximately 1 in 700–800 people is IgA-deficient (18), but, as shown by Sandler et al. (who looked at 97 asymptomatic IgA-deficient individuals), only approximately 22% of IgA-deficient people will make anti-IgA antibodies (21). Other possible causes for anaphylactic transfusion reactions include various undefined plasma-soluble antigens, plasticizers and sterilizing agents used during blood bag production (22), passive transfer of donor IgE antibody (23,24), passive transfer of donor allergens (25), HLA-incompatible platelet transfusions (26), and even the use of leukocyte reduction filters (27).

Fortunately, the incidence of anaphylactic transfusion reactions is very low, with two different series putting it at 1 in 20,000 and 1 in 47,000 units transfused, respectively (28,29). Still, the morbidity, with resultant increased hospital stays, associated with this form of transfusion reaction is not inconsiderable. And although most patients do recover completely, a few do not. For example, Sazama found anaphylaxis to be implicated in 8 of 256 non-AIDS/hepatitis transfusion–related deaths that occurred between 1976 and 1985. Interestingly, anti-IgA was demonstrated in only 1 of the 8 cases (30).

When an anaphylactic transfusion reaction is suspected, the transfusion should be discontinued immediately, and the intravenous line kept open (e.g., with saline) in order to treat any ensuing hypotension. What follows is an example of the typical treatment for an adult patient who is having an anaphylactic transfusion reactions: For mild-to-moderate reactions, 0.3–0.5 mg of epinephrine (0.3–0.5 mL of a 1:1000 solution) can be given subcutaneously every 15–30 minutes, as needed, for a maximum of three doses. For severe reactions, 0.1–0.5 mg epinephrine (1–5 mL of a 1:10,000 solution) should be slowly given intravenously and repeated every 5–15 minutes as needed. Sublingual or endotracheal epinephrine administration may be used when an IV line is not available. Intravenous aminophylline is often administered to treat bronchospasm (loading dose of 6 mg/kg, followed by 0.5–1 mg/kg/h). Volume expansion, using crystalloids, is also recommended for the treatment of hypotension. A vasopressor, such as dopamine, may be necessary if the hypotension does not respond to volume expansion alone. Intravenous hydrocortisone, at a dose of 500 mg every 6 hours, should be given for severe reactions; it is important to remember, however, that this is not the first drug to administer, as it takes 6–12 hours to reach maximal effect and probably plays a greater role in preventing the redevelopment of anaphylaxis. Antihistamines, such as diphenhydramine hydrochloride, while having little value in the treatment of acute symptoms, may reduce the duration of the reaction and keep it from redeveloping. And, finally, airway protection and oxygen administration are sometimes needed. After the diagnosis of anaphylaxis has been made, the patient should be observed for at least 6 hours, assuming he or she makes a rapid and complete recovery (31). Also, the patient should be provided a Medi-Alert bracelet documenting his or her susceptibility to these reactions to prevent a reoccurrence.

Pretransfusion specimens from any patient who has had a suspected anaphylactic reaction should be analyzed for the presence of serum IgA. If the patient is IgA-deficient, it is important to document the presence or absence of anti-IgA antibody in his or her serum. When such patients have evidence of anti-IgA antibodies, prevention of subsequent anaphylactic reactions is accomplished by transfusing only IgA-deficient blood components. In the case of RBC transfusions, it is often possible to remove sufficient quantities of IgA via either deglycerolization or extensive washing of the units. When platelets are needed, various "washing" protocols have been established; however, all cause some degree of platelet activation and loss, and some may not remove sufficient quantities of IgA to prevent subsequent reactions. Fortunately, IgA-deficient units may be obtained through the American Association of Blood Banks (AABB) Rare Donor Registry and other sources. It is important to note though that, because of the precious nature of such components, these units should be used only when absolutely necessary.

IV. TRANSFUSION-RELATED ALLOIMMUNIZATION

Sensitization to RBC antigens following transfusions occurs commonly. After excluding the ABO system, the most immunogenic of the RBC antigens is the D antigen, followed, in descending order, by K, E, Fy^a, and Jk^a (32). Rosse et al. demonstrated a direct correlation between the number of RBC transfusions and the percentage of sickle cell disease (SCD) patients sensitized (33). Hoeltge et al. formed a similar conclusion based upon their retrospective study looking at RBC alloantibodies in 159,262 transfused patients with varying diagnoses (34). Lostumbo et al. determined that the risk of alloimmunization is additive, at a rate of "approximately 1 per cent per unit of transfused blood" (35). This cumulative RBC alloimmunization risk is of particular importance to frequently transfused patients. Coles et al. observed that of multiply transfused SCD and thalassemia patients, 23 of 99 (23%) and 4 of 39 (10%), respectively, became alloimmunized (36). Others have found similarly high rates of RBC alloimmunization, with the incidence in SCD patients ranging from 8% in pediatric populations to 50% in multiply transfused adults (37). This translates into significantly higher rates of delayed hemolytic transfusion reactions in these patient populations, the results of which, particularly in patients who receive RBC exchange transfusions (e.g., SCD patients), can sometimes be devastating (38,39).

Another very important form of alloimmunization is that which occurs against antigens in the HLA system. These generally occur in multiply transfused and/or multiparous individuals and, in the transplant setting, can be minimized through leukoreduction techniques (40). Approximately 30–70% of patients who are exposed to multiple, unmodified (e.g., nonleukoreduced or ultraviolet B–treated) RBC and platelet transfusions will become alloimmunized to HLA antigens (41). The consequences of HLA alloimmunization can include FNHTRs (see earlier), platelet transfusion refractoriness (when antibodies against HLA class I antigens are involved), and a reduced likelihood for successful solid organ and bone marrow transplants. The Trial to Reduce Alloimmunization to Platelets (TRAP) looked at approximately 600 acute myelogenous leukemia patients, comparing alloimmunization rates in patients who received unmodified, pooled platelet concentrates (controls) versus rates in patients enrolled in three different experimental arms. The three arms separated patients into those who received only leukoreduced platelet concentrates (filtered) versus those who received only leukoreduced plateletpheresis units (filtered) versus those who received only ultraviolet B–irradiated, pooled platelet concentrates. All patients in the study received leukoreduced (filtered) RBC units. Rates of HLA alloimmunization and refractoriness in the control group were approximately 45 and 13%, respectively. Alloimmunization and refractoriness rates for all three of the experimental arms were similar (and significantly less than those for the control group), at 17–21 and 3–5%, respectively (i.e., regardless of the type of platelet treatment) (40).

Transfusion-associated alloimmunization may also occur against platelet-specific antigens. Antibodies have been observed against antigens in each of the five human platelet antigen systems (HPA-1 through 5) and are the cause of neonatal alloimmune thrombocytopenia and posttransfusion purpura. They can also, in some cases, lead to platelet transfusion refractoriness, although less commonly than is seen with antibodies to the HLA system (42). Neutrophil antigen alloimmunization also occurs, with the resultant antibodies rarely leading to neonatal alloimmune granulocytopenia (less than 1% incidence). These antibodies are also causal in the development of FNHTRs; however, their role is considered to be far less important than that of HLA antibodies (42,43). Neutrophil-specific antibodies have also been shown to cause TRALI (44);

however, their relative importance in the pathogenesis of TRALI, vis-à-vis HLA antibodies, is not entirely known (45).

V. TRANSFUSION-ASSOCIATED CIRCULATORY OVERLOAD

Rapid increases in blood volume are poorly tolerated in many patients with cardiac, pulmonary, or renal failure, as well as in chronically anemic patients with expanded plasma volumes and in very young or old patients (4,46). Manifestations of transfusion-associated circulatory overload (TACO) include dyspnea, rapid increases in systolic blood pressure, coughing, orthopnea, severe headache, and peripheral edema. The reaction is not so much related to the blood component itself as it is to the *volume* infused. In other words, the problem is primarily a physiological one.

The incidence of TACO is difficult to determine, largely because of the problem of underreporting. In a series from the Mayo Clinic, Popovsky and Taswell (47) found that when the formal diagnosis of TACO was made by the clinicians alone, only 1 in 3168 patients transfused with RBCs was reported as being affected (as observed by a retrospective review looking at all transfusions for a 7-year period). When they then set up a more structured consultation service, that rate increased to 1 in 708. A recent study of elderly orthopedic surgery patients revealed that over 1% of this population developed TACO. Not surprisingly, the patients who developed TACO were older (mean of 84 vs. 77 years) than those who did not, and each was in positive fluid balance (mean of 2480 mL) prior to administration of the offending transfusions (46). A final note regarding the importance of TACO as a cause of patient morbidity and mortality is that of 355 transfusion-associated deaths that occurred between 1976 and 1985, 39 were caused by acute pulmonary injury. This was the third most common cause of death after acute hemolysis (158 deaths) and non-A, non-B hepatitis (42 deaths). Anaphylaxis accounted for 8 of the acute pulmonary injury-related deaths, with the remaining 31 (9% of total deaths) caused by the acute onset of pulmonary edema or respiratory insufficiency (30). While no distinction could be made between TACO and TRALI as the cause of these, it is likely that at least some (and perhaps many) were due to TACO.

Treatment of TACO is to stop the transfusion, sit the patient up as much as possible, and give a diuretic (e.g., 40 mg intravenous furosemide for a typical adult) and oxygen. In rare cases, such as when marked pulmonary edema occurs, phlebotomy of 200–400 mL whole blood, with the concomitant slow transfusion of packed RBCs, may be useful (this is actually faster than plasmapheresis). Prevention may be accomplished by transfusing the at-risk patient with very small volumes of the required component, as slowly as possible. Generally, the transfusion rate should not exceed 1 mL per kilogram body weight per hour (18,48). Also, consideration should be given to administering a diuretic prior to the transfusion of an at-risk individual. In rare cases, partial RBC exchange (i.e., removing whole blood and replacing with packed RBCs) may be utilized in order to reduce the patient's plasma volume while increasing his or her hemoglobin concentration.

VI. TRANSFUSION-INDUCED IRON OVERLOAD

A single unit of RBCs contains approximately 200–250 mg of iron. Most transfused patients never receive sufficient quantities of RBCs to cause iron overload (Table 2). However, some individuals, such as those who require chronic transfusion (e.g., thalassemic patients), may, over time, receive literally hundreds of RBC transfusions, placing them at risk for developing secondary hemochromatosis. This can potentially lead to significant organ damage, with the end result in some patients being dysfunction of the liver, heart, kidneys, and/or multiple other organs. There is a multifaceted approach to prevention. First, only the minimum required number of RBC units should be transfused. Second, when possible, pharmacological means should be used to reduce the need for RBC transfusions. For instance, erythropoietin may be used to treat anemia in chronic renal failure and zidovudine-treated HIV-infected patients. Third, patients who are expected to require long-term chronic transfusions, such as those with thalassemia, and some sickle cell anemia patients, should be treated with an iron-chelating agent (e.g., desferoxamine). And, fourth, in certain instances (e.g., some sickle cell anemia and paroxysmal nocturnal hemoglobinuria patients), the use of RBC exchange procedures is warranted, as this approach serves both to introduce new, healthy RBCs into the patient and to remove the patient's pathological RBCs that would otherwise be rapidly hemolyzed and broken down into additional unwanted storage iron (49). One more approach that has been used in a few facilities is to transfuse young RBCs (neocytes), so as to provide more longer-lived RBCs, thus minimizing the number of required transfusions (50).

Table 2 Prevention of Transfusion-Induced Iron Overload

1. Minimization of RBC transfusions
2. Pharmacological therapy (e.g., erythropoietin), when appropriate
3. Iron chelation agents (e.g., desferoxamine)
4. RBC exchange (in some cases)
5. Neocyte transfusions (if available)

VII. HYPOTHERMIA AND ARRHYTHMIAS RELATED TO TRANSFUSIONS

The rapid transfusion of large volumes of cold blood may cause ventricular arrhythmias, especially in a patient who is predisposed to arrhythmias or whose central venous catheter (CVC) is positioned in close proximity to the cardiac conduction system. Various means for treatment and prevention exist. These include pulling the CVC slightly back, reducing the rate of infusion (not always possible), using ultra-efficient blood warmers that are capable of rapidly warming (without overheating) large volumes of blood, and adding warmed saline directly to the RBC component prior to transfusion.

Another cause of arrhythmias is the transfusion of hyperkalemic RBC units. Over time, the red cell storage lesion contributes to increasingly elevated levels of potassium in the supernatant plasma/anticoagulant/preservative. The leakage rate is further increased by irradiation of the component. Although hyperkalemia is rarely a problem for most transfusion recipients (because of rapid uptake of extracellular potassium by RBCs after transfusion, as well as dilution in the circulation), it can, on occasion, cause morbidity, and even mortality, particularly in premature infants and newborns, massively transfused patients, and acidotic patients (51,52). Cardiac manifestation of hyperkalemia can include bradycardia (which can progress to asystole), complete heart block, and ventricular fibrillation (73). Generally, no special prophylactic approach is needed to prevent these reactions; however, when transfusing relatively large volumes of RBCs to susceptible patients, many authorities recommend the use of fresh (<7–10 days old) packed RBCs, or, if fresh components are unavailable, saline-washed packed RBCs (51).

VIII. TRANSFUSION-ASSOCIATED CITRATE TOXICITY

When large volumes of blood are transfused rapidly (e.g., at rates exceeding 100 mL/min), the result may be increased plasma citrate levels in the recipient. These may produce transient hypocalcemia, with resultant perioral paresthesia, chills, nausea, vomiting, muscular twitching, chest pressure, and, finally, tetany (especially if there is concomitant hyperkalemia). Treatment and prevention are aimed at either slowing the rate of transfusion (not always possible) or, in certain instances, administering intravenous calcium solutions. When the latter method is used, it is important to (a) avoid infusing so much calcium as to cause iatrogenic hypercalcemia; and (b) administer the calcium through a line other than the one through which the transfusion is being administered (so as to prevent the calcium from causing the blood to clot in the line).

IX. TRANSFUSION-ASSOCIATED AIR EMBOLISM

Air emboli related to conventional transfusion are virtually never seen anymore now that glass bottles are no longer used for the storage of blood components, although it has been reported in association with intraoperatively or post-operatively recovered blood (54). However, when blood is transfused under pressure while using an open system, it is possible for air to enter the system and cause significant morbidity, and possibly mortality. Likewise, if air enters while containers or blood administration sets are being changed, an air embolism may result. Symptoms include coughing, dyspnea, chest pain, and shock. Treatment is to place the patient on his left side with his head down. If this is not effective, intracardiac aspiration (to remove the air bubble) may be necessary.

X. HYPOTENSIVE PLATELET TRANSFUSION REACTIONS

In 1993 the AABB was alerted by one of its members that several clusters of severe hypotensive reactions had been associated with the transfusions of leuko-cyte-reduced (filtered) platelets. These appeared to be unrelated to the anaphylac-tic reactions described in Section III.B of this chapter. Hume et al. surveyed all AABB institutional members and looked in detail at 17 reactions that had similar findings (i.e., primarily characterized by hypotension and occurring in association with platelet transfusions). Some 88% of these reactions occurred within one hour of beginning the transfusions; 82% were associated with respiratory distress; 82% rapidly resolved after stopping the transfusion; and 88% of the implicated platelet units had been given through leukocyte reduction filters (55). While this uncon-trolled study lends some support for the existence of hypotensive reactions to platelet transfusions, it would also be important to look for these reactions during/after transfusions of other components before ascribing them to platelet transfusions alone (i.e., no detailed search for hypotensive reactions related to, say, RBC or plasma transfusions has yet been made). Also, other possible causes for these reactions (unrelated to transfusion) must be ruled out. For instance, 2 of the 17 hypotensive reactions in this study occurred in patients who were taking angiotensin-converting enzyme (ACE) inhibitors, which are known to be associ-ated with hypotensive reactions during therapeutic apheresis with albumin re-placement (56). Moore, in his editorial accompanying Hume's article, therefore asks, "Do we know enough about all medications taken by all of these patients to be sure that the concomitant administration of some other medications or combination of medications might not have an even stronger association (than ACE inhibitors) with hypotensive reactions?" (57). In other words, clinical and basic science research must be performed before we can say whether or not hypotensive platelet transfusion reactions truly exist, or are merely the "by-

Table 3 Treatment of Some Adverse Consequences of Transfusions

Type of reaction	Recommended treatment
FNHTRs	Stop transfusion; administer acetaminophen 500–1000 mg PO; do not restart transfusion with same unit
Allergic—*urticarial*	Stop transfusion; administer diphenhydramine hydrochloride 50 mg PO/IM/IV; rarely, hydrocortisone will also be needed; if reaction is mild and symptoms subside, transfusion may be restarted
Allergic—*anaphylactic*	Stop transfusion; depending upon severity of anaphylaxis, administer epinephrine, aminophylline, fluid and vasopressor support (e.g., colloid/crystalloid and dopamine); hydrocortisone, diphenhydramine, oxygen, and airway protection (see text for details) may also be necessary.
Circulatory overload	Stop transufsion; sit patient up as much as possible and administer diuretic (e.g., furosemide 40 mg PO/IV) and oxygen; phlebotomy, with concomitant slow transfusion of packed RBCs (or partial RBC exchange), may rarely be necessary
Citrate toxicity	Slow down or temporarily stop transfusion; oral or parenteral calcium salts (e.g., calcium gluconate 1 g IV) may occasionally be needed

FNHTRs = Febrile, nonhemolytic transfusion reactions.

products" of other types of transfusion reactions, *or* are simply caused by confounding factors.

XI. TRANSFUSION-ASSOCIATED "RED EYE SYNDROME"

In 1997/1998, a series of unusual reactions was reported to the Centers for Disease Control and Prevention (CDC) (58). Collectively, they were referred to as transfusion-associated "red-eye syndrome." The name derives from the severe conjunctival erythema and/or conjunctival hemorrhage that all affected patients experienced, as well as the fact that all the reactions occurred within 24 hours of red blood cell transfusion. The first case was reported in late 1997. As of early 1998, 14 states had reported a total of 106 similar reactions in 74 patients.

CDC looked closely at a subset of 49 of these reactions involving 38 patients in Michigan, Oregon, and Washington. The patients ranged in age from 28 to 84 years (median age: 59 years). Twenty-two (58%) were male, and all were diagnosed previously with an hematological or oncologic illness. All of the reactions manifested between one and 24 hours of the initiation of transfusion (median: 20 hours) and were characterized by: severe conjunctival erythema and/or conjunctival hemorrhage (100%); eye pain (62%); headache (25%); periorbital edema (23%); arthralgias (19%); nausea (15%); dyspnea (6%); and rash (6%). Time to resolution ranged from 2 to 21 days (median: 5 days). Intriguingly, all 38 patients had been transfused with leukocyte-reduced red blood cells. Moreover, it was discovered that, in 45 of 46 reactions for which information was available, the prestorage system used to leukoreduce the (presumably) offending red blood cell units was the same. The mechanism by which these reactions occurs has not been deduced; however, prime suspects include an allergic response to an unknown allergen in—or a toxic reaction to a chemical or material used to produce—the collection-filtration system (Table 3).

REFERENCES

1. Heddle NM, Klama LN, Griffith L, Roberts R, Shukla G, Kelton JG. A prospective study to identify the risk factors associated with acute reactions to platelet and red cell transfusions. Transfusion 1993; 33:794–797.
2. Heddle NM, Klama L, Singer J, Richards C, Fedak P, Walker I, Kelton JG. The role of plasma from platelet concentrates in transfusion reactions. N Engl J Med 1994; 331:625–628.
3. Payne R. The association of febrile transfusion reactions with leuko-agglutinins. Vox Sang 1957; 2:233–241.
4. Litty C. A review: Transfusion reactions. Immunohematology 1996; 12:72–79.
5. Meryman HT, Hornblower M. The preparation of red cells depleted of leukocytes. Transfusion 1986; 26:101–106.
6. Mangano MM, Chambers LA, Kruskall MS. Limited efficacy of leukopoor platelets for prevention of febrile transfusion reactions. Am J Clin Pathol 1991; 95:733–738.
7. Dzik WH. Is the febrile response to transfusion due to donor or recipient cytokines? Transfusion 1992; 32:594.
8. Muylle L, Joos M, Wouters E, De Bock R, Peetermans ME. Increased tumor necrosis factor alpha (TNF-alpha), interleukin 1 (IL-1), and interleukin 6 (IL-6) levels in the plasma of stored platelet concentrates: relationship between TNF-alpha and IL-6 levels and febrile transfusion reactions. Transfusion 1993; 33:195–199.
9. Ferrara JLM. The febrile platelet transfusion reaction: a cytokine shower. Transfusion 1995; 35:89–90.
10. Aye MT, Palmer DS, Giulivi A, Hashemi S. Effect of filtration of platelet concentrates on the accumulation of cytokines and platelet release factors during storage. Transfusion 1995; 35:117–124.
11. Stack G, Snyder EL. Cytokine generation in stored platelet concentrates. Transfusion 1994; 34:20–25.
12. Federowicz I, Barrett BB, Anderson JW, Urashima M, Popovsky MA, Anderson KC. A characterization of reactions after transfusion of cellular blood components that are white cell reduced before storage. Transfusion 1996; 36:21–28.

13. Muylle L, Wouters E, Peetermans ME. Febrile reactions to platelet transfusion: the effect of increased interleukin 6 levels in concentrates prepared by the platelet-rich plasma method. Transfusion 1996; 36:886–890.

14. Widmann FK. Controversies in transfusion medicine: Should a febrile transfusion reaction occasion the return of the blood component to the blood bank? Pro. Transfusion 1994; 34:356–358.

15. Oberman HA. Controversies in transfusion medicine: Should a febrile transfusion response occasion the return of the blood component to the blood bank? Con. Transfusion 1994; 34:353–355.

16. Ryden SW, Oberman HA. Compatibility of common intravenous solutions with CPD blood. Transfusion 1975; 15:250–255.

17. Kevy S, Schmidt PJ, McGinniss MH, Workman WG. Febrile nonhemolytic transfusion reactions and the limited role of leukoagglutinins in their etiology. Transfusion 1962; 2:7–16.

18. Vengelen-Tyler V, ed. Noninfectious complications of blood transfusion. In: Technical Manual. 12th ed. Bethesda, MD: American Association of Blood Banks, 1996:543–562.

19. Vesilind GW, Simpson MB, Shifman MA, Colman RE, Kao KJ. Evaluation of a centrifugal blood cell processor for washing platelet concentrates. Transfusion 1988; 28:46–50.

20. Silvergleid AJ, Hafleigh EB, Harabin MA, Wolf RM, Grumet FC. Clinical value of washed-platelet concentrates in patients with non-hemolytic transfusion reactions. Transfusion 1977; 17:33–37.

21. Sandler SG, Eckrich R, Malamut D, Mallory D. Hemagglutination assays for the diagnosis and prevention of IgA anaphylactic transfusion reactions. Blood 1994; 84:2031–2035.

22. Poothullil J, Shimizu A, Day RP, Dolovich J. Anaphylaxis from the product(s) of ethylene oxide gas. Ann Intern Med 1975; 82:58–60.

23. Branch DR, Gifford G. Allergic reaction to transfused cephalothin antibody. JAMA 1979; 241:495–496.

24. Stern A, van Hage-Hamsten M, Sondell K, Johansson SGO. Is allergy screening of blood donors necessary? Vox Sang 1995; 69:114–119.

25. Michel J, Sharon R. Non-hemolytic adverse reaction after transfusion of a blood unit containing penicillin. Br Med J 1980; 1:152–153.

26. Take H, Tamura J, Sawamura M, Murakami H, Naruse T, Tsuchiya, Miyawaki S, Hirabayashi H. Severe anaphylactic transfusion reaction associated with HLA-incompatible platelets. Br J Haematol 1993; 83:673–674.

27. Sano H, Koga Y, Hamasaki K, Furuyama H, Itami N. Anaphylaxis associated with white-cell reduction filter. Lancet 1996; 347:1053.

28. Bjerrum OJ, Jersild C. Class-specific anti-IgA associated with severe anaphylactic transfusion reactions in a patient with pernicious anemia. Vox Sang 1971; 21:411–424.

29. Pineda A, Taswell HF. Transfusion reactions associated with anti-IgA antibodies: Report of four cases and review of the literature. Transfusion 1975; 15:10–15.

30. Sazama K. Reports of 355 transfusion-associated deaths: 1976 through 1985. Transfusion 1990; 30:583–590.

31. Lippman M, Rumley W. Medical emergencies. In: Dunagan WC, Ridner ML, eds.

Manual of Medical Therapeutic. 26th ed. Boston: Little, Brown and Company, 1989:482–503.

32. Shirey RS, Ness PM. Alloimmunization to blood group antigens. In: Anderson KC, Ness PM, eds. Scientific Basis of Transfusion Medicine: Implications for Clinical Practice. Philadelphia: W.B. Saunders Company, 1994:507–516.

33. Rosse WF, Gallagher D, Kinney TR, Castro O, Dosik H, Moohr J, Wang W, Levy PS, and the Cooperative Study of Sickle Cell Disease. Transfusion and alloimmunization in sickle cell disease. Blood 1990; 76:1431–1437.

34. Hoeltge GA, Domen RE, Rybicki LA, Schaffer PA. Multiple red cell transfusion and alloimmunization—experience with 6996 antibodies detected in a total of 159,262 patients from 1985 to 1993. Arch Pathol Lab Med 1995; 119:42–45.

35. Lostumbo MM, Holland PV, Schmidt PJ. Isoimmunization after multiple transfusions. N Engl J Med 1966; 275:141–144.

36. Coles SM, Klein HG, Holland PV. Alloimmunization in two multitransfused patient populations. Transfusion 1981; 21:462–466.

37. Wayne AS, Kevy SV, Nathan DG. Transfusion management of sickle cell disease. Blood 1993; 81:1109–1123.

38. Diamond WJ, Brown FL, Bitterman P, Klein HG, Davey RJ, Winslow RM. Delayed hemolytic transfusion reaction presenting as sickle-cell crisis. Ann Intern Med 1980; 93:231–234.

39. Milner PF, Squires JE, Larison PJ, Charles WT, Krauss JS. Posttransfusion crisis in sickle cell anemia: role of delayed hemolytic reactions to transfusion. Southern Med J 1985; 78:1462–1469.

40. The Trial to Reduce Alloimmunization to Platelets Study Group. Leukocyte reduction and ultraviolet B irradiation of platelets to prevent alloimmunization and refractoriness to platelet transfusions. N Engl J Med 1997; 337:1861–1869.

41. Williamson LM, Wimperis JZ, Williamson P, Copplestone JA, Gooi HC, Morgenstern GR, Norfolk DR. Bedside filtration of blood products in the prevention of HLA alloimmunization—A prospective randomized study. Blood 1994; 83:3028–3035.

42. von dem Borne AEGK, Simsek S, van der Schoot CE, Goldschmeding R. Platelet and neutrophil alloantigens: their nature and role in immune-mediated cytopenias. In: Garratty G, ed. Immunobiology of Transfusion Medicine. New York: Marcel Dekker Inc., 1994:149–171.

43. Puig N, de Haas M, Kleijer M, Montoro JA, Perez A, Villalba JV, Gomez I, von dem Borne AEJK. Isoimmune neonatal neutropenia caused by FcgammaRIIIb antibodies in a Spanish child. Transfusion 1995; 35:683–687.

44. Van Buren NL, Stroncek DF, Clay ME, McCullough J, Dalmasso AP. Transfusion-related acute lung injury caused by an NB2 granulocyte-specific antibody in a patient with thrombotic thrombocytopenic purpura. Transfusion 1990; 30:42–45.

45. Popovsky MA, Chaplin HC, Moore SB. Transfusion-related acute lung injury: a neglected, serious complication of hemotherapy. Transfusion 1992; 32:589–591.

46. Popovsky MA, Audet AM, Andrzejewski Jr. C. Transfusion-associated circulatory overload in orthopedic surgery patients: a multi-institutional study. Immunohematology 1996; 12:87–89.

47. Popovsky MA, Taswell HF. Circulatory overload: an underdiagnosed consequence of transfusion. Transfusion 1985; 25:469.

48. Marriott HL, Kekwick A. Volume and rate in blood transfusion for the relief of anemia. Br Med J 1040; 1:1043–1046.

49. Kim HC, Dugan NP, Silber JH, Martin MB, Schwartz E, Ohene-Frempong K, Cohen AR. Erythrocytapheresis therapy to reduce iron overload in chronically transfused patients with sickle cell disease. Blood 1994; 83:1136–1142.

50. Propper RD, Button LN, Nathan DG. New approaches to the transfusion management of thalassemia. Blood 1980; 55:55–60.

51. Hall TL, Barnes A, Miller JR, Bethencourt DN, Nestor L. Neonatal mortality following transfusion of red cells with high plasma potassium levels. Transfusion 1993; 33:606–609.

52. Brown KA, Bissonnette B, MacDonald M, Poon AO. Hyperkalemia during massive blood transfusion in paediatric craniofacial surgery. Can J Anaesth 1990; 37:401–408.

53. Kohan DE. Fluid and electrolyte management. In: Dunagan WC, Ridner ML, eds. Manual of Medical Therapeutics. 26th ed. Boston: Little, Brown and Company, 1989:52–71.

54. Linden JV, Kaplan HS, Murphy MT. Fatal air embolism due to postoperative blood recovery. Anesthesia Analgesia 1997, 84:422–426.

55. Hume HA, Popovsky MA, Benson K, Glassman AB, Hines D, Oberman HA, Pisciotto PT, Anderson KC. Hypotensive reactions: a previously uncharacterized complication of platelet transfusion? Transfusion 1996; 36:904–909.

56. Owen HG, Brecher ME. Atypical reactions associated with use of angiotensin-converting enzyme inhibitors and apheresis. Transfusion 1994; 34:891–894.

57. Moore AB. Hypotensive reactions: Are they a new phenomenon? Are they related solely to transfusion of platelets? Does filtration of components play a role? Transfusion 1996; 36:852–853.

58. Adverse ocular reactions following transfusion—United States, 1997–1998. MMWR 1998; 47:49–50.

4

Managing Error for System Improvement

Harold S. Kaplan
New York-Presbyterian Hospital, New York, New York

James B. Battles
University of Texas, Southwestern Medical Center, Dallas, Texas

The safety of blood transfusion has long been an area of concern and study (1). However, with the intense public and legislative scrutiny following the discovery of the potential for human immunodeficiency virus (HIV) transmission by blood transfusion, there has been an exceptional increase in the investigative and regulatory interest directed at a broad range of blood safety issues.

In an effort to minimize undesirable variations in the "manufacturing" aspect of transfusion medicine, i.e., the recruitment, collection, testing, and processing of units of donated blood, there is an increased regulatory emphasis on rigorous process control coupled with training to protocols of standard operating procedures (2). This approach, contained within the Current Good Manufacturing Practices (CGMPs), clearly contributes to more reliable processes. However, even with the long-established CGMPs in the biopharmaceutical man-ufacturing industry, there is a documented persistence of human error even with strict adherence to CGMPs (3). Similar problems are seen with the process of transfusion to the intended recipient.

I. METHODS TO IDENTIFY ERROR

There are a number of methods to identify and reduce the contribution of human error to the risks of transfusion.

A. Observation/Audit

One approach has been direct observation by skilled observers in the actual operating environment. This is a well-established way to address human error in its actual setting (4). Shulman and coworkers (5) developed a multidisciplinary team approach to quality assurance and improvement directed at reducing patient identification errors by improving compliance with standard procedures. The program involved periodic concurrent audits, which included direct observation of procedures. With feedback of deviations from protocol and active educational efforts, adherence to patient identification protocols improved gradually from 50% during a pilot study to nearly 100% by the 125th audit (5). Although the authors found in-service education to be effective in increasing compliance with protocol and reducing the risk of error, observation may itself alter the circumstances studied, as may observer error and limitation in controlling all relevant variables. In addition, the enduring effect of such improvement may be difficult to maintain given employee turnover and the need for sustained intensive effort.

B. Accident Analysis

The second approach to error identification and prevention is the analysis of accident data. This approach has been an important source of information used by the National Transportation Safety Board (NTSB) in aviation (4). However, hindsight bias and incomplete data lead to distortion. Additionally, although human error has often been identified as a cause of an accident, little insight has been provided as to why an error occurred.

Despite these limitations, analysis of accident data has been an important source of information in blood transfusion. In 1975, the Food and Drug Administration (FDA) first mandated the reporting of transfusion-associated fatalities, and by 1980, the Health Care Finance Administration agreed to investigate these fatalities in greater depth. The file of these reports is accessible under the Freedom of Information Act. This database has been extensively studied by a number of investigators (6–10).

Mummert and Tourault (11) reviewed 150 transfusion-associated fatalities reported to the FDA from 1990 to 1992. They concluded that nearly one third of these fatalities could have been prevented by adherence to proper procedure. Interestingly, a failure to follow procedures is also responsible for one third of major air carrier accidents. However, as pointed out by Nagle (4), even with categorization of error data, if it is not known *why* someone "failed to follow standard procedures," development of an effective preventive strategy remains problematic. In this regard, Nagle has stressed the need for a model of human error to be used in conjunction with error data collection and classification.

Mummert and Tourault also noted that improper transfusion of ABO-incompatible red blood cells due to error continues to be a primary cause of preventable death. They also reported that failure to identify a reaction in progress contributed to many of the fatalities. Again, in analogy with other error-critical areas, such as nuclear power and aviation, delay in detecting a problem, improperly identifying its cause, and delay in implementing corrective actions are recognized as critical issues (12).

The management of error to limit adverse outcomes or unplanned effects is now recognized to be of fundamental importance in system design and training in error-critical activities, particularly since the Three Mile Island accident (12). Although the importance of this has also been appreciated in transfusion medicine, its proper emphasis has not been carried through to all critical operational areas. In some cases analyzed by Mummert and Tourault (11), signs or symptoms were treated, but the transfusion was not identified as the cause and was continued. These authors also reported that in several cases signs such as hemoglobinuria were noted without being recognized as a transfusion reaction.

In an extensive analysis of fatalities reported to the FDA over a 10-year period, Sazama (10) reviewed 355 reports and studied 256 (99 did not involve transfusion, 68 related to transfusion-associated hepatitis, 3 related to transfusion-associated acquired immune deficiency syndrome, and one report recorded could not be located). Acute hemolytic transfusion reaction resulting from ABO incompatibility accounted for the majority of fatalities. Sazama found one third of all deaths and two thirds of incompatible red cell transfusions to be attributable to error and therefore preventable. She estimated that 124 fatal ABO errors occurred in approximately 100,000,000 transfusions, or 1/800,000 units. Sazama also reported that 5 of the 26 hepatitis B deaths resulted from error, with three seropositive units labeled properly but released in error, and two seropositive units labeled improperly as negative. Additionally, of 12 reported donor deaths, one related to an O-positive plasma donor who received A red cells from another donor. Sazama determined that errors leading to fatality were most often "managerial" or system errors, rather than isolated human error.

In a 2-year period from 1990 through 1991, transfusion-related incidents reported to the New York State Department of Health (NYSDOH) also included errors that as precursor events could have but did not necessarily result in harm (13). The reported incidence of administration of the wrong unit of blood, or of blood given to the wrong recipient, was estimated at 1/12,000 units transfused. Of these mistakes, ABO-incompatible red cell transfusions had an estimated incidence of 1/33,000. Three of the ABO-incompatible transfusions resulted in death, yielding a fatal transfusion error rate of 1/600,000 units (13).

The importance of management and system contributions to human error identified in the 10-year study of FDA reports (10) and in the NYSDOH's demonstration of the importance of "benign" precursor events (50 times greater occurrence rate than errors resulting in fatal accidents) (13) parallel the experience in other error-critical fields (4).

C. Simulation

A third method of error analysis for development of prevention strategies is the study of error in the laboratory and by simulation. This approach has also proven useful since laboratory circumstances allow simplification and control of confounding variables. Simplification, however, may itself be an important shortcoming in understanding inherently complex situations (4).

The laboratory approach has not been generally applied to transfusion error analysis, although the announced introduction of simulated benign errors into transfusion operations has been an effective means for increasing error detection. Taswell et al. (14) demonstrated that by modifying work to demand staff attention in looking for known introduced errors and by providing positive feedback when they were found, the blood bank not only achieved an increased detection of the introduced errors, but also increased the detection of real, previously undetected errors from 4 in the first 3 months to 73 in the final 3 months of the study.

D. Record Review/Chart Audit

A fourth approach to identifying errors is to review records, including donor and laboratory records and patient charts. The review of such records has been the most traditional means of performing quality assurance checks and documenting patient outcome. The chart or record is a documentation of actions performed or missing information. This auditing of charts or records against predetermined criteria can be a valuable method of identifying errors and near-miss events. Classen and colleagues (15,16) have successfully used a sophisticated automated hospital information and record system to identify adverse drug events that would have otherwise gone unreported. The limitation of record review and chart audit is determined by whether information necessary to detect an error is part of the record.

E. Event Reporting

A fifth approach to compiling information for the study of error is the event report, including self-reporting as exemplified by the Aviation Safety Reporting

System (ASRS) operated by NASA for the Federal Aviation Administration (FAA) (17). Commercial airline accidents are very rare events, with approximately one accident (defined as aircraft hull loss or by one or more fatalities) per million departures by U.S. carriers (4). Despite this excellent record, human error is identified as the causal factor in more than one half of all airline accidents and as much as 90% in general aviation (4). The ASRS has been operational for almost two decades. More than 250,000 reports (18) have been archived, analyzed, and made available for research and study by interested professionals as well as by regulatory and investigative bodies. An advisory group representing the major U.S. aviation operations organizations oversees and monitors the ASRS. This a no-fault, confidential, voluntary, self-reporting system, in which pilots and controllers report noncalamitous mistakes, including caught or trapped errors, occurrences/situations. The ASRS philosophy recognized that post hoc analysis (which is what the study of incident reports necessarily is) cannot prove causation—it can only observe a significant association of certain possibly causal factors with a class of occurrence (4).

Confidentiality and immunity from prosecution for noncriminal acts are important features of this or any system intended to capture operational data. There is no disincentive to report, and this approach also optimizes access to information from the incident reporters themselves. The no-fault confidential nature of this system has led to an increased frankness in reporting and completeness of invaluable data (15). This eminently successful voluntary reporting system has provided a rich database from which valuable improvements in safety have been made possible (15).

One drawback of the voluntary reporting system is the variability of reporting by different individuals. This sampling variability makes any quantification problematic and leads to more reliable qualitative than quantitative data. There is a better idea of what errors occur, but relatively little is known about their frequency.

The preponderance of "benign" error in transfusion medicine leads to a deceptively low morbidity from failure to follow safe practice (19). This obscures the frequency and potential of these errors for hemolytic reaction and increased risk of disease transmission. Even though such errors are an important source of information for improving transfusion safety, there has been no means for their systematic collection and analysis. The study of the "benign" or "caught" errors (i.e., potential errors trapped by the system) could provide a rich database for improving the safety of the blood supply (20). As demonstrated in studies of safety incidents in commercial aviation, these near-miss events are very similar to those associated with full-blown disasters. Since there are many more near misses than there are events with major adverse outcomes, there is a need to collect near-miss event data in addition to accident data (21). The relationship between near misses and accidents has been compared to a pyramid or iceberg

(22), which represents a continuum from the rare visible accident to the much more frequent near misses. Linden et al.'s (13) data from New York State can illustrate this relationship with the iceberg in Figure 1. The fatalities from hemolytic reactions due to ABO-incompatible blood transfusions are the visible tip of the iceberg, the number of adverse reactions reported as being just below the waterline, the number of incorrect units transfused by nurses as next, and the unreported near misses as unknown.

A fundamental aspect of any event-reporting system is the identification or detection of events that occur within an organization. Zapt and Reason (23) indicate that error detection is the first step in error management. If an error is not detected, it cannot be managed. They go on to point out that, from an organizational point of view, it is very important that the error detection rate

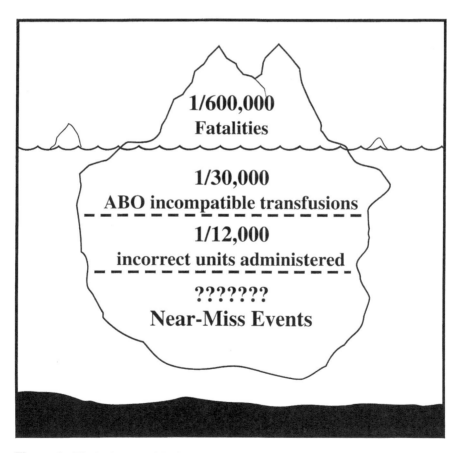

Figure 1   The iceberg model of accidents and near-miss events.

is high; errors that are not detected for a long time could have disastrous consequences. Thus, the goal of error management should be to *increase* error detection or reporting rate. The number of events reported is an indicator of an organization's *detection sensitivity level* (DSL). High reporting rates indicate a high DSL; few reported events indicate a low DSL. A low DSL might be considered an indicator of an inadequate error-detection and reporting approach. While the DSL should remain high, the *event severity level* (ESL) of the incidents detected should decrease over time as corrective actions are implemented (24).

In order to achieve a high DSL, an organization must remove any impediments to reporting an event. Confidential no-fault reporting is one of the best ways to encourage event reporting. Since the purpose of the event-reporting system is to learn about how systems are operating, there must be separation between event reporting and employee performance assessment approaches. Research literature indicates that organizational encouragement such as confidential no-fault reporting significantly increases error detection and reporting (24).

Table 1 is a review of the strengths and limitations of the five error analysis methods previously discussed.

II. CLASSIFICATION OF EVENTS

Regardless of the method that one chooses to identify error, there is a need to classify them once they are discovered. Just what are the elements of events, both near misses and major misadventures, that should be studied? In essence all events are nested within the context of what happened, where in the process it occurred, when it happened, and who was involved in the event. Although it is necessary to investigate all of these elements of an event for complete understanding, most existing approaches to event analysis concentrate on describing *what* happened. Little information is found as the causes or description of *why* the event occurred. A review of 200 cases obtained from reports submitted to the FDA found an almost total lack of information regarding the root causes of the events. The lack of in-depth investigation of the root causes of transfusion events could indicate that the corrective actions that are taken may be inappropriate or unrelated to the actual cause of the event (24).

A. Causes of Errors

Reason (12) has identified two major categories of failures or errors that occur in complex systems: active and latent. The distinction hinges on both who initiated the failure and how long it took to have an adverse effect (25,26). *Active failures* are committed by people in direct contact with the human/system interface, i.e.,

Table 1 Methods for Identifying Errors

Method	Advantage	Limitations
Observation/Audit	Accurate method to identify performance of individuals compared to standards	Labor intensive and limited lasting value with employee turnover
Accident analysis	Used to determine error rates and understanding major misadventures and is required to be performed when such events occur	Limited by hindsight and delays in investigation; often lack of information as to causes
Simulation	An accurate way to assess team and individual performance and decision making; has the ability to introduce known errors or events to be identified and managed	Difficult to create and can only simulate some aspects of the transfusion process
Record review/ Chart audit	Standard method of documenting outcomes and many processes; normal activity which can provide valuable information	Only as good as the information recorded; always after the fact
Event reporting	Captures near-miss events and deviations as perceived by individuals; gives perspective of individuals involved	Subject to underreporting because individuals do not feel comfortable reporting errors

health professionals. The consequences of these failures are usually readily apparent almost immediately. It is the active failure that we most often associate with human error. Latent failures are the delayed-action consequences of technical design or organizational issues and decisions. These latent failures often are initiated at the upper levels of an organization. Accidents or major misadventures with adverse outcomes occur when latent errors or system considerations combine with an active human error, as illustrated in Figure 2. Error researchers stress the importance of examining both human or active failures as well as the underlying latent or system failures.

B. Human Active Failures

As discussed previously, active or human failures are most commonly associated with human error. These errors are associated with the individuals who are at what Reason (12) calls the "sharp end" of the system. In the case of transfusion medicine, these are the people responsible for collecting, processing, and trans-

Misadventures Happen When:

- Latent underlying conditions
- ✚ An active human error
- = Misadventure

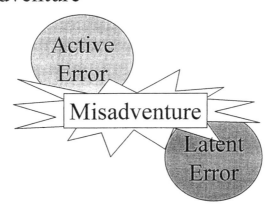

Figure 2   The relationship between latent and active failures and misadventures.

fusing blood products. We can moderate human fallibility, but we can never eliminate it completely. Active errors are tied to human cognitive processes and associated behaviors. Rasmussen (27,28) gives us a useful taxonomy for identifying and classifying these different types of human behavior underlying human errors:

> *Skill-based behavior* refers to routine tasks requiring little or no conscious attention during task execution.
>
> *Rule-based behavior* refers to familiar procedures applied to frequent decision-making situations.
>
> *Knowledge-based behavior* refers to problem-solving activities such as when one is confronted with new situations for which no readily available standard solutions exist.

1. Skill-Based Behavior

Most health professionals operate in a skill-based behavioral mode for all of the routine tasks that are carried out, from drawing blood to the transfusion process itself. These highly skilled activities become routine and can be executed without conscious thought. It is like riding a bicycle—once you learn you can do it automatically. Driving a car is another example—we can drive while listening to the radio or talking to a passenger. It is because these skills are so often used that one can perform with a very high level of reliability. We operate almost as if we were on automatic pilot, performing virtually without thinking about what we are doing, at almost an unconscious level. However, there are opportunities for failures when one operates in the skill-based mode. If we are distracted or something interrupts the smooth flow of a skill-based routine, a skill-based failure can occur—called a slip. An example of a slip is being distracted by someone in the parking lot and inadvertently locking the keys in the car or arriving home only to discover that you forgot to stop at the store and buy milk on the way home. Slips are unintended errors caused by either not doing some part of the routine, an error of omission, or doing something that one should not have done, like a repeating step in the process twice, which would be a failure of commission. Slips cannot effectively be remediated by retraining an individual. It is a waste of time because the individual already knows how to perform the task at a very high level of accuracy and retraining is often insulting and ineffective. Counseling employees to be more careful is equally ineffective as a means of remediation. However, slips can be prevented by redesign of equipment or procedures so that it is harder to make a slip. For example, feedback mechanisms can be designed into the process that give clues to the individual as soon as they have made a slip. Job aids such as a template for reviewing donor records that highlight omissions or inconsistencies can help to prevent slips in the skill-based mode.

2. Rule-Based Behavior

Rule-based behavior occurs at the conscious level within the context of the situation that exists. Rule-based behavior involves recognizing the situation, then selecting the proper routine or protocol that is called for in a given situation. For example, if we are driving and come to a stop sign, we must decide what rules to apply in this situation. If it is a two-way stop, then there is a given set of traffic rules to follow, but if it is a four-way stop then there are different rules of the road that we must follow. Rule-based behavior is an if-then condition. Failure in rule-based behavior can occur at the different stages in this conscious decision and action process. These failures are often referred to as mistakes. A mistake can occur under two conditions: selecting the wrong rule for a given situation, or selecting the correct rule but carrying it out incorrectly. Rule-based failures can occur when someone carries out a procedure that they are not qualified to perform. Another type of rule-based failure is inadequately assessing or verifying the situation, which can result in a mistake in selecting the correct rule. An example of verification would be failing to check the patient's identity before transfusion. While most rule-based failures are unintended, some are not. In some instances an individual can consciously choose to apply a different rule or carry out a task differently than is proscribed by standard operating procedures. This type of action is a violation. Violations can be either routine, a work around of an inadequate procedure, or a cultural artefact of the organization—i.e., "everyone does it this way." Routine violations often occur when procedures are changed and individuals continue to apply the old procedure. In rare cases an individual may choose to freelance and carry out tasks in a manner contrary to standard procedures. Rule-based failures are subject to remediation through training in many instances. In addition they can be reinforced through clearly written procedures and protocols and job aids. Rule-based failures of verification can be prevented in some cases by redesigning the task to place a forcing function, like the blood lock that prevents a transfusion from being started until the patient's identify has been matched to the unit.

3.   Knowledge-Based Behavior

Knowledge-based behavior involves solving unique problems or selecting a plan of action in a new or unfamiliar setting. Knowledge-based behavior most often occurs with new employees. They do not have the depth of experience to operate in the skill-based mode or to draw from past experience to select the appropriate rule or protocol to carry out a task or to solve a problem. Learners such as medical residents and other trainees often operate in the knowledge-based mode because the number of unique or new situations for them is significant compared to the experienced individual or expert. Experienced individuals only rarely operate in the knowledge-based mode. Thus, the expert and the novice are likely to make different types of errors. The expert is most likely to make a slip or an occasional rule-based error, while the novice is most likely to have knowledge-based failures. If is possible for the expert to encounter unique conditions and be placed in a situation where they can be subject to knowledge-based failures. The procedures, equipment, and situation are all slightly different, and their set of skills and rules may be inadequate for the new situation. Examples of such conditions would be expert pilots moving from one type of aircraft to another. The skills and rules used in operating a Boeing 737 are not the same as for a Boeing 757. While it may not take an expert long to become familiar with a new setting, there is a need for orientation and knowledge transfer from the previous setting to the new one. This is why it is good practice to have individuals recertified or credentialed when moving to a new job or assuming new responsibilities.

Figure 3 summarizes the three levels of human behavior associated with such common activity as driving a car.

Skill Based
- Perform routine tasks
  e.g. driving while
  listening to the radio,
  holding a conversation

Rule Based
- Perform familiar
  tasks, experience
  e.g. approach
  familiar stop sign
  access stored info
  slow car down,
  look both
  directions, etc.

Knowledge Based
- Novel situation,
  problem solving at
  conscious level e.g.
  traffic lights broken at
  busy junction,
  consciously generate
  solution proceed or
  stop ?

Figure 3   Rasmussen's model of human behavior.

C. Latent Failures

While we may never totally eliminate human or active errors, we can eliminate the technical or organizational aspects that might set the person up for an active failure. Latent or system failures include both technical and organizational aspects. The technical aspects associated with latent failure include such things as the design of equipment and software, the construction of facilities, including mobiles, and materials. One aspect of organizational failures stems from normal management considerations including the structure of the organization, planning and scheduling, forecasting, budgeting, and allocating resources. The policies and procedures in place in an organization can also be a source of latent failure, as are the orientation, training, and selection of employees. The informal but very real culture of an organization can be another source of latent failure. These latent failures have the potential of setting up the individuals for failure. The adverse safety consequences of normal technical and organizational decisions may lie dormant for a very long time. Reason (12) has referred to latent error as organizational pathogens, which wait to combine with the right active human failure to have an adverse consequence.

It is difficult to recognize a latent error before the fact and to predict how it will present itself in the future, since there are so many possible outcomes of technical and management decisions. However, since an event represents a fixed outcome, one is often able to identify the responsible latent error by reasoning backward from the event. Once latent failures are recognized, they can be diagnosed and corrected before they combine with an active error to produce a bad outcome.

III. ASSIGNING BLAME

One of the major problems with the management of error is detecting that an error has occurred. This is particularly true if one tries to move from dealing with only the rare visible events to major adverse consequences. Perper (29) has noted that there is substantial underreporting of medical misadventures, which is in part attributable to the very strong tendency in the health care field to blame the individual or individuals associated with an active failure, the individuals at the sharp end of an error chain. This produces a climate where individuals are reluctant to report events where there may be an adverse consequence to reporting, i.e., losing one's license to practice. As Reason (25) has pointed out, blaming people is universal, natural, and emotionally satisfying. In addition, in a litigious environment it is easier to blame the person involved. In fact, the willingness of individuals to accept blame for their actions is almost universal among health-care professionals.

Health professionals all share one common professional focus, and that is to take personal responsibility for applying their particular skills to solve the patient's health problems either directly or indirectly. This sense of personal responsibility and accountability for patient care is ancient, stemming in the Hippocratic oath that physicians recite to this day on graduation. Nurses are at the sharp end in the transfusion process; as Curtain (30) has stated, "in the end, nurses are the patient's last line of defense against system errors." Curtain goes on to relate a statement made by one of her instructors in nursing school: "and you, you alone, stand responsible for it (giving the correct medication)—before God, the patient and the state board of nursing." Since the consequence—causing harm or failing to protect the patient—has such potentially grave outcomes, including death, a physician or nurse can lose his or her license to practice and, in rare cases, may face criminal charges. In the health care field the norm is to expect perfect performance at all times; anything less could be considered as being careless or negligent. This sense of perfectionism has become a professional norm and has been codified in law.

There are some obvious unwanted consequences of perfectionism in terms of overall safety and event reporting. One consequence is a personal sense of guilt when patient harm has occurred. This guilt focuses on one's own professional behavior and diminishes one's ability to find underlying system or latent causes for an error. Within the organization there is a desire to focus event investigations on finding the guilty party(s) who were negligent and committed the error. The system searches for those negligent or less than perfect health professionals to eliminate them and, in so doing, reduce error from the system. Human resource policies encourage or mandate recording the number of errors or adverse events within an employee's personnel record. Such policies can lead to denial that errors have occurred. If an error is caught and is not revealed and if no harm was caused to the patient, then it is rationalized that it did not matter and need not be revealed. Both conditions tend to result in underreporting of events. Despite the illusion of perfect performance, Paget (31) points out that health care is error-ridden, inexact, uncertain, and is practiced on the human body.

Reason (25) points out that the blaming individuals leads to ineffective countermeasures: disciplinary action, exhortations to be more careful, retraining, and writing new procedures to proscribe those actions implicated in some recent event. He goes on to point out that these measures can have an impact at the outset of some necessary safety program, but they have little or no value when applied to a well-qualified and highly motivated work force. Figure 4 illustrates the issue of assigning blame.

Figure 4 Blaming traditions and consequences.

IV. DEVELOPING A SAFETY CULTURE

To avoid the blaming of individuals and its negative consequences, both Berwick (32) and Lucas (33,34) have emphasized the importance of creating an environment within an organization where events can be reported in an open and free manner. It is essential that there be no adverse consequences applied to those submitting reports of events. In order for this to be accomplished, there should be a decoupling of discovery error from individual employee performance. Error management efforts should be directed at learning how the system actually operates as opposed to how management thinks it is operating. Therefore, a separation between event reporting and employee assessment should be made. Everyone in the organization should be encouraged to report events that have the potential for adverse outcome for products or patient/donor safety. It is important that feedback be provided to blood center or hospital employees on any changes that result from events reported. Such information is essential for continued reporting and for employees to feel that they have a degree of ownership in the system.

If there is truly a concerted effort to create a positive safety culture in the organization and to have individuals capture all events including near-miss events, then a significant increase in the number of known events is likely to occur. In a medical setting in which there is a strong, positive safety culture and employees are encouraged to voluntarily report events, there may be as much as a 10-fold increase in reporting (35). The authors found that when an event reporting system was established within the blood bank at a large indigent care public hospital, this same 10-fold increase in events reported.

V. CAUSAL CLASSIFICATION MODEL

A root cause classification model has been developed for the field of transfusion medicine as part of a medical event reporting system for transfusion medicine (31). This classification approach was based on the Eindhoven Classification Model (21,24,36). It has three major categories of causes, which are grouped as (a) technical (equipment, software, and forms), (b) organizational (policies procedures, and protocols), and (c) human causes (knowledge-based, rule-based, and skill-based). The classification of human failures is consistent with the theoretical framework of Rasmussen (27,28), and the latent technical and organizational factors are consistent with the framework of Reason (12,25). Table 2 is the Eindhoven Classification Model, medical version for transfusion medicine.

To illustrate how this classification model works, we have selected a transfusion event that was reported, investigated, and diagrammed as to what happened and for which a root cause analysis was performed.

Table 2 Eindhoven Classification Model for Medical Domain

Category	Code	Definition
1. *Latent Errors*		*Errors that result from underlying system failures*
A. **Technical**		Refers to physical items such as equipment, physical installations, software, materials, labels, and forms
External	TEX	Technical failures beyond the control and repsonsibility of the investigating organization
Design	TD	Failures due to poor design of equipment, software, labels or forms
Construction	TC	Correct design was not followed accurately during construction
Materials	TM	Material defects not classified under TD or TC
B. **Organizational**		
External	OEX	Failures at an organizational level beyond the control and responsibility of the investigating organization
Transfer of knowledge	OK	Failures resulting from inadequate measures taken to ensure that situational or domain specific knowledge or information is transferred to all new or inexperienced staff
Protocols/Procedures	OP	Failures related to the quality and availability of the protocols with the department (too complicted, inaccurate, unrealistic, absent, or poorly presented)
Management Priorities	OM	Internal management decisions in which safety is relegated to an inferior position when faced with conflicting demands or objectives; a conflict between production needs and safety (e.g., decisions made about staffing levels)
Culture	OC	Failures resulting from collective approach and its attendant modes of behavior to risks in the investigating organization
2. *Active Errors*		*Errors or failures that result from human behavior*
A. **Human**		
External	HEX	Human failures originating beyond the control and responsibility of the investigation organization

Knowledge-based		
Knowledge-based errors	HKK	The inability of an individual to apply existing knowledge to a novel situation
Rule-based		
Qualifications	HRQ	Incorrect fit between an individual's qualification, training, or education and a particular task
Coordination	HRC	A lack of task coordination within a health-care team in an organization
Verification	HRV	Failures in the correct and complete assessment of a situation including relevant conditions of the patient and materials to be used before starting the intervention
Intervention	HRI	Failures that result from faulty task planning (selecting the wrong protocol) and/or execution (selecting the correct protocol but carrying it out incorrectly)
Monitoring	HRM	Failures during monitoring of process or patient status during or postintervention
Skill-based		
Slips	HSS	Failures in performance of fine motor skills
Tripping	HST	Failures in whole body movements
3. *Other*		
A. **Patient-related factor**	PRF	Failures related to patient characteristics or conditions beyond the control of staff and influence treatment
B. **Unclassifiable**	X	Failures that cannot be classified in any other category

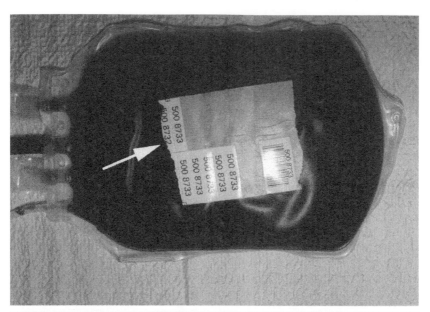

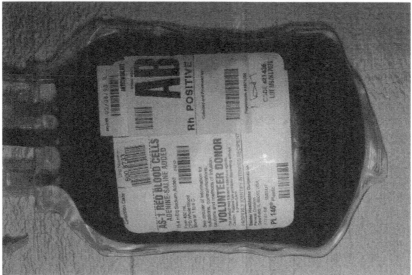

Figure 5 Photograph of a unit of red cells with an out-of-sequence transfer label.

A medical technologist on the second shift in a blood bank was releasing units from quarantine to inventory when she noticed an out-of-sequence number on the back of a unit of red blood cells (see Fig. 5). The unit was isolated until the labels were corrected. It was determined that no incorrect labels had been used either in testing or in component production, therefore no harm was done. Clearly this event was a near miss.

Figure 6 is a causal tree diagramming this event. When classifying this event, the first question to ask would be: Were there any technical failures? The separation markings between different number sequence labels were not prominent, providing unclear guidance as to where to tear the roll of labels in order to separate adjacent blocks of numbers. In addition, the markings provided little feedback when the tear had been done incorrectly (allowing little chance for recovery from the error). Clearly, there was a design failure in the label itself, classified as a TD. Next we looked for any organizational failures. There might have been a failure in the procedure for checking the accuracy or consistency of the label on the unit prior to placing it into quarantine. These procedures should be reviewed. If the procedure is not clearly written, another contributing root cause would be classified as OP. However, even a very clear and explicit procedure might not be effective if the detectability of the error (feedback) is poor. The phlebotomist made a slip by tearing separate labels at the wrong place. This action would be classified as an HSS skill-based behavioral error. However, without redesigning the label, this event would likely recur.

VI. SUMMARY

The safety of transfusion can be improved if one can identify errors that are an indication of a system's weak points before they result in an adverse outcome to a donor or a patient. Doing this requires a focus not only on adverse events, but on the capture and recording of near-miss events as well. In order to capture near-miss events, it is necessary for everyone in an organization to identify and report those conditions and actions that have the potential to adversely affect patient safety. It is also necessary to avoid assigning blame when an error is identified, but rather to find the root causes of the error. Without an adequate understanding of the causes of error, there is little likelihood the error can be corrected and prevented in the future. It is essential to look for and to eliminate those things that set up humans for failure. A useful goal is to create a safety culture where everyone seeks to identify and report conditions that may compromise transfusion safety.

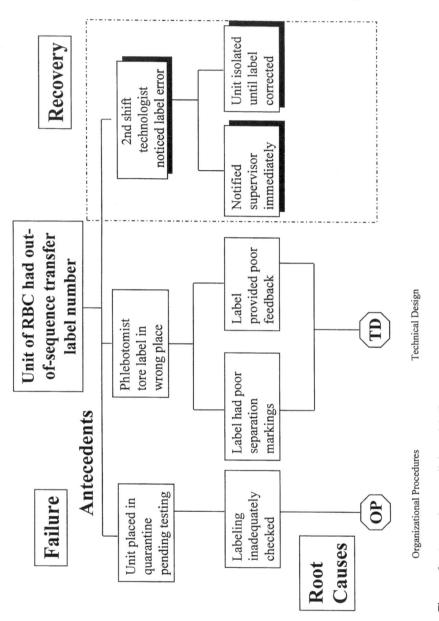

Figure 6   A causal tree outlining a labeling error.

REFERENCES

1. Linden JV, Kaplan HS. Transfusion errors: causes and effects. Transfus Med Rev 1994; 8(3):169–183.
2. Guidelines for Good Manufacturing Practices. U.S. Food and Drug Administration, 1993.
3. Monger P. Packaging security in the pharmaceutical industry: an MCA inspector's viewpoint. Pharmaceut Technol 1993; 4:81.
4. Nagel D. Human error in aviation operations. In: Wiener EL, ed. Human Factors in Aviation. San Diego, CA: Academic Press, 1988:
5. Shulman IA, Lohr K, Derdiarian AK, Picukaric JM. Monitoring transfusion practices a strategy for improving transfusion practices. J Bone Joint Surg 1992; 74-A:652–658.
6. Honig CL, Bove JR. Transfusion-associated fatalities: review of Bureau of Biologics reports 1976–1978. Transfusion 1980; 20:653–661.
7. Myhre B. Fatalities from blood transfusion. JAMA 1980; 244:1333–1335.
8. Camp FR, Monaghan WP. Fatal blood transfusion reactions: an analysis. Am J Forensic Med Pathol 1981; 2:143–150.
9. Edinger S. A closer look at fatal transfusion reactions. Med Lab Obs 1985; 4:41–45.
10. Sazama K. Reports of 355 transfusion-associated deaths: 1976 through 1985. Transfusion 1990; 30:583–590.
11. Mummert TB, Tourault MA. Review of transfusion related fatalities: many preventable. Hosp Technol Scanner 1993; 4:1–3.
12. Reason J. Human Error. New York: Cambridge University Press, 1990.
13. Linden JV, Paul B, Dressler KP. A report of 104 transfusion errors in New York State. Transfusion 1992; 32:601–660.
14. Taswell HF, Smith AM, Sweatt MA, Pfaff KJ. Quality control in the blood bank: a new approach. Am J Clin Pathol 1974; 62:491–495.
15. Classen DC, Pestotnik SL, Evans RS, Burke JP. Computerized surveillance of adverse drug events in hospitalized patients. JAMA 1991; 266:2817–2851.
16. Classen DC, Pestotnik MS, Evans RS, Lloyd JF, Burke JP. Adverse drug events in hospitalized patients. JAMA 1997; 277:301–306.
17. Reynard WD, Billings CE, Cheaney ES, Hardy R. The Development of the NASA Aviation Safety Reporting System. Moffett Field, CA: National Aeronautics and Space Administration Science and Technology Branch, 1986.
18. Billings, CE. Personal communication
19. Murphy WG, McClelland DBL. Deceptively low morbidity from failure to practice safe blood transfusion: an analysis of serious blood transfusion errors. Vox Sang 1989; 57:59–62.
20. Gambino R, Mallon P. Near misses: an untapped data base to find root causes. Lab Rep 1991; 13:41–44.
21. Van der Schaaf TW. Near miss reporting in the chemical process industry. Ph.D. thesis, Eindhoven University of Technology, 1992.
22. Heinrich HW. Industrial Accident Prevention. New York: McGraw-Hill, 1931.
23. Zapt D, Reason JT. Introduction to error handling. Appl Psychol 1994; 43:427–432.
24. Kaplan HS, Battles JB, Van der Schaaf TW, Shea CE, Mercer SQ. Identification and

classification of the causes of events in transfusion medicine. Transfusion 1998; 38:1071–1081.

25. Reason JT. Forward. In: Bogner MS, ed. Human Error in Medicine. Hillsdale, NJ: Lawrence Erlbaum Associates; 1994:vii–xv.

26. Reason JT. Managing the Risks of Organizational Accidents. Aldershot: Ashgate, 1997.

27. Rasmussen J. The definition of human error and a taxonomy for technical system design. In: Rasmussen J, Duncan K, Lepant J, eds. New Technology and Human Error. London: John Wiley & Sons LTD, 1987:23–30.

28. Rasmussen J. Information processing and human-machine interaction: an approach to cognitive engineering. New York: Elsevier, 1986.

29. Perper JA. Life-threatening and fatal therapeutic misadventures. In: Bogner MS, ed. Human Error in Medicine. Hillsdale, NJ: Lawrence Erlbaum Associates, 1994:27–52.

30. Curtain LL. When negligence becomes homicide. Nursing Manage 1997; 2:7–8.

31. Paget MA. The Unity of Mistakes: A Phenomenological Interpretation of Medical Work. Philadelphia: Temple University Press, 1988.

32. Berwick DM. Continuous improvement as an ideal in health care. N Engl J Med 1989; 32:53–56.

33. Lucas DA. Organizational aspects of near miss reporting. In: van der Schaaf TW, Lucas DA, Hale AR, eds. Near Miss Reporting as a Safety Tool. Oxford: Butterworth-Heinemann, 1991:

34. Lucas DA. Understanding the human factors in disasters. Interdisciplinary Sci Rev 1992; 17:185–190.

35. Leape LL, Bates DE, Cullen DJ, et al. System analysis of adverse drug event: ADE prevention study group. JAMA 1995; 274:35–43.

36. Battles JB, Kaplan HS, Van der Schaaf TW, Shea CE. Attributes of medical event reporting systems. Arch Pathol Lab Med 1998; 122:132–139.

5
Graft-Versus-Host Disease

Iain J. Webb and Kenneth C. Anderson
Dana-Farber Cancer Institute and Harvard Medical School, Boston, Massachusetts

I. INTRODUCTION

The clinical course of allogeneic bone marrow and peripheral blood stem cell transplant patients is frequently complicated by graft-versus-host disease (GVHD). This condition results when lymphocytes in the donor hematopoietic stem cell (HSC) component recognize the HLA antigens of the recipient as foreign, generating a characteristic immune response (1,2). Fever, diarrhea, liver function test (LFT) abnormalities, and a characteristic cutaneous rash are the major clinical manifestations of this condition. However, GVHD may also result from the infusion of viable T lymphocytes within cellular blood components. This condition, which is accompanied by marrow aplasia and pancytopenia, was first described in 1966 (3). In the following decades, subsequent reports established transfusion-associated graft-versus-host disease (TA-GVHD) as a distinct disease entity. TA-GVHD is resistant to most immunosuppressive therapeutic modalities. Consequently, treatment is rarely successful, making the recognition of patient groups warranting preventive measures essential.

Recently, new therapeutic strategies utilizing the potential graft-versus-leukemia (GVL) effect of allogeneic lymphocytes have been developed, emphasizing the need to further understand the pathogenesis of TA-GVHD. Adoptive immunotherapy, the infusion of allogeneic lymphocytes in patients who have relapsed following allogeneic hematopoietic progenitor cell (HPC) transplantation, has been shown to produce both remissions and a clinical syndrome similar to TA-GVHD (4). Whether the GVL effect is separable from GVHD is the object of ongoing laboratory and clinical studies.

II. CLINICAL PRESENTATION AND COMPLICATIONS

Symptoms and signs of TA-GVHD typically appear 8–10 days posttransfusion, with death typically occurring 3–4 weeks posttransfusion (5). As seen in cases of GVHD following HPC transplantation, a characteristic cutaneous eruption appears, associated with watery diarrhea, LFT abnormalities, and fever. Watery diarrhea may be profuse, and LFT elevations may be marked and accompanied by extensive hepatocellular damage. Nonspecific manifestations include anorexia, nausea, and vomiting. The maculopapular exanthem typically develops centrally, then progresses to involve the extremities. In severe cases, generalized erythroderma and bullae may appear.

The development of marrow aplasia distinguishes TA-GVHD from GVHD occurring following allogeneic HPC transplantation. Thrombocytopenia and leukopenia are late features. Complications of pancytopenia such as hemorrhage and infection ensue and lead to patient death. The time course is rapid, with death occurring 1–3 weeks following development of clinical symptoms.

III. DIFFERENTIAL DIAGNOSIS

There are no pathognomonic features to differentiate TA-GVHD from a variety of viral illnesses and drug reactions (6). Patients who are receiving transfusions typically suffer from comorbid conditions, which may obscure the clinical features of TA-GVHD, particularly should the clinician have a low index of suspicion. Characteristic pathological changes in the skin, liver, and bone marrow may aid diagnosis, but only the documentation of donor-derived lymphocytes in the recipient circulation and/or tissues will confirm it. Techniques used to detect donor-derived lymphocytes in the patient will be discussed below. Pathological examination of a skin biopsy may reveal degeneration of the epidermal basal cell layer with vascuolization; dermal-epithelial layer separation and bullae formation; mononuclear cell migration into, and infiltration of, the upper dermis; hyperkeratosis; and degenerative dyskeratosis (7,8). Liver biopsies reveal degeneration and eosinophilic necrosis of the small bile ducts with intense periportal inflammation and mononuclear (lymphocytic) infiltration. Bone marrow aspirates reveal lymphocytic infiltration, pancytopenia, and possibly fibrosis.

IV. INCIDENCE

The epidemiological data on TA-GVHD are derived from analysis of reports of single or very small groups of patients. A prospective study on the development of TA-GVHD has never been undertaken and would be very difficult to perform. Estimates of the incidence and identification of patient groups at risk are therefore subject to the limitations of retrospective data. Cases of TA-GVHD are most certainly underreported, with at least two factors contributing to the underreporting: lack of recognition and the absence of definitive diagnostic studies in many instances. Thus, while over 200 cases of presumed TA-GVHD have been reported or referenced in the Japanese- and English-language literature, definitive diagnostic tests have been performed in only a handful of cases. Lists of published case reports and small series have been compiled in several articles (9,10). Rare survivors have been documented, but the overall reported mortality is approximately 90% (5,11,12).

V. PATIENT GROUPS AT RISK

TA-GVHD has been reported in patients with hematological or solid malignancies or congenital immunodeficiency states, as well as in infants and adults with apparently intact immune systems, but not in patients afflicted with the acquired immune deficiency syndrome (AIDS). In addition, the disease has also only rarely been reported in recipients of organ transplants or in patients on immunosuppressive medications.

Initially, cases of TA-GVHD were reported in patients with severe combined immunodeficiency or Wiskott-Aldrich syndromes (Table 1), in newborns with erythroblastosis fetalis (Table 2), and in patients with Hodgkin's disease or non-Hodgkin's lymphoma, acute myelocytic or lymphoblastic leukemia, or chronic lymphocytic leukemia (Table 3) (13). Although its true incidence remains unknown, TA-GVHD is estimated to occur in 0.1–1.0% of patients with hematological malignancies or lymphoproliferative diseases, and patients carrying the above diagnoses are felt to be at risk for TA-GVHD. Certain subgroups of patients with hematological malignancies, including those suffering from chronic lymphocytic leukemia who are treated with fludarabine, may be at higher risk because of the prolonged effects of this purine analog on cell-mediated immune function (14–16).

Table 1 TA-GVHD in Patients with Congenital Immunodeficiency Syndromes: Clinical Setting

Severe combined immunodeficiency syndrome
Thymic hypoplasia
Wiskott-Aldrich syndrome
Lenier's disease
5'-Nucleotidase deficiency
Nonspecified immunodeficiency

Table 2   TA-GVHD in Patients with
Immunodeficiency States: Clinical Setting

Hemolytic disease of the fetus or newborn
Premature newborns
Neonatal alloimmune thrombocytopenia
Neonatal immunosuppressive medication

Cytotoxic drugs and irradiation may be related to the development of
TA-GVHD (17). TA-GVHD was originally recognized in patients with solid
tumors receiving intensive therapy for neuroblastoma (18,19). In one series, 4 of
34 patients with solid tumors (lung and germ cell cancer) who were treated with
high doses of chemotherapy and autologous marrow infusions and subsequently
received transfusions of nonirradiated blood cells developed TA-GVHD (20). In
addition, case reports documenting TA-GVHD in patients with cervical, renal,
esophageal, lung, bladder, or prostate carcinoma who did not receive aggressive
chemotherapy indicated that a broader spectrum of patients with solid tumors may
be at risk.

TA-GVHD has also been documented in premature infants who received
unirradiated blood products in the setting of hyaline-membrane disease, suspected
sepsis, and respiratory distress syndrome, but also in infants without these

Table 3   Posttransfusion GVHD in Patients with
Malignancies: Clinical Setting

Hematological
  Hodgkin's disease
  Non-Hodgkin's lymphoma
  Acute myelocytic leukemia
  Acute lymphocytic leukemia
  Chronic lymphocytic leukemia
  Aplastic anemia
Solid tumors
  Neuroblastoma
  Lung carcinoma
  Glioblastoma
  Rhabdomyosarcoma
  Cervical carcinoma
  Esophageal carcinoma
  Renal adenocarcinoma
  Autologous hematopoietic progenitor cell transplantation

complications (10,21). Such patients did not have congenital immunodeficiency syndromes or erythroblastosis fetalis.

Finally, TA-GVHD has been reported in apparently immunocompetent adults (Table 4). Clinical settings in which TA-GVHD has been reported in immunologically normal hosts include pregnancy; cardiac, vascular, and abdominal surgeries; alpha thalassemia; rheumatoid arthritis; trauma; and short-course glucocorticoid therapy (22,23). The syndrome was initially described in 1986 following blood transfusion to a patient in Japan who had surgery for an aortic aneurysm and was not recognized to be immunodeficient (24). A survey of 340 Japanese hospitals documented "postoperative erythroderma," identical to TA-GVHD, in 96 of the 63,257 patients who underwent cardiac surgery, with a mortality rate of 90% (25).

More recently, fatal GVHD has been reported in a number of HLA-heterozygous transfusion recipients who received a transfusion with a "one-way HLA match" (26,27). These recipients shared a haplotype with related or unrelated HLA-homozygous donors. Directed donations from immediate family members increase the likelihood of TA-GVHD because such donors share HLA antigens with recipients; homozygosity for HLA types is likely to be present among not only first-degree relatives but also all related recipient-donor pairs (28). The frequency of one-way HLA matches has been calculated in different countries (29). The reported risk varies from 1:16,835 in France to 1:874 in Japan, where there is less diversity in HLA antigen expression and, consequently, TA-GVHD cases have been more frequently reported (9,10,29).

The transfusion of platelets from donors sharing at least two antigens at the HLA-A and B loci (HLA-matched platelets) has been demonstrated to result in satisfactory platelet increments in alloimmunized patients refractory to standard platelet therapy (30). However, the provision of platelets from donors sharing HLA antigens may also predispose to TA-GVHD (31).

Table 4 TA-GVHD in
Immunocompetent Patients:
Clinical Setting

Pregnancy
Cholecystectomy
Cardiac surgery
Vascular surgery
Gastrointestinal surgery
Abdominal surgery
Alpha thalassemia
Liver transplantation
Pancreosplenic transplantation

The risk factors predisposing to TA-GVHD are only partially defined. TA-GVHD does not always occur in immunodeficient patients receiving unirradiated blood components, while it may affect individuals with apparently normal immune function, particularly in the setting of a one-way HLA match. Blood transfusion itself may be immunosuppressive (32). Hence, an argument can be made that almost every patient who requires transfusion of a blood component is potentially immunocompromised in some way that could facilitate the development of TA-GVHD. The low incidence of TA-GVHD in presumably immunocompetent patients may result from underrecognition of the syndrome, but likely also reflects effective defense mechanisms in individuals with truly intact immune function.

VI. PATHOGENESIS

The immune status of the host and the extent of HLA mismatch between donor and recipient together determine the extent of any host-versus-graft response. The ability of the transfusion recipient to mount an immune response against donor T lymphocytes is fundamental to the pathogenesis of TA-GVHD. Thus, Billingham (33) has proposed three requirements for the development of GVHD: (a) differences in histocompatibility (HLA) antigens between the donor and the recipient, (b) the presence of immunocompetent cells in the graft, and (c) inability of the host to reject these immunocompetent cells. Usually the larger number of immune cells in the immunocompetent host will eliminate the donor-derived T cells via a host-versus-graft reaction. However, if an immunocompetent HLA-heterozygous individual is transfused with even a small number of functional T lymphocytes derived from a donor who is homozygous for one of the recipient's HLA haplotypes, the recipient's immune system does not recognize the major histocompatibility antigens on the donor cells as being foreign and is therefore incapable of eliminating them. Some of the donor-derived T cells will recognize those host HLA antigens that are encoded by the unshared haplotype as being foreign, undergo clonal expansion, and establish TA-GVHD (26). The TA-GVHD expressed under these circumstances may be expected to occur regardless of the host's immune status since the failure to eliminate donor-derived T lymphocytes is based on the genetics of the HLA system rather than on variables that contribute to immune competence per se.

Fast et al. (34) have provided important insights into the pathogenesis of TA-GVHD, implicating recipient CD4$^+$, CD8$^+$, and natural killer cells in controlling TA-GVHD. In a mouse model, varying numbers of parental lymphoid cells were injected into unirradiated F1 hybrid recipients, providing donor lymphocytes homozygous for an HLA haplotype present in the recipient. The effect of selective depletion of recipient CD4$^+$, CD8$^+$, and natural killer cells on the regulation of

TA-GVHD was assessed. Depletion of CD4$^+$ cells increased the number of donor cells necessary to induce TA-GVHD, while depletion of recipient CD8$^+$ cells or natural killer cells decreased the number of door cells required to produce TA-GVHD. Thus, CD4$^+$ cells may be involved in the pathogenesis of TA-GVHD, and CD8$^+$ and natural killer cells may be protective. According to this model, patients at high risk for TA-GVHD would be those with impaired CD8 and natural killer cell function, especially if they receive blood products with a "one-way HLA match."

No cases of TA-GVHD have been reported in individuals with AIDS, further emphasizing the role of CD4$^+$ and CD8$^+$ lymphocytes in the pathogenesis of TA-GVHD. It is possible that TA-GVHD may account for some of the nonspecific signs and symptoms presently attributed to infections, drug reactions, and other coexistent medical conditions in AIDS patients. Alternatively, it may be that some qualitative aspect of the human immunodeficiency virus (HIV)–related immune deficit may alter the predisposition of AIDS patients to develop TA-GVHD. The murine study reported by Fast et al. (34) suggests that the latter explanation may be valid, as CD4$^+$ lymphocyte function declines early while CD8$^+$ function is preserved until late in the course of HIV disease. In the mouse model, both of these features would be expected to decrease the likelihood of developing TA-GVHD. In contrast, it has been proposed that reactive recipient CD8$^+$ T cells are required for the development of GVHD (35). Activated HIV-1–infected CD4$^+$ T cells express an HLA class 2–derived peptide mimicked by the carboxy-terminus of the HIV-1 envelope. It is hypothesized that the activation of CD8$^+$ T cells against the HIV-infected CD4$^+$ T cells may preclude the development of GVHD. Consequently, clarification of the role of both CD4$^+$ and CD8$^+$ cells in AIDS will likely provide further insight into the pathogenesis of GVHD and vice versa.

In recipients of allogeneic HPC transplants, the spectrum between GVHD and HLA alloimmunization and the extent of mononuclear cell microchimerism depend on the dose of allogeneic cells transfused, the immune competence of the recipient, as well as the extent of HLA similarity between donor and recipient (36). For example, in an animal model of post–bone marrow transplant GVHD, reducing the number of cells transplanted resulted in a stepwise increase in rejection rates of donor cells; conversely, reduction in the size of the marrow innoculum could be compensated by increasing host immunosuppression (37).

Since transfused cellular blood products are rarely HLA-antigen tested or matched, the first of Billingham's three requirements (33)—that there be differences in HLA between the donor and recipient—is almost always present in the setting of blood component transfusion. TA-GVHD is mediated by the viable T lymphocytes that inevitably contaminate nonirradiated transfused cellular blood components. The naturally or iatrogenically immunosuppressed recipient has only a limited capacity to generate an effective host-versus-graft reaction, and greater HLA disparity increases the probability that donor lymphocytes will attack host tissues.

VII. DIAGNOSIS

The differential diagnosis for TA-GVHD is broad: myriad factors such as infections and drug reactions can result in the development of fevers, skin rashes, and LFT abnormalities. Histological findings in the skin and gastrointestinal tract may suggest the diagnosis of TA-GVHD, but are not pathognomonic. The only definitive approach to the diagnosis of TA-GVHD is the identification of donor-derived lymphocytes in the circulation or tissues of the affected host (Table 5). This requires either careful HLA typing or some other technique that reliably distinguishes between host and donor cells (38–41). Blood samples adequate for HLA typing are frequently not available, since circulating host blood cells are rapidly eliminated. Polymerase chain reaction–based methods for HLA typing may be a useful substitute (40–43). Otherwise, the patient's HLA type may be deduced from those of surviving first-degree relatives (26). Cytogenetics have been employed in the event that donor and recipient have been of different gender or when the disease has followed transfusion of granulocytes donated by individuals with Philadelphia chromosome-positive chronic myeloid leukemia (44). Increasingly sophisticated techniques for confirming the diagnosis of TA-GVHD have included the detection of polymorphisms for restriction fragment lengths and human microsatellite markers (27,41). Even so, this syndrome is still frequently diagnosed only at autopsy.

VIII. THERAPY

Treatment of TA-GVHD is only rarely effective. Attempted immunosuppressive therapies have included glucocorticoids, antithymocyte globulin, cyclosporine, cyclophosphamide, and anti-T-cell monoclonal antibodies (8,23,25,45–47). Al-

---

Table 5 Methods Used to Diagnose or Document TA-GVHD

Conventional HLA typing
Deduction of patient's HLA type from those of family members
DNA-based HLA typing using the polymerase chain reaction (PCR)
Cytogenetics
Restriction fragment length polymorphism
Polymorphism of human microsatellite markers
Identification of donor T cells by above techniques in skin biopsies

---

though some of these agents have been successful in the treatment of post-HPC transplant GVHD, they have been ineffective for TA-GVHD. Rare responses to some of the commonly used agents have been reported (7,48), contributing to anecdotal experiences from which it is difficult to extract guidelines for clinical practice. A therapeutic trial of glucocorticoids or other immunosuppressive agents is often attempted but is frequently ineffective in this serious and increasingly frequent disease. There appears to be no advantage to early diagnosis and treatment, as patients diagnosed early in the course of the disease fare no better than those diagnosed later. Thus, prevention is critically important.

IX. PREVENTION: GAMMA IRRADIATION

Irradiation of blood components is indicated in patient groups at high risk for the development of TA-GVHD (Table 6). The relatively low frequency of TA-GVHD in immunocompetent patients receiving blood from unrelated donors has thus far precluded the extension of gamma-irradiation to all transfused cellular blood components. Issues relating to cost, the logistics of irradiation in emergency and small clinic settings, and the exceedingly low risk of TA-GVHD in most cases

Table 6 Patient Groups at Risk for Developing TA-GVHD

Clearly supported
Patients with selected immunodeficiencies:
  Congenital immunodeficiencies
  Hodgkin's disease
  Chronic lymphocytic leukemia treated with fludarabine
Newborns with erythroblastosis fetalis
Intrauterine transfusions
Recipients of hematopoietic progenitor cell transplants
Recipients of blood products donated by relatives
Recipients of HLA-selected (matched) platelets or platelets known to be
  homozygous
Probably at risk
Patients with:
  Other hematological malignancies
  Solid tumors treated with cytotoxic agents
Recipient-donor pairs from genetically homogeneous populations
Premature and, possibly, term neonates
No defined risk
Patients with:
  Acquired immunodeficiency syndrome (AIDS)
  Immunosuppressive medications

have also been raised (49,50). However, irradiation is likely indicated within genetically homogeneous populations, since transfusion of unirradiated components between unrelated donor-recipient pairs may be expected to result in TA-GVHD when a one-way HLA match occurs by chance.

The American Association of Blood Banks (AABB) currently recommends the irradiation of blood components at 2.5 Gy to the center of the component, with no area receiving less than 1.5 Gy (51). This irradiation dose is in excess of the levels found to abrogate mixed lymphocyte culture (MLC) reactivity, as this dose is inadequate to prevent TA-GVHD (52,53). Instead, the recommended 2.5 Gy dose is based on limiting dilution assays (LDAs) using visual assessment of T-cell proliferation, which demonstrate a greater than 5 log reduction in viable T cells. However, levels of host cytotoxic T-lymphocyte precursors (pCTLs) and interleukin-2–secreting helper T-lymphocyte precursors (pHTLs), which are not measured in LDAs, may be more predictive of GVHD development following allogeneic BMT (54–58).

Significant variability in irradiation practice exists between centers. For example, blood component irradiation practice was examined in a survey of 2250 blood centers, hospital blood banks, and transfusion services that are institutional members of the AABB (59). Only 12.3% of the institutions had on-site facilities for the irradiation of blood components. Of 9,397,516 components transfused in 1989, 952,516 (10.1%) were irradiated, and 44 cases of TA-GVHD were identified. There was marked variability in blood component irradiation practice, even among groups in whom the risk of TA-GVHD was well defined. For example, 12, 19, and 32% of institutions did not provide irradiated components to recipients of allogeneic BMT, patients receiving autologous BMT, and those with congenital immunodeficiencies, respectively. Irradiated blood components were provided by 51.4, 34, 32, and 20% of institutions to patients with leukemias, Hodgkin's disease, non-Hodgkin's lymphoma, and solid tumors, respectively, and 24.5% provided irradiated blood products to patients with AIDS.

X. NEW DIRECTIONS

A. Leukoreduction to Prevent TA-GVHD

In theory, leukoreduction of cellular blood components could be used to decrease TA-GVHD. However, since neither the number nor quality of T cells that mediate GVHD are presently defined, targets for leukoreduction to prevent TA-GVHD cannot be established. Further, TA-GVHD has been reported in both immunocompetent and immunodeficient recipients of transfusions leukoreduced by filtration, suggesting that standard leukoreduction procedures cannot completely prevent TA-GVHD (60,61). Newer technologies appear capable of decreasing the number of contaminating leukocytes (62); whether the levels of leukoreduction achieved will be adequate to prevent TA-GVHD remains to be established. Leukoreduction could theoretically deplete sufficient numbers of T-helper lymphocyte precursors (pHTL) and cytotoxic T-lymphocyte precursors (pCTL) to avoid TA-GVHD. However, the effect of neither gamma irradiation nor leukoreduction on these cell populations has yet been determined. Until data demonstrate adequate highly efficient removal of pHTL and pCTL by leukoreduction, gamma irradiation of all cellular blood components should be utilized to prevent TA-GVHD in patient groups judged to be at risk.

B. Donor Lymphocyte Infusions and TA-GVHD

Patients with leukemia relapsing following allogeneic bone marrow transplantation may respond to infusions of lymphocytes from the original bone marrow donor, without receiving chemotherapy or other treatment. For example, the European Group for Blood and Marrow Transplantation (EGBMT) documented complete remissions in 73% of 84 patients with relapsed chronic myelogenous leukemia (CML) (4). Eighty-seven percent of patients remained in remission at 3 years. GVHD of Grade II or greater developed in 41% of patients, and myelosuppression occurred in 34% of patients. The development of these features associated with TA-GVHD was associated with the attainment of remission, suggesting a potential relationship between TA-GVHD and the GVL effect of the lymphocyte infusions.

The donor lymphocyte populations responsible for GVL, TA-GVHD, and post-HPC transplantation GVHD have not been determined. CD4+ cells have been implicated in GVL (63,64), while it has been observed that the depletion of either CD6+ or CD8+ T lymphocytes from donor bone marrow can prevent GVHD at the time of allogeneic transplantation (65,66). Further experiments to identify the role of both donor and host lymphocyte populations in TA-GVHD and GVL are necessary. These studies will be important to determine how best to prevent TA-GVHD and optimize the GVL effect of lymphocytes while minimizing GVHD.

REFERENCES

1. Ferrara JL, Deeg HJ. Graft versus host disease. N Engl J Med 1991; 324:667–764.
2. Antin JH, Ferrara JLM. Cytokine dysregulation and acute graft-versus-host disease. Blood 1992; 80:2964–2968.
3. Hathaway WE, Brangle RW, Nelson TL, Roeckel IE. Aplastic anemia and alymphocytosis in an infant with hypogammaglobulinemia: Graft-versus-host reaction? J Ped 1966; 68:713–722.
4. Kolb HJ, Schattenberg A, Goldman JM, Hertenstein B, Jacobsen N, Arcese W, Ljungman P, Ferrant A, Verdonck L, Niederwieser D, van Rhee F, Mittermueller J,

de Witte T, Holler E, Ansari H. Graft-versus-leukemia effect of donor lymphocyte transfusions in marrow grafted patients. European Group for Blood and Marrow Transplantation Working Party Chronic Leukemia. Blood 1995; 86:2041–2050.

5. Anderson KC. Clinical indications for blood component irradiation. In: Baldwin ML, Jefferies LC, eds. Irradiation of Blood Components. Bethesda, MD: American Association of Blood Banks, 1992:31–49.

6. Shivdasani RA, Anderson KC. Transfusion-associated graft-versus-host disease: scratching the surface. Transfusion 1993; 33;696–697.

7. Prince M, Szer J, van der Weyden MB, Pedersen JS, Holdsworth RF, Whyte G. Transfusion associated graft-versus-host disease after cardiac surgery: response to antithymocyte-globulin and corticosteroid therapy. Aust NZ J Med 1991; 21:43–46.

8. O'Connor NTJ, Mackintosh P. Transfusion associated graft versus host disease in an immunocompetent patient. J Clin Pathol 1992; 45:621–622.

9. Ohto H, Anderson KC. Survey of transfusion-associated graft-versus-host disease in immunocompetent recipients. Transfusion Med Rev 1996; 10:31–43.

10. Ohto H, Anderson KC. Posttransfusion graft-versus-host disease in Japanese newborns. Transfusion 1996; 36:117–123.

11. Andersen CB, Ladefoged SD, Taaning E. Transfusion-associated graft-versus-graft and potential graft-versus-host disease in a renal allotransplanted patient. Hum Path 1992; 23:831–834.

12. Mori S, Matsushita H, Ozaki K, Ishida A, Tokuhira M, Nakajima H, Kizaki M, Sugiura H, Kikuchi A, Handa M, et al. Spontaneous resolution of transfusion-associated graft-versus-host disease. Transfusion 1995; 35:431–435.

13. von Fliedner V, Higby DJ, Kim U. Graft-versus-host reaction following blood product transfusion. Am J Med 1982; 72:951–961.

14. Briz M, Cabrera R, Sanjuan I, Fores R, Diez JL, Herrero M, Regidor C, Algora M, Fernandez MN. Diagnosis of transfusion-associated graft-versus-host disease by polymerase chain reaction in fludarabine-treated B-chronic lymphocytic leukaemia. Br J Haematol 1995; 91:409–411.

15. Briones J, Pereira A, Alcorta I. Transfusion-associated graft-versus-host disease (TA-GVHD) in fludarabine-treated patients: is it time to irradiate blood component? Br J Haematol 1996; 93:739–741.

16. Williamson LM, Wimperis JZ, Wood ME, Woodcock B. Fludarabine treatment and transfusion-associated graft-versus-host disease. Lancet 1996; 348:472–473.

17. Kessinger A, Armitage J, Klassen L, Landmark J, Hayes J, Larsen A, Purtilo D. Graft versus host disease following transfusion of normal blood products to patients with malignancies. J Surg Oncol 1987; 36:206–209.

18. Woods WG, Lubin BH. Fatal graft-versus-host disease following a blood transfusion in a child with neuroblastoma. Paediatrics 1981; 67:217–221.

19. Kennedy J, Ricketts R. Fatal graft versus host disease in a child with neuroblastoma following a blood transfusion. J Ped Surg 1986; 21:1108–1109.

20. Postmus PE, Mulder NH, Elema JD. Graft versus host disease after transfusions of non-irradiated blood cells in patients having received autologous bone marrow: a report of 4 cases following ablative chemotherapy for solid tumors. Eur J Cancer Clin Oncol 1988; 24:889–894.

21. Berger RS, Dixon SL. Fulminant transfusion-associated graft-versus-host disease in a premature infant. J Am Acad Dermatol 1989; 9:205–207.

22. Sheehan T, McLaren KM, Brettle R, Parker AC. Transfusion-induced graft versus host disease in pregnancy. Clin Lab Haematol 1987; 9:205–207.

23. Otsuka S, Kunieda K, Kitamura F, Misawa K, Sasaoka I, Hirose M, Kasuya S, Saji S, Noma A. The critical role of blood from HLA-homozygous donors in fatal transfusion-associated graft-versus-host disease in immunocompetent patients. Transfusion 1991; 31:260–264.

24. Hathaway WE, Fulginit VA, Pierce CW, Githens JH, Pearlman DS, Muschenheim F, Kempe CH. Graft-vs-host reaction following a single blood transfusion. J Am Med Assoc 1967; 201:1015–1020.

25. Juji T, Takahashi K, Shibata Y, Ide H, Sakakibira T, Ino T, Mori S. Posttransfusion graft-versus-host disease in immunocompetent patients after cardiac surgery. N Engl J Med 1989; 321:56.

26. Shivdasani RA, Haluska FG, Dock NL, Dover JS, Kineke EJ, Anderson KC. Graft-versus-host disease associated with transfusion of blood from unrelated HLA-homozygous donors. N Engl J Med 1993; 328:766–770.

27. Petz LD, Calhoun L, Yam P, Cecka M, Schiller G, Faitlowicz AR, Herron R, Sayah D, Wallace RB, Belidegrun A. Transfusion-associated graft-versus-host disease in immunocompetent patients: report of a fatal case associated with transfusion of blood from a second-degree relative, and a survey of predisposing factors. Transfusion 1993; 33:742–750.

28. Kantre MH. Transfusion-associated graft-versus-host disease: Do transfusions from second-degree relatives pose a greater risk than those from first-degree relatives? Transfusion 1992; 32:323–327.

29. Ohto H, Yasuda H, Noguchi M, Abe R. Risk of transfusion-associated graft-versus-host disease as a result of directed donations from relatives. Transfusion 1992; 32:691–693.

30. Yankee RA, Grumet FC, Rogentine GN. Platelet transfusion therapy: The selection of compatible platelet donors for refractory patients by lymphocyte HLA typing. N Engl J Med 1969; 281:1208–1212.

31. Benson K, Marks AR, Marshall MJ, Goldstein JD. Fatal graft-versus-host disease associated with transfusions of HLA-matched, HLA-homozygous platelets from unrelated donors. Transfusion 1994; 34:432–437.

32. Perkins HA. Transfusion-induced immunologic unresponsiveness. Transfusion Med Rev 1988; 2:196–203.

33. Billingham RE. The biology of graft-versus-host reactions. Harvey Lectures 1966-67; 62:21–78.

34. Fast LD, Valeri CR, Crowley JP. Immune responses to major histocompatibility complex homozygous lymphoid cells in murine F1 hybrid recipients: implications for transfusion-associated graft-versus-host disease. Blood 1995; 86:3090–3096.

35. Habeshaw JA, Dalgleish AG, Hounsell EF. Absence of GVH in AIDS. J AIDS 1994; 7:1287–1289.

36. Dzik WH. Mononuclear cell microchimerism and the immunomodulatory effect of transfusion. Transfusion 1994; 34:1007–1012.

37. Uharek L, Gassmann W, Glass B, Steinmann J, Loeffler H, Mueller-Ruchholtz W.

Influence of cell dose and graft-versus-host disease on rejection rates after allogeneic transplantation. Blood 1992; 79:1612–1620.

38. Kunstmann E, Bocker T, Roewer L, Sauer H, Mempel W, Epplen JT. Diagnosis of transfusion-associated graft-versus-host disease by genetic fingerprinting and polymerase chain reaction. Transfusion 1992; 32:766–770.

39. Suzuki K, Akiyama H, Takamoto S, Maruyama Y, Sakamaki H, Akagi K, Maeda Y, Takenaka M, Onozawa Y. Transfusion-associated graft-versus-host disease in a presumably immunocompetent patient after transfusion of stored packed red cells. Transfusion 1992; 32:358–360.

40. Hayakawa S, Chishima F, Sakata H, Fuji K, Ohtani K, Kurashina K, Hayakawa J, Suzuki K, Nakabayashi H, Esumi M, Nemoto N, Sakurai I, Satoh K. A rapid molecular diagnosis of posttransfusion graft-versus-host disease by polymerase chain reaction. Transfusion 1993; 33:413–417.

41. Wang L, Juji T, Tokunaga K, Takahashi K, Kuwata S, Uchida S, Tadokoro K, Takai K. Brief Report: Polymorphic microsatellite markers for the diagnosis of graft-versus-host disease. N Engl J Med 1994; 330:398–401.

42. Saito M, Takamatsu H, Nakao S, Shiobara S, Matsuda T, Tajika E, Nakamura T, Kaji T, Yoshida T. Transfusion-associated graft-versus-host disease after surgery for bladder cancer. Blood 1993; 82:326–330.

43. Uchida S, Wang L, Yahagi Y, Tokunaga K, Tadokoro K, Juji T. Utility of fingernail DNA for evaluation of chimerism after bone marrow transplantation and for diagnostic testing for transfusion-associated graft-versus-host disease [letter]. Blood 1996; 87:4015–4016.

44. Matsushita H, Shibata Y, Fuse K, Kimura M, Iinuma K. Sex chromatin analysis of lymphocytes invading host organs in transfusion-associated graft-versus-host disease. Virchows Archiv B Cell Pathol 1988; 55:237–239.

45. Arsura EL, Bertelle A, Minkowitz S, Cunningham J, Jr., Grob D. Transfusion-associated-graft-versus-host disease in a presumed immunocompetent patient. Arch Int Med 1988; 148:1941–1944.

46. Otsuka S, Kunieda K, Hirose H, Takeuchi H, Mizutani M, Nagaya G, Sato G, Kasuya S, Matsutomo K, Noma A, Saji S. Fatal erythroderma (suspected graft-versus-host disease) after cholecystectomy. Transfusion 1989; 29:544–548.

47. Vogelsang GB. Transfusion-associated graft-versus-host disease in nonimmunocompromised hosts. Transfusion 1990; 30:101–103.

48. Cohen D, Weinstein H, Mihm M, Yankee R. Nonfatal graft-versus-host disease occurring after transfusion with leukocytes and platelets obtained from normal donors. Blood 1979; 53:1053–1059.

49. Lind SE. Has the case for irradiating blood products been made? Am J Med 1985; 78:543–544.

50. Perkins H. Should all blood from related donors be irradiated? Transfusion 1992; 32:302–303.

51. Preparation of blood components. In: Klein H, ed. Standards for Blood Banks and Transfusion Services. Bethesda, MD: American Association of Blood Banks, 1996:14.

52. Sproul AM, Chalmers EA, Mills KI, Burnett AK, Simpson E. Third party mediated

graft rejection despite irradiation of blood products. Br J Haematol 1992; 80:251–252.

53. Lowenthal RM, Challis DR, Griffiths AE, Chappell RA, Goulder PJ. Transfusion-associated graft-versus-host disease: report of an occurrence following the administration of irradiated blood. Transfusion 1993; 33:524–529.

54. Kaminski E, Hows J, Man S, Brookes P, Mackinnon S, Hughes T, Avakian O, Goldman JM, Batchelor JR. Prediction of graft versus host disease by frequency analysis of cytotoxic T cells after unrelated donor bone marrow transplantation. Transplantation 1989; 48:608–613.

55. van Els CA, Bakker A, Zwinderman AH, Zwaan FE, van Rood JJ, Goulmy E. Effector mechanisms in graft-versus-host disease in response to minor histocompatibility antigens. II. Evidence of a possible involvement of proliferative T cells. Transplantation 1990; 50:67–71.

56. Irschick EU, Hladik F, Niederwieser D, Nussbaumer W, Holler E, Kaminski E, Huber C. Studies on the mechanism of tolerance or graft-versus-host disease in allogeneic bone marrow recipients at the level of cytotoxic T-cell precursor frequencies. Blood 1992; 79:1622–1628.

57. Theobald M, Nierle T, Bunjes D, Arnold R, Heimpel H. Host-specific interleukin-2-secreting donor T-cell precursors as predictors of acute graft-versus-host disease in bone marrow transplantation between HLA-identical siblings. N Engl J Med 1992; 327:1613–1617.

58. Schwarer AP, Jiang YZ, Brookes PA, Barrett AJ, Batchelor JR, Goldman JM, Lechler RI. Frequency of anti-recipient alloreactive helper T-cell precursors in donor blood and graft-versus-host disease after HLA-identical sibling bone-marrow transplantation. Lancet 1993; 341:203–205.

59. Anderson KC, Goodnough LT, Sayers M, Pisciotto PT, Kurtz SR, Lane TA, Anderson CS, Silberstein LE. Variation in blood component irradiation practice: implications for prevention of transfusion-associated graft-versus-host disease. Blood 1991; 77:2096–2102.

60. Akahoshi M, Takanashi M, Masuda M, Yamashita H, Hidano A, Hasegawa K, Kasajima T, Shimizu M, Motoji T, Oshimi K, et al. A case of transfusion-associated graft-versus-host disease not prevented by white cell-reduction filters. Transfusion 1992; 32:169–172.

61. Hayashi H, Nishiuchi T, Tamura H, Takeda K. Transfusion-associated graft-versus-host disease caused by leukocyte-filtered stored blood. Anesthesiology 1993; 79:1419–1421.

62. Webb IJ, Schott DM, Cook J, Anderesen JW, Barrett BB, Anderson KC. Cobe Spectra LRS for preparation of leukoreduced single donor apheresis platelets without laboratory filtration. Blood 1996; 88:335a (Abstr 1327).

63. Faber LM, van Luxemburg-Heijs SAP, Veenhof WFJ, Willemze R, Falkenburg JHF. Generation of CD4+ cytotoxic T-lymphocyte clones from a patient with severe graft-versus-host disease after allogeneic bone marrow transplantation: implications for graft-versus-leukemia reactivity. Blood 1995; 86:2821–2828.

64. Giralt S, Hester J, Huh Y, Hirsch-Ginsberg C, Rondon G, Seonh D, Lee M, Gajewski J, Van Besien K, Khouri I, Mehra R, Przepiorka D, Korbling M, Talpaz M, Kantarjian H, Fischer H, Deisseroth A, Champlin R. CD8-depleted donor lymphocyte infusion

as treatment for relapsed chronic myelogenous leukemia after allogeneic bone marrow transplantation. Blood 1995; 86:4337–4343.

65. Champlin R, Ho W, Gajewski J, Feig S, Burnison M, Holley G, Greenberg P, Lee K, Schmid I, Giorgi J, Yam P, Petz L, Winston D, Warner N, Reichert T. Selective depletion of CD8+ T lymphocytes for prevention of graft-versus-host disease after allogeneic bone marrow transplantation. Blood 1990; 76:418–423.

66. Soiffer RJ, Murray C, Mauch P, Anderson KC, Freedman AS, Rabinowe SN, Takvorian T, Robertson MJ, Spector N, Gonin R, Miller KB, Rudders RA, Freeman A, Blake K, Coral F, Nadler LM, Ritz J. Prevention of graft-versus-host disease by selective depletion of CD6-positive T lymphocytes from donor bone marrow. J Clin Oncol 1992; 10:1191–1200.

6
Transfusion-Related Acute Lung Injury

Mark A. Popovsky
American Red Cross Blood Services—New England Region;
Harvard Medical School; and Beth Israel Hospital, Boston,
Massachusetts

I. INTRODUCTION

Although more than three centuries have passed since the recognition that transfusion can be associated with deadly complications, it is only in the last 10–15 years that pulmonary injury has been generally appreciated as a possible transfusion outcome. In fact, before the mid-1980s the only well-recognized manifestations of pulmonary injury from transfusion were anaphylactic reactions and circulatory overload. Unfortunately, the respiratory system can be compromised by another, immunologically driven type of reaction. Such reactions were originally designated by a variety of descriptive terms, including non-cardiogenic pulmonary edema (1), allergic pulmonary edema (2), hypersensitivity reaction (3), and leukoagglutinin transfusion reaction (4). Only in the last decade has there been a broader appreciation that this type of lung injury has an immunological basis.

II. CLINICAL PRESENTATION

Transfusion-related acute lung injury (TRALI) is a life-threatening complication that, when it presents fulminantly, is indistinguishable from the adult respiratory distress syndrome (ARDS) secondary to other etiologies (e.g., sepsis, aspiration,

Table 1 Signs and Symptoms of TRALI

Acute respiratory distress
Acute pulmonary edema
Hypotension
Hypoxemia
Fever
Setting: transfusion of plasma-containing blood products within 1–2 hours

toxic inhalation) (5,6). As with ARDS, TRALI is a syndrome characterized by acute respiratory distress.

The symptoms of TRALI include severe bilateral pulmonary edema, severe hypoxemia (arterial oxygen tensions of 30–50 torr are frequently observed) (5–7), and cyanosis. The respiratory distress may first be manifested as dyspnea or cyanosis (peripheral or central). Although the edema may first be confined to the lower lung fields, over several hours it usually involves the entire lung. Roentgenograms classically demonstrate "white-out" by interstitial and alveolar infiltrates (3,5,6), but in the first few hours a patchy pattern may be observed. For patients who are in a decubitus condition in the operating room, the edema may initially manifest itself in only the dependent areas of the lung (Table 1).

Other frequent manifestations include fever (1–2°C elevation) and mild to moderate hypotension, although infrequently, hypertension may be observed. When hypotension occurs, it is usually unresponsive to intravenous fluid administration.

All of these symptoms arise in the setting of recent transfusion of plasma-containing blood components, always within 1–6 hours and usually within 1–2 hours. In contrast to circulatory overload, patients with TRALI have normal central venous pressure and normal or low pulmonary wedge pressures.

While this discussion addresses the severe, classic presentation, many patients may present with milder forms of respiratory distress that still represent this syndrome.

III. COMPLICATIONS

TRALI differs from ARDS in several important ways. Unlike ARDS with its attendant morbidity and mortality (death rate of approximately 40–50%), approximately 80% of patients with TRALI improve both clinically and physiologically within 48–96 hours of the original insult, provided there is prompt and vigorous respiratory support (5–8) While in many ARDS patients the lung injury is irreversible, in TRALI the pulmonary lesion is typically transient. The pO_2 levels return to their pretransfusion levels. Roentgenograms demonstrate rapid clearing of the edema fluid. In one large study of this syndrome 100% of 36 patients required oxygen support, while 72% required short term mechanical ventilation (8). There was a subset of patients, however, with a more prolonged course. In about 20% of cases, pulmonary infiltrates persisted for at least 7 days, but even these patients show no evidence of permanent sequelae (8). Although data are limited, it appears that 5–8% of patients die from complications related to the pulmonary insult (5,6,8). As more cases are reported, there is a growing appreciation of the risk of death. In a recent report two children with malignant osteopetrosis died of TRALI following transfusion of single donor platelets (9). For obvious reasons, TRALI is an important clinical diagnosis.

IV. DIFFERENTIAL DIAGNOSIS

A. Circulatory Overload

Respiratory distress, cyanosis, and tachypnea are prominent features of circulatory overload (7,10). Tachycardia and hypertension are usually present. Symptoms begin within several hours of transfusion of any type of blood component. The setting is often rapid infusion in either very young or old patients.

B. Bacterial Contamination

Fever, hypotension, and vascular collapse are prominent features of bacterial contamination (11). Respiratory distress is infrequently observed. Patients may present with disseminated intravascular coagulation. The onset of symptoms is within 1–2 hours of transfusion of cellular or plasma-containing blood components. Although platelet concentrates or apheresis platelets are the most frequently implicated components (12), red cell concentrates may be involved.

C. Anaphylactic Transfusion Reactions

Respiratory distress, cyanosis related to laryngeal edema, and bronchospasm, not pulmonary edema, are the dominant symptoms of this complication (13,14). Erythema and urticarial eruption are prominent and typically involve conflunaries of the trunk, face, and neck. Hypertension is usually severe and frequently occurs within seconds to minutes after the initiation of transfusion of a plasma protein–containing blood component or derivative (as little as a few milliliters). Fever is not a manifestation of anaphylactic reactions.

V. INCIDENCE

The incidence rate of TRALI is unknown. In one study from the mid-1980s, 1 in 5000 plasma-containing transfusions were associated with this reaction (6,8). This study took place during a period in which blood banks in the United States were converting to red cell concentrates containing significantly less plasma (reduced from an average of 100 to approximately 40–60 mL); therefore, one might assume that the frequency has decreased. On the other hand, the number of reports in the literature has increased dramatically. From 1951 when the syndrome was first described until 1985, there were fewer than 40 case reports in the English language literature (15–31). Since then descriptions of at least 94 recipient reactions have appeared in the literature (8,9,32–48,52,53,67–69), and the author is aware of an additional 65 unpublished cases.

In a study by Clarke et al. (41), 46 (0.34%) of 14,602 transfusion were associated with severe respiratory reactions to random donor platelets over a 2-year period in a single general hospital. Rare reactions were also seen in recipients of red cells. The reactions are most frequently seen in patients with hematological malignancies. The average age of the platelets at transfusion was 4.5 days, significantly greater than that of the controls.

Other investigators have failed to find an at-risk population, although recurring cases have been rarely described (39). The male:female ratio among reactors is approximately 1:1 Cases have been described in both very young and elderly transfusion recipients (from one month to 87 years) (8,39). Most patients had no history of transfusion reactions, and there are no common denominators, disease associations, or underlying conditions that necessitated the transfusions.

A report from New Zealand found an incidence of 0.001% of ARDS reactions from 1981 to 1987 from a total of 440,000 transfused blood components (49). The nearly 20-fold difference in reported incidents in these studies may reflect the level of awareness at a medical center, rather than changes in incidence. At the Mayo Clinic, for instance, transfusions are often administered under the supervision of blood bank staff who are trained to identify transfusion reactions.

There is reason to believe that TRALI may be significantly underdiagnosed. In a series of 40 patients with pulmonary edema in the operative setting, Cooperman and Price (50) found that 50% of cases were attributed to circulatory overload or an unknown cause. It is conceivable that some of these cases represented TRALI. Culliford and colleagues (25) described a type of non-cardiogenic pulmonary edema in three patients following cardiopulmonary by-pass that is consistent with this diagnosis, but tests that might have supported it were not performed.

In an analysis of transfusion-associated fatalities reported to the U.S. Food and Drug Administration from 1976 to 1985, acute pulmonary injury was implicated in 12.1% (31) of 256 cases (51). In this study, respiratory death from acute-onset pulmonary edema was the third most common cause of death from transfusion. This type of complication was more frequent than bacterial contamination or anaphylaxis. The relative importance of TRALI may increase as other important complications, specifically transfusion-transmitted hepatitis, recede as a consequence of improved blood donor screening and testing.

Finally, in a recent study of hypotensive reactions associated with platelet-containing products, 3 of 24 reactions were consistent with, but unrecognized as TRALI (52). This report underscores two points: (a) that TRALI remains underdiagnosed and (b) that it may be confused with other complications of transfusion.

VI. IMPLICATED BLOOD COMPONENTS

As stated previously, TRALI is associated with transfusion of blood components containing plasma. These components include whole blood, red blood cells (prepared in citrate-phosphate-dextrose or citrate-phosphate-dextrose-adenine 1) as well as protein-poor anticoagulant-preservative solutions (such as Additive Solution-1 or Additive Solution-3), granulocytes collected by apheresis, platelet concentrates, and platelets collected by apheresis and cryoprecipitate (1–6,15–28). In most instances the implicated blood component contains more than 60 mL of plasma, but it is apparent that in some instances smaller quantities (e.g., cryoprecipitate contains only 10–15 mL of plasma and platelet concentrate, 40–50 mL of plasma) are sufficient to initiate the pulmonary events described above. It is noteworthy that commercially available plasma derivatives, such as albumin, plasma protein fraction, intravenous immune globulin, and gamma globulin, that manufactured from large pools of plasma donors using Cohn fractionation procedures have not been associated with any case reports.

VII. MECHANISM

Although the precise mechanism of TRALI is unknown, there are sufficient clues to assume that it is an immune-mediated event. Unlike most immunologically triggered transfusion reactions, in TRALI pathological antibodies are typically of donor, rather than recipient, origin (Table 2). Numerous reports have documented the presence of human leukocyte antigen (HLA)–specific antibodies or leukoagglutinins in the plasma of the donors of implicated blood components (3,4,8,18,26,29–35,37–39,42).

Popovsky and Moore (8) found such antibodies in 89% of 36 cases in one series. In about half of the cases studied, the HLA-A or HLA-B antibodies of the implicated donor corresponded with one or more HLA epitopes of the recipient

Table 2 Immunological
Findings in TRALI

Donor plasma
  HLA-specific antibodies
  Granulocyte-specific antibodies
  Leukoagglutinins
Recipient plasma
  HLA-specific antibodies
  Granulocyte-specific antibodies
  Leukoagglutinins

(8,26). Goeken and colleagues (29) as well as others have confirmed these findings (31). In other cases, neutrophil-specific antibodies (anti-NA2, anti-5b, and anti-NB2) have been identified in the serum of implicated units (27,32,37). These antibodies are usually found in the blood of multiparous donors. On the other hand, in 5% of reported cases, similar specificities of antibodies are found in the pretransfusion serum of the transfusion recipient (5,7,8). Finally, in 5–15% of cases, no antibody has been identified in either the patient or the donor.

The likely explanation of antibodies in the donor, rather than antibodies in the recipient, as the causative agent is that the "substrate" with which the leukocyte antibodies can react—namely, the recipient's entire circulating and marginated pool of leukocyte—is far larger than the quantity of donor leukocytes present in a single transfused component. It appears that TRALI begins with passive transfer of antibody from donor plasma to the recipient (5,7), which sets off a chain of reactions.

Underscoring the primacy of the antibody-mediated theory are a handful of case reports of TRALI associated with interdonor incompatibility. In a recent report, a 67-year-old male with acute myelogenous leukemia received a pool of four platelet concentrates and developed the signs and symptoms of classic TRALI. In the ensuing workup, one of the platelet donors was found to have anti-A2 and anti-A28 in the plasma. The recipient tissue type was negative for both A2 and A28, and the plasma did not contain HLA granulocyte antibodies. One of the other donors of the platelets used in the pool was found to be A28 positive (53).

What is the relationship of these antibodies to this reaction? Much of the current understanding is gleaned from studies of ARDS. Although the mechanisms involved in the development of ARDS are complex, there is considerable evidence to support a major role for complement activation in neutrophil influx into the lung, causing damage to the pulmonary microvasculature. When complement is activated, C5a promotes neutrophil aggregation, margination, and seque-stration in the microvasculature of the lung (54,55), which is at least partially related to increased granulocyte adhesion (56). Experimental studies in rabbits, as well as observations in ARDS patients, suggest that when complement-activated neutrophils release their proteases, oxygen radicals, and acidic lipids, the underlying pulmonary vascular endothelium is damaged, with subsequent extravasation of protein-laden fluid into the adjacent interstitium and alveoli (57,58). Larsen et al. (59) demonstrated that C5 fragments consistently produced lung inflammation characterized by neutrophil accumulation and edema. In all likelihood, these pathological changes account for the radiographic and clinical findings seen in TRALI. Brittingham (20) noted that when 50 mL of blood known to contain leukoagglutinins was transfused to a healthy person, the result was a severe pulmonary reaction characterized by hypoxemia, pulmonary edema, hypo-tension, and fever. This study suggested that passive transfer of leukocyte antibodies may play an important, if not decisive, role in triggering the action (7). As lymphocytotoxic (i.e., HLA) antibodies readily fix complement, passive transfusion of these antibodies probably accounts for complement activation of the sequence of events described previously.

Seeger et al. (60) have described a powerful model for understanding the relation between donor antibodies and the development of TRALI. Using an ex vivo rabbit lung model, these investigators found that acute lung injury charac-terized by severe lung edema resulted from the infusion of an admixture of complement, anti-5b, and 5b-positive human neutrophils. These changes were seen 3–6 hours after infusion, which parallels the clinical presentation in humans. Other investigators have documented a similar pathological timeline (58). When complement, anti-5b, or 5b-positive granulocyte antigen was deleted from the experiments, no pathological changes occurred. While these data suggest that the correspondence of antibody specificity for a recipient epitope is important in the pathogenesis of the respiratory decompensation observed in TRALI, cases are left unexplained in which the HLA or neutrophil-specific antibody does not share epitopes of the recipient. Despite the fact that approximately 1–2% of blood donors have HLA-specific antibodies, TRALI is an infrequent result of transfu-sion. Although there is a report of two episodes of TRALI involving the same recipient and the same antibody-positive donor (39), current understanding does not allow for a characteristic profile of at-risk blood recipient.

In all likelihood, other factors such as the character of the antibody, the nature and distribution of the related antigen, the extent of complement activation, and the immune status of the recipient are important variables that determine the final clinical response (47,61). Silliman et al. (45) identified a cohort of TRALI patients in whom no HLA or leukocyte antibodies were found. Rather, they describe the presence of a neutrophil priming agent—a lipid in the blood components given to the patients who developed TRALI. They postulated that this lipid developing during routine storage of blood components and that it primes polymorphonuclear oxidase. These investigators (48) found that at the time blood components (e.g., whole blood, red blood cells, platelet concentrate) become outdated, they contain a priming agent that enhance polymorphonuclear NADPH-oxidase activity by 2.1 to 2.8 fold. As this study represents the first description of an alternative, non–antibody-mediated model of TRALI, other laboratories will need to confirm these findings.

In a retrospective study from the same laboratory reporting the work described above, 10 consecutive patients suspected of TRALI were evaluated for PMN priming activity (62). These investigators used as controls patients having febrile or urticarial reactions. They found that postreaction sera from TRALI patients demonstrated a significant increase in PMN priming activity (2.1-fold) compared with the patients' prereaction sera as well as that of the control group. In all cases the priming activity from serum samples was inhibited by pretreatment of the isolated PMNs with 400 μM WEB 2170, an inhibitor of the platelet-activating factor receptor. Silliman and colleagues found that PMN-generating lipids have a significant effect on lung function in an isolated, perfused rat lung model (63). When lipopolysaccharide formed at day 42 of red blood cell storage was infused, significant changes in pulmonary artery pressure and lung weight were observed.

One other mechanism that merits discussion involves cytokines. Numerous laboratories have shown that cytokines play a central role in the modulation of inflammatory immune responses. Several reports implicate cytokines, including tumor necrosis factor (TNF) and interleukin-8 in the pathogenesis of IgG-mediated hemolytic transfusion reactions (HTRS) (64,65). Of interest is the observation that patients experiencing HTRs may have hypoxemic or hypercapnic respiratory failure or both (66). It may be relevant that during HTRs the concentrations of TNF increase and TNF has been implicated in the development of septic ARDS (66). It has been suggested that the release of significant quantities of TNF from degranulating neutrophils may contribute to the injury of pulmonary capillary endothelium seen in ARDS. How these observations precisely relate to TRALI remains a matter of conjecture.

VIII. DIAGNOSIS

Because there is no diagnostic test or pathognomonic sign, TRALI remains a diagnosis of exclusion. One must rule out other causes of respiratory distress and pulmonary edema in the transfusion setting: myocardial infarction, circulatory overload, and bacterial infection. Normal central venous and pulmonary wedge pressures are consistent with TRALI. The demonstration of lymphocytotoxic, HLA-or granulocyte-specific antibodies in donor or recipient serum is strongly suggestive of the diagnosis (7). The presence of a positive reverse lymphocyte crossmatch between donor serum and the patient's lymphocytes provides important, supportive results, as does correspondence of antibody and antigen.

IX. TREATMENT

While the earlier reports of TRALI described a fulminant picture of respiratory distress, it is clear that not all cases are associated with life-threatening complications. Respiratory support should be as intensive as dictated by the clinical picture. In almost all cases oxygen supplementation is necessary, and if the hypoxemia is severe, intubation and mechanical ventilation are important interventions (6,8). Once a diagnosis is seriously entertained, therapeutic measures should be started promptly. Pressor agents may be useful in case of sustained hypertension. Corticosteroids are probably of marginal value, and diuretics have no role because the underlying pathology involves microvascular injury, rather than fluid overload (36).

X. MANAGEMENT OF FUTURE TRANSFUSIONS

In the majority of cases in which a donor or antibody has been implicated, no special measures are necessary to manage future transfusions of plasma-containing components. However, if antibody in the recipient has been identified, it has been suggested that filters that significantly reduce leukocyte content be used for transfusion of cellular components. However, given the low reported incidence of TRALI, no data are available to either support or refute this approach.

XI. PREVENTION

Strategies aimed at reducing the incidence of reactions are complicated by the absence of a profile of those recipients at greatest risk and by the lack of a diagnostic test. Any effort will suffer for lack of sensitivity or specificity. Therefore, measures must focus on limiting exposure. As a consequence, there is no consensus on the subject, and few blood collectors have taken specific steps. However, some investigators have made recommendations that include the following (5):

1. Donors who have been implicated in TRALI should be permanently deferred or subsequent donations limited to the production of frozen-deglycerolized or washed red blood cells. Such steps will prevent the use of plasma from blood components prepared from these donors.

2.   Multiparous donors (two or three pregnancies as a suggested threshold number) should be prospectively identified and their blood either screened for HLA or granulocyte antibodies or diverted for uses other than whole blood, fresh frozen plasma, or single donor apheresis platelets.

If the second group of recommendations were followed, these measures would be expected to decrease the frequency of TRALI by limiting any components containing large amounts of plasma from donors most likely to have produced these antibodies. However, there are significant weaknesses to this approach. First, donor histories are not necessarily accurate, and women having had alloimmunizing exposures to fetal leukocytes through either abortion or ectopic pregnancy may neglect to report this part of their medical history. Second, this fails to address the donor who has been immunized by transfusion, unless the donor's blood was tested for HLA or granulocyte-specific antibodies. Third, red blood cells, random donor platelet concentrates, and cryoprecipitate contain less than 50 mL of plasma, but such components have been associated with TRALI. To make this approach more effective, one would need to defer all blood component production from multiparous donors (estimated to be 5–30% of donor bases), but this would result in a significant loss of many "safe" blood donors. Finally, tests for HLA and granulocyte antibodies are time consuming and are not routinely available in many blood centers or hospital blood banks. Clearly, more sensitive and specific measures are needed for a more effective strategy to prevent TRALI.

XII. CONCLUSION

TRALI is an important, life-threatening transfusion complication, the incidence rate of which is unknown but is most likely underrecognized. There may be several mechanisms that lead to a common pathway of microvascular insult and alveolar injury. In most cases, this syndrome is reversible, particularly with rapid diagnosis and treatment.

REFERENCES

1.   Carilli AD, Ramanamurty MV, Chang YS, et al. Noncardiogenic pulmonary edema following blood transfusion. Chest 1978; 74:310–312.
2.   Kernoff PBA, Durrant IJ, Rizza CR, Wright FW. Severe allergic pulmonary oedema after plasma transfusion. Br J Haematol 1972; 23:777–781.
3.   Wolf CFW, Canale VC. Fatal pulmonary hypersensitivity reaction to HLA-incompatible blood transfusion: report of a case and review of the literature. Transfusion 1976; 16:135–140.

4. Ward HN. Pulmonary infiltrates associated with leukoagglutinin transfusion reactions. Ann Intern Med 1970; 73:689–694.

5. Popovsky MA, Chaplin HC Jr, Moore SB. Transfusion-related acute lung injury: a neglected, serious complication of hemotherapy. Transfusion 1992; 32:589–592.

6. Popovsky MA. The role of leukocyte depletion in prevention of transfusion-related acute lung injury. In: Sweeney J, Heaton A, eds. Clinical Benefits of Leukodepleted Blood Products. Austin, TX: R.G. Landes, 1995.

7. Popovsky MA. Transfusion-related acute lung injury. In: Popovsky M, ed. Transfusion Reactions. Bethesda, MD: American Association of Blood Banks, 1996.

8. Popovsky MA, Moore SB. Diagnostic and pathogenetic considerations in transfusion related acute lung injury. Transfusion 1985; 25:573–577.

9. Jeter EK, Madysatha P, Rodriguiz RM, Key LL. Transfusion-associated acute lung injury induced by granulocytebound cytophilic IgG (abstr). Transfusion 1994; 34(suppl):65S.

10. Stack G, Judge JV, Snyder EL. Febrile and non-immune transfusion reactions. In: Rossi EC, Simon TL, Moss GS, Gould SA, eds. Principles of Transfusion Medicine. 2d ed. Baltimore, MD: Williams & Wilkins, 1996.

11. Goldman M, Blajchman MA. Blood product-associated bacterial sepsis. Transfus Med Rev 1991; 5:73-83.

12. Blajchman MA, Ali AM. Bacteria in the blood supply: an overlooked issue in transfusion medicine. In: Nance SJ, ed. Blood Safety: Current Challenges. Bethesda, MD: American Association of Blood Banks, 1992:213–228.

13. Vengelen-Tyler V, ed. Technical Manual. 12 ed. Bethesda, MD: American Association of Blood Banks, 1996:549.

14. Pineda AA, Taswell HF. Transfusion reactions associated with anti-IgA antibodies: report of four cases and review of the literature. Transfusion 1975; 15:10–15.

15. Barnard RD. Indiscriminate transfusion: a critique of case reports illustrating hypersensitivity reactions. NY State J Med 1951; 51:2399–2401.

16. Ward HN, Lipscomb TS, Cawley LP. Pulmonary hypersensitivity reaction after blood transfusion. Arch Intern Med 1968; 122:362–366.

17. Byrne JP, Dixon JA. Pulmonary edema following blood transfusion reaction. Arch Surg 1971; 102:91–94.

18. Andrews AT, Zmijewski CM, Bowman HS, Reihart JK. Transfusion reaction with pulmonary infiltration associated with HLA-specific leukocyte antibodies. Am J Clin Pathol 1976; 66:483–487.

19. Philipps E, Fleischner FG. Pulmonary edema in the course of a blood transfusion without overloading the circulation. Dis Chest 1966; 50:619–623.

20. Brittingham TE. Immunologic studies on leukocytes. Vox Sang 1957; 2:242–248.

21. Silver H. Non-cardiac pulmonary edema following blood transfusion. Hartford Hosp Bill 1973; 28:336–338.

22. Thompson JS, Severson CD, Parmely MJ, et al. Pulmonary "hypersensitivity" reactions induced by transfusion of non-HLA leukoagglutinins. N Engl J Med 1971; 284:1120–1125.

23. Felbo M, Jensen KG. Death in childbirth following transfusion of leukocyte-incompatible blood. Acta Haematol (Basel) 1962; 27:113–119.

24. Dubois M, Lotze MT, Diamond WJ, et al. Pulmonary shunting during leuko-agglutinin-induced non-cardiac pulmonary edema. JAMA 1980; 244:2186–2189.
25. Culliford AT, Thomas S, Spencer FC. Fulminating noncardiogenic pulmonary edema. A newly recognized hazard during cardiac operations. J Thorac Cardiovasc Surg 1980; 80:868–875.
26. Popovsky MA, Abel MD, Moore SM. Transfusion-related acute lung injury associated with passive transfer of antileukocyte antibodies. Am Rev Respir Dis 1983; 128:185–189.
27. Yomtovian R, Kline W, Press C, et al. Severe pulmonary hypersensitivity associated with passive transfusion of a neutrophil-specific antibody. Lancet 1984; 1:244–246.
28. Reese EP Jr, McCullough JJ, Craddock PR. An adverse pulmonary reaction to cryoprecipitate in a hemophiliac. Transfusion 1975; 15:583–588.
29. Goeken NE, Schulak JA, Nghiem DD, et al. Transfusion in donor-specific blood transfusion patients resulting from transfused maternal antibody. Transplantation 1984; 38:306–307.
30. Dhainaut JF, Brossard Y, Dimercurio JP, et al. Oedeme pulmonaire lesionnel gravissime au cours du 20° echange plasmatique pour incompatibilite Rhesus. In: Hemoperfusion, Echanges Plasmatique en Reanimation. Paris: Expansion Scientifique Francaise, 1981:291–298.
31. Campbell DA, Swartz RD, Waskeritz JA, Turcotte JG. Leukoagglutination with interstitial pulmonary edema (letter). Transplantation 1982; 34:300–301.
32. VanBuren NL, Stroncek DF, Clay MA, et al. Transfusion-related acute lung injury caused by an NB2 granulocyte-specific antibody in a patient with thrombotic thrombocytopenic purpura. Transfusion 1990; 30:42–45.
33. Eastlund T, McGrath PC, Britten A, Propp R. Fatal pulmonary transfusion reaction to plasma containing donor HLA antibody. Vox Sang 1989; 56:63–66.
34. Eastlund DT, McGrath PC, Burkart P. Platelet transfusion reaction associated with interdonor HLA incompatibility. Vox Sang 1988; 55:157–160.
35. O'Connor JC, Strauss RG, Goeken NE, Knox LB. A near-fatal reaction during granulocyte transfusion of a neonate. Transfusion 1988; 28:173–176.
36. Levy GJ, Shabot MM, Hart ME, et al. Transfusion-associated noncardiogenic pulmonary edema: Report of a case and a warning regarding treatment. Transfusion 1986; 26:278–281.
37. Nordhagen R, Conradi M, Dromtorp SM. Pulmonary reaction associated with transfusion of plasma containing anti-5b. Vox Sang 1986; 51:102–107.
38. DeWolf AM, Van Den Berg BW, Hoffman HJ, Zundert AA. Pulmonary dysfunction during one-lung ventilation caused by HLA-specific antibodies against leukocytes. Anesth Analg 1987; 66:463–467.
39. Leaman B, Anderson D, Walker I, Heddle N. Two episodes of non-cardiogenic pulmonary edema in a patient caused by the same donor's blood (abstr). Transfusion 1994; 34(suppl):26S.
40. Win N, Kaye T, Jones L, Knowles S. Transfusion-related acute lung injury (TRALI) (abstr). Transfus Med 1995; 5(suppl 1):33.
41. Clarke G, Podlosky L, Petrie L, Boshkov L. Severe respiratory reactions to random donor platelets: an incidence and nested case-control study (abstr). Blood 1994; 84(suppl 1):465a.

42. Lin M, Chen CC, Hong CC, et al. Transfusion-associated respiratory distress in Taiwan. Vox Sang 1994; 67:372–376.
43. Reissman P, Manny N, Shapira SC, et al. Transfusion-related adult respiratory distress syndrome. Isr J Med Sci 1993; 29:303–307.
44. Popovsky MA, Chaplin HC, Moore SB. Transfusion-related acute lung injury (letter). Transfusion 1993; 33:444–445.
45. Silliman C, Pitman J, Thurman G, Ambruso DR. Neutrophil (PMN) priming agents develop in patients with transfusion-related acute lung injury (abstr). Blood 1992; 80:(suppl 1):261a.
46. Bux J, Hoch J, Bindl L, et al. Transfusionassoziierte acute Lungeninsuffizienz. Dtsch Med Wochenschr 1994; 119:19–24.
47. Gans ROB, Duurkens VAM, van Zundert AA, Hoorntje SJ. Transfusion-related acute lung injury. Intensive Care Med 1988; 14:654–657.
48. Silliman CC, Thurman GW, Ambruso DR. Stored blood components contain agents that prime the neutrophil NADPH oxidase through the platelet-activating-factor receptor. Vox Sang 1992; 53:133–136.
49. Henderson RA. Acute transfusion reactions. NZ Med J 1990; 103:509–511.
50. Cooperman LH, Price HL. Pulmonary edema in the operative and postoperative period: a review of 40 cases. Ann Surg 1970; 172:833–891.
51. Sazama K. Reports of 355 transfusion-associated deaths: 1976 through 1985. Transfusion 1990; 14:654–670.
52. Hume HA, Popovsky MA, Benson K, Glasman AB, et al. Hypotensive reactions: a previously uncharacterized complication of platelet reaction? Transfusion. In press.
53. Virchis AE, Contreras M, Novarrete C, Jan-Mohamed R, et al. Transfusion-related acute lung injury (TRALI) due to inter-donor incompatibility (abstr). Blood. In press.
54. Jacob JS, Craddock PR, Hammerschmidt DE, Moldow CF. Complement-induced granulocyte aggregation: an unsuspected mechanism of disease. N Engl J Med 1980; 302:789–794.
55. Hammerschmidt DE, Jacob HS. Adverse pulmonary reactions to transfusion. Adv Intern Med 1982; 27:511–530.
56. Craddock PR, Hammerschmidt DE, Moldow CF, et al. Granulocyte aggregation as a manifestation of membrane interactions with complement: possible role in leukocyte margination microvascular occlusion, and endothelial damage. Semin Hematol 1979; 16:140–147.
57. Shasby DM, Van Benthuysem KM, Tate RM, et al. Granulocytes mediate acute edematous lung injury in rabbits and in isolated rabbits lungs perfused with phorbol myristate acetate: role of oxygen radicals. Am Rev Respir Dis 1982; 125:443-447.
58. Sznajder JI, Fraiman A, Hal JB, et al. Increased hydrogen peroxide in the expired breath of patients with acute hypoxemic respiratory failure. Chest 1989; 96:606–612.
59. Larsen GL, McCarthy K, Webster RO, et al. A differential effect of C5a and C5a des Arg in the induction of pulmonary inflammation. Am J Pathol 1980; 100:179–192.
60. Seeger W, Schneider U, Kreusler B, et al. Reproduction of transfusion-related acute lung injury in an ex vivo lung model. Blood 1990; 76:1438–444.
61. Westaby S. Mechanisms of membrane damage and surfactant depletion in acute lung injury. Intensive Care Med 1986; 12:2–5.
62. Silliman CC, Paterson A, Dickey WO, Stroncek D, Popovsky MA, Caldwell SA,

Ambruso DR. The association of biologically active lipids with the development of transfusion-related acute lung injury: a retrospective study. Transfusion. In press.

63. Silliman C, Allard J, Voelkel N, Ambruso D. Plasma and lipids from stored packed red cells (PRBCs) cause acute lung injury in an animal model (abstr). Blood 1996.

64. Davenport RD, Polak TJ, Kunkel SL. White cell-associated procoagulant induced by ABO incompatibility. Transfusion 1994; 34:943–949.

65. Davenport RD, Streiter RM, Sandiford TJ, Kunkel SL. Interleukin-8 production in red blood cell incompatibility. Blood 1990; 76:2439–2442.

66. Capon SM, Goldfinger D. Acute hemolytic transfusion reaction, a paradigm of the systemic inflammatory response: new insights into pathophysiology and treatment. Transfusion 1995; 35:513–520.

67. Boshkov L, Silliman C, Clarke G, Dickey W, Ambruso D. Transfusion-related acute lung injury (TRALI) following platelet transfusion (abstr). Blood 1995; 86:1403.

68. Lindgren L, Ylihankala Å, Holme L, Koskimies S, et al. Transfusion-related acute lung injury (TRALI) after fresh-frozen plasma in a patient with a coagulopathy. Acta Anaesthes Scand 1996; 40:641–644.

69. Bux J, Becker F, Seeger W, Kilpatrick D, et al. Transfusion-related acute lung injury due to HLA-A2-specific antibodies in recipient and NB1-specific antibodies in donor blood. Br J Haem 1996; 93:707–713.

7

Clinical Effects of the Immunomodulation Associated with Allogeneic Blood Transfusions

José O. Bordin
Escola Paulista de Medicina, São Paulo, Brazil

Morris A. Blajchman
McMaster University and Hamilton Centre Canadian Red Cross Society, Hamilton, Ontario, Canada

I. INTRODUCTION

Considerable data have accumulated over the past two decades suggesting that allogeneic blood transfusions (ABTs) may be associated with immunomodulation in recipients (1,2). Depending on patient category, this immunomodulatory effect can be clinically detrimental or beneficial (Table 1). Thus, it has been suggested that the ABT-associated immunomodulation might adversely affect the overall clinical outcome in patients undergoing curative surgery for a variety of malignant tumors by downregulating the recipient's immune system permitting unregulated tumor cell growth (3–5). In addition, many observational studies have implicated this ABT-associated immunomodulatory effect with an increased prevalence of postoperative bacterial infection episodes after abdominal, open-heart, and orthopedic surgery (6–9). These adverse clinical effects, however, have yet to be proven to be associated with ABT. In contrast, there is clear evidence that ABT-associated immunomodulation can be beneficial for selected categories of patients, such as: increasing allograft survival in renal allograft recipients (10); decreasing the recurrence rate in women with recurrent spontaneous abortion (11); and possibly reducing the relapse rate in patients with Crohn's disease (12).

Table 1 Potential Clinical Effects of Immunomodulation Associated with Allogeneic Blood Transfusions

---

1. Adverse
     Increase in cancer recurrence rate
     Increase in prevalence of postoperative bacterial infection
2. Beneficial
     Improvement of renal allograft survival
     Reduction in prevalence of spontaneous recurrent abortion
     Decrease in relapse rate of Crohn's disease
     Adoptive immunotherapy in chronic myelogenous leukemia reducing the relapse
          rate after bone marrow transplantation

This chapter summarizes the currently available evidence relating to the clinical effects of ABT-associated immunomodulation.

II. ALLOGENEIC BLOOD TRANSFUSIONS AND CANCER RECURRENCE

The possible association between perioperative ABT and increased cancer recurrence was first suggested by Gantt in 1981 (13). Since then, over 100 retrospective and prospective studies evaluating the effect of perioperative ABT on cancer recurrence and/or overall outcome in patients with a malignancy undergoing cancer surgery have been published (14–16). However, because the available data are mostly from retrospective or prospective observational studies, they are not regarded as being conclusive, and the question as to whether or not ABTs influence tumor growth is still unresolved.

Evidence for a possible adverse effect of ABT in patients with a malignancy has been reported in approximately 60% of observational studies evaluating patients with a large variety of malignancies, including breast, lung, kidney, prostate, stomach, cervix, vulva, head and neck, larynx, soft tissue, bone, and liver metastases; the remaining 40% showing no deleterious effect (3,14).

Since 1993, three prospective, randomized, controlled clinical trials (RCTs) have been published that investigated the association of perioperative ABT with colorectal cancer recurrence (17–19) (Table 2). An RCT conducted in Rotterdam, The Netherlands, randomized 475 colorectal cancer patients to receive either allogeneic or autologous blood products perioperatively (17). This study reported no difference in either the cancer-specific survival rate at 4 years (68% vs. 64%, $p = 0.60$) or the cancer recurrence rate at 4 years (62% vs. 56%, $p = 0.50$). However, the data showed that the relative risk (RR) of cancer recurrence was increased in transfused patients who had received either allogeneic (RR =

Table 2 Results of Prospective, Randomized Clinical Trials Analyzing the Effect of Perioperative Blood Transfusions on Clinical Outcome (recurrence rate and/or overall prognosis) in Patients with Malignant Tumors

	A[a]	B[b]	C[c]
Tumor site	Colorectal	Colorectal	Colorectal
Number of patients	475	120	697
Number of subjects per arm	(1) 133 (2) 112	(1) 48 (2) 52	(1) 337 (2) 360
Type of blood transfusion per arm	(1) Autologous BC-PRBCs (2) Allogeneic BC-PRBCs	(1) Autologous BC-PRBCs (2) Allogeneic BC-PRBCs	(1) LR-Allogeneic PRBCs (2) Allogeneic BC-PRBCs
Rate of tumor recurrence per arm	(1) 62% (2) 56% $p = 0.50$	(1) 16.7% (2) 28.9% $p = 0.11$	Transfused[d] = 30% No. transfused = 26% $p = 0.22$
Relative risk of tumor recurrence compared with untransfused patients	Arm (1) 1.8; $p = 0.04$ Arm (2) 2.1; $p = 0.01$	Arm (1) 0.96; $p = 0.96$ Arm (2) 7.01; $p = 0.006$	Arm (1) 0.91; $p = 0.53$
Cancer-specific survival rate	(1) 68% (2) 64% $p = 0.60$	(1) vs (2) $p = 0.20$	Transfused[d] = 69% Not transfused = 81% $p < 0.001$

PRBCs = Packed red blood cells; BC-PRBCs = buffy coat–reduced PRBCs; LR-Allogeneic PRBCs = leukocyte-reduced (≤48 hours old) allogeneic PRBCs.
[a]From Ref. 17.
[b]From Ref. 18.
[c]From Ref. 19.
[d]Patients transfused with either LR-PRBCs or BC-PRBCs.

2.1, $p = 0.01$) or autologous (RR = 1.8, $p = 0.04$) blood, compared to subjects that had not been transfused (17). Since this study actually compared outcomes among patients receiving autologous blood versus recipients of buffy coat–reduced allogeneic blood, it is possible that the degree of leukocyte removal resulting from buffy coat reduction may have diminished the ABT-associated immunomodulatory effect that might have been observed had unmodified allogeneic blood been used. Buffy coat–reduced allogeneic blood represents the removal of approximately 80% of the leukocytes present in a unit of whole blood. Interestingly, this level of leukocyte reduction has been shown to prevent donor-specific T-cell responsiveness associated with non–buffy coat–reduced blood (20). Thus it is possible that the widespread use in Western Europe of buffy-coat–reduced allogeneic cellular blood components may significantly lessen the immunomodulatory risk of cellular blood component transfusions in Western Europe compared to that occurring in allogeneically transfused patients in North America (20).

The second RCT, from Munich, Germany, randomized 120 patients with potentially curative colorectal carcinoma to receive either leukocyte-reduced allogeneic blood or predeposited autologous blood. After a median follow-up of 22 months, tumor recurrence was detected in 28.9% of the patients transfused with allogeneic blood compared with 16.7% of the subjects transfused with autologous blood ($p = 0.11$). The authors also reported that the need for allogeneic blood was an independent predictor of cancer recurrence (RR = 7.01; 95% Cl = 1.77–27.75; $p = 0.006$) (18).

The third prospective RCT was also from The Netherlands and compared recipients of leukocyte-reduced allogeneic packed red blood cells (PRBCs) with buffy coat–reduced allogeneic PRBC transfusions in patients also undergoing curative surgery for colorectal cancer. This study did not detect a difference in patient survival between the two transfusion arms. As in the Rotterdam study, transfused patients who received either allogeneic or autologous blood had a significantly lower 3-year survival than untransfused study subjects (69% vs. 81%, $p < 0.001$) (19). Interestingly, recurrence rates appeared not to be affected by the need for transfusion (30% vs. 26% $p = 0.22$).

In 1993, the results of the available observational studies of patients with colorectal carcinoma were subjected to meta-analysis by two groups of investigators independently (4,5). The literature-based meta-analysis from the first team of investigators reported that the RRs of cancer recurrence, cancer-associated death, and death from any cause in subjects transfused with allogeneic blood were 1.80, 1.76, and 1.63, respectively (4). These authors concluded that their analysis supported the hypothesis that perioperative ABT was associated with an increased risk of cancer recurrence and death from this disease (4). The second team of meta-analysts concluded that perioperative ABT increased the RR of cancer recurrence by 37% (95% Cl = 20–56%) (5).

A third meta-analysis, performed to try to show a quantitative synthesis of the published observational studies by the random-effects method before any adjustment for all known confounders, concluded that the risk of ABT-related adverse outcome ranged from 6% in breast cancer to 262% in head and neck carcinoma. In this analysis, the ABT-associated adverse outcome was found to be statistically significant for all cancer sites, except breast (15).

The results of the three RCTs mentioned above (17–19) were subjected recently to yet another meta-analysis (16). For the latter meta-analysis, subjects receiving buffy coat–reduced allogeneic RBC transfusions were allocated to the treatment group, while the control subjects were those assigned to receive either autologous or leukocyte-reduced allogeneic PRBCs. The results of this analysis gave an RR very close to unity, not supporting the hypothesis that ABT was associated with a deleterious effect. However, it is important to point out that this analysis could not rule out an ABT effect smaller than a 33% increase in risk of cancer recurrence (16).

The association of transfusion history and cancer risk has also been evaluated in approximately 37,000 cancer-free women aged between 55 and 69 years. The results of this study indicate that the RR is 2.20 (95% Cl = 1.35–3.58) for non-Hodgkin's lymphoma and 2.53 (95% Cl = 1.34 – 4.78) for renal carcinoma (21). Thus, despite considerable advances in our knowledge over the past decade about risk factors associated with malignancy, the issue of the association between ABT and cancer recurrence is still unclear (22).

III. ALLOGENEIC BLOOD TRANSFUSIONS AND BACTERIAL INFECTION

The relationship between ABT-associated immunomodulation and postoperative bacterial infectious complications has been reviewed recently by several authors (1,9,16,23). Again, most of the available clinical data are from uncontrolled studies, and unequivocal evidence for the existence of an adverse ABT effect relating allogeneic transfusions as an independent prognostic factor for postoperative septic complications has not yet been established.

Over the past 5 years, six prospective RCTs have evaluated the impact of blood transfusions on the prevalence of postoperative bacterial infections in blood transfusion recipients (7,8,17,24–26) (Table 3). In 1992, an RCT from Denmark reported on 197 patients who underwent curative colorectal surgery (7). Study subjects were assigned randomly to receive either leukocyte-reduced allogeneic whole blood or non–leukocyte-reduced allogeneic whole blood (7). The results showed that patients transfused with non–leukocyte-reduced allogeneic whole blood had a significantly higher prevalence of postoperative infections

Table 3 Results of Prospective, Randomized Clinical Studies Analyzing the Effect of Perioperative Allogeneic, Leukocyte-Reduced Allogeneic and Autologous Transfusions on the Prevalence of Postoperative Bacterial Infections in Recipients

	A[a]	B[b]	C[c]	D[d]	E[e]	F[f]
Type of surgery Number of patients	Colorectal 197	Colorectal 475	Colorectal 120	Cardiac 914	Colorectal 589	Colorectal 697
Number of patients per study arm	(1) 48 (2) 56	(1) 133 (2) 112	(1) 53 (2) 37	(1) 285 (2) 287 (3) 294	(1) 118 (2) 142 (3) 155	(1) 215 (2) 231 (3) 251
Type of blood component transfusion per study arm	(1) LR-WB (stored) (2) Whole Blood	(1) Autologous BC-PRBCs (2) Allogeneic BC-PRBCs	(1) Autologous PRBCs (2) Allogeneic BC-PRBCs	(1) LR-BC-PRBCs (fresh) (2) LR-BC-PRBCs (stored) (3) BC-PRBCs	(1) LR-BC-PRBCs (stored) (2) BC-PRBCs (3) Not transfused	(1) LR-Allogeneic PRBCs (2) Allogeneic BC-PRBCs (3) Not transfused
Prevalence rate of infection per study arm	(1) 2% (2) 23%	(1) 25% (2) 27%	(1) 12% (2) 27%	(1) 16.7% (2) 17.7% (3) 22.7%	(1) 0% (2) 18.3% (3) 1%	(1) 42% (2) 36% (3) 24%
Statistical significance	(1) vs. (2); $p < 0.01$	(1) vs. (2); NS	(1) vs. (2); $p < 0.05$	(1) vs. (2); NS (1) and (2) vs. (3); $p < 0.05$	(1) vs. (2), $p < 0.0001$ (1) vs. (3); $p < 0.0001$	(1) vs. (2), $p < 0.75$ (1) and (2) vs. (3); $p < 0.01$

PRBCs = packed red blood cells; LR-WB (stored) = leukocyte-reduced whole blood filtered after storage; Autologous BC-PRBCs = autologous buffy coat-reduced PRBCs; Allogeneic BC-PRBCs = allogeneic buffy coat-reduced PRBCs; NS = not significant.
[a] From Ref. 7.
[b] From Ref. 17.
[c] From Ref. 8.
[d] From Ref. 24.
[e] From Ref. 25.
[f] From Ref. 26.

than patients who received 99.98% leukocyte-reduced allogeneic blood (23% vs. 2%; $p < 0.01$).

In another RCT, which had been designed to measure cancer-related prognosis, no difference was detected in the prevalence of postoperative infection in study patients who were transfused with allogeneic buffy coat–reduced PRBCs compared to those who received autologous whole blood (17). In this study, however, transfused subjects who received either allogeneic or autologous red blood cell transfusions had a higher prevalence of postoperative infection than those who were not transfused (17).

In the RCT from Munich, in which study subjects were assigned to receive either autologous PRBCs or buffy coat–reduced PRBCs, a significantly higher postoperative infection rate in patients transfused with buffy coat–reduced PRBCs was seen compared to that in subjects transfused with autologous PRBCs (27% vs. 12% $p = 0.036$) (8). Using multivariate regression analysis to adjust for other risk factors, the RR of postoperative infections in the allogeneic group versus that in the autologous transfusion group was 2.84 ($p = 0.047$; 95% Cl = 1.02–7.98). The observed number of noninfectious complications was similar in the two groups of patients. In contrast to that seen in the study of Busch et al. (17), autologous blood recipients did not have a greater prevalence of postoperative infectious complications than that seen in those who were not transfused (8).

A three-arm RCT including 914 cardiac surgery patients has been reported from Leiden, The Netherlands (24). In this study, patients were assigned randomly to receive allogeneic leukocyte-reduced buffy coat–reduced PRBCs filtered within 24 hours of collection, allogeneic leukocyte-reduced buffy coat–reduced PRBCs filtered after storage, or non–leukocyte-reduced buffy coat–reduced PRBCs. Patients who received allogeneic leukocyte-reduced buffy coat–reduced PRBCs showed a lower prevalence of both postoperative infection (22.7% vs. 17.3%; $p < 0.05$) and mortality rate than those transfused with non–leukocyte-reduced buffy coat–reduced PRBCs. This study, however, detected no difference in mortality or in the prevalence of postoperative infection (16.7% vs. 17.7%) between the two leukocyte-reduced groups of study subjects (24).

Another RCT randomly assigned 589 colorectal carcinoma patients to receive either allogeneic poststorage leukocyte-reduced buffy coat–reduced PRBCs or allogeneic buffy coat–reduced PRBCs (25). The results indicated that patients transfused with allogeneic poststorage leukocyte-reduced buffy coat–reduced PRBCs had a significantly lower prevalance of postoperative bacterial infections than subjects who received allogeneic buffy coat–reduced PRBCs (0% vs. 18.3%, $p < 0.001$) (25).

Recently, yet another large multicenter RCT randomly assigned 697 patients undergoing colorectal surgery to receive either allogeneic leukocyte-reduced buffy coat–reduced PRBCs or allogeneic buffy coat–reduced PRBCs. Leukocyte reduction was performed within 48 hours of blood collection. No difference was detected in the prevalence of postoperative bacterial infection in the study subjects in the two transfusion arms. There was, however, a higher number of bacterial infectious episodes in patients who received a transfusion (allogeneic or autologous) compared with those who did not (39% vs. 24%, $p >$ 0.01) (26).

The results of three of these RCTs (8,17,19) were subjected recently to a meta-analysis (16). The results did not support the hypothesis that a deleterious ABT-associated effect occurred; however, the author could not rule out an ABT effect of a <33% increase in infectious risk (16).

It has been suggested that the risk of postoperative infection might increase with the number of allogeneic blood units transfused. In a study of patients who underwent surgery for a penetrating colonic injury, the calculated risk of a bacterial infection was 7.5% for untransfused patients and 25, 37, and 57%, respectively, for patients transfused with 1–5, 6– 9, or ≥10 allogeneic blood units (27). Similarly, a retrospective analysis of patients undergoing surgery for gastric carcinoma reported that those patients who developed postoperative infections had received a higher number of allogeneic blood products compared to those who did not (28). Using multiple logistic and receiver operating characteristic (ROC) curve analysis, a recent prospective study in 267 patients with colorectal cancer reported that the incidence of infection was significantly higher in patients transfused with allogeneic blood (28.8%) than in either patients transfused with autologous blood (8.0%) or those who had not been transfused (6.3%) ($p =$ 0.001). These results also showed a significant trend associated with an increasing number of allogeneic blood units transfused and risk of infection ($p < 0.0002$) (6). In a recently reported RCT, colorectal cancer patients transfused perioperatively with more than three units of PRBCs had a higher corrected RR for postoperative infections than patients transfused with one to three units (3.6 vs. 1.6; $p <$ 0.05) (26).

Based on the available observational studies, the postoperative bacterial infection rate in allogeneically transfused patients varied from 20 to 30% compared to 5–10% for either untransfused or autologous blood recipients (1). The definition of the term "infection" in such patients, however, is crucially important. Limiting the definition of infection complication to positive cultures underestimates prevalence, while extending the definition to include fever probably overestimates prevalence.

In conclusion, the six available European RCTs have contributed importantly to our understanding about a possible association between perioperative blood transfusion and bacterial complications; however, they give contradictory results. In an effort to resolve controversies about causal relationships, some investigators have recommended the use of meta-analysis. Two types of meta-analysis can be done: one is a meta-analysis of the literature (MAL) and the other is meta-analysis of individual patient data (MAP). In this instance, a MAL cannot be done because of heterogeneity of the data from the six RCTs (29). It may, however, be possible to do a MAP. Such an international collaborative individual patient-based meta-analysis might allow for a definitive conclusion to be reached as to whether ABTs increase susceptibility to postoperative infection. Such a study has been proposed recently (23).

IV. OTHER CLINICAL MANIFESTATIONS OF ALLOGENEIC BLOOD TRANSFUSION–ASSOCIATED IMMUNOMODULATION

A. Blood Transfusion and Allograft Transplantation

Since the report from Opelz et al. over 25 years ago, it is widely accepted that ABTs improve renal allograft survival (30,31). In spite of the fact that human leukocyte antigen (HLA) matching is one of the most important predictors for the continuing long-term function of cadaveric renal allografts, patients receiving ABTs have a significantly better allograft survival rate than those not transfused, regardless of the number of HLA-A, HLA-B, and HLA-DR locus mismatches (10,32). Even with HLA-identical sibling renal allografts, about 30% of allogeneically transfused recipients experience graft rejection compared to 75% of untransfused recipients (33).

Because of the availability of improved treatment regimens for rejection episodes and the potent action of the currently available immunosuppressive drugs, the ABT effect on renal allograft survival has declined over the last decade (10,34,35). Nevertheless, a collaborative multicenter study reporting on the outcome of more than 58,000 cadaveric renal transplantation since the advent of the use of cyclosporine reports that subjects receiving ABTs are still more likely to have successful renal allografts than those who did not (10). This study reported that the one-year renal allograft survival rate of subjects receiving pretransplant ABTs was 3–5% higher than that observed in untransfused patients (10). Similar results have been obtained also in patients receiving living-related-donor renal transplants (36).

For renal allograft recipients, the following still need to be defined: the optimal number of allogeneic blood units necessary to achieve the optimal ABT-associated effect; the allogeneic blood component required to produce such an effect; the optimal volume of blood required with each transfusion; the optimal timing of the ABT to produce the effect; the coexisting hazards of the ABT-associated immunomodulatory effect; and whether ABTs are even still needed (32). Nonetheless, patients receiving larger numbers of ABTs have been shown to have better one-year allograft survival rates than subjects transfused with few. Interestingly, subjects transfused with more than 10 units show poorer overall graft survival rates, suggesting that multitransfused patients are more likely to develop cytotoxic antibodies and thus are at greater risk for earlier and more severe allograft rejection (36).

Patients given leukocyte-reduced blood components such as washed RBC concentrates or frozen-deglycerolized RBCs have been shown to have poorer one-year cadaveric graft survival than recipients of whole blood or unmodified RBC concentrates, indicating that the allogeneic leukocytes present in the donor blood participate in the production of the ABT-associated beneficial effect (37). Further studies are required to understand how ABTs induce their clinical effect in renal transplantation; however, ABT is still considered an efficacious intervention that can be useful in the management of some patients scheduled for kidney transplantation. This treatment modality continues to be used in donor-directed renal allograft transplantation.

B. Blood Transfusion and Recurrent Spontaneous Abortions

The maintenance of a pregnancy depends on the immunological equilibrium between the fetus and the maternal immune response to the fetus. When the two spouses share HLA antigens, this immunological balance may be modified and maternal blocking antibodies may not be formed, predisposing the woman to recurrent abortions. Based on this theory, the use of allogeneic leukocyte transfusions has been proposed as a form of immunotherapy to treat women with recurrent spontaneous abortions (38). Overall, the results of prospective non-randomized studies of women with recurrent spontaneous abortions indicate a success rate of about 75% with the use of either paternal or third-party leukocytes compared to a success rate of only 50% receiving autologous or no leukocytes (1,38).

Because the therapeutic efficacy of allogeneic leukocyte infusions in women with recurrent spontaneous abortion became increasingly controversial and also because of the lack of a large RCT of sufficient sample size to indicate the most appropriate treatment method for such patients, the American Society for Reproductive Immunology (ASRI) initiated the conduct of a worldwide collaborative individual patient–based meta-analysis to evaluate all the available patient data relating to the efficacy of allogeneic leukocyte immunotherapy for women with recurrent spontaneous abortion (12). This meta-analysis of individual patient data was done by two separate and independent analytic teams. Both agreed that leukocyte immunotherapy represented an effective treatment for patients with recurrent spontaneous abortion. Even though such an effect appears to be small, with only 8–10% of affected women likely to achieve one additional live birth, allogeneic leukocyte immunotherapy is now widely accepted as an efficacious form of treatment for women with recurrent spontaneous abortion (11,38).

The use of allogeneic leukocyte immunotherapy has been associated with various transfusion risks, including alloimmunization to leukocyte antigens, neonatal graft-versus-host-disease, and congenital anomalies. Nonetheless, such side effects are rare, and the number of affected infants (3%) in the treated group was similar to the number of affected newborns seen in the control group (11,38).

C. Blood Transfusion and Inflammatory Bowel Disease

Following surgery in patients with Crohn's disease, the recurrence rate of a bowel obstruction or perforation has been estimated at about 50% at 10 years. Because immunological mechanisms might be involved in the pathogenesis of this disease, several clinical studies have analyzed whether the postoperative recurrence rate is affected by the immunomodulatory effects associated with ABTs administered perioperatively. The results from the available studies indicate that the recurrence rate in the two groups is similar (37.5% in the ABT-transfused group vs. 40.5% in the untransfused group) (1). However, all the data pooled in this evaluation had been generated by retrospective observational studies that evaluated patients subjected to different surgical treatments for different follow-up periods.

ABTs have also been proposed as a major risk factor in the development of postoperative bacterial infections in Crohn's disease patients in one study (39). Such an association did not reach statistical significance in a similar study (40). Multiple ABTs have been also associated with a significantly lower peripheral total lymphocyte and T-cell counts following surgery in Crohn's disease patients (12). Many factors might affect the recurrence rates in patients with Crohn's disease as well as the prevalence of bacterial infections following the surgical treatment; therefore, large well-designed RCTs are needed to ascertain the impact of ABT in the clinical activity of patients with Crohn's disease.

V. TRANSFUSION AND IMMUNE FUNCTION

The immunogenicity of soluble, particulate, or cellular antigens associated with the major histocompatibility complex (MHC) molecules (in humans, the HLA antigens) present in transfused blood products depends on the ability of antigen-presenting cells (APCs) to present them to recipient T cells. In addition, co-stimulatory signals are required to make possible the generation and amplification of antigen-specific T-cell responses and effector function (42,41). The CD28 receptor is the major costimulatory signal for T cells, and CD28/B7 interaction represents a critical pathway for transplantation tolerance and immune reactivity (42,43). Currently, T-helper cells are categorized into two major subsets: Th1 and Th2. CD28 costimulation enables the development of Th2 cytokine–producing cells and in the absence of CD28 costimulation, T cells will not be primed to produce Th2 cytokines. This could result in the failure to produce the Th1 subset (43). The Th1 subset when activated produces interleukin-2 (IL-2), interferon-γ (IFN-γ), tumor necrosis factor-α (TNF-α), and lymphotoxin (LT), but not IL-4 or IL-5. On the other hand, the Th2 sub-set of helper cells produces IL-4, IL-5, IL-6, and IL-10, but not IL-2, IFN-γ, TNF-α, or LT. Th1 cells stimulate those cells involved in the cellular immune response, while Th2 cells are associated with the humoral immune response. The B7-1 protein delivers a costimulatory signal through CD-28 and CTLA-4 T cell receptors, which regulate IL-2 secretion, while the B7-2 protein provides a critical early costimulatory signal that results in T-cell clonal proliferation (42). Impairment of one of the costimulatory pathway signals thus could result in T-cell anergy (41,44).

ABTs have been shown to be associated with various alterations in *in vitro* measurements of immunological responsiveness in recipients. The most commonly observed functional modification is a lowering in the helper: suppressor (CD4:CD8) lymphocyte ratio. Such an abnormality has also been shown to occur in patients with hemophilia A after treatment with factor VIII concentrates (45). Recently, two prospective clinical trials have reported that the use of very high-purity factor VIII concentrates retards the decline in CD4 counts over time compared with intermediate purity factor VIII concentrates (46–48). Moreover, CD4 cell counts were shown to remain relatively stable in HIV-infected hemophiliacs treated exclusively with recombinant factor VIII for 3.5 years (49). However, the use of high-purity factor VIII products was shown to neither retard the development of AIDS nor decrease the risk of death in HIV-infected patients with hemophilia (50). In addition to quantitative alterations of T–cell subsets, functional abnormalities in lymphocytes have also been described in patients with hemophilia. These include decreased proliferative responses to mitogens, decreased natural killer (NK) cell activity, diminished cell-mediated immunity, hypergammaglobulinemia due to polyclonal B cell activation, T-cell activation, and inadequate monocyte function (45,51). It has been suggested that some of these functional immunological alterations could be prevented with the use of very high-purity factor VIII concentrates (52).

Other functional immunological alterations associated with ABT include suppression of lymphocyte blastogenesis, decreased antigen presentation, and reduction in delayed-type hypersensitivity (53).

VI. MECHANISMS OF ALLOGENEIC TRANSFUSION–ASSOCIATED IMMUNOMODULATION

Although the mechanisms of the ABT-associated immunomodulatory effect remain to be elucidated, it is generally accepted that this biological phenomenon is mediated by the allogeneic leukocytes present in transfused cellular blood products (1). The Class ll HLA antigens present in transfused allogeneic leukocytes appear to elicit an immune response by recipients' T cells, but HLA compatibility between blood donor and recipient may result in the persistence of circulating donor mononuclear cells in the recipient (54,55). In this context, it has been demonstrated, using the polymerase chain reaction technique, that transfused male leukocytes can persist for 1–6 days in female patients receiving multiple ABTs (56). This prolonged survival of small numbers of transfused allogeneic leukocytes within the recipient's circulation, a phenomenon known as mononuclear microchimerism, can downregulate the immune response of the recipient, inducing tolerance for donor alloantigens and predisposing the recipient to the development of a chronic transfusion-associated graft-versus-host disease (54,55).

In vitro investigations have suggested that leukocytes lose their immunogenicity during blood storage. Consequently, it has been hypothesized that the transfusion of allogeneic blood, stored for prolonged periods of time, could result in transfusion-associated immunomodulation due to recipient T-cell anergy (44).

The hypothesis that the immunomodulatory effect of ABT is related to the presence of allogeneic leukocytes has also been supported by research involving experimental animals. Data from such studies indicate that ABTs accelerate tumor growth and enhance metastatic nodule formation in both inbred and outbred experimental animals (57,58). In such studies, it has been shown that allogeneically transfused experimental animals (mice and rabbits) inoculated with syngeneic tumor cells develop significantly higher numbers of pulmonary nodules than animals given syngeneic blood (57,58). These studies show that animals receiving allogeneic buffy-coat leukocytes develop significantly higher numbers of pulmonary nodules than animals given either plasma or prestorage leukocyte-reduced whole blood (58). Conceivably, the prestorage removal of allogeneic leukocytes prevented the accumulation of the soluble biological mediators synthesized and released by the donor allogeneic leukocytes during storage. It is possible that such biologically active substances are involved in the ABT-associated immunomodulation induced. Relevantly, allogeneic leukocytes have been recognized as the blood component responsible for the increased susceptibility to gut-derived infection in a murine model (59).

Further clues about the mechanism of ABT-associated immunomodulation have been provided by experimental data showing that the ABT-associated tumor growth–promoting effect can be adoptively transferred. In these experiments, naive animals that had received spleen cells from allogeneically transfused animals (inbred and outbred) developed a greater number of pulmonary metastatic nodules than was observed in animals that had received spleen cells from animals, transfused with syngeneic blood. This ABT-associated tumor growth–promoting effect could not be adoptively transferred using spleen cells derived from animals that had been transfused with prestorage leukocyte-reduced allogeneic blood (57). Additionally, it has been observed that the ABT-associated immunomodulatory effect occurred following the infusion of ABT-conditioned splenic T cells but was not seen after the infusion of ABT-conditioned splenic B cells, even though the presence of the B cells enhanced the extent of the tumor growth–promoting effect of the ABT-conditioned splenic T cells.

The ABT-associated tumor growth–promoting effect also was observed in adoptive-transfer experiments in which ABT-conditioned spleen cells were instilled intraperitoneally in diffusion chambers that allowed only the release of soluble substances. The results of these latter experiments suggest that the ABT-associated tumor growth–promoting effect might be mediated by biologically active substances released by conditioned T cells. The nature of these substances still needs to be defined.

The mechanism of the ABT-associated immunomodulatory effect thus is still unresolved. It is probably due to a combination of mechanisms involving active immunosuppression, host anergy and clonal deletion. With regard to clonal deletion, the infusion of foreign MHC antigens could result in the deletion of recipient's T-cell clones, whose T-cell receptor is directed against foreign MHC antigens. The development of an active suppressor cell network following ABT thus may result in shift towards a Th2-type immune response. Preliminary clinical data have recently suggested that ABTs elicit a Th2-type response predominantly (60). Relevantly, a significant increase in soluble IL-2R and IL-6 concentration has been detected in colorectal carcinoma patients receiving allogeneic whole blood transfusions but not in patients transfused with leukocyte-reduced allogeneic blood (61).

Several in vitro studies have shown that low molecular weight components found in factor VIII products inhibit the proliferative response of mononuclear cells to phytohemaglgutinin (52). In these studies, high-purity factor VIII concentrates have been shown to reduce the induced expression of T-cell activation molecules such as the IL-2 receptor (CD25), the transferrin receptor (CD71), CD38, CD11a/CD18, and HLA-DR (52). This inhibitory action of factor VIII concentrates may, at least in part, be due to contamination with transforming growth factor-β (TGF-β) (62). TGF-β may also be involved in mechanisms by which veto cells downregulate the immune responsiveness of the host (63).

In contrast to active suppression, anergy refers to nonreactivity by the host. As outlined earlier, the absence of costimulatory signals may result in T-cell unresponsiveness. Of interest, it has been shown that IL-10, a Th2-type cytokine, prevents in vitro expression of the CD80 family of costimulatory molecules, on macrophages (64).

VII. SUMMARY

The potential clinical importance of the immunomodulatory effects associated with ABT is one of the major current concerns in transfusion medicine. Many questions relating to this phenomenon remain to be elucidated. Data from both retrospective and prospective studies, including three RCTs, addressing the issue of immunomodulatory effects of perioperative ABT on cancer prognosis have yielded contradictory results. The conclusions from six RCTs examining the prevalence of postoperative septic complications following ABTs also have been contradictory. In contrast, there is clear-cut evidence that ABT-associated immunomodulation might be beneficial for selected groups of patients. Accordingly, transfusions of allogeneic cellular blood components have been shown to improve renal allograft survival as well as reducing the recurrence rate in women with recurrent spontaneous abortions.

The immunomodulatory effect of ABT is generally accepted as being mediated by the allogeneic leukocytes and/or their products present in transfused cellular allogeneic blood products. The presence of the allogeneic leukocytes in these products has thus been associated with diverse adverse biological activities, including febrile transfusion reactions, graft-versus-host disease, alloimmunization to leukocyte antigens causing platelet refractoriness, and immunomodulation.

Data from animal-based research suggest that the ABT-associated immunomodulatory effect is immunologically mediated and that this effect is due to the presence of allogeneic leukocytes in the transfused blood products. Accordingly, the experimental animal data show that prestorage leukocyte reduction might prevent the ABT-associated growth enhancement of animal tumors. A similar protective effect of leukocyte reduction has also been observed in some human studies of ABT-associated postoperative bacterial infections, but clear-cut evidence for the clinical benefit of leukocyte reduction is not yet available.

Addendum: Subsequent to completion of this chapter, many publications have appeared relevant to the topic of immunomodulation and allogeneic blood transfusions. These are summarized in an editorial in Transfusion published in 1999 (65). In this editorial, the issue of transfusion-associated immunomodulation and the case for universal white cell reduction is discussed in some detail (65). In addition, E. C. Vamvakas and M. A. Blajchman have co-edited a book entitled "The Immunomodulatory Effects of Blood Transfusion," recently published by the AABB Press (1999). This volume contains 13 chapters, in which most of the published data relating to the issue of the immunomodulatory effect of allogenic blood transfusions are reviewed in some detail (66). Thus, for the latest information relating to the topic of this chapter, the reader is referred to these two recent publications.

REFERENCES

1. Bordin JO, Heddle NM, Blajchman MA. Biologic effects of white blood cells present in transfused cellular blood products. Blood 1994; 84:1703–1721.
2. Meryman HT. Transfusion induced alloimmunization and immunosuppression and the effect of white blood cell depletion. Transfus Med Rev 1989; 3:180–193.
3. Francis DMA. Relationship between blood transfusion and tumour behaviour. Br J Surg 1991; 78:1420–1428.
4. Chung M, Steinmetz OK, Gordon PH. Perioperative blood transfusion and outcome after resection for colorectal carcinoma. Br J Surg 1993; 80:427–432.
5. Vamvakas EC, Moore SB. Perioperative blood transfusion and colorectal cancer recurrence: a qualitative statistical overview and meta-analysis. Transfusion 1993; 33:754–765.
6. Vignali A, Braga M, Gianotti L, Radaelli G, Gentilini O, Russo A, Di Carlo V. A single unit of transfused allogeneic blood increases postoperative infections. Vox Sang 1996; 71:170–175.
7. Jensen LS, Andersen AJ, Christiansen PM, et al. Postoperative infection and natural killer cell function following blood transfusion in patients undergoing elective colorectal surgery. Br J Surg 1992; 79:513–516.
8. Heiss MM, Mempel W, Jauch KW, et al. Beneficial effect of autologous blood transfusion on infectious complications after colorectal cancer surgery. Lancet 1993; 342:1328–1333.
9. Vamvakas EC, Moore SB. Blood transfusion and postoperative septic complications. Transfusion 1994; 34:714–727.
10. Opelz G. The role of HLA matching and blood transfusions in the cyclosporine era. Transplant Proc 1989; 21:609–612.
11. Coulam CB, Clark DA, Collins J, et al. Worldwide collaborative observational study and meta-analysis on allogeneic white blood cell immunotherapy for recurrent spontaneous abortion. Am J Reprod Immunol 1994; 32:55–72.
12. Tartter PI, Heimann TM, Aufses, Jr, AH. Blood transfusion, skin test reactivity, and lymphocytes in inflammatory bowel disease. Am J Surg 1986; 151:358–361.
13. Gantt CL. Red blood cells for cancer patients. Lancet 1981; 2:363.
14. Bordin JO, Blajchman MA. Immunosuppressive effects of allogeneic blood transfusions: Implications for the patient with a malignancy. Hematol Oncol Clin North Am 1995; 9:205–218.
15. Vamvakas EC. Perioperative blood transfusion and cancer recurrence: meta-analysis for explanation. Transfusion 1995; 35:760–768.
16. Vamvakas EC. Transfusion-associated cancer recurrence and postoperative infection: meta-analysis of randomized, controlled clinical trials. Transfusion 1996; 36:175–186.
17. Busch ORC, Hop WCJ, van Papendrecht MAWH, Marquet RL, Jeekel J. Blood transfusions and prognosis in colorectal cancer. N Engl J Med 1993; 328:1372–1376.
18. Heiss MM, Jauch KW, Delanoff C, Mempel W, Schildberg FW. Blood transfusion modulated tumor recurrence—a randomized study of autologous versus allogeneic blood transfusion in colorectal cancer surgery. J Clin Oncol 1994; 12:1859–1867.

19. Houbiers JGA, Brand A, van de Watering LMG, et al. Randomised controlled trial comparing transfusion of leucocyte-reduced or buffy-coat-reduced blood in surgery for colorectal cancer. Lancet 1994; 344:573–578.

20. van Prooijen HC, Aarts-Riemens MI, van Oostendorf WR, Hene RJ, Gmelig-Meyling FHJ, de Weger RA. Prevention of donor-specific T-cell unresponsiveness after buffy-coat-reduced blood transfusion. Br J Haematol 1995; 91:219–223.

21. Cerhan JR, Wallace RB, Folsom AR, Potter JD, Munger RG, Prineas RJ. Transfusion history and cancer risk in older women. Ann Inter Med 1993; 119:8–15.

22. Dzik S, Blajchman MA, Blumberg N, Kirkley SA, Heal JM, Wood K. Current research on the immunomodulatory effect of allogeneic blood transfusion. Vox Sang 1996; 70:187–194.

23. Blajchman MA. Allogeneic blood transfusions, immunomodulation, and postoperative bacterial infection: Do we have the answers yet? Transfusion 1997; 37:121–125.

24. van de Watering LM, Houbiers JG, Hermans J, et al. White blood cell depletion reduces postoperative mortality in patients undergoing cardiac surgery (abstract #SY3DI-06). Proceedings of the 24th Congress of the International Society of Blood Transfusion, Mukuhari, Japan, 1996, p. 37.

25. Jensen LS, Kissmeyer-Nielsen P, Wolff B, Qvist N. Randomised comparison of white blood cell-reduced versus buffy-coat-poor transfusion and complications after colorectal surgery. Lancet 1996; 348:841–845.

26. Houbiers JG, van de Velde CJ, van de Watering LM, Hermans J, Schreuder S, Bijnen AB, Pahplatz P, Schattenkerk ME, Wobbes T, de Vries JE, Klementschitsch P, van de Maas, AH, Brand A. Transfusion of red blood cells is associated with increased incidence of bacterial infection after colorectal surgery: a prospective study. Transfusion 1997; 37:126–134.

27. Dawes LG, Aprahamian C, Condon RE, Malongi MA. The risk of infection after colon injury. Surgery 1986; 100:796–803.

28. Pinto V, Baldonedo R, Nicolas C, Barez A, Perez A, Aza J. Relationship of transfusion and infectious complications after gastric carcinoma operations. Transfusion 1991; 31:114–118.

29. Vamvakas EC, Blajchman MA. A proposal for an individual patient data-based meta-analysis of randomized controlled trials of allogeneic transfusion and postoperative bacterial infection. Transfus Med Rev 1997; 11:180–194.

30. Opelz G, Sengar DPS, Mickey MR, Terasaki PI. Effect of blood transfusions on subsequent kidney transplants. Transplant Proc 1973; 5:253–259.

31. Opelz G, Terasaki PI. Improvement of kidney-graft survival with increased numbers of blood transfusions. N Engl J Med 1978; 299:799–803.

32. Blajchman MA, Singal DP. The role of red blood cell antigens, histocompatibility antigens, and blood transfusions on renal allograft survival. Transfus Med Rev 1989; 3:171–179.

33. Norman DJ, Wetzsteon P, Barry JM, Fischer S. Blood transfusions are beneficial in HLA–identical sibling kidney transplants. Transplant Proc 1985; 17:2347–2348.

34. van Twuyver E, Mooijaart RJD, ten Berge IJM, et al. Pretransplantation blood transfusion revisited. N Engl J Med 1991; 325:1210–1213.

35. Ross WB, Yap PL: Blood transfusion and organ transplantation. Blood Rev 1990; 4:252–258.

36. Sells RA, Scott MH, Prieto M, Bone JM, Evans GM, Millar R, Hillis AN. Early rejection following donor-specific transfusion prior to HLA-mismatched living related renal transplantation. Transplant Proc 1989; 21:1173–1174.

37. Horimi T, Terasaki PI, Chia D, Sasaki B. Factors influencing the paradoxical effect of transfusions on kidney transplants. Transplantation 1983; 35:320–323.

38. Unander AM. The role of immunization treatment in preventing recurrent abortion. Transfus Med Rev 1992; 6:1–16.

39. Tartter PI, Driefuss RM, Malon AM, Heimann TM, Aufses AH. Relationship of postoperative septic complications and blood transfusions in patients with Crohn's disease. Am J Surg 1988; 155:43–48.

40. Peters WR, Fry RD, Fleshman JW, Kodner IJ. Multiple blood transfusions reduce the recurrence rate of Crohn's disease. Dis Col Rect 1989; 32:749–753.

41. Mincheff MS, Meryman HT. Costimulatory signals necessary for induction of T cell proliferation. Transplantation 1990; 49:768–772.

42. Guinan EV, Gribben JG, Boussiotis VA, Freeman GJ, Nadler LM. Pivotal role of the B7:CD28 pathway in tranplantation tolerance and tumor immunity. Blood 1994; 84:3261–3282.

43. Webb LMC, Feldmann M. Critical role of CD28/B7 coestimulation in the development of human Th2 cytokine–producing cells. Blood 1995; 86:3479–3486.

44. Mincheff MS, Meryman HT, Kapoor V, Alsop P, Wotzel M. Blood transfusion and immunomodulation: a possible mechanism. Vox Sang 1993; 65:18–24.

45. Watson HG, Ludlam CA. Immunological abnormalities in haemophiliacs. Blood Rev 1992; 6:26–33.

46. de Biasi R, Rocino A, Miraglia E, Mastrullo L, Quirino AA. The impact of a very high purity factor VIII concentrate on the immune system of human immunodeficiency virus-infected hemophiliacs: a randomized, prospective, two-year comparison with an intermediate purity concentrate. Blood 1991; 78:1919–1922.

47. Seremetis SV, Aledort LM, Bergman GE, et al. Three-year randomised study of high-purity or intermediate-purity factor VIII concentrates in symptom-free HIV–seropositive haemophiliacs: effects on immune status. Lancet 1993; 342:700– 703.

48. Hilgartner MW, Buckley JD, Operskalski EA, Pike MC, Mosley JW. Purity of factor VIII concentrates and serial CD4 counts. Lancet 1992; 341:1373–1374.

49. Mannucci PM, Brettler DB, Aledort LM, et al. Immune status of human immunodeficiency virus seropositive and seronegative hemophiliacs infused for 3.5 years with recombinant factor VIII. Blood 1994; 83:1958–1962.

50. Goedert JJ, Cohen AR, Kessler CM, et al. Risks of immunodeficiency, AIDS, and death related to purity of factor VIII concentrate. Lancet 1994; 344:791–792.

51. Blumberg N, Heal JM. Effects of transfusion on immune function: cancer recurrence and infection. Arch Pathol Lab Med 1994; 118:371–379.

52. Vermont-Desroches C, Rigal D, Blourde C, Bernaud J. Immunosuppressive property of a very high purity antihaemophilic preparation: a low molecular weight component inhibits an early step of PHA induce cell activation. Br J Haematol 1992; 80:370–377.

53. Blajchman MA, Bordin JO. Mechanisms of transfusion-associated immunosuppression. Curr Opin Hematol 1994; 1:457–461.

54. Dzik WH. Mononuclear microchimerism and the immunomodulatory effect of transfusion. Transfusion 1994; 34:1007–1012.

55. Nusbacher J. Blood transfusion is mononuclear cell transplantation. Transfusion 1994; 34:1002–1006.

56. Adams PT, Davenport RD, Reardon DA, Roth MS. Detection of circulating donor white blood cells in patients receiving multiple transfusions. Blood 1992; 80:551–555.

57. Blajchman MA, Bardossy L, Carmen R, Sastry A, Singal DP. Allogeneic blood transfusion-induced enhancement of tumor growth: two animal models showing amelioration by WBC-depletion and passive transfer using spleen cells: Blood 1993; 81:1880–1882.

58. Bordin JO, Bardossy L, Blajchman MA. Growth enhancement of established tumors by allogeneic blood transfusion in experimental animals and its amelioration by WBC-depletion: the importance of the timing of the leukodepletion. Blood 1994; 84:344–348.

59. Gianotti L, Pyles T, Alexander JW, Fukushima R, Babcock GF. Identification of the blood component responsible for increased susceptibility to gut-derived infection. Transfusion 1993; 33:458–465.

60. Kirkley SA, Cowles J, Pellegrini VD, Harris CM, Boyd AD, Blumberg N. Cytokine secretion after allogeneic or autologous blood transfusion. Lancet 1995; 345:527.

61. Jensen LS, Hokland M, Nielsen HJ. A randomized controlled study of the effect of bedside white blood cell depletion on the immunosuppressive effect of whole blood transfusion in patients undergoing elective colorectal surgery. Br J Surg 1996; 83:973–977.

62. Wadhwa M, Dilger P, Tubbs J, Mire-Sluis A, Barrowcliffe T, Thorpe R. Identification of transforming growth factor-b as a contaminant in factor VIII concentrates: a possible link with immunosuppressive effects in hemophiliacs. Blood 1994; 84:2021–2030.

63. Verbanac KM, Carver FM, Haisch CE, Thomas JM. A role for transforming growth factor-beta in the veto mechanism in transplant tolerance. Transplantation 1994; 57:893–900.

64. Ding L, Linsley PS, Huang LY, Germain RN, Shevach EM. IL-10 inhibits macrophage costimulatory activity by selectively inhibiting the up-regulation of B7 expression. J Immunol 1993; 151:1224–1234.

65. Blajchman MA. Transfusion-associated immunomodulation and universal white cell reduction: Are we putting the cart before the horse? Transfusion 1999; 39:665–670.

66. Vamvakas EC, Blajchman MA. Immunomodulatory Effects of Blood Transfusion. Bethesda, MD: AABB Press; 1999.

8
Overview of Infectious Disease

Roger Y. Dodd
Holland Laboratory, American Red Cross, Rockville, Maryland

I. INTRODUCTION

Infection has always been an adverse outcome of blood transfusion. A great deal of effort has been directed towards reducing the risk of this outcome, and these efforts have been extraordinarily successful, so that it is true that, in objective terms, the blood supply is safer than it has ever been (1–3). Nevertheless, the issue of blood safety continues to attract a great deal of attention from the media, politicians, and professionals. As a natural consequence of this attention, there continues to be interest in further reduction of the frequency of transfusion-transmitted infection. However, an important component of any program designed to improve safety is an assessment of the current level of risk, along with the benefits attributable to the proposed intervention. This should form a basis for logical decision making and appropriate use of resources. In addition, it is important that responsible and accurate information about risk be freely available to those who prescribe or receive blood components. At the same time, it must be recognized that public sentiment will not always support decisions made purely upon the basis of costs and benefits. It is clear, for example, that there is little tolerance for failure to take actions that may prevent transmission of HIV, whereas there is much less concern about the greater risk of transfusion-associated bacterial sepsis.

Transfusion-transmitted disease occurs because our measures to assure blood safety are not perfect. At interview, donors may be unaware of their own risk of infectivity or deny it. Laboratory errors may occur, and even if they do not, current serological tests cannot identify all infectious individuals, since virus may circulate prior to the development of detectable levels of antibodies or of viral antigens.

This chapter will address the means that can be used to estimate the residual risk of infection from blood components and will provide estimates that are current at the time of writing. It will also introduce some upcoming measures that are anticipated to provide further reductions in risk.

II. APPROACHES FOR ASSESSING INFECTION RISK

A number of different approaches have been used to measure or estimate the residual risk of transfusion-transmitted infection or disease. Each has advantages and disadvantages and includes sources of error. Consequently, at this time, assessment of transfusion risk is an inexact process. Ideally, the outcomes of a variety of measures should be considered in order to arrive at an appropriate synthesis. A problem with almost all approaches actually stems from the very success of those measures designed to assure blood safety. That is, the frequency of adverse outcomes is extremely low, resulting in estimates with large confidence intervals or a need for extremely large studies or both.

A. Surveillance

Surveillance is an organized approach to collecting and reviewing data about posttransfusion disease or infection. It is an important tool but cannot necessarily be used to generate useful estimates of risk. Two aspects of surveillance are applicable. In the first, the blood provider or some other agency actively solicits reports of posttransfusion disease from establishments that have used the blood. This procedure requires a high degree of attention from the medical community and effective record keeping across institutions. Even so, a reporting system will only capture cases that are recognized, usually as a result of overt sickness, although some cases come to light as a result of serological investigation. Thus, even when successful in identifying disease, reporting is an insensitive measure of the frequency of posttransfusion infection. Also, it suffers from the disadvantage that there is not necessarily a causal linkage between transfusion and disease; this is particularly true when, as is the case for many infections, incidence rates in the community exceed those among blood recipients.

Formal programs of surveillance for posttransfusion disease have been established at the national level in at least two countries. The hemovigilance system in France involves a formal mechanism of reporting and assessing adverse outcomes, as does the English SHOT (Serious Hazards of Transfusion) program. These programs have been productive but suffer from the fact that there is really no control over the initial recognition and reporting of posttransfusion disease.

In the United States, adverse effects of transfusion (with special focus on deaths) must be reported to the Food and Drug Administration (FDA).

The second aspect of surveillance relates to follow-up investigation of locally or nationally reportable disease. For example, in the United States, viral hepatitis and acquired immunodeficiency syndrome (AIDS) are reportable. In some states human immunodeficiency virus (HIV) infection is also reportable. Further studies are performed to assess risk factors associated with these reported diseases; for AIDS, all cases are investigated, whereas for hepatitis, only a proportion are evaluated. It is reasonable to suppose that the majority of AIDS cases are reported, but more intensive local surveillance clearly shows that hepatitis is underreported (4,5). Again, surveillance mechanisms will only identify disease, and even in the case of HIV, where every infection will likely result in disease, the length of the incubation period precludes contemporaneous estimates of infection rates. Nevertheless, surveillance studies do demonstrate temporal variation. They have effectively demonstrated a continuing reduction in the incidence of hepatitis that is epidemiologically linked to transfusion (6–8) and have revealed that, by December 1998, only 39 of the total of 8760 transfusion-associated AIDS cases in the United States could be linked to transfusions given after the implementation of anti-HIV testing (9). It should be noted that great care is necessary in attributing infection to transfusion, and many cases of apparent transfusion AIDS were not confirmed upon careful follow-up (10). In some cases, surveillance data may be the only available way to estimate risk, as is the case for transfusion-associated malaria in the United States.

B. Prospective Studies

Conceptually, the most satisfactory way to define the risk of transfusion-associated infection is to perform a prospective study on a population of blood recipients, thus providing a direct measure of the frequency of infection. This necessitates the identification of a suitable recipient population, collection of pretransfusion samples, and posttransfusion follow up with sampling over a sufficient time period for evolution of markers of infection. The study population should be selected to avoid confounding factors and with the expectation that the recipients will survive for a reasonable amount of time after transfusion. A good example of such a study is the series of investigations performed by Nelson and colleagues on cardiac surgery patients in Baltimore and Houston (11–14). Much greater value is gained by retaining samples of all donations along with sufficient information to access the donors again in the future. In the context of posttransfusion follow-up studies, the classic examples are the hepatitis studies performed in the late 1970s, particularly in the United States (15–18). Such studies have proven to be a rich mine of information over many years, although it should be emphasized that great caution must be taken in extrapolating all of the data to current times. However, Alter's study (17) continues to the present day. Even further value may be obtained from prospective studies that include a controlled evaluation of an intervention. For example, the posttransfusion study reported by Blajchman and colleagues assessed the impact of surrogate markers [alanine aminotransferase (ALT) and hepatitis B core antibody (anti-HBc)] in reducing the incidence of posttransfusion hepatitis (19). Similarly, studies by Bowden and colleagues compared the frequency of cytomegalovirus (CMV) infection and disease in bone marrow transplant patients receiving CMV-seronegative or leuko-reduced blood components (20).

The major advantage of a properly conducted prospective study is that each posttransfusion infection may be unequivocally identified and that proper attention to follow-up testing of the donors can clearly establish that the infection was indeed acquired by transfusion of a given donor's blood. Ideally, such investigation should include serological or genomic characterization of the specific strain of the isolates from donor and recipient. The size of the recipient population is known, along with the number of products transfused, so infection rates can be defined, along with confidence intervals.

The major disadvantages of prospective studies are their complexity and cost. In fact, as will be shown below, the frequency of residual infections is now such that enormous studies have to be performed even to identify a single infection. Nelson's studies, for example, included up to 9294 transfused, and 2238 untransfused patients, involving transfusion of 120,312 components (13). Even if one or two infections are identified, the confidence intervals for the resulting risk estimates are large. More useful data on the risk of hepatitis C were, however, obtained from this study, with the earliest report showing transmission of HCV from 0.45% of donations before testing was initiated and 0.19 and 0.03% risks after the respective initiation of surrogate testing and version 1.0 anti-HCV tests (12). The resources needed to mount comprehensive prospective studies are no longer available, and in any case it could be argued that the expenditure would not be justified. Another difficulty is the extent to which a study can be regarded as representative. As pointed out above, the posttransfusion hepatitis studies of the 1970s, although still widely quoted, cannot be regarded as representative of today's situation, as they involved very different donor populations (some of which were paid) and less comprehensive procedures for donor screening and collection of medical histories. Nelson's study was performed in two metropolitan areas that could not be presumed to be representative of the country as a whole. Finally, the tests involved may not be adequate to provide the best measure; the ALT tests used in the original post transfusion hepatitis (PTH) studies were neither specific nor sensitive, and reevaluation of Nelson's study on HCV seroconversion, using a newer test procedure, essentially doubled the per-unit incidence estimate (12,14).

Another direct measure of the risk of infectivity for HIV was developed by Busch et al. (21) and Vyas et al. (22) who pooled samples of blood donations and used viral culture and PCR technology to look directly for evidence of HIV in blood, tested and issued as seronegative. Ultimately, this study yielded one isolate from an investigation representing the equivalent of 160,000 donations (21,22). Clearly, this represented an enormous effort, which was potentially subject to criticism about the sensitivity or specificity of the methods involved. In addition, this heroic study generated but a single data point, with its resultant wide confidence interval.

Finally, in cases where a diagnostic test is available, but is not used for donor screening, it is possible to perform a seroprevalence study among blood donors. If there is some knowledge about the frequency of transmission of the agent from seropositive donors, then it is possible to make a reasonable estimate of the risk of recipient exposure and infection in the absence of the test. Once a test is implemented, however, the problem becomes the measurement of efficacy of the test and other methods must be used. At this time, donor seroprevalence studies of this type are being performed in order to assess the risk of exposure to *Trypanosoma cruzi,* the agent of Chagas' disease, in the United States (23,23a).

C. Other Means of Estimating Risk

A variety of techniques may be used to estimate residual risk: all require some assumptions, which are a possible source of error. Perhaps the simplest approach is to measure, or estimate, the true sensitivity of the serological screening test(s) used and to multiply this by the prevalence of the marker in the donor population. If necessary, the risk can then be adjusted to reflect the anticipated infectivity of the false-negative samples. In this way Alter has recently estimated that the residual risk of HBV infection in the United States is about 1:250,000 (24,25). She based this calculation on HBsAg and anti-HBc seroprevalence rates of 0.03 and 1.0% respectively, along with sensitivities of 99.9 and 99% for the two tests. She assumed that all HBsAg false negatives would be infectious but estimated that only 4% of anti-HBc false negatives would be infectious. The critical assumption for this estimate is the value for test sensitivity, which may be affected by a number of factors, particularly if window period donations are a major source of posttransfusion infection. In some cases, sensitivity can be estimated from other, prospective studies.

In the case of posttransfusion HIV infection, it is generally accepted that tests are highly sensitive and that laboratory errors are rare. Consequently, collection of blood during the window period is probably the most important source of such infections (26–29). Thus, the risk of donor infectivity translates to the probability of collecting a donation during the window period. Assuming that there is no association between exposure to HIV and desire to give blood, then the risk is simply stated as: incidence of infection × probability of being in window period. The probability of being in the window period is length of window period ÷ time between donations. As discussed below, it is possible to estimate the window period with reasonable accuracy, but the other assumptions require some caution. It is known that some HIV-positive donors do acknowledge that they donated blood in order to obtain a test result (30,31), and it seems likely that such individuals might be more likely to seek testing shortly after risk behavior. Also, it is not clear that first-time donors are equivalent to habitual donors. Some give only once, and at the initiation of testing the prevalence rates for HIV antibodies were higher among first time donors, even though none of the donors had been previously tested (32). Some estimates of risk incorporate an adjustment for this difference (28). Ward and colleagues were the first to use this approach (26), and subsequently Cumming and colleagues developed a more exhaustive estimate, refining many of Ward's original estimates (32). More recently, Busch and colleagues have used insensitive ("detuned") assays for anti-HIV to identify and quantitate the frequency of seropositive donations collected within 6 months following seroconversion. In this way, it is possible to estimate the incidence of HIV infection among first-time donors, which proved to be 2.4-fold greater than that for repeat donors (32a).

Given that HIV incidence rates and donation frequency can be observed, the most sensitive component of this type of estimate is the length of the window period. The concept of using lookback information for this purpose was introduced by Kleinman and Secord (33) and was subsequently developed further by Petersen and colleagues (27) and formed the basis for current estimates of risk (28, 29). Briefly, a population of repeat blood donors who had seroconverted was identified. The disposition of the last donation before seroconversion was determined and the HIV status of the recipient(s) of that donation was established. It was found that there was an inverse relationship between the risk of infection and the time between the seropositive and previous, seronegative, donation. This relationship was fitted to a mathematical model, which clearly indicated that the infectious window period was on the order of 45 days. Further, the observed data fit the model so well that it was clear that there was relatively little variation in the length of the window period, and additionally this suggested that the observed infections were not dominated by laboratory errors resulting in false-negative findings. Had this been the case, a strong time relationship would not be expected. It should be noted that these studies support the concept that HIV infection does not result in extraordinarily lengthy preseroconversion periods. This lookback approach provides a good measure of the infectious window period, which probably differs from the overall period between exposure to HIV and the appearance of detectable serological markers.

Petersen's original study relates to data collected up to the end of 1990 and thus defines a window period that reflects the sensitivity of the tests in use at that time. Anti-HIV tests have increased in sensitivity, as demonstrated by their ability to identify seroconversion earlier; the test in most common use in the United

States detects seroconversion some 23 days earlier than those in use in 1990 (34). These data have been used to arrive at an estimate of risk of 1:340,000 per component in the United States as of the beginning of 1995. This estimate is reduced to 1:420,000 if an adjustment is made for the impact of other tests (28). Schreiber et al. estimated the decrease in the window period attributable to the increased sensitivity of a variety of tests, including those that detect the HIV genome (29).

The use of window period estimates along with the incidence of new infection is also applicable to other transfusion-transmitted agents, as exemplified by the analysis published by the Retrovirus Epidemiology in Donors Study (REDS) group (29). Lookback studies on other agents have not yet been performed or if performed, have not been analyzed in a way that provides an estimate of the window period.

D. Infection and Disease

For many agents, infection does not necessarily result in disease. Consequently estimates of the risk of infection may not provide useful information about the long-term outcomes of posttransfusion infection or the eventual resource usage. Therefore, it is important to understand the natural history of posttransfusion disease in order to establish a complete assessment of risk. In general, this has not proven simple, and some prospective estimates do not appear to have been supported by subsequent findings. Although it is clear that essentially all individuals who are infected with HIV will develop AIDS, the outcome of transfusion-transmitted infection with human T-cell lymphotrophic virus (HTLV), hepatitis B virus (HBV), or hepatitis C virus (HCV) is less clear. Early prospective studies on blood recipients with non-A, non-B hepatitis (NANB) suggested that up to 60% had histological evidence of serious or severe liver disease (35,36). However, long-term follow-up studies have suggested that, despite these pathological findings, symptomatic disease is uncommon and there does not appear to be excess mortality after 18–20 years of observation (37). It now appears likely, however, that up to 20% of chronically infected patients may eventually develop symptomatic and potentially severe liver disease (38).

III. QUANTITATIVE RISK ESTIMATES

A. HIV

Table 1 outlines key estimates for the residual risk of HIV infection from the fully screened and tested voluntary blood supply in the United States. The methodology is noted along (where appropriate) with the number of observations that generated the estimate. At first glance, the risk estimates appear to be widely

Table 1 Published Risk of HIV Infection from Fully Screened and Tested Blood in the United States

Risk/Unit	Observations	Method	Publication year	Ref.
1:40,000	NA	Estimate	1988	26
1:68,000	3	Lookback	1988	33
1:153,000	NA	Estimate	1989	32
1:61,000	1	Viral culture	1991	21
1:60,000	2	Recipient seroconversion	1992	13
1:160,000	1	Viral culture and PCR	1994	22
1:210,000	36	Lookback, window	1994	27
1:420,000	NA	Estimate	1995	28
1:493,000	NA	Estimate	1996	29
1:676,000[a]	NA	Estimate	1996	29

NA = Not applicable—estimate based upon window period and population figures.
[a]Estimate adjusted to include the effect of testing for HIV p24 antigen.

disparate. However, all of the estimates (prior to the implementation of HIV p24 antigen screening) fall within one order of magnitude. Further, there is a clear trend over time towards lower risk estimates, commensurate with improvements in test sensitivity and reductions in the frequency of test-positive donations. What is in fact remarkable is the similarity of the estimates, particularly when those made during the same time interval are compared. In addition, recent studies show, as might be expected, that there is considerable regional variation in the residual risk in the United States, implying that national estimates will vary from those developed for limited regions. One recent national estimate of 1:420,000 (28) includes an adjustment for components infectious but seronegative for HIV, but that would nevertheless be withheld from transfusion because of other test markers. This estimate is based upon a window period of 25 days, derived from lookback studies, subsequently corrected for the improved sensitivity of current tests, and an incidence rate of 3.7 infections per 100,000 donations from repeat donors, representing 78% of donations. For first-time donors, an estimate of 6.6 incident HIV infections per 100,000 was made. Schreiber et al. (29) came up with a remarkably similar estimate of 1:493,000, based upon careful studies in five large blood centers. Additionally, they estimated the impact of additional testing, including that for HIV p24 antigen, implying a current risk of 1:676,000 (29). As pointed out above, the risk of disease and ultimately death from HIV infection is 100%. Consequently, every potential infection may also be regarded as a potential death, albeit many years after the original transfusion.

B. Hepatitis Viruses

One estimate of the risk of posttransfusion HBV infection (1:250,000 per unit) in the United States is outlined above; it should be noted that this contrasts with a reporting rate of one acute, clinical case per 30,000 recipients. In a preliminary report from his study of cardiac surgery patients in Baltimore and Houston, Nelson et al. suggest that the recipient seroconversion rate for anti-HBc implies a per unit risk of about 1:2,500 after implementation of surrogate testing (ALT and anti-HBc), with a further reduction to 1:25,000 after anti-HCV was implemented (39). However, these findings have not been confirmed by additional testing (particularly among the donors). Also, within the same study, there were five seroconversions among 2,334 nontransfused patients. This rate did not differ significantly from the overall seroconversion rate of 39 among the 9,449 transfused patients. There are no contemporary prospective studies that define the frequency of posttransfusion HBV infection. Surveillance studies now suggest that only 1% of reported cases of hepatitis B have prior transfusion as a risk factor (8).

Risk estimates based upon seroconversion rates and a window period of 59 days suggest that one unit in every 63,000 may be infectious for HBV (29). This estimate is, however, dependent upon a window period that does not necessarily reflect the true period of infectivity and upon adjustments that reflect the transient nature of HBs antigenemia. Thus, this estimate should be regarded with some caution—it seems likely that the risk is lower. Reasonable estimates of the outcomes of HBV infection are that there will be clinically apparent acute disease in 35% of cases, of which less than 0.5% will be fulminant, but of these, 60% may result in death. Chronic disease appears to be very rare for adults, with a long-term outcome in fewer than 5% of those infected.

The studies of Nelson et al. have been most instructive in the early development of risk estimates for HCV infection. In their evaluation of transfused cardiac surgery patients, they observed an incidence of one HCV infection per 3300 transfused components. This study represented donations tested by a first-generation (c100-3) anti-HCV test and for anti-HBc and ALT elevations (12). Subsequently, the study was extended and recipients (but not donations) were tested using a so-called second-generation, multiantigen procedure. On this basis, the residual risk was one infection per 1672 components (14) Kleinman and others made an estimate of the potential improvement attributable to second-generation testing. They based their estimate upon the increased frequency of detection of HCV antibodies among donors and suggested that the residual risk was between 1:2000 and 1:6000 (40). In Blajchman et al's study, the frequency of hepatitis C infection after the introduction of the first-generation test was 1.6 and 2.7 cases per thousand recipients of surrogate tested and nontested components, respectively (19). A recent paper (41) points out that, as with HBV, care must be taken in attributing iatrogenic HCV infection to transfusion. Careful molecular studies of isolates from 17 apparent posttransfusion HCV cases among recipients of blood screened by second-generation tests showed that the source was not transfusion, but was likely patient-to-patient transmission.

Schreiber et al. (29) estimated the current risk of residual posttransfusion HCV infection as one in 103,000 units if all risk is attributable to window period infections. In this case it is clear that the incidence of new infections is low, but the window period of 82 days has been estimated from prospective studies of blood recipients and may not necessarily reflect the true period of infectivity (29). Another concern about this estimate is that of immunosilent HCV infection. Alter has pointed out that there are individuals who are HCV antibody negative but positive for HCV RNA by PCR (5). Accordingly, she has developed a different estimate based upon her estimate of the sensitivity of so-called version 2 tests, along with the seroprevalence rate for anti-HCV among donors. She concluded that the test sensitivity was 90% and the residual risk was about 1:4000, based upon a prevalence rate of 0.24% (25). However, newer tests are more sensitive, and this estimate is no longer appropriate. More interestingly, as data from genome amplification testing of blood donations are emerging, it is becoming apparent that most, if not all donors identified as HCV RNA positive but antibody negative are actually in the early stages of seroconversion. In the United States, there have been no major prospective posttransfusion hepatitis studies that generate meaningful risk data since the introduction of multiantigen anti-HCV tests. Those that have been presented or discussed have not identified any cases among several hundred patients evaluated.

At the time of writing, blood agencies in Europe and in the United States are implementing nucleic acid–based testing of donor samples for HIV and/or HCV RNA. In general, such testing is being achieved using amplification technology (primarily the reverse transcriptase-polymerase chain reaction [RT-PCR], and transcription-mediated amplification [TMA]) on small to moderate-sized (16–128) pools of samples. These techniques should provide further information about the incidence of infection and window period risk. Early experience has suggested that the frequency of positive findings is either compatible with, or lower than, predictions made from incidence and window period estimates.

One of the greatest concerns about posttransfusion HCV infection is the frequency and severity of long-term outcomes. Although there is little disagreement about the frequency of chronic infection, the frequency of long-term elevations of serum transaminases, or even the frequency of significant pathological change on biopsy, these figures do not appear to be congruent with the frequency or severity of clinically apparent disease. Overall, a synthesis of current data suggests that among those infected with HCV, almost all will develop chronic infection, as shown by circulating HCV RNA. Perhaps 25% of infected individuals will have some acute, symptomatic disease, albeit mild. Fewer than

0.25% suffer fatal acute disease. Some 70% of infected individuals will have chronic manifestations of infection. However, of all those infected, it appears that up to 15% may eventually be diagnosed with liver failure and perhaps 3.5% overall will die of liver disease after an incubation period of 20 years (38). There does not seem to be any significant excess mortality during 18–20 years of follow-up of individuals originally diagnosed with posttransfusion NANB (37). Follow-up studies do not provide reliable data beyond this period, although it must be noted that in Japan some individuals have been shown to progress to liver cancer (42).

There continues to be discussion about additional forms of viral hepatitis that may be transmitted by transfusion. Although enteric viruses (such as HAV) may be transmitted very infrequently as a result of collection of blood during an asymptomatic preacute phase (43,44), there is also some evidence that post-transfusion hepatitis (or at least, serum transaminase elevation) occurs in the absence of any markers to known viruses (5,45,46). Most studies suggest that these events are self-limited and that maximum ALT levels tend to be low. Of great interest is Blajchman et al.'s observation that this form of posttransfusion hepatitis appears to occur among recipients of autologous transfusions as frequently as it does among allogeneic blood recipients (19). Thus, great caution should be used in attributing all (or perhaps any) such cases to an infectious agent.

An HCV-like virus, variously termed hepatitis G virus (47) or GB virus type C (48), has been identified by molecular cloning and has been shown to be associated with a minority (about 15%) of cases of residual posttransfusion hepatitis. The agent is clearly transmissible by transfusion, but appears to have little, if any, clinical relevance (49–51).

Similarly, a DNA virus identified among three individuals with hepatitis and termed TT virus (after one of the patients) has been shown to occur with relatively high frequency and to be transmissible by transfusion. Again, however, it has not proven possible to associate this virus with any evidence of liver disease, and it appears to offer little, if any, risk to blood recipients (51a,51b).

C. Other Agents

The risk of HTLV infection was originally defined in Nelson's studies. In his cohort, one infection was noted among the recipients of almost 70,000 tested components (13). However, anti-HTLV-I tests are improving, particularly in their ability to detect infection with HTLV-II, and as of 1997 two tests have been licensed with a specific claim for detection of HTLV-II. The REDS group estimated that window period infections would present a residual risk of about 1:641,000 (29). It is generally accepted that individuals who are seropositive for HTLV-I have only about a 4% lifetime chance of developing either HTLV-associated myelopathy or adult T-cell leukemia lymphoma (ATL). Although the former disease has been found in association with transfusion, this does not appear to be the case for ATL. Published window period risk estimates for key agents are outlined in Table 2.

Malaria is infrequently transmitted by transfusion in the United States: in a 1991 review, Nahlen et al. showed that the average reporting rate for clinically apparent malaria is approximately one per 3–4 million units transfused (52); surveillance data show that these rates have not changed appreciably through the surveillance report of 1997 (53). The risk may be higher in countries with populations having closer ties and more frequent travel to malarious areas. An additional concern is the possibility of reestablishment of malaria in countries from which it had previously been eliminated.

Infection with CMV is a relatively frequent outcome of transfusion, with some studies indicating that 1–2% of blood units may be capable of transmitting CMV. In almost all cases, however, such infection has little impact upon immunologically competent recipients but often has profound or fatal consequences for immunocompromised patients. The risk of such outcomes is not well defined, and increasing concentration on the provision of CMV seronegative or leuko-reduced products has largely eliminated the concern for those patient populations most at risk (20,54).

Another disease that has attracted some recent attention is Creutzfeldt-Jakob disease (CJD). This is a prion disease with an extended incubation period. It occurs with an incidence rate of about one case per million population annually, and concern arises when a person with a history of blood donation is diagnosed with this disease. The agent is clearly transmissible, although there is no current evidence to show that it can be transmitted by transfusion. Indeed, case-control

Table 2 Estimated Risk of Infection by Selected Transfusion-Transmissible Agents, United States, 1998, and Potential Impact of Genome Amplification Testing (GAT)

Agent	Window period (days)	Infection risk per unit	
		Serological tests	Serological tests + GAT
HBV	59	1:63,000	1:110,000
HCV	82	1:103,000	1:368,000
HIV	16	1:676,000	1:990,000
HTLV	51	1:641,000	NA
Malaria	NA	1:3,000,000	NA
T. cruzi	NA	<1:48,000[a]	NA

NA = Not applicable.
[a]See text.
Source: Adapted from Refs. 29, 52.

and lookback studies have failed to show any evidence of such transmission (55–57). Animal studies suggest that the transmissible agent, when obtained from brain tissue, may be infectious by parenteral inoculation. Conversely, intracranial inoculation of blood from infected animals can also transmit disease. Recognition that CJD had been transmitted by certain lots of human-derived growth hormone has generated concern, and donors who received this material are now permanently deferred (58), even though blood-to-blood transmission does not appear to have been noted. This concern has been extended to recipients of dura mater and to those with a family history of CJD. Despite the absence of any evidence of transmission of CJD by transfusion, stringent requirements are now in place for donor deferral and for recall of components of manufactured products collected from donors subsequently found to be affected by, or judged to be at risk of, CJD. These requirements are based solely upon the theoretical possibility of transmission. Additional concern has arisen, at least in the United Kingdom, as a result of the apparent association between bovine spongiform encephalopathy (BSE) and new variant CJD (nv CJD) in humans. Because the characteristics of the BSE agent are not well known, specific measures have been proposed to reduce the possible risk of transmission.

In the United Kingdom and some other countries, uniform leukoreduction of components has been introduced, as it is thought that the agent of nvCJD is more likely to be associated with leukocytes. In the United Kingdom, domestically obtained plasma is no longer used for the manufacture of plasma derivatives. This has led in the United States and Canada to consideration of procedures to defer donors who have spent enough time in the British Isles to be considered at some increased risk for nvCJD infection.

Finally, routine testing for markers of syphilis infection continues in most countries. There appears to be essentially no risk of syphilis transmission by transfusion at this time, and consequently no estimate is provided.

D. Bacterial Contamination

Since the adoption of closed plastic bag collection systems, bacterial contamination has not generally been regarded as a serious problem in transfusion medicine. It is indeed true that bacterial contamination of red cell concentrates and fresh frozen plasma is infrequent (59–62). The major concern with red cells has been sepsis or endotoxin shock resulting from transfusion of products with accumulated high counts of *Yersinia enterocolitica*. In United States, such events occur with a frequency of about one case per 3 million units transfused (63). A similar rate of contamination with pseudomonads has been reported (64). These events usually involve red cells that stored for 20 days or more. Bacterial outgrowth is limited to organisms that can multiply at the 4°C storage temperature of red cells. It seems likely that the source of *Y. enterocolitica* is enteric infection in the donor, with a concomitant low-level bacteremia. Interestingly, a number of cases of *Yersinia* sepsis have been noted among autologous blood recipients, providing an exception to the general rule that you cannot be infected by your own blood (65). Because autologous units tend to be stored for prolonged periods, the risk may actually be greater than for allogeneic units.

Platelet concentrates are stored at 20–22°C and rapid outgrowth of a variety of bacterial species can occur. There are many estimates of the frequency of contamination of platelet units, with very wide variation, depending upon the actual measure used. For example, careful sterility cultures suggest that one to two platelet concentrates in every thousand may contain bacteria (59). Although much higher rates have been reported, such studies may not have been adequately corrected for false-positive cultures. Quantitative evaluation suggests that many such contaminants may only be present at very low levels, even at platelet outdate (66). In contrast, prospective studies looking for sepsis among platelet recipients have indicated that as many as one platelet concentrate in every 12,000 may contain pathogenic levels of contaminants (67). This appeared to hold for random donor platelets and for apheresis products; the per patient risk is, of course, greater for the former, given that five to six packs constitute a therapeutic dose. It is not yet clear whether these rates are truly representative, since passive and active surveillance suggests that posttransfusion sepsis is much less frequent when a large number of institutions are included. Again, as a result of the dynamics of bacterial growth, the risk of sepsis does increase with the time the concentrate has been stored.

There are a number of sources of bacteria that may contaminate platelets. It is likely that a variety of enteric bacteria that contaminate platelet units are actually derived from the donor's circulation; it is also known that bacteria can enter the bloodstream as a result of dental or other manipulation of the teeth. Others may be accidental environmental or skin contaminants. It should be noted that there is no easy solution to this problem, since it is essentially impossible to render skin aseptic at more than the most superficial level. Recently, an outbreak of *Serratia marcescens* sepsis was reported; it apparently resulted from accidental external contamination of the blood containers during manufacturing (68). One comprehensive review notes that the overall fatality rate for transfusion-associated sepsis is about 25% (59). Unlike most other outcomes described in this chapter, death occurs shortly after transfusion: it is possible that it has gained a lower degree of public concern because it is seen as but one of the many mishaps that can occur during hospitalization.

E. Laboratory Errors

As indicated above, laboratory errors are a possible source of risk to blood recipients, inasmuch as improper performance of a test could lead to a false-negative finding, but there is no clear measure of the frequency of such errors. Systematic errors that might result in the failure of a complete test run are unlikely to occur because of the need to obtain satisfactory results with test calibrators and (where used) external controls, along with routine quality assurance measures. Random errors such as sample transposition or omission may occur, although modern, automated systems in place in blood centers should preclude such problems. In order to affect a recipient, such an error would have to coincide with the presence of an infectious sample. On the other hand, Young reported that 18, 27, and 55 HBsAg testing errors were reported to FDA in 1985, 1986, and 1988, respectively (69). If every one of these reflected failure to identify an EIA-positive product (which is by no means clear), then the error rate could have been as high as 18–55 per 18,000, assuming 18 million collections of whole blood and plasma per year and an EIA-reactive rate of 0.1%. This would translate to an overall error rate of 0.1–0.3%. In order to assess the risk of transmission of disease, this error rate would have to be multiplied by the prevalence of true-positive results. Thus, an error rate of 0.1% might lead to a risk of infection of about one in 14 million for HIV (with a prevalence of six per hundred thousand); the figure for HCV, with a prevalence of 0.16% would, however, be about one in 600,000. It is reasonable to assume that increased attention to transfusion safety and quality assurance in testing over the past years will have resulted in low rates of laboratory errors. Consequently, laboratory testing errors probably have no significant contribution to the risk of infection from transfusion. Other widely publicized errors certainly do occur but most often reflect failure to withhold a safe, test-negative product because of a prior false-positive test result on the donor of that unit (70).

IV. EMERGING INFECTIONS

One of the lessons of the AIDS epidemic is that there is always potential for new diseases that may impact the safety of transfusion. While it is clearly not possible to predict the outbreak of an entirely new disease, it does imply a need to be alert to the implications of newly described diseases. More important, not all emerging infections are novel; in most cases an old disease appears in a new environment. At least three examples are relevant. First, immunocompromised patients have become a population at singular risk of adverse outcomes from otherwise benign infections. Thus, as immunocompromising or immunoablative therapies increase, so does the risk of disease, even if the risk of infection does not change. In this context, consider the impact of CMV or B19 infection on bone marrow transplant recipients (20,71). Second, population movements are now more common than they have ever been, and infections move with their hosts. The risk of transfusion-transmitted Chagas' disease is now apparent in the United States and elsewhere solely as a result of emigration from countries in which human infection with *T. cruzi* is endemic (72). Finally, changes in ecology may have a profound and unexpected impact. Changes in the relationship between humans and the countryside have resulted in major increases in the population and range of hosts and vectors of the agents of Lyme disease, babesiosis, ehrlichiosis, and other tickborne infections in the United States (73,74).

Of necessity, it is difficult to provide risk estimates for emerging diseases. However, if the potential threat is significant, it may be appropriate to mount studies to define such a threat as a means to assist in rational decision making. Such a process was used for HTLV in the United States (75), and at the time of writing studies to define the risk of *T. cruzi* infection are under way (23). Estimates of the number of potentially infected individuals have been published: there may be at least 100,000 *T. cruzi*–infected legal immigrants in the United States (72). Even if only 1% were to donate, this would generate a tangible donor prevalence rate of about 1:12,000—a figure that has, at least in part, been supported by seroprevalence studies reported to date, in which one in 7000–9000 donations are seropositive in some parts of the United State (23). Even so, there has been no evidence of infection from lookback studies on these seropositive donors. To date, a worst-case estimate of infectivity of 1:48,000 could be derived from the seroprevalence rates of around 1:8,000 in Miami and Los Angeles and an infectivity of one out of six, which would represent the upper 95% confidence interval of zero infections among 18 lookbacks. However, other information suggests that national seroprevalence rates would be less than 1:33,000 and that infectivity would also be lower. Some estimates for the frequency of infection with *Babesia microti* have also been made for areas of known endemicity—indeed, one study reported one transmission among 600 units in Connecticut. It appears that this agent is becoming more widespread and additional species of piroplasms are being recognized in unexpected localities (74,76,77).

V. SURVIVAL AFTER TRANSFUSION

One other component of the overall estimation of risk of infectious disease relates to the likelihood that the blood recipient will actually survive long enough to be affected by the disease resulting from the infection. While this has no effect upon the definition of the risk of infection for any patient, it does affect the estimation of the societal costs of posttransfusion infection. For many years it has been recognized that individuals who are transfused are quite likely to die of their underlying disease. Additionally, the majority of transfusions are given to those aged 65 years or more. Early studies in which attempts were made to identify recipients of blood from donors who were potentially infected with HIV showed that any given component had a 50% chance of having been transfused to an individual who died within one year of the transfusion (26). This does not necessarily mean that 50% of patients die, since those who did die may have received more blood components. As discussed above, the overall mortality among patients originally entered into posttransfusion hepatitis studies was around 50% after 18 years of follow-up. However, a recent publication from Vamvakas and Taswell suggests that posttransfusion mortality was not this high in a community hospital system. However, posttransfusion mortality did vary significantly according to age at transfusion (78). In summary, then, economic estimates that define the overall costs of transfusion-associated disease should recognize that up to 50% of the chronic disease outcomes will not contribute, since the patients will have died before disease can be manifested.

VI. POOLED PLASMA PRODUCTS

The issue of risk from pooled plasma products is complex and will merely be outlined here. Therapeutic products are derived from plasma by industrial-scale fractionation procedures requiring the pooling of large numbers (perhaps tens of thousands) of individual units. As a consequence, even a modest risk of residual infectivity per unit may translate to a high risk of contamination of the pool itself, albeit with significant dilution. Some fractionated products, such as albumin, which incorporate a pasteurization step, have always been regarded as safe. In general, immune globulins have also been regarded as safe, although the mechanism underlying such safety has been unclear. Recently, some intravenous immunoglobulin preparations have been shown to transmit HCV, perhaps as a result of gentler fractionation procedures, in association with the absence of anti-HCV, resulting from the implementation of sensitive screening tests (79). Viral inactivation procedures for immunoglobulin preparations are now being implemented. Of much more concern, labile clotting factor concentrates have, in the past, offered an almost uniform risk of infection for HBV, HCV, and HIV. Fortunately, procedures for viral inactivation of labile plasma products were under development around the time that transfusion-associated AIDS was recognized. Unfortunately, these procedures came too late to prevent HIV infection among a majority of users of these products. Progressive improvements in these inactivation procedures involving the use of heat and of solvent-detergent methods have essentially eliminated the risk of infection with HIV, HCV, and HBV, the last of which has also been affected by the use of HBV vaccine.

One concern about the solvent-detergent approach to viral inactivation is that it is ineffective against nonenveloped viruses. Although transfusion-associated infection with nonenveloped viruses is unusual, this concern was illustrated by outbreaks of HAV infection among recipients of solvent detergent-treated antihemophilic factor concentrates in Europe (80). The source of the viral contamination remains unclear, but there have been no further reports of any outbreaks. The B19 parvovirus is also nonenveloped and has been readily transmitted by concentrates that had been subject to early, and less stringent, heat-treatment regimens (81). It is unclear whether these transmissions led to any clinically apparent disease. Currently, in some countries, fresh frozen plasma is also being subjected to inactivation, either by methylene blue photoinactivation or solvent-detergent treatment (82–84). A possible disadvantage of the solvent-detergent procedure is that it must be performed on a pooled product, consequently, risk from enveloped viruses will be reduced or eliminated but at the cost of some increase in the risk of exposure to HAV or B19. A solvent-detergent–treated frozen plasma product has also been licensed and is in use in the United States. Phase 4 (postlicensure) clinical studies showed that this product could indeed transmit B19 parvovirus, as some lots were contaminated with a relatively high titer of the virus. Preventive measures, including testing for viral DNA in final products, have been implemented.

VII. OPTIONS FOR RISK REDUCTION

As with any other aspect of life, blood transfusion is not without risk of adverse effects. A proportion of these adverse effects are due to infectious agents. The risk of incapacitating disease or death from such infection is very low compared to other everyday or medical risks. For example, one study showed that adverse events occurred in 3.7% of all hospitalizations; of these, 6.5% led to permanent disability and 13.6% to death. In other words, the risk of dying in hospital is about one in 200: about half of these deaths were attributable to negligent acts and were thus preventable (85,86). McCullough reviewed some other medical risks: a 1:50,000 annual risk of death from oral contraceptives, for example (2). Nevertheless, there is little tolerance for even rare transfusion mishaps, and there is thus pressure to continue to try to reduce the risk to some as-yet-to-be-defined tolerable level. Perhaps one perceptual problem is that the risk is not diffuse, as is the risk of reacting to a drug; rather, it is focused in a single blood unit. Thus, it is perhaps natural to believe that the offensive unit should be identifiable.

As pointed out above, none of the multiple layers of blood safety is impregnable and perfection will not be achievable, but there may be some room for improvement. Some donors with positive test results for anti-HIV acknowledge, on further questioning, that they were aware of risk factors or behaviors (30,31), so behavioral research may define ways to improve the screening process. Indeed, as tests improve and the window periods narrow, it will be more and more important to focus on recent risk exposures rather than those in the distant past. At the same time, a greater proportion of seropositive donors are unable to recognize their risk, so there will be clear limits to the improvement that can be gained, particularly for infections such as HCV where 40% or more of the cases may be unaccompanied by identifiable risk (5,87).

Serological testing is unlikely to improve greatly, although it might be possible to test for additional markers, as was the case for the HIV p24 antigen. There is widespread anticipation that genome-based testing will offer significant benefits. Indeed, the benefits of such testing have been projected (see Table 2). It seems unlikely that any procedure for genome amplification testing of individual donations will be available in the immediate future but testing of pooled samples has been implemented on a broad scale in Europe and the United States. Although this application was implemented to reduce viral load in plasma for further manufacture, it is clear that testing in small pools of 16–24 will have sufficient sensitivity to achieve significant improvement in the detection of HCV window period donations and has the potential to detect at least some of the remaining HIV window period donations. It will probably not have significant effect upon HBV safety, however.

There may be some prospect for viral inactivation of cellular products, but such procedures will almost certainly require the addition of chemicals or drugs to the components; these, of course, will have their own risks, such as genotoxicity. These risks may not outweigh the benefits to be gained. Finally, it will be very important to consider emerging diseases in order to determine whether interventions are necessary or appropriate. Ultimately, it must to be recognized that the marginal gains that might be achieved by additional measures may not justify the resources required to implement them.

REFERENCES

1. Dodd RY. The risk of transfusion-transmitted infection. N Engl J Med 1992; 327:419–421.
2. McCullough J. The nation's changing blood supply system. JAMA 1993; 269:2239–2245.
3. AuBuchon JP, Birkmeyer JD, Busch MP. Safety of the blood supply in the United States: opportunities and controversies. Ann Intern Med 1997; 127:904–909.
4. Alter MJ, Mares A, Hadler SC, Maynard JE. The effect of underreporting on the apparent incidence and epidemiology of acute viral hepatitis. Am J Epidemiol 1987; 125:133–139.
5. Alter MJ, Margolis HS, Krawczynski K, Judson FN, Mares A, Alexander WJ, Hu PY, Miller JK, Gerber MA, Sampliner RE, Meeks EL, Beach MJ. The natural history of community-acquired hepatitis C in the United States. N Engl J Med 1992; 327:1899–1905.
6. Alter MJ, Hadler SC, Margolis HS, Alexander WJ, Hu PY, Judson FN, Mares A, Miller JK, Moyer LA. The changing epidemiology of hepatitis B in the United States. Need for alternative vaccination strategies. JAMA 1990; 263:1218–1222.

7. CDC. Hepatitis Surveillance Report No. 55. Atlanta: Centers for Disease Control and Prevention, 1994: 1–36.

8. CDC. Hepatitis Surveillance Report No. 56. Atlanta: Centers for Disease Control and Prevention, 1995: 1–33.

9. CDC. HIV/AIDS surveillance Report Vol. 10, No 2. Atlanta: Centers for Disease Control and Prevention, 1999: 1–43.

10. Selik RM, Ward JW, Buehler JW. Trends in transfusion-associated acquired immune deficiency syndrome in the United States, 1982 through 1991. Transfusion 1993; 33:890–893.

11. Cohen ND, Munoz A, Reitz BA, Ness PK, Frazier OH, Yawn DH, Lee H, Blattner W, Donahue JG, Nelson KE, Polk BF. Transmission of retroviruses by transfusion of screened blood in patients undergoing cardiac surgery. N Engl J Med 1989; 320:1172–1176.

12. Donahue JG, Muñoz A, Ness PM, Brown DE, Jr, Yawn DH, McAllister HA, Jr, Reitz BA, Nelson KE. The declining risk of post-transfusion hepatitis C virus infection. N Engl J Med 1992; 327:369–373.

13. Nelson KE, Donahue JG, Muñoz A, Cohen ND, Ness PM, Teague A, Stambolis VA, Yawn DH, Callicott B, McAllister H, Reitz BA, Lee H, Farzadegan H, Hollingsworth CG. Transmission of retroviruses from seronegative donors by transfusion during cardiac surgery. A multicenter study of HIV–1 and HTLV-I/II infections. Ann Intern Med 1992; 117:554–559.

14. Nelson KE, Donahue JG, Stambolis V. Post-transfusion hepatitis C virus infection. Reply. N Engl J Med 1992; 327:1601–1602.

15. Aach RD, Szmuness W, Mosley JW, Hollinger FB, Kahn RA, Stevens CE, Edwards VM, Werch J. Serum alanine aminotransferase of donors in relation to the risk of non-A, non-B hepatitis in recipients. The Transfusion-Transmitted Viruses Study. N Engl J Med 1981; 304:989–994.

16. Koziol DE, Holland PV, Alling DW, Melpolder JC, Solomon RE, Purcell RH, Hudson LM, Shoup FJ, Krakauer H, Alter HJ. Antibody to hepatitis B core antigen as a paradoxical marker for non-A, non-B hepatitis agents in donated blood. Ann Intern Med 1986; 104:488–495.

17. Alter HJ, Purcell RH, Holland PV, Alling DW, Koziol DE. Donor transaminase and recipient hepatitis. Impact on blood transfusion services. JAMA 1981; 246:630–634.

18. Stevens CE, Aach RD, Hollinger FB, Mosley JW, Szmuness W, Kahn R, Werch J, Edwards V. Hepatitis B virus antibody in blood donors and the occurrence of non-A, non-B hepatitis in transfusion recipients. An analysis of the Transmission-Transmitted Viruses Study. Ann Intern Med 1984; 101:733–738.

19. Blajchman MA, Bull SB, Feinman SV. Post-transfusion hepatitis: Impact of non-A, non-B hepatitis surrogate tests. Lancet 1995; 345:21–25.

20. Bowden RA, Slichter SJ, Sayers M, Weisdorf D, Cays M, Schoch G, Banaji M, Haake R, Welk K, Fisher L, McCullough J, Miller W. A comparison of filtered leukocyte-reduced and cytomegalovirus (CMV) seronegative blood products for the prevention of transfusion-associated CMV infection after marrow transplant. Blood 1995; 86:3598–3603.

21. Busch MP, Eble BE, Khayam-Bashi H, Heilbron D, Murphy EL, Kwok S, Sninsky J, Perkins HA, Vyas GN. Evaluation of screened blood donations for human

immunodeficiency virus type 1 infection by culture and DNA amplification of pooled cells. N Engl J Med 1991; 325:1–5.

22. Vyas GN, Rawal BD, Babu G, Busch MP. Diminishing risk of HIV infection from transfusion of seronegative blood (abstr). Transfusion 1994; 34:63S

23. Leiby DA, Read EJ, Lenes BA, Yund AJ, Stumpf RJ, Kirchhoff LV, Dodd RY. Seroepidemiology of *Trypanosoma cruzi*, etiologic agent of Chagas' disease, in US blood donors. J Infect Dis 1997; 176:1047–1052.

23a. Leiby DA, Fucci MH, Stumpf RJ. Trypanosoma cruzi in a low-to moderate-risk blood donor population: seroprevalence and possible congenital transmission. Transfusion 1999; 39:310–315.

24. CDC. Public Health Service inter-agency guidelines for screening donors of blood, plasma, organs, tissues, and semen for evidence of hepatitis B and hepatitis C. MMWR 1991; 40 (RR-4):1–17.

25. Alter MJ. Residual Risk of transfusion-associated Hepatitis. Bethesda, MD: National Institutes of Health, 1995: 23–27.

26. Ward JW, Holmberg SD, Allen JR, Cohn DL, Critchley SE, Kleinman SH, Lenes BA, Ravenholt O, Davis JR, Quinn MG, et al. Transmission of human immunodeficiency virus (HIV) by blood transfusions screened as negative for HIV antibody. N Engl J Med 1988; 318:473–478.

27. Petersen LR, Satten GA, Dodd R, Busch M, Kleinman S, Grindon A, Lenes B, HIV Seroconversion Study Group. Duration of time from onset of human immunodeficiency virus type 1 infectiousness to development of detectable antibody. Transfusion 1994; 34:283–289.

28. Lackritz EM, Satten GA, Aberle-Grasse J, Dodd RY, Raimondi VP, Janssen RS, Lewis WF, Notari EP, Petersen LR. Estimated risk of transmission of the human immunodeficiency virus by screened blood in the United States. N Engl J Med 1995; 333:1721–1725.

29. Schreiber GB, Busch MP, Kleinman SH, Korelitz J. The risk of transfusion-transmitted viral infections. N Engl J Med 1996; 334:1685–1690.

30. Doll LS, Petersen LR, White CR, Ward JW, HIV Blood Donor Study Group. Human immunodeficiency virus type 1-infected blood donors: behavioral characteristics and reasons for donation. Transfusion 1991; 31:704–709.

31. Williams AE, Thomson RA, Schreiber GB, Watanabe K, Bethel J, Lo A, Kleinman SH, Hollingsworth CG, Nemo GJ. Estimates of infectious disease risk factors in US blood donors. JAMA 1997; 277:967–972.

32. Cumming PD, Wallace EL, Schorr JB, Dodd RY. Exposure of patients to human immunodeficiency virus through the transfusion of blood components that test antibody-negative. N Engl J Med 1989; 321:941–946.

32a. Janssen RS, Satten GA, Stramer SL, Rawal BD, O'Brien TR, Weiblen BJ, Hecht FM, Jack N, Cleghorn FR, Kahn JO, et al, New testing strategy to detect early HIV-1 infection for use in incidence estimates and for clinical and prevention purposes. JAMA 1998; 280:42–48.

33. Kleinman S, Secord K. Risk of human immunodeficiency virus (HIV) transmission by anti-HIV negative blood. Estimates using the lookback methodology. Transfusion 1988; 28:499–501.

34. Busch MP, Lee LLL, Satten GA, Henrard DR, Farzadegan H, Nelson KE, Read S,

Dodd RY, Petersen LR. Time course of detection of viral and serologic markers preceding human immunodeficiency virus type 1 seroconversion: Implications for screening of blood and tissue donors. Transfusion 1995; 35:91–97.

35. Alter HJ. You'll wonder where the yellow went: a 15-year retrospective of post-transfusion hepatitis. In: Moore SB, ed. Arlington, VA: AABB, 1987:53–86.

36. Aledort LM. Consequences of chronic hepatitis C: a review article for the hematologist. Am J Hematol 1993; 44:29–37.

37. Seeff LB, Buskell-Bales Z, Wright EC, Durako SJ, Alter HJ, Iber FL, Hollinger FB, Gitnick G, Knodell RG, Perrillo RP, Stevens CE, Hollingsworth CG, NHLBI Study Group. Long-term mortality after transfusion-associated non-A, non-B hepatitis. N Engl J Med 1992; 327:1906–1911.

38. Koretz RL, Abbey H, Coleman E, Gitnick G. Non-A, non-B post-transfusion hepatitis: Looking back in the second decade. Ann Intern Med 1993; 119:110–115.

39. Nelson KE, Ahmed F, Stambolis V, Ness PM, Yawn D, McAllister H. Incident hepatitis C virus (HCV) and hepatitis B virus (HBV) infections in transfused cardiac surgery patients: infection rates during different methods of donor screening. Bethesda, MD: NIH Consensus Development Conference on Infectious Disease Testing for Blood Transfusions. National Institutes of Health, 1995: 67–69.

40. Kleinman S, Alter H, Busch M, Holland P, Tegtmeier G, Nelles M, Lee S, Page E, Wilber J, Polito A. Increased detection of hepatitis C virus (HCV)-infected blood donors by a multiple-antigen HCV enzyme immunoassay. Transfusion 1992; 32:805–813.

41. Allander T, Gruber A, Naghavi M, Beyene A, Soderstrom T, Bjorkholm M, Grillner L, Persson MAA. Frequent patient-to-patient transmission of hepatitis C virus in a haematology ward. Lancet 1995; 345:603–607.

42. Kiyosawa K, Sodeyama T, Tanaka E, Gibo Y, Yoshizawa K, Nakano Y, Furuta S, Akahane Y, Nishioka K, Purcell RH, Alter HJ. Interrelationship of blood transfusion, non-A, non-B hepatitis and hepatocellular carcinoma: analysis by detection of antibody to hepatitis C virus. Hepatology 1990; 12:671–675.

43. Hollinger FB, Khan NC, Oefinger PE, Yawn DH, Schmulen AC, Dreesman GR, Melnick JL. Posttransfusion hepatitis type A. JAMA 1983; 250:2313–2317.

44. Noble RC, Kane MA, Reeves SA, Roeckel I. Posttransfusion hepatitis A in a neonatal intensive care unit. JAMA 1984; 252:2711–2715.

45. Alter HJ, Purcell RH, Shih JW, Melpolder JC, Houghton M, Choo Q-L, Kuo G. Detection of antibody to hepatitis C virus in prospectively followed transfusion recipients with acute and chronic non-A, non-B hepatitis. N Engl J Med 1989; 321:1494–1500.

46. Alter HJ. New kit on the block: evaluation of second-generation assays for detection of antibody to the hepatitis C virus. Hepatology 1992; 15:350–353.

47. Linnen J, Wages J, Jr., Zhang-Keck ZY, Fry KE, Krawczynski KZ, Alter H, Koonin E, Gallagher M, Alter M, Hadziyannis S, Karayiannis P, Fung K, Nakatsuji Y, Shih JWK, Young L, Piatak M, Jr, Hoover C, Fernandez J, Chen S, Zou JC, Morris T, Hyams KC, Ismay S, Lifson JD. Molecular cloning and disease association of hepatitis G virus: a transfusion-transmissible agent. Science 1996; 271:505–508.

48. Simons JN, Leary TP, Dawson GJ, Pilot-Matias TJ, Muerhoff AS, Schlauder GG, Desai SM, Mushahwar IK. Isolation of novel virus-like sequences associated with human hepatitis. Nature Med 1995; 1:564–569.

49. Miyakawa Y, Mayumi M. Hepatitis G virus—true hepatitis virus or an accidental tourist? N Engl J Med 1997; 336:795–796.

50. Alter HJ, Nakatsuji Y, Melpolder J, Wages J, Wesley R, Shih JWK, Kim JP. The incidence of transfusion-associated hepatitis G virus infection and its relation to liver disease. N Engl J Med 1997; 336:747–754.

51. Alter MJ, Gallagher M, Morris TT, Moyer LA, Meeks EL, Krawczynski K, Kim JP, Margolis HS. Acute non-A-E hepatitis in the United States and the role of hepatitis G virus infection. N Engl J Med. 1997; 336:741–746.

51a. Nishizawa T, Okamoto H, Konishi K, Yoshizawa H, Miyakawa Y, Mayumi M. A novel DNA virus (TTV) associated with elevated trasaminase levels in post-transfusion hepatitis of unknown etiology. Biochem Biophys Res Commun 1997; 241:92–97

51b. Simmonds P, Davidson F, Lycett C, Prescott LE, MacDonald DM, Ellender J, Yap PL, Ludlam CA, Haydon GH, Gillon J, et al. Detection of a novel DNA virus (TTV) in blood donors and blood products. Lancet 1998; 352:191–195.

52. Nahlen BL, Lobel HO, Cannon SE, Campbell CC. Reassessment of blood donor selection criteria for United States travellers to malarious areas. Transfusion 1991; 31:798–804.

53. CDC. Malaria surveillance—United States, 1994. MMWR 1997; 46 (suppl):1–18.

54. Preiksaitis JK. Indications for the use of cytomegalovirus-seronegative blood products. Transf Med Rev 1991; 5:1–17.

55. Esmonde TFG, Will RG, Slattery JM, Knight R, Harries-Jones R, De Silva R, Matthews WB. Creutzfeldt-Jakob disease and blood transfusion. Lancet 1993; 341:205–207.

56. Klein R, Dumble LJ. Transmission of Creutzfeldt-Jakob disease by blood transfusion. Lancet 1993; 341:768–768.

57. Dodd RY, Sullivan MT. Creutzfeldt-Jakob disease and transfusion safety: tilting at icebergs? Transfusion 1998; 38:221–223.

58. Holland PV. Why a new standard to prevent Creutzfeldt-Jakob disease? Transfusion 1988; 28:293–294.

59. Goldman M, Blajchman MA. Blood product-associated bacterial sepsis. Transfus Med Rev 1991; 5:73–83.

60. Wagner SJ, Friedman LI, Dodd RY. Transfusion-associated bacterial sepsis. Clin Microbiol Rev 1994; 7:290–302.

61. Sazama K. Bacteria in blood for transfusion: review. Arch Pathol Lab Med 1994; 118:350–365.

62. Klein HG, Dodd RY, Ness PM, Fratantoni JA, Nemo GJ. Current status of microbial contamination of blood components: summary of a conference. Transfusion 1997; 37:95–101.

63. Tipple MA, Bland LA, Murphy JJ, Arduino MJ, Panlilio AL, Farmer JJ, III, Tourault MA, Macpherson CR, Menitove JE, Grindon AJ, Johnson PS, Strauss RG, Bufill JA, Ritch PS, Archer JR, Tablan OC, Jarvis WR. Sepsis associated with transfusion of red cells contaminated with *Yersinia enterocolitica*. Transfusion 1990; 30:207–213.

64. Lifson AR, Stanley M, Pane J, O'Malley PM, Wilber JC, Stanley A, Jeffery B, Rutherford GW, Sohmer PR. Detection of human immunodeficiency virus DNA

using the polymerase chain reaction in a well-characterized group of homosexual and bisexual men. J Infect Dis 1990; 161:436–439.

65. Richards C, Kolins J, Trindade CD. Autologous transfusion-transmitted *Yersinia enterocolitica*. JAMA 1992; 268:1541–1542.

66. Leiby DA, Kerr KL, Campos JM, Dodd RY. A retrospective analysis of microbial contaminants in outdated random-donor platelets from multiple sites. Transfusion 1997; 37:259–263.

67. Morrow JF, Braine HG, Kickler TS, Ness PM, Dick JD, Fuller AK. Septic reactions to platelet transfusions. A persistent problem. JAMA 1991; 266:555–558.

68. Gong J, Högman CF, Hambraeus A, Johansson CS, Eriksson L. Transfusion-associated *Serratia marcescens* infection: studies of the mechanism of action. Transfusion 1993; 33:802–808.

69. Young FE. Efficacy of new tests and the safety of the blood supply. Transfusion 1990; 30:4–5.

70. Dodd RY, Houlihan K, Lamberson HV. The specificity of enzyme immunoassays for antibodies to human immunodeficiency virus: impact on record and donor management [letter]. Transfusion 1993; 33:693.

71. Cohen BJ, Beard S, Knowles WA, Ellis JS, Joske D, Goldman JM, Hewitt P, Ward KN. Chronic anemia due to parvovirus B19 infection in a bone marrow transplant patient after platelet transfusion. Transfusion 1997; 37:947–952.

72. Schmuñis GA. *Trypanosoma cruzi*, the etiologic agent of Chagas' disease: status in the blood supply in endemic and nonendemic countries. Transfusion 1991; 31:547–557.

73. Gerber MA, Shapiro ED, Krause PJ, Cable RG, Badon SJ, Ryan RW. The risk of acquiring Lyme disease or babesiosis from a blood transfusion. J Infect Dis 1994; 170:231–234.

74. Herwaldt BL, Kjemtrup AM, Conrad PA, Barnes RC, Wilson M, McCarthy MG, Sayers MH, Eberhard ML. Transfusion-transmitted babesiosis in Washington state: first reported case caused by a WA1-type parasite. J Infect Dis 1997; 175:1259–1262.

75. Williams AE, Fang CT, Slamon DJ, Poiesz BJ, Sandler SG, Darr WF, Shulman G, McGowan El, Douglas DK, Bowman RJ, Peetoom F, Kleinman SH, Lenes B, Dodd RY. Seroprevalence and epidemiological correlates of HTLV-1 infection in U.S. blood donors. Science 1988; 240:643–646.

76. Persing DH, Herwaldt BL, Glaser C, Lane RS, Thomford JW, Mathiesen D, Krause PJ, Phillip DF, Conrad PA. Infection with a Babesia-like organism in northern California. N Engl J Med 1995; 332:298–303.

77. Herwaldt BL, Persing DH, Précigout EA, Goff WL, Mathiesen DA, Taylor PW, Eberhard ML, Gorenflot AF. A fatal case of babesiosis in Missouri: identification of another piroplasm that infects humans. Ann Intern Med 1996; 124:643–650.

78. Vamvakas EC, Taswell HF. Mortality after blood transfusion. Transf Med Rev 1994; 8:267–280.

79. CDC. Outbreak of hepatitis C associated with intravenous immunoglobulin administration—United States, October 1993;–June 1994. MMWR 1994; 43:505–509.

80. Mannucci PM, Gdovin S, Gringeri A, Colombo M, Mele A, Schinaia N, Ciavarella N, Emerson SU, Purcell RH, Italian Collaborative Group. Transmission of hepatitis

A to patients with hemophilia by Factor VIII concentrates treated with organic solvent and detergent to inactivate viruses. Ann Intern Med 1994; 120:1–7.

81. Azzi A, Ciappi S, Zakvrzewska K, Morfini M, Mariani G, Mannucci PM. Human parvovirus B19 infection in hemophiliacs first infused with two high-purity, virally attenuated Factor VIII concentrates. Am J Hematol 1992; 39:228–230.

82. Lambrecht B, Mohr H, Knüver-Hopf J, Schmitt H. Photoinactivation of viruses in human fresh plasma by phenothiazine dyes in combination with visible light. Vox Sang 1991; 60:207–213.

83. Wieding JU, Hellstern P, Köhler M. Inactivation of viruses in fresh-frozen plasma. Ann Hematol 1993; 67:259–266.

84. Horowitz B, Bonomo R, Prince AM, Chin SN, Brotman B, Shulman RW. Solvent/detergent-treated plasma: a virus-inactivated substitute for fresh frozen plasma. Blood 1992; 79:826–831.

85. Leape LL, Brennan TA, Laird N, Lawthers AG, Localio AR, Barnes BA, Hebert L, Newhouse JP, Weiler PC, Hiatt H. The nature of adverse events in hospitalized patients. Results of the Harvard Medical Practice Study II. N Engl J Med 1991; 324:377–384.

86. Brennan TA, Leape LL, Laird NM, Hebert L, Localio AR, Lawthers AG, Newhouse JP, Weiler PC, Hiatt HH. Incidence of adverse events and negligence in hospitalized patients. Results of the Harvard Medical Practice Study I [see comments]. N Engl J Med 1991; 324:370–376.

87. Alter MJ, Hadler SC, Judson FN, Mares A, Alexander WJ, Hu PY, Miller JK, Moyer LA, Fields HA, Bradley DW, Margolis HS. Risk factors for acute non-A, non-B hepatitis in the United States and association with hepatitis C virus infection. JAMA 1990; 264:2231–2235.

9

Blood Donor Screening and Supplemental Testing
Principles, Procedures, and Consequences

Jay E. Valinsky
New York Blood Center, New York, New York

I. INTRODUCTION

Blood transfusion has become increasingly safe worldwide since the introduction of screening tests for transfusion-transmitted infectious diseases (TTD) (1) and an extensive series of other measures to minimize the risk to recipients of blood, blood components, and derivatives. Two events triggered dramatic improvements in blood safety in the United States in the 1970s: the conversion to all-volunteer, unpaid donors of blood for transfusion (2) and the widespread introduction of tests for hepatitis B surface antigen that could be applied at the level of mass screening (3). Cases of posttransfusion hepatitis dropped from about 25% of recipients to about 5% of recipients.

The repertoire of blood screening tests for TTD expanded following the introduction of tests for HIV-1 in the mid-1980s, screening tests for HIV, HTLV, HCV, and HIV-1 p24 antigen, and tests of "surrogate" markers for liver damage/disease (ALT and anti-HBc). Incremental improvements in blood safety accompanied the initial implementation of each of these tests, and further improvements were seen with increasingly more sensitive generations of tests. Nucleic acid amplification testing (NAT) for HCV and HIV, and potentially other transfusion-transmitted infectious agents, promises to reduce the already low prevalence of these markers in the donor population and, by extension, the exposure of transfusion recipients even further.

It should be emphasized that the ongoing improvements in blood safety did not result solely from the introduction of new screening tests, but also by (a) more carefully defining donor eligibility; (b) directly questioning donors about risk behavior; (c) the establishment of registries of deferred donors; (d) the quarantine of products until analysis of test results was complete and process controls permitted labeling and release to inventory; (e) the introduction and enforcement of current good manufacturing practices (cGMP); and (f) extensive monitoring and investigation of adverse incidents, errors, and accidents (4).

All blood and plasma collected in the United States is screened for a variety of infectious disease markers as well as ABO group and Rh type (up to 14 screening tests). A list of current screening tests is provided in Table 1. The U.S. Food and Drug Administration (FDA) requires many of these screening tests for the qualification of products and donors. Others, like assays for alanine amino-transferase (ALT) and anti-hepatitis B core antibody, are still in use as surrogate tests for non–A-E hepatitis or as product qualification tests for plasma destined for further manufacture to blood derivatives. Still others (e.g., cytomegalovirus, sickle cell trait) are used at the discretion of the blood centers as a means of identifying products that may have specific clinical or therapeutic applications.

Table 1 Current Blood Screening and Supplemental Tests

Screening tests	Supplemental tests
HIV-1/HIV-2 EIA[a]	HIV-1/HIV-2 Algorithm[b] (HIV-1 Western blot,[b] or Immunofluorescence Assay[b] (I FA, HIV-2 EIA,[b] HIV-2 Western blot)
HIV-1 p24 Antigen EIA[a]	
HTLV-I/II EIA[a]	HIV-1 p24 antigen neutralization[b]
Hepatitis B surface Ag EIA[a]	HTLV-I/II Western blot, alternative EIA[b] or PCR
Hepatitis C EIA (HCV 2.0 or 3.0)[a]	HCV-RIBA slot immunoblot assay[b]
Anti-hepatitis B core EIA[a]	HBsAg neutralization[b]
Alanine aminotransferase (ALT)[c]	Syphilis (FTA-ABS)[b]
Syphilis (PK-TP or RPR)[a]	
ABO/Rh[a]	
NAT-HCV/HIV[d]	
Cytomegalovirus (CMV)[c,e]	
Sickle cell[c,e]	
Antibody screen[c,e]	
Extended antigen typing[c,e]	
HLA match[c,e]	

[a]Denotes required test.
[b]FDA-approved confirmatory test.
[c]Test not required.
[d]Currently being performed under Investigational New Drug applications (IND).
[e]Test routinely performed by most blood centers on a portion of inventory to identify products for which there are specific clinical or therapeutic indications.

The focus of this chapter will be on the tests currently employed in the United States for screening of volunteer blood doors for TTD and on the disposition of donors and products as determined by test results. Other chapters in this volume will directly address the issues of blood safety. General information about the test algorithms, test kit qualification, controls, sensitivity and specificity, and quality control will be followed by more specific information about the performance and outcomes of each of the individual tests. The discussions in this chapter are not intended to compare tests from different vendors nor to endorse the use of specific tests. The tables that follow describe donor and product disposition reflect requirements described in various FDA guidances and memoranda.

II. GENERAL TECHNIQUES FOR BLOOD SCREENING

A. Test Devices, Test Kits, and Test Performance

The screening of donated blood for markers of TTD is typically performed on samples of serum or plasma using serological tests for diagnostic antigens, antibodies, or enzymes. Blood screening tests are generally enzyme-linked immunosorbent assays (EIA/ELISA), agglutination tests (e.g., ABO/Rh screening, syphilis), or chemistry tests (e.g., ALT). The serological tests employed in donor screening are qualitative or semi-quantitative and are generally used to detect the presence or absence of a particular analyte.

While donor screening tests may be performed using a sequence of manual steps on a variety of devices, mass screening of blood donors in the contemporary setting is routinely conducted on automated or semi-automated devices. Automated testing platforms have similar properties, namely: (a) positive identification of specimens and reagents by bar-code scanning; (b) robotic aliquoting of specimens, controls, and reagents; (c) temperature-controlled incubators that are integral parts of the system; (d) spectrophotometric detection systems; and (e) computerized systems to calculate test results, manage the testing process, provide batch records, and reinforce current good manufacturing practices (cGMP). Current testing platforms are designed to provide relatively rapid throughput of samples and turnaround of test results, typically in 5–8 hours.

Rapid tests (5) for infectious disease markers have also been developed. These are typically self-contained devices that use flow-through or other techniques to trap analytes and reagents on a membrane and produce a color reaction that indicates whether the result is positive or negative. These tests may prove valuable in regions of the world where automated technologies are prohibited by cost or local conditions (6), but they may be limited in sensitivity and specificity and, in the context of mass screening, may be difficult to quality control.

In most cases, blood screening tests are provided in the form of test kits containing all of the reagents necessary for test performance, including solid phases for performing EIA/ELISA, buffers, test reagents, and controls. Each kit component is identified with a part number and has a defined expiration date. The components are linked to a manufacturing "master lot" number with an independent expiration date. Components from different kit lots should not be interchanged, since test performance is based in part on the set of components linked to a given master lot. Sample age, storage, and transport conditions are specified in the manufacturer's instruction circulars to ensure optimal test performance.

The EIA/ELISA tests used for detection of TTD markers use antigen or antibody capture techniques (7). The antigen or antibody capture reagents (e.g., purified antibodies, monoclonal antibodies, purified antigens, cell or viral lysates, or combinations thereof) are bound to a solid phase, typically a plastic support. Different vendors have deployed a variety of test matrices, including 96-well plastic microtiter/microwell plates, plastic beads, and microparticles, but the basic principles are the same.

The EIA/ELISA tests are performed in sequential steps. Samples of plasma or serum are incubated with matrix-bound capture reagents for a sufficient period, at an appropriate temperature, to allow optimal binding of the analyte present in the test sample to occur. Test controls (see below) are incubated simultaneously. The matrix is then washed to remove unbound serum or plasma. The wash step is followed by the addition of a conjugate reagent in one or several steps. These reagents are typically enzyme-linked (e.g., horseradish peroxidase, alkaline phosphatase) anti-human Ig antibodies, enzyme-conjugated antigens, or biotin-avidin-enzyme conjugates. During this incubation, the conjugate binds to the analyte bound in the first step to the solid phase by the capture reagent. The matrix is washed again to remove unbound conjugate. In the last step, or detection step, reporter molecules or substrates that react with the bound enzyme conjugates are added. Detection occurs as the specifically bound conjugates convert substrates to chromogenic, fluorogenic, or chemiluminescent products or react with other reporter molecules that can be detected spectrophotometrically. The signal (e.g., absorbance, relative fluorescence) produced in the test is proportional to the amount of analyte initially present in the test sample. In qualitative tests, the signal is evaluated relative to a threshold or "cut-off" value computed from control values (see below).

B. Positive and Negative Kit Controls, Calculation of Assay Cut-Off Values, and the Use of External Controls

Control samples are included in, and are an integral part of, assay kits ("manufacturer's kit controls"). Like other components of the kits, the controls are linked to the master kit lot number. Both positive and negative controls are typically analyzed in replicate as part of the test procedures. The results of the replicate tests are averaged. The averages can then be used to assess kit performance by comparing the actual results to ranges described in the manufacturer's package inserts. If the controls do not meet the performance characteristics defined in the package insert, the test is invalid.

Positive kit controls are typically prepared from known antibody- or antigen-positive specimens and are designed to react strongly in the test. The positive controls are generally not used as kit calibrators but, rather, are controls that show that the test procedure is working and that the reagents used in the test perform within the limits described in the package insert.

Negative controls are usually prepared from normal human serum or plasma. In most current assays, negative control values are used as kit calibrators. The negative control is typically used to calculate the test "cut-off" (CO) or threshold value. The cut-off calculation is test specific. Calculation of the cut-off usually entails computing the mean of the negative control values and then adding a constant factor to the mean, or alternatively, multiplying the mean by a constant factor. Thus, the cut-off for a specific test is variable and related to the performance of the test in a given test run. The constants are determined by the manufacturer and specified in the package insert. The cut-off calculation method is set during development of the test to optimize the differences between reactive and nonreactive samples, thereby balancing sensitivity and specificity.

If the signal (e.g., absorbance) (S) produced by a given test sample is equal to or greater than the calculated cut-off value, the specimen is considered to be reactive in the test. This may also be expressed as the signal-to-cut-off ratio (S/CO). If the S/CO ratio is ≥ 1.0, the specimen is considered reactive. The use of the S/CO ratio rather than the absolute absorbance value for reporting results is valuable, since it normalizes the test results, thereby permitting inter- and intra-assay comparisons.

In addition to the manufacturer's kit controls, external or run controls should also be analyzed with each test run. By definition, external controls are not part of the test kit or linked to the master lot. Positive external controls are generally prepared from weakly reactive specimens or from strongly reactive specimens diluted to react near the cut-off. Since this control is intended to mimic a weakly reactive test sample, even small changes in test conditions or performance (e.g., temperature fluctuations, sampling errors, time variances) might result in this control giving a false-negative result. Thus, if the external control fails, it may be an indicator that actual samples tested in that run, with similar near-cut-off reactivity, might also have given false-negative findings in the test. Negative external controls are useful to monitor the performance of the kit negative control. These reagents are prepared from negative human serum or plasma. Unlike the negative kit controls, they cannot be used to calculate the kit cut-off. Failure of the external control may also invalidate the test run. If an external control fails, the test run is suspect, whether or not the manufacturer's kit controls are in range.

The use of external controls has been somewhat controversial (8) because:

1. The performance characteristics of some of the external control reagents in current use are not well defined. There is presently no requirement for FDA clearance of these reagents, nor is there an absolute requirement that they be manufactured under cGMP conditions.
2. External control values are sometimes used to define test performance characteristics that exceed the manufacturer's specifications. For example, quantitative criteria for external control performance (e.g., controls must perform within certain ranges of S/CO to be valid) have been applied to semi-quantitative or qualitative tests.
3. There remain questions about how frequently external controls should be run during the day (e.g., with each set of manufacturer's controls, with a batch of specimens, twice daily).

The Health Care Financing Administration (HCFA) has recently published rules for the use of positive and negative external controls for in vitro diagnostic tests (9). In commenting on these rules, FDA notes that the Clinical Laboratory Improvement Amendments rules for use of these controls should be followed but cautions that the use of external controls goes beyond the claims of the manufacturer's package inserts, that the manufacturer's guidelines must be followed, and that external controls must not be used as substitutes for the calibrators included in the test kits (10).

C. Quality Control for Screening Tests

Quality control (QC) measures must be incorporated into the daily operation of laboratories performing blood donor screening tests. QC provides a quantitative or semi-quantitative approach to evaluation of test performance and verifies that the tests are operating within the limits described in the manufacturer's package inserts. QC as defined herein addresses neither the issue of accuracy of the tests nor the correct reporting of test results. These issues should be addressed in periodic audits as part of an overall quality improvement plan.

The performance of the manufacturer's positive and negative kit controls is the first measure of adequacy of the test. If these controls perform within the ranges described by the vendor and all test parameters are met, the test run is considered valid, and the results for all samples tested on that run are considered valid. If the manufacturer's controls are out of range, the test is invalid and should be repeated. This is obviously the case when the calibrator (e.g., negative control) fails and the cut-off value cannot be calculated as well as when the positive control fails.

Failure of the external control(s) when manufacturer's kit controls are in range also renders the test run suspect. The results for reactive (positive) specimens must be retained and the samples subjected to the rest of the test algorithm. The nonreactive (negative) samples should be retested (10). The procedure used to assess the validity of the external control should be designed cautiously, so as not to exceed the specifications of the test set by the manufacturer. Several attempts have been made to establish performance rules for external controls [e.g., Westgard rules (11) or other standard deviation rules]. However, these statistical process control methods are not strictly applicable to the semi-quantitative or qualitative tests used in donor screening. If the limits are too stringent (e.g., values for the external control must be within 2 standard deviations of mean), the frequency of failed runs due to random error alone is unreasonably high (nearly 5%). If the limits are too relaxed (e.g., 3 standard deviations from the mean), it is likely that a considerable percentage of run failures may go undetected. Thus, it is more appropriate to apply a "pass/fail" system to qualify external control performance for a particular run. Nonetheless, statistical process control methods (e.g., control charts) should be applied rigorously to track shifts or trends in laboratory performance using both the external and manufacturer's control values.

Lot acceptance criteria should also be established in each laboratory. Upon receipt, a new master lot of test reagents should be quarantined pending qualification for use. Lot acceptance may involve testing the new lot of reagents against a panel of specimens that challenges the performance of the new lot in the specific laboratory environment. The current lot should be tested in parallel. This is an important step, since considerable variation in sensitivity is often observed among master lots, even though they all meet manufacturing and FDA specifications. The external controls should be included in the lot acceptance panel. This is most important for the positive external control, since it is weakly reactive and may give false-negative results if the sensitivity of the new lot is lower than the current lot. For purposes of tracking and trending the performance of the external controls, it is also recommended that they be requalified with each new master lot of reagents and that statistical parameters (e.g., mean, standard deviation) be recalculated. This may be done conveniently, for example by testing 20 replicates of the controls as part of lot validation. As part of a quality improvement plan and to complement these quality control measures, laboratories should actively participate in certified proficiency testing programs managed by external organizations (e.g., College of American Pathologists, state health departments).

D. Test Sensitivity, Specificity, Window Period, Efficiency, and Predictive Values

Two commonly used indices of assay performance are test sensitivity and specificity. Sensitivity often has two interpretations. In comparing two tests, for example, one test may be considered more sensitive if it is able to detect the presence of an analyte in a sample when the other does not. On the other hand, one test may be considered more sensitive if it can detect an analyte at higher dilution. While the less sensitive of the two tests may detect the presence of low levels of analyte, it may still not detect all infected individuals, thereby leading to false-negative results. Thus, while both definitions apply, sensitivity, in the context of donor screening, is the ability of the assay to identify true positives (TP) (e.g., infected individuals) in the test population, while minimizing the number of false negatives (FN). The sensitivity of most commercially available test kits currently exceeds 98%. Because the emphasis is on the detection of as many positive donors as possible, most existing EIA tests for donor screening produce a significant number of false-positive results (see below).

As test sensitivity increases, the ability to identify individuals at earlier stages of infection also improves. This reduces the time between exposure/infection and detection [i.e., the window period (12)]. It is important to note that the length of the window period is more a function of the sensitivity of the test than it is of the disease. This has been shown clearly in the cases of HIV (13) and HCV (14,15), in which the window period has decreased markedly with improvements in test sensitivity in progressive generations of test kits.

The counterpoint of test sensitivity is specificity. Specificity can be defined as the ability of a test to identify noninfected individuals in a population (true negatives, TN), thereby avoiding false positives (FP). The specificity of most commercially available EIA test kits exceeds 99%. It should be remembered that sensitivity and specificity are essentially reciprocal values.

A convenient means of comparing tests, which takes both sensitivity and specificity into account, is test efficiency. This is the ability of an assay to correctly identify positives *and* negatives in the test population.

The predictive value (positive or negative) of a test is a semi-quantitative assessment of the value of the test that takes the actual population prevalence into account. Thus, for a given specificity and sensitivity, the value of tests may differ depending on the populations tested, e.g., low-risk blood donors versus high-risk populations in a sexually transmitted disease clinic. In the case of blood donor testing, the negative predictive value of a test may be the more valuable parameter, since it estimates the ability of the test to detect false negatives.

Equations for the calculation of the parameters defined in this section are found in Table 2.

The ability of these serological assays for infectious disease markers to detect antibodies or antigens may vary regionally, reflecting the genotypic distribution of the infectious agent (16,17). In some instances it has been

Table 2 Calculation of Sensitivity, Specificity, Efficiency, and Predictive Values

Parameter	Calculation
Sensitivity	$(TP/TP + FN) \times 100\%$
Specificity	$(TN/TN + FP) \times 100\%$
Efficiency	$(TP/TP + FN) \times 100\%$
Positive predictive value (PPV)	$(TP + TN/TP + FP + TN + FN) \times 100\%$
Negative predictive value (NPV)	$TN/(TN + FN) \times 100\%$

TP = True positives; TN = true negatives; FP = false positives; FN = false negatives.

shown that mutations in the infectious agent may go undetected in some tests (18,19).

E. Screening Test Algorithms

The same basic algorithm applies to all serological screening tests. Serum or plasma samples are subjected to an initial screening test. If the initial result is nonreactive (NR) or negative (NEG), the donated blood unit is considered acceptable for the individual test. If the initial screening result is reactive (R) or positive (POS), the sample is considered initially reactive (IR) and the test is repeated in duplicate. When repeat tests are performed, the final interpretation is derived from the analysis of the three test results. If two or three results are reactive, the sample is considered repeatedly reactive (RR). If only one of the three tests is reactive, the specimen is considered initially reactive only and classified as nonreactive (NR).

Exceptions to this general algorithm include: (1) ALT testing, in which a single determination is made and the activity, expressed in international units (IU), is reported as normal or elevated; (b) NAT for HCV and HIV, in which specimens are tested in pools and positive pools are resolved to the individual samples (see below) and; (c) syphilis testing on some automated platforms in which an indeterminate (IND) result is possible. IND results are treated operationally as positive results in this case.

Three consequences arise from a repeatedly reactive screening test result on the current donation. First, the labeling of the implicated unit of blood, and therefore its placement into inventory for transfusion, is interdicted. Second, the donor is placed in a deferral registry that may affect future donations. Third, supplemental testing is ordered where appropriate and available to confirm the screening test result. The outcomes for donors and products based on screening test results are summarized in Table 3.

Table 3 Product and Sample Disposition—Implications of Screening Test Results

Analyte	Screening result		Result interpretation	Suitable for transfusion	Interdict shipment	Sample to confirmation	Product label	Product disposition
	Initial	Repeat						
HBc	NR	None	NR	Yes	No	N/A	ABO/Rh	Inventory
	R	1 or 2 R[a]	RR	No	Yes	N/A	Biohazard	Discard RBC/PLT; plasma to manufacture
HBsAg HIV-1/2 HCV	NR	None	NR	Yes	No	No	ABO/Rh	Inventory
HTLV-I/II HIV-1 p24 Ag	R	1 or 2 R	RR	No	Yes	No	Biohazard	Discard
Syphilis	NR or NEG R/POS/IND[b]	None R/POS/IND	NR/NEG R/POS/IND	Yes No	No Yes	No Yes	ABO/Rh Biohazard	Inventory Discard
ALT[c]	N E or S	None None	N E or S	Yes No	No Yes	N/A N/A	ABO/Rh Biohazard	Inventory Discard

[a]Each IR sample is tested in duplicate. If either one or both of the repeat tests is reactive, the interpretation is repeatedly reactive (RR).
[b]Indeterminate syphilis results are treated as positive.
[c]Results for ALT testing are linked to International Units of enzyme activity.

III. SUPPLEMENTAL AND CONFIRMATORY TESTING

Additional, more specific supplemental or confirmatory tests are used to verify a reactive result in the screening tests (Table 1). As noted above, screening tests are not 100% specific. The balance between sensitivity and specificity in the design of screening tests is critical, since even small changes in sensitivity can have large consequences for the absolute number of donors deferred and units lost as a consequence of false-positive results. This is illustrated in Table 4. In the low prevalence U.S. blood donor population, for example, the ratio of confirmed (i.e., true) positives to total number of repeatedly reactive samples detected in the screening tests ranged from about 0.8 (HCV) to essentially zero (HIV-1 p24 antigen). The sensitivity of supplemental tests must be at least as good as the screening tests to which they are linked. Generally, supplemental tests use a different methodology than do the associated screening test (e.g., HIV-1 Western blot instead of HIV-1/2 EIA).

The results of supplemental testing have no implications for labeling, shipment of blood products, or placement of the donor in the deferral registry for the current donation. Rather, these results are utilized for donor notification, counseling, reentry, in-date product retrieval, and lookback. However, the donor deferral status may be modified based on subsequent test results. Donor and product dispositions, dictated by the screening and confirmatory test results, are summarized in Tables 5 and 6.

A. Supplemental Testing Methods

Supplemental tests in current use include Western blots (WB), microscope-based immunofluorescence assays (IFA), immunoblots, EIA/ELISA neutralization techniques, and molecular methods, such as PCR.

Table 4 Prevalence of Serological Markers Among Blood Donors

Marker	EIA RR (%)	Confirmed (%)	Ratio Conf/RR
Hepatitis B surface antigen	0.055	0.025	0.45
Hepatitis C antibody	0.195	0.156	0.80
HIV-1/2 antibody	0.080	0.012	0.15
HIV-1 p24 antigen	0.030	$<1/10^7$	~0
HTLV-I/II antibody	0.11	0.006	0.55
Anti-hepatitis B core antibody	0.665	N/A	N/A
ALT	0.200	N/A	N/A
Syphilis	0.240	0.200	0.83

Source: Summary of New York Blood Center screening and confirmatory test results 1998–1999. N = ~700,000; see Ref. 28 For HIV-1 p24 antigen data.

Table 5 Donor Disposition—Implications of Test Results

Screening test result	Confirmatory result	Surveillance	Deferral type	Reentry available
Syphilis RR or Indeterminate	FTA Pos	No	Permanent	Yes
	FTA-NEG	No	None	N/A
HBsAg RR	Positive	No	Permanent	No
	Not neutralized	Yes	1st occurrence—temporary 8 wk 2nd occurrence—permanent	1st occurrence—Yes 2nd occurrence—No
HBc RR	N/A	Yes 1st hit	2 hits permanent	No
HCV RR	Negative	Yes	Permanent	1st occurrence—Yes: 2nd—No
	Indeterminate	No	Permanent	No
	Positive	No	Permanent	No
ALT Elevated	N/A	Temporary 1 yr for 1st moderate elevation	1 yr, 2nd occurrence moderate elevation or 1st occurrence super elevated	Yes—automatic after 1 yr
HIV-1/2 RR	Negative/HIV-2 NR	Yes	Permanent	1st occurrence—Yes; 2nd—No
	Negative/HIV-2 RR	No	Permanent	No
	Indeterminate	No	Permanent	No
	Positive	No	Permanent	No
HIV p24 Antigen RR	Indeterminate	Yes	1st occurrence temporary 8 wk 2nd occurrence permanent	2nd occurrence—No
	Positive	No	Permanent	No
HTLV-1/2 RR HTLV-I/II	Negative	Yes	Permanent if 2nd occurrence negative or indeterminate	No
	Indeterminate	Yes	Permanent if 2nd occurrence negative or indeterminate	No
	Positive (WB or EIAs)	No	Permanent	No

The combination of a HIV-1/2 RR and a HIV-1 p24 antigen RR on any single or combination of donations will prevent reentry.
The combination of a HBsAg RR and HBc RR on any single or combination of donations will result in permanent deferral.

Table 6 Hospital In-Date Product Retrieval and Lookback

Screening test result	Confirmatory result	Lookback	In-date product retrieval
Syphilis RR or indeterminate	FTA Positive or negative	N/A	N/A
HBsAg RR	Not neutralized	N/A	5 years
	Positive	6 months	
HBc RR	N/A	N/A	5 years
HCV RR	Negative	N/A	Earliest available records
	Indeterminate HCV RIBA 3.0	N/A	
	Positive	Earliest available records	
ALT Reactive	N/A	N/A	N/A
HIV-1/2 RR	Negative/HIV2 NR	N/A	5 years
	Negative/HIV 2 RR	5 years	
	Indeterminate/HIV 2 NR	N/A	
	Indeterminate/HIV 2 RR	5 years	
	Positive	5 years	
HIV p24 Antigen RR	Indeterminate	N/A	3 months
	Positive	3 months	
HTLV-1/2 RR	WB negative	N/A	5 yr—cellular products only
	WB indeterminate	N/A	
	WB positive	5 yr—cellular products only	
	Positive in 2 EIAs	5 yr—cellular products only	

1. Western Blots

The Western blot is one of the most widely used tests for the confirmation of the presence of antibodies to retroviruses. A Western blot assay is typically prepared from partially purified viral proteins derived from viral lysates, recombinant proteins, peptides, or combinations thereof. The viral proteins are separated by SDS-polyacrylamide gel electrophoresis according to apparent molecular weight. Following electrophoretic separation, the proteins are arrayed in the gel as concentrated "bands." The proteins are then transferred electrophoretically from the polyacrylamide to strips of nitrocellulose paper, where the proteins/peptides are stabilized and stored until use. The nitrocellulose strips, therefore, contain an image of the proteins as originally displayed in the polyacrylamide gel.

To perform the test, samples of serum or plasma are incubated with the nitrocellulose test strips and processed in a manner similar to an EIA. Antibodies in the test sample bind to specific proteins or antigens arrayed on the nitrocellulose strip. Binding is revealed through a series of reactions with enzyme-antibody conjugates and substrates. Colored products produced by the enzymatic reaction precipitate and bind to the nitrocellulose strips. The identity of the antibody binding sites is established both by the position of the stained protein band on the strip (i.e., apparent molecular weight) and by the reactivity estimated by the staining intensity. The specificity of the test arises from this specific binding of antibody to recognizable virus-associated antigens, and the sensitivity of the test arises, in part, from the concentration of the viral antigens in electrophoretic bands. The test kits include positive and negative control samples that give predictable patterns of antibody binding and intensity that can be used to calibrate the position and reactivity of the test samples.

Typically results are reported as positive (POS) if there is a pattern of antibody binding to diagnostic bands specific for the virus in question or negative (NEG) if there are no specific binding patterns or no antibody binding at all. Results may also be indeterminate (IND) if there are binding patterns that do not meet the criteria for positive. Failure of the control reagents to produce the expected pattern of binding and/or intensity invalidates the entire run. A discussion of Western blot tests for particular viral markers can be found in subsequent sections.

2. Immunofluorescence Assays

An alternative to the Western blot for the detection of viral antibodies is the Immunofluorescence assay (IFA). Unlike the Western blot, IFA does not identify specific antibodies. A positive result simply indicates whether antibodies to the virus in question were present in the test sample. Immunofluorescence assays have been used as confirmatory tests for HIV, HTLV, and syphilis.

In this test, which is basically an indirect immunofluorescence assay, cells infected with a particular virus are deposited and fixed in wells etched or circumscribed on a glass microscope slide. The fixed cells are then incubated with test serum or plasma. After a series of washes to remove unbound test sample, the cells are incubated with a fluorescently tagged anti-human IgG. Viral antigens present intracellularly are revealed by fluorescence microscopy. The specificity of the test is assessed by comparing the immunofluorescence intensity and patterns in the infected cells with those observed in noninfected cells treated with the same test sample. Staining intensity and patterns produced by the test samples can also be compared with those produced by the positive and negative controls. The fluorescence intensity is usually scored on an arbitrary scale of 0 to 4+. Additional quality controls include evaluation of patterns of fluorescence (e.g., membrane vs. ctyoplasmic, hazy vs. well-demarcated fluorescence).

3. Immunoblot (Slot Immunoblot)

The immunoblot assays are similar to Western blots in that the test is performed on a strip of nitrocellulose paper and follows the general principles for incubation and deposition of a colored enzymatic product at the site of binding of a specific antibody. The difference is in the preparation of the nitrocellulose strip. In this case, the antigens are purified recombinant, synthetic, or viral peptides and are applied, rather than electrophoresed, to the nitrocellulose strip. One advantage of this methodology is that the concentration of antigen applied to any given location on the strip can be optimized for sensitivity and specificity. The readout of the strip is essentially cleaner, since there are no extraneous, nonspecific, or nonviral proteins present. In addition, this format may result in a reduction of indeterminate results relative to the Western blot (20–22). In the current immunoblot assays (e.g., RIBA tests, see below), two concentrations of human immunoglobulin are also transferred to the strip. These are methodological controls that show whether or not the anti-human IgG-developing reagents are functional. The test sample must react positively with these internal strip controls in order for the strip to be valid. In addition, positive and negative controls must react appropriately for the entire test run to be valid. A detailed discussion of the application of this format to confirmatory testing for HCV follows in a later section.

4. EIA Neutralization Tests

Neutralization tests are generally used to confirm the presence of viral antigens in samples repeated reactive in EIA tests.

The principle of the neutralization test is competition for binding of antigen in the test sample between antibody free in solution and antibody bound to the solid phase. The test is usually performed in two parts. One aliquot of the test specimen is preincubated with a known amount of antibody to the antigen in question ("neutralizing antibody"). A second aliquot is incubated with a nonreactive antibody ("control antibody"). The EIA test is performed following these

Valinsky

incubations. If the antigen is present in the "neutralized sample," some or all will bind to the antibody in solution and form an antigen-antibody complex. Antigen in the complex will be unavailable for binding to the antibody on the solid phase. The signal in the EIA reaction will be reduced relative to the sample incubated with the control antibody. The percentage of inhibition or neutralization can then be determined by comparing the neutralized and nonneutralized values. The sample is considered confirmed positive if assay-specific threshold values are achieved (see below). It has recently been shown that neutralization assays may be prone to artifacts that produce false-positive (23,24) and/or indeterminate results (25).

B. Quality Control for Supplemental and Confirmatory Tests

The procedures described above for quality control of screening tests apply equally to confirmatory or supplemental tests. Positive and negative kit controls must meet criteria defined in the manufacturer's package inserts. Failure of the controls invalidates the test run. Any positive results stand, and specimens must be reported as confirmed positive. Negative or indeterminate results should be repeated. External controls should also be included as in screening tests with the same consequences in the event of control failures. Lot acceptance panels should also be used. Lot validation for EIA-based confirmatory tests is managed in the same way as for screening tests. In the case of blot-type assays, or IFA, lot validation involves preparation of panels for lot-to-lot comparisons that contain manufacturer's kit controls and external controls only.

IV. NUCLEIC ACID AMPLIFICATION TESTING

In 1999, nucleic acid amplification testing (NAT) ushered in a new era for screening of donated blood. Unlike the serological blood screening tests currently in use, NAT is a molecular technology used to detect nucleic acids rather than antibodies or antigens. Using NAT methods [e.g., PCR or transcription-mediated amplification (TMA)], nucleic acid sequences can be amplified in vitro up to 10^7-fold. By combining the process of nucleic acid amplification with the appropriate detection systems (e.g., liquid hybridization, biotinylated probes, chemiluminescence), high-sensitivity, high-specificity tests for viral infections have been created that are amenable to mass screening. Because amplification of the target sequences can be effected in vitro, NAT ostensibly increases the sensitivity of tests for viral markers, in contrast to current serological tests for antibodies or antigens. The latter are limited by the degree to which antibody production had been amplified in vivo and the amount of viremia in the blood.

The principal objective of the introduction of NAT was to implement assays that would effectively reduce the window period for certain TTD. Recent data suggest that this is feasible for HCV and HIV (26) (i.e., reduction from 70–80 days to 10–30 days for HCV and from 22 days to 11 days for HIV). It is also inferred that the implementation of NAT will reduce the residual risk for HCV from ~1.100,000 to 1/500,000-1/1 million and HIV from 1/677,000 to 1/1 million (27). Therefore, the focus has been on the implementation of tests for these two viruses. Thorough reviews of the implications of NAT with regard to improvements in blood safety and the ramifications for blood availability have been presented (27,28). NAT for HIV and HCV were the initial tests implemented for donor screening.

In this section, general procedures for NAT will be discussed. The application to blood donor screening will be addressed in the section on specific test performance. Specific guidelines for the design of these tests have been provided by FDA in a recent guidance (28).

Two of several available NAT technologies have recently been employed for blood screening on a massive scale. Both depend on the extraction of RNA from samples of plasma. The first is polymerase chain reaction (PCR) (29). In the application to blood screening, viral RNA is first isolated from EDTA-plasma samples. This is accomplished by concentration of viral particles by high-speed centrifugation of the plasma and lysis of virus particles with a chaotropic agent followed by alcohol precipitation. The assay then proceeds through several steps: (a) reverse transcription of the RNA to cDNA; (b) amplification of the target cDNA by thermocycling in the presence of target specific complementary primers, DNA polymerase, deoxynucleoside triphosphates (dNTP), and Mg^{2+}; (c) hybridization of the amplified products ("amplicons") to oligonucleotide probes specific to the targets; and (d) detection of the probe-bound amplified products. Positive and negative control samples and an internal method control are analyzed simultaneously. In addition, an external control with a known number of copies of RNA is analyzed to check the sensitivity of the method.

An alternative method, transcription-mediated amplification (TMA) is also currently being used for blood screening. In this assay format, viral genomic RNA is extracted from plasma samples. Target-specific oligonucleotides are hybridized to viral sequences, and the hybrids are captured on a magnetic microparticles. Reverse transcriptase is used to generate cDNA corresponding to the target sequences, and then RNA polymerase is used to generate multiple RNA amplicons from this DNA template. The reaction is carried out isothermally at 41.5°C. In the next steps, the amplicons are hybridized to acridinium ester-labeled probes that are detected by chemiluminescence (30,31). Controls similar to those used in the PCR assays are employed as well.

IV. SPECIFIC TESTING ALGORITHMS

The following sections contain detailed descriptions of test algorithms applied to specific TTD markers. Tables 3, 5, and 6 can be used to aid in tracking the disposition of both donors and products following positive or reactive test results. These tables reflect the intent of a variety of FDA memoranda and guidances. The administration of these policies and procedures for donor deferral, confidential unit exclusion, in-date product retrieval, and lookback may vary in the details from center to center.

A. HIV Testing (Antibodies to HIV-1 and HIV-2 and HIV-1 p24 Antigen)

Both FDA (32) and AABB standards (33) require that all units of blood intended for use in transfusion be screened for the presence of antibodies to HIV-1 and HIV-2. Additionally, AABB standards require, and FDA recommends, testing for the presence of HIV-1 p24 antigen. The EIA antibody test is typically performed as a so-called "combined" test in which HIV-1 and HIV-2 antibodies are detected simultaneously in an antibody capture assay. This combined test was introduced in the United States in 1992. The test in most widespread use employs recombinant HIV-1 *env* and *gag* and HIV-2 *env* proteins bound to the solid phase. Binding of anti-HIV antibodies is detected by incubation of the immobilized antigen anti-body complex with HIV-1 *env* and *gag* and HIV-2 *env* proteins conjugated to horseradish peroxidase. Color formation following incubation with substrates is proportional to the amount of HIV-specific antibody bound.

Confirmation of HIV-1/HIV-2 screening test results is accomplished using a combination of Western blot or IFA (34) and ELISA assays. Because the initial screening test was a combination test for HIV-1 and HIV-2, the confirmatory algorithm uses an approach that may lead to the discrimination between these two analytes.

The most commonly used algorithm employs an FDA-approved HIV-1 Western blot performed on donor samples repeatedly reactive in the HIV-1/HIV-2 combined EIA. The interpretations in the manufacturer's package inserts conform to recommendations made by the Centers for Disease Control (35). Valid test results for the HIV-1 Western Blot are:

> **POSITIVE**—The sample contains antibodies specific for HIV-1. The sample is positive for HIV-1 antibodies if any two of the following bands are present: p24, gp41, and/or gp120/160. Several studies (36,37) indicate that false-positive results are not uncommon. Therefore, counseling of donors with such patterns requires careful interpretation of the results as well as an evaluation of risk.

NEGATIVE—For HIV-1, NO bands of any kind may be visible on the test strips. If this is the case, the interpretation is that the sample does not contain detectable antibodies to HIV-1 but may contain antibodies to HIV-2. Supplemental testing using an FDA-approved test for HIV-2 is recommended.

INDETERMINATE—In this case, any combination of bands not consistent with the positive pattern results in an interpretation of indeterminate. No conclusive determination about the presence of antibodies to HIV-1 or HIV-2 antigens can be made on this sample. Supplemental testing using an FDA-approved test for HIV-2 is recommended.

Table 7 summarizes these band patterns and HIV-1 Western blot interpretative standards currently in use.

Alternatively, an FDA-approved HIV-1 IFA can be used in place of the Western blot in the initial step of the confirmatory algorithm. The valid results for this test are (34,38):

Table 7 Interpretation of HIV-1 Western Blots

	Gene product			
env	gag[a]	pol[a]	Nonviral bands[a]	Interpretation
gp41 gp120 gp160	p24	p31	(e.g. p70)	
None	None	None	None	Negative
Any	p24	Any	Any or none	
Any	p24	Any	Any or none	Positive
Any 2	None	Any or none	Any or none	
Any	Other	Pattern	Any or none	Indeterminate
None	None	None	Any	Indeterminate

[a]Additional reactivities for *gag* (e.g., p17, p26, and p55) and *pol* (e.g., p56 and p66) gene products may also be present in band patterns associated with a fully reactive specimen. However, these are not diagnostic bands defined in the CDC criteria nor in the manufacturers' package inserts. Nonviral bands (NVB) commonly appear in the p70 region of the Western blot strip but may also appear in other regions. NVBs do *not* appear to be associated with HIV-specific antigens. Nonetheless, they are recorded during the reading of the strips. Their appearance can affect the interpretation of the strip in only one case, namely that instance in which NVBs appear on a strip devoid of HIV diagnostic bands. Under current guidelines, this strip must be interpreted as "Indeterminate."

POSITIVE—Specific cytoplasmic fluorescence staining is observed in the HIV-1–infected cells and that there is a significant difference in the intensity of fluorescent staining and the pattern of staining between the infected and noninfected cells.

NEGATIVE—Both the uninfected and infected cells treated with test sample have an appearance similar to the uninfected and infected cells treated with the negative control serum and the uninfected cells treated with positive control serum.

INDETERMINATE—An interpretation of indeterminate pertains when: (a) there is fluorescent staining in both infected and uninfected cells; (b) one cannot distinguish differences in staining intensity between infected and uninfected cells; or (c) duplicates are discordant. The interpretation of indeterminate cannot lead to any conclusions about the presence or absence of antibodies to HIV-1.

Regardless of whether WB or IFA was used as the primary supplemental test, HIV-2 assays are performed on all samples with indeterminate or negative results. This step is introduced to address the possibility that an HIV-2–positive sample escaped detection in the HIV-1 confirmatory tests. In the case of the Western blot, there is extensive crossreactivity of antibodies with HIV-1 (p24) and HIV-2 (p26) *gag* proteins. It should be noted that in the United States only three HIV-2–positive blood donors have been identified since 1992 (39). An FDA-licensed EIA for antibodies to HIV-2 is used in this portion of the algorithm. The valid results are:

REPEATEDLY REACTIVE—The presence of antibodies to HIV-2 antigens is suspected. Additional supplemental tests (e.g., HIV-2 Western blot) are recommended.

NONREACTIVE—Antibodies to HIV-2 are not detectable in the sample.

Samples that are reactive in the HIV-2 EIA may be subjected to an HIV-2 Western blot. Currently these blots are available for research use only. Valid test results for this assay are:

POSITIVE—Antibodies to p26 (*gag*) and gp34 (*env* transmembrane) or gp105 (gp34 trimer) are present in the sample. It is likely, therefore, that the specimen is positive for HIV-2 antibodies.

NEGATIVE—The sample does not contain detectable antibodies to HIV-2.

INDETERMINATE—Any pattern of reactivity that does not produce a positive result. The results are inconclusive regarding the presence of HIV-2 antibodies.

The algorithm for final interpretation of the HIV-1/2 testing, based on the combined results of the Western blot or IFA and EIA tests, is presented in Table 8.

B. HIV-1 p24 Antigen

Screening for HIV-1 p24 antigen, required by AABB (33) and recommended by FDA (40), was implemented in the United States in March 1996 (41). The purpose of this test was to reduce the window period through the earlier detection of donors who were antigenemic but who had not yet produced anti-HIV antibodies. The test is an antigen capture assay in an EIA format. For the tests in common use, monoclonal antibodies to HIV-1 p24 antigen are coated onto a solid phase. Virus particles present in the test sample are lysed in a specific buffer. Binding of the HIV-1 p24 antigen released by this process is revealed in several steps following binding of antibody-enzyme conjugates and substrate. This test is a qualitative test for the presence of HIV-1 p24 antigen. The reactivity of test samples from specimens that also contain antibodies to HIV-1 p24 antigen may be significantly reduced as a result of the formation of antigen-antibody complexes. The qualitative tests approved for donor screening do not incorporate an antigen-antibody dissociation step.

Table 8 Final Interpretation of HIV-1/2 Test Results

HIV-1/2 EIA	HIV-1 WB or IFA	HIV-2 EIA	HIV-2 WB	Final interpretation
NR	N/A	N/A	N/A	Negative
RR	POS	N/A	N/A	HIV positive
RR	IND	RR	POS	HIV-2 positive[a]
	IND	RR	IND	Indeterminate
	IND	RR	NEG	Indeterminate
	IND	NR	N/A	Indeterminate
RR	NEG	RR	POS	HIV-2 positive
	NEG	RR	IND	Indeterminate
	NEG	RR	NEG	Negative on supplemental tests[b]
	NEG	NR	N/A	Negative on supplemental tests[c]

[a]In some cases it is not possible to differentiate between HIV-1 and HIV-2 using this algorithm because of extensive antibody cross-reactivity.
[b]Donor is *not* eligible for reentry.
[c]Donor *may be* eligible for reentry.

Samples repeatedly reactive in the screening test are confirmed using a neutralization test. In this case, one set of test specimens is preincubated with purified human anti-HIV globulins (neutralizing antibody), and a second set is incubated with control, nonneutralizing antibody. If the reactivity of the "neutralized sample" is at least 40% of the control, nonneutralized sample, the test sample is considered confirmed positive for HIV-1 p24 antigen. Valid test results for this test are:

> **POSITIVE**—the sample treated with the nonneutralizing antibody is reactive in the test, and, in the case of the sample treated with neutralizing antibody, the signal is reduced by greater than or equal to 40%. This result implies that in the absence of anti-HIV antibodies, or other signs of HIV infection, that the donor may be in a preseroconversion phase.
>
> **INDETERMINATE**—An indeterminate result may be obtained in two ways: (a) specimens are reactive in the screening test but neutralization is less than 40%, or (b) the neutralization test is invalid (e.g., the result of the sample treated with the nonneutralizing antibody is nonreactive). In both of these cases, the donor status is unclear. Retesting of the original or fresh specimens is recommended as is follow-up after 8 weeks, to determine whether seroconversion has occurred.

It should be noted that extensive follow-up of donors with positive HIV-1 p24 antigen neutralization results by RT-PCR and by monitoring over time revealed that the vast majority are false positive. The donors are routinely PCR negative and do not show evidence of HIV-1 seroconversion. All observations to date indicate that the prevalence of true positives (HIV-1 p24 antigen-positive, antibody-negative) is $<1/10^7$ donations (41).

C. Human T-Lymphotropic Virus Types I and II

Screening of U.S. blood donors for human T-lymphotrophic virus I (HTLV-I) was implemented in 1988. The original screening tests had package insert intended use claims for HTLV-I only. Nonetheless, HTLV-II antibodies were also detected in these tests as a consequence of cross-reactivity with HTLV-I antigens. The sensitivity of these tests for HTLV-II was limited. (It is likely that <50% of HTLV-II infections were detected.) In 1997, FDA recommended the implementation of donor screening tests that specifically detected HTLV-II (42). The tests in current use are combined tests for HTLV-I and II that contain viral *env* and *gag* antigens specific for HTLV-I and II bound to the solid phase. The sensitivity of these test for HTLV-II is markedly enhanced (43,44).

Until recently, most supplemental testing for HTLV-I/II was performed using investigational or research use only assays, typically Western blots. Early on, the difficulty with these Western blots was their relative insensitivity for HTLV *env* antibodies and, in some cases, the inability to clearly distinguish between HTLV-I/II. Radioimmunoprecipitation assays (RIPA) (45) or IFA tests (46) were also added to the repertoire of HTLV supplemental tests to overcome some of the sensitivity issues. The difficulty in performing tests like RIPA and IFA, quality control issues, and the lack of commercial success of some assays has limited the alternatives. There are currently no FDA-approved supplemental tests for HTLV. Since the implementation of the requirement for HTLV-II screening tests, there are no tests available for routine use that distinguish between HTLV-I and HTLV-II. This raises the complexity of donor notification and counseling.

One "investigational/research use only" Western blot is still in use, however. This Western blot strips contain HTLV-I viral lysate and a recombinant HTLV-I *env* protein (rp21e). The inclusion of this recombinant protein enhances the sensitivity for envelope antibodies. In some cases it is possible to discriminate between HTLV-I and HTLV-II based on band intensities of rp21e, p19, and p24 in these blots (43). For this test, the presence of nonviral bands on a strip that does not elicit diagnostic bands does not affect an interpretation of negative. Common nonviral bands are in the molecular weight ranges of 70, 51–55, and 43 kDa. These bands are likely to be related to HLA antigens.

The valid test results for this Western blot are:

POSITIVE—The sample contains, at a minimum, antibodies to p24 (*gag*) and gp46 or p21*env* (*env*). Some specimens may contain p19 (*gag*) and p21*env* only and no p24. These may be early seroconversion cases that should be verified by follow-up testing or by PCR.

NEGATIVE—No viral bands detected.

INDETERMINATE—Viral-specific bands are present but do not meet the criteria for positive. Up to 70% of repeatedly reactive specimens may elicit indeterminate test results.

Recent data suggest that many donors described as "positive" for HTLV using these algorithms may be false positive (47,48). Because of this, and because of the unavailability of licensed confirmatory tests, an algorithm was proposed in which a second FDA-licensed EIA test is used to confirm the presence of HTLV antibodies in a given specimen (49). This test algorithm is based on results that suggest that many specimens repeatedly reactive in one EIA may not be reactive in a second licensed test. Thus, only those specimens that are reactive in both tests are considered "positive" for HTLV. Although it is not an obligatory part of the algorithm, additional testing using the investigational or research use only Western blot is suggested for those samples positive in the two EIAs. This algorithm does *not* allow discrimination of HTLV-I and HTLV-II. Additional testing using research use only PCR tests may be valuable in this regard.

D. Hepatitis B Surface Antigen

The hepatitis B virus (HBV) tests employed in donor screening are not comprehensive and cannot necessarily be used to diagnose the status of infection (50). Screening for HBV consists of tests for hepatitis B surface antigen and antibodies to hepatitis B core antigen (see below). The donor screening algorithms do not include tests for antibodies to hepatitis B surface antigen (anti-HBsAg) or for hepatitis B e-antigen (HBeAg or anti-HBe). The current HBSAg assays are sensitive to ~0.1–0.2 ng/mL, corresponding to about 10^7–10^8 virus particles. Consequently, detection of both early phase acute infections as well as chronic carriers is possible with the conventional serological assays. The use of HBV NAT or more sensitive serological tests is currently the subject of intense discussion (27,28). Current antigen capture EIA/ELISA for HBsAg can be performed either in qualitative or quantitative modes, but the qualitative tests are used in blood screening. Monoclonal anti-HBsAg antibodies are typically used as the capture reagents. Binding of antigens is detected using antibody enzyme conjugates and a chromogenic substrate.

Confirmation of the presence of hepatitis B surface antigen in serum or plasma is performed using a neutralization test. In this instance, a specimen is confirmed positive if the reduction of a specific absorbance is at least 50% upon addition of neutralizing antibody and the nonneutralized control generates a signal greater than or equal to the cutoff of the assay. The valid test results are:

POSITIVE—The test is reactive for the sample incubated with the control, nonneutralizing antibody (S/CO ≥ 1) and neutralization is greater than or equal to 50%. High concentrations of antigen in a sample may lead to a "prozone" effect. Samples that produce absorbance values greater than the cut-off, but which are weakly neutralized (<50%), should be diluted and retested until a valid result is obtained.

NEGATIVE or NOT NEUTRALIZABLE—The test is nonreactive for the sample incubated with the control, nonneutralizing antibody (S/CO < 1). The neutralization can assume any value.

It should be noted that there are a significant number of samples weakly reactive in the EIA that are weakly neutralized in the confirmatory test but nonetheless are confirmed positive. These anti-HBc nonreactive and PCR-negative samples are likely to be false positives (50). Despite this finding, donors must be indefinitely deferred.

E. Antibodies to Hepatitis C Virus

Screening tests for hepatitis C virus (HCV) were introduced as single antigen EIA tests in 1990. Multiantigen tests were introduced in 1992 (HCV 2.0) and in 1996 (HCV 3.0). The difference in sensitivity between the HCV 3.0 and HCV 2.0 test is small but significant (51); nonetheless both tests are licensed by FDA and remain in common use. The HCV EIA tests are antibody capture assays based on recombinant proteins bound to the solid phase. These proteins represent various regions of the HCV genome. Peptides representing the core (c22-3), NS3 and NS4 (c200 or c33c/c100-3), and, in some cases, NS5 regions of the HCV genome are included in the test. Antibody binding is detected using enzyme-conjugated antibodies and the appropriate substrates.

HCV EIA reactivity is confirmed with a slot immunoblot assay (recombinant immunoblot assay, RIBA). In this assay, HCV recombinant and synthetic peptides representing several regions of the HCV genome are deposited on nitrocellulose strips. In the current version of this test (RIBA 3.0), the peptides included are c100 (p)/5-1-1(p) (NS-4), c33c (NS3), c22 (p) (core), and NS5. In addition to these HCV-specific peptides, two internal IgG controls and a control for the presence of antibodies to superoxide dismutase (SOD) are included on the strip. The latter is included because the recombinant peptides used in this test and in the EIA are expressed as fusion proteins with SOD. The SOD control is used to eliminate the possibility that antibody reactivity might be due to anti-SOD antibodies and not to HCV-specific antibodies. Detection of anti-HCV antibodies is revealed using an anti-human IgG-enzyme conjugate and a chromogenic enzyme substrate system (52). Bands are scored for presence of antibody and for binding intensity (0–4+). Failure of the high and/or low concentration IgG controls or the kit positive or negative controls invalidates the test run. Valid test results for the HCV RIBA 3.0 assay are:

> **POSITIVE**—At least 2 HCV bands having 1+ or greater reactivity are present.
>
> **NEGATIVE**—No HCV bands having 1+ or greater reactivity are present or the SOD band having 1+ or greater reactivity is present alone.
>
> **INDETERMINATE**—A single HCV band having a reactivity of 1+ or greater is present or the SOD band with at least 1+ reactivity is present in conjunction with any combination of HCV bands of 1+ reactivity or greater.

F. Antibodies to Hepatitis B Core Antigen

Screening for antibodies to hepatitis core antigen (anti-HBc) was implemented in the mid-1980s as a surrogate marker for non-A, non-B hepatitis and, somewhat more controversially, as a surrogate marker for HIV. The value of anti-HBc screening was reduced following the introduction of specific and sensitive tests for HCV (53). It nonetheless remains a required test. In some quarters, it is still considered valuable in reducing the risk of HBV infections both in the transplant setting and in some instances in which HBsAg tests are negative, but the risk of HBV transmission nonetheless exists (54).

The tests currently in use for donor screening detect both IgM and IgG and thus have limited diagnostic value in detecting current infections. Approximately 1% of donors tested with the current anti-HBc EIAs are repeatedly reactive. Most of these donors are negative for HBsAg, and most never develop HBV infections. In all likelihood these are false-positives. There are currently no confirmatory tests in routine use for anti-HBc. Thus a significant number of these donors are deferred, and in-date products must be retrieved (Tables 5,6), perhaps unnecessarily. It should be noted that the deferral status of donors is affected by the combination of HBsAg and anti-HBc test results.

G. Alanine Aminotransferase

Alanine aminotransferase (ALT) an enzyme involved in amino acid metabolism, is found in highest concentrations in the liver and kidney. The enzyme catalyzes the conversion of alanine and α-aminoglutaric acid to pyruvic acid and glutamic acid.

The appearance of the enzyme in the serum is often taken as an indicator of tissue damage. ALT testing of blood donors was initiated as a surrogate marker for non-A, non-B hepatitis in the mid- to late 1980s. Its value has been reduced significantly following the introduction of specific tests for HCV (55). Neither AABB nor FDA requires donor screening for ALT. However, ALT screening is a requirement for the shipment of recovered plasma for further manufacture in the countries of the European Union (56).

A variety of tests have been used to measure the ALT activity in serum. These generally take advantage of coupled enzyme reactions utilizing the products of the ALT reaction in subsequent enzymatic reactions, which, in turn, lead to the formation of chromogenic products that can be detected spectrophotometrically. Both kinetic and endpoint tests have been used. The cut-off for acceptable ALT activity is defined in terms of either studies on the distribution of ALT activities in the test population or by using the normal values defined by the manufacturer's package insert (57). The valid results for the ALT test are:

NORMAL—ALT activities, expressed in international units (IU), <60–120 IU.
ELEVATED—ALT activities are ≥60–120 IU.
SUPERELEVATED—ALT activities are ≥120 IU.

H. Syphilis Testing

Serological tests for syphilis (STS) were the first infectious disease marker tests applied to blood for transfusion. Syphilis testing was essentially the first test for transfusion-transmitted diseases. Currently the STS employed for screening blood donors include manual reagin tests [e.g., rapid plasma reagin tests (RPR)] or microhemagglutination (MHA) tests antibodies to *Treponema pallidum*. These tests appear in large measure to identify biological false positives—individuals who retain antibodies for many years following exposure and a much smaller subset of individuals who may have active or untreated syphilis (58). Transmission of syphilis by blood transfusion is an extremely rare occurrence. STS is still required for donor screening.

The RPR test detects the presence of "reagin" in the serum or plasma of infected individuals using a cardiolipin "antigen" bound to carbon particles. When the reagin is present, an agglutination reaction occurs, which can be scored visually. Test results are either reactive or nonreactive. Reactive results should be interpreted cautiously, should be confirmed in a quantitative test and should be reviewed in the context of health history. Confirmation using a quantitative test is typically not part of the screening algorithm, but rather a treponemal test, FTA-ABS (see below), is used.

Alternative tests, either EIA or MHA-TP tests, have been automated for mass screening and are more appropriately deployed in the context of donor screening than the reagin tests. The MHA-TP type tests, which are in wide use, analyze serum or plasma samples for the presence of antibodies to *T. pallidum*. The presence of antibody is detected in an agglutination reaction measured by light scattering or other photometric methods. The results are typically reported as reactive or nonreactive (59). In some cases, results may be reported as indeterminate. These are technically treated as reactive, and samples are reflexed to the confirmatory algorithm.

Reactive findings in the screening tests are confirmed using the fluorescent treponemal antibody absorption test (FTA-ABS). In this assay, test serum is treated with a sorbent derived from a Reiter strain culture of *T. pallidum* to absorb nonspecific antibodies. This absorbed sample is then incubated with *T. pallidum* fixed to microscope slides. If the sample contains antibody, it will bind to the fixed cells. Specific antibody binding is detected by fluorescence microscopy following incubation with FITC-conjugated anti-human antibody. Test results are compare to positive and negative control sera. Valid results are reactive or nonreactive based on staining intensity. Because the false-positive rate for blood donor samples is significant (60–62), additional testing, using RPR or other assays, may be employed for counseling purposes. The composite of interpretations of syphilis results can be found in Table 9.

I. Nucleic Acid Amplification Testing

U.S. blood centers embarked on nucleic acid amplification testing (NAT) for HCV and HIV in the spring of 1999. Testing is currently being performed under Investigational New Drug (IND) applications. All allogeneic whole blood, directed, and apheresis donors are being tested. The TMA-based multiplex assays and a PCR-based assay are being evaluated in the INDs. The first objective of the IND is to assess the operational aspects of NAT, evaluate test performance in a mass screening setting, and assess the impact of NAT on blood availability. During this phase of the study (Phase 1), there was no requirement to release blood for transfusion based on NAT results. In Phase 2 of the study, it is expected that there will be a requirement for the release of blood based on NAT results. Most importantly, data will be collected throughout to assess the efficacy of NAT in reducing the window period.

NAT is currently being conducted in pools of 16–24 samples ("primary pool"). Testing is being conducted in this manner since, at this writing, the technology for single unit testing is not available. Sample pools are constructed by robotic transfer of sample aliquots to tubes in which the extraction of RNA is carried out. Amplification and detection of the target sequences then follow

Table 9 Interpretation of Syphilis Confirmatory Test Results

Screening test result	FTA-ABS result	RPR result	Interpretation
Nonreactive	N/A	N/A	Negative
Repeatedly reactive	Nonreactive	Nonreactive	Negative, false-positive screen
Repeatedly reactive	Reactive	Reactive	Positive syphilis serology, suggests current infection
Repeatedly reactive	Nonreactive	Reactive	Negative, false-positive screen
Repeatedly reactive	Reactive	Nonreactive	Positive syphilis serology, suggests past infection

standard protocols in manual or semi-automated systems. FDA has defined requirements for the sensitivity of the tests in sample pool (~100 copies/mL in the pool, at a 95% detection rate) as well as in individual samples (5000 copies/mL, at a 95% detection rate) (28). These levels conform to those proposed by the European Union (63).

The NAT algorithms are dependent upon the testing format used. In each case, however, positive primary pools must be resolved to identify the implicated samples and donors. For the PCR-based assay in current use, primary pools of 24 samples are currently being tested. After the RNA extraction step, amplification and detection are carried out independently for HCV RNA and HIV RNA. If the pool is negative for HCV or HIV, the units represented in that pool are considered negative. If the pool is positive for HCV or HIV or both, four mini-pools ("secondary pools") containing six samples each are created and tested using the same methodology. Units represented in negative secondary pools are reported as negative. If a positive secondary pool is detected, the six samples contained therein are tested individually in the third stage of pool resolution. Negative individual samples are exonerated, while donors associated with positive samples are deferred, units are discarded, and the donors invited to participate in follow-up studies that test for seroconversion. This algorithm applies equally to HCV and HIV tests.

The TMA-based assays are multiplex tests in which HCV and HIV RNA are assessed simultaneously. In addition, the current test configuration permits a more direct resolution of positive primary pools. Primary pools of 16 samples each are tested. Units represented in a negative pool are considered negative for both HCV and HIV RNA. Samples in a positive pools are tested individually. Units associated with negative results on the individual samples are exonerated for both HCV and HIV RNA. Positive samples are considered NAT positive and are reflexed to discriminatory TMA assays tests that determine whether the reactivity was due to HCV, HIV, or both. Donor deferral, unit discard and follow-up studies are also performed in the INDs employing the TMA-based test. Both PCR and TMA tests can give rise to inconclusive results. This is the case, for example, when primary or secondary pools are positive, but the result cannot be confirmed in tests on the individual samples. This is also true in the case of positive multiplexed TMA tests in which the discriminatory tests do not reveal a definitive result.

Preliminary data suggest that the sensitivity and specificity of the PCR and TMA tests are comparable, but that there may be some differences in test performance characteristics (FDA Workshop on Implementation of NAT, December 14, 1999). The algorithms for disposition of products and donors based on NAT results are presented in Table 10.

Table 10 Nucleic Acid Amplification Testing for HCV and HIV RNA

1. Possible Results

NAT HCV or HIV Result	Interpretation	Suitable for transfusion
PCR Assay[a]		
NEG	Negative	Yes
POS	Positive	No
Pos Pool/Indiv. Neg[b]	Inconclusive	No
Pos Pool/QNS[c]	Inconclusive	No
TMA Assay[d]		
NEG	Negative	Yes
POS	Positive	No
HIV POS	Positive for HIV-1 RNA	No
HCV POS	Positive for HCV RNA	No
NAT POS	Positive—no discrimination between HIV and HCV	No

[a]Specimens are tested in primary pools of 24 plasma samples. If the primary pool is negative, all 24 samples are reported negative. If the primary pool is positive, specimens are retested in 4 pools of 6 samples each. If a positive pool(s) is (are) identified, specimens are retested as individual samples. The result reported is the final result. Hold implies that test results during the pool resolution were inconclusive. QNS implies that the pool resolution could not be completed.
[b]This result reflects a positive test on the primary pool, but negative results in testing of individual samples in the pool.
[c]This result occurs when the pool testing algorithm cannot be completed because of technical or other reasons.
[d]Specimens are tested in primary pools of 16 plasma samples. If the primary pool is negative, all 16 samples are reported negative. If the primary pool is positive, all 16 specimens are retested individually. If one or more specimens are positive, they are subjected to discriminatory TMA assays to distinguish between HIV and HCV. All negative samples are released. The result reported is the final result following discriminatory testing. In those cases where the discriminatory assay fails, the result is reported as positive.

2. Disposition of Blood Products According to Test Results

Result interpretation	Interdict shipment	Product label	Product disposition	
			RBC/PLT	Plasma
Negative	No	For transfusion	Inventory	Inventory
Positive	Yes	Biohazard	Discard	Study[a]
Inconclusive	Yes	Biohazard	Discard	Study[a]
QNS	Yes	Biohazard	Discard	Discard

[a]Specimens in this category are submitted for further analysis as part of the IND studies.

3. Management of Donor Deferral Entries

NAT result for	Deferral type	Donor notification	Recipient lookback
HCV			
Negative	None	None	No
Positive	1 yr unless seroconverts to HCV antibody POS	In person	Yes
Pos pool/Indiv neg	Surveillance	In person	No
Pos pool/QNS	1 yr or until retest negative	In person	No
HIV			
Negative	None	None	No
Positive	6 mo unless seroconverts to HIV antibody POS	In person	Yes
Pos pool/Indiv. neg	Surveillance	In person	No
Pos. pool/QNS	6 mo or until retest negative	In person	No

Note: In those cases where the TMA discriminatory assay is inconclusive, the donors are managed as if the result were positive.

REFERENCES

1. Busch M, Chamberland M, Epstein J, et al. Vox Sang 1999; 77:67–76.
2. Eastlund T. Monetary blood donation incentives and the risk of transfusion transmitted diseases. Transfusion 1998; 38:874–882.
3. Alter HJ, Holland PV, Purcell RH, et al. Post-transfusion hepatitis after exclusion of commercial hepatitis B antigen positive donors. Ann Int Med 1972; 77:691–699.
4. U.S. Food and Drug Administration. Guidance for Industry. Quality assurance in blood establishments. Rockville, MD: CBER Office of Communication, Training and Manufacturer's Assistance, 1995.
5. Giles RE, Perry KR, Parry JV. Simple rapid test devices for anti-HIV screening: Do they come up to the mark? J Med Virol 1999; 59:104–109.
6. Mvere D, Constantine M, et al. Rapid and simple hepatitis assays: encouraging results from a blood donor population in Zimbabwe. Bull WHO 1996; 74:19–24.
7. Constantine NT, Callahan JD, Watts DM. Retroviral Testing: Essentials for Quality Control and Laboratory Diagnosis. Boca Raton, FL: CRC Press, 1992.
8a. Linden JV, Wethers J, Dressler KP. Controversies in Y medicine: use of external controls in transmissible disease testing: pro. Transfusion 1994; 34:550–551.
8b. Epstein JS. Controversies in transfusion medicine: use of external controls in transmissible disease testing: con. Transfusion 1994; 34:552–553.
9. Code of Federal Regulations, 42CFR Part 493. Washington, DC: U.S. Government Printing Office, 2000.
10. U.S. Food and Drug Administration. Draft Guidance for Industry: revised recommendations for the invalidation of test results when using licensed and 510(k) cleared

blood borne pathogen assays to test donors. Rockville, MD: CBER Office of Communication, Training and Manufacturer's Assistance, 1999.

11. Green GA 4th, Carey RN, Westgard JO, et al. Quality control for qualitative assays: quantitative QC procedure designed to assure analytical quality required for an ELISA of hepatitis B surface antigen. Clin Chem 1997; 43:1618–1621.

12. Schreiber GB, Busch MP, Kleinman SH, Korelitz JJ. The risk of transfusion-transmitted viral infections. The Retrovirus Epidemiology Donor Study. N Engl J Med 1996; 334:1685–1690.

13. Busch MP, Lee LL, Satten GA, et al. Time course of detection of viral and serologic markers preceding human immunodeficiency virus type 1 seroconversion: implications for screening of blood and tissue donors, Transfusion 1995; 35:91–97.

14. Kleinman S, Busch MP, Korelitz JJ, Schreiber GB. The incidence/window period model and its use to assess the risk of transfusion-transmitted human immunodeficiency virus and hepatitis C virus infection. Transfus Med Rev 1997; 11:155–172.

15. Vrielink H, Reesink HW, van den Burg PJ, et al. Performance of three generations of anti-hepatitis C virus enzyme-linked immunosorbent assays in donors and patients. Transfusion 1997; 37:845–849.

16. Lee JH, Roth WK, Zeuzem S. Evaluation and comparison of different hepatitis C virus genotyping and serotyping assays. J Hepatol 1997; 26:1001–1009.

17. Cheingsong-Popov R, Osmanov S, Pau CP, et al. Serotyping of HIV type 1 infections: definition, relationship to viral genetic subtypes, and assay evaluation. UNAIDS Network for HIV-1 Isolation and Characterization. AIDS Res Hum Retroviruses 1998; 14:311–318.

18. Schable C, Zekeng L, Pau CP, et al. Sensitivity of United States HIV antibody tests for detection of HIV-1 group O infections. Lancet 1994; 344:1333–1334.

19. Jongerius JM, Webster M, Cuypers HT, et al. New hepatitis B virus mutant form in a blood donor that is undetectable in several hepatitis B surface antigen screening assays. Transfusion 1998, 38:56–59.

20. Zaaijer HL, van Rixel T, van Exel-Oehlers P, et al. New anti-human immunodeficiency virus immunoblot assays resolve nonspecific western blot results. Transfusion 1997; 37:193–198.

21. Kleinman SH, Busch MP, Stramer SL, Watanabe K. Use of HIV-1/HIV-2 recombinant immunoblot assay (RIBA) to resolve infection status of donors with possible false positive HIV Western blot (WB) (abstract). Transfusion 1997; 37(suppl):47S.

22. Vrielink H, Zaaijer HL, van der Poel CL, et al. New strip immunoblot confirmation of HTLV-I/II infection. Vox Sang 1996; 70:114–116.

23. Kleinman S, Busch M, Rawal B, Glynn S. Evaluation of HBsAg neutralization test positive (Neut POS) donors with negative (NEG) anti-HBc (abstract). Transfusion 1998; 38(suppl):92S.

24. Stramer SL, Aberle-Grasse J, Bordsky JP, et al. US blood donor screening with p24 antigen (Ag): one year experience (abstr). Transfusion 1997; 37 (suppl):1S.

25. Strauss D, Valinsky JE, Kessler D, et al. Specificity of HIV-1 p24 antigen neutralization (abstract). Transfusion 1996; 36(suppl):38S.

26. Murthy KK, Henrard DR, Eichberg JW, et al. Redefining the HIV-infectious window period in the chimpanzee model: evidence to suggest that viral nucleic acid testing can prevent blood-borne transmission. Transfusion 1999; 39:688–693.

27. Busch MP, Kleinman SH, Jackson B, et al. Committee report. Nucleic acid amplification testing of blood donors for transfusion-transmitted infectious diseases: report of the Interorganizational Task Force on Nucleic Acid Amplification Testing of Blood Donors. Transfusion 2000; 40:143–145.

28. U.S. Food and Drug Administration. Guidance for Industry: in the manufacture and clinical evaluation of in vitro tests to detect nucleic acid sequences of human immunodeficiency viruses types 1 and 2. Rockville, MD: CBER Office of Communication, Training and Manufacturer's Assistance, 1999.

29. Tilston P, Morris DJ, Klapper PE, Corbitt G. Commercial assay for hepatitis C virus RNA. Lancet 1994; 344:201–202.

30. MacDonough SH, Giachetti C, Yang Y, et al. High throughput assay for the simultaneous or separate detection of human immunodeficiency virus-1 (HIV-1) and hepatitis type C virus (HCV). Infusionther Transfusionmed 1998; 25:164–9.

31. Myers TW, Gelfand DH. Reverse transcription and DNA amplification by a Thermus termophilus DNA polymerase. Biochemistry 1994; 30:7661–7666.

32. Code of Federal Regulations, Title 21 CFR Part 610. §610.45. Washington, DC: U.S. Government Printing Office.

33. Menitove J, ed. Standards for Blood Banks and Transfusion Services. 19th ed. Bethesda, MD: American Association of Blood Banks, 1999.

34. Food and Drug Administration. Memorandum: use of Fluorognost HIV-1 immunofluorescent assay (IFA). Rockville, MD: CBER Office of Communication, Training and Manufacturer's Assistance, 1992.

35. Centers for Disease Control. Interpretive criteria used to report Western blot results for HIV-1 antibody testing, MMWR 1991; 40:692–695.

36. Kleinman S, et al. False-positive HIV-1 test results in a low risk screening setting of voluntary blood donation. Retrovirus Epidemiol Donor Study, JAMA 1998; 280:1080–1085.

37. Sayre KR, Dodd RY, Tegtmeier G, et al. False-positive human immunodeficiency virus type 1 western blot tests in non-infected blood donors. Transfusion 1996; 36:45–52.

38. Human Immunodeficiency Virus Type 1 (HIV-1) Fluorognost HIV-1 IFA. Manufacturer's package insert. Vienna, Austria: Waldheim Pharmazeutika, Ges.m.b.H, 1992.

39. Centers for Disease Control and Prevention. Update: HIV-2 infections among blood and plasma donors—United States. JAMA 1995; 274:1007–1008.

40. U.S. Food and Drug Administration. Memorandum: recommendations for donor screening with a licensed test for HIV-1 antigen. Rockville, MD: CBER Office of Communication, Training, and Manufacturer's Assistance, 1995.

41. Stramer S, Aberle-Grasse J, Bordsky J, et al. United States blood donor screening with p24 antigen: (one year experience) (abstract). Transfusion 1997; 37(suppl):1S.

42. Food and Drug Administration. Guidance for industry: donor screening for antibodies to HTLV-II. Rockville, MD: CBER Office of Communication, Training and Manufacturer's Assistance, 1997.

43. Vrielink J, Reesink HW, Zaaijer JL, et al. Sensitivity and specificity of four assays to detect human T-lymphotropic virus type I or type I/II antibodies. Transfusion 1996; 36:344–346.

44. Liu H, Sha M, Stramer S, et al. Sensitivity and specificity of human T-lymphotropic virus (HTLV) types I and II polymerase chain reaction and several serologic assays in screening a population with a high prevalence of HTLV-II. Transfusion 1999; 39:1185–1193.

45. Anderson DW, Epstein JS, Lee TH, et al. Serological confirmation of human T-lymphotrophic virus Type I infections in healthy blood and plasma donors. Blood 1989; 74:2585–2591.

46. Gallo D, Penning LM, Hanson CV. Detection and differentiation of antibodies to human T-cell lymphotropic virus types I and II by the immunofluorescence method. J Clin Micro 1991; 29:2345–2347.

47. Busch MP, Kleinman SH, Stramer SL. False positive HTLV-I/II supplemental test results in blood donors (abstr). Transfusion 1999; 39:105S.

48. Stramer SL, Layug L, Trenbeath J, et al. Use of a second EIA in an HTLV-1/HTLV-2 algorithm (abstr). Transfusion 1998; 38(suppl):81S.

49. American Association of Blood Banks. Association bulletin #99-9. Dual enzyme immuno assay (EIA) approach for deferral and notification of anti-HTLV-I/II EIA reactive donors. Bethesda, MD: American Association of Blood Banks, 1999.

50. Strauss D, Valinsky JE, Kessler D, Bianco C. Decreased specificity of HBsAg confirmation as a result of decreased specificity of the screening test (abstract). Transfusion 1994; 34(suppl):34S.

51. Busch MP, Tobler LH, Stramer S, et al. Yield of HCV EIA 3.0 vs EIA 2.0 in screening of US blood donors (abstr). Transfusion 1997; 37(suppl):111S.

52. Skidmore S. Recombinant immunoblot assay for hepatitis C antibody. Lancet 1990; 335:1346.

53. Schifman RB, Rivers SL, Sampliner RE, Kramer JE. Significance of isolated hepatitis B core antibody in blood donors. Arch Int Med 1993; 153:2261–2266.

54. Lok A. Hepatitis B infection: pathogenesis and management. J Hepatol 2000; 32(suppl):89–97.

55. Cable R, Badon S, Pray C, Popovsky MA. Limited utility of alanine aminotransferase screening of hepatitis C antibody screened blood donors. Transfusion 1997; 37:206–210.

56. Committee for Proprietary Medicinal Products. Plasma derived medicinal products: position paper on ALT testing, CPMP/BWP/385/99, 1999.

57. American Association of Blood Banks. Association bulletin #95-7. FDA notification requirement: ALT procedure change, change to the circular of information. Bethesda, MD: American Association of Blood Banks, 1995.

58. Orton S, Liu H, Cable R, et al. Prevalence of circulating *T. pallicum* in STS+/F TA-Abs+ blood donors (abstr). Transfusion 1999; 39(suppl):2S.

59. Larsen SA, Hunter EF, Kraus SJ. A manual of tests for syphilis. Washington, DC: American Public Health Association, 1990.

60. Win N, Islam SI, Peterkin MA, Walker ID. Positive direct antiglobulin test due to antiphospholipid antibodies in normal healthy blood donors. Vox Sang 1997; 72:182–184.

61. Fosdick M, Winslow D, Larsen S. Clinical significance of MHATP as a confirmatory test for the Olympus PK™-TP system (abstr). Transfusion 1994; 34(suppl):49S.

62. Strauss D, Del Valle C, Valinsky JE, et al. Donor screening for syphilis using the Olympus PK-TP assay—implications for donor notification and re-entry. Transfusion 1993; 33(suppl):38S.

63. Committee for Proprietary Medicinal Products. The introduction of nucleic acid amplification technology (NAT) for detection of hepatitis C virus RNA in plasma pools, addendum CPMP/BWP/390/97 to CP/BWP/269/95, 1998.

10
Bacterial Contamination

Laura L. Spinelli and Mark E. Brecher
University of North Carolina, Chapel Hill, North Carolina

Transfusion-transmitted bacterial infection remains a persistent complication of transfusion. Currently the aggregate risk of contracting a viral infection [hepatitis B virus (HBV), hepatitis C virus (HCV), human immunodeficiency virus types 1 and 2 (HIV-1/2), of human T-cell lymphotrophic virus types I and II (HTLV-I/II)] is estimated at 1 in 34,000 (1), while the incidence of platelet bacterial contamination is approximately 1 in 1000 and is thought to cause severe morbidity or death in as many as 150 people per year in the United States (2). While much attention has been focused by the public and the media on transfusion-transmitted disease (particularly HIV), increasing awareness and improved testing and direct questioning of donors have significantly decreased the transmission of hepatitis, retroviruses, and other viruses. Bacterial contamination of blood products, however, has been largely overlooked and is now thought to be the major cause of mortality from transfusion-transmitted disease. The risk of receiving a bacterially contaminated platelet may be 50- to 250-fold higher than the risk of transfusion-related infection per unit associated with HIV-1, HBV, and HTLV-I/II (2).

I. TRANSFUSION-TRANSMITTED BACTERIAL INFECTION OF PLATELETS

Sepsis due to transfusion of bacterially contaminated platelets is the most common transfusion-transmitted disease, principally because of the fact that platelets are stored for up to 5 days at 20–24°C (3). In the years 1986–1991 there was a total of 182 transfusion-related deaths reported to the U.S. Food and Drug Administration, (FDA) 29 of which were due to bacterially contaminated blood products. Some 21 (72%) of these deaths were associated with the transfusion of bacterially contaminated platelets (2). Five fatalities were reported in both 1990 and 1991. Five to six million random platelet concentrates and single donor apheresis are transfused per year in the United States (4–6). This would mean that there is at least a one in a million chance of death due to sepsis per unit transfused. However, it is widely suspected that platelet bacterial sepsis is frequently unrecognized and thus underreported.

The contamination rate for platelets is approximately 1 in 1000 per individual unit (7,8). Single unit contamination is similar for both platelet concentrates made from whole blood and single-donor apheresis concentrates, but the ultimate risk of sepsis is likely to be 6–10 times greater with pooled random units, as there is a 6- to 10-fold increased donor exposure (7,9). It has been estimated that as many as 150 people per year in the United States suffer severe morbidity and or mortality as a consequence of a platelet transfusion (2).

In a recent study of symptomatic bacteremia following platelet transfusion in 161 bone marrow transplant recipients in Hong Kong, it was found that 1 in 2000 units of platelet concentrates were bacterially contaminated. This translated to 1 in 350 pooled platelets being contaminated. Of those patients who were febrile (elevation of temperature of $\geq 1°C$) following platelet transfusion, 1 in 4 (27%) were found to have received a bacterially contaminated unit. Of those found to have a $\geq 2°C$ rise in temperature following a platelet transfusion, 50% were found to have received a bacterially contaminated unit (10). In this multiply transfused patient population, the chance of receiving a bacterially contaminated platelet was 1 in 16. Of the 10 patients who are known to have received a bacterially contaminated unit, 4 suffered from septic shock.

It is felt that the incidence of sepsis due to red cell transfusions has decreased over the last 30 years (11), most likely due to the introduction of disposable collection sets and bags in the 1960s. Yet, the frequency of bacterial sepsis due to platelet transfusion has increased, largely due to increasing use of this component and prolonged storage time at 20-24°C.

A. Organisms and Source

Skin commensals such as *Staphylococcus epidermidis* and *Bacillus cereus* are the organisms most often implicated in platelet bacterial contamination (12). These organisms typically do not grow at 0–6°C but survive and multiply readily at 20–24°C, the storage temperature of platelets. In descending order, the organisms most commonly implicated in fatalities (Table 1) are *Staphylococcus aureus*, *Klebsiella pneumoniae*, *Serratia marcescens*, and *S. epidermidis* (13). Other isolated organisms include *Salmonella*, *Escherichia coli*, *Pseudomonas aeruginosa*, and *B. cereus* (13–19). Fatalities due to platelet contamination tend to be equally divided between gram-positive and gram-negative organisms (13). Potential sources of contaminant organisms include contamination of the collec-

Table 1 Reported Fatalities Due to Platelet Sepsis in the United States, 1989–1991

Year	No.	Associated bacteria	Gram stain result
1987	4	*Klebsiella oxytoca*	Negative
		Serratia marcescens	Negative
		Klebsiella pneumoniae	Negative
		Staphylococcus epidermidis	Positive
1988	2	*Alpha-hemolytic streptococci*	Positive
		Serratia marcescens	Negative
1989	3	*Salmonella cholera Livingston*	Negative
		Staphylococcus warneri	Positive
		Enterobacter aerogens	Negative
1990	5	*Staphylococcus aureus* (4)	Positive
		Streptococcus mitis	Positive
1991	5	*Pseudomonas aeruginosa*	Negative
		Staphylococcus aureus (2)	Positive
		Escherichia coli	Negative
		Klebsiella pneumoniae	Negative

tion bag, tubing, or anticoagulant and donor-related factors such as transient bacteremia. However, contamination of platelets is thought to occur principally during phlebotomy because of inadequate sterilization and or skin core removal by the collection needle. Despite excellent technique, one cannot assure a sterile venipuncture, because organisms harbored in sebaceous glands and hair follicles cannot be completely disinfected. Scarring or dimpling of the venipuncture site due to prior donations has also been recognized as a risk factor for aseptic venipuncture, as these areas frequently contain recessed pits that are difficult to adequately sterilize (20,21). One percent iodine solution is the only topical cleanser that has been shown to be 100% effective in providing donor skin sterility. Donors who are allergic to iodine are often cleansed with some type of acetone alcohol solution, which has been shown to effect only a 50% reduction in skin microbials (22). It would seem prudent not to prepare platelets from such donors.

B. Clinical Presentation

The clinical sequelae of the transfusion of bacterially contaminated platelets may range from asymptomatic to mild fever (which may be indistinguishable from a nonhemolytic transfusion reaction) to acute sepsis, hypotension, and death. The presentation is much more varied and often less severe than that of patients infected by transfusion of bacterially contaminated red cells (9). In fact, it is felt that sepsis due to transfusion of contaminated platelets is vastly underrecognized and underreported. Patients in need of platelet transfusion are often leukopenic, and fever can be readily attributed to other infectious causes (36). Much of the underreporting may occur because the organisms most frequently found in platelet contamination are skin commensals that are the same organisms implicated in catheter sepsis. Therefore, sepsis, which in these patients is often attributed to catheters, may very well have its origin in platelets transfused several hours before. The overall mortality rate of platelet-associated sepsis reported in the literature is 26% (12). Any patient who develops fever within 6 hours of platelet infusion should be started on empiric broad-spectrum antibiotics (10,23).

II. TRANSFUSION-TRANSMITTED BACTERIAL INFECTION OF RED CELLS

Of the 29 fatalities due to transfusion of bacterially contaminated blood products reported to the FDA from 1986 to 1991, 8 (28%) were associated with transfusion of red cells (2). Considerable attention has been paid to red cell–associated sepsis because of the unusual organisms and the high mortality associated with these episodes. Yet, data from the Centers for Disease Control and Prevention (CDC) for 1987–1994 suggest a contamination rate of less than one per million red cell units (22 cases per 28 million units of red cells) (2).

A. Organisms and Source

The most commonly implicated organism in bacterial contamination of red cells is *Yersinia enterocolitica*, usually serotype 0:3 (24–26). Seven of the eight fatalities due to sepsis secondary to transfusion of contaminated red cells reported to the FDA in the years 1986–1991 were caused by *Y. enterocolitica* (2). This organism grows readily in the presence of dextrose and iron at 4°C, the temperature at which red cells are stored. Contamination is attributed to transient bacteremia in asymptomatic infected donors. On retrospective analysis, up to 50% of donors implicated in contamination of products recalled gastrointestinal symptoms in the weeks prior to and surrounding donation (23,27–30). White cells of infected persons contain viable organisms that multiply during storage. These cells lose membrane integrity and disintegrate, releasing bacteria into the stored units (31,32). Consequently, contamination is directly related to storage time, with a significantly higher incidence as units age more than 25 days (24). In fact, all seven cases of *Yersinia* contamination reported to the CDC in the years between

1986 and 1991 were older than 25 days (2). However, cases of *Yersinia* red cell sepsis have been reported following as little as 7–14 days of storage (29,33).

Serratia marcescens has been implicated in the contamination of plastic blood containers manufactured in a plant in Belgium, which affected several Danish and Swedish transfusion centers. The outbreak was thought to involve the manufacturing process and resulted in the closing of a blood bag manufacturing plant (34,35). *Serratia liquefaciens* has been recently recognized as both a red cell and a platelet contaminant in the United States (L. Bland, personal communication). Other gram-negative organisms that have been repeatedly associated with red cell contamination are *Pseudomonas* and *Enterobacter* spp. (12,24,36,37).

B. Infection of Autologous Red Cell Units

Although autologous blood is generally considered a "safer" blood product, to date there have been at least five cases of bacterial contamination of autologous red cell units, four due to *Y. enterocolitica* and one due to *S. liquefaciens* (38–42; S. Cookson, personal communication). Fortunately, all recipients survived. Upon retrospective questioning, all patients infected by *Yersinia* recalled gastrointestinal symptoms in days prior to donation. In the case of *Serratia* contamination, the patient's infected toe ulcer was presumed to be the source.

C. Clinical Presentation

Symptoms associated with transfusion of contaminated red cells are more severe and rapid in onset than those caused by an infected platelet transfusion. Patients frequently develop high fever (temperatures as high as 109°F have been observed) and chills during or immediately following transfusion (42,43). From 1987 to February 1996, 20 recipients of *Yersinia*-infected red cells in 14 states were reported to the CDC. Twelve of the 20 recipients died in 37 days or less following transfusion. The median time to death was 25 hours! Of the 7 who developed disseminated intravascular coagulation (DIC), 6 died. Signs, symptoms, and complications are summarized in Table 2 (44).

In an anesthetized patient, hypotension, oozing, oliguria/anuria, and fever should alert the anesthesiologist to the problem. Affected recipients may also experience nausea, vomiting, and diarrhea. In severe instances, DIC, vascular collapse, and death can rapidly ensue. If a septic transfusion reaction is suspected, the transfusion should be discontinued immediately and not restarted. The minimum number of organisms necessary to cause clinical symptoms is not known, but concentrations of 10^8 CFU/mL or greater have been associated with severe reactions and death (11).

Table 2 Morbidity and Mortality Associated with *Yersinia*
enterocolitica–Contaminated Red Blood Cells

Signs, symptoms, and mortality	Number	Percentage
Chills	16	80
Fever	14	70
Hypotension	13	65
DIC	7	35
Death	12	60

Source: Ref. 60.

III. TRANSFUSION-TRANSMITTED BACTERIAL INFECTION OF PLASMA AND CRYOPRECIPITATE

Cell-free products such as plasma and cryoprecipitate are stored in the frozen state and thus are rarely associated with contamination. However, in some cases *Pseudomonas cepacia* and *P. aeruginosa* have been cultured from cryoprecipitate and plasma thawed in contaminated water baths (45,46).

IV. TRANSFUSION-TRANSMITTED BACTERIAL INFECTION OF PLASMA PROTEIN CONCENTRATES

Human serum albumin is a good culture medium and preserves viability. The heating step (60°C for 10 hours) in the manufacturing of albumin is performed to inactivate certain viruses, not to assure bacterial sterility (47). Achieving bacterial sterility would require autoclaving; albumin would denature at these extreme temperatures. On occasion, specific lots of albumin product have been found to be contaminated with bacteria, typically *Pseudomonas* species. These lots have produced transient bacteremias, hypotension, and febrile reactions in recipients (48). Most recently, two patients in two different hospitals developed *Enterobacter cloacae* septicemia after receiving albumin (47,49,50). This resulted in a worldwide recall of 5, 20, and 25% albumin, Monoclate-P (antihemophilic factor), and plasma protein fraction. It is suspected that cracks in the seal may have been responsible for the contamination.

A. Detection

There is no universally accepted test, method, or device used in the detection of bacterially contaminated blood product. Ideally, the test must be sensitive (preferably to 10^4–10^5 CFU/ml), specific, inexpensive, simple to use, capable of detecting the commonly implicated organisms, adaptable for new bacterial threats, and usable in a hospital environment. Approaches currently under investigation are summarized below.

1. Bacterial Staining

Stain of a smear immediately prior to transfusion is sensitive to approximately 10^6 CFU/mL for gram-positive and 10^8 CFU/mL for gram-negative organisms (51,52). Gram stain is most often employed, although Wright's stain and acridine orange have also been recommended (53,54). This test lacks the necessary sensitivity to detect all clinically significant bacterial contamination and has been associated with both high false-positive and false-negative rates (53).

Acridine orange stains have a sensitivity of 10^4 CFU/mL, but require a fluorescent microscope for visualization (55,56). While there is an increased rate of detection, the cost and time required have precluded any further interest in this approach.

2. Bacterial Culture

Because only 0.1–1 mL of product is typically cultured on an agar plate, the sensitivity of this method is limited. This may be overcome in part by the use of automated blood culture systems (57,58). This procedure generally requires greater than 24 hours for the culture to grow and often is fraught with false positives resulting from inoculation/culture technique.

3. Endotoxin Assays

The *Limulus* amebocyte lysate (LAL) assay is the most sensitive, detecting 10^4 mg of endotoxin per 0.1 mL of plasma, or 10^4 CFU/mL (59). However, this test is not widely available and is of limited value; gram-positive bacteria are not detected by this method because they do not contain endotoxin in their cell walls.

4. Bacterial Ribosomal Assays

A technique that is sensitive to 10^5 CFU/mL is the use of rRNA (ribosomal RNA) chemiluminescence linked probes. This technique utilizes a single-stranded (DNA) probe complementary to a highly conserved bacterial rRNA found in all bacterial species. Requiring only 2–3 hours to perform, this method has detected 100–1000 CFU/mL of *S. aureus* and the majority of *B. cereus*, *P. aeruginosa*, *S. aureus*, and *S. epidermidis* discontaminants exceeding 10^4 CFU/mL (60,61). The probe assay is depicted in Figure 1. The bacteria are enzymatically lysed, which causes bacterial rRNA to be released. A labeled DNA probe that combines with the complementary rRNA to form a stable DNA:RNA hybrid is then added. Any unhybridized probe is selectively hydrolyzed by the addition of base.

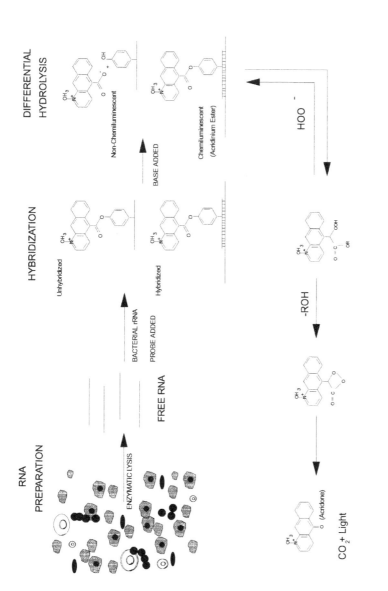

Figure 1 The rRNA chemiluminescence linked probe assay is schematically represented in four stages. (1) RNA preparation: bacteria are enzymatically lysed and the rRNA is released. (2) Hybridization: a labeled DNA probe combines with the complementary rRNA to form a stable DNA:RNA hybrid. (3) Differential hydrolysis: the unhybridized probe is selectively hydrolyzed by base. (4) Detection: a chemiluminescence reaction is initiated in the presence of base and hydrogen peroxide. The amount of luminesence is quantitated in relative light units (RLU). (From Ref. 23.)

A chemiluminescent reaction is then initiated in the presence of base and hydrogen peroxide, and the resulting amount of luminescence is quantitated in relative light units (RLU). Recently the use of probe technology to bacterial rRNA has been applied to detect bacterial contamination of food. DuPont has developed two machines (the Riboprinter Microbial Characterization System and the Bax system), which, in a matter of hours, can scan a sample for dangerous bacteria. In the future, this technology might be applied not only to detection of food contamination, but also to detection of blood product contamination and prevention of resultant catastrophic events (62).

5. Polymerase Chain Reaction

The polymerase chain reaction (PCR) has been evaluated in the detection of *Yersinia*. Feng et al. were able to detect 10^3 organisms in 100 µL (5×10^3 CFU/mL) of blood (63). Unfortunately, this technique, as described, is time consuming, identifies only *Yersinia*, and is subject to problems of contamination, thereby compromising specificity.

6. Altered Biochemistry

Bacterial metabolism during storage alters certain biochemical properties, namely glucose, pCO_2, pO_2, and pH (64–67). As bacteria proliferate, they consume oxygen and glucose, causing a decrease in these analytes, and CO_2 is transiently increased (Fig. 2). Changes in glucose can be rapidly and inexpensively detected by the use of glucometry (Fig. 3) (65). Two groups have studied the utilization of dipstick reagents to detect decreased glucose and pH in contaminated platelet concentrates (64,65). In platelets contaminated with $\geq 10^7$ CFU/mL, the overall sensitivity and specificity were 94% and 98%, respectively (65). In some cases, *S. aureus* and *K. pneumoniae* were detected in the 10^3–10^5 CFU/mL range (65). Change in pH has been detected using a CO_2-sensitive label placed on the outside surface of platelet containers. During aerobic growth of bacteria, CO_2 diffuses through the wall of the container and the color in the label changes. Unfortunately, platelets themselves release CO_2 in relation to their number and metabolism, limiting the utility of this method (68). An alternative technique is the use of CO_2-sensitive labels on gas-permeable plastic bags with culture medium, transferring only part of the platelet component into it. Unfortunately, this procedure is also quite insensitive, requiring large numbers of bacteria for detection (69).

7. Visual Inspection

An important observation made by Kim et al. was that grossly contaminated addition solution (AS) red cell units were darker in appearance than their attached segmented tubing. As a result of bacterial growth and metabolism, red cells are

Log 10 CFU per mL

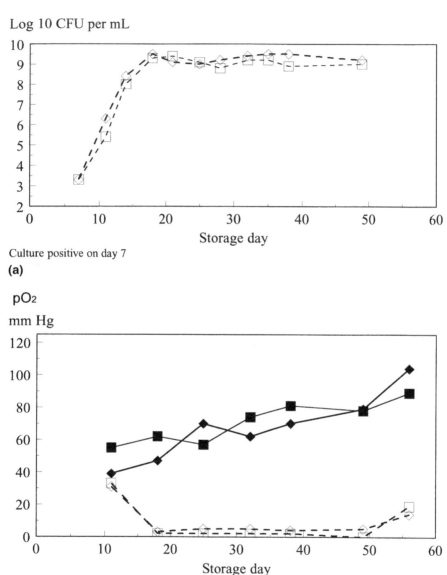

Culture positive on day 7

(a)

(b)

Figure 2 Growth of *Yersinia enterocolitica* in AS red cells. (a) Growth curves of two inoculated units indicated by dashed lines. (b) Oxygen tension plotted over storage time for two sterile (culture negative) and the two inoculated (culture positive) AS3 red cell units. (c) CO_2 tension plotted over storage time for two sterile and the two inoculated AS3 red cell units. (d) Free supernatant hemoglobin over storage time for the same two sterile and two inoculated AS red cell units. (Figures 2a, b, and d modified from Ref. 23.)

pCO₂
mm Hg

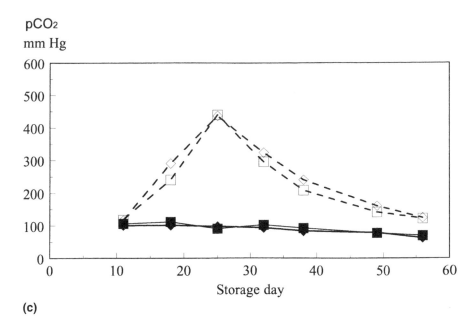

(c)

Free HgB mg/dL

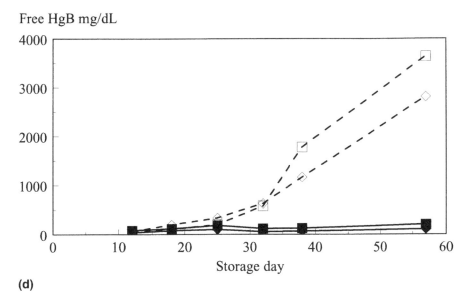

(d)

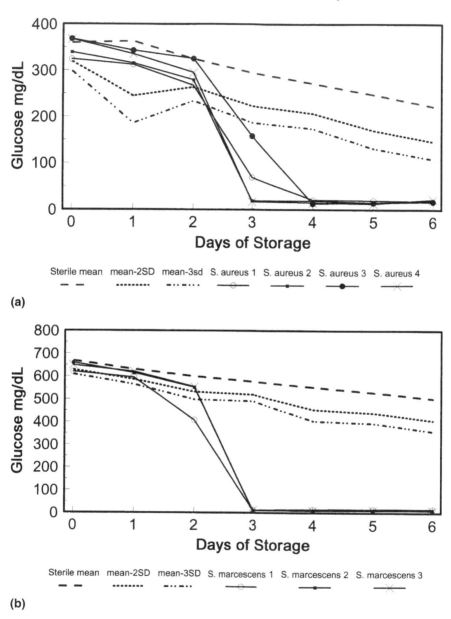

Figure 3   (a) Glucose analysis of sterile platelets stored in PL-732 bags (mean, mean -2SD, and mean -3SD) versus platelets stored red in PL-732 bags with CPD and inoculated with *S. aureus* (day 0). (b) Glucose analysis of sterile platelets stored in CLX bags (mean, mean -2SD, and mean-3SD) versus platelets stored in CLX bags with CP2D ("double" dextrose) and inoculated with *S. marcescens* (day 0).

lysed and oxygen consumed, causing a decrease in the oxygen saturation of hemoglobin and a darkening of the bag compared to the attached segmented tubing (Fig. 2) (70,71). In contaminated red cells, as a rule, the bacteria can be isolated only from the bags, and the segmented tubing attached to the bag is invariably sterile. While the same concentration of bacteria would be expected to be present in the bag and segmental tubing, most of the bacteria are actually killed. Since only a very few survive, the greater volume found in the bag compared with the volume in the segmented tubing favors growth in the bag. We have observed this color change as early as day 24 of storage with *Y. enterocolitica* and day 20 of storage with *S. liquefaciens* (unpublished observations). Careful inspection of units, comparing the color of the bag to that of the segments, is a quick and easy screening tool.

The use of visual inspection is more difficult with platelets. One proposed way to detect contamination is the observation of decreased "swirling" or "streaming" in platelet bags (37,54,72). This method is based on the observation that viable, intact platelets are discoid in shape and produce a "swirling" phenomenon when gently squeezed and visualized against a light source. Platelets do not "swirl" if the pH is low or they have been exposed to cold (73–80). Platelet concentrates contaminated with bacteria frequently have a decreased pH as the bacteria respire and produce CO_2, thus causing a decreased "swirling" effect when visualized. However, several investigators remain skeptical as to the clinical utility of this method. Significantly, a recent study found that more than one third of "swirling-negative" platelets had a normal pH and as many as 18% of 5-day-old platelet concentrates did not swirl and thus would be unnecessarily destroyed (81). Aggregated platelet concentrates can also be indicative of bacterial contamination (particularly with gram-negative organisms) and should not be infused.

B. Prevention

Many methods have been proposed to aid in the prevention of bacterial contamination of blood products. While many show great promise, there has not been wide acceptance and institution of any one technique.

1. Donor Questioning

Most cases of red cell contamination are thought to be attributed to transient asymptomatic bacteremia in donors. Questions are asked prior to donation to tease out prospective bacteremic donors (24,82). Histories of recent dental procedures, gastrointestinal or genitourinary manipulation, and breast feeding may all be associated with bacteremia and would cause a potential donor to be deferred. Some have suggested asking donors about a recent history of diarrhea or abdominal pain to help identify persons infected with *Y. enterocolitica* (82). Unfortunately, this does not appear to be a specific method of prevention, as this would defer approximately 9.7% of potential donors, most of whom are not infected (83). In addition, this method lacks sensitivity, as only 13 of 20 donors associated with *Y. enterocolitica*–contaminated red cells recalled a history of gastrointestinal symptoms (44). Of patients with gastrointestinal symptoms who have a stool culture performed, only 2% grow *Yersinia* (84–86).

2. Skin Core Contamination

Most cases of platelet contamination arise as the result of inadequate skin sterilization prior to donation. In addition, skin fragments are drawn up into the collection bag during the initial phase of donation and provide a source of infection (20,21). A variety of simple methods to prevent skin core contamination are under investigation. Possibilities include the use of a trochar instead of a large-bore needle for collection, placement of a filter screen at the base of the collection bag, and disposal of the first few milliliters of blood (87,88). A study performed on 22,000 blood donations by the Red Cross in the Netherlands in which the first 10 mL of donor blood were diverted from the primary bag showed that 16 of the first 5 mL aliquots were bacterially contaminated, while only 2 of the second 5 mL aliquots were culture positive. Similar reports have been documented in vitro studies of collection needles (22,23,88,89,102).

3. Prestorage Culture

Prestorage culture as a preventive measure against the transfusion of bacterially contaminated products is problematic. It has been found that 0.2–0.5% of units are culture positive (57). As a result of artifactual contamination during culturing, the rate of positive cultures may be higher than the amount of bacterial contamination actually present in stored blood products. A high number of false positives would likely result in the unnecessary disposal of noncontaminated units. Additionally, as numerous studies in our and other laboratories have demonstrated, even with known bacterially inoculated units, units are frequently culture negative for several days before later cultures become positive (24,90,91). This is likely due to the antibacterial effects of plasma and granulocytes. Alternatively, breakdown of granulocytes or skin plugs may lead to a late release of bacteria; thus, many cases may not be detected by prestorage culture.

4. Bacteriocidal Techniques

The use of antibiotics to assure a sterile product, while effective, is not felt to be an acceptable solution. Fears of the selection and development of antibiotic-resistant strains of bacteria and of merely trading one rare event (drug anaphylaxis) for another (bacterial sepsis) preclude such use (37,51). A promising approach is the use of light or ionizing radiation to produce not only nonimmunogenic, but also sterile, blood products (92–95). A photochemical decontamination system for platelet concentrates using long-wavelength ultraviolet radiation and 8-methoxypsoralen has been shown to inactivate 25–30 logs/h of *E. coli* or *S. aureus* (96). The techniques that utilize light are restricted to nonopaque products such as plasma and possibly platelets. With regard to platelets, there has been concern as to the effects this technology might have on metabolic and functional properties as well as concerns of mutagenicity, logistics, and cost (97). Because of such concerns and technical hurdles, such methodology has, to date, been limited to the research laboratory.

5. Storage Time

In 1991, the Blood Product Advisory Committee (BPAC) of FDA reviewed all cases of *Yersinia* sepsis from red cell units reported to either FDA or the CDC during the late 1980s. At that time all reported cases of red cell–associated *yersinia* sepsis in the United States had occurred in units older than 25 days. As a result of the time necessary for the bacteria to attain a lethal concentration, the BPAC proposed reducing the storage time of red cells from 42 to 25 days (98). This recommendation was subsequently rejected for the following reasons:

1. A questionnaire distributed at the time revealed that 20% of red cell units in stock at over 1500 blood banks and transfusion services were more than 28 days old (98). Discarding such units would have severely compromised the nations blood supply.
2. A shorter outdate would then require recruitment of new donors; it was estimated that the addition of a quarter of a million donations per year would be required to replace the losses due to outdates (98,99). This would involve additional risk since first-time donors are known to be at a greater risk of carrying disease because their blood has not been repeatedly tested, as has the blood of veteran donors (98,99).
3. Units less than 25 days old can also cause sepsis. While decreasing the storage time may lessen the problem, it would not eliminate it entirely (29,33,59,100).
4. Older units are less likely to transmit viruses such as HIV (101).

Increased platelet storage time has also been associated with increased probability of contamination. At present, the allowable storage time for platelets is 5 days, although in 1983 the shelf life of platelets was increased to 7 days (Fig. 4). This increase was associated with an increase in the number of sep-

Figure 4   Platelet shelf life timeline.

tic events in older platelets, and the shelf life was again reduced to 5 days in 1986 (102). Unfortunately, merely decreasing the shelf life did not eliminate the problem of bacterial contamination. We and other laboratories have shown that even a moderate inoculate (10–50 CFU/mL) of certain bacteria, such as B. cereus and P. aeruginosa, can have a minimal lag phase with a doubling time of 1–2 hours (60). This can lead to a bacterial load of 108 CFU/mL in just 1–2 days. One approach to minimize platelet associated sepsis taken by the Oncology Center of Johns Hopkins was to limit the transfusion of platelets to 4 days of storage (103). It is unlikely that there will be further national reductions in storage time of platelets because this would cause severe shortages of this component.

Other concerns within the blood banking community are also affecting platelet availability. Because of the increased complexity of viral screening of blood products, an increasing awareness of the potential for errors, and a need to minimize cost and maximize efficiency of operations, many blood collection organizations such as the American Red Cross are attempting to centralize or regionalize disease marker testing. While commendable in concept, this centralization of testing can, because of the transport time of samples, result in the decreased availability of one-day-old platelets. In 1982, the mean age of distributed platelets was 1.6 days, in 1983 (after extension of the dating period to 5 days) it was 2.0 days, and in 1992 (after addition of increased laboratory testing) it was 2.5 days. In 1983, only 5% of issued platelets were older than 3 days. In 1992, just 10% were older than 3 days. But with the introduction of centralized testing by the Red Cross, the mean age of issued platelets increased to 2.7 days, with 20% older than 3 days (89). Not only can this decrease the available shelf life of an already precariously limited supply of platelets, it can also decrease the availability of fresh platelets, the most hemostatically effective and the least likely to be bacterially contaminated.

6.   Storage Temperature and Separation of Components

After inoculation of whole blood with *Y. enterocolitica*, there is an initial rapid decline in the number of viable organisms, followed by a resumption of growth after a lag phase of approximately 5 days (55,56,104–106). When whole blood is placed immediately at 4°C, growth occurs more rapidly than if held at 10°C for 24 hours prior to 4°C storage (107). Bacterial growth of most pathogens is inhibited by cold temperatures, but host defense mechanisms present in fresh whole blood are also inhibited by storage at 4°C. *Yersinia* with plasmid-encoded complement resistance can become complement sensitive when blood is transiently stored at 20°C (105). Because phagocytosis and complement activation are impaired by storage at 4°C, it may be advantageous to allow red blood cells to remain in contact with plasma for several hours prior to separation and storage of components.

Platelets are stored for a maximum of 5 days at 20–24°C because of concern regarding the potential for bacterial contamination and progressive decline in platelet function (storage lesion) if platelets are stored for longer periods of time at these temperatures (108,109). While storage of platelets at 4°C results in a significantly lower rate of bacterial contamination, it also causes a temperature-induced activation of platelets and a rapid decline in functional ability and in vitro viability. In a recent study, cold storage of platelets was performed, mimicking the endogenous inhibition of platelet activation through the addition of specific second-messenger stimulators. It was reported that the platelets stored at 4°C for 9 days displayed no loss in cell number, and that the study platelets recovered partial functional ability and viability compared with control platelets stored at 22°C for 5 days (110). If a practical method for storing platelets at 4°C is perfected, it would have the potential to reduce the risk of bacterial contamination of this component.

7. Leukoreduction

Because of concern regarding the accumulation of leukocyte and platelet break-down products in stored blood, as well as the immunogenicity of white cell fragments, there has been considerable emphasis placed on the potential benefits of prestorage versus poststorage leukoreduction (111,112). However, this posed a potential dilemma, as it was possible that prestorage filtration would cause an increase in bacterial contamination of blood products and septic complications because of removal of the phagocytic leukocytes that would normally remove low levels of bacteria present in these components. Fortunately, in the case of *Y. enterocolitica* contamination of red cells, prestorage leukoreduction actually is associated with a decrease in bacterial growth in inoculated red blood cells (Table 3) (56,104,106,113,114). The mechanism by which leukoreduction re-moves bacteria is multifactorial. Bacteria that have been phagocytized (Fig. 5) but not killed are removed with the white blood cells. Alternatively, organisms may be adsorbed to leukocytes or activated complement, to then be bound indirectly to the filter, or the bacteria may directly adhere to the filter fibers (116,117). Studies on leukoreduction of platelets have not shown such promising results. Unlike the decrease in *Y. enterocolitica* growth in prestorage leukoreduced

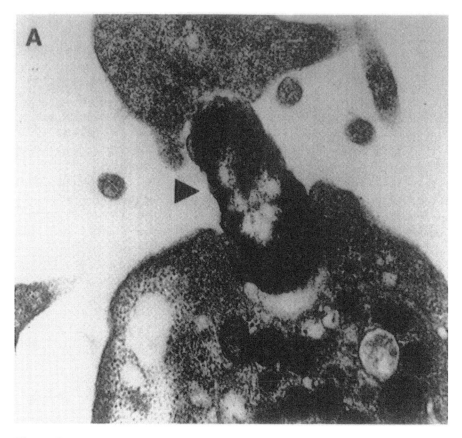

Figure 5 Transmission electron micrograph showing (A) penetration and engulfment and (B) internalization of *Yersinia enterocolitica* in leukocytes from a buffy coat preparation of a normal blood donor. The innoculation dose was 10^9 CFU added to 100 mL of a buffy coat preparation. The unit was stored for 2 hours at room temperature before sampling. The microorganisms are indicated by arrowheads. (From Ref. 115.)

red cells, neither a positive nor a negative effect on bacterial growth has been demonstrated in prestorage leukoreduction of platelets (60,118,119).

8. Frozen Components

Contamination of blood components has occurred during the thawing process (45,46). Use of a plastic overwrap that prevents outlet ports from direct exposure to water from the warming bath is an easy and effective method to prevent contamination (120). Disinfectants and frequent changing of water baths have not been shown to prevent growth of bacterial species (11,37).

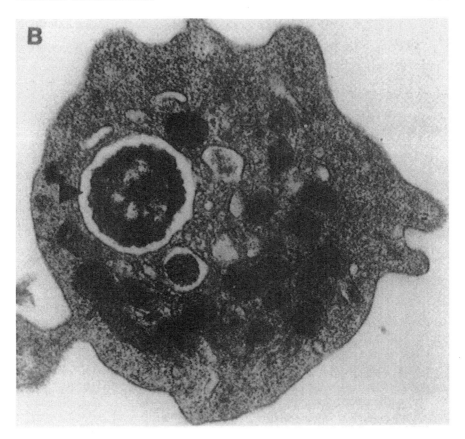

9. Immunoassay

The Red Cross is currently developing an immunochromatographic technique with Binax, Portland, ME (22,89). This method is intended to be applied immediately prior to issuance of the blood component. The goals of this effort are to detect the 8–10 bacteria that account for 95% of bacterially infected platelets, to detect $>10^5$ CFU/mL, to be performed in less than 20 minutes, to be simple and require no special equipment, and to have a distinct yes or no answer. As yet, it has not entered clinical trials.

Recently a monoclonal antibody (MAb900) has been described that detects a prokaryotic elongation factor (EF-Tu). EF-Tu is one of the most abundant proteins in prokaryotes and is not present in eukaryotic cells. As such, it is hoped that the use of anti EF-Tu may make a very rapid (4–6 h) and effective screening tool possible (121).

Table 3 *Yersinia enterocolitica* Growth and Prestorage Leukocyte Reduction
by Filtration

Inoculating concentration (CFU/mL)	Filtered growth/total (%)	Control growth/total (%)	Filter type	Ref.
100	0/10 (0)	10/10 (100)	Sepacell PL-5N	31
65	1/5 (20)	4/4 (100)	Leukotrap	58
65	1/5 (20)	4/4 (100)	Leukotrap RC (Pall RC300)	58
10/150	3/8 (37)	8/8 (100)	Pall BPF4	113
0.3–132	3/24 (12)	16/24 (67)	Sepacell R-500	106
20–30,000	6/30 (20)	22/30 (73)	Cellselect, NPBI	108
1.5	2/6 (33)	6/6 (100)	Leukotrap RC (Pall RC300)	72
Total	16/88 (18)	70/86 (81)		

V. TRANSFUSION-TRANSMITTED SYPHILIS

Treponema pallidum, the agent that causes syphilis, is a thin–walled, motile, spirochete. This organism cannot be visualized with Gram stain, nor does it grow on bacteriological media or cell culture, yet it is considered to be a bacterium, and infection is treated with penicillin. Although it is a bacterium, it is often treated as a distinct entity, different from other transfusion-transmitted bacterial infection and is thus addressed in this separate section of the text. Donors infected with *T. pallidum* may be asymptomatic with negative serology during periods of spirochetemia (122). We are only aware of three cases of transfusion–transmitted syphilis in the past 27 years (123–125). While the organism is killed by storage at 4°C, it may live for 1–5 days at these cold temperatures (126,127). Subsequently, a rare posttranfusion infection may be associated with transfusion of a very fresh unit of red blood cells from a donor who was in the seronegative phase at the time of donation. There is greater concern with platelet transfusion, since this component is stored at 20–24°C, temperatures suitable for growth of this organism. The cardiolipin test is used in screening donated blood, but this test lacks sensitivity for detecting an acute infection. Nevertheless, there is an extremely low rate of transfusion–transmitted syphilis infection for a number of reasons:

1. Many infected donors are screened with donor questioning.
2. Although an insensitive test in the acute post infections setting, the cardiolipin assay does pick up a number of infected donors.
3. Refrigerator storage results in the death of spirochetes.
4. Most patients receiving platelets are on antibiotics at the time of transfusion, which would be bactericidal for any transmitted viable organisms.

5. Because there is a high correlation between infection with *T. pallidum* and viruses such as HIV (128–131) and hepatitis B and C (132,133), donors in the seronegative phase of syphilis may be excluded as a result of a positive test for one of these viruses.

VI. INVESTIGATION, THERAPY, AND REPORTING

When transfusion-related sepsis is suspected, one should obtain the residual blood in the bag for culture and stain. One should also culture the patient's blood and compare its isolates with the blood bag isolates. Antibiotic sensitivities may be helpful in confirming that an organism isolated from a blood bag is the same organism isolated from a patient's blood. We recommend that antibiotic therapy be considered if the patient is not already receiving broad-spectrum antibiotics.

It may be critical to locate other blood components from the same donor since other liquid-stored components may also be bacterially contaminated. In such cases, liquid components from the same donation should be identified, quarantined, tested for contamination, and destroyed. If blood components from the same donation have already been administered to other patients, the clinicians caring for those patients should be notified.

Confirmed cases should be reported to:

Investigations and Prevention Branch
Hospital Infections Program, A-07
Centers for Disease Control and Prevention
(404) 639-1550
FAX (404) 639-3770

Fatalities must be reported to:

Office of Compliance
Center for Biologics Evaluation and Research
Food and Drug Administration
(301) 594-1191

VII. CONCLUSION

Bacterial contamination of blood components remains a problem today. While the bacterial contamination of red cells, fresh frozen plasma, and cryoprecipitate occur rarely, it is estimated that approximately 1 in 1000 platelet units are contaminated as a consequence of storage at 20–24°C. Thus, the risk of receiving a bacterially contaminated platelet transfusion exceeds the combined risk of receiving an HIV-, hepatitis B–, or hepatitis C–contaminated blood component. Unfortunately, recognition of bacterial sepsis is problematic because patients often do not become symptomatic until several hours following a contaminated platelet transfusion and the spectrum of organisms overlaps those seen in catheter sepsis. It is therefore suspected that cases of platelet-related bacterial sepsis go undiagnosed and are often falsely attributed to catheter sepsis.

Ironically, those patients who are the most ill equipped to handle a bolus of intravenous bacteria are the ones most often exposed (Table 4). Recipients of platelets tend to be the sickest patients, often having received chemotherapy with resultant temporary marrow aplasia. It is in these patients who are immuno-suppressed that sepsis from platelet contamination most often occurs.

Unlike testing for viruses, which only needs to be performed once at the time of donation, testing of blood components for bacterial contamination due to bacterial growth during storage must be performed close to the time of transfusion. Methods are now being described for the rapid and sensitive testing of blood components for bacterial contamination. Such methods may have the added benefit of prolonging the shelf life of platelets, which is currently time limited because of the increasing risk of bacterial contamination over extended storage times.

Every year documented cases of fatalities from bacterially contaminated blood components (principally platelets) are reported. It may be more cost-effective to implement platelet bacterial testing than the currently implemented tests for syphilis, anti HIV–2, HIV p24 antigen, anti HTLV–I/II, and antibody to hepatitis B core antigen (anti-HBC) routinely performed on all donations in the United States. Recent studies demonstrating high concentrations of cytokines (TNF-α, IL–1β, IL-8, and IL-1β) following transfusion-associated sepsis offer a glimmer of hope for possible future prospects for therapy with anticytokines or cytokine antagonists (134). Efforts to perfect a method of refrigerated storage of platelets also remain a possibility (110). However, our duty as blood bankers

Table 4 Factors Affecting Outcome of Transfusion of Bacterially Contaminated Blood Products

Virulence of the organism
Immune status and general condition of the recipient
Concentration and bolus dose of bacteria transfused
Timely recognition and therapeutic intervention
Intensity of patient monitoring—i.e., inpatient vs. outpatient
Medicines the patient is receiving—i.e., antibiotics

and clinicians is to assure the safest blood product possible for both today and tomorrow.

There remains some controversy regarding the actual risk of bacterial contamination of blood, and no perfect screening or prevention methodology currently exists. The perfect should not be the enemy of the good, and implementation of partial solutions that have little risk of causing harm should be encouraged (135). Rapid bacterial screening of platelets will likely be available in the near future.

REFERENCES

1. Schreiber GB, Busch MP, Kleinman SH, Korelitz. The risk of tranfusion-transmitted viral infections. N Engl J Med 1996; 334:1685–1690.
2. Association Bulletin 96-6. Bacterial Contamination of Blood Components. AABB Faxnet, No. 294, August 1996. American Association of Blood Banks.
3. Dodd RY. Adverse consequences of blood transfusion—quantitative risk estimates. In: Blood Supply Risks, Perceptions, and Prospects for the Future. Bethesda, MD: American Association of Blood Banks, 1994:1–24.
4. Devine P, Linden JV, Hoffstadter LK, et al. Blood donor-, apheresis-, and transfusion-related activities: results of the 1991 American Association of Blood Banks Institutional Membership Questionnaire. Transfusion 1993; 33:770–782.
5. Devine P, Postoway N, Hoffstadter L, et al. Blood donation and transfusion practices: the 1990 American Association of Blood Banks Institutional Membership Questionnaire. Transfusion 1992; 32:683–687.
6. Surgenor DM, Wallace EL, Hao SHS, et al. Collection and transfusion of blood in the United States, 1982-1988. N Engl J Med 1990; 322:1646–1651.
7. Barrett BB, Andersen JW, Anderson KC. Strategies for the avoidance of bacterial contamination of blood components. Transfusion 1993; 33:228–233.
8. Halpin TJ, Kilker S, Epstein J, Tourault M. Bacterial contamination of platelet pools—Ohio, 1991. MMWR 1992; 41:36–)37.
9. Morro JF, Braine HG, Kickler TS, Ness PM, Dick JD, Fuller AK. Septic reactions to platelet transfusions. A persistent problem. JAMA 1991; 266:555–558.
10. Chiu EKW, Yuien KY, Lie AKW, Liang R, Lau YL, Lee ACW, Kwong YL, Wong S, Ng MH, Chan TK. A prosective study of symptomatic bacteremia following platelet transfusion and its management. Transfusion 1994; 34:950–954.
11. Wallas CH. Transfusion of blood components contaminated with bacteria. Transfusion transmitted infections. In: Smith DM, Dodd RY, eds. Transfusion Transmitted Infections. Chicago: ASCP Press, 1991:195–206.
12. Goldman M, Blajchman MA. Blood product-associated bacterial sepsis. Transfusion Med Rev 1991; 5(1):73–83.
13. BPAC discusses invalidation of test results, platelet usage. Blood Bank Week 1992; 9:1–3.
14. Rhame FS, Root RK, MacLowry JD, Dadisman TA, Bennett JV. Salmonella

septicemia from platelet transfusions. Study of an outbreak traced to a hemato-genous carrier of Salmonella cholerae-suis. Ann Intern Med 1973; 78:633–641.

15. Heal JM, Jones ME, Forey J, Chaudhry A, Stricof RL. Fatal Salmonella septicemia after platelet transfusion. Transfusion 1987; 27:2–5.

16. Arnow PM, Weiss LM, Weil D, Rosen NR. Escherichia coli sepsis from contami-nated platelet transfusion. Arch Intern Med 1986; 146:321–324.

17. Yomtovian R, Lazarus HM, Goodnough LT, Hirschler NV, Morrissey AM, Jacobs MR. A prospective microbiologic surveillance program to detect and prevent the transfusion of bacterially contaminated platelets. Transfusion 1993; 33:902–909.

18. Buchholz DH, Young VM, Friedman NR, Reilly JA, Mardiney MR. Detection and quantitation of bacteria in platelet products stored at ambient temperature. Transfu-sion 1973; 13(5):268–275.

19. Halpin TJ, Kilker S, Epstein J, Tourault M. Bacterial contamination of platelet pools—Ohio, 1991. MMWR 1992; 41(3):36–37.

20. Gibson T, Norris W. Skin fragments removed by injection needles. Lancet 1958; 2:983–985.

21. Lilly HA, Lowbury EJL, Wilkins MD. Limits to progressive reduction to resident skin bacteria by disinfecion. J Clin Pathol 1979; 32:382–385.

22. NIH workshop examines bacterial contamination of blood components. CCBC Newslett 1995; 13:16.

23. Krishnan LS, Brecher ME. Transfusion transmitted bacterial infection. Hematol/Oncol Clin North Am 1995; 9:167–185.

24. Tipple MA, Bland LA, Murphy MF, et al. Sepsis associated with transfusion of red cells contaminated with *Yersinia enterocolitica*. Transfusion 1990; 30:207–213.

25. Update: *Yersinia enterocolitica* bacteremia and endotoxin shock associated with red blood cell transfusion—United States, 1987-1988. MMWR 1991; 37:577–578.

26. Update: *Yersinia enterocolitica* bacteremia and endotoxin shock associated with red blood cell transfusions—United States, 1991. MMWR 1991; 40:176–178.

27. Bjune G, Rund T, Eng J. Bacterial shock due to transfusion with *Yersinia en-terocolitica* infected blood. Scand J Infect Diss 1984; 16:411–412.

28. Wright DC, Selss IF, Vinton KF, et al. Fatal *Yersinia enterocolitica* sepsis after blood transfusion. Arch Pathol Lab Med 1985; 109:1040–1042.

29. Jacobs J, Jamaer D, Vandeven J, et al. *Yersinia enterocolitica* in donor blood: a case report and review. J Clin Microbiol 1989; 27:1119–1121.

30. Update: *Yersinia enterocolitica* bacteremia and endotoxin shock associated with red blood cell transfusion—United States, 1987-1988. MMWR 1988; 37:577–578.

31. Hogman CF, Gong J, Hambraeus A, Johansson CS, Eriksson L. The role of white cells in the transmission of *Yersinia enterocolitica* in blood products. Transfusion 1992; 32:654–657.

32. Pollack C, Straley SC, Klempner MS. Probing the phagolysosomal environment of human macrophages with a Ca2+-responsive operon fusion in *Yersinia pestis*. Nature 1986; 22:834–683.

33. Jensenius M, Hoel T, Heier HE. *Yersinia enterocolitica* septicemia after blood transfusion. Tidsskr Nor Laegeforen 1995; 115:940–942.

34. Hogman CF, Fritz H, Sandberg L. Post-transfusion *Serratia marcescens* septicemia (editorial). Transfusion 1993; 33:189–191.

35. Heltberg O, Show F, Gerner-Smidt P, Kolmos HJ, Dybkjer E, Gutschik E, Jerne D, Jepsen OB, Weischer M, Frederiksen W, Sorensen H. Nosocomial epidemic of *Serratia marcescens* septicemia ascribed to contaminated blood transfusion bags. Transfusion 1993; 33:221–227.

36. Sazama K. Bacteria in blood for transfusion: a review. Arch Pathol Lab Med 1994; 18:350–365.

37. Wagner SJ, Friedman LI, Dodd RY. Transfusion associated sepsis. Clin Microbiol Rev 1994; 7:290–302.

38. Richards C, Kolins J, Trindale CD. Autologous transfusion-transmitted *Yersinia enterocolitica* (letter). JAMA 1992; 268:1541–1542.

39. Sire JM, Michelet C, Mesnard R, et al. Septic shock due to *Yersinia enterocolitica* after autologous transfusion (letter). Clin Infect Dis 1993; 17:954–955.

40. Duncan KL, Ransley J, Elterman M. Transfusion-transmitted *Serratia liquefaciens* from an autologous blood unit (letter). Transfusion 1994; 34:738–739.

41. Haditsch M, Binder L, Gabriel C, et al. *Yersinia enterocolitica* septicemia in autologous blood transfusion. Transfusion 1994; 34:907–909.

42. Braude AI, Williams D, Siemienski J, Murphy R. Shock-like state due to transfusion of blood contaminated with gram-negative bacilli. Arch Intern Med 1953; 92:75–84.

43. Sazama K. Reports of 355 transfusion-associated deaths: 1976-1985. Transfusion 1990; 30:583–590.

44. Cookson ST, Arduino MJ, Aguero SM, Jarvis WR, and the *Yersinia* Study Group. *Yersinia enterocolitica*-contaminated red blood cells (RBCs)—an emerging threat to blood safety. 1996; ICAAC.ABS:2352.

45. Rhame FS, McCullough JJ, Cameron S, et al. *Pseudomonas cepacia* infections caused by thawing cryoprecipitate in a contaminated water bath (abstr). Transfusion 1979; 19:653.

46. Casewell MW, Slater NGP, Cooper JE. Operating theatre water-baths as a cause of *Pseudomonas* septicemia. J Hosp Infect 1981; 2:237–240.

47. Albumin recall. Lancet 1996; 348:1026.

48. Sgouris JT, Rene A, eds. Proceedings of the Workshop on Albumin, 1975. Bethesda, MD: National Heart and Lung Institute, National Institutues of Health, Department of Health, Education and Welfare, 1976:284.

49. Recalls issued for Centeon products. AABB Regulatory Update, October 1996; 3:6.

50. Centeon issues world wide recall of albumin and PPF. America's Blood Centers Newslett 1996; 39:1–2.

51. Food and Drug Administration: Blood Products Advisory Committee, Center for Biologist Evaluation and Research, 36th Meeting, Rockville, MD, May 29, 1992, Publication No. 92-026824, pp. 440–445.

52. Walter CW, Kundsin RB, Button LN. New technique for detection of bacterial contamination in a blood bank using plastic equipment. N Engl Med 1957; 257:364–369.

53. Barrett BB, Andersen JW, Anderson KC. Strategies for the avoidance of bacterial contamination of blood components. Transfusion 1993; 33:228–233.

54. Yomtovian R, Lazarus HM, Goodnough LT, et al. A prospective microbiologic surveillance program to detect and prevent the transmission of bacterially contaminated platelets. Transfusion 1993; 33:902–909.

55. Arduino MJ, Bland LA, Tipple MA, et al. Growth and endotoxin production of *Yersinia enterocolitica* and *Enterobacter agglomerans* in packed erythrocytes. J Clin Microbiol 1989; 27:1483–1485.

56. Kim DM, Brecher ME, Bland LA, et al. Prestorage removal of *Yersinia entercolitica* from red cells with white cell-reduction filters. Transfusion 1992; 32:658–662.

57. Blajchman MA, Ali AM. Bacteria in the blood supply: an overlooked issue in transfusion medicine. In: Nance SJ, ed. Blood safety: Current Challenges. Bethesda, MD: American Association of Blood Banks, 1992:213–228.

58. Myhre BA, Nakusako YY, Schott R. A rapid method for determining the sterility of frozen-reconstituted blood. Transfusion 1977; 17:195–202.

59. Arduino MJ, Bland LA, Tipple MA, et al. Growth and endotoxin production of *Yersinia enterocolitica* and *Enterobacter agglomerans* in packed erythrocytes. J Clin Microbiol 1989; 27:1483–1485.

60. Brecher NE, Hogan JJ, Boothe G, et al. The use of a chemiluminescence-linked universal bacterial ribosomal RNA gene probe and blood gas analysis for the rapid detection of bacterial contamination in white cell reduced and nonreduced platelets. Transfusion 1993; 33:450–457.

61. Brecher ME, Hogan JJ, Boothe G, et al. Platelet bacterial contamination and the use of a chemiluminescence-linked universal bacterial ribosomal RNA gene probe. Transfusion 1994; 34:750–755.

62. Sullivan A. Machines speed testing of food for bacteria, Wall Street 1996; (July 15):

63. Feng P, Keasler SP, Hill WE. Direct identification of *Yersinia enterocolitica* in blood by polymerase chain reaction amplification. Transfusion 1992; 32:850–854.

64. Wagner SJ, Robinette D. Evaluation of swirling, pH, and glucose tests for the detection of bacterial contamination of platelet concentrates. Transfusion 1996; 36:989–993.

65. Burstain JM, Brecher ME, Workman K, Foster M, Faber GH, Mair D. Rapid identification of bacterially contaminated platelets using reagent strips. Transfusion 1997;

66. Myhre BA, Demainew SH, Yoshimori RN, Nelson E, Carmen RA. pH changes caused by bacterial growth in contaminated platelet concentrates. Ann Clin Lab Sci 1985; 15:509–514.

67. Arpi M, Bremmelgaard A, Abel Y, Olsson K, Hansen L. A novel screening method for the detection of microbial contamination of platelet concentrates (letter). Vox Sang 1993; 65:335–336.

68. Arpi M, Bremmelgaard A, Abel Y, Olsson K, Hansen L. A novel screening method for the detection of microbial contamination of platelet concentrates. An experimental pilot study. Vox Sang 1993; 65:335–336.

69. Hogman CF, Gong J. Studies of one invasive and two noninvasive methods for detection of bacterial contamination of platelet concentrates. Vox Sang 1994; 67:351–355.

70. Kim DM, Estes TJ, Brecher ME et al. WBC filtration, blood gas analysis and plasma hemoglobin in *Yersinia enterocolitica* contaminated red cells. Transfusion 1992; 32:41S.

71. Kim DM, Brecher ME, Bland LA, Estes TJ, Carmen RA, Nelson EJ. Visual identification of bacterially contaminated red cells. Transfusion 1992; 32:221–225.

72. Myre BA, Walker LJ, White ML. Bacteriocidal properties of platelet concentrates. Transfusion 1974; 14:116–123.

73. Murphy S, Kahn RA, Holme S, et al. Improved storage of platelets for transfusion in a new container. Blood 1982; 60:194–200.

74. Holme S, Murphy S. Quantitative measurements of platelet shape by light transmission studies: application to storage of platelets for transfusion. J Lab Clin Med 1978; 92:53–64.

75. Holme S, Murphy S. Platelet storage at 22°C for transfusion: interrelationship of platelet density and size, medium pH, and viability after in vivo infusion. J Lab Clin Med 1983; 101:161–174.

76. Lindberg JE, Slichter SJ, Murphy S, et al. In vitro function and in vivo viability of stored platelet concentrates. Effect of a secondary plasticizer component of PVC storage bags. Transfusion 1983; 23:294–299.

77. Murphy S, Sayar SN, Gardner FH. Storage of platelet concentrates at 22°C. Blood 1970; 35:549–557.

78. White JG, Krivit W. Ultrastructural basis for shape change induced in platelets by chilling. Blood 1967; 30:625–635.

79. Murphy S, Gardner FH. Platelet preservation. Effect of storage temperature on maintenance of platelet viability—deleterious effect of refrigerated storage. N Engl J Med 1969; 280:1094–1098.

80. Holme S, Vaidja K, Murphy S. Platelet storage at 22°C: effect of type of agitation on morphology, viability, and function in vitro. Blood 1978; 52:425–435.

81. Bertolini F, Murphy S. A multicenter inspection of the swirling phenomenon in platelet concentrates prepared in routine practice. Transfusion 1996; 36:128–132.

82. Grossman BJ, Kollins P, Lau PM, et al. Screening blood donors for gastrointestinal illness: a strategy to eliminate carriers of *Yersinia entercolitica*. Transfusion 1991; 31:500–501.

83. Katz L, MacPherson JL, Zuck TF. *Yersinia* and blood donation (letter). Transfusion 1992; 32:191.

84. Hoogkamp-Korstanje JA, de Koning J, Samsom JP. Incidence of human infection with *Yersinia enterocolitica* serotypes 03, 08 and 09 and the use of indirect immunofluorescence in diagnosis. J Infect Dis 1986; 153:138–141.

85. Marks MI, Pai CH, Lafleur L, Lackman L, Hammerberg O. *Yersinia enterocolitica* gastroenteritis: a prospective study of clinical, bacteriologic, and epidemiologic features. J Pediatr 1980; 96:26–31.

86. Mingrone MG, Fantasia M, Figura N, Guglielmetti P. Characteristics of *Yersinia enterocolitica* isolated form children with diarrhea in Italy. J Clin Microbiol 1987; 25:1301–1304.

87. Olthuis H, Putlaert C, Verhagen C, Valk L. Method for removal of contaminating bacteria during venapuncture (abstract). Int Soc Blood Transf Regional Congress 1995; 77.

88. Figueroa PI, Yoshimori R, Nelson E, Macabasco G, Carmen R. Distribution of bacteria in fluid passing through an inoculated collection needle (abstr). Transfusion 1995; 35(suppl):11S.

89. Bacterial detection device. Blood Bank Week 1995; (Sept. 29):2.

90. Stenhouse MAE, Milner LV. *Yersinia enterocolitica*: a hazard in blood transfusion. Transfusion 1982; 22:396–398.

91. Van Noyen R, Vandepitte J, Wauters G, Selderslaghs R. *Yersinia enterocolitica*: its isolation by cold enrichment from patients and healthy subjects. J Clin Pathol 1981; 34:1052–1056.

92. Lin L, Wiesehahn GP, Morel PA, et al. The use of 8-methoxypsoralen and long-wavelength ultraviolet radiation for decontamination of platelet concentrates. Blood 1989; 74:515–525.

93. Matthews JL, Newman JT, Sogandares-Bernal F, et al. Photodynamic therapy of viral contaminants with potential for blood banking applications. Transfusion 1988; 28:81–85.

94. Pamphilon DH, Corbin SA, Saunders J, Tandy NP. Applications of ultraviolet light in the preparation of platelet concentrates. Transfusion 1989; 29:379–383.

95. Prince AM, Stephan W, Brotman B. B-propiolactone/ultraviolet irradiation; a review of its effectiveness for inactivation of viruses in blood derivatives. Rev Infect Dis 1983; 5:92–107.

96. Lin L, Wiesehahn GP, Morel PA, Corash L. Use of 8-methoxypsoralen and long-wavelength ultraviolet radiation for decontamination of platelet concentrates. Blood 1989; 74:517–525.

97. Johnson RB, Napychank PA, Murphy S, Snyder EL. In vitro changes in platelet function and metabolism following increasing doses of ultraviolet-B irradiation. Transfusion 1993; 33:249–255.

98. FDA committee endorses education and research to combat rare bacterial reaction: rejects operational changes for now. Council Commun Blood Centers (CCBC) Newslett 1991; (May 10):1–4.

99. FDA Blood Products Advisory Committee supports educational efforts on *Yersinia enterocolitica*. Blood Bank Week 1991; 20:1–3.

100. Kostreski F. Don't change storage rules, blood bankers warn. CAP Today 1991; 5, 45.

101. Donegan E, Lenes BA, Tomasulo PA, et al. Transmission of HIV-1 by component type and duration of shelf storage before transfusion (letter). Transfusion 1991; 30:851–852.

102. Braine HG, Kickler TS, Charache P, et al. Bacterial sepsis secondary to platelet transfusion: an adverse effect of extended storage at room temperature. Transfusion 1986; 26:391–393.

103. Food and Drug Administration: Blood Products Advisory Committee, Center for Biologist Evaluation and Research, 36th Meeting, Rockville, MD, May 29, 1992, Publication No. 92-026824, p. 433.

104. Buchholz DH, AuBuchon JP, Snyder EL, et al. Removal of *Yersinia enterocolitica* from AS-1 Red cells. Transfusion 1992; 32:667–672.

105. Gibb AP, Martin Km, Davidson GA, et al. Modeling the growth of *Yersinia enterocolitica* in donated blood. Transfusion 1004; 34:304–310.

106. Pietersz RNI, Reesink HW, Pauw W, et al. Prevention of *Yersinia enterocolitica* growth in red blood cell concentrates. Lancet 1992; 340:755–756.

107. Pietersz RNI, Reesink HW, Dekker MA, et al. Elimination of *Yersinia enterocolitica*

by a 20h hold of whole blood and removal of leukocytes by filtration (abstr). Transfusion 1992; 32(suppl):253S.

108. Lazarus HM, Herzig RH, Warm SE, Fishman DJ. Transfusion experience with platelet concentrates stored for 24 to 72 hours at 22°C: importance of storage time. Transfusion 1982; 22:39–43.

109. Punsalang A, Heal JM, Murphy PJ. Growth of gram-positive and gram-negative bacteria in platelet concentrates. Transfusion 1989; 29:596–599.

110. Connor J, Currie LM, Allan H, Livesey SA. Recovery of in vitro functional activity of platelet concentrates stored at 4°C and treated with second-messenger effectors. Transfusion 1996; 36:691–698.

111. Blajchman MA. The effect of leukodepletion on allogenic donor platelet survival and refractoriness in an animal model. Semin Hematol 1991; 28(suppl):14–17.

112. Brecher ME, Pineda AA, Torloni AS, et al. Prestorage leukocyte depletion: effect on leukocyte and platelet metabolities, erythrocyte lysis, metabolism and in vivo survival. Semin Hematol 1991; 28(suppl):3–9

113. Wenz B, Burns ER, Freundlich LF. Prevention of growth of *Yersinia enterocolitica* in blood by polyester fiber filtration. Transfusion 1992; 32:663–666.

114. Kim DM, Estes TJ, Brecher ME, et al. WBC filtration, blood gas analysis and plasma hemoglobin in *Yersinia enterocolitica* contaminated red cells. Transfusion 1992; 32:41S.

115. Hogman CF, Engstrand L. Factors affecting growth of *Yersinia enterocolitica* in cellular blood products. Transfus Med Rev 1996; 10:259–275.

116. Goldman M, Delage G. The role of leukodepletion in the control of transfusion-transmitted disease. Transfus Med Rev 1995; 9:9–19.

117. AuBuchon JP, Pickard C. White cell reduction and bacterial proliferation (letter). Transfusion 1993; 33:533–534.

118. Sherburne B, McCullough A, Dzik WH, et al. Bacterial proliferation in platelet concentrates is unaffected by pre-storage leukocyte depletion. Blood 1991; 78(suppl):350a.

119. Wenz B, Ciavarella D, Freundlich L. Effect of prestorage white cell reduction on bacterial growth in platelet concentrates. Transfusion 1993; 33:520–523.

120. Smith DA, Monaghan WP, Orcult RM et al. A presealed overwrap method of protecting frozen blood components during water immersion thawing. Transfusion 1981; 21:447–449.

121. Weber S, Lottspeich F, Kohl J. An epitope of elongation factor Tu is widely distributed within the bacterial and archaeal domains. J Bacteriol 1995; 177:11–19.

122. Seidl S. Syphilis screening in the 1990s. Transfusion 1990; 30:773–774.

123. Soendjojo A, Boedisantoso M, Ilias MI, et al. Syphilis d'emblee due to a blood transfusion. Br J Veneral Dis 1982; 58:149–150.

124. Risseeuw-Appel IM, Kothe FC. Transfusion syphilis: a case report. Sex Transm Dis 1983; 10:200–201.

125. Chambers RW, Foley HT, Schmidt PJ. Transfusion of syphilis by fresh blood components. Transfusion 1969; 9:32–34.

126. Van der Sluis JJ, Onvlee PC, Kothe FCHA, et al. Transfusion syphilis, survival of *Treponema pallidum* in donor blood I. Report of an orientating study. Vox Sang 1984; 47:197–204.

127. Van der Sluis JJ, ten Kate FJW, Vuzevski VD, et al. Transfusion syphilis, survival

of *Treponema pallidum* in donor blood II. Dose dependence of experimentally determined survival times. Vox Sang 1985; 49:390–399.

128. Quinn TC, Cannon RO, Glasser D, et al. The association of syphilis with risk of human immunodeficiency virus infection in patients attending sexually transmitted dissease clinics. Arch Intern Med 1990; 150:1297–1302.

129. Nelson KE, Vlahov D, Cohn S, et al. Sexually transmitted diseases in a population of intravenous drug users: association with seropositivity to the human immunodeficiency virus (HIV). J Infect Dis 1991; 164:457–463.

130. Potterat JJ. Does syphilis facilitate sexual acquisition of HIV? (letter). JAMA 1987; 258:473.

131. Otten MW Jr, Zaidi AA, Peterman TA, et al. High rate of HIV seroconversion among patients attending urban sexually transmitted disease clinics. AIDS 1994; 8:549–553.

132. Rosenblum L, Darrow W, Witte J, et al. Sexual practices in the transmission of hepatitis B virus and prevalence of hepatitis delta virus infection in female prostitutes in the United States. JAMA 1992; 267:2477–2481.

133. Thomas DL, Cannon RO, Shapiro CN, et al. Hepatitis C, hepatitis B, and human immunodeficiency virus infections among non-intravenous drug-using patients attending clinics for sexually transmitted diseases. J Infect Dis 1994; 169:990–995.

134. McAllister SK, Bland LA, Arduino MJ, et al. Patient cytokine response in transfusion-associated sepsis. Infect Immun 1994; 62:2126–2128.

135. Leveton LB, Sox HC, Stoto MA. HIV and blood supply: an analysis of crisis decisionmaking, executive summary. Transfusion 1996; 36:919–927.

11
HIV and Blood Transfusion

Celso Bianco and Maria Rios
New York Blood Center, New York, New York

I. INTRODUCTION

Human immunodeficiency virus (HIV) transmission by transfusion of blood and blood products has been the biggest driver of change in the history of transfusion medicine. Most of the medical world in the 1970s and the early 1980s was celebrating the control of infectious diseases. The hemophilia community was celebrating the enjoyment of a normal life provided by the use of plasma-derived clotting factor concentrates. In this environment of excitement and trust in the power of medical science and pharmaceuticals, the initial reactions to the news that the acquired immunodeficiency syndrome (AIDS) could possibly be transmitted by transfusion were denial and disbelief. The first report suggesting that clotting factor concentrates might transmit HIV was published in July 1982 (1). It described three hemophilia patients who developed immunosuppression and opportunistic infections. By December 1992, four more cases had been identified among patients with hemophilia A (2). The first case of suspected transmission of AIDS by blood transfusion was also reported at that time—a 20-month-old child who developed AIDS after receiving multiple transfusions, including a transfusion of platelets derived from blood donated by a male who subsequently was found to have AIDS (3). The findings about AIDS and blood transfusions prior to the identification of the etiological agent were reviewed intensively (4,5), and both the medical community and the patient community had no choice but to accept the growing evidence that AIDS was transmitted by a bloodborne infectious agent (6).

Assays for blood donor screening for HIV were licensed by the U. S. Food and Drug Administration (FDA) in March 1985 and led to a remarkable reduction in the transmission of HIV by transfusion. The development of viral inactivation technologies applicable to plasma derivatives stemmed the spread of AIDS through the large pools required for the manufacture of clotting factor concentrates. Unfortunately, the development was not smooth and six hemophilia patients previously seronegative for HIV seroconverted between September 1986 and September 1987. None had risk factors for HIV infection other than hemophilia. The implicated lots had been produced from plasma that had been screened for HIV and then heated at 60°C for 30 hours in the lyophilized state. Subsequently, concentrates produced by this process were removed from distribution (7). A similar event was identified by the Transfusion Safety Study (8).

More recently the Institute of Medicine of the National Academy of Sciences reviewed the history of the first few years of AIDS and transfusion in a landmark report. This report concluded that the AIDS epidemic was mismanaged by the blood-collecting agencies, professional organizations, hemophilia organizations, and the federal government. The report was vehemently criticized by the blood banking community for "judging history in hindsight" and for acceptance of allegations and opinions "as facts without critical examination and without placement in the context of contemporary knowledge" (9).

The tragedy of the first few years led to the development of successful programs for the prevention of transmission of AIDS by transfusion that included donor education, adequate medical history, physical examination, and mechanisms that allowed exclusion of individuals at risk in a confidential manner (10). The current screening tests for HIV antibodies are highly sensitive, and the Western blot confirmatory test is highly specific. Finally, additional screening tests capable of detecting antibodies to HIV variants, HIV-1 p24 antigen, and HIV RNA in the plasma of infected individuals have made blood transfusion extremely safe. In addition, all plasma derivatives are virally inactivated by chemical and physical methods and therefore do not transmit lipid-enveloped viruses such as HIV, hepatitis B virus (HBC), hepatitis C virus (HCV), and human T-cell lymphotropic virus (HTLV). For instance, the solvent detergent process was licensed in 1985 and became extremely successful (11).

II. THE VIRUS

The first retroviruses associated with human disease were HTLV-I and HTLV-II, discovered in 1980 and 1982, respectively (these viruses are the subject of another chapter in this book). Human immunodeficiency virus type 1 (HIV-1, formerly called LAV and HTLV-III) was first recognized in 1983 and identified as a lentivirus, the most complex group of retroviruses. In 1985 another virus closely related to HIV-1 was characterized and named HIV-2. Soon thereafter the simian immunodeficiency virus (SIV) was isolated from a captive macaque monkey. The biology and structure of HIV-1 and HIV-2 have been extensively reviewed (12,13). The genome of retroviruses is contained in two strands of RNA that must be transcribed into complementary DNA (cDNA) and integrate into the host viral genome for completion of its life cycle. All have a characteristic genome arrangement: they have a *gag* (group antigen) gene, a *pol* (polymerase) gene, and an *env* (envelope) gene flanked by two long terminal repeats (LTR). In addition, they have genes that regulate proviral gene expression both temporally and quantitatively. HIV contains more than six genes not found in other retroviruses. The *tat* gene encodes for the TAT protein. TAT binds to transactivating transcription elements and induces the synthesis of proviral RNA transcripts that encode for structural proteins of the virus. The *rev* gene codes for the REV protein, which increases expression of structural proteins. HIV proviral gene expression utilizes mRNA splicing to generate several viral proteins. In the absence of REV, these mRNA are only spliced into those that encode for regulatory proteins. The *nef* gene encodes for the NEF protein. NEF-negative strains replicate more rapidly than NEF-positive strains. Two other genes, *vif* and *vpu*, are required for virion assembly and maturation. Finally, a second transactivator gene supplementing *tat* is *vpr*. Its product, the VPR protein, accelerates the rate of production of viral proteins. Reduction of TAT levels downregulates overall viral gene expression. The balance between TAT and REV is the major event determining the viral latency/expression switch and subsequent disease development. HIV-2 has all the regulatory genes present in HIV-1 but differs from it in genomic organization. HIV-2 infection predominates in West Africa, and there is evidence that it is less virulent.

The most important HIV proteins are briefly described in Table 1. Figure 1 shows the HIV-1 genes and corresponding proteins.

III. GENETIC VARIATION

Genetic variation is the hallmark of the HIV infection. Diversity leads to the existence of major groups (Group M, or main, and Group O, outlier). The Group M viruses can be divided into at least eight distinct clades (A through H). Clades differ among themselves in 20–30% of their amino acid sequences of the gp120 protein. Isolates within clades (and within the same individuals) vary by 5–20% and are called quasispecies. Diversity can represent a problem for diagnostic tests. This issue is further discussed in the testing section of this chapter.

Diversity enables the virus to escape surveillance by the immune system. The virus establishes a persistent infection without being cleared by the immune system and induces immunodeficiency that allows its survival. Most of the

Table 1 Major Genes and Proteins of HIV-1 and HIV-2

Gene	Virus type	
	HIV-1	HIV-2
gag		
Precursor	p55	p56
Core	p24	p26
Matrix	p17	p16
Nucleocapsid	p9	
Nucleocapsid	p7	
pol		
Reverse transcriptase	p66, p51	p68, p53
Endonuclease	p31	p34
env		
Precursor	gp160	gp140
Surface	gp120	gp105 (125)
Trans-membrane	gp41	gp36 (41)
Regulatory		
Vif	p23	
Vpr	p15	
Tat	p14	
Rev	p19	
Vpu	p16	
Nef	p27	

diversity in HIV is generated during the reverse transcription of RNA into cDNA. The HIV reverse transcriptase (RT) lacks $3'$ exonuclease proofreading activity allowing the occurrence of errors during the transcription process. The overall mutation rate is very high, in the order of 3.4×10^{-5} per base per replication cycle. The degree of genetic variation observed in HIV infection is phenomenal—up to 20% within an infected individual (14,15). This high degree of diversity is particularly seen in patients receiving antiprotease therapy, reaching more than 7% by week 60 (16,17). Diversity is observed even within the same tissue. HIV-1 genomes infecting different regions of the brain of one study subject with HIV encephalitis (HIVE) had a mosaic structure, being assembled from different combinations of evolutionarily distinct lineages in p17 (gag), pol, individual hypervariable regions of gp 120 (V1/V2, V3, V4, and V5), and gp41/nef (18). Antigenic stimulation influences the dynamics of HIV replication, including the relative expression of different HIV variants (19). Naturally occurring recombinant HIV strains have been found in infected patients in regions of the world where multiple genotypic variants coexist (20).

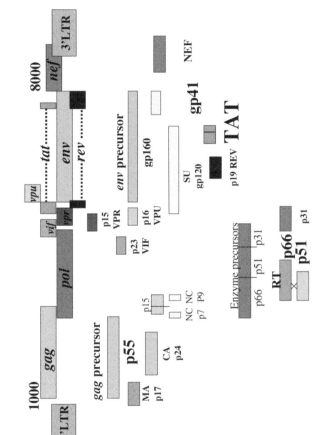

Figure 1 Graphic representation of the HIV genome and respective gene products. 5'LTR-*gag-pol-vpr-vpu-env-tat-rev-nef*-LRT3' HIV-1 gene products—the *gag* (group antigen) region encodes for the structural proteins: p17 (matrix), p24 (capsid), and p15 (p7, p9 nucleocapsid). The *pol* region encodes for the nonstructural proteins protease (physically part of the *pol* open reading frame), p31 (integrase), and p66/p51 (heterodimer reverse transcriptase). The *env* (envelope) region encodes for the envelope proteins gp120 (exposed to the external surface of the virus) and for gp41 (envelope trans-membrane). The genes *vpr*, *tat*, *rev*, and *nef* encode for p15, p14, p19, and p27, respectively, these are regulatory proteins involved in viral replication. The genes *vif* and *vpu* encode for p23 and p16, respectively.

IV.   HIV-1 (HIV M AND HIV O) AND HIV-2

The strains of HIV-1 that have caused the worldwide pandemic of AIDS have been designated as group M viruses. Another group of HIV-1 viruses character-ized by extensive genetic divergence from group M strains have been identified recently and classified as group O viruses. Group O viruses are rare but have been reported in patients from West and Central Africa (Cameroon, Gabon, Niger, Nigeria, Senegal, and Togo), nationals of these countries living in Europe, and one French national (21). The first case of Group O infection in the United States was identified in April 1996 in a woman who had come to the United States from Africa (22). Enzyme immunoassay (EIA) kits commercially available in the United States do not consistently detect antibodies elicited by infection with HIV-1 group O strains. For this reason, until FDA-licensed assays are able detect Group O variants, individuals who have emigrated from West and Central Africa are deferred from donating blood and tissue. Tests capable of detecting HIV Group O variants have been licensed and in use in European countries for several years (23).

HIV is found worldwide, with distribution ranging from 0.01 to 5.6% of the population. The prevalence may be even higher in some African countries. The prevalence of HIV-1 infection among blood donors in the United States is approximately 1:20,000. The prevalence of HIV infection among the general population has been estimated at 1:250. Currently, 33 U.S. states require reporting of HIV infection in addition to AIDS. It is expected that a more precise measure of incidence with increased reporting will allow better monitoring of the effect of the epidemic because of the therapies that have reduced AIDS incidence.

The major modes of transmission are either homosexual or heterosexual intercourse, parenteral transmission through needle sharing among injecting drug users (IDU), and through transfusion of contaminated blood or blood products. HIV is also transmitted from mother to infant, either intrapartum, perinatally, or via breast-feeding. By December 1998, 679,739 cases of AIDS had been reported to CDC since the beginning of the epidemic. Of these, 48% occurred among men who had sex with men and 26% among injection drug users. Men who had sex with men and also injected drugs constituted 10% of the reported cases. Ten percent of the cases occurred in heterosexual contacts of individuals at risk (sex with an injection drug user, a bisexual male, a transfusion recipient, or a person with hemophilia) (24).

HIV is present in seminal fluid, cervical mucus, and vaginal fluid. There is a stronger association of efficacy of HIV transmission with receptive anal intercourse, but the virus can also be transmitted during vaginal intercourse. The probability of a woman becoming infected by an HIV-positive male partner during vaginal intercourse is estimated at 0.2% per encounter, and probability is even lower for infection from a woman to a man in vaginal intercourse.

Maternal transmission of HIV accounts for over 90% of HIV infections in infants and children. The efficiency of transmission from mother to child ranges from 13 to 42% in the absence of intervention (HIV treatment). Between 50 and 70% of the mother-to-child transmissions occur late in pregnancy or during birth, when maternal blood may enter the fetal circulation, or by neonatal mucosal exposure to the virus during labor or delivery. Breast-feeding increases the risk of HIV transmission by 14% over the risk of HIV infection during pregnancy or delivery (13).

V. HIV AND DISEASE

Because CD4$^+$ T cells and macrophages are the only cells found to be infected consistently in vivo, these are considered critical for viral replication. However, HIV has been found in B cells, natural killer (NK) cells, CD8$^+$ T cells, peripheral and follicular dendritic cells, eosinophils, precursors of CD4$^+$ bone marrow cells, Langerhans cells, megakariocytes, astrocytes, oligodendrocytes, renal epithelial cells, cervical cells, gastrointestinal epithelial cells, and cells from organs such as liver, lungs, salivary glands, eyes, prostate, testes, and adrenal glands (13). The CD4 molecule is the primary receptor for HIV, and essentially any cells that express this molecule, even in a transient stage, may be susceptible to infection. The viral gp 120 binding CD4 is the first step in viral infection. That CD4 binding is critical, but not sufficient, for viral infection is clearly demonstrated by the fact that human brain and skin cells expressing the CD4 molecule bind to HIV envelope but their membranes fail to fuse. This observation indicates a requirement for other components (co-receptors) for proper fusion and consequent cell infection.

The two most important co-receptors are the chemokine receptors CXCR4 (receptor for SDF-1) and CCR5 (receptor for MIP-1α, MIP-β, and RANTES). The chemokines that bind to these receptors can block HIV infection, and natural resistance to infection is observed in individuals who have defect in the gene encoding for the CCR5 (25,26). Mutant CCR5 co-receptors can confer resistance to HIV-1 infection. p120 binds to CD4 (T4) on T lymphocytes and other cells and leads to infection. Co-receptors on T cells (fusin) and macrophages (CCR5) also play a role in the binding and penetration of the virus. A polymorphism in the CCR5 gene (with a 32 bp deletion) reduces the ability of HIV to enter cells, slows decline in CD4 cells, and leads to a reduced (>100×) viral load. About 50% of long-term survivors of HIV are heterozygous for CCR5 deletion (27). HIV resistance has also been observed in individuals with a combination of two separate CCR5 mutations (28). The distribution of the homozygous deleted CCR5 genotype among 566 persons with hemophilia and 97 transfusion recipients known to have been exposed to HIV indicated that the lack of CCR5 expression protected persons from infection. Only individuals who are homozygous for CCR5 are protected, and there is no difference in the rate of progression to AIDS between infected heterozygous and homozygous wild-type subjects (29).

VI. CELL TROPISM AND CONSEQUENCE OF INFECTION

The tropism of the virus for monocyte/macrophage (M-tropic) or CD4$^+$ T cell (T-tropic) is determined by the co-receptor used for entry. M-tropic virus can only use CCR5, and T-tropic virus uses CXCR4. There are isolates capable of using both CCR5 and CXCR4. In the course of infection of CD4$^+$ T cells, virions are released almost exclusively to the plasma surrounding the cells and there is extensive cell death. In the course of infection of monocytes and macrophages, the virions are often released into intracytoplasmic vacuoles and there is less cell death. The tropism for macrophages or CD4$^+$ T cells seems to be determined by changes in *env* genes. Other CD4$^+$ cells like microglia and follicular dendritic cells can also be infected and function as anatomical "reservoirs," protecting the virus from antiretroviral drugs.

VII. PATHOGENY

The evidence demonstrating that HIV-1 and HIV-2 cause AIDS is overwhelming. This evidence has been contested by a small number of prominent scientists (30), but this opinion has been totally rejected by others on the basis of availability of sound scientific data.

Primary HIV infection is followed by a retroviral syndrome that develops in 40–90% of cases (31). Usual symptoms are "flu"-like and include fever, fatigue, pharyngitis, weight loss, myalgias, headache, and nausea. About 50% of the patients present lymphadenopathy and night sweats. These symptoms disappear after a few weeks. During this period, HIV-1 RNA concentrations vary widely (10^4–10^6 molecules/mL). Because of the difficulty in identifying the date of exposure to HIV-1 infection in persons other than transfusion recipients, studies of the incubation periods for AIDS have been limited. One study based on a cohort of 84 homosexual and bisexual men showed that the maximum likelihood estimate for the proportion of infected homosexual men developing AIDS was 0.99 (90% CI, 0.38–1). Furthermore, the maximum likelihood estimate for the mean incubation period for AIDS in homosexual men was 7.8 years (90% CI, 4.2–15.0 years), which was close to the estimate of 8.2 years for adults developing transfusion-associated AIDS (32). European data on transfusion-associated (TA) AIDS cases reported in 1989 estimated the median incubation period in adults from 6.5 to 11 years (33).

HIV infection results in progressive elimination of helper T lymphocytes with consequent immunodeficiency. Most individuals remain asymptomatic for several years prior to development of AIDS. The definition of AIDS is based on the presence of low CD4$^+$ counts (CD4 < 200/μL or CD4$^+$ T cells < 14% of total lymphocytes) or opportunistic infections. The normal concentration of CD4$^+$ T cells ranges between 800 and 1400/L. AIDS-defining illnesses include tuberculosis, atypical mycobacteria, fungal infection, cytomegalovirus retinitis, (CMV) *Pneumocystis carinii* pneumonia, oral and esophageal candidiasis, Herpes simplex infection, cryptosporidia, isospora, cryptococcal meningitis, toxoplasmosis, Kaposi's sarcoma, and non-Hodgkin lymphomas. A number of neurological diseases also occur. Among them are encephalitis, aseptic meningitis, progressive multifocal leukoencephalopathy (PML), central nervous system (CNS) lymphoma, and AIDS dementia. Thrombocytopenia is very common in late HIV and responds poorly to usual therapy. Parvovirus B19 may be an important infection in AIDS patients. However, aggressive antiretroviral treatment may effectively diminish transfusion requirements among HIV-infected individuals with pure red blood cell (RBS) aplasia resulting from parvovirus B19 infection (34). The course of HIV infection and progression to AIDS has been extensively reviewed (13). Until the recent past the prognosis of AIDS was bleak, and death usually occurred within 8–12 years of diagnosis. Recent therapeutic advances have changed this picture entirely, with substantial reduction in mortality. HIV mortality has decreased from 29.4 to 8.8 per 100 person-years from 1995 to 1997 (35).

The hypothesis that blood transfusions could directly accelerate progression to AIDS through activation of HIV-1 expression and/or transfusion-related immunosuppression was proposed several years ago. In essence, allogeneic leukocytes would present an antigenic challenge to HIV-infected mononuclear cells, which would then proliferate and increase viral production. In vitro incubation of HIV-infected mononuclear cells with allogeneic blood components (mainly leukocytes) results in increased viral replication. However, preliminary data suggest that leukocyte reduction prior to RBC transfusion does not alter viral replication compared with standard packed RBC transfusions (33)

VIII.   HIV TRANSMISSION BY TRANSFUSION OF BLOOD AND BLOOD PRODUCTS

Most recipients of HIV-infected blood become seropositive (37). HIV transmission by transfusion was also recognized through testing of repositories in clinical laboratories. For instance, 18 of 211 patients with leukemia who had been multiply transfused before the availability of screening for HIV antibody were found to be seropositive for HIV (38). Life-table analysis of 116 seropositive recipients suggested that AIDS develops in 49% (95% CI, 36–62%) within 7 years after infection (39). By December 1998 there were 8,760 cases of AIDS among recipients of blood, blood components, or tissue and 5,145 among patients with hemophilia or other coagulation disorders among the 688,200 cases of AIDS reported to CDC (24). This number is somewhat smaller than that predicted by modeling studies suggesting a total of 15,000 eventual cases of AIDS attributable to infection by blood transfusion prior to July 1985 (40,41). The incidence of transfusion-associated HIV-1 infection in San Francisco was estimated to have risen rapidly from the first occurrence in 1978 to a peak in late 1982 of approximately 1.1% per transfused unit. The decrease after 1982 coincided with the implementation of high-risk donor deferral measures. It is estimated that, overall, approximately 2,135 transfusion recipients were infected with HIV-1 in the San Francisco region alone (37). By December 1998, 39 cases of AIDS had been reported among recipients of blood that had screened negative for HIV antibody (transfused after introduction of screening tests in 1985). The number of transfusion-associated AIDS cases will certainly be affected by the newer HIV therapies. Accurate data about transmission will not be available until reporting of HIV infection (instead of AIDS) is required for the entire United States.

One of the most important sources of information about HIV transmission by transfusion was a repository of approximately 200,000 sera from blood donors established in late 1984 and early 1985 by the Transfusion Safety Study (TSS), which was sponsored by the National Heart, Lung, and Blood Institute (NHLBI). Collections were made in the four metropolitan areas with the highest prevalence of AIDS prior to the availability of screening tests for antibodies to HIV in March 1985. Retrospective testing of this repository showed an overall anti-HIV-1 prevalence of 16 cases per 10,000 donations (42). The vast majority of individuals who received transfusion of blood from seropositive donors became positive for antibodies to HIV, and many developed AIDS. This was documented by extensive "lookback" studies. Essentially, a seropositive donation triggered a search for records of all prior donations made by that donor and notification of recipients and testing whenever possible. One of the earliest studies identified seropositive donors among the units transfused to each of 19 patients who developed AIDS and were seropositive for HIV (43). HIV-1 was isolated from the blood of blood donors and HIV-positive blood recipients for months after the transfusion event— clear documentation that HIV viremia was persistent (44). In one rather informative case, blood components harvested from a single, asymptomatic, seropositive donor were transfused into a group of cancer patients. Of 10 living recipients, 9 had antibodies to the virus. Cultures for HIV were positive in 7 of the 9 seropositive recipients. Six seropositive recipients had developed immunological and clinical sequelae of HIV infection (45). A similar case of transmission occurred in a bone marrow transplant recipient (46).

In the study of a cohort of pediatric patients in a large private metropolitan hospital, of the 775 children identified as having received transfusions during the project period, 644 (83%) were located, and 443 (69%) were evaluated for HIV-1 infection. Among those evaluated, 33 (7%) had antibody to HIV-1 (47).

IX. LOOKBACK FOR HIV

These studies were so effective at identifying patients exposed to HIV prior to the availability of blood donor screening tests that "lookback" for HIV became part of the routine of blood collecting facilities and was ultimately mandated by FDA. Some authors found that an expanded "lookback" could help identify recipients at risk. They cross-referenced blood donor lists with case reports of AIDS made to the Department of Health and identified several seropositive recipients of blood donated by these individuals (48). This approach was not widely utilized because of ethical questions and concerns about confidentiality.

One of the most tragic aspects of transfusion-associated HIV was the inadvertent transmission of the virus to spouses and sexual partners. One CDC study verified that 7 of 32 (21.9%) female partners of male recipients were themselves infected with HIV-1, as compared with none of 14 male partners of female recipients ($p = 0.08$). Transmission was not associated with frequency of unprotected vaginal intercourse (49). In another study, blood recipients who transmitted HIV-1 to their sexual partners had higher mean viral RNA levels than did nontransmitting recipients (4.3 vs. 3.6 $\log_{10}$ copies/mL; $p = 0.05$), suggesting that viral load contributed to heterosexual infectivity (50). The most important factor associated with transmission of HIV in a review of 132 recipients who tested positive for antibody to HIV-1 as part of the Transfusion Safety Study was viremia (51). Review of data also suggested that older RBC units were less likely to transmit HIV than fresher units, probably because of the viability of lymphocytes (52).

Another sad aspect of the AIDS epidemic took place in less developed countries in Latin America, Africa, and Asia. For instance, plasmapheresis banks reusing needles played a major role in the dissemination of HIV infection in Mexico, where paid donors provided a third of the blood used in 1986 (53). By 1996, 9 of the 12 Central and South American countries studied screened all donors for HIV (54). However, donor screening is spotty at best in many areas of the Middle East, India, and Africa. Although the contribution of transfusion-transmitted infection to the HIV epidemic has not been accurately assessed, an estimated 5–10% of HIV infections in developing countries are due to blood transfusion. In a study conducted one year after implementation of HIV blood screening in the largest hospital in the capital city of the Democratic Republic of the Congo, an estimated 25% of pediatric HIV infections and 40% of infections among children over one year of age were due to transfusion (55).

X. IDIOPATHIC CD4$^+$ T-CELL LYMPHOCYTOPENIA,
OR AIDS WITHOUT HIV

In the course of the International Conference on AIDS in 1992, there were several case reports of patients with profound immunosuppression without serological or molecular evidence of infection by HIV. The general media immediately published these reports and raised substantial concerns about a potential new epidemic of immunosuppression caused by an unknown infectious agent (56,57). The case definition of idiopathic CD4$^+$ T-cell lymphocytopenia (ICL) was broad: a CD4$^+$ cell count lower than 400/L in an individual who was negative for HIV serology. Follow-up studies demonstrated that transmissible agents did not cause this condition (58,59). A CDC task force reviewed more than 230,000 cases of AIDS and 47 patients with ICL. It confirmed that the disorder was rare and represented various clinical and immunological states not associated with a transmissible agent (60). The best explanation for the ICL phenomenon came from a study of the distribution of CD4$^+$ cells in normal individuals. Individuals with a low CD4$^+$ count are at the tail end of the normal distribution. Essentially, ICL appeared to be an artifact of the normal statistical distribution of CD4$^+$ values (61).

XI. DONOR SELECTION

In the absence of screening assays prior to 1985, a large amount of effort was developed in donor screening procedures and potential surrogate tests. In early 1983, the New York Blood Center (NYBC) introduced confidential unit exclusion (CUE). The procedure was designed to allow members of groups at increased risk of AIDS to confidentially designate their donations for laboratory studies and not for transfusion. AIDS-related questions in medical history led to a 2% increase in donor rejections; 97% of donors said their blood could be used for transfusions; 1.4% said their blood could be used for laboratory studies only; and 1.6% did not respond (62). CUE has been less effective recently in the detection of HIV-positive individuals than in the early days of donor screening for HIV. A study performed in Canada showed that only 1.7% of individuals positive on HIV Western blot used CUE (63). In the last few years none of the HIV-positive donors to NYBC have used CUE (C. Bianco, personal communication).

About 50% of the donors who tested positive for HIV in 1985 used CUE. This high degree of effectiveness may have been unique to NYBC (64). Overall, only 3–5% of units donated by window-period donors were not transfused because of the CUE option. Although donors who confidentially exclude their blood from transfusion were 21 times more likely to have HIV antibody, the rarity of window-period donors and the infrequency of confidential exclusion by window-period donors cause the CUE option to have minimal impact on transfusion safety. Only a miniscule number of HIV-positive donors identified by NYBC in the last 10 years opted for CUE (C. Bianco, personal communication).

A major effort has been dedicated to understanding why HIV-positive individuals donate blood despite the educational materials provided to donors and questions asked during medical history. Of 388 seropositive men who donated between 1988 and 1989, 56% had had sex with men, 10% had used drugs intravenously, 8% had had sex with intravenous drug users, and 27% had no identified risk. Of 124 seropositive women, 58% had had sex with men at risk for HIV (81% of whom used drugs intravenously), 5% had used drugs intravenously, and 41% had no identified risk. Racial and ethnic minorities made up 68% of seropositive donors (black, 38%; Hispanic, 30%) (65). More recent data from the study show an increase in individuals with no identified risk and in minorities. A study sponsored by FDA in the early 1990s suggested that direct questions about risk behavior would be effective in the identification of individuals with risk behavior (66). Direct oral questions were reasonably well accepted by potential blood donors (67). On April 23, 1992, FDA recommended adoption of the direct questioning approach to medical history by all regulated blood establishments (68).

XII. TESTING

The history of introduction of HIV screening tests for blood donor screening has been extensively reviewed (69).

A. Surrogate Testing

Prior to the availability of a specific screening test for HIV, there were many attempts to identify surrogate assays that could assist in donor screening. For instance, some scientists at CDC proposed the use of the antibody to the hepatitis B core antigen (HBcAb) and the detection of urinary neopterin for identification of donors at risk (70). Others proposed the use of levels of $CD4^+$ cells for the screening of blood donors (71). However, a study of the correlation of HBcAb and $CD4^+$ cell counts with use of CUE (a correlate of risk behavior) suggested that the contribution of these assays in the absence of a specific screening assay for HIV would be relatively small (72). In addition, determination of T-helper/T-suppressor cell ratios, HBcAb, and immune complexes among 18 sets of blood donors who donated blood to recipients who subsequently developed AIDS could not distinguish suspected transmitters from controls. None of the assays was as sensitive and specific as the later developed tests for antibody to HIV (73).

B.   Specific Tests

The first specific tests for antibodies to HIV became available in March 1985. Within several weeks, the entire blood supply was being screened using the first-generation assays. These assays had a number of recognized problems, such as lack of specificity and known cross-reactivity with antibodies to HLA antigens that were present on the cell line used to grow the virus. There was so much concern about lack of specificity that the FDA Memorandum to Blood Establishments published in February 1995 determined that a sample was reactive only when, after an initial reactive screen, it was repeated in duplicate and one of the duplicates was reactive. There were no confirmatory assays available, and there was widespread concern about notifying donors of reactive test results in the absence of adequate sensitivity and specificity data. Most blood-collecting facilities delayed notification of reactive blood donors until the first quarter of 1987, when the Western blot confirmatory assay was licensed (74). Despite these caveats, the early HIV screening assays contributed immensely to the safety of the blood supply. The development of blood donor screening tests for HIV has been extensively reviewed in the past (75).

C.   Testing for HIV-2, HIV-1 Group O

FDA recommended that screening of blood donors for HIV-2 be implemented by June 1, 1992, a few months after licensing a combined test for antibodies to HIV-1 and HIV-2 (76). Between June 1992 and June 1995, there were two HIV-2–positive donors identified among an estimated 74 million blood and plasma donations that had been screened for HIV-2 (77). The next version of screening assays for HIV-1 must also be able to detect HIV-1 Group O variants, as discussed previously (21–23).

D.   Confirmation and Indeterminates

The licensure of the Western blot assay for antibodies to HIV in 1987 introduced the then new concept of indeterminate test results. Fearful that test results that were not clearly negative could be associated with risk of HIV transmission to recipients, FDA determined that donors with reactive results on screening tests that were not negative (a blank strip) on Western blot could not be accepted as blood donors. Several subsequent studies documented the lack of specificity of these EIA assays and have clearly shown that individuals with indeterminate test results do not constitute a risk to the safety of the blood supply. For instance, donors with indeterminate supplemental test results for HIV identified between 1990 and 1993 were tested by EIA, Western blot, and peptide assays for antibodies to HIV-2 and HIV-1 subtype O. Peripheral blood mononuclear cells and/or plasma from the follow-up samples were also tested for HIV-1 DNA and/or RNA by polymerase chain reaction. The study concluded that contemporary blood donors classified as indeterminate in supplemental HIV testing are infrequently infected with HIV and recommended that donors whose follow-up samples test negative in anti-HIV-1/2 EIAs and negative or persistently indeterminate in Western blots be considered eligible for reinstatement (78). Another study addressed donors who were positive for HIV-1 by Western blot but were possibly falsely positive because they lacked reactivity to p31. Many of these individuals were tested by PCR and shown not to be infected with HIV-1. The false-positive rate of Western blot–positive donors was 4.8% of the EIA reactive donors and 0.0004% (1 in 251,000) of all donors (95% CI, 1 in 173,000 to 1 in 379,000 donors) (79).

E. Addressing the Window of Seroconversion for HIV

As mentioned above, the introduction of screening tests for antibodies to HIV led to a substantial reduction of transmission by blood and blood products. However, a small number of cases continued to occur, mostly because of the window of seroconversion, that is, the period between the first presence of infectious virus in the circulation of a recently infected individual and the ability of the screening assay to detect the HIV infection. Reducing or closing the window has been the ultimate goal of every assay improvement and new assay technology implemented since 1985, as shown in Table 2. The first well-documented cases of transmission to 13 blood recipients who had received blood from 7 donors who screened negative for antibody to HIV at the time of donation were published in 1988. All 7 donors seroconverted (80).

Table 2 Evolution of Blood Donor Screening Assays for HIV

Date	Test	HIV per million transfusions	Window (days)
Pre-1985	N.A.	2400	—
1985–1987	HIV-1 (1.0)	7.7	56
1987–1990	HIV-1 (1.0+)	5.7	42
1991–1992	EIA-2 (2.0)	4.5	33
1992–1996	HIV-1/2 (3.0)	1.8	22
1996–	P24 Ag	1.3	16
(?)	DNA PCR	(1.3)	(16)
1999	RNA PCR	0.9	11

Estimates of risk associated with the window of seroconversion for HIV in the 1980s were derived from studies of donor-recipient pairs. In a study of 4,163 adults undergoing cardiac surgery who received 36,282 transfusions of blood components, the investigators found one case of HIV-1 transmission by transfusion of screened blood components or 0.003% per unit (81). This large multicenter study among cardiac surgery patients was updated in 1992 and included 11,532 patients who received 120,312 units in three hospitals. Two new HIV infections were detected, for a rate of 0.0017% with an upper limit of the 95% Cl of 0.0053% (82). The study of 179 seropositive donors and 39 recipients of blood also addressed the issue of seroconversion from these donors. The window period averaged 45 days, with few, if any, donors remaining infectious and seronegative for longer than 6 months (83).

Transfusion risk estimated based on the window period of assays in use for donor screening was 1:153,000 per unit transfused in 1989 (84). More recently, two major studies generated more accurate and up-to-date estimates of window-period transmission. A collaboration between the Centers for Disease Control and Prevention (CDC) and the American Red Cross estimated that in 1992–1993 one donation in every 360,000 (95% CI, 210,000–1,140000) was made during the window period. In addition, it estimated that 1 in 2,600,000 donations was HIV seropositive but was not identified as such because of an error in the laboratory. The study also estimated that 15–42% of window-period donations were discarded because they were seropositive on laboratory tests other than the HIV-antibody test. The final estimated risk for a transfusion recipient was 1:450,000–660,000 donations of screened blood (85). The other study was based on incidence data collected through the Retroviral Epidemiology Donor Study supported by the National Heart, Lung and Blood Institute (86). It estimated the risk of donations made by donors whose units passed all screening tests during an infectious window as 1:493,000 (95% CI, 202,000–2,778,000).

Improvement in the sensitivity of anti-HIV assays has resulted in significant shortening of the preseroconversion window period. A study comparing the sensitivity of early screening assays with current generation assays showed days of shortening of the HIV window period as follows: contemporary anti-HIV-1/2 EIAs, 20.3 days (95% Cl, 8.0–32.5); p24 antigen and DNA PCR, 26.4 days (95% Cl, 12.6–38.7); and RNA PCR, 31.0 days (95% Cl, 16.7–45.3) (87).

Testing donor specimens with both a sensitive HIV-1 EIA (3A11 assay) and a less sensitive modification of the same EIA (3A11-LS assay) allows for the differentiation between individuals with early HIV-1 infection from those infected for longer periods. This is a result of the increase in the affinity of antibodies that accompanies development of the immune response in the infected individual. This approach allowed estimation of incident infections among first-time donors as 7.18 per 100,000 per year (95% CI, 4.51–11.20/100,000) versus repeat blood donors with 2.95/100,000 per year (95% CI, 1.14–6.53/100,000). Thus, the incidence of HIV infection among first-time donors is 2.4 times higher than that of repeat donors (88). Interestingly, concern over the theoretical possibility of disease transmission via blood from donors who develop Creutzfeldt-Jakob disease has led to proposals for the deferral of donors who are 50 years of age or older. This would require recruitment of a higher number of first-time donors to replace the deferred individuals. The estimated increase in the risk of infected units would be 12% for HIV, 21% for HCV, and 22% for HBsAg (89). The potential effects of the introduction of research assays for HIV RNA will be discussed later in this chapter.

F. Blood Donor Screening for HIV-1 p24 Antigen

The desire to shorten the window of seroconversion for HIV led to the development of a test for HIV-1 p24 antigen that could identify viral particles in circulation, very much like the very effective HBsAg assays. Unfortunately, large clinical trials showed that the contribution of the HIV-1 p24 antigen assays would be miniscule. For instance, a large trial carried out in 1989 among over 500,000 volunteer blood donors in the United States failed to identify a single individual positive for HIV-1 p24 antigen and negative on the screening test for antibodies to HIV-1. The finding suggested that the available HIV-1 p24 antigen test would not add substantially to the safety of the U.S. blood supply (90).

However, concerns about the risk of transmission of HIV by donations made in the window of seroconversion continued to rise with the infrequent, but periodic, identification of cases of transmission of HIV by transfusion (91,92). The incidence rate of HIV in certain populations was also extremely high. In one study of 2300 emergency room patients, 180 (7.8%) were Western blot (WB)–positive for HIV-1 antibodies. Of 2120 antibody-negative or WB-indeterminate patients, none of whom were identified on clinical grounds as having primary HIV-1 infection, 6 (0.28%) were HIV-1 p24 antigen–positive and had serologies consistent with primary HIV-1 infection. Of these 6, 3 were seronegative even with third-generation antibody ELISA assays. Thus 3 of 183 individuals showing up at an emergency room in a large metropolitan area were positive for HIV p24 antigen and negative for antibodies for HIV-1 (93).

The issue of HIV-1 p24 antigen screening was addressed by the FDA Blood Products Advisory Committee (BPAC). After extensive discussion, the committee decided not to recommend its introduction. The decision was based on two major issues: lack of cost benefit, considering the miniscule number of individuals that would be detected, and fear of the "magnet" effect, that is, fear that individuals at risk may be tempted to donate blood in order to obtain confidential test results (94,95). Following the meeting, FDA received a letter from a U.S. congressman questioning BPAC's decision. The FDA commissioner reconstituted BPAC. On August 8, 1995, FDA issued a Memorandum to Registered Establishments recommending adoption of the HIV-1 p24 antigen screening assay as soon as licensed (96). The first test was licensed on March 14, 1996, and implemented overnight by the blood banking community. By March 1999, with almost 40 million units screened, there had been five cases of individuals positive on the HIV-1 p24 antigen test and negative on the antibody test, for a rate of 1:8,000,000. This rate is much smaller than that predicted at the time of test introduction (about seven cases per year). The most accepted explanation is that recently infected individuals have a viral syndrome, do not feel well, have a fever, and do not donate.

G. Blood Donor Screening by Nucleic Acid Amplification Technologies

Obviously, HIV-1 p24 antigen screening could not "close" the window of seroconversion for HIV. In an attempt to further address this issue, FDA convened a meeting in September 1994 to discuss the feasibility of "closing the window" through nucleic acid amplification technologies (NAT) (97). That meeting concluded that NAT was promising, but that the technology was not practical for mass donor screening. In October 1996 NHLBI awarded contracts to manufacturers for the development of tests and equipment that would allow mass screening of blood donors HCV and HIV RNA using cGMP-compliant automated methodology.

The availability of commercial assays based on (NAT) encouraged the development of approaches for screening blood donors even before automated equipment became available. One of these approaches was to use pools of donor samples. Pools would reduce the number of specimens that needed to be tested because the vast majority of blood donors are negative for HIV (and for HCV). Pools had already been used successfully to determine risk of HIV transmission in a study carried out in San Francisco. In that study, 1530 pools of leukocytes from 50 donors each were tested for HIV by culture, by PCR, or by both. One pool was positive for both, and the calculated risk of HIV transmission for the donor population (November 1987–December 1989) was estimated at 1:61,171 (98).

In 1999, U.S. blood centers implemented NAT screening of blood donors under Investigational New Drug (IND) applications submitted to FDA as clinical research studies in collaboration with the manufacturers. The study objectives are to determine the specificity and reproducibility of the NAT test systems on pooled samples in high volume blood donor screening laboratories, to assess the impact of NAT testing on blood component availability, and to evaluate the use of NAT tests to improve the safety of the blood supply. Two test systems are being used: the Roche Molecular Systems' COBAS AMPLISCREEN for HCV and HIV and the GenProbe Pooled Plasma HIV-1/HCV Amplified Assay. The Roche COBAS

AMPLISCREEN system is based on PCR amplification of target cDNA using virus-specific complementary primers, that is, hybridization of the amplified products to oligonucleotide probes specific to the target. The entire test process takes approximately 6 hours. The GenProbe HIV-1/HCV test, which detects HIV-1 and/or HCV RNA in a single tube multiplex format, is based on transcription-mediated amplification (TMA), which utilizes two enzymes to produce RNA amplicons via DNA intermediates. These assays are being carried out in pools of plasma samples that include 16–24 donors. If the pool is positive in NAT, it is broken down into smaller pools and retested until the positive sample is identified. Although data from preclinical studies are encouraging, in that several donors positive on NAT and negative for antibodies to HCV have been identified, specificity, sensitivity, reproducibility, and run validity data for these test systems are unknown in the donor screening laboratory setting. To date, with over 2 million units screened, only one donor positive for HIV-1 on NAT and negative for antibodies to HIV-1 or p24 antigen has been confirmed to have been identified.

Similar systems have been implemented by manufacturers of plasma derivatives and by several countries in Europe, and recent experience suggests that NAT testing reduces the window of seroconversion for HCV. The data for HIV are not as encouraging (99–101).

Experimental data obtained in chimpanzees indicate that NAT may actually completely close the window of seroconversion for HIV. Apparently, the initial replication of HIV occurs in cells of the immune system that are not circulating. When viral particles appear in the circulation, NAT becomes positive. There was no demonstrable infectivity in either plasma or peripheral blood mononuclear cells obtained before molecular markers were detectable. This suggested that the infectious window is considerably shorter than the total window as measured from exposure and that NAT might not only shorten the seronegative window, but also totally prevent transfusion-transmitted HIV infection (102).

One issue highlighted by the introduction of NAT under a research protocol was the appropriateness of using postexposure prophylaxis (PEP) against HIV in case a donated unit was transfused and HIV-1 NAT test results became available only after the transfusion. CDC has issued extremely useful guidelines for PEP that are applicable to recipients of potentially infected blood products and to health care workers inadvertently exposed to HIV-positive materials (103).

XIII. DONOR NOTIFICATION AND COUNSELING

A fundamental piece of the prevention of disease transmission by transfusion is donor notification and counseling. During this process, donors with positive results for infectious disease markers are notified of test results and are educated about the risk of transmitting infections to recipients of their donations (104). Unfortunately, the donor counseling process for the majority of the other donors, that is, those with repeatedly reactive results for HIV on EIA or on HIV-1 p24 antigen with negative or indeterminate supplemental test results, is not very effective.

Donor notification has been trivialized by the bureaucratic approach of FDA guidances: (a) all donors with repeatedly reactive results are deferred from donating blood even if negative on subsequent donations; (b) donors with indeterminate test results, that is, with any bands in Western blot even if clearly nonviral bands, are never acceptable as blood donors again; (c) donors who had repeatedly reactive test results on more than one donation in the past, even in the first generation of nonspecific EIAs, are not acceptable; and (d) there are no negative results for HIV-1 p24 antigen supplemental tests. Results are either positive or indeterminate. Thus, regulations have created a cadre of individuals in limbo. These donors cannot be cleared even after years of negative screening test results and negative NAT results. Donors are extremely frustrated by these rules. Blood centers are very frustrated by these rules. They do not contribute to the safety of the blood supply.

XIV. COST/BENEFIT CONSIDERATIONS

There have been many attempts to identify strategies that facilitate the implementation of blood donor screening assays for HIV in third world countries. Most of these approaches have been rejected outright, despite evidence that they would have contributed substantially to the safety of the blood supply in these countries. One study showed a reduction of 70% in costs when pools of 10 samples were used for initial EIA screen (105). Another study reused wells on EIA plates that had tested negative on previous rounds and concluded that there was no significant reduction in sensitivity of the test samples or controls when run in parallel with new plates (106). Obviously, these procedures are unacceptable in the United States or Europe. They have rarely been used in third world countries because of concerns about tests that are less sensitive than those used in industrialized countries.

A review of the addition of newer blood donor screening tests for HIV since 1992 (HIV-2, HIV-1 p24 antigen, requirement for HIV-1 type O sensitivity, research NAT) show that their contribution to prevention of HIV transmission by transfusion of blood and blood products is miniscule, if any. This impression is confirmed by studies designed to estimate the cost-effectiveness of expanding the HIV testing protocol for donated blood by adding HIV-1 p24 antigen detection or RNA PCR (at costs of $5/unit and $8/unit, respectively). The addition of p24 antigen testing would prevent eight more cases at a net additional cost of $60 million annually ($2.3 million/quality-adjusted life-year); RNA PCR testing would prevent 16 more cases at a net additional cost of $96 million annually ($2.0 million/quality-adjusted life-year). The authors concluded that the cost-effectiveness of these additions was far below that of most medical interventions. On the other hand, HIV antibody testing prevents 1568 cases of transfusion-acquired HIV infection each year at a modest cost of $3,600 per quality-adjusted year of life saved (107). [This study of test efficacy projected based on anticipated window-period reductions (6 days for p24 antigen, 11 days for RNA PCR) and donor seroconversion rates derived from the Retrovirus Epidemiology Donor Study on the basis of current estimates of HIV prevalence rates in blood donors (1/10,000) and 16 million annual transfusions in the United States.]

XV. CONCLUSION

The control of HIV transmission by transfusion of blood and blood products is one of the biggest success stories of science and medicine. We certainly will benefit from the study of all the efforts applied by many people in many different areas to address this major issue. The major issue that still remains unresolved for the transfusion medicine community is how to effectively transmit information about the safety of the blood supply instead of the risks associated with blood transfusions.

REFERENCES

1. Centers for Disease Control and Prevention. Epidemiologic notes and reports: *Pneumocystis carinii* pneumonia among persons with hemophilia A. MMWR 1982; 31:365–367,
2. Centers for Disease Control and Prevention. Update on acquired immunodeficiency syndrome (AIDS) among patients with hemophilia A. MMWR 1982; 31:644–646,
3. Centers for Disease Control and Prevention. Epidemiologic notes and reports: possible transfusion-associated acquired immune deficiency syndrome (AIDS)—California. MMWR 1982; 31:652–654,
4. Jett JR, Kuritsky JN, Katzmann JA, Homburger HA. Acquired immunodeficiency syndrome associated with blood-product transfusions. Ann Int Med 1983; 99:621–624,
5. Curran JW, Lawrence DW, Jaffe, H, Kaplan JE, et al. Acquired immuno-deficiency syndrome (AIDS) associated with transfusions. N Engl J Med 1984; 310:69–75,
6. Bove, JR. Transfusion associated AIDS—a cause for concern. N Engl J Med 1984; 310:115–116,
7. Remis RS, O'Shaughnessy MV, Tsoukas C, Growe GH, Schechter MT, Palmer RW, Lawrence DN. HIV transmission to patients with hemophilia by heat-treated, donor-screened factor concentrate. CMAJ 1990; 142:1247–1254.

8. Dietrich SL, Mosley JW, Lusher JM, Hilgartner MW, Operskalski EA, Habel L, Aledort LM, Gjerset GF, Koerper MA, Lewis BH, et al. Transmission of human immunodeficiency virus type 1 by dry-heated clotting factor concentrates. Transfusion Safety Study Group. Vox Sang 1990; 59:129–135.

9. Zuck TF, Eyster ME. Blood safety decisions, 1982 to 1986: perceptions and misconceptions. Transfusion 1996; 36:928–931.

10. Bianco C. Protecting the blood supply. Transfus Med Rev 1989; 3 (suppl 1):9–12,

11. Horowitz B, Prince AM, Hamman J, Watklevicz C. Viral safety of solvent/detergent-treated blood products. Blood Coagul Fibrinolysis 1994; (suppl 3)S21–28.

12. Martin MA. The molecular and biological properties of the human immunodeficiency virus. In: Stamatoyannopoloulos G, Neinhuis AW, Majerus PW, Varmus H, eds. The Molecular Basis of Blood Diseases. 2d ed. Philadelphia: W.B. Saunders Company, 1994:863–908.

13. Fauci AS, Desrosiers RC. Pathogenesis of HIV and SIV. In: Coffin JM, Hughes SH, Varmus HE, eds. Retroviruses. Plainview, NY: Cold Spring Harbor Laboratory Press, 1997: 587–635.

14. Wain-Hobson S. Running the gamut of retroviral variation. Trends Microbiol 1996; 4:135–141.

15. Vartanian JP, Sala M, Henry M, Wain-Hobson S, Meyerhans A. Manganese cations increase the mutation rate of human immunodeficiency virus type 1 ex vivo. J Gen Virol 1999; 80:1983–1986.

16. Berkhout B. HIV-1 evolution under pressure of protease inhibitors: climbing the stairs of viral fitness. J Biomed Sci 1999; 6:298–305.

17. Brown AJ, Korber BT, Condra JH. Associations between amino acids in the evolution of HIV type 1 protease sequences under indinavir therapy. AIDS Res Hum Retroviruses 1999; 15:247–255.

18. Morris A, Marsden M, Halcrow K, Hughes ES, Brettle RP, Bell JE, Simmonds P. Mosaic structure of the human immunodeficiency virus type 1 genome infecting lymphoid cells and the brain: evidence for frequent in vivo recombination events in the evolution of regional populations. J Virol 1999; 73:8720–8731.

19. Ostrowski MA, Krakauer DC, Li Y, Justement SJ, Learn G, Ehler LA, Stanley SK, Nowak M, Fauci AS. Effect of immune activation on the dynamics of human immunodeficiency virus replication and on the distribution of viral quasispecies. J Virol 1998; 72:7772–7784.

20. Burke DS. Recombination in HIV: an important viral evolutionary strategy. Emerg Infect Dis 1997; 3:253–259.

21. De Leys R, Vanderborght B, Vanden Haesevelde M, et al. Isolation and partial characterization of an unusual human immunodeficiency retrovirus from two persons of West-Central African origin. J Virol 1990; 64:1207–1216.

22. Centers for Disease Control and Prevention. Identification of HIV-1 Group O Infection—Los Angeles County, California, 1996. MMWR 1996; 45:561–565.

23. van Binsbergen J, Keur W, v d Graaf M, Siebelink A, Jacobs A, de Rijk D, Toonen J, Zekeng L, Afane Ze E, Gurtler LG. Reactivity of a new HIV-1 group O third generation A-HIV-1/-2 assay with an unusual HIV-1 seroconversion panel and HIV-1 group O/group M subtyped samples. J Virol Methods 1997; 69:29–37.

24. Centers for Disease Control and Prevention. HIV AIDS Surveillance Report 1998; 10:14.

25. Cao Y, Qin L, Zhang L, Safrit J, Ho DD. Virologic and immunologic characterization of long-term survivors of human immunodeficiency virus type 1 infection. N Engl J Med 1995; 332:201–208.

26. Pantaleo G, Menzo S, Vaccarezza M, Graziosi C, Cohen OJ, Demarest JF, Montefiori D, Orenstein JM, Fox C, Schrager LK, et al. Studies in subjects with long-term nonprogressive human immunodeficiency virus infection. N Engl J Med 1995; 332:209–216.

27. de Roda Husman AM, Koot M, Cornelissen M, Keet IP, Brouwer M, Broersen SM, Bakker M, Roos MT, Prins M, de Wolf F, Coutinho RA, Miedema F, Goudsmit J, Schuitemaker H. Association between CCR5 genotype and the clinical course of HIV-1 infection. Ann Intern Med 1997; 127:882.

28. Quillent C, Oberlin E, Braun J, et al. HIV-1-resistance phenotype conferred by combination of two separate inherited mutations of CCR5 gene. Lancet 1998; 351:14–18.

29. Wilkinson DA, Operskalski EA, Busch MP, Mosley JW, Koup RA. A 32-bp deletion within the CCR5 locus protects against transmission of parenterally acquired human immunodeficiency virus but does not affect progression to AIDS-defining illness. J Infect Dis 1998; 178:1163–1166.

30. Duesberg P, Rasnick D. The AIDS dilemma: drug diseases blamed on a passenger virus. Genetica 1998; 104:85–132.

31. Quinn TC. Acute primary HIV infection. JAMA 1997; 278:58–62.

32. Lui KJ, Darrow WW, Rutherford GW 3d. A model-based estimate of the mean incubation period for AIDS in homosexual men. Science 1988; 240:1333–1335.

33. Kalbfleisch JD, Lawless JF. Estimating the incubation time distribution and expected number of cases of transfusion-associated acquired immune deficiency syndrome. Transfusion 1989; 29:672–676.

34. Mylonakis E, Dickinson BP, Mileno MD, Flanigan T, Schiffman FJ, Mega A, Rich JD. Persistent parvovirus B19 related anemia of seven years' duration in an HIV-infected patient: complete remission associated with highly active antiretroviral therapy. Am J Hematol 1999; 60:164–166.

35. Palella FJ Jr, Delaney KM, Moorman AC, et al. Declining morbidity and mortality among patients with advanced human immunodeficiency virus infection. HIV Outpatient Study Investigators. N Engl J Med 1998; 26 (338):853–860.

36. Groopman JE. Impact of transfusion on viral load in human immunodeficiency virus infection. Semin Hematol 1997; 34 (suppl 2):27–33.

37. Busch MP, Young MJ, Samson SM, Mosley JW, Ward JW, Perkins HA. Risk of human immunodeficiency virus (HIV) transmission by blood transfusions before the implementation of HIV-1 antibody screening. The Transfusion Safety Study Group. Transfusion 1991; 31:4–11.

38. Minamoto GY, Scheinberg DA, Dietz K, Gold JW, Chein N, Gee T, Reich LM, Hoffer J, Mayer K, Armstrong D, et al. Human immunodeficiency virus infection in patients with leukemia. Blood 1988; 71:1147–1149.

39. Ward JW, Bush TJ, Perkins HA, Lieb LE, Allen JR, Goldfinger D, Samson SM, Pepkowitz SH, Fernando LP, Holland PV, et al W, Bush TJ, Perkins HA, Lieb LE,

Allen JR, Goldfinger D, Samson SM, Pepkowitz SH, Fernando LP, Holland PV, et al. The natural history of transfusion-associated infection with human immunodeficiency virus. Factors influencing the rate of progression to disease. N Engl J Med 1989; 321:947–952.

40. Kalbfleisch JD, Lawless JF. Estimating the incubation time distribution and expected number of cases of transfusion-associated acquired immune deficiency syndrome. Transfusion 1989; 29:672–676.

41. Selik RM, Ward JW, Buehler JW. Trends in transfusion-associated acquired immune deficiency syndrome in the United States, 1982 through 1991. Transfusion 1993; 33:890–893.

42. Kleinman SH, Niland JC, Azen SP, Operskalski EA, Barbosa LH, Chernoff Al, Edwards VM, Lenes BA, Marshall GJ, Nemo GJ, et al. Prevalence of antibodies to human immunodeficiency virus type 1 among blood donors prior to screening. The Transfusion Safety Study/NHLBI Donor Repository. Transfusion 1989; 29:572–580.

43. Jaffe HW, Sarngadharan MG, DeVico AL, Bruch L, Getchell JP, Kalayanaraman VS, Haverkos HW, Stoneburner RL, Gallo RC, Curran JW. Infection with HTLV-III/LAV and transfusion-associated acquired immunodeficiency syndrome. Serologic evidence of an association. JAMA 1985; 254:770–773.

44. Feorino PM, Jaffe HW, Palmer E, Peterman TA, Francis DP, Kalyanaraman VS, Weinstein RA, Stoneburner RL, Alexander WJ, Raevsky C, et al. Transfusion-associated acquired immunodeficiency syndrome. Evidence for persistent infection in blood donors. N Engl J Med 1985; 312:1293–1296.

45. Anderson KC, Gorgone BC, Marlink RG, Ferriani R, Essex ME, Benz PM, Groopman JE. Transfusion-acquired human immunodeficiency virus infection among immunocompromised persons. Ann Intern Med 1986; 105:519–527.

46. Antin JH, Smith BR, Ewenstein BM, Arceci RJ, Lipton JM, Page PL, Rappeport JM. HTLV-III infection after bone marrow trasplantation. Blood 1986; 67:160–163.

47. Lieb LE, Mundy TM, Goldfinger D, Pepkowitz SH, Brunell PA, Caldwell MB, Ward JW. Unrecognized human immunodeficiency virus type 1 infection in a cohort of transfused neonates: a retrospective investigation. Pediatrics 1995; 95:717–721.

48. Samson S, Busch M, Ward J, Garner J, Salk S, Fernando L, Holland P, Rutherford G, Benjamin R, Perkins H. Identification of HIV-infected transfusion recipients: the utility of cross-referencing previous donor records with AIDS case reports. Transfusion 1990; 30:214–218.

49. O'Brien TR, Busch MP, Donegan E, Ward JW, Wong L, Samson SM, Perkins HA, Altman R, Stoneburner RL, Holmberg SD J. Heterosexual transmission of human immunodeficiency virus type 1 from transfusion recipients to their sex partners. J AIDS 1994; 7:705–710.

50. Operskalski EA, Stram DO, Busch MP, Huang W, Harris M, Dietrich SL, Schiff ER, Donegan E, Mosley JW. Role of viral load in heterosexual transmission of human immunodeficiency virus type 1 by blood transfusion recipients. Transfusion Safety Study Group. Am J Epidemiol 1997; 146:655–661.

51. Busch MP, Operskalski EA, Mosley JW, Lee TH, Henrard D, Herman S, Sachs DH, Harris M, Huang W, Stram DO. Factors influencing human immunodeficiency virus

type 1 transmission by blood transfusion. Transfusion Safety Study Group. J Infect Dis 1996; 174:26–33.

52. Donegan E, Lenes BA, Tomasulo PA, Mosley JW. Transmission of HIV-1 by component type and duration of shelf storage before transfusion. Transfusion 1990; 30:851–852.

53. Volkow P, Perez-Padilla R, del-Rio C, Mohar A. The role of commercial plasma-pheresis banks on the AIDS epidemic in Mexico. Rev Invest Clin 1998; 50:221–226.

54. Schmunis GA, Zicker F, Pinheiro F, Brandling-Bennett D. Risk for transfusion-transmitted infections diseases in Central and South America. Emerg Infect Dis 1998; 4:5–11.

55. Lackritz EM. Prevention of HIV transmission by blood transfusion in the developing world: achievements and continuing challenges. AIDS 1998; 12 (suppl A):S81–86.

56. Duncan RA, von Reyn CF, Alliegro GM, Toossi Z, Sugar AM, Levitz SM. Idiopathic CD4+ T-lymphocytopenia—four patients with opportunistic infections and no evidence of HIV infection. N Engl J Med 1993; 328:393–398.

57. Laurence J. T-cell subsets in health, infectious disease, and idiopathic CD4+ T-lymphocytopenia. Ann Intern Med 1993; 119:55–62.

58. Ho DD, Cao Y, Zhu T, Farthing C, Wang N, Gu G, Schooley RT, Daar ES. Idiopathic CD4+ T-lymphocytopenia—an analysis of five patients with unexplained opportunistic infections. N Engl J Med 1993; 328:386–392.

59. Spira TJ, Jones BM, Nicholson JK, Lal RB, Rowe T, Mawle AC, Lauter CB, Shulman JA, Monson RA. Idiopathic CD4+ T-lymphocytopenia—immunodeficiency without evidence of HIV infection. N Engl J Med 1993; 328:380–385.

60. Smith DK, Neal JJ, Holmberg SD. Unexplained opportunistic infections and CD4+ T-lymphocytopenia without HIV infection. An investigation of cases in the United States. The Centers for Disease Control Idiopathic CD4+ T-lymphocytopenia Task Force. N Engl J Med 1993; 328:373–379.

61. Busch MP, Valinsky JE, Paglieroni T, Prince HE, Crutcher GJ, Gjerset GF, Oper-skalski EA, Charlebois E, Bianco C, Holland PV, et al. Screening of blood donors for idiopathic CD4 + T-lymphocytopenia. Transfusion 1994; 34:192–197.

62. Pindyck J, Waldman A, Zang E, Oleszko W, Lowy M, Bianco C. Measures to decrease the risk of acquired immunodeficiency syndrome transmission by blood transfusion. Evidence of volunteer blood donor cooperation. Transfusion 1985; 25:3–9.

63. Chiavetta JA, Nusbacher J, Wall A. Donor self-exclusion patterns and human immunodeficiency virus antibody test results over a twelve-month period. Transfusion 1989; 29:81–83.

64. Petersen LR, Lackritz E, Lewis WF, Smith DS, Herrera G, Raimondi V, Aberle-Grasse J, Dodd RY. The effectiveness of the confidential unit exclusion option. Transfusion 1994; 34:865–869.

65. Petersen LR, Doll LS and The HIV Blood Donor Study Group. Human immunodeficiency virus type 1-infected blood donors: epidemiologic, laboratory, and donation characteristics. Transfusion 1991; 31:698–703.

66. Mayo DJ, Rose AM, Matchett SE, Hoppe PA, Solomon JM, McCurdy KK. Screening potential blood donors at risk for human immunodeficiency virus. Transfusion 1991; 31:466–474.

67. Gimble JG, Friedman LI. Effects of oral donor questioning about high-risk behaviors for human immunodeficiency virus infection. Transfusion 1992; 32(5):446–449.

68. Food and Drug Administration. Memorandum to all registered blood establishments. Revised recommendations for the prevention of HIV transmission by blood and blood products. (http//:www.fda.gov/cber/publications).

69. Busch MP. Transfusion associated AIDS. In: Rossi EC, Simon TL, Moss GS, Gould SA, eds. Principles of Transfusion Medicine Baltimore: Williams & Wilkins, 1996: 699–708.

70. Fuchs D, Hausen A, Reibnegger G, Reissigl H, Schonitzer D, Spira T, Wachter H. Urinary neopterin in the diagnosis of acquired immune deficiency syndrome. Eur J Clin Microbiol 1984; 3:70–71.

71. Galel SA, Lifson JD, Engleman EG. Prevention of AIDS transmission through screening of the blood supply. Annu Rev Immunol 1995; 13:201–227.

72. Pindyck J, Waldman A, Oleszko W, Zang E, Bianco C. Prevalence of viral antibodies and leukocyte abnormalities among blood donors considering themselves at risk of exposure to AIDS. Ann NY Acad Sci 1984; 437:472–484.

73. McDougal JS, Jaffe HW, Cabridilla CD, Sarngadharan MG, Nicholson JK, Kalyanaraman VS, Schable CA, Kilbourne B, Evatt BL, Gallo RC, et al. Screening tests for blood donors presumed to have transmitted the acquired immunodeficiency syndrome. Blood 1985; 65:772–775.

74. The Consortium for Retrovirus Serology Standardization. Serological diagnosis of human immunodeficiency virus infection by Western blot testing. JAMA 1988; 260:675–679.

75. Groopman JE, Chen FW, Hope JA, Andrews JM, Swift RL, Benton CV, Sullivan JL, Volberding PA, Sites DP, Landesman S, et al. Serological characterization of HTLV-III infection in AIDS and related disorders. J Infect Dis 1986; 153(4):736–742.

76. Centers for Disease Control and Prevention. Testing for antibodies to human immunodeficiency virus type 2 in the United States. MMWR 1992; 41 (RR-no.12).

77. Centers for Disease Control and Prevention. Update: HIV-2 infection among blood donors and plasma donors—United States, June 1992-June 1995. MMWR 1995; 44:603–606.

78. Busch MP, Kleinman SH, Williams AE, Smith JW, Ownby HE, Laycock ME, Lee LL, Pau CP, Schreiber GB. Frequency of human immunodeficiency virus (HIV) infection among contemporary anti-HIV-1 and anti-HIV-1/2 supplemental test-indeterminate blood donors. The Retrovirus Epidemiology Donor Study. Transfusion 1996; 36:37–44.

79. Kleinman S, Busch MP, Hall L, Thomson R, Glynn S, Gallahan D, Ownby HE, Williams AE. False-positive HIV-1 test results in a low-risk screening setting of voluntary blood donation. Retrovirus Epidemiology Donor Study. JAMA 1998; 280:1080–1085.

80. Ward JW, Holmberg SD, Allen JR, Cohn DL, Critchley SE, Kleinman SH, Lenes BA, Ravenholt O, Davis JR, Quinn MG, et al. Transmission of human immunodeficiency virus (HIV) by blood transfusions screened as negative for HIV antibody. N Engl J Med 1988; 318:473–478.

81. Cohen ND, Munoz A, Reitz BA, Ness PK, Frazier OH, Yawn DH, Lee H, Blattner W, Donahue JG, Nelson KE, et al. Transmission of retroviruses by transfusion of

screened blood in patients undergoing cardiac surgery. N Engl J Med 1989; 320:1172–1176.

82. Nelson KE, Donahue JG, Munoz A, Cohen ND, Ness PM, Teague A, Stambolis VA, Yawn DH, Callicott B, McAllister H, et al. Transmission of retroviruses from seronegative donors by transfusion during cardiac surgery. A multicenter study of HIV-1 and HTLV-I/II infections. Ann Intern Med 1992; 117:554–559.

83. Petersen LR, Satten GA, Dodd R, Busch M, Kleinman S, Grindon A, Lenes B. Duration of time from onset of human immunodeficiency virus type 1 infectiousness to development of detectable antibody. Transfusion 1994; 34:283–289.

84. Cumming PD, Wallace EL, Schorr JB, Dodd RY. Exposure of patients to human immunodeficiency virus through the transfusion of blood components that test antibody-negative. N Engl J Med 1989; 321(14):941–946.

85. Lackritz EM, Satten GA, Aberle-Grasse J, Dodd RY, Raimondi VP, Janssen RS, Lewis WF, Notari EP 4th, Petersen LR. Estimated risk of transmission of the human immunodeficiency virus by screened blood in the United States. N Engl J Med 1995; 333:1721–1725.

86. Schreiber GB, Busch MP, Kleinman SH, Korelitz JJ. The risk of transfusion-transmitted viral infections. The Retrovirus Epidemiology Donor Study. N Engl J Med 1996; 334:1685–1690.

87. Busch MP, Lee LL, Satten GA, Henrard DR, Farzadegan H, Nelson KE, Read S, Dodd RY, Petersen LR. Time course of detection of viral and serologic markers preceding human immunodeficiency virus type 1 seroconversion: implications for screening of blood and tissue donors. Transfusion 1995; 35:91–97.

88. Janssen RS, Satten GA, Stramer SL, Rawal BD, O'Brien TR, Weiblen BJ, Hecht FM, Jack N, Cleghorn FR, Kahn JO, Chesney MA, Busch MP. New testing strategy to detect early HIV-1 infection for use in incidence estimates and for clinical and prevention purposes. JAMA 1998; 280:42–48.

89. Busch MP, Glynn SA, Schreiber GB. Potential increased risk of virus transmission due to exclusion of older donors because of concern over Creutzfeldt-Jakob disease. Transfusion 1997; 37(10):996–1002.

90. Alter HJ, Epstein JS, Swenson SG, VanRaden MJ, Ward JW, Kaslow RA, Menitove JE, Klein HG, Sandler SG, Sayers MH, et al. Prevalence of human immunodeficiency virus type 1 p24 antigen in U.S. blood donors—an assessment of the efficacy of testing in donor screening. The HIV-Antigen Study Group. N Engl J Med 1990; 323:1312–1317.

91. Roberts CR, Longfield JN, Platte RC, Zielmanski KP, Wages J, Fowler A. Transfusion-associated human immunodeficiency virus type 1 from screened antibody-negative blood donors. Arch Pathol Lab Med 1994; 118:1188–1192.

92. Centers for Disease Control and Prevention. Persistent lack of detectable HIV-1 antibody in a person with HIV infection—Utah, 1995. MMWR 1996; 45:181–185.

93. Clark SJ, Kelen GD, Henrard DR, Daar ES, Craig S, Shaw GM, Quinn TC. Unsuspected primary human immunodeficiency virus type 1 infection in seronegative emergency department patients. J Infect Dis 1994; 170:194–197.

94. Busch MP, Alter HJ. Will human immunodeficiency virus p24 antigen screening increase the safety of the blood supply and, if so, at what cost? Transfusion 1995; 35:536–539.

95. Korelitz JJ, Busch MP, Williams AE. Antigen testing for human immunodeficiency virus (HIV) and the magnet effect: Will the benefit of a new HIV test be offset by the numbers of higher risk, test-seeking donors attracted to blood centers? Retrovirus Epidemiology Donor Study. Transfusion 1996; 36:203–208.

96. Centers for Disease Control and Prevention. U.S. Public Health Service guidelines for testing and counseling blood and plasma donors for human immunodeficiency virus type 1 antigen. MMWR 1996; 45 (No. RR-2):1–9.

97. Hewlett IK, Epstein JS. Food and Drug Administration conference on the feasibility of genetic technology to close the HIV window in donor screening. Transfusion 1997; 37:346–351.

98. Busch MP, Eble BE, Khayam-Bashi H, Heilbron D, Murphy EL, Kwok S, Sninsky J, Perkins HA, Vyas GN. Evaluation of screened blood donations for human immunodeficiency virus type 1 infection by culture and DNA amplification of pooled cells. N Engl J Med 1991; 325:1–5.

99. Yerly S, Pedrocchi M, Perrin L. The use of polymerase chain reaction in plasma pools for the concomitant detection of hepatitis C virus and HIV type 1 RNA. Transfusion 1998; 38:908–914.

100. Cardoso MS, Koerner K, Kubanek B. Mini-pool screening by nucleic acid testing for hepatitis B virus, hepatitis C virus, and HIV: preliminary results. Transfusion 1998; 38:905–907.

101. Schottstedt V, Tuma W, Bunger G, Lefevre H. PCR for HBV, HCV and HIV-1 experiences and first results from a routine screening programme in a large blood transfusion service. Biologicals 1998; 26:101–104.

102. Murthy KK, Henrard DR, Eichberg JW, Cobb KE, Busch MP, Allain JP, Alter HJ. Redefining the HIV-infectious window period in the chimpanzee model: evidence to suggest that viral nucleic acid testing can prevent blood-borne transmission. Transfusion 1999; 39:688–693.

103. Centers for Disease Control and Prevention. Public Health Service Guidelines for the Management of Health-Care Worker Exposures to HIV and Recommendations for Postexposure Prophylaxis. MMWR 1998; 47(RR-7):1–28.

104. Bianco C, Kessler D. Donor notification and counseling. Management of blood donors with positive test results. Vox Sang 1994; 67(suppl 3):255–259.

105. Emmanuel JC, Bassett MT, Smith HJ, Jacobs JA. Pooling of sera for human immunodeficiency virus (HIV) testing: an economical method for use in developing countries. J Clin Pathol 1988; 41:582–585.

106. Smillie JM, Ala FA. Reducing the cost of anti-HIV screening. J Virol Methods 1988; 19:181–184.

107. AuBuchon JP, Birkmeyer JD, Busch MP. Department of Pathology. Cost-effectiveness of expanded human immunodeficiency virus-testing protocols for donated blood. Transfusion 1997; 37:45–51.

12
Hepatitis Viruses and Blood Transfusion

Alfred M. Prince
Lindsley F. Kimball Research Institute, New York Blood Center, New York, New York

This review will summarize our expanding understanding of the transmission of hepatitis viruses by blood transfusion. In addition to the well-known hepatitis B virus (HBV) and hepatitis C virus (HCV), the recently identified hepatitis G virus, not yet definitively identified as a hepatitis-causing agent, and the most recently identified TT virus (TTV) agent will be reviewed.

I. HEPATITIS B VIRUS

The classic studies of Krugman at the Willowbrook School were the first to identify two distinct hepatitis agents, originally termed MS-1 and MS-2, now known as hepatitis A and hepatitis B virus (1). This made it possible to identify an antigen discovered in liver tissue in 1967 by immunofluorescence as a hepatitis B–specific antigen, (HBsAg) first called the S.H. antigen (2). Blumberg identified an antigen in the serum of an Australian aborigine that was originally interpreted as a genetic marker conferring susceptibility to a variety of diseases: leukemia, leprosy, and all forms of hepatitis (3). However, eventually it became clear that the Australia antigen was the surface coat of HBV and thus was hepatitis B specific (4).

Numerous studies revealed a statistical asociation between HBsAg and hepatocellular carcinoma (e.g., Ref. 5). That these reflected an etiological relationship was shown when prospective follow-up of HBsAg carriers and matched controls revealed that the relative risk of development of hepatocellular carcinoma was about 224:1 (6), establishing HBV as the leading oncogenic virus in the world.

A. Modes of Transmission of HBV

HBV is readily transmitted by sexual (7) and parenteral routes, such as unsterilized syringes and needles. Primate experiments using HBV-susceptible gibbons (8) and chimpanzees (9) have revealed that semen and saliva can transmit HBV infection when administered subcutaneously and intravaginally (8).

In addition to the above modes of transmission, horizontal transmission (i.e., that occurring without apparent parenteral, sexual, or perinatal exposure,) is common, especially in the developing world (10). In Africa most children are infected with HBV by the age of 5, and transmission from infected mothers is rare (11). Horizontal transmission between uninfected and infected infants is the likely mechanism. In institutions for the mentally retarded the virus is readily transmitted between carriers, patients, and staff (12). The virus is also readily transmitted from carrier mothers to their infants, especially in Asia. Both transplacemental and intravaginal routes have been postulated. Thus, numerous modes of transmission exist other than blood transfusion.

B. Infectivity of Blood Containing HBsAg

Following the studies indicating an association between HBsAg (formerly called Australia antigen, SH antigen, hepatitis-associated antigen), numerous studies were carried out to assess the infectivity of HBsAg-containing blood. Holland et al. reported that 50% of transfused patients receiving at least 1 HBsAg unit developed icteric posttransfusion hepatitis, as compared to only 7% of control patients receiving no HBsAg (13). These findings led to rapid institution of screening for HBsAg in the developed world. Numerous assays have been used to screen blood donors for HBsAg. The first of these was the Ouchterlony, or agar gel diffusion, assay. The New York Blood Center was the first to screen all blood for this antigen using this relatively insensitive assay. Subsequently a series of more sensitive assays was introduced: counterelectrophoresis, passive hemagglutination inhibition, radioimmunoassay, and enzyme immunoassays. The first radioimmunoassay was stated to be 10 times as sensitive as the agar gel diffusion test; however, it soon became clear that much of this increase was due to nonspecificity of the radioimmune assay (14).

C. Use of Anti-HBc for the Detection of HBsAg-Negative, HBV-Infective Blood

In a report that remains provocative and controversial, Hoofnagle et al. found four cases of posttransfusion hepatitis B in which no HBsAg- or anti-HBs–containing blood had been transfused, although each had received a unit with antibody to the hepatitis core (HBcAg) (15). This study raised the possibility that anti-HBc alone could be a marker of infectivity. This hypothesis was supported recently by Chung et al., who found that exclusion of donors with isolated anti-HBc had the highest sensitivity and specificity (66.7 and 96.1%, respectively) for prevention of posttransfusion B (16). This hypothesis is also in accord with a more recent finding. Rehermann et al. reported that HBV DNA is detectable up to decades after a primary, apparently self-limited, HBV infection (17). It would not be surprising that HBV DNA, which is largely if not entirely in the HBV virion (the Dane particle), would be a marker of infectivity.

Although anti-core testing may detect donors who are HBsAg negative and infectious, this involves considerable loss to the blood supply. It has been estimated that the prevalence of anti-HBc in the U.S. blood supply averages 2.6%, ranging from 0.55 to 6.38% in different geographic regions (18). The loss would be approximately 300,000 units per year in the United States. Nevertheless, this test is now in use, primarily as a surrogate maker for HIV and for prevention of transmission of HBV (19). The radioimmunoassay (Corab, Abbott Labs, North Chicago, IL) is at least twice as specific as the more widely used enzyme immunoassay method (Corzyme, Abbott Labs, North Chicago, IL) and thus would reduce blood wastage (20).

D. The Estimated Risk of Transmission of HBV Infection in the United States

Schreiber et al. have reported a very sophisticated approach for estimating the risk of transmission of bloodborne agents in 1996, when second- and third-generation screening assays were in place (21). Using data from 586,507 blood donors who donated more than once between 1991 and 1993, they estimated the incidence of each of the infections screened for in subjects negative when initially tested. These were then adjusted for the duration of the window period, i.e., the period while the infection is incubating but serological markers are not yet positive. Using this approach they estimated that the risk of donating blood during the HBV incubation period was 1 in 63,000 (31,000–147,000). It was estimated that addition of polymerase chain reaction (PCR) to routine screening would reduce the window period by 25% and that this would reduce the overall risk by 42% or 81 cases per 12 million units transfused. These estimates may be low, especially if HBV DNA persisting for decades after acute infections, as demonstrated by the results of Rehermann et al. (17), is infectious.

E. Impact of PCR Screening on the Transmission of HBV

As indicated above, Schreiber et al. (21) estimated that PCR screening would reduce the transmission of HBV by 42%. Sankary et al. tested 375 units of plasma with alanine aminotransferase (ALT) elevations and negative HBsAg tests and estimated that these would be derived from 47,500 blood donations having both normal and abnormal ALT levels (22). Only one unit tested positive by PCR, and even in this case contamination could not be excluded since seroconversion did not occur and PCR testing was negative on follow-up. If the PCR result is correct, one positive in 47,500 donations would correspond to 252 PCR positives in the 12 million units of blood transfused in the United States annually. This would be a higher estimate than the 81 cases preventable by PCR testing given by Schreiber et al. (21).

II. HEPATITIS C VIRUS

By 1974 a prospective posttransfusion follow-up study had provided definitive evidence that most transfusion-related hepatitis was not related to HBV. The authors somewhat prematurely coined the term hepatitis C virus for the agent of these infections (23). The non-B cases did not resemble hepatitis A epidemiologically and were subsequently shown not to be hepatitis A by immune electron microscopy (24). The generally accepted terminology for these cases became non-A, non-B (NANB) hepatitis, recognizing that more than one agent could be involved. Investigators at Chiron undertook to clone the genome from an NANB agent (25). After 5 years of discouragement they succeeded in cloning the first NANB-specific clone (5-1-1) using expression cloning and a human source of antibody. Because the sequence of the clone was unique, calling the cloned virus HCV was justified. These workers rapidly cloned and sequenced most of the viral genome, revealing it to have close similarity in genome organization, and in hydrophilicity, to the flaviviruses. Ligation of four different cloned sequences and expression of these provided the first generation (C100-3) of anti-HCV diagnostic tests. Addition of capsid (C22), NS3, and NS5 proteins provided the second- and third-generation assays generally used today for diagnosis and for blood screening. A prospective posttransfusion follow-up study estimated that first-generation assays reduced the incidence of HCV infection by 86%, with a further reduction due to the use of second-generation assays of 57% (26). These improved assays dramatically reduced the incidence of posttransfusion transmission of HCV (27), but the usefulness of the NS5 component has been questioned, because its inclusion did not yield additional positives confirmable by PCR and by peptide assays (28). PCR assays are useful for confirmation of the results of the serological assays, although only 93% of serologically confirmed assays are PCR positive (29). Presumably the PCR-negative cases were self-limited. A large posttransfusion study in which 50 probable and 11 possible cases of non-B were observed was retrospectively analyzed by testing of antibody to C100-3, capsid polypeptides, and RT-PCR (23,30). All of the probable cases and five of the possible cases were shown to be due to HCV infection. This study suggested that all bloodborne non-A, non-B infections in the population studied were likely due to HCV.

Application of anti-HCV tests rapidly confirmed the importance of these assays: 80% of cases of chronic posttransfusion hepatitis from different parts of the world were anti-C100-3 positive (25). Self-limited cases tended to show transient or no antibody by this assay (31,32). HCV infections are characterized by a high rate (60–80%) of chronic infections. Chronic liver disease in HCV infections may be manifested as chronic active hepatitis, cirrhosis, and hepatocellular carcinoma (33). HCV infections differ in that respect from HBV infections, where only about 5% of adult infections become chronic.

A strip radio immunoblot assay (RIBA) was manufactured by Chiron to provide some measure of confirmatory specificity for the ELISA assays. The concordance between third-generation enzyme immunoassays and the third-generation immunoblot assay was 96% (34). The third-generation assay is considerably more sensitive than the second-generation assays. Fifty-seven sera with indeterminate results with the second-generation assay were retested with the third-generation assay. Thirty-three (57.9%) showed at least one additional band with the third-generation assay and thus were classified as positive (35).

A. Should ALT Testing Be Used for the Prevention of HCV Posttransfusion Hepatitis?

It has been estimated that ALT testing would detect about three window-phase donations per million units of blood transfused after institution of second-generation screening assays. This contrasts with ALT elevations of approximately 1800 units per million units prior to anti-HCV testing. Only 8 of 10,000 units with ALT elevations and negative anti-HCV tests are estimated to be infected with HCV. The cost of ALT testing per year of life saved was calculated to be $7.9 million. The authors concluded that ALT screening of volunteer blood donors should be stopped (36). A policy that ALT could be discontinued was adopted in the United States (19), but European fractionators are still required to use plasma with normal ALT levels, thus U.S. blood centers still test for ALT in order to comply with European requirements for plasma shipped to European fractionators.

B. Sources of HCV Infection Other than Transfusion

In most cases transfused individuals who develop HCV infection will have been infected by transfused blood; however, this is not always the case. Probably the most common source of HCV infection worldwide is intravenous drug abuse (37). If a transfused patient is a drug user or the spouse of a drug user, this could give rise to HCV infection in a transfusion recipient. Surprisingly, drug use in donors who had denied drug use during predonation questioning was found to be a major factor in HCV transmission (38). Intrafamilial transmission of HCV among spouses has been documented in some (39,40) but not all studies (41). Sex partners whose spouses were anti-HCV positive were 3.7 times as likely to be anti-HCV positive as partners of seronegative spouses (42). HCV RNA has been detected, albeit in very low concentration, in both saliva and urine (43) and rarely in breast milk (44). Vertical transmission from infected mothers appears to be extremely rare, except when the mother is coinfected with HIV (45,46). Surgical intervention, use of nondisposable needles or syringes, and dental therapy have been implicated in the transmission of HCV (47,48). All of the above possible routes of transmission need to be evaluated in the analysis of posttransfusion cases, especially in cases where blood has been screened with second- and third-generation assays. It should be remembered that over 90% of HCV infections have been acquired outside the transfusion setting and current testing has reduced transfusion-transmitted HCV to an extremely low level (33).

C. Impact of PCR Screening on Transmission of HCV

Cases negative by ELISA and RIBA assays, but positive by PCR, were identified (34). Such cases were reported to be identifiable among blood donors (49), but a subsequent study including the sera tested in the first study failed to confirm this finding, suggesting PCR contamination in the first study (50).

Window period analysis has suggested that the risk of HCV transmission of blood tested by second-generation assays is 1:103000 (28,000–288,000) and that this would be reduced by 72% following introduction of PCR testing (21). This would seem to be a very minimal estimate.

PCR testing for HCV was introduced in the United States in 1999 under Investigational New Drug (IND) protocols. Samples from 16–128 units are pooled before testing. Positive pools are then resolved to find the individual positive sample.

D. Immunity in HCV Infections

Both in humans and in rechallenged chimpanzees, there is evidence of absent or weak immunity after repeated exposure to even the same isolate of HCV (51). Wyatt et al. analyzed this phenomenon in the extreme situation of homologous challenge of chronically infected chimpanzees (52). Two factors were identified as playing a role in the reinfection of these animals. In some cases immunity seemed to be limited to major quasispecies in the inoculum, thus reinfection was accompanied by emergence of minor quasispecies present in the inoculum. In other cases "fitness" of certain quasispecies emerging after challenge was postulated. The lack of immunity in HCV infections must be taken into consideration when postulating "reactivation" of chronic HCV infection because many such cases probably represent dual infections.

E. Course of Hepatitis C

Hepatitis C viremia, as detected by the presence of HCV RNA, occurs within 1–3 weeks after exposure. About 90% of patients will have detectable anti-HCV 3 months after infection. Chronic hepatitis C is a common clinical syndrome in the United States and is now the most common reason for liver transplantation. At least 70% of patients have persistent or intermittent ALT elevations on long-term follow-up, with liver biopsies showing chronic inflammatory changes. The virus persists because it continuously evolves into differing variants (quasispecies) as neutralizing antibodies are developed by the host. About 80% of patients with chronic HCV will eventually develop cirrhosis and 1–5% will develop hepato-cellular carcinoma after 20 years. It is not understood why 15% of those infected with HCV spontaneously recover or why patients with chronic disease may have markedly different clinical courses.

Interferon-α has been used in the treatment of HCV for several years. Unfortunately, the treatment results in a sustained response in only 10–20% of patients. Almost all patients who receive interferon experience an uncomfortable flu-like syndrome early in the course of treatment. More recently, interferon-α and the antiviral agent ribavirin have been given as combined therapy. Sustained response rates have approximately doubled (to 40–50%) using this combination. There is some controversy about which patients should be treated. However, most clinicians agree that patients with a persistently elevated ALT, positive HCV RNA, and a liver biopsy showing portal or bridging fibrosis should be treated.

III. NON-ABC HEPATITIS

In recent years there has been considerable interest in attempting to characterize a putative non-A, non-B, non-C, non-D, non-E virus causing posttransfusion hepatitis. Some have termed this elusive entity hepatitis F. In a very careful study, Japanese workers tested the hypothesis that this entity reflected silent HBV infection. PCR for HBV identified this agent in 18 of 20 cases of acute and 17 of 20 chronic cases of putative hepatitis F. Sequencing revealed T-to-C mutations in DR2 and an eight nucleotide deletion of the 3′ terminus of the X gene–coding region. These mutations were thought to lead to suppression of replication and expression of the HBV DNA (53). Clearly, this was not the elusive hepatitis G or F.

Alter and Bradley (54) summarized the evidence for the existence of a non-ABC form of hepatitis: Bradley's chimpanzee studies revealed a putative chloroform-resistant agent that did not induce tubular ultrastructural changes, such as those produced by HCV. This observation was, however, never confirmed. Furthermore, HCV sometimes resists the effects of chloroform, presumably because the chloroform does not always penetrate to all parts of the infectious material (Prince and Brotman, unpublished data). The chloroform-resistant agent appeared to have a diameter of 27 nm, which is very similar to that of the core of HCV. The 27 nm agent was not shown to be a human hepatitis agent by development of antibodies in inoculated chimpanzees. Putative clinical evidence for the existence of an additional non-ABC agent was the observation of multiple episodes of hepatitis in patients. This cannot be taken as evidence for a non-ABC agent in the light of the weak or absent immunity to HCV, described above.

Further putative evidence for the existence of non-ABC agent(s) was drawn from posttransfusion follow-up studies. In three such studies 40, 12, and 11% of NANB cases were classified as non-ABC by serlogical exclusion (reviewed in Ref. 54). These observations may reflect lenient criteria for the diagnosis of hepatitis because when the incidence of non-ABC hepatitis was compared in patients receiving allogeneic and autologous transfusions, the incidence was found to be almost identical (0.55 vs. 0.51%). Thus, a high proportion, or even all, of the non-ABC cases may represent cases with low levels of transaminase elevation related to surgery and hospitalization, rather than to viral infection. An additional factor is that most of these cases were diagnosed by the relatively insensitive first-generation assays and PCR was not done.

Additional evidence supporting the conclusion that posttransfusion studies did not identify non-ABC cases is the fact that, in a retrospective posttransfusion follow-up study in which very strict criteria were used to define "probable viral hepatitis," each of 50 such cases could be identified as HCV based on serology and PCR (23,30).

In an ongoing study, Alter and Bradley (54) review cases of chronic hepatitis that serologically appear to be due to a non-ABC agent. These cases are less severe than HCV cases clinically, except in reports from Greece, and have a lower rate of development of long-term chronicity. These findings could reflect infection with a non-ABC agent or, alternatively, could reflect very mild HCV cases, which are known to have a tendency to be HCV seronegative, or only transiently seropositive, and which tend to be self-limited and thus unlikely to progress to chronicity (31).

IV. HEPATITIS G VIRUS

A viral agent of putative human origin, the GB agent, was passaged into tamarins and marmosets, producing severe short incubation hepatitis by the sixth passage.

Investigators from Abbott Laboratories used representational difference analysis and this material to isolate clones from two flavi-like viruses, GBV-A and GBV-B (55). Both of these agents turned out to be of tamarin origin. Shortly therafter these investigators isolated a novel human flavivirus GB virus C (56). A similar, if not identical, virus termed hepatitis G virus (HGV) was independantly isolated by another group of investigators (57). These viruses (reviewed in Ref. 58) are positive single-stranded RNA viruses containing about 9400 nucleotides, have the genomic organization of flaviviruses, and are distantly related to HCV. GB virus C and HGV share 96% of their deduced amino acid sequences and may thus be considered different isolates of the same virus. One to two percent of voluntary blood donors have HGV RNA (59), and the infection is clearly transmissible by transfusion. HGV frequently exists as a mixed infection with HBV, HCV, or HIV but does not appear to intensify disease caused by the other viruses.

It is not yet clear whether HGV itself causes hepatitis. In Alter's study there were 35 HGV infections among 357 transfusion recipients. Only three had hepatitis with HGV as the sole viral marker, and in these the hepatitis was mild (59). Long-term follow-up of HGV infections has revealed that 75–100% became chronically infected (60) but that chronic hepatitis did not develop in any patient infected with HGV alone (61). The findings of this study did not support HGV as an etiological agent of non-ABC hepatitis. However, it has been reported that HGV sequences were detected by PCR in three of six cases of fulminant hepatitis (62). This observation must be pursued, especially since most cases of fulminant hepatitis are serologically non-ABC.

It is of interest that both HCV and HGV associate with lipoproteins and are therefore largely precipitated by antibodies to B lipoprotein but not by anti-IgG (63). This property provides a defense against antibody-mediated neutralization and may contribute to the high rate of chronic infection by these viruses.

V. THE TTV AGENT

A surprising and possibly important finding was recently reported from the laboratory of M. Mayumi in Japan. Using representational difference analysis, these workers isolated a viral clone (N22) of 500 nucleotides from a patient with posttransfussion non-ABC hepatitis (64). Primers made to the sequence of the clone permitted detection of the clone in serum and characterization of the density of the associated virions, designated the TT virus (1.26 g/cm^2). The nucleic acid of this particle was sensitive to DNase I and was equally amplified with and without reverse transcription, thus indicating the genome to contain DNA. The TTV DNA sequence was not detectable by PCR in human leukocytes or human placenta. Thus the TTV sequence was not of host origin. This conclusion was also drawn from the fact that no homology to the TTV sequence was found among 1,731,752 DNA sequences and 154,072 protein sequences in the National Institute of Genetics (Mishima, Japan) database.

TTV DNA was detected in three of five patients with non-A to G post-transfusion hepatitis. This virus may belong to the parvovirus group. Its role in posttransfusion hepatitis deserves further study. The data so far presented suggest that TTV is an extremely common infection, and that it is not associated with acute or chronic hepatitis.

VI. APPROACHES TO REDUCTION IN THE COST OF ANTIVIRAL SCREENING

The cost of antiviral screening in the developed world is high and renders these tests beyond the reach of many developing world countries. One approach that could be considered is the simpification of the screening tests themselves and their manufacture in selected centers in the developing world. Dipstick assays lend themselves to this kind of application (65). The Program for Appropriate Health Care (PATH) in Seattle, Washington, has instituted development of dipstick diagnostics for use in blood screening and transfers the manufacturing responsibility to sites in the developing world. PATH maintains responsibility for quality control.

It is clearly desirable that alternate and less expensive assays approach the sensitivity and reliability of present second- and third-generation assays, if possible. However, if the choice is "no testing" versus a slight reduction in sensitivity, this should be made at the level of the developing country. In all cases panels of test sera should be provided by international organizations to assess test performance.

One means of cost reduction is to use two sequential ELISA assays and to limit the use of confirmatory assays, or PCR, to those samples positive in both screening assays (66). An evaluation of this strategy found no samples with discordant screening results to be positive in RIBA or PCR tests.

VII. RESIDUAL RISK OF POSTTRANSFUSION HEPATITIS IN THE DEVELOPED WORLD

There has been an extraordinary decline in the risk of posttransfusion hepatitis during the past 20 years. This has been due to largely better donor selection including avoidance of paid commercial donors and avoidance of high-risk donors through thorough questioning and self-exclusion policies. Further reductions have been due to specific serological tests for HCV and the progressive improvement of these tests and those for HBsAg.

To what extent will PCR tests, shortly to be introduced, prevent all residual posttransfusion hepatitis? This important question will doubtless be clarified in the next few years. It is not unlikely that posttransfusion hepatitis will soon be eliminated. Reviews such as the present will then, at best be of only historical interest.

REFERENCES

1. Krugman S, Giles JP, Hammond J. Infectious hepatitis. Evidence for two distinctive clinical, epidemiological and immunological types of infection. JAMA 1967; 200:365–373.
2. Prince AM, Fiji H, Gershon RK. Immunohistochemical studies on the etiology of anicteric hepatitis in Korea. Am J Hyg 1964; 79:365–381.
3. Blumberg BS, Gerstley BJS, Hungerford DA, London WT Sutnick AI. A serum antigen (Australia antigen) in Down's syndrome, leukemia and hepatitis. Ann Int Med 1967; 66:924–931.
4. Prince AM. An antigen detected in the blood during the incubation period of serum hepatitis Proc Natl Acad Sci USA 1968; 60:814–821.
5. Prince AM, Szmuness W, Michon J, Demaille J, Diebolt G, Linhard J, Quenum C, Sankale M. A case/control study of the association between primary liver cancer and hepatitis B infection in Senegal. Int J Cancer 1975; 16:376–383.
6. Beasley RP, Lin CC, Hwang L-Y, Chien C-S. Risk of hepatocellular carcinoma in hepatitis B infection: a prospective study in Taiwan. In: Szmuness W, Alter HJ, Maynard JE, eds. Viral Hepatitis. 1981 International Symposium. Franklin Institute Press, 1982:261–272.
7. Szmuness W, Much MI, Prince AM, Hoofnagle JH, Cherubin CE, Harley EJ, Block GH. On the role of sexual behavior in the spread of hepatitis B infection. Ann Int Med 1975; 83:489–495.
8. Scott RM, Snitbhan R, Bancroft WH, Alter HJ, Tingpalapong M. Experimental transmission of hepatitis B virus by semen and saliva. J Infec Dis 1980; 142:67–71.
9. Alter HJ, Purcell RH, Gerin JL, London WT, Kaplan PM, McAuliffe WJ, Wagner J, Holland PV. Transmission of hepatitis B to chimpanzees by hepatitis B surface antigen-positive saliva and semen. Infect Immun 1977; 16:928–933.
10. Davis LG, Weber DJ, Lemon SM. Horizontal transmission of hepatitis B virus. Lancet 1989; i:889–893.
11. Prince AM, White T, Pollock N, Riddle N, Brotman B, Richardson L. The epidemiology of hepatitis B infections in Liberian infants. Infect Immun 1981; 32:675–680.
12. Breuer B, Friedman SM, Millner ES, Kane MA, Synder RH, Maynard JE. Transmission of hepatitis B virus to classroom contacts of mentally retarded carriers. JAMA 1985; 254:3190–3195.
13. Holland PV, Alter HJ, Purcell RH, Walsh JH, Morrow AG. The infectivity of blood containing the hepatitis associated antigen. In: Prier JE, Freidman H, eds. Australia Antigen. Baltimore: University Park Press, 1973:191–203.

14. Prince AM, Brotman B, Jass D, Ikram H. Specificity of the direct radioimmunoassay for the detection of hepatitis B antigen. Lancet 1973; i:1346–1350.

15. Hoofnagle JH, Seeff LB, Bales ZB, Zimmerman HJ, Veterans Administration Hepatitis Cooperative Study Group. Type B hepatitis after transfusion with blood containing antibody to hepatitis B core antigen. N Engl J Med 1978; 298:1379–1383.

16. Chung HT, Lee JSK, Lok ASF. Prevention of posttransfusion hepatitis B and C by screening for antibody to hepatitis C virus and antibody to HBcAg. Hepatology 1993; 18:1045–1049.

17. Rehermann B, Ferrari C, Pasqunelli C, Chisari FV. The hepatitis B virus persists for decades after recovery from acute viral hepatitis despite active maintenance of a cytotoxic T lymphocyte response. Nature Med 1996; 2:1104–1108.

18. Kline WE, Bowmann RJ, McCurdy KKE, O'Malley JP, Sandler SG. Hepatitis B core antibody (anti-HBc) in blood donors in the United States: implications for surrogate testing programs. Transfusion 1987; 27:99–102.

19. Infectious disease testing for blood transfusions. Consensus development conference statement. National Institutes of Health, June 9–11, 1995.

20. Hanson MR, Polesky HF. Evaluation of routine anti-HBc screening of volunteer blood donors: a questionable surrogate test for non-A, non-B hepatitis. Transfusion 1987; 27:107–108.

21. Schreiber GB, Busch MP, Kleinman SH, Korelitz JJ. The risk of transfusion-transmitted viral infections. N Engl J Med 1996; 334:1685–1690.

22. Sankary TM, Yang G, Romeo JM, Ulrich PP, Busch MP, Rawal BD, Vyas GN. Rare detection of hepatitis B and hepatitis C virus genomes by polymerase chain reaction in seronegative donors with elevated alanine aminotransferase. Transfusion 1994; 34:656–660.

23. Prince AM, Brotman B, Grady GF, Kuhns WJ, Hazzi C, Levin RW, Millian SJ. Long incubation posttransfusion hepatitis without serological evidence of exposure to hepatitis B virus. Lancet 1974; ii:241–246.

24. Feinstone SM, Kapikian AZ, Purcell RH, Alter HJ, Holland PV. Transfusion associated hepatitis not due to viral hepatitis type A or B. N Engl J Med 1975; 292:767–770.

25. Choo Q-L, Weiner AJ, Overby LR, Kuo G, Houghton M, Bradley DW. Hepatitis C virus: the major causative agent of viral non-A, non-B hepatitis. Br Med Bull 1990; 46:423–441.

26. Gonzalez A, Esteban JI, Madoz P, Viladomiu L, Genesca J, Muniz E, Enriquez J, Torras X, Hernández JM, Quer J, Vidal X, Alter HJ, Shih JW, Esteban R, Guardia J. Efficacy of screening donors for antibodies to the hepatitis C virus to prevent transfusion-associated hepatitis: final report of a prospective trial. Hepatology 1995; 22:439–445.

27. Donahue JG, Munoz A, Ness PM, Brown DE Jr, Yawn DH, McAllister HA Jr, Reitz BA, Nelson KE. The declining risk of post-transfusion hepatitis C virus infection. N Engl J Med 1992; 327:369–373.

28. Uyttendaele S, Claeys H, Mertens H, Verhaert H, Vermylen C. Evaluation of third-generation screening and confirmatory assays for HCV antibodies. Vox Sang 1994; 66:122–129.

29. Silva AE, Hosein B, Boyle RW, Fang CT, Shindo M Waggoner JG, Hoofnagle JH,

DiBisceglie AM. Diagnosis of chronic hepatitis C: comparison of immunoassays and the polymerase chain reaction. Am J Gastroenterol 1994; 89:493–496.

30. Prince AM, Brotman B, Inchauspé, Pascual D, Nasoff M, Hosein B, Wang CY. Patterns and prevalence of hepatitis C virus infection in posttransfusion non-A, non-B hepatitis. J Infect Dis 1993; 167:1296–1301.

31. Prince AM, Brotman B, Huima T, Kraduledat P, Houghton M, Kuo G, Choo Q-L, Polito A, diNello R, Nelles MJ. Distinction between chronic and self-limited forms of hepatitis C infection. In: Shikata T, Purcell RH, Uchida Y, eds. Viral Hepatitis C, D, and E. Amsterdam: Elsevier Science Publishers, 1991:7–16.

32. Yuki N, Hayashi N, Kasahara A, Hagiware H, Ohkawa K, Fusamoto H, Kamada T. Hepatitis C virus replication and antibody responses toward specific hepatitis C virus proteins. Hepatology 1994; 19:1360–1365.

33. Alter MJ. Review of serologic testing for hepatitis C virus infection and risk of posttransfusion hepatitis C. Arch Path Lab Med 1994; 118:342–345.

34. Craxi A, Valenza M, Fabiano C, Magrin S, Fiorentino G, Diquattro O, Pagliaro L. Third-generation hepatitis C virus tests in asymptomatic anti-HCV-positive blood donors. J Hepatol 1994; 21:730–734.

35. Buffet C, Charnaux N, Laurent-Puig P, Chopineau S, Quichon JP, Briantais MJ, Dussaix E. Enhanced detection of antibodies to hepatitis C virus by use of a third-generation recombinant immunoblot assay. J Med Virol 1994; 43:259–261.

36. Busch MP, Korelitz JJ, Kleinman SH, Lee SR, AuBuchon JP, Schreiber GB, Retrovirus Epidemiology Donor Study. Declining value of alanine aminotransferase in screening of blood donors to prevent posttransfusion hepatitis B and virus infection. Transfusion 1995; 35:903–910.

37. Verbaan H, Andersson K, Eriksson S. Intravenous drug abuse—the major route of hepatitis C virus transmission among alcohol-dependent individuals. Scand J Gastroenterol 1993; 28:714–718.

38. Conry-Cantilena C, VanRaden M, Gibble J, Melpolder J, Shakil AO, Viladomiu L, Cheung L, DiBisceglie A, Hoofnagle J, Shih JW, Kaslow R, Ness P, Alter HJ. Routes of infection, viremia, and liver disease in blood donors found to have hepatitis C virus infection. N Engl J Med 1996; 334:1691–1696.

39. Oshita M, Hayashi N, Kasahara A, Yuki N, Takehara T, Hagiwara H, Hayakawa Y, Yasumatsuya Y, Kishida Y, Fusamoto H, Kamada T. Prevalence of hepatitis C virus in family members of patients with hepatitis C. J Med Virol 1993; 41:251–255.

40. Lissen E, Alter HJ, Abad MA, Torres Y, Perez-Romero M, Lcal M, Pineda JA, Torronteras R, Sánchez-Quijano A. Hepatitis C virus infection among sexually promiscuous groups and the heterosexual partners of hepatitis C virus infected index cases. Eur J Clin Microbiol Infect Dis 1993; 12:827–831.

41. Bresters D, Mauser-Bunschoten EP, Reesink HW, Roosendall G, van der Poel CL, Chamuleau RAFM, Jansen PLM, Weegink CJ, Cuypers HTM, Lelie PN, van den Berg HM. Sexual transmission of hepatitis C virus. Lancet 1993; 342:210–211.

42. Thomas DL, Zenilman JM, Alter Shih JW, Galai N, Carella AV, Quinn TC. Sexual transmission of hepatitis C virus among patients attending sexually transmitted diseases clinics in Baltimore—an analysis of 309 sex partnerships. J Infect Dis 1995; 171:768–775.

43. Numato N, Ohori H, Hayakawa Y, Saitoh Y, Tsunoda A, Kanno A. Demonstration of

hepatitis C virus genome in saliva and urine of patients with type C hepatitis. J Med Virol 1993; 41:120–128.

44. Zimmermann R, Perucchini D, Fauchere J-C, Joller-Jemelka H, Geyer M, Huch R, Huch A. Hepatitis C virus in breast milk. Lancet 1995; 345:928.

45. Roudot-Thoraval F, Pawlotsky J-M, Thiers V, Deforges L, Girollet P-P, Guillot F, Huraux C, Aumont P, Brechot C, Dhumeaux D. Lack of mother-to-infant transmission of hepatitis C virus in human immunodeficiency virus-seronegative women: a prospective study with hepatitis C virus RNA testing. Hepatology 1993; 17:772–777.

46. Zanetti AR, Tanzi E, Paccagnini S, Principi N, Pizzocolo G, Caccamo ML, D'Amico E, Cambié G, Vecchi L, Lombardy Study Group on Vertical HCV Transmission. Mother-to-infant transmission of hepatitis C virus. Lancet 1995; 345:289–291.

47. Mele A, Sagliocca L, Manzillo G, Converti F, Amoroso P, Stazi MA, Ferrigno L, Rapicetta M, Franco E, Adamo B, Palumbo F, Sbreglia C, Paná A, Pasquini P, SEIVA Collaborating Group. Risk factors for acute non-A, non-B hepatitis and their relationship to antibodies for hepatitis C virus: a case-control study. Am J Public Health 1994; 84:1640–1643.

48. Chen T-Z, Wu J-C, Yen F-S, Sheng W-Y, Hwang S-J, Huo T-I, Lee S-D. Injection with nondisposable needles as an important route for transmission of acute community-acquired hepatitis C virus infection in Taiwan. J Med Virol 1995; 46:247–251.

49. Sugitani M, Inchauspe G, Shindo M, Prince AM. Sensitivity of serological assays for detection of HCV viremic blood donors. Lancet 1992; 339:1018–1019.

50. Prince AM, Scheffel JW, Moore B. A search for hepatitis C virus polymerase chain reaction positive but seronegative subjects among blood donors with elevated aminotransferase. Transfusion 1997; 37:211–214.

51. Prince AM, Brotman B, Huima T, Pascual D, Jaffery M, Inchauspe G. Immunity in hepatitis C infection. J Infect Dis 1992; 165:438–443.

52. Wyatt CA, Andrus L, Brotman B, Huang F, Lee D-H, Prince AM. Immunity in chimpanzees chronically infected with hepatitis C virus: role of minor quasispecies in reinfection. J Virol 1998; In Press.

53. Uchida T, Shimojima M, Gotoh K, Shikata T, Tanaka E, Kiyosawa K. "Silent" hepatitis B virus mutants are responsible for non-A, non-B, non-C, non-D, non-E hepatitis. Microbiol Immunol 1994; 38:281–285.

54. Alter HJ, Bradley DW. Non-A, non-B hepatitis unrelated to the hepatitis C virus (non-ABC) Semin Liver Dis 1995; 15:110–120.

55. Simons JN, Pilot-Matias TJ, Leary TP, Dawson GJ, Desai SM, Schlauder GG, Muerhoff AS, Erker JC, Buijk SL, Chalmers ML, Van Sant CL, Mushahwa IK. Identification of two flavivirus-like genomes in the GB hepatitis agent. Proc Natl Acad Sci USA 1995; 92:3401–3405.

56. Simons JN, Leary TP, Dawson GJ, Pilot-Matias TJ, Muerhoff AS, Schlauder GG, Desai SM. Isolation of novel virus-like sequences associated with human hepatitis. Nat Med 1995; 1:564–569.

57. Linner J, Wages J, Jr, Zhang-Keck ZY, Fry KE. Molecular cloning and disease association of hepatitis G virus: a transfusion transmissible agent. Science 1996; 271:505–508.

58. Miyakawa Y, Mayumi M. Hepatitis G virus—a true hepatitis virus or an accidental tourist? N Engl J Med 1997; 336:795–796.

59. Alter HJ, Nakatsuji Y, Melpolder J, Wages J, Wesley R, Shih JW-K, Kim JP. The incidence of transfusion-associated hepatitis G virus infection and its relation to liver disease. N Engl J Med 1997; 336:747–754.

60. Lefrere J-J, Loiseau P, Maury J, Lasserre J, Mariotti M, Ravera N, Lerable J, Lefevre G, Morand-Joubert L, Girot R. Natural history of GBV-C/hepatitis G virus infection through the follow-up of GBV-C/hepatitis G virus-infected blood donors and recipients studied by RNA polymerase chain reaction and anti-E2 serology. Blood 1997; 90:3776–3780.

61. Alter MJ, Gallagher M, Morris TT, Moyer LA, Meeks EL, Krawczynski K, Kim IP, Margolis HS, Sentinel Counties Viral Hepatitis Study Team. Acute non-A-E hepatitis in the United States and the role of hepatitis G virus infection. N Engl J Med 1997; 336:741–746.

62. Yoshiba M, Okamoto H, Mishiro S. Detection of the GBV-C hepatitis virus genome in serum from patients with fulminant hepatitis of unknown aetiology. Lancet 1995; 346:1131–1132.

63. Sato K, Tanaka T, Okamoto H, Miyakawa Y, Mayumi M. Association of circulating hepatitis G virus with lipoproteins for a lack of binding with antibodies. Biochem Biophys Res Commun 1996; 229:719–725.

64. Nishizawa T, Okamoto H, Konishi K, Yoshizawa H, Miyakawa Y, Mayumi M. A novel DNA virus (TTV) associated with elevated transaminase levels in posttransfusion hepatitis of unknown etiology. Biochem Biophy Res Comm 1997; 241:92–97.

65. Mulyanto DR, Suwignya S, Tsauri S, Itoh K, Mizui M, Tsuda F, Okamoto H, Yoshizawa H, Mishiro. An easy dipstick assay for anti-core antibodies to screen donors for hepatitis C virus viremia. Vox Sang 1996; 70:229–231.

66. Allain JP, Kitchen A, Aloysius S, Reeves I, Petrik J, Barbara JAJ, Williamson LM. Safety and efficacy of hepatitis C virus antibody screening of blood donors with two sequential screening assays. Transfusion 1996; 36:401–405.

13
Human T-Cell Leukemia Virus

Maria Rios and Celso Bianco
New York Blood Center, New York, New York

I. THE VIRUS: ISOLATION, CHARACTERIZATION, AND BIOLOGICAL PROPERTIES

The human T-cell leukemia viruses type I (HTLV-I) and type II (HTLV-II) are human retroviruses in the oncornavirus family. This family includes the human immunodeficiency virus (HIV), the bovine leukemia virus (BLV), and the simian T-cell leukemia virus (STLV) (1). HTLV-I was first isolated from a patient with cutaneous T-cell lymphoma (2,3). The virus was quickly associated with human diseases, such as adult T-cell leukemia, leading to the addition of the retrovirus family to the category of human pathogens (2–7). HTLV-II was isolated from a patient with a T-cell variant hairy cell leukemia (8).

Retroviruses are enveloped viruses that need to be transcribed into DNA and integrated into the host cell genome in order to replicate. The viral particles carry the enzyme reverse transcriptase (RT), which transcribes the viral RNA into complementary DNA (cDNA). The cDNA is subsequently converted into double-stranded DNA (dsDNA) and integrated into the host cell genome as proviral DNA (9). The genomic material of retroviruses is composed of three major regions: *gag* (group antigen), which encodes for structural proteins; *pol*, which encodes for nonstructural proteins, such as polymerase and proteases; and *env*, which encodes for envelope proteins. HTLV-I and HTLV-II also have a set of genes named *tax/rex* that encode for proteins that regulate viral replication. The genomic sequence of the virus is flanked by two long terminal repeats (LTR) with elements that regulate transcription and join the host cell genome after integration (Fig. 1). The *tax* protein increases the rate of transcription initiation by acting on the promoter located in the 5'LTR. The *tax* protein also transactivates heterologous

295

HTLV Genome

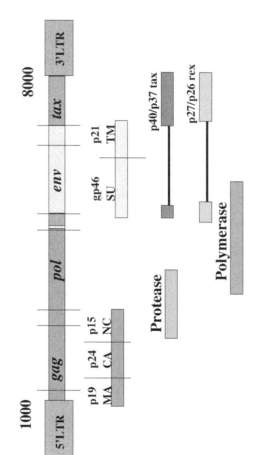

Figure 1 Graphic representation of the HTLV genome and respective gene products. 5′LTR-*gag-pol-env-tax/rex*-LRT3′HTLV gene products—the *gag* (group antigen) region encodes for the following structural proteins: p19 (matrix), p24 (capsid), and p15 (nucleocapsid). The *pol* region encodes for the nonstructural proteins protease and reverse transcriptase. The *env* (envelope) region encodes for the envelope proteins gp46 (exposed to the external surface of the virus) and for p21 (envelope transmembrane). The *tax/rex* region encodes for p40 (*tax*) a regulatory, nonstructural protein that regulates activation of viral transcription by interacting with LTR, and for the p27 (*rex*) nonstructural protein that regulates viral replication at postranscriptional level. (From Refs. 11,12.)

promoters such as the IL-2 and IL-2R promoter, the GM-CSF promoter, the c-fos and c-cis promoter. The *rex* protein controls HTLV gene expression at the post transcriptional level (10,11). Retroviruses infect a wide range of cellular types in vitro. Fortunately, their ability to transform these cells is limited.

Unlike other retroviruses, HTLV has highly conserved genomic sequences (12). The rate of base substitutions is estimated at approximately 1% per 1000 years (13,14). The diversity of the entire collection of HTLV sequences identified to date is lower than that observed within a single patient in late stage of HIV infection (14–17).

II. EPIDEMIOLOGY

HTLV-I is found worldwide. However, it clusters preferentially around the equatorial belt (Table 1). The prevalence of HTLV-I/II infection in the United States is approximately 0.0004%, based on blood donor screening. About half of the positive individuals are infected with HTLV-II (37).

The epidemiology of HTLV-II is not as well known as that of HTLV-I. Infection is highly prevalent among intravenous drug users (IVDUs) in the United States and in Europe (43–46). Infection with HTLV-II is also frequent among Native American populations from North, Central, and South America (45–56), and the prevalence can be as high as 20–30% (54,57).

The major routes of transmission for HTLV-I and HTLV-II are sexual contact and from mother to child through breast-feeding, leading to clear familial clustering of HTLV-I carriers (56,58). HTLV-I infection has also been reported in children who have not been breast-fed, indicating that other perinatal routes of transmission have to be considered (60). Vertical transmission (mother-to-child) occurs with a frequency of 10–30% (29,58,61). HTLV-I/II and HIV share the same routes of infection. However, HTLV-I/II appears to be less infectious than HIV. This difference has been attributed to viral load in the course of infection and to the fact that, in the host, HTLV-I always remain cell-associated while HIV-1 is both cell-associated and cell-free (62–64). The rate of infection among females is higher than that among males (24,29). Studies involving steady heterosexual couples documented significant concordance of HTLV-I serological status (65). The efficacy of sexual transmission has been estimated at 53% (44). Serologically discordant couples were predominantly female positive and male negative, indicating higher efficiency of transmission from males to females than from females to males (59,64,65). HTLV-I has been isolated from semen (66). Transmission from females to males may be associated with other factors, such as sexual intercourse during menses and bleeding during intercourse (44).

The modes of transmission of HTLV-II are less well documented than that of HTLV-I. Sexual transmission of HTLV-II has been difficult to study because

Table 1 Prevalence of HTLV-I Infection in Various Regions of the World

Region	Countries	Prevalence (%)	Ref.
Africa	Cameroon, Gabon, Ivory Coast, Kenya, Tanzania, Zaire	1–10	18–21
Caribbean islands	Barbados, Guadeloupe, Haiti, Jamaica, Martinique, Tobago	1–7	21–25
Europe	France, Italy, United Kingdom, Spain	~0.1	19,26–28
Japanese islands	Kyushu, Okinawa	1–30	29
South and Central America	Argentina, Brazil, Bolivia, Colombia, Honduras, Paraguay, Peru, Venezuela, Uruguay	0.3–10	30–36
North America	United States, Canada	<0.1	37
Pacific islands	Australia, Malaysia, Taiwan, Vietnam	1.7–14	38–42

of the frequent coincidence of intravenous drug abuse. For instance, studies of female prostitutes have shown that intravenous drug abuse is the major risk factor for seropositivity (43–46). Studies of Guaymi Indians from Panama and Native Americans from New Mexico show concordance of seropositivity among married couples, similar to what has been observed with HTLV-I (47). Vertical transmission of HTLV-II through breast-feeding has also been reported (67,68). Parenteral transmission through contaminated needles is observed among IVDUs (44–46) and in countries without disposable needles where sterilization of multiple use needles is inadequate.

Transmission by blood and blood products will be discussed later in this chapter.

III. ASSOCIATION OF HTLV-I INFECTION WITH DISEASE

The first two diseases identified as associated with HTLV-I were the hematological malignancy known as adult T-cell leukemia (ATL) and the progressive neurodegenerative disease known as tropical spastic paraparesis (TSP) in the Caribbean and Africa (69,70), and as HTLV-I–associated myelopathy (HAM) in Japan. Other diseases reported to be associated with HTLV-I infection are infectious dermatitis (71), uveitis (72), opportunistic infections of the lungs, chronic renal insufficiency, and lymphadenopathy (73,74). It has been suggested that malignant diseases are caused by monoclonal proliferation of cells containing integrated provirus and that nonmalignant diseases result from polyclonal proliferation of HTLV-I–infected cells or are a consequence of the host's immunological reaction to the virus (75–77).

A. Adult T-Cell Leukemia

Adult T-cell leukemia was first described in Japan in 1974 and recognized as a specific disease in 1977 (78,79). The virus was first isolated in the United States from leukocytes from an ATL patient in 1980 (1) and called HTLV. The virus was also isolated in Japan in 1981 from a cell line derived from an ATL patient (MT-I) and called adult T-cell leukemia virus (ATLV) (80). Documentation that the U.S. and Japanese isolates were identical led to the agreement that the newly identified retroviruses should be called HTLV-I (81,82).

ATL is a mature T-cell lymphoma characterized by monoclonal integration of the virus into the leukemic cell genome (81,83). The leukemic phase of ATL is characterized by circulating $CD4^+/CD25^+$ T cells (79). ATL develops after a long incubation period. In Japan, the age of onset of ATL ranges from 24 to 85 years, with an average of 58 years, but in the Caribbean and South America onset occurs at an average of 40 years (81,83–85). A proportion of HTLV-I–infected individuals develop ATL after an extraordinary long period of incubation, 20–30 years (86,87). The lifetime risk for individuals infected before the age of 20 is 5% (84). The male-to-female ratio is 1.4:1, opposite to that HTLV-I of asymptomatic carriers. The major clinical findings at onset are enlargement of peripheral lymph nodes, hepatomegaly, splenomegaly, and skin lesions. Hypercalcemia is present in 32% of the patients. Immunosuppression accompanied by opportunistic infections is also common. The white blood cell count varies from normal up to $5 \times 10^5/\mu L$. Leukemic cells have cleaved or multilobular nuclei known as "flower cells" (79). There are four clinical forms of ATL according to their clinical course: acute, chronic, lymphomatous, and smoldering (82). The prognosis of ATL is very poor, with a mean survival time in Japan of 6.2, 10.2, and 24.3 months, respectively, for acute, lymphomatous, and chronic ATL. ATL does not respond well to chemotherapy. Recent reports suggest that treatment with zidovudine and interferon-alpha may be effective (86,88,89).

B. Tropical Spastic Paraparesis/
HTLV-I–Associated Myelopathy

Tropical spastic paraparesis/HTLV-I–associated myelopathy (TSP/HAM) was first associated with HTLV-I in 1985 in Martinique (69) and in 1986 in Africa (70) and Japan (87). In Japan, this disease is strongly associated with history of blood transfusions (90). The lifetime risk of development of TSP/HAM among HTLV-I–infected individuals is less than 2% (91). The main neurological features of TSP/HAM are spasticity or hyperreflexia of the legs, disturbances of bladder function, weakness of leg muscles, and sensory disturbances. Spinal cord atrophy, signs of funicular demyelinization, axonal loss, and gliosis are often found in the lower thoracic spinal cord. Sometimes the white matter presents lesions in magnetic resonance imaging.

Analysis of the cerebrospinal fluid shows pleocytosis, high titer of IgG, and oligoclonality (92). Neuropathologically it appears as a typical immune-inflammatory disease with infiltration of the parenchyma by CD4$^+$ and CD8$^+$ T cells. In later stages, the number of inflammatory cells diminishes and they are almost exclusively CD8$^+$ T-cells. TSP/HAM patients have a very intense immunological response to HTLV-I antigens. The relationship between the immune response and damage to the central nervous system is unclear. There is indication that HTLV-I proviral load may be a factor, because TSP/HAM patients have 50 times more HTLV-I proviral DNA in peripheral blood lymphocytes than asymptomatic carrier (93). Patients with TSP/HAM show some improvement after treatment with oral corticosteroids.

C. Infective Dermatitis

Infective dermatitis was described in 1966 in Jamaican children. The association with HTLV-I infection was made in 1990 by detection of viral genome in skin biopsies (71). Infective dermatitis is characterized by crusted scabies, corneal opacities, chronic bronchiectasis, parasitic worm infestation, and progression to more severe HTLV-I–associated diseases such as ATL and TSP/HAM (94,95).

D. HTLV-I–Associated Uveitis

HTLV-I–associated uveitis is characterized by moderate to severe cellular infiltration of the vitreous body (vitreous opacity), mild iritis, and moderate retinal vasculitis (72). Virological and molecular biological findings suggest that cytokines produced by HTLV-I–infected T cells in the eye play a central role in the pathogenesis of the disease. The proviral load in blood lymphocytes from patients with uveitis is higher than that of asymptomatic carriers (72). The inflammation responds to topical and systemic treatment with corticosteroids and reoccurs in about 60% of the cases after therapy is discontinued. Some patients present typical Sjögren's syndrome (96–98).

E. Other Diseases

Other diseases observed in HTLV-I–infected individuals are opportunistic infections of the lungs, chronic renal insufficiency, lymphadenopathy, arthropathy, and autoimmune diseases (99–101). HTLV-I–associated infiltrating pneumonitis has also been reported in some individuals in Japan (100–102).

IV. DISEASE ASSOCIATED WITH HTLV-II

HTLV-II has not been clearly associated with any disease. The original isolate of HTLV-II came from a patient with hairy cell leukemia. Large surveys of patients with hairy cell leukemia have identified only sporadic examples of HTLV-II seropositivity (103–105). Subsequently, several cases of large granular lympho-cytic leukemia (LGLL), a T-cell malignancy with natural killer cell phenotype, have been reported (106). However, several surveys of LGLL did not show clear excess prevalence of HTLV-I antibodies or sequences of the HTLV-II genome in these patients (107–111).

New Mexico has a large Native American population with high prevalence of HTLV-II infection. The incidence of lymphoproliferative disorders among these individuals is not higher than that of the normal population. However, this lack of association cannot be directly documented because the HTLV-II status of the registered cases has not been determined (112). One case of HTLV-II–associated mycosis fungoides positive by PCR and negative for antibodies has been reported (113). A syndrome of severe skin disease, eosinophilia, and dermatopathic lymphadenopathy has been reported among intravenous drug abusers co-infected with HTLV-II and HIV-1 (114). A growing number of TSP/HAM cases associated with HTLV-II are being reported (115–121). Some of the case reports had features reminiscent of the ataxic form of TSP/HAM reported from Jamaica. Cases have had oligoclonal bands in the CSF reminiscent of what has been observed in HTLV-I–positive cases.

An increased incidence of infectious diseases was observed during prospec-tive follow-up of human T-lymphotropic virus type II– and I–infected blood donors. Compared with seronegative controls, HTLV-II infection was associated with an increased incidence of bronchitis, bladder and/or kidney infections, and oral herpes. HTLV-I infection was associated with increased incidence of bladder and/or kidney infection (122). Other possible conditions identified in medical surveys of the Guaymi Indians, drug abuser and transfusion cohorts that are being evaluated in association with HTLV-II are an adult polyarthritis, eczema of the skin, and asthma.

V. TRANSMISSION OF HTLV-I AND HTLV-II BY BLOOD AND BLOOD PRODUCTS

Retrospective studies performed in Japan have clearly documented the transmis-sion of HTLV-I by transfusion of cellular components of blood, but not by plasma or by plasma derivatives. The estimated frequency of infection by transfusion of a seropositive cellular component was 63% (123). This study led to the im-plementation of screening of United States blood donors for antibodies to HTLV-I/II in December 1988 (124). The previously observed rate of transmission was confirmed by a large donor-recipient study performed in Jamaica prior to the availability of screening tests. That study showed that the median time to seroconversion among infected recipients was 51 days and that infectivity was inversely proportional to the age of the transfused product, suggesting that the loss of infectivity was associated with loss of viability of leukocytes (125). Transmission of HTLV-I/II by transfusion seems to be rare and has been estimated at 1:641,000 based on large studies of seroconversion among blood donors at four major U.S. blood centers (126).

Transmission of HTLV-II by transfusion of cellular products has also been documented (127,128). Retrospective studies based on lookback programs lead to the identification of recipients infected by HTLV-II through the transfusion of blood that had tested negative on an HTLV-I screening assay, showing the lower sensitivity of HTLV-I based screening assays to detect antibodies to HTLV-II (47,128,129). More sensitive assays containing specific HTLV-II epitopes have since been licensed and are in use for blood donor screening (130).

While transmission of HTLV-I/II infection by transfusion is well documented in the literature, transmission of disease has been infrequent. There is one report suggesting that two long-term survivors of hematological malignancies, one with Hodgkin's and one with acute promyelocytic leukemia, developed ATL 6 months and 11 years after blood transfusions, respectively (131). There are several reported cases of TSP/HAM attributed to transfusion in the literature. The incubation time varied from 6 to 24 months, with an average of 15 months (132–138).

VI. LABORATORY ASSAYS FOR HTLV-I/II

Blood donor screening for HTLV-I and HTLV-II was recommended by the U.S. Food and Drug Administration (FDA) in December 1988, as screening assays for antibodies to these viruses became licensed (124). All antibody-screening assays licensed in the United States contain, in addition to HTLV-I antigens, HTLV-II specific proteins (130) and are based on enzyme immunoassay (EIA) principles (microtiter plates, beads, or microparticles containing antigens that are incubated with serum or plasma of the prospective blood donor). Japan uses particle agglutination assays based on the same principles and similar reagents.

Every year, 10,000–15,000 U.S. blood donors are found to be repeatedly reactive on commercial EIA screening assays for HTLV-I/II and require performance of additional, more specific tests for confirmation of screening test results. They include Western blots (WB), radioimmunoprecipitation assay (RIPA), recombinant immunoblot (RIBA), and immunofluorescence. Unfortunately, the sensitivity and specificity of these assays is poorly defined. At present, there is no "gold standard." None of these supplemental assays has been licensed by FDA. In addition, because of miniscule demand, it is unlikely that they will ever be licensed.

The Western blot is the most used supplemental assay for HTLV-I/II. A sample is positive when it reacts with at least two gene products (*gag*, p24, and *env*, p21 or gp46). In the most commonly available Western blot (Cambridge Biotech), *gag* encoded proteins (p19 and p24) are well represented, while the envelope protein gp46 is not. Therefore other supplemental assays such as RIPA are used to increase sensitivity for *env* products. RIPA is performed with a lysate of MT-2 cells and is positive when antibodies to gp61/68 are detected.

Supplemental assays generate a large number of indeterminate test results and provide poor type discrimination between HTLV-I and HTLV-II due to high homology between the two viral types. (See Fig. 2.) FDA approved in June 1999 the use of a second licensed test for antibodies to HTLV-I/II (manufactured by a different supplier) on samples that test repeatedly reactive on a screening test for

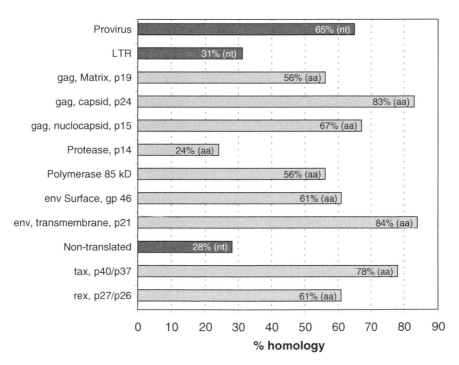

Figure 2 Degree of homology between HTLV-I and HTLV-II at the nucleotide (nt) and amino acid levels.

antibodies to HTLV-I/II. It appears that more than 60% of these samples test nonreactive in the second assay. Donors with discordant EIA reactivity remain eligible to donate as long as the screening assay for the next donation tests nonreactive. The dual EIA strategy facilitates donor counseling by removing false-positive test results and avoiding indeterminate Western blot test results on a substantial number of donors.

Amplification of specific viral sequences through the polymerase chain reaction has been the most productive approach for confirmation of EIA results and for the discrimination HTLV type (43–47, 128,129). Unfortunately, nucleic acid amplification technologies for HTLV-I/II are not readily available to most blood-collecting facilities and clinical laboratories.

VII.   DONOR NOTIFICATION AND COUNSELING

The lack of accuracy of confirmatory results, together with the unclear consequences of viral infection, have made donor notification, counseling, and follow-up of donors with repeatedly reactive results of EIA for antibodies to HTLV-I and HTLV-II a difficult task. Counseling of donors for HTLV-I/II has been the subject of an extensive review by the public health authorities and the blood banking community. The outcome was published in 1993 (139). Counseling should stress the difference between HTLV-I/II and HIV. Counseling should also be tailored to viral type because of differences in disease association (or lack thereof) between the two viral types. In addition, the low frequency of disease development over the lifetime of infected individuals (2–5%) should be emphasized.

Donors with positive test results are told not to donate blood or tissues in the future and to use precautions for the prevention of transmission of the virus by blood or by sexual contact. HTLV-I/II–positive mothers are discouraged from breast-feeding when practicable to prevent mother-to-child transmission. However, this approach should be avoided in countries where breast-feeding is critical to child survival, e.g., in areas where diarrheal disease leads to high mortality. Use of condoms is recommended for couples in which one of the partners is HTLV-I/II positive. In case these couples desire to have babies, unprotected sex should be limited to the period of fertility. Such decisions require careful discussions between physician and patient, and no clear guidelines have been defined.

Counseling of donors with indeterminate test results is always difficult because of the undefined messages that must be conveyed. These donors are told that they are probably not infected. However, they are strictly barred from donating blood.

REFERENCES

1. Poiesz BJ, Sherman M, Saksena N, et al. The biology and epidemiology of the human T-cell lymphoma/leukemia viruses. In: Neu HC, Levy JA, Weiss RA, eds. Frontiers of infectious diseases: Focus on HIV London: Churchill Livingston, 1993: 189–205.

2. Poiesz BJ, Ruscetti FW, Gazdar AF, Bunn PA, Gallo RC. Detection and isolation of type C retrovirus particles from fresh and cultured lymphocytes of a patient with cutaneous T-cell lymphoma. Proc Natl Acad Sci USA 1980; 77:7415–7419,

3. Yoshida M, Miyoshi I, Hinuma Y. Isolation and characterization of retrovirus from cell lines of human adult T-cell leukemia and its implication in the disease. Proc Natl Acad Sci 1984; 79:2031–2035.

4. Popovic M, Reitz MS, Jr, Sarngadharan MG. The virus of Japanese adult T-cell leukemia is a member of the human T-cell leukemia/lymphoma virus Group. Nature 1982; 300:63–66.

5. Watanabe T, Seiki M, Yoshida M. ATLV (Japanese isolate) and HTLV (US isolate) are the same strain of retroviruses. Virology 1984; 133:238–241.

6. Blattner WA, Kalyanaram VS, Robert-Guroff M, Lister A, Galton DAG, Sarin PS, Crawford MH, Catovsky D, Greaves M, Gallo R. The human type-C retrovirus, HTLV, in blacks from the Caribbean region, and relationship to adult T-cell leukemia/lymphoma. Int J Cancer 1982; 30:257–264.

7. Doski H, Denic S, Patel N, Krishnamurthy M, Levine P, Clark JW. Adult T-cell Leukemia/Lymphoma in Brooklyn. JAMA 1988; 259:2255–2257.

8. Kalyanaraman VS, Sarngadharan MG, Robert-Guroff M. A new subtype of human T-cell leukemia virus (HTLV-II) associated with a T-cell variant of hairy cell leukemia. Science 1982; 218:571–573.

9. Weiss R, Teich N, Varmus H, Coffin J, eds. RNA Tumor Viruses. Cold Spring Harbor, NY: Cold Spring Harbor Laboratory, 1985.

10. Inoue J, Seiki M, Yoshida M. The second pX product p27xIII of HTLV-I is required for gag gene expression. FEBS 1986; 209:187–190.

11. Inoue J, Yoshida M, Seiki M. Transcriptional (p40x) and post-transcriptional (p27xIII) regulators are required for the expression and replication of human T-cell leukemia virus type I genes. Proc Natl Sci USA 1987; 84:3653–3657.

12. Holland J J, ed. Genetic Diversity of RNA Viruses. Berlin: Spring-Verlag, 1992.

13. Sherman MP, Saksena NK, Dube DK, Yanangihara R, Poiesz BJ. Evolutionary insights in the origin of human T-cell lymphoma/leukemia virus type I (HTLV-I) derived from sequence analyses of a new HTLV-I variant from Papua New Guinea. J Virol 1992; 66:2556–2563.

14. Gessain A, Gallo RC, Franchini G. Low degree of human T-cell leukemia virus type I genetic drift in vivo as means of monitoring viral transmission and movement of ancient human populations. J Virol 1992; 66:2288–2295.

15. Sherman MP, Saksena NK, Dube DK, Yanangihara R, Poiesz BJ. Evolutionary insights in the origin of human T-cell lymphoma/leukemia virus type I (HTLV-I) derived from sequence analyses of a new HTLV-I variant from Papua New Guinea. J Virol 1992; 66:2556–2563.

16. Myers G, Korber B, Wain-Hobson S, Smith RF, Pavlakis GN. Human retroviruses and AIDS. 1993. Los Alamos, NM:Los Alamos National Laboratory, 1993.

17. Pedrosa Martins L, Chenciner N, Wain-Hobson S. 1992. Complex intra-patient sequence variation in the V1 and V2 hypervariable regions of the HIV-1 gp120 envelope sequences. Virology 64:837–845.

18. Verdier M, Denis F, Sangare A, et al. Prevalence of antibody to human T cell leukemia virus type I (HTLV-I) in populations of Ivory Coast, West Africa. J Infect Dis 1989; 160:363–370.

19. Touzé E, Gessain A, Lyon-Caen O, Gout O. Tropical spastic paraparesis/HTLV-I-associated myelopathy in Europe and Africa: clinical and epidemiological aspects. JAIDS Hum Retrov 1996; 13(S1):S38–45.

20. Wiktor SZ, Piot P, Mann JM, et al. Human T-cell lymphotropic virus type I (HTLV-I) among female prostitutes in Kinshasa, Zaire. J Infect Dis 1990; 161:1073–1077.

21. Blattner WA, Saxinger C, Riedel D. A study of HTLV-I and its associated risk factors in Trinidad and Tobago. J AIDS 1990; 90:1102–1108.

22. Blattner WA, Blaney DW, Robert-Guroff M, Sarngadharan MG, Kalyanaraman VS, Sarin PS, Jaffe ES, Gallo, RC. Epidemiology of human T-cell leukemia/lymphoma virus. J Infect Dis 1983 147:406–416.

23. Riedel D, Evans AS, Saxinger C, Blattner WA. A historical study of human T-lymphotropic virus type I transmission in Barbados. J Infect Dis 1989; 159:603–609.

24. Murphy EL, Figueroa JP, Gibbs WN, et al. Human T-lymphotropic virus type I (HTLV-I) seroprevalence in Jamaica: I. Demographic determinants. Am J Epidemiol 1991; 133(11):1114–1124.

25. Maloney EM, Murphy EL, Figueroa JP, Gibbs WN, Cranston B, Hanchard B, Holding-Cobham M, Malley K, Blattner WA. Human T-lymphotropic virus type-I (HTLV-I) seroprevalence in Jamaica II. Geographic and ecological determinants. Am J Epidemiol 1991; 133:1125–1134.

26. Taylor GP. The epidemiology of HTLV-I in Europe. JAIDS Hum Retrov 1996; 13(S1):S8–14.

27. Hale A, Leung T, Sivasubramaniam S, Kenny J, Sutherland S. Prevalence of antibodies to HTLV in antenatal clinic attendees in south east London. J Med Virol 1997; 52:326–329.

28. Voevodin A, Gessain A. Common origin of human T-lymphotropic virus type-I from Iran, Kuwait, Israel, and La Reunion Island. J Med Virol 1997; 52:77–82.

29. Yamaguchi K. Human T-lymphotropic virus type I in Japan. Lancet 1994; 343:213–216.

30. Gabbai AA, Bordin JO, Vieira-Filho JBP, Kuroda A, Oliveira ASB, Cruz MV, Ribeiro AAF, Delaney SR, Henrard DR, Rosario J, Roman GC. Selectivity of human T-lymphotropic virus type-I (HTLV-1) and HTLV-2 infection among different populations in Brasil. Am J Trop Med Hyg 1993; 49:664–671.

31. de Rivera IL, Amador L, Mourra S, Li S, Rasheed S. Geographical clustering of human T-cell lymphotropic virus type 1 infection in Honduras. J Clin Microbiol 1995; 33:2999–3003.

32. Maloney EM, Ramirez H, Levine A, Blattner WA. A survey of the human T-cell

lymphotropic virus type I (HTLV-I) in south-western Colombia. Int J Cancer 1989; 44:419–423.

33. Gotuzzo E, Sanchez J, Escamilla J, Carrillo C, Phillips IA, Moreyra L, Stamm W, Ashley R, Roggen EL, Kreiss J, Piot P, Holmes KK. Human T cell lymphotropic virus type I infection among female sex workers in Peru. J Infect Dis 1994; 169:54–59.

34. Pino N, Peralta LM, Pampuro S, Pimental E, Libonatti O. HTLV-I/II seroprevalence and co-infection with other pathogens in blood donors in Buenos Aires. J AIDS 1994; 7:206–207.

35. Vasquez P, Sanchez G, Volante C, Ramirez E, Soto G, Lee H. Human T-lymphotropic virus type I: new risk for Chilean population. Blood 1991; 78:850.

36. Merino F, Robert-Guroff M, Clark J, Bundo-Barcho M, Blattner WA, Gallo RC. Natural antibodies to human T-cell leukemia/lymphoma virus in healthy Venezuelan population. Int J Cancer 1984; 34:501–506.

37. Khabbaz RF, Heneine W, Grindon A, Hartley TM, Shulman G, Kaplan J. Indeterminate HTLV serologic results in U.S. blood donors: are they due to HTLV-I or HTLV-II? J AIDS 1992; 5:400-404.

38. Bastian I, Gardner J, Webb D, Gardner I. Isolation of a human T-lymphotropic virus type-I strain from Australian aboriginals. J Virol 1993; 67:843–851.

39. Doherty RR. HTLV-I in Australia and Oceania: long-term resident or recent immigrant? Med J Aust 1996: 164:84–86.

40. Yang Y-C, Hsu T-Y, Liiu M-Y et al. Molecular subtyping of T-lymphotropic virus type I (HTLV-I) by a nested polymerase chain reaction-restriction fragment polymorphism analysis of the envelope gene: two distinct lineages of HTLV-I in Taiwan. J Med Virol 1997; 51:25–31.

41. Yanagihara R, Jenkins CL, Alexander SS, et al. Human T lymphotropic virus type I infection in Papua New Guinea: high prevalence among the Hagahai confirmed by Western blot analysis. J Infect Dis 1990; 162:649–654.

42. Yamashita M, Achiron A, Miura T et al. HTLV-I from Iranian Mashhadi Jews in Israel is phylogenetically related to that of Japan, India, and South America rather than that of Africa and Melanesia. Virus Genes 1995; 10:85–90.

43. Khabbaz RF, Hartel D, Lairmore M, Horsburgh CR, Schoenbaum EE, Roberts B, Hartley TM, Frieldland G. Human T lymphotropic virus type II (HTLV-II) infection in a cohort of New York intravenous drug users: an old infection? J Infect Dis 1990; 163:252.

44. Khabbaz RF, Onorato IM, Cannon RO, et al. 1992 Seroprevalence of HTLV-I and HTLV-II among intravenous drug users and persons in clinics for sexually transmitted diseases. N Engl J Med 1992; 326:375–380.

45. The HTLV European Research Network. Seroepidemiology of the human T-cell leukaemia/lymphoma viruses in Europe. J Acquir Immune Defic Syndr Hum Retrovirol 1996; 13(1):68–77.

46. Lee H, Sawanson P, Shorty VS, Zack JA, Rosenbalt JD, Chen IS-Y. High rate of HTLV-II infection in seropositive drug abusers in New Orleans. Science 1989; 244:471.

47. Hjelle B, Wilson C, Cyrus S, Bradshaw P, Schammel C, Wiltbank T, Alexander S.

Human T-cell leukemia virus type II infection frequently goes undetected in contemporary US blood donors. Blood 1993; 81:1641–1644.

48. Laimore MD, Jacobson S, Garcia F, et al. Isolation of human T-cell lymphotropic virus type 2 from Guaymi Indians in Panama. Proc Natl Acad Sci USA 1990; 87:8840–8844,

49. Lal RB, Povoa M, Lal AA. Seroprevalence of HTLV-II in Paragaminos, state of Para, Brazil. Lett J AIDS 1992; 5:634–636.

50. Fujiyama C, Fujiyoshi T, Mivra T, Yashiki S, Matsumoto D, Zaninovic V, Blanco O, Harrington Jr W, Byrnes JJ, Hayami M, Sonoda S. A new endemic focus of T-cell lymphotropic virus type among Ornico natives in Colombia. J Infect Dis 1992; 168:1075–1077.

51. Hjelle B, Cyrus S, Swenson SG. Evidence for sexual transmission of human T lymphotropic virus type II. Ann Intern Med 1992; 116:90–91.

52. Biglone M, Gessain A, Quiruelas S, Fay O, Taborda MA, Fernandez E, Lupo S, Panzita A, de Thé G. Endemic HTLV-II infection among Tobas and Matacos Amerindians from North of Argentina. J AIDS 1993; 6:631–633.

53. Lavine PH, Jacobson S, Elliot R, Cavallero A, Colclough G, Stephenson C, Knigge RM, Drumond J, Iishimura M, Taylor ME, Wiktor S, Shaw GM. HTLV-II in Florida Indians. AIDS Res Hum Retrov 1993; 9:123–128.

54. Maloney EM, Biggar RJ, Neel JV, et al. Endemic human T-cell lymphotropic virus type II infection among isolated Brazilian Amerindians. J Infect Dis 1992; 166:100–107.

55. Lairmore MD, Jacobson S, Gracia F, et al. Isolation of human T-cell lymphotropic virus type 2 from Guaymi Indians in Panama. Proc Natl Acad Sci USA 1990; 87:8840–8844.

56. Ijichi S, Zaninovic V, Leon FE et al. Identification of human T-cell leukemia virus type IIb infection in the Wayu, an aboriginal population of Colombia. Jpn J Cancer Res 1993; 84:1215–1218.

57. Ishak R, Harrington WJ, Azevedo VN, et al. Identification of human T cell lymphotropic virus type IIa infection in the Kayapo, an indigenous population of Brazil. AIDS Res Hum Retrovir 1995; 11:813–821.

58. Kajiyama W, Kashiwagi S, Ikematsu H, Hayashi J, Nomura H, Okochi K. Intrafamilial transmission of adult T cell leukemia virus. J Infect Dis 1986; 154:851–857.

59. Ichimaru M, Ikeda S, Kinoshita K, Hino S, Tsuji Y. Mother-to-child transmission of HTLV-1. Cancer Detect Prev 1991; 15:177–181.

60. Fujino T, Fujiyoshi T, Yashiki S, Sonoda S, Otsuka H, Nagata Y. HTLV-I transmission from mother to fetus via placenta (letter). Lancet 1992; 340:1157.

61. Tajima K, Cartier L. Epidemiological features of HTLV-I and adult T-cell leukemia. Intervirology 1995; 38:238–246.

62. Bartolomeu C, Saxinger WC, Clark JW, et al. Transmission of HTLV-I and HIV among homosexual men in Trinidad. JAMA 1987; 257:2604–2608.

63. Figureoa JP, Ward E, Morris J, et al. Incidence of HIV and HTLV-I infection among sexually transmitted disease clinic attendees in Jamaica. J AIDS Hum Retrovir 1997; 15:232–237.

64. Bulterys M, Landesman S, Burns DN, Rubinstein A, Goedert JJ. Sexual behavior

and injection drug use during pregnancy and vertical transmission of HIV-1. J AIDS Hum Retrovir 1997; 15:76–82.

65. Kaplan JK, Khabbaz RF, Murphy EL, Hermansen S, Roberts C, Lal R, Heneine V, Wright D, Matijas L, Thomson R, Rudolph D, Switzer WM, Kleinman S, Busch M, Schreiber GB, and the Retrovirus Epidemiology Donor Study Group. Male-to-female transmission of human T-cell lymphotropic virus type I and II: association with viral load. J AIDS 1996; 12:193–201.

66. Iwahara Y, Takehara N, Kataoka R, Sawada T, Ohtsuki Y, Nakachi H, Maehama T, Okayama T, Miyoshi I. Transmission of HTLV-I to rabbits via semen and breast milk from serositive healthy persons. Int J Cancer 1990; 45:980–983.

67. Lal RB, Gongora-Biachi RA, Pardi D, Switzer WM, Goldman I, Lal AA. Evidence for mother-to-child transmission of human T lymphotropic virus type II. J Infect Dis 1993; 586–591.

68. Heneine V, Woods T, Green D, Fukuda K, Giusti R, Castillo L, Armien B, Garcia F, and Kaplan J E. Detection of HTLV-II in breast milk of HTLV-II infected mothers (letter). Lancet 1992; 340:1157–1158.

69. Gessain A, Vernant JC, Maurs L. Antibodies to human T-lymphotropic virus type I in patients with tropical spastic paraparesis. Lancet 1985; ii:407–409.

70. Gessain A, Francis H, Sonan T. HTLV-I and tropical spastic paraparesis in Africa. Lancet 1986; ii:698.

71. La Grenade L. HTLV-I-associated infective dermatitis: past, present, and future. J AIDS Hum Retrov 1996; 13(S1):S46–49.

72. Mochizuki M, Ono A, Ikeda E, Hikita, Watanabe T, Yamaguchi K, Sagawa K, Ito K. HTLV-I uveitis. J AIDS Hum Retrov 1996; 13(S1):S50–56.

73. Osato M, Yamaguchi K, Yamasaki H, Suzushima H, Asou N, Sakata K, Kawakita M, Takatsuki K. A human T-cell lymphotropic virus type-I carrier with chronic renal failure, aplastic anaemia, myelopathy, uveitis, Sjogren syndrome and panniculitis. Int Med 1996; 35(9):742–745.

74. Yamaguchi K, Takatsuki K. Adult T cell leukemia-lymphoma. Baillieres Clin Hematol 1993; 6:899–915.

75. Franchini, G. Molecular mechanisms of human T-cell leukemia/lymphotropic virus type I infection. Blood 1995; 86:3619–3639.

76. Blattner WA, Pombo-de-Oliveira, MS. HTLV-I and HTLV-II. In: Merigan C, Bartlett JG, Bolognesi D, eds. Textbook of AIDS Medicine, 1998: 1003–1029.

77. Manns A, Hisada M, La Grenade L Human T-lymphotropic virus type I infection. Lancet 1999; 353:1951–1958.

78. Yodoi J, Takatsuki K, Masuda T. N Engl J Med 1974; 290:572–574.

79. Uchiyama T, Yodoi J, Sagawa, K., Takatsuki K, Uchino, H. Adult T-cell leukemia: clinical and hematological features of 16 cases. Blood 1977; 50:481–492.

80. Hinuma Y, Nagata K, Hanaoka M, et al. Adult T-cell leukemia: antigen in adult T-cell leukemia cell line and detection of antibodies to the antigen in human sera. Proc Natl Acad Sci USA 1981; 78:6476–6480.

81. Yodoi J, Uchiyama T. Diseases associated with HTLV-I: virus, IL-2 receptor deregulation and redox regulation. Immunol Today 1992; 13:405–410.

82. Shimoyama M, members of Lymphoma Study Group. The fourth nationwide study

of T-cell leukemia/lymphoma (ATL) in Japan: estimates of risk of ATL and its geographical and clinical features. Br J Hematol 1991; 79:428–439.

83. Yoshida M, Seiki M, Yamaguchi K, Takatsuki K. Monoclonal integration of human T-cell leukemia provirus in all primary tumors of adult T-cell leukemia suggests causative role of human T-cell leukemia virus in the disease. Proc Natl Acad Sci USA 1984; 81:2534–2537.

84. Cleghorn FR, Manns A, Falk R, et al. Effect of human T-cell leukemia virus type I infection on non-Hodgkin's lymphoma incidence. J Natl Cancer Inst 1995; 87:1009–1014.

85. Pombo de Oliveira MS, Matutes E, Schulz T, et al. T-cell malignancies in Brazil. Clinico-pathological and molecular studies of HTLV-I-positive and -negative cases. Int J Cancer 1995; 60:823–827.

86. Tajima K, Kuroishi T. Estimation of rate of incidence of ATL among ATLV (HTLV-I) carriers in Kyushu, Japan. Jpn J Clin Oncol 1985; 15:423–430.

87. Takatsuki K, Matsuoka M, Yamaguchi K. Adult T-cell leukemia/lymphoma in Japan. J AIDS Hum Retrovir 1996; 13 (suppl 1):s15–19.

88. Gill PS, Harrington W, Kaplan M, et al. Treatment of T-cell leukemia-lymphoma with a combination of interferon alpha and zidovudine. N Engl J Med 1995; 332:1744–1748.

89. Hermine O, Bouscary D, Gessain A, et al. Brief report: treatment for adult T-cell leukemia-lymphoma with zidovudine and interferon alpha. N Engl J Med 1995; 332:1749–1751.

90. Osame M, Izumo S, Igata A. Blood transfusion with HTLV-I associated myelopathy. Lancet 1986; ii:104–105.

91. Maloney EM, Cleghorn FR, Morgan OS, et al. Incidence of HTLV-I associated myelopathy/Tropical spastic paraparesis (HAM/TSP) in Jamaica and Trinidad. J AIDS Human Retrovir 1998; 17:167–170.

92. Link H, Cruz M, Gessain A, Gout O, de The G, Kam-Hansen S. Chronic progressive myelopathy associated with HTLV-I; oligoclonal IgG and anti-HTLV-I IgG antibodies in the cerebrospinal fluid and serum. Neurology 1989; 39:1566–1572.

93. Kira J, Koyanagi Y, Yamada T, et al. Increased HTLV-I proviral DNA in HTLV-I-associated myelopathy: a quantitative polymerase chain reaction study. Ann Neurol 1991; 29:194–201.

94. Tsukasaki K, Yamada Y, Ikeda S, Tomonaga M. Infective dermatitis among patients with ATL in Japan. Int J Cancer 1994; 57:293.

95. Hanchard B, LaGrenade L, Canberry C, et al. Childhood infective dermatitis evolving into adult T-cell leukaemia after 17 years [letter]. Lancet 1991; 338:1593–1594.

96. Ohba N, Matsumoto M, Sameshima Y, et al. Ocular manifestations in patients with human T-lymphotropic virus type I. Jpn J Ophthalmol 1989; 33:1–12.

97. Mochizuki M, Tajima K, Watanabe T, Yamaguchi K. Human T lymphotropic virus type-I uveitis. Br J Ophthalmol 1994; 78:149–154.

98. Sagawa K, Mochizuki M, Masuoka K, et al. Immunopathological mechanisms of human T lymphotropic virus type-I (HTLV-I) uveitis. Detection of HTLV-I infected T cells in the eye and their constitutive cytokine production. J Clin Invest 1995; 95:852–858.

99. Ohshima K, Kikuchi M, Masuda Y, et al. HTLV-I associated lymphoadenopathy. Cancer 1992; 69:239–248.

100. Nishioka K, Maruyama I, Sato K, Kitajima I, Nakajima Y, Osame M. Chronic inflamatory arthropathy associated with HTLV-I. Lancet 1989; 1:441.

101. Nakada K, Yamaguchi K, Furugen S, et al. Monoclonal integration of HTLV-I proviral DNA in patients with strongyloidiasis. Int J Cancer 1987; 40:145–148.

102. Mita S, Sugimoto M, Nakamura M, et al. Increased human T lymphotropic virus type-I (HTLV-I) proviral DNA in peripheral blood mononuclear cells and broncho-alveolar lavage cells from Japanese patients with HTLV-I-associated myelopathy. Am J Trop Med Hyg 1993; 48:170–177.

103. Rosenblatt JD, Gasson JC, Glaspy J, et al. Relationship between human T-cell leukemia virus-II and atypical hairy cell leukemia: serologic study of hairy cell leukemia patients. Leukemia 1987; 1:397–401.

104. Hjelle B, Mills R, Swenson S, Mertz G, Key C, Allen S. Incidence of hairy cell leukemia, mycosis fungoides, and chronic lymphocytic leukemia in a first known HTLV-II-endemic population. J Infect Dis 1991; 163:435–440.

105. Kalyanaraman VS, Sarngadharan MG, Robert-Guroff M, et al. A new subtype of human T-cell leukemia virus (HTLV-II) associated with a T-cell variant of hairy cell leukemia. Science 1982; 218:571–573.

106. Hjelle B, Appenzeller O, Mills R, et al. Chronic neurodegenerative disease associated with HTLV-II infection. Lancet 1992; 339:645–646.

107. Pombo de Oliveira MS, Matutes E, Schulz T, et al. T-cell malignancies in Brazil. clinico-pathological and molecular studies of HTLV-I positive and negative cases. Int J Cancer 1995; 60:823–827.

108. Pawson R, Schulz TF, Matutes E, Catovsky D. The human T-cell lymphotropic viruses types I/II are not involved in T-prolymphocytic leukemia and large granular lymphocytic leukemia. Leukemia 1997; 11:1305–1311.

109. Jacobson S, Lehky T, Nishimura M, Robinson S, McFarlin D, Dhib-Jalbut S. Isolation of HTLV-II from a patient with chronic, progressive neurological disease clinically indistinguishable from HTLV-I-associated myelopathy/tropical spastic paraparesis. Am Neur Assoc 1993; 14:392–396.

110. Loughran TP, Sherman MP, Ruscetti FW, et al. Prototypical HTLV-I/II infection is rare in patients with large granular lymphocyte leukemia. Leukemia Res 1994; 18:423–429.

111. Loughran TP, Coyle T, Sherman MP, et al. Detection of human T-cell leukemia/lymphoma virus, type II, in patient with large granular lymphocyte leukemia. Blood 1992; 80:1116–1119.

112. Hjelle B, Mills R, Swenson S, Mertz G, Key C, Allen S. Incidence of hairy cell leukemia, mycosis fungoides, and chronic lymphocytic leukemia in a first known HTLV-II-endemic population. J Infect Dis 1991; 163:435–440.

113. Zucker-Franklin D, Hooper WC, Evatt BL. Human lymphotropic retroviruses associated with mycosis fungoides: evidence that human T-cell lymphotropic virus type II (HTLV-II) as well as HTLV-I may play a role in the disease. Blood 1992; 80:1537–1545.

114. Kaplan MH, Hall WW, Susin M, et al. Syndrome of severe skin disease, eosinophilia

and dermatopathic lymphadenopathy in patients with HTLV-II complicating human immunodeficiency virus infection. Am J Med 1991; 91:300–309.

115. Martin MP, Biggar RJ, Hamlin-Green G, Staal S, Mann D. AIDS Res Hum Retrovir 1993; 9:715–719.

116. Semmes OJ, Majone F, Cantemir C, Turchetto L, Hjelle B, Jeang K-T. HTLV-I and HTLV-II tax: differences in induction of micronuclei in cells and transcriptional activation of viral LTRs. Virology 1996; 217:313–379.

117. Fouchard N, Flaguel B, Bagot M, Avril MF, Hermine O, Sigaux F, Merle-Beral H, Troussard X, Delfraissy JF, de The G. Lack of evidence of HTLV-I/II infection in T CD8 malignant or reactive lymphoproliferative disorders in France: a serological and/or molecular study of 169 cases. Leukemia 1995; 9:2087–2092.

118. Woods TC, Graber JM, Hershow RC, Khabbaz RF, Kaplan JE, Heineine W. Investigation of proviral load in individuals infected with human T-lymphotropic virus type II. AIDS Res Hum Retrovir 1995; 11:1235–1239.

119. Lehky TJ, Flerlage N, Katz D, Houff S, Hall WH, Ishii K, Monken C, Dhib-Jalbut S, McFarland HF, Jacobson S. Human T-cell lymphotropic virus type II-associated myelopathy: clinical and immunologic profiles. Ann Neurol 1996; 40:714–723.

120. Doeneief G, Marlink R, Bell K, Marder K, Renjifo B, Sern Y, Mayeux R. Neurological consequences of HTLV-II infection in injection-drug users. Neurology 1996; 46: 1556–1560.

121. Yokoi K, Kawai H, Akaike M, Mine H, Saito S. Presence of human T-lymphotropic virus type II-related genes in DNA of peripheral leukocytes from patients with autoimmune thyroid diseases. J Med Virol 1995; 45:392–398.

122. Murphy EL, Glynn SA, Fridey J, Smith JW, Sacher RA, Nass CC, Ownby HE, Wright DJ, Nemo GJ. Increased incidence of infectious diseases during prospective follow-up of human T-lymphotropic virus type II- and I-infected blood donors. Retrovirus Epidemiology Donor Study. Arch Intern Med 1999; 159(13):1485–1491.

123. Okochi K, Sato H, Hinuma Y. A retrospective study on transmission of adult T-cell leukemia virus by blood transfusion: seroconversion in recipients. Vox Sang 1984; 46:245–253.

124. Public Health Service Working Group. Licensure of screening tests for antibodies to human T-lymphotropic virus type I. MMWR 1988; 37:736–747.

125. Manns A, Wilks RJ, Murphy EL, et al. A prospective study of transmission by transfusion of HTLV-I and risk factors associated with seroconversion. Int J Cancer 1992; 51:886–891.

126. Schreiber GB, Busch MP, Kleinman SH, Korelitz JJ, the risk of transfusion-transmitted viral infections. N Engl J Med 1996; 334:1685–1690.

127. Sullivan MT, Williams AE, Fang CT, Grandinett T, Poiesz BJ, Ehrlich GD. Transmission of human T-lymphotropic virus types I and II by blood transfusion. Arch Intern Med 1991; 151:2043–2048.

128. Rios M, Khabbaz RF, Kaplan JE, Hall WW, Kessler D, Bianco C. Transmission of human T-cell leukemia virus type II by transfusion of human T-cell lymphotropic virus type I screened blood products. J Infect Dis 1994; 170:206–210.

129. Nelson KE, Donahue JG, Munoz A, et al. Transmission of retroviruses from seronegative donors by transfusion during cardiac surgery. A multicenter study of HIV-1 and HTLV-I/II infections. Ann Intern Med 1992; 117:554–559.

130. Food and Drug Administration (CBER). Guidance for Industry: Donor Screening for Antibodies to HTLV-II. August 1997

131. Chen YC, Wang CH, Su IJ, Hu CY, Chou MJ, Lee TH, Lin DT, Chung TY, Liu CH, Yang CS. Infection of human T-cell leukemia virus type I and development of human T-cell leukemia lymphoma in patients with hematologic neoplasms: a possible linkage to blood transfusion. Blood 1989; 74(1):388–394.

132. Bartholomew C, Jack N, Edwards J, Charles W, Corbin D, Cleghorn FR, Blattner WA. HTLV-I serostatus of mothers of patients with adult T-cell leukemia and HTLV-I-associated myelopathy/tropical spastic paraparesis. J Hum Virol 1998; 1(4):302–305.

133. Domingues RB, Muniz MR, Jorge ML, Mayo MS, Saez-Alquezar A, Chamone DF, Scaff M, Marchiori PE. Human T cell lymphotropic virus type-1-associated myelopathy/tropical spastic paraparesis in Sao Paulo, Brazil: association with blood transfusion. Am J Trop Med Hyg 1997; 57(1):56–59.

134. Kuroda Y, Takashima H, Yukitake M, Sakemi T. Development of HTLV-I-associated myelopathy after blood transfusion in a patient with aplastic anemia and a recipient of a renal transplant. J Neurol Sci 1992; 109(2):196–199.

135. Saxton EH, Lee H, Swanson P, Chen IS, Ruland C, Chin E, Aboulafia D, Delamarter R, Rosenblatt JD. Detection of human T-cell leukemia/lymphoma virus type I in a transfusion recipient with chronic myelopathy. Neurology 1989; 89(6):841–844.

136. Kaplan JE, Litchfield B, Rouault C, Lairmore MD, Luo CC, Williams L, Brew BJ, Price RW, Janssen R, Stoneburner R, et al. HTLV-I-associated myelopathy associated with blood transfusion in the United States: epidemiologic and molecular evidence linking donor and recipient. Neurology 1991; 41(2 Pt 1):192–197.

137. Kurosawa M, Machii T, Kitani T, Tokumine Y, Kawa K, Maekawa I, Kawamura T, Miyake T, Kanda M. HTLV-I associated myelopathy (HAM) after blood transfusion in a patient with CD2+ hairy cell leukemia. Am J Clin Pathol 1991; 95(1):72–76.

138. Delamarter RB, Carr J, Saxton EH. HTLV-I viral-associated myelopathy after blood transfusion in a multiple trauma patient. Clin Orthop 1990; (260):191–194.

139. Khabbaz RF, Fukuda K, Kaplan JE, Bianco C, Blattner W, Busch M, Dodd R, Epstein J, Gilcher R, Jackson C, Katz L, Kleinman S, Murphy EL, Nemo G, Poiesz BJ, Rios M, Sloand E, Sullivan M, William AE. Guidelines for counseling persons infected with human T-lymphotropic virus type I (HTLV-I) and type II (HTLV-II) Ann Int Med 1993; 118:448–454.

14

Transfusion-Acquired Cytomegalovirus Infection
Approaching Resolution

Gary E. Tegtmeier
Community Blood Center of Greater Kansas City, Kansas City, Missouri

I. INTRODUCTION

Cytomegalovirus (CMV) is one of the human herpesviruses; all are highly successful intracellular parasites of humans. With the exception of varicella virus, they cause asymptomatic or mild primary infections, establish latent infections in their hosts, can periodically reactivate and infect other susceptible hosts, and persist lifelong. As long as the host's immune system is uncompromised, the balance between virus and host is maintained. However, immunosuppression induced by disease or therapy can alter the balance between virus and host, resulting in systemic virus infection and concomitant disease.

CMV's disease-producing potential was first recognized in infants who were infected in utero (1). Although posttransfusion CMV infections were first described in 1966 (2), it was not until the 1980s that severe CMV disease was unequivocally linked to the transfusion of CMV-seropositive blood in premature infants (3).

The high frequency and serious consequences of CMV infection in immunocompromised patients was documented in solid organ and bone marrow transplant (BMT) patients in the mid- to late 1970s (1). The dominant role of the donor organ versus blood product in CMV transmission was quickly established in solid organ transplantation (4). It was more gradually recognized that transfused blood might be the source of CMV in BMT patients (5), particularly seronegative patients receiving marrow from CMV-negative donors (6). The efficacy of CMV-seronegative blood products in reducing the risk of transfusion-acquired (TA) CMV infection in such patients was soon established (6–8).

The use of leukoreduced blood products to lower the risk of TA CMV infection was established subsequently, first in neonates (9), then in BMT patients (10).

Progress in controlling TA CMV infections has been achieved, but an intractable, low level of risk persists in BMT patients (11). Effective surveillance for early CMV infections using sensitive laboratory tests such as the pp65 antigenemia test and the availability of effective antiviral agents have reduced morbidity and mortality in this patient population. Nevertheless, prevention remains the ultimate goal, one that will certainly be realized in the context of ongoing research on CMV latency, molecular methods for CMV detection, and progress in viral inactivation technology.

The aim of this chapter is to review the following areas: (a) recent progress in understanding the sites of CMV latency and the natural history of CMV infection as they relate to TA CMV infections; (b) the epidemiology of TA CMV in recipients; (c) the epidemiology of CMV in donors; and (d) the interventions currently available to prevent TA CMV infections. The focus will be on the transmission of CMV by blood components to the seronegative recipient.

II. CMV LATENCY AND THE NATURAL HISTORY OF CMV INFECTION: RECENT FINDINGS

CMV is a highly evolved infectious agent. By virtue of persistent shedding after primary infection and a capacity to induce latent infection with periodic reactivation, CMV maximizes its potential to spread. CMV is transmitted both vertically from mother to her unborn or newborn child and horizontally by exposure to body fluids, sexual contact, transplantation, and blood transfusion.

CMV can cause disease in immunocompromised patients, an outcome that varies in severity with the degree of the patient's immunosuppression, whether disease-induced, iatrogenic, or due to prematurity. Disease manifestations in immunocompromised patients include pneumonitis, retinitis, and gastritis.

CMV has the largest genome of any known animal virus. It codes for 220–230 open reading frames, 62 of which have been shown to be unnecessary for virus growth in cell culture. It is, therefore, likely that the proteins encoded by the latter are involved in modulating CMV infection in vivo, including the establishment of latent infection (12).

Our understanding of the site(s) and mechanism(s) of CMV latency and how the virus is reactivated is incomplete. However, recent experimental data have established the monocyte–macrophage lineage as the likely site of CMV latency in the bone marrow and peripheral blood. CMV DNA was found in five of six seropositive subjects, predominantly in the non–T-cell population, and specifically in adherent cells and CD14+ cells. CMV DNA was also detected in three of nine seronegative subjects (13).

CMV has been successfully reactivated in vitro by means of allogeneic stimulation of progenitor or peripheral blood mononuclear cells (14,15). Virus was recovered after long-term culture from macrophages expressing dendritic cell markers (14).

In a recent study (16), CMV genomes were detected in 0.004–0.01% mononuclear cells from granulocyte colony-stimulating factor—mobilized peripheral blood from 7 of 10 seropositive donors at copy numbers of 2–13 genomes per infected cell. Genome-positive cells were found in one of two seronegative donors. The application of the in situ detection and quantitation methods used in this study will permit a comprehensive analysis of the distribution of latent viral genomes and transcripts in various cell populations. Such work will be crucial to understanding the transmission and the pathogenesis of CMV infections in blood and organ transplant recipients.

Evidence that actively infected donors might be the source of infectivity in some blood products dates back to a report from Rumania describing the isolation of CMV from buffy coats of 2 of 35 "healthy" blood donors (17). Numerous studies followed that attempted to isolate CMV from blood of over 1400 donors without success (1). Retrospective (18,19) and prospective (19) testing of blood donors for IgM anti-CMV also support the notion that actively infected donors may transmit CMV.

A study of recently infected pregnant women demonstrated white blood cell–associated CMV DNA by PCR in 100% of samples during the first month of infection, which fell to 90% during the second month and to 0% by 6 months (20). Viral load fell even more rapidly: at month 1, 60% of positive samples at viral loads of >10 genome equivalents (GE) per 10^5 white blood cells (WBCs) compared to 3.3% of the positive samples at month 2.

Similar findings were reported from a study of seroconverting adolescents where 75–85% of WBC samples were positive by PCR within 16 weeks of infection, declining to 0–25% 48 weeks after infection (21). CMV DNA in plasma was also monitored and was detected at a lower frequency, 25–40%, at 8–16 weeks. However, some WBC and plasma samples were positive as late as 60 weeks after infection.

Further evidence that actively or recently infected donors may be responsible for some TA CMV infections comes from a study of 168 seroconverting blood donors, whose plasma samples were tested for CMV DNA by PCR both pre- and postseroconversion (22). Three (1.6%) were found positive, one in a preseroconversion sample and two in postseroconversion samples. Viral load ranged from 400 to 1000 copies/mL. No attempt was made to demonstrate the possible infectivity of the detected DNA in vitro.

Whether CMV DNA can be detected in remotely infected seropositive donors or in seronegative donors is a subject of controversy. Publications have appeared reporting the detection of CMV DNA at high frequency in monocytes or WBC from both seropositive and seronegative donors (13,23–25). By contrast, other reports have either failed or only occasionally identified CMV DNA by PCR from seropositive or seronegative donors (26,27). Preliminary results from a large multilaboratory study (28) indicate that the disparate findings among different labs appear not to be due to lack of assay sensitivity; rather, the reports of positive results among seronegative donors are more likely due to amplicon contamination or lack of assay specificity.

III. EPIDEMIOLOGY OF TA CMV

That CMV can be transmitted by leukocytes contaminating blood products has been suspected for a long time (29,30). The association of transmission with seropositive donors was firmly established in the 1980s (3). However, it is still uncertain whether all seropositive donors can transmit infection, or whether infectivity is restricted to a subset of donors who either have experienced a recent primary infection or a reactivated infection. Circumstantial evidence favors the former hypothesis in that high infection frequencies were seen in exchange-transfused infants (31), recipients of fresh whole blood (1), and patients receiving granulocyte transfusions (29,30).

Other donor-related variables in CMV transmission include the type of blood product transfused and the age of the blood product. Whereas cellular-containing blood products such as whole blood, red blood cells, platelets, and granulocytes have been associated with CMV transmission, no evidence has been published implicating fresh-frozen plasma in TA CMV infections (32). The very high rates of TA CMV infection seen in the early prospective studies of cardiac surgery patients also suggested that fresh blood may be more infectious than stored blood, although this has never been proven in controlled studies.

Studies of immunocompetent, CMV-seronegative cardiac surgery patients carried out in the 1960s and 1970s showed high rates of TA infection, ranging from 8.3 to 66.7% (1). These studies were carried out primarily in patients who had received large volumes of fresh heparinized whole blood. These early findings contrast markedly with more recently published data in seronegative immunocompetent recipients showing TA infection rates in the range of 0.9–1.2% (1,33,34).

The transmission of CMV by transfused blood is influenced by a multiplicity of factors. Clearly, infectious virus, free or cell associated, and/or latently infected cells must be present in donor blood. In theory, one virion or latently infected cell should suffice, but at present the infectious dose of cell-free virus or latently infected cells is unknown. If latently infected cells are the vehicle for transmission, they must survive long enough in the recipient for viral activation and release of virions to occur.

If recently infected donors are the source of infection, they may have low-level viremia and/or larger numbers of latently infected cells than seropositive donors who were infected at a more remote time. Because leukocytes are not distributed evenly across different blood components, both the kind and number of components a patient receives affects the level of risk. Recipient factors that play a role in transmission are the degree of HLA matching between donor and recipient, iatrogenic or disease-induced immunosuppression, and the cytokine environment in the recipient.

Patient populations known to be at risk for severe TA CMV morbidity and mortality include infants, especially premature infants, pregnant women, solid organ transplant patients, BMT patients, HIV-infected patients, and patients with malignancy.

Rates of infection in transfused CMV-seronegative premature infants were shown to be quite high in early studies, ranging from 24.0 to 31.8% (3,35). Later investigations failed to corroborate the high rates originally seen; infection rates varied from 0 to 8.7% (19,36–38). No clear explanations for these differences in rates could be discerned; these studies were carried out in different geographic regions. The observed differences in rates were not readily correlated with donor anti-CMV prevalence, the amount or age of the blood transfused, or infant birth weight.

Seronegative pregnant women undergoing primary CMV infection transmit the infection with high efficiency to the fetus, often with devastating consequences (39). Although the risk of TA CMV in this patient group has not been rigorously assessed, a recent study failed to show CMV conversions in 162 CMV-seronegative pregnant women, 8 of whom were transfused prior to delivery (38).

The risk of TA CMV infections in CMV-seronegative allogeneic BMT patients receiving marrow from CMV seronegative donors and routine blood product support has been assessed in three studies. The infection rates ranged from 31.8 to 50.0% (6,8,10) not dissimilar to the 21.4% rate seen in CMV-seronegative autologous BMT patients receiving routine blood products after transplantation (10).

Highly variable levels of risk have been reported in CMV-seronegative solid organ transplant recipients who received organs from CMV-seronegative donors, as summarized in Table 1 (40–56). An extraordinary number of variables influencing the potential TA risk combine to account for the heterogeneous results seen in this setting. The variables include the incidence of CMV infections in the donor population, the CMV antibody test employed, the age of the transfused blood, and the methods of blood component preparation.

At the recipient level, the potential of TA CMV infection and disease in organ transplant patients is influenced by the following factors: the immunosuppressive regimen employed; the immunogenicity of the transplanted organs;

Table 1 Posttransfusion CMV Infections in
Seronegative Recipients Receiving Seronegative Organs

Type of transplant	Range of PT CMV infections (%)	Ref.
Kidney	0–20	40–44
Heart	0–26	45,46
Heart/Lung	4.5–33	46–49
Liver	7.1–100	50–56

posttransfusion sepsis; and graft leukocytes that establish microchimeras and thereby induce tolerance to transfused leukocytes.

TA CMV infections in seronegative oncology patients have been monitored in several studies and range in incidence from 0 to 22% (57–59). Symptomatic CMV disease, however, is rare outside of the bone marrow transplant setting. The American Association of Blood Banks (AABB) has recommended the use of either CMV-seronegative or leukoreduced blood products for CMV-seronegative patients who receive chemotherapy intended to produce severe neutropenia (60). The rationale is to prevent potential candidates for BMT from acquiring an infection that could result in serious morbidity after transplantation.

The risk of TA CMV infections in HIV-infected patients who are CMV seronegative is not known. Given the devastating clinical consequences CMV can effect in HIV-infected patients and the possibility that it may hasten the progression of AIDS, the use of CMV-seronegative or leukoreduced blood products for CMV-seronegative patients infected with HIV has been recommended (60). Although transmission of second strains to CMV seropositive, HIV-infected patients is possible, provision of "CMV-safe" products has not been recommended. With the recent public presentation of the data from the Viral Activation Transfusion Study (VATS), which showed no benefit to CMV-infected patients with HIV-1 infection from leukocyte reduction of red blood cells, this concern may be allayed.

IV. PREVENTION OF TA CMV INFECTION BY DONOR ANTIBODY SCREENING

A 1971 study of exchange-transfused infants in Germany was the first to suggest that CMV-seropositive donors might transmit the infection and that seronegative donors might be less likely to transmit (31). Eight of 15 seronegative infants (53%) receiving CMV-seropositive donor blood became infected, while none of 20 seronegative infants receiving seronegative blood became infected. This was the first published data suggesting that CMV-seronegative donor blood posed a reduced risk of CMV transmission.

A large prospective study conducted in 1976 further suggested that CMV-seronegative blood products posed a lesser risk of CMV transmission than those from seropositive donors (61). Three of 86 seronegative recipients (3%) receiving seronegative blood became infected compared to 13 of 54 seronegative recipients (24%) receiving seropositive blood.

The seminal study demonstrating the efficacy of CMV-seronegative blood products in preventing neonatal CMV infections appeared in 1981 (3). None of 90 seronegative infants given CMV-seronegative blood products became infected. In contrast, 10 of 74 (13.5%) seronegative infants given unscreened blood products (some of which were seropositive) became infected, 5 with serious or fatal infections. All serious or fatal infections occurred in infants who weighed less than 1500 g.

Seropositive infants in both the 1971 and 1981 studies showed evidence of posttransfusion CMV infection at varying frequencies whether they received CMV-seropositive or seronegative blood. Although it is not known whether the infections were transfusion acquired or maternally derived, none were symptomatic.

Adding further credibility to the 1981 study from Stanford was a 1983 publication from the Medical College of Virginia, which reported on 178 transfused neonates (35). Eight (4%) infants became infected, all of whom weighed less than 1050 g. Three of these infants died of CMV-related syndromes, and three others had symptomatic CMV infections. Infected infants received more blood products than uninfected infants, a greater percentage of which were CMV antibody positive, and infected infants were more likely to be born to seronegative mothers.

The combined weight of these studies led to the implementation of donor screening for antibodies to CMV (anti-CMV) to provide an inventory of CMV-seronegative blood products with a reduced risk of CMV transmission to sero-negative low birth weight infants. This became an AABB standard in the mid-1980s.

It is unclear whether the use of seronegative blood products has been restricted to seronegative at-risk infants despite a subsequent study from the Stanford group showing that the use of CMV-seronegative blood products might place low birth weight infants born to seropositive mothers at risk for developing CMV disease (62). This was thought to be a consequence of iatrogenic blood loss with replacement by CMV-seronegative blood, catabolic loss of remaining maternally acquired antibody, and CMV infection acquired from maternal secretions during birth or from breast milk.

The impetus for providing CMV-seronegative blood products to CMV-seronegative BMT recipients with CMV-seronegative marrow donors was generated by studies from Seattle (6), Glasgow (7), and Minneapolis (8). The Minnesota and Seattle studies demonstrated that those recipients had greatly reduced rates of primary CMV infections compared to recipients who were given unscreened blood products. The results of these investigations are summarized in Table 2.

Prevention of TA CMV infection in CMV-seronegative solid organ transplant patients receiving CMV-seronegative organs by the use of "CMV-safe" blood products has been recommended (60). Due to the limited transfusion requirements of renal transplant patients, provision of CMV-seronegative blood products is feasible. However, the more intensive use of blood in heart, heart-lung, and liver transplants may outstrip the available CMV-screened inventory. Fortunately, filtered products can be supplied under these circumstances.

A. Antibody Screening Tests

Early studies documenting the efficacy of anti-CMV negative blood in preventing TA CMV infections included complement fixation and indirect hemagglutination (3,31,61). The assays used in these studies were in-house, unstandardized assays of undefined sensitivity and specificity. An indirect hemagglutination test based on the one used in the 1981 Stanford study became the first commercially available assay in 1983.

Other commercially available assays soon appeared including solid-phase fluorescence, enzyme immunoassay (EIA), and passive latex agglutination. Comparative evaluation of these assays followed, which reported test sensitivities and specificities ranging from 89 to 100% (63–66). However, these evaluations were carried out in the 1980s, and no reliable supplemental test was available to corroborate the specificity of reactive screening test results, i.e., no gold standard existed then or now.

Table 2   Posttransplant CMV Infections in CMV
Seronegative BMT with CMV Seronegative Marrow Donors
According to CMV Serological Status of Blood Products

	No. infected/No. transfused (%)	
Study	CMV-seronegative blood products	CMV unscreened blood products
Miller (8)	2/45 (4)	14/44 (32)
MacKinnon (7)	0/22[a] (0)	N.D.
Bowden (6)	1/32[b] (3)	8/25 (32)

[a]Six recipients given marrow from CMV seropositive donors.
[b]$p < 0.007$.

Currently available commercial assays for anti-CMV are listed in Table 3. Both the Hemagen hemagglutination test and Olympus particle agglutination test are automated assays that can be run on the Olympus PK7200. The Immucor solid phase red cell adherence assay is semi-automated, as is the enzyme immunoassay from Abbott. The latex agglutination test from Becton Dickinson is manual. No comparative evaluations of these contemporary anti-CMV assays have been published.

Despite the probable high quality of currently available commercial tests, breakthrough infections continue to occur with low frequency in high-risk patients. The possible explanations for the failure of antibody screening are several. The donor could be in the window period, i.e., the period of time when a newly infected donor is infectious, but antibody negative. Strain variation may also account for false-negative antibody tests in donors, but given the broad reactivity of strain AD169, which serves as the basis for most commercial tests, this explanation is not likely. Finally, donor antibody levels may fall to undetectable levels. One publication has shown evidence for this phenomenon (67). However, given that CMV is thought to reactivate periodically, it is doubtful that most infected individuals would lose detectable antibody.

Although accurate data on the percentage of the U.S. blood supply being screened for anti-CMV are unavailable, it is thought that 20–25% of allogeneic donations are screened each year to provide anti-CMV negative blood products for high-risk patients. The extent to which FDA guidance to provide leukoreduced blood products to all patients in the United States by 2002 will affect the use of anti-CMV negative blood is not clear. However, a majority of the panelists at a recent Canadian consensus conference (68) recommended the continued use of CMV-seronegative blood components to high-risk patients despite the fact that all cellular containing blood products in Canada are now leukoreduced.

Table 3 CMV Antibody Tests for Blood Donor Screening

Manufacturer	Test name	Type of test
Olympus (Fujirebio)	PK^{TM} CMV-PA	Particle agglutination
Abbott	CMV Total Ab EIA	Enzyme immunoassay
Becton Dickinson	CMV Scan®	Latex agglutination
Immucor	Capture-CMV®	Solid phase red cell adherence
Hemagen	PK CMV	Hemagglutination

B. Epidemiology of CMV in Blood Donors

The wide variation in anti-CMV prevalence in blood donors around the world was highlighted by a 1973 study (69), which reported prevalences ranging from 40% in Western Europe to 100% in third world countries. Although a systematic study of anti-CMV prevalence in U.S. blood donors has not been published, the previous report showed prevalences of 45% and 79% for donors from Albany and Houston, respectively. A 1985 telephone survey of seven U.S. blood centers yielded anti-CMV prevalence rates ranging from 30 to 70% (70).

In the United States CMV antibody prevalence varies according to age and gender. Younger donors have lower rates than older donors, and at any given age, female donors show higher rates than males. These relationships are illustrated in Fig. 1. Donors 17–25 years of age had a 30% prevalence, while donors over 65 years of age were 80% positive. A steady, age-related increase in prevalence can be seen between these extremes. With the exception of the over 65 group, females have higher prevalence rates than males.

Ethnic variations in anti-CMV prevalence seen in Kansas City donors are summarized in Table 4. Caucasians showed the lowest prevalence (46%), while African-American and Asian donors had higher prevalence of 64% and 76%, respectively. Thus, the intersecting variables of geography, age, gender, and ethnicity will determine the relative ease or difficulty that a given blood center will have in providing an adequate inventory of CMV-seronegative blood products for high-risk patients.

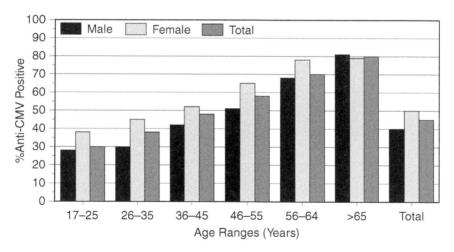

Figure 1 Prevalence of anti-CMV by gender and age in Kansas City blood donors from 1992 to 1995. Data from 20,000 donors screened for the first time by enzyme immunoassay.

Table 4 Prevalence of Anti-CMV in Kansas
City Blood Donors by Ethnicity

	Number (%)	
Ethnicity	Tested	Positive[a]
Caucasian	50,243	23,275 (46)
African-American	1,291	826 (64)
Asian	59	45 (76)

[a]By enzyme immunoassay.

V. LEUKOREDUCTION

A 1977 publication from Duke was the first to suggest leukoreduction as a means
of reducing the risk of TA CMV infections (71). Leukocyte-poor units prepared
by inverted centrifugation of whole blood were given to eight cardiac surgery
patients, one of whom became infected compared to four of six controls who were
given unmanipulated whole blood.

The reduced risk of CMV transmission of frozen deglycerolized red cells
was demonstrated in two studies. One from Boston followed renal dialysis
patients (72). None of 21 seronegative recipients became infected after receiving
frozen blood compared to 3 seronegative recipients who became infected after
receiving conventional blood. One hundred and six seronegative neonates in
Houston were given frozen, deglycerolized red cells, none of which showed
evidence of posttransfusion CMV infection (9).

Later studies employed saline washing to reduce the leukocyte count of red
cell units. Despite this intervention, one published in 1986 reported 6 of 54
neonates (11%) with posttransfusion CMV infection (73). A second reported
seroconversion of one infant of 76 transfused (1.5%) with at least one saline-
washed CMV-seropositive unit (74). No contemporary controls were available
for comparison.

An Australian study was the first to demonstrate the effectiveness of
leukoreduction by filtration (75). Nine of 42 infants (21%) receiving unfiltered
seropositive blood became infected compared to 0 of 30 infants given filtered
blood.

None of 48 premature neonates given filtered blood in three Connecticut
intensive care nurseries became infected with CMV (76). No control population
was followed by these investigators. It should be noted that only the studies from
Duke and Australia included controls.

Six additional studies (10,58,77–80) using either filtration and/or centrifugation to leukocyte-reduce red blood cells and platelets given to patients with

hematological malignancies or to BMT patients have further documented the efficacy of leukoreduction as a means of preventing TA CMV infections. The results are summarized in Table 5. Two of these studies were randomized (10,58), one was a cohort study (77), two represented case series (78,79), and one compared leukoreduction to prior experience using CMV-seronegative blood products (80).

The collective weight of the evidence from these investigations support the conclusion that leukoreduced blood components carry a much reduced risk of CMV transmission. In 1997, the Ad Hoc Committee on Prevention of CMV Transmission of the AABB concluded that the leukocyte reduction level currently accepted for the prevention of alloimmunization to HLA molecules reduces CMV transmission to a level at least equivalent with that observed with CMV-seronegative components (60).

Identical standards have been set by AABB and FDA to qualify blood components as leukoreduced. Red blood cells and apheresis platelets must contain $<5 \times 10^6$ WBCs per unit. Platelets derived from whole blood must contain $<8.3 \times 10^5$ WBC per unit or $<5 \times 10^6$ WBC per pool of six.

Quality control of leukoreduced products is essential. It is clear that more consistent results are obtained when blood components are filtered in the laboratory rather than at the bedside. Moreover, bedside filters have yielded results at odds with those generated by manufacturers (81), and, until recently, counting the number of residual WBCs has been difficult. Filter failures have been reported in

Table 5 Prevention of TA CMV Infections in BMT Patients and Patients with Hematological Malignancies by Leukoreduction

Author (Ref.)	Year	No. with CMV infection (%)/ No. transfused	
		Control	LR[a]
Murphy (58)	1988	2/9 (22)	0/11
DeGraan-Hentzen (77)	1989	10/86 (12)	0/59
DeWitte (78)	1991	None	0/28
Bowden (10)	1991	7/30 (23)	0/35
Van Prooijen (79)	1994	None	0/60
Pamphilon (80)	1999	0/114[b]	0/62

[a]LR = Leukoreduced.
[b]Experience in patients given CMV-seronegative blood.

donors with hemoglobin AS (82,83), and adverse recipient reactions have surfaced recently, e.g., red-eye syndrome (84).

VI. ARE LEUKOREDUCTION AND ANTIBODY SCREENING EQUALLY EFFECTIVE?

Only one prospective, randomized, controlled trial has been carried out to date that has sought to answer this question (11). Bedside filters from one manufacturer were used to provide leukoreduced blood components to patients randomized to one arm of this study, while CMV-seronegative blood components were supplied to the other. Recipients were CMV-seronegative BMT patients who received marrow from CMV-seronegative donors.

In the primary analysis, defined as infections occurring after day 21 posttransplant, there was no significant difference between the probability of CMV infection or disease in patients receiving CMV-seronegative blood (0.8%; 95% CI 0.1–28%) compared to patients receiving leukoreduced blood components (1.2%; 95% CI 0.3–5.0%). No patients in the former group and three patients in the latter group developed CMV disease.

A secondary analysis was performed that included all infections diagnosed between day 0 and day 100. Similar rates of CMV infection were seen in the CMV-screened group (1.6%) and the leukoreduced group (2.4%). However, no CMV disease was observed in patients receiving CMV-seronegative blood components compared to 2.4% in patients given leukoreduced components. All six infected patients in the filtered arm died, whereas the four infected patients in the CMV-screened arm survived without evidence of disease.

The results of the secondary analysis were surprising. The 100% mortality of infected patients in the filtered arm has been ascribed to a statistical anomaly. The authors of this paper also pointed out that four of five patients who developed CMV infection before day 21 had discrepant or equivocal CMV antibody tests at randomization and suggested that these patients may have been infected prior to the receipt of blood components in the study. Some believe this study overestimates the rate of CMV infection and disease in patients who received leukoreduced components.

At the conclusion of this trial, CMV-seronegative blood products were again given to seronegative patients with CMV-seronegative donors in Seattle. Of 117 patients followed, two became infected and one developed CMV-related disease. Based on this experience, it was concluded that CMV infection occurs in 2–3% of patients regardless of the interventions employed to prevent it and that CMV disease occurs in 1–2%. Since 1994, both CMV-seronegative and leukoreduced blood products have been used to support transplant patients in Seattle (85).

Since 1997 apheresis platelets that qualify as leukoreduced have been part of the "CMV-safe" product mix used to support BMT patients in Seattle. Of 387 patients transplanted during this interval, 4% have experienced primary CMV infection. It is unclear whether pheresis platelets carry a higher risk of CMV transmission compared to filtered products, but the question begs to be answered. Thus, there remains an intractable low level of risk for primary CMV infection in CMV-seronegative transplant patients who are supported with "CMV-safe" blood products (85).

VII. WHAT IS THE SOURCE OF RESIDUAL RISK?

The limitations of CMV antibody screening and leukoreduction techniques have been outlined previously. A plausible, but yet unproved, hypothesis is that the residual risk posed by "CMV-safe" blood products is a consequence of window period donations. Data presented earlier have documented high levels of cell-associated CMV DNA and lower levels of CMV DNA in plasma of recently infected immunocompetent individuals who experienced asymptomatic CMV infections. If plasma DNA is infectious, and this remains to be proven, then individuals early in the course of an asymptomatic infection would be seronegative and potentially infectious. Such donors would not be identified by antibody testing, and although infected cells would be retained by a filter, CMV DNA in plasma is not likely to be retained. Molecular testing of donor blood may soon provide the means of finally resolving the problem of TA CMV infections.

REFERENCES

1. Ho M, Cytomegalovirus: Biology and Infection. 2nd ed. New York: Plenum, 1991.
2. Kaariainen L, Klemola E, Paloheimo J. Rise of cytomegalovirus antibodies in an infectious mononucleosis-like syndrome after transfusion. Br Med J 1966; 1:1270–1272.
3. Yeager AS, Grumet FC, Hafleigh EB, Arvin AR, Bradley JS, Prober CG. Prevention of transfusion-acquired cytomegalovirus infections in newborn infants. J Pediatr 1981; 98:281–287.
4. Ho M, Suwansirikul S, Dowling JN, Youngblood LA, Armstrong JA. The transplanted kidney as a source of cytomegalovirus infection. N Engl J Med 1975; 293:1109–1112.
5. Meyers JD, Flournoy N, Thomas ED. Risk factors for cytomegalovirus infection after human marrow transplantation. J Infect Dis 1986; 153:478–488.
6. Bowden RA, Sayers M, Flournoy N, Newton B, Banaji M, Thomas ED, Meyers JD. Cytomegalovirus immune globulin and seronegative blood products to prevent primary cytomegalovirus infection after marrow transplantation. N Engl J Med 1986; 314:1006–1010.
7. Mackinnon S, Burnett AK, Crawford RJ, Cameron S, Leask BG, Sommerville RG.

Seronegative blood products prevent primary cytomegalovirus infection after bone marrow transplantation. J Clin Pathol 1988; 41:948–950.

8.   Miller WJ, McCullough J, Balfour HH Jr, Haake RJ, Ramsay NK, Goldman A, Bowman R, Kersey J. Prevention of cytomegalovirus-infection following bone marrow transplantation: a randomized trial of blood product screening. Bone Marrow Transplant 1991; 7:227–234.

9.   Brady MT, Milam JD, Anderson DC, Hawkins EP, Speer ME, Seavy D, Bijou H, Yow MD. Use of deglycerolized red blood cells to prevent posttransfusion infection with cytomegalovirus in neonates. J Infect Dis 1984; 150:334–339.

10.   Bowden RA, Slichter SJ, Sayers MH, Mori M, Cays MJ, Meyers JD. Use of leukocyte-depleted platelets and cytomegalovirus-seronegative red blood cells for prevention of primary cytomegalovirus infection after marrow transplant. Blood 1991; 79:246–250.

11.   Bowden RA, Slichter SJ, Sayers M, Weisdorf D, Cays M, Schoch G, Banaji M, Haake R, Welk K, Fisher L, McCullough J, Miller W. A comparison of filtered leukocyte-reduced and cytomegalovirus (CMV) seronegative blood products for the prevention of transfusion-associated CMV infection after marrow transplant. Blood 1995; 86:3598–3603.

12.   Mocarski Jr. ES. Cytomegaloviruses and their replication. In: Fields BN, Knipe DM, Howley PM, eds. Virology. Philadelphia: Lippincott, Raven, 1996:2447–2492.

13.   Taylor-Wiedeman J, Sissons JGP, Sinclair JH. Monocytes are a major site of persistence of human cytomegalovirus in peripheral blood mononuclear cells. J Gen Virol 1991; 72:2059–2064.

14.   Söderberg-Nauclér C, Fisk KN, Nelson JA. Reactivation of latent human cytomegalovirus by allogeneic stimulation of blood cells from healthy donors. Cell 1977; 91:119–126.

15.   Hahn G, Jores R, Mocarski ES. Cytomegalovirus remains latent in a common precursor of dendritic and myeloid cells. Proc Natl Acad Sci 1998; 95:3937–3942.

16.   Slobedman B, Mocarski ES. Quantitative analysis of latent human cytomegalovirus. J Virol 1999; 78:4806–4812.

17.   Diosi P, Moldovan E, Tomescu N. Latent cytomegalovirus infection in blood donors. Br Med J 1969; 4:660–662.

18.   Beneke JS, Tegtmeier GE, Alter JH, Luetkemeyer RB, Solomon R, Bayer WL. Relation of titers of antibodies to CMV in blood donors to the transmission of cytomegalovirus infection. J Infect Dis 1984; 150:883–888.

19.   Lamberson Jr. HV, McMillan JA, Weiner LB, Williams ML, Clark DA, McMahon CA, Lentz EB, Higgins AP, Dock NL. Prevention of transfusion-associated cytomegalovirus (CMV) infection in neonates by screening blood donors for IgM to CMV. J Infect Dis 1988; 157:820–823.

20.   Revello MG, Zavattoni M, Sarasini A, Percivalle E, Simoncini L, Gerna G. Human cytomegalovirus in blood of immunocompetent persons during primary infection: prognostic implications for pregnancy. J Infect Dis 1998; 177:1170–1175.

21.   Zhanghellini F, Boppana SB, Emery VC, Griffiths PD, Pass RF. Asymptomatic primary cytomegalovirus infection: virologic and immunologic features. J Infect Dis 1999; 180:702–707.

22.   Tegtmeier GE, Henderson SE, Blosser JK, Drew WL, Miner R. CMV DNA in plasma

of seroconverting and anti-CMV seroprevalent blood donors (abstract). Transfusion 1999; 39:116S.

23. Stanier P, Taylor DL, Kitchen AD, Wales N, Tryhorn Y, Tyms AS. Persistence of cytomegalovirus in mononuclear cells in peripheral blood from blood donors. Br Med J 1989; 299:897–898.

24. Bevan IS, Daw RA, Day PJ, Ala FA, Walker MR. Polymerase chain reaction for detection of human cytomegalovirus infection in a blood donor population. Br J Haematol 1991; 78:94–99.

25. Larsson S, Soderberg-Nauclér C, Wang FZ, Moller E. Cytomegalovirus DNA can be detected in peripheral blood mononuclear cells from all seropositive and most seronegative healthy blood donors over time. Transfusion 1998; 38:271–278.

26. Bitsch A, Kirchner H, Dupke R, Bein G. Failure to detect human cytomegalovirus DNA in peripheral blood leukocytes of healthy blood donors by the polymerase chain reaction. Transfusion 1992; 32:612–617.

27. Nolte FS, Emmens RK, Thurmond C, Mitchell PS, Pascuzzi C, Devine SM, Saral R, Wingard JR. Early detection of human cytomegalovirus viremia in bone marrow transplant recipients by DNA amplification. J Clin Microbiol 1995; 33:1263–1266.

28. Roback JD, Hillyer CD, Drew WL, Luka J, Mocarski ES, Soderberg-Naucler C, Woxenius S, Busch MP. Comparison of 7 PCR assays for detection of cytomegalovirus (CMV) DNA in PBMCS of blood donors: results of a blinded multicenter study (abstr). Blood 1999; 94:246a.

29. Winston DJ, Ho WG, Howell CL, Miller MJ, Mickey R, Martin WJ, Lin CH, Gale RP. Cytomegalovirus infections associated with leukocyte transfusions. Ann Intern Med 1980; 93:671–675.

30. Hersman J, Meyers JD, Thomas ED, Buckner CD, Clift R. The effect of granulocyte transfusions on the incidence of cytomegalovirus infection after allogeneic marrow transplantation. Ann Intern Med 1982; 96:149–152.

31. Luthardt T, Siebert H, Lösel I, Quevedo M, Todt R. Cytomegalovirus-infektionen bei Kindern mit Blutaustausch-transfusion im Neugeborenenalter. Klin Wochenschr 1971; 49:81–86.

32. Bowden R, Sayers M. The risk of transmitting cytomegalovirus infection by fresh frozen plasma. Transfusion 1990; 30:762–763.

33. Wilhelm JA, Matter L, Schopfer K. The risk of transmitting cytomegalovirus to patients receiving blood transfusion. J Infect Dis 1986; 154:169–171.

34. Preiksaitis JK, Brown L, McKenzie M. The risk of cytomegalovirus infection in seronegative transfusion recipients not receiving exogenous immunosuppression. J Infect Dis 1988; 157:523–529.

35. Adler SP, Chandrika T, Lawrence L, Baggett J. Cytomegalovirus infections in neonates acquired by blood transfusions. Pediatr Infect Dis 1983; 2:114–118.

36. Smith D Jr, Wright P, Estes W, Krueger L, Wallas C, Moldovan R, Tanley P. Posttransfusion cytomegalovirus infection in neonates weighing less than 1250 grams (abstr). Transfusion 1983; 23:420.

37. Tegtmeier GE. The use of cytomegalovirus-screened blood in neonates. Transfusion 1988; 28:201–203.

38. Preiksaitis JK, Brown L, McKenzie M. Transfusion-acquired cytomegalovirus infection in neonates. A prospective study. Transfusion 1988; 28:205–209.

39. Stagno S. Cytomegalovirus. In: Remington J, Klein G, eds. Infectious Diseases of the Fetus and Newborn. Philadelphia: WB Saunders, 1995:312–353.

40. Marker SC, Howard RJ, Simmons RL, Kalis JM, Connelly DP, Najarian JS, Balfour Jr. HM. Cytomegalovirus infection: A quantitative prospective study of three hundred consecutive renal transplants. Surgery 1981; 89:660–671.

41. Harris KR, Saeed AA, Digard NJ, Whiteford K, Geoghegan TA, Lee HA, Slapak M. Cytomegalovirus titers in kidney transplant donor and recipient: influence of cyclosporine A. Transplant Proc 1984; 16:31–33.

42. Rubin RH, Tolkoff-Rubin NE, Oliver R, Rota TR, Hamilton J, Betts RF, Pass RF, Hillis W, Szmuness W, Farrel ML, Hirsch MS. Multi-center seroepidemiologic study of the impact of cytomegalovirus infection on renal transplantation. Transplantation 1985; 40:243–249.

43. Boyce NW, Hayes K, Gee D, Holdsworth SR, Thomson NM, Scott D, Atkins RC. Cytomegalovirus infection complicating renal transplantation and its relationship to acute transplant glomerulopathy. Transplantation 1988; 45:706–709.

44. Chou S, Norman DJ. The influence of donor factors other than serologic status on transmission of cytomegalovirus to transplant recipients. Transplantation 1988; 46:89–93.

45. Preiksaitis JK, Rosno S, Grumet C, Merigan TC. Infections due to herpesviruses in cardiac transplant recipients: role of the donor heart and immunosuppressive therapy. J Infect Dis 1983; 147:974–981.

46. Wreghitt TG, Hakim M, Gray JJ, Kucia S, Wallwork J, English TA. Cytomegalovirus infections in heart and heart and lung transplant recipients. J Clin Pathol 1988; 41:660–667.

47. Dummer JS, Montero CG, Griffith BP, Hardesty RL, Paradis IL, Ho M. Infections in heart-lung transplant recipients. Transplantation 1986; 41:725–729.

48. Wreghitt T. Cytomegalovirus infections in heart and heart-lung transplant recipients. J Anti-Microb Chem 1989(suppl E); 23:49–60.

49. Smyth RL, Scott JP, Borysiewicz LK, Sharples LD, Steart S, Wreghitt T, Gray JJ, Higenbottam TW, Wallwork J. Cytomegalovirus infection in heart-lung transplant recipients: risk factors, clinical associations and response to treatment. J Infect Dis 1991; 164:1045–1050.

50. Singh N, Dummer JS, Kusne S, Breinig MK, Armstrong JA, Makowka L, Starzl TE, Ho M. Infections with cytomegalovirus and other herpesviruses in 121 liver transplant recipients: transmission by donated organ and the effect of OKT3 antibodies. J Infect Dis 1988; 158:124–131.

51. Barkholt LM, Ericzon B-G, Ehrnst A, Forsgren M, Anderson JP. Cytomegalovirus infections in liver transplant patients: incidence and outcome. Transplant Proc 1990; 22:235–237.

52. Gorensek MJ, Carey WD, Vogt D, Goormastic M. A multivariate analysis of risk factors for cytomegalovirus infection in liver transplant recipients. Gastroenterology 1990; 98:1326–1332.

53. Pillay D, Charman H, Burroughs AK, Smith M, Rolles K, Griffiths PD. Surveillance for CMV infections in orthotopic liver transplant recipients. Transplantation 1992; 53:1261–1265.

54. Sutherland S, Bracken P, Wreghitt TG, O'Grady J, Calne R, Williams R. Donated

organ as a source of cytomegalovirus in orthotopic liver transplantation. J Med Virol 1992; 37:170–173.

55. Manez R, Kusne S, Martin M, Linden P, Irish W, Torre-Cisneros J, Kramer D, Ho M, Starzl TE. The impact of blood transfusion on the occurrence of pneumonitis in primary cytomegalovirus infection after liver transplantation. Transfusion 1993; 33:594–597.

56. Falagas ME, Snydman DR, Ruthazer R, Griffith J, Werner BG. Primary cytomegalovirus infection in liver transplant recipients: comparison of infections transmitted via donor organs and via transfusions. Clin Infec Dis 1996; 23:292–297.

57. Cox F, Hughes WT. Cytomegaloviremia in children with acute leukemia. J Pediatr 1975; 87:190–194.

58. Murphy MF, Grint PC, Hardiman AE, Lister TA, Waters AH. Use of leukocyte-poor blood components to prevent primary cytomegalovirus (CMV) infection in patients with acute leukemia (letter). Br J Haematol 1988; 70:253–254.

59. Preiksaitis JK, Desai S, Vaudry W, Roberts S, Akabutu J, Grundy P, Wilson B, Boshkov L, Hannon J, Joffres M. Transfusion- and community-acquired cytomegalovirus infection in children with malignant disease: a prospective study. Transfusion 1997; 37:941–946.

60. American Association of Blood Banks, Association Bulletin #97-2, Leukocyte reduction for the prevention of TA cytomegalovirus. Bethesda, MD: American Association of Blood Banks, 1997.

61. Monif GRG, Daicoff GI, Flory LF. Blood as a potential vehicle for the cytomegaloviruses. Am J Obstet Gynecol 1976; 126:445–448.

62. Yeager AS, Palumbo PE, Malachowski N, Ariagno RL, Stevenson DK. Sequelae of maternally derived cytomegalovirus infections in premature infants. J Pediatr 1983; 102:918–922.

63. Phipps PH, Gregoire L, Rossier E, Perry E. Comparison of five methods of cytomegalovirus antibody screening of blood donors. J Clin Microbiol 1983; 18:1296–1300.

64. Beckwith DG, Halstead DC, Alpaugh K, Schweder A, Blount-Fronefield DA, Toth K. Comparison of a latex agglutination test with five other methods for determining the presence of antibody against cytomegalovirus. J Clin Microbiol 1985; 21:328–331.

65. Adler SP, McVoy M, Biro VG. Detection of cytomegalovirus antibody with latex agglutination. J Clin Microbiol 1985; 22:68–70.

66. Taswell HF, Reisner RK, Rabe DE, Shelley CD, Smith TF. Comparison of three methods for detecting antibody to cytomegalovirus. Transfusion 1986; 26:285–289.

67. Waner JL, Weller TH, Kevy SV. Patterns of cytomegalovirus complement fixing antibody activity: A longitudinal study of blood donors. J Infect Dis 1973; 127:538–543.

68. Canadian Blood Services, Canadian Blood and Marrow Transplant Group, Consensus Conference: Prevention of Post-Transfusion CMV in the Era of Universal Leukoreduction, Toronto, Canada, January 7–8, 2000.

69. Krech U. Complement-fixing antibodies against cytomegalovirus in different parts of the world. Bull WHO 1973; 49:103–106.

70. Tegtmeier GE. Transfusion-transmitted cytomegalovirus infections: significance and control. Vox Sang 1986; 51(suppl1):22–30.

71. Lang DJ, Ebert PA, Rodgers BM, Boggess HP, Rixse RS. Reduction of postperfusion

cytomegalovirus infections following the use of leukocyte-depleted blood. Transfusion 1977; 17:391–395.

72. Tolkoff-Rubin NE, Rubin RH, Keller EE, Baker GP, Stewart JA, Hirsch MS. Cytomegalovirus infection in dialysis patients and personnel. Ann Intern Med 1978; 89:625–628.

73. Demmler GJ, Brady MT, Bijou H, Speer ME, Milam JD, Hawkins EP, Anderson DC, Six H, Yow MD. Posttransfusion cytomegalovirus infection of neonates: role of saline-washed red blood cells. J Pediatr 1986; 108:762–765.

74. Luban NL, Williams AE, MacDonald MG, Mikesell GT, Williams KM, Sacher RA. Low incidence of cytomegalovirus infection in neonates transfused with washed red blood cells. Am J Dis Child 1987; 141:416–419.

75. Gilbert GL, Hayes K, Hudson IL, James J. Prevention of transfusion-acquired cytomegalovirus infection in infants by blood filtration to remove leukocytes. Lancet 1989; 2:1228–1231.

76. Eisenfeld L, Silver H, McLaughlin J, Klevjer-Anderson P, Mayo D, Anderson J, Herson V, Krause P, Savidakis J, Lazar A. Prevention of transfusion-associated cytomegalovirus infection in neonatal patients by the removal of white cells from blood. Transfusion 1992; 32:205–209.

77. de Graan-Hentzen YC, Gratama JW, Mudde GC, Verdonck LF, Houbiers JG, Brand A, Sebens FW, van Loon AM, The TH, Willemze R. Prevention of primary cytomegalovirus infection in patients with hematologic malignancies by intensive white cell depletion of blood products. Transfusion 1989; 29:757–760.

78. De Witte T, Schattenberg A, Van Dijk BA, Galama J, Olthuis H, Van der Meer JW, Kunst VA. Prevention of primary cytomegalovirus infection after allogeneic bone marrow transplantation by using leukocyte-poor random blood products from cytomegalovirus-unscreened blood bank donors. Transplantation 1990; 50:964–968.

79. van Prooijen HC, Visser JJ, van Oostendorp WR, de Gast GC, Verdonck LF. Prevention of primary transfusion-associated cytomegalovirus infection in bone marrow transplant recipients by the removal of white cells from blood components with high-affinity filters. Br J Haematol 1994; 87:144–147.

80. Pamphilon DH, Rider JR, Barbara JA, Williamson LM. Prevention of transfusion-transmitted cytomegalovirus infection. Transf Med 1999; 9:115–123.

81. Ledent E, Berlin G. Inadequate white cell reduction from red cell concentrates by filtration. Transfusion 1994; 34:765–768.

82. Bodensteiner D. White cell reduction in blood donors with sickle trait (letter). Transfusion 1994; 34:84.

83. Ould Amar AK, Cesaire R, Kérob-Bauchet B, Robert P, Maier H, Bucher B. Altered filterability of fresh sickle trait donor blood (letter). Vox Sang 1997; 73:55–56.

84. Centers for Disease Control and Prevention. Adverse ocular reactions following transfusion-United States, 1997–1998. MMWR 1998; 47:49–50.

85. Nichols G. Is leukoreduction a suitable alternative to CMV screening? Are there alternate methods? Canadian Blood Services, Canadian Blood and Marrow Transplant Group Consensus Conference, Prevention of Post-Transfusion CMV in the Era of Universal Leukoreduction, Toronto, Canada, January 7–8, 2000.

15

Creutzfeldt-Jakob Disease, Other Human Transmissible Spongiform Encephalopathies, and Transfusion of Blood and Blood Products

Celso Bianco
New York Blood Center, New York, New York

I. INTRODUCTION

This chapter addresses human transmissible spongiform encephalopathies (TSEs) and the theoretical possibility of transmission of these diseases by the transfusion of blood and blood products. TSEs are rapidly progressing, fatal diseases, characterized by mental deterioration, cerebellar dysfunctions, involuntary movements, and psychiatric alterations. The brains of these patients show spongiform degeneration and deposition of an amyloid protein called prion protein (PrP^{res}). This protein is the protease-resistant form of a cellular protein called PrP^c, which is enclosed by a gene designated PRNP. PrP^{res} is pathognomonic for this group of illnesses. The diagnosis of human TSE can be strongly suspected on clinical grounds (e.g., by a characteristic electroencephalogram in a number of cases), but it can be only confirmed by histological or biochemical investigations of brain material after biopsy or autopsy. Over 85% of the cases of human TSEs are sporadic, appearing in individuals without family history. About 10% of the cases are familial. More than 80 cases of iatrogenic transmission of human TSEs have been reported. A new form of Creutzfeldt-Jakob disease (CJD) named new variant CJD (nvCJD) was described in 1996, and there is evidence indicating that it is related to bovine spongiform encephalopathy (BSE). These issues have been reviewed (1–3).

II. NATURE OF THE TRANSMISSIBLE AGENT

The causative agent of TSEs is controversial. Initially, the etiology of TSE was attributed to a slow virus infection. However, transmission studies performed in the scrapie model indicated that the infective material was devoid of measurable amounts of nucleic acid. The evidence for an infectious protein, the prion, was carefully reviewed (4). Essentially, the prion is a conformationally altered form of a normal cellular membrane protein called PrP^c. Abnormal PrP, PrP^{sc}, or PrP^{res} can induce conformational changes in normal PrP and is consequently "infectious." These conformational changes may require cofactors. PrP^{sc} and PrP^{res} are highly resistant to proteases and form rod-shaped multimers that precipitate as amyloid-causing spongiform alterations in the brain (5). Some authors still favor a viral etiology for CJD or believe that the cofactor for the alterations of PrP is a virus (6). Currently, the majority of investigators in the area accept the prion etiology for TSEs.

III. TSEs

The major human TSEs are kuru, sporadic CJD, iatrogenic CJD, nvCJD, familial CJD, Gerstmann-Straüssler-Scheinker syndrome (GSS), and fatal familial insomnia (FFI). Animal TSEs have been known for many years and are useful models for the human disease. Among them are scrapie in sheep and goats, transmissible mink encephalopathy (TME), chronic wasting disease of elks, and bovine spongiform encephalopathy (BSE), also known as "mad cow disease." TSEs appear to be transmitted by the ingestion of infected tissues from diseased animals. This has been documented for both TME and BSE (2,3).

A. Kuru

Kuru was the first TSE ever recognized. It occurred among the Fore peoples inhabiting the Central Highlands of Papua-New Guinea. It was apparently spread by cannibalism performed as a rite of respect and mourning for the dead. Since the cessation of cannibalism in the 1950s, the disease has nearly disappeared. The incubation time exceeded 40 years. The disease was transmitted experimentally to different species of Old and New World monkeys and apes in classic experiments by Asher, Gibbs, and Gajdusek. Brain contained the highest amount of infectivity, while serum and blood did not transmit the infection (7). Occasionally, spleen and lymph nodes transmitted disease after intracerebral inoculations, but not by administration through a nasogastric tube (four attempts with chimpanzees) (7). Clinically, Kuru is characterized by a preponderance of cerebellar symptoms; mental deterioration appears later in the course of the disease. In histological sections, relatively large deposits of PrP (so-called kuru plaques) can be observed.

B. Sporadic CJD

The sporadic form of CJD is the most common type of human TSE. CJD was first described in 1920–21. Most affected individuals die within one year of onset of symptoms (reviewed in Refs. 4,5). In many cases, a characteristic electroencephalogram with periodic triphasic waves can be observed. The human disease can be transmitted to nonhuman primates (7) and less regularly to nonprimates (cats, guinea pigs, mice, and hamsters) (8).

The incidence of CJD has been extensively analyzed by Schonberger et al. from the CDC. There were 3642 deaths between 1979 and 1994, or 228 deaths/year, for a rate of about one case per million inhabitants per year in the United States. The average annual age-adjusted death rate during the study period was 0.95 deaths per million persons, ranging from 0.78 in 1980 to 1.11 in 1987 (9). The incidence was zero among 5- to 19-year-olds, and reached 3.6–5.8/1,000,000 among individuals over 60 years of age. The incidence has remained constant over the years and was the same in all U.S. states. There are no reports of transmission of CJD by sexual or casual contact. The overall mortality rate in Europe is 0.69 at one year (10). Interestingly, the phenotypic expression of the disease may be linked to polymorphism at codon 129 of PrP. In contrast to the normal population, 69% of CJD patients were homozygous for methionine at codon 129 (vs. 42% of controls). Homozygosity on codon 129 is considered to be a genetic predisposing factor for CJD (11).

Clinically, sporadic CJD it is characterized by an early onset of mental dysfunctions (e.g., memory loss or behavioral abnormalities). However, in a substantial proportion of cases (15% in a large study of confirmed CJD cases), cerebellar symptoms are the first signs of the disease (12). The most extensive experience of experimental transmission of TSEs was reported by Brown et al. (12) The most effective route of transmission is intracerebral inoculation, and the highest infectivity is found in the brain of infected individuals, followed by spinal cord, cerebrospinal fluid, and eye.

C. Iatrogenic CJD

The possibility of iatrogenic transmission of TSEs was first raised in 1974, with the association of a case of CJD with a corneal transplant performed 18 months earlier (13). A second case was described more recently with onset of disease 30 years after a corneal transplant (14). However, these cases are not well documented, and transmission of CJD by corneal transplants is unlikely. Silver electrodes used for stereotactic electroencephalograms during neurosurgery transmitted CJD to two patients, although the electrodes had been cleaned and sterilized by 70% ethanol and formaldehyde vapor between uses (15). No other transmissions by either of these routes have been reported.

Starting in 1985, CJD was identified among 7 of 6284 recipients of human pituitary-derived growth hormone prepared from human cadaveric pituitary glands (16). Concerned about the theoretical possibility of transmission by transfusion, the U.S. Food and Drug Administration (FDA) recommended as a precautionary measure that individuals who received human pituitary-derived growth hormone be deferred from donating blood (November 25, 1987). In Europe, development of CJD among recipients of human pituitary-derived growth hormone was also a serious problem. By November 1994, 11 cases had been reported in the United States, 14 in the United Kingdom, and 32 in France (L. Schonberger, personal communication). Large batch sizes contributed to the spread. Duration of the disease was significantly longer than that observed in sporadic CJD. Estimated mean incubation time was 8.9 years in France and more than 10 years in the United Kingdom and the United States. Clinical symptoms consisted mainly of cerebellar ataxia. Homozygosity for codon 129 of the PRNP gene, the main genetic determinant for susceptibility to CJD, was significantly associated with disease. The mean incubation time was significantly longer in heterozygous individuals than in homozygous individuals (11 vs. 8.95 years). There have been four transmissions traceable to gonadotropin use in Australia. Gonadotropin was also prepared from cadaveric human pituitary glands but has had a far more limited use than human growth hormone.

Iatrogenic transmission of CJD has also been documented among recipients of human dura mater transplants (17). Incubation times were less than 2 years for some patients. Most, but not all, of the dura mater transmissions have been associated with use of a single product manufactured in large batches by a single manufacturer. To date approximately 60 cases have been traced to this source. Recently, Japan identified 43 additional cases associated with transplants of dura mater (18). Most of the transmissions occurred in codon 129 homozygous individuals.

D. New Variant CJD

A new variant of CJD was first described in 1996 (19,20). By July 1999 there had been 39 cases identified in the United Kingdom, one in France, and one in the Republic of Ireland. The major characteristic of nvCJD is the age of onset: all patients have been under the age of 50, while sporadic CJD occurs mainly in the elderly, with a peak of incidence at an age of 70 (9). The histological picture is characterized by relatively large and abundant deposits of PrP (kuru-like plaques) surrounded by prominent vacuoles ("florid" plaques) in the neutrophil. In contrast to sporadic CJD, PrP deposits have been found in peripheral lymphoid organs (tonsils, spleen) (21). This disease seems to be associated with BSE for several reasons: the geographical distribution, the clinical presentation, the molecular similarity of the nvCJD- and BSE-associated PrPs (22), and the biological properties of the infectious agents (23).

E. Familial TSEs

Three types of CJD, namely familial CJD, GSS (24), and FFI (25), are hereditary diseases. They are associated with mutations in the normal cellular gene that codes for the prion protein. GSS evolves very slowly, over a period of years. Patients with FFI are unable to sleep. Transmission of these TSEs to animals has been occasionally successful (12).

F. Animal TSEs

Scrapie in sheep has been known for more than 200 years. In 1961, scrapie was successfully transmitted to laboratory mice (26). Gajdusek and Gibbs were able to transmit the disease to New and Old World monkeys (reviewed in Refs. 27,28). In 1975, Manuelidis described the transmission of CJD to guinea pigs by intracerebral injection of brain tissue (29). These observations were extended to hamsters, mice, and rats (29,30). The exact route of natural transmission of scrapie has not been elucidated. Animal experiments are complicated by the "species barrier," i.e., an animal species is less sensitive to a TSE agent isolated from another species than the originally infected species. In addition, intracerebral injections accept only a limited sample volume (30–50 μL), raising the possibility that infectivity is frequently underestimated. Mad cow disease, or bovine spongiform encephalopathy has been attributed to the practice of feeding cattle with sheep offal.

IV. RELATIONSHIP BETWEEN nvCJD AND MAD COW DISEASE

A cluster of nvCJD cases with a unique neuropathological picture among young patients was reported in 1996 (31). The authors of the report suggested that these patients were infected by a new strain of prions related to "mad cow disease." The molecular characteristics of the variant strains have been determined (32). One case of variant CJD has been reported in France (33), and another appears to have been identified in the Republic of Ireland (commentary in Lancet, June

26, 1999). The public concern was so intense that it led the European Community to ban importation of British beef until measures designed to control the spread of the infection were instituted. The ban was lifted as of August 1,1999. Little is known about the relative efficiency of various routes of infection by the BSE or the nvCJD agent. However, the spread of the disease in cattle and its transmission to other species, presumably through food, suggests that the oral route may be efficient. In the United States, the Centers for Disease Control and Prevention (CDC) established surveillance systems for CJD and CJD variants (34). No cases of BSE have so far been identified. In addition, an analysis of CJD between 1979 and 1994 found no evidence of the variants form of CJD (35). Unfortunately, because of the very low incidence of CJD and the long incubation period, there will be a long period before more definitive answers become available.

V. CJD AND BLOOD TRANSFUSION

On October 18, 1994, the American Red Cross (ARC) reported to FDA that a 64-year-old blood donor who had donated more than 90 times over more than 30 years had died with a clinical diagnosis of CJD. Plasma from his donations was often pooled for further manufacture of plasma derivatives. On October 27, 1994, ARC voluntarily recalled components of the last four donations made by the donor. On November 17, 1994, Baxter and ARC initiated voluntary market withdrawal of implicated lots of IVIG, Factor VIII AHF, albumin, and plasma protein fraction. Soon, Miles withdrew alpha$_1$-proteinase inhibitor lots and Sandoz withdrew IVIG that contained donations made by this donor. In November 1994 hemophilia treaters in New York initiated notification of patients who had received implicated lots of Factor VIII AHF that they had received products that contained plasma from a donor who later developed CJD. This set of events triggered worldwide concerns about transmissibility of CJD by blood and blood products.

VI. EXPERIMENTAL ATTEMPTS TO TRANSMIT TSEs BY BLOOD

The initial concerns about transmissibility of CJD by transfusion were raised by Manuelidis (36), who inoculated buffy coat cells from peripheral blood of two CJD patients into the brains of rodents. After 200–500 days, these animals showed spongiform degeneration of the brain, while control experiments "never resulted in CJD." In 1993, these investigators inoculated buffy coat cells from normal volunteers with no family history of dementia into the brains of hamsters. After a long period of observation, 26 of 30 buffy coats (86.7%) induced CJD-like changes in the animal's brains. The investigators concluded that the CJD agent "endemically infects humans but only infrequently produces dementia" (37). This interpretation is highly controversial, because these are the logical controls for the early experiments performed with CJD buffy coats and raise serious questions about assay specificity. Transmission of classical CJD to animals by intracerebral inoculation was attempted in other studies (38,39). Data presented in these papers are conflicting. For instance, one author finds CJD infectivity in blood clots injected intracerebrally into mice in one out of three patients (38). Another author injected plasma of a pregnant woman with CJD intracerebrally into mice (39). The neat plasma was noninfectious, but after threefold concentration it was highly infectious. In addition, the patients' leukocytes were negative, while cord blood was infective. Another author described transmission of iatrogenic CJD by buffy coat injected into hamsters but provides no details of dose, route, or development of alterations in the animal (40). The group of Manuelidis also reported transmission of CJD by buffy coat from a patient with an unclear neurological disease (41), from patients with Alzheimer's disease (42), and from healthy individuals (37). Those results could not be repeated (43,44). Rohwer attributed the experimental results to the occurrence of a late-onset wasting disease associated with *Clostridium difficile* in the hamsters (45). In addition, two studies with goats as donor and indicator animals could not demonstrate any infectivity in blood (46,47). Studies in minks inoculated with the TME agent did not reveal any infectivity in serum or any other component of blood (48,49). Purified and concentrated lymphocytes from peripheral blood did not transmit the disease while spleen and mesenteric lymph nodes were clearly infectious. No infectivity could be found in serum or in blood clots of scrapie-infected goats and sheep (50–52). In addition, no infectivity has been detected in buffy coat of cattle infected orally with the BSE agent up to 18 months postinoculation (53,54).

A number of long-term, well-controlled experiments have failed to demonstrate transmission of disease by blood from kuru and CJD patients into monkeys and apes (7,12). In addition, Gajdusek transfused blood (>300 mL) from three different CJD patients into three chimpanzees. None of these animals developed TSE after an observation period of more than 20 years (7,12). It should be noted that transmission of CJD by routes other than the intracerebral route has rarely been successful, and the reproducibility of the phenomenon has often been questioned.

VII. LACK OF CORRELATION BETWEEN TSEs AND TRANSFUSION OF BLOOD AND BLOOD PRODUCTS

Several investigators have examined the theoretical possibility of CJD transmissions by transfusion in humans. A study of the transfusion histories of 202 definite and probable cases of CJD performed in England and Wales between 1980–84 and 1990–92 showed that 21 of the patients had received blood transfusions and 29 had donated blood (55). The frequency of blood transfusions or donations did not differ between CJD cases and matched controls, leading the investigators to conclude that the evidence did not suggest that transfusion was a major risk factor for development of CJD (55).

No cases of CJD among persons with hemophilia had been reported in the medical literature until October 1994. The Medline database contained 1485 references on CJD and 6385 references on hemophilia between January 1976 and October 1994. None of these references linked CJD and hemophilia. Unfortunately, this type of search cannot be repeated because of the high number of articles addressing the theoretical possibility of transmission of CJD by blood transfusion. An extensive review of mortality data between 1979 and 1994 performed by CDC did not identify a single CJD death in individuals with a clotting disorder or hemoglobinopathy (35).

A recent multicenter European case control study found no significant risk of CJD associated with surgery and blood transfusions (56). In a follow-up of one CJD patient who was a frequent blood donor, none of the blood recipients developed CJD. Eighteen blood recipients have died of nonneurological disorders; nine were alive at the time of the investigation. The time periods for follow-up ranged from 1 to 22 years after the blood transfusions.

The distribution of infectivity in plasma derivatives in experimental TSE models was studied by spiking normal plasma with trypsinized cells from a scrapie-infected hamster. The plasma was fractionated using the classical Cohn method and fractions injected intracerebrally into animals. The study showed a potential but minimal risk of acquiring CJD from the administration of plasma protein concentrates (57).

VIII. LOOKBACK STUDIES

Studies of recipients who received blood and blood products from donors who later developed CJD have not yet led to a documented case of CJD. A collaborative lookback study performed by the American Red Cross, the New York Blood Center, and the CDC tracked 178 recipients of blood units derived from donors who developed CJD. Nine of these recipients lived between 13 and 24 years after transfusion, and 41 lived more than 5 years. No CJD was revealed in any of these recipients (58). However, only 2 patients had been followed for more than 20 years after the transfusion.

CJD has not been identified among patients who received large amounts of blood or blood products (35,59). CDC has examined tissues from 30 patients with severe hemophilia who died with CNS symptoms since 1983 and found no evidence of CJD. These patients had received clotting factor concentrates for 15–23 years. In addition, none of 101 hemophilia A patients, 76 of whom lived 11–17 years after receiving more than 100 units of cryoprecipitate, developed CJD (60). Another study carried out by the Veterans Administration involved review of records of 8614 inpatient episodes of care and 543 death certificates of veterans who received plasma products from a donor who later developed CJD. It did not yield any cases of potential transmission after 7 years of follow-up (61). One case of potential transmission to a liver transplant recipient who also received transfusions of albumin has recently been reported. One of the albumin donors died 3 years later from a dementia clinically characterized as CJD (62). Obviously, the liver transplant recipient was exposed to a variety of drugs and biologics, making it difficult to determine the exact source of disease.

IX. MEASURE TO PREVENT THE THEORETICAL TRANSMISSION OF THE TSE AGENT BY TRANSFUSION OF BLOOD AND BLOOD PRODUCTS

A. Market Withdrawals and Recalls

On December 15, 1994, the issue of CJD and transfusion was reviewed by the FDA Blood Products Advisory Committee. After extensive discussion, the Committee recommended that in-date cellular products of blood from donors who later develop CJD should be withdrawn from distribution. In cases in which these products had been transfused, the Committee recommended that physicians and recipients be notified. In the case of plasma pooled for further manufacture, the Committee recommended against recall of manufactured products because of the lack of evidence for transmission. The hemophilia community, extremely concerned about the theoretical potential for transmission of CJD, was quite dissatisfied with this recommendation, leading FDA to convene a new advisory committee to review the possibility of transmission of CJD by plasma derivatives. The special advisory committee met on June 22, 1995, and recommended that all plasma products containing donations from individuals who later died of CJD be withdrawn from the market. This recommendation was based on "precautionary principles," despite the lack of evidence for transmissibility of CJD by these products. FDA issued a memorandum to blood establishments on August 8, 1995, recommending quarantine of these products. FDA also indicated that release of these products might need to occur because of shortages and that the released products should bear a warning disclosing risks and benefits. However, this clause has not been invoked because of lack of acceptability of such products by the patients.

B. Deferral of Older Donors

The American Red Cross announced on December 5, 1996, that it would only use plasma from donors under the age of 60 as a source of plasma for the manufacture of plasma derivatives. This step was taken "to lessen major market withdrawals of plasma derivatives manufactured from volunteer donors because of rare reports of older donors developing CJD." This policy was also adopted by some collectors of source plasma who deferred donors over the age of 50. Interestingly, Busch et al. have shown, based on data from the Retroviral Epidemiology Donor Study, that a blanket removal of donors age 50 and over increases the risk of human immunodeficiency virus (HIV) transmission by 12% hepatitis C virus (HCV) by 21%, and hepatitis B virus (HBV) by 22% (63).

C. Deferral of Donors with Family History or Potential Exposure to Infectious Materials

Since 1987, individuals who had received human growth hormone of human pituitary origin have been deferred from donating blood according to an FDA recommendation. An FDA memorandum issued on August 8, 1995, advised that individuals who had a family history of CJD or had received dura mater transplants be deferred from donating blood or plasma. The deferral policies were extended with the issuance of another memorandum on December 11, 1996, entitled "Revised Precautionary Measures to Reduce the Possible Risk of Transmission of Creutzfeldt-Jakob Disease (CJD) by Blood and Blood Products." It defined the categories of iatrogenic, familial, and possibly familial risks. It added dura mater transplants to the deferrals and defined three questions to be asked during the donor history. It also elaborated on actions to be taken when donors were identified as at increased risk of developing CJD or were subsequently diagnosed with CJD. Blood donors with one "blood relative" with history of CJD were to be deferred and the collected unit discarded. If there were two or more "blood relatives," the family was considered a family at risk for CJD, and in-date products from prior donations were to be placed in quarantine. In order to address concerns about large amounts of blood products placed in quarantine, FDA indicated that donors could be subjected to genetic testing for familial forms of PrP. If the tests were negative (i.e., no mutations associated with increased susceptibility were identified), products could be released from quarantine. If the tests were not performed or the donors tested positive, recipients of products from these donors were to be notified and counseled. The same applied for donors who subsequently died of CJD.

The American Association of Blood Banks issued Bulletin #96-4 containing guidance for recipient notification. This bulletin was published in the AABB News Briefs issue of June 1996. The guidance suggested that appropriate committees within an institution (Internal Review Board, Ethics Committee, etc.) review the issues and define criteria for recipient notification.

On September 8, 1998, FDA changed its policy regarding classic CJD. Deferral of donors with family history of CJD (two or more family members) was retained. However, withdrawal of products was restricted to products made with plasma from donors who later developed nvCJD, not classic CJD. The latter was retained as a precautionary measure because of the limited follow-up of individuals exposed to BSE. So far, there have been no cases of nvCJD identified in the United States. The European Community has had a similar policy: "given the lack of specific information on nvCJD, as a precautionary measure it would be prudent to withdraw batches of plasma-derived medicinal products from the market if a donor to a plasma pool is subsequently strongly suspected, by the reference center, of having nvCJD." In addition, FDA and the U.S. Department of Agriculture have established rigid criteria for the importation of products that could be used for manufacture of drugs or for human consumption. These include fetal bovine serum, gelatin, and prepared foods.

D. Deferral of Donors Who Have Spent 6 Months or More in the U.K.

In June 1999, the TSE Advisory Committee of FDA recommended that persons who had been in the United Kingdom for an aggregate amount of 6 months or more between 1980 and 1996 should be deferred from donating blood. This represents 2% of all blood donors in the United States and 3.1% of all donors in New York (A. Williams et al. personal communication). The Committee reflected concerns about nvCJD and about the fact that the United Kingdom had been discarding the plasma donated by their own donors and was using plasma from paid United States blood donors to use in their plasma fractionation plants. The Committee was not swayed by arguments expressed by the transfusion medicine community indicating that the policy would lead to major shortages. In addition, the Committee rejected indications that replacement of these regular blood donors with first-time donors with much higher prevalence of HIV, HCV, and HBV would increase the risk for diseases known to be transmitted by transfusion. The Committee preferred to adhere to the "precautionary principles" adopted by their British counterparts. This deferral policy will be reviewed every 6 months. A similar policy is currently under consideration in Canada.

E. Leukoreduction

The argument that leukoreduction, a process that removes the vast majority of leukocytes from blood and blood components, may decrease CJD infectivity of blood is derived from two different types of observation. First Klein et al. (64)

demonstrated that mice lacking mature B lymphocytes do not develop clinical symptoms of scrapie when inoculated with infectious material outside the brain (i.e., intravenously and intraperitoneally). Second, PrP Sc has been detected in tonsils and appendices of patients with nvCJD (21). In addition, PrP^c is expressed at different stages of leukocyte differentiation from CD34$^+$ stem cells to mature lymphocytes and monocytes but not granulocytes (65). Because infectivity could be present in circulating leukocytes, leukoreduction would be a practical way to reduce the risk of nvCJD. Several countries have implemented leukoreduction or have committed to implementation of leukoreduction procedures based on these theoretical arguments. It should be noted that the arguments are based on observations made in experimental models that may bear no relevance to nvCJD transmission.

As of July 1999, France, Portugal, Ireland, Luxembourg, and Canada had implemented universal leukoreduction. The United Kingdom had decided that leukoreduction for all blood for transfusion should be extended as soon as practically possible, and the FDA Blood Products Advisory Committee recommended implementation of universal leukoreduction, regardless of its role in the prevention of CJD transmission. The Committee indicated that that universal, prestorage leukoreduction would benefit recipients of blood components.

While leukoreduction has a number of well-documented benefits, it is difficult to assess the role it would play in the prevention of transmission of nvCJD. For instance, the degree of leukoreduction required to prevent transmission is unknown (particularly because transmission has not yet been observed). In addition, the subclass of white blood cells that may carry the nvCJD agent has not been determined. Prestorage leukoreduction has not yet been applied universally. Thus infrequent allergic reactions, rare hypotensive reactions (FDA letter dated may 4, 1999, http:/www.fda.gov/cdrh/safety/hypoblrf.htm), and a "red eye syndrome" observed among recipients of one filter brand raise some concerns (66).

The arguments that have been presented for implementing this practice in the context of nvCJD include the suggestion that white blood cells may be involved in the transport of the CJD and nvCJD agents. It is not yet clear what proportion of the bloodborne infectivity is distributed into white blood cells and which subtype classes of white blood cells (T, B, or dendritic cells) carry infectivity for CJD or nvCJD. Furthermore, there is no evidence to date suggesting that CJD/nvCJD is spread by blood transfusion. Consequently, implementation of universal leukoreduction to prevent CJD/nvCJD transmission is not based on epidemiological or experimental data.

F. Screening Tests for CJD/nvCJD

There are no assays currently available for the screening of blood donations for CJD or nvCJD. Thus, in the absence of cases of transmission of CJD and nvCJD by blood, it is impossible to assess the influence of any of the current preventive measures on the risk of transmission of CJD and nvCJD. However, various assays based on monoclonal antibodies to PrP have been developed. Discrimination between normal PrP and PrP^{sc} or PRP^{res} is based on resistance to digestion by proteinase K (67,68). These assays are useful in the identification of cows with BSE and in the diagnosis of sick patients (71,72).

G. Inactivation/Removal of the Agent from Blood and Plasma

The infectivity of various cellular blood components and plasma derivatives has been studied through "spiking" human blood with the scrapie agent and by intracerebral, intravenous, and intraperitoneal inoculation of a mouse-adapted strain of human CJD using hamsters and mice as assay animals. The data of such studies suggest that when CJD is present (at low concentration) in blood of infected animals, partitioning into various cellular and plasma compartments occurs. In cellular blood components, CJD is present in leukocytes and platelets. In plasma CJD is recovered from cryoprecipitate and fractions I, II, and III of the Cohn fractionation method, but not in fractions IV and V and albumin (57,69). These experiments have shown that fractionation reduces the infectious load of plasma.

H. Reduction of the Size of Pools Used for Manufacture of Derivatives

The pool size of plasma for fractionation varies from 1,000 to 10,000 units when source plasma collected by aphersis is used; for recovered plasma the pool size is also quite variable (30,000–60,000 donor units from whole blood donations). The question has been raised whether reduction of the pool size may decrease the risk of CJD transmission. The probability that pooled donor plasma will contain a donation from an individual with a disease has been analyzed for a range of disorders and different pool sizes (70). Using this analysis, the probability that a CJD patient has contributed to a pool of 10,000 donors is 0.8%; if the pool size increases to 100,000 donors, the probability increases to 7.6%. However, it is unlikely that a person with symptoms of CJD will donate blood. Using mathematical modeling, Brown et al. (57) concluded that the chance of contracting CJD from a pooled blood product to which a patient with CJD has contributed would be extremely small, no matter what the size of the donor pool. Limitation of the pool size is not likely to reduce such a risk, because the infectivity does not saturate the pool.

Other diagnostic tools (e.g., detection of brain proteins in the cerebrospinal fluid or in the peripheral blood) are under development (68,69). A specific immune response, often the basis for a diagnostic test, has not been observed. Tests indicative of the disease before the onset of clinical symptoms do not yet exist.

X. OVERALL ASSESSMENT

The assessment of the potential risk of TSE transmission by transfusion has been a very difficult task. The reality of the AIDS tragedy hit the transfusion medicine community after years of dismissive statements that minimized risks. In addition, the hemophilia community, devastated by the transmission of HIV and HCV, has exerted substantial political pressure, demanding safety and compensation. Now both the scientific and the blood banking community are afraid of repeating the same mistakes. The phenomenon could be called the "fear of another AIDS mistake." Medical experts do not want to risk a statement such as "there is sufficient evidence to indicate that the transmission of TSEs by transfusion of blood and blood products is unlikely" out of fear of being proven wrong. In September 1998 FDA suspended a recall of plasma products that had been manufactured from pools containing a unit donated by an individual who later developed classical CJD. They retained recalls for nvCJD and the discard of components from these donors. These derivative recalls had caused substantial shortages of plasma derivatives all over the world. However, the "fear of another AIDS mistake" prevented the regulators from accepting the overwhelming evidence that individual components also do not transmit classical CJD. Another interesting observation is the adoption of leukoreduction by several European countries and Canada despite the lack of epidemiological or experimental evidence that it will contribute to the prevention of CJD transmission. The action was based on the experiments of Klein et al. (64) suggesting that B cells played a role in dissemination scrapie in a mouse model quite distant from nvCJD. However, evidence that blood and plasma have very low infectivity, derived from the same model, has been summarily ignored.

Despite the evidence against the transmission of classical CJD by transfusion, many of the restrictions, geographic deferrals, recommendations for leukoreduction, etc. continue to be applied because the period of follow-up for nvCJD has been relatively short. The peak of BSE in England occurred in 1990, the first case of nvCJD was identified in 1996, and as of May 31, 1999, there were 42 definite and probable cases of nvCJD.

The most solid recent assessment has been made by Paul Brown, from the National Institutes of Health at a meeting in February 1999, "Although experimental studies indicate that blood donations from individuals with CJD might be capable of transmitting disease, the available epidemiological evidence indicates that bloodborne infection does not occur." He attributed the disparity to (a) very low to absent levels of blood infectivity in patients with CJD; (b) dilution of infectivity in large donor pools; (c) loss of infectivity (1–3 logs) during plasma fractionation; and (d) the comparative inefficiency of transmission of the infectious agent by parenteral routes. Items b and c are only applicable to plasma derivatives.

ACKNOWLEDGMENTS

The author thanks Maria Rios for assistance in the preparation of this manuscript. The author also wants to credit the report to the Scientific Committee on Medicinal Products and Medical Devices of the European Community led by Dr. J. Löwer, dated October 21, 1998, for its insights into the subject. The report is posted at the following internet site: http://europa.eu.int/comm/dg24/health/sc/scmp/outcome_en.html.

REFERENCES

1. Haywood A M. Transmissible spongiform encephalopathies. N Engl J Med 1997; 337:1821–1828.
2. Johnson RT, Gibbs CJ Jr. Creutzfeldt-Jakob disease and related transmissible spongiform encephalopathies. N Engl J Med 1998; 339:1994–2004.
3. Knight R. The relationship between new variant Creutzfeldt-Jakob disease and bovine spongiform encephalopathy. Vox Sang 1999; 79:203–208.
4. DeArmond SJ, Prusiner SB. Etiology and pathogenesis of prion diseases. AM J Pathol 1995; 146:785.
5. Gajdusek DC. Nucleation of amyloidogenesis in infectious and non-infectious amyloidoses of the brain. Ann NY Acad Sci 1994; 724:173.
6. Manuelidis L. The dimensions of Creutzfeldt-Jakob disease. Transfusion 1994; 34:915.
7. Asher DM, Gibbs CJ Jr, Gajdusek DC. Pathogenesis of subacute spongiform encephalopathies. Ann Clin Lab Sci 1976; 6:84–103.
8. Manuelidis EE, Kim JH, Mericangas JR, Manuelidis L. Transmission to animals of Creutzfeldt-Jakob disease from human blood. Lancet 1985; ii:896.
9. Holman RC, Khan AS Belay ED, Schonberger LB. Creutzfeldt-Jakob disease in the United States, 1979-1994: using national mortality data to assess the possible occurrence of variant cases. Emerg Infect Dis 1996; 2:333–337.
10. Will RG, Alperovitch A, Poser S, Pocchiari M, Hofman A, Mitrova E, de silva R, D' Alessandro M, Delasnerie-Laupretre N, Zerr I, van Duijn C. Descriptive epidemiology of Creutzfeldt-Jakob disease in six European countries, 1993-1995. Ann Neurol 1998; 43:763–767.
11. Parchi P, Castellani R, Capellari S, Ghetti B, Young K, Chen SG, et al. Molecular basis of phenotypic variability in sporadic Creutzfeldt-Jakob disease. Ann Neurol 1998; 39:767–778.

12. Brown P, Gibbs CJ Jr, Rodgers-Johnson P, Asher DM, Sulima MP, Bacote A, Goldfarb LG, Gajdusek DC. Human spongiform encephalopathy: the National Institutes of Health series of 300 cases of experimetally transmitted disease. Ann Neurol 1994; 35:513–529.

13. Duffy P, Wolf J, Collins G, DeVoe A G, Steeten B, Cowen D. Possible person-to-person transmission of Creutzfeldt-Jakob disease. N Engl J Med 1974; 290:692–693.

14. Heckmann JG, Lang CJG, Petruch F, Druschky A, Erb C, Brown P, Neundrfer B. Transmission of Creutzfeldt-Jakob disease via corneal transplant. J Neurol Neurosurg Psychiatry 1997; 63:388–390.

15. Bernoulli C, Siegfried J, Baumgartner G, Regli F, Rabinowicz T, Gajdusek DC, Gibbs CJ Jr. Danger of accidental person-to-person transmission of Creutzfeldt-Jakob disease by surgery. Lancet 1977; i:478–479.

16. Fradkin JE, Schonberger LB, Mills JL, et al. Creutzfeldt-Jakob disease in pituitary growth hormone recipients in the United States. JAMA 1991; 265:880.

17. Martinez-Lage JF, Poza M, Sola J, Tortosa JG, Brown P, Cervenakova L, Esteban JA, Mendonza A. Accidental transmission of Cretzfeldt-Jakob disease by dural cadaveric grafts. J Neurol Neurosurg Psychiatry 1994; 57:1091–1094.

18. Centers for Disease Control. Cretzfeldt-Jakob disease associated with cadaveric dura mater grafts—Japan, January 1979-May. MMWR 1996; 46:1066–1096.

19. Will RG, Ironside JW, Zeidler M, Cousens SN, Estibeiro K, Alperovitch A, Poser S, Pocchiari M, Hofman A, Smith PG, A new variant of Cretzfeldt-Jakob disease in the UK. Lancet 1996; 347:921–925.

20. Will RG, Knight RSG, Zeidler M, Ironside JW, Cousens SN, et al. Reporting of suspect new variant Creutzfeldt-Jakob disease. Lancet 1997; 349:847.

21. Hill AF, Butterworth RJ, Joiner D, Rossor MN, Thomas DJ, Frosh A, Tolley N, Bell JE, Spencer M, King A, Al-Sarraj S, Ironside JW, Iantos PL, Collinge J. Investigation of variant Cretzfeldt-Jakob disease and other human prion diseases with tonsil biopsy samples. Lancet 1999; 353:183–189.

22. Collinge J, Sidle KCL, Meads J, Ironside J, Hill AF. Molecular analysis of prion strain variation and the etiology of 'new variant' CJD. Nature 1999; 383:685–690.

23. Bruce ME, Will RG, Ironside JW, McConnell I, Drummond D, Suttie A, McCardle L, Chree A, Hope J, Birkett C, Cousens S, Fraser H, Bostock CJ. Transmissions to mice indicate that new variant CJD is caused by the BSE agent. Nature 1997; 389:498–501.

24. Gerstmann J, Sträussler E, Scheinker I. Über eine eigenartige hereditär-familiäre Erkrankung des Zentralnervensystems. Zugleich ein Beitrag zur Frage des vorzeitigen lokalen Alterns. Z Ges Neurol Psych 1936; 154:736–762.

25. Lugaresi E, Medori R, Montagna P, Baruzzi A, Cortelli P, Lugaresi A, et al. Fatal familial insomnia and dysautonomia with selective degeneration of thalamic nuclei. N Engl J Med 1986; 315:997–1003.

26. Chandler R L. Encephalopathy in mice produced by inoculation with scrapie brain material. Lancet 1961; i:107–108.

27. Gibbs CJ Jr, Gajdusek DC, Morris JA. Viral characteristics of the scrapie agent in mice. In: Gajdusek DC, Gibbs, CJ, Alper M, eds Slow, Latent and Temperate Virus Infections. National Institute of Neurologic Diseases and Blindness, 1965:195–202.

28. Gibbs CJ Jr, Gajdusek DC. Isolation and characterization of the subacute spongiform

virus encephalopathies of man:kuru and Creutzfeldt-Jakob disease. J Clin Pathol 1972; 25(suppl. 6):84–96.

29. Manuelidis EE, Angelo JN, Gorgacz EJ, Manuelidis L. Transmission of Creutzfeldt-Jakob disease to Syrian hamster. Lancet 1977; i:479–479.

30. Tateishi J, Ohta M, Koga M, Sato Y, Kuroiwa Y. Transmission of chronic spogiform encephalopathy with kuru plaques and leukomalacia to small rodents. Ann Neurol 1979; 5:581–584.

31. Will RG, Ironside JW, Zeidler M, Cousens SN, Estibeiro K, Alperovitch A, et al. A new variant of Creutzfeldt-Jakob disease in the UK. Lancet 1996; 347:921–925.

32. Collinge J, Sidie KCL, Meads J, Ironside J, Hill AF. Molecular analysis of prion strain variation and the etiology of "new variant" CJD. Nature 1996; 383:685–690.

33. Chazot, G, Broussoille, E, Lapras C, Blattler C, Aguzzi A, Koop N. New variant of Creutzfeldt-Jakob disease in a 26-year old French man (letter). Lancet 1996; 347:1181.

34. Reingold A, Rothrock G, Starr M, et al. Surveillance for Creutzfeldt-Jakob disease— United States. MMWR 1996; 45:665–668.

35. Holman RC, Kahn AS, Belay ED, Schonberger LB. Creutzfeldt-Jakob disease in the United States, 1979-1994: using national mortality data to assess the possible occurence of variant cases. Emerg Infect 1996; 2:333–337.

36. Manuelidis EE. Transmission of Creutzfeldt-Jakob disease from man to guinea pig. Science 1975; 190:571–572.

37. Manuelidis L, Manuelidis EE. A transmissible Creutzfeldt-Jakob disease-like agent is prevalent in the human population. Proc Natl Acad Sci 1993; 90:7724–7728.

38. Tateishi J. Transmission of Creutzfeldt-Jakob disease from human blood and urine into mice. Lancet 1985; ii:1074–1074.

39. Tamai Y, Kojima H, Kirajima R, Taguchi F, Ohtani Y, Kawaguchi T, Miura S, Sato M, Ishihara Y. Demonstration of the transmissible agent in tissue from a pregnant woman with Creutzfeldt-Jakob disease. N Engl J Med 1992; 327:649–649.

40. Deslys JP, Lasmézas C, Dormont D. Selection of specific strains in iatrogenic Creutzfeldt-Jakob disease (letter). Lancet 1994; 343:848–849.

41. Manuelidis EE, Manuelidis L, Pincus JH, Collins WF. Transmission, from man to hamster, of Creutzfeldt-Jakob disease with clinical recovery. Lancet 1978; ii:40–42.

42. Manuelidis EE, de Figueiredo JM, Kim JH, Fritch WW, Manuelidis L. Transmission studies from blood of Alzheimer disease patient and healthy relatives. Proc Natl Acad Sci USA 1988; 85:4898–4901.

43. Godec MS, Asher DM, Master CL, Rubi JU, Payne JA, Rubi-Villa DJ, Wagner EE, Rapoport SI, Schapiro MB. Evidence against the transmissibility of Alzheimer's disease. Neurology 1992; 41:1320–1320.

44. Godec MS, Asher DM, Kozachuk WE, Masters CL, Rubi JU, Payne JA, Rubi-Villa DJ, Wagner EE, Rapoport SI, Schapiro MB. Blood buffy coat from Alzheimer's disease patients and their relatives does not transmit spongiform encephalopathy to hamsters. Neurology 1994; 44:1111–1115.

45. Rohwer RG. Alzheimer's disease transmission: possible artifact due to intercurrent illness. Neurology 1992; 42:287–288.

46. Pattison IH, Millson GC. Distribution of scrapie agent in the tissues of experimentally inoculated goats. J Comp Pathol Ther 1962; 72:233–244.

47. Pattison IH, Millson GC, Smith K. An examination of the action of whole blood, blood cells or serum on the goat scrapie agent. Res Vet Sci 1964; 5:116–121.

48. Marsh RF, Burger D, Hanson RP. Transmissible mink encephalopathy: behavior of the disease agent in mink. Am J Vet Res 1969; 30:1637–1642.

49. Marsh RF, Miller JM, Hanson RP. Transmissible mink encephalopathy: studies on the peripheral lymphocyte. Infect Immun 1973; 7:352–355.

50. Hadlow WJ, Eklund CM, Kennedy RC, Jackson TA, Whitford HW, Boyle CC. Course of experimental scrapie virus infection in the goat. J Infect Dis 1974; 129:559–567.

51. Hadlow WJ, Kennedy RC, Race RE, Eklund CM. Virologic and neurohistologic findings in dairy goats affected with natural scrapie. Vet Pathol 1980; 17:187–199.

52. Hadlow WJ, Race RE, Kennedy RC. Temporal distribution of transmissible mink encephalopathy virus in mink inoculated subcutaneously. J Virol 1987; 61:3235–3240.

53. Wells GAH, Dawson M, Hawkins SAC, Austin AR, Green RB, Dexter I, Horigan MW, Simmons MM. Preliminary observations on the pathogenesis of experimental bovine spongiform encephalopathy. In: Gibbs CJ Jr, ed. Bovine Spongiform Encephalopathy: The BSE Dilemma. New York: Springer-Verlag, 1996:28–44.

54. Wells GAH, Hawkins SAC, Green RB, Austin AR, Dexter I, Spencer YI, Chaplin MJ, Stack MJ, Dawson M. Preliminary observations on the pathogenesis of experimental bovine spongiform encephalopathy (BSE): an update. Vet Rec 1998; 142:103–106.

55. Esmonde TFG, Will RG, Slattery JM, Knight R, Harries-Jones R, de Silva R, Matthews WB. Creutzfeldt-Jakob disease and blood transfusion. Lancet 1993; 341:205–207.

56. van Duijn CM, Delasnerie-Lauprêtre N, Masullo C, Zerr I, de Silva R, Wientjens DPWM, Brandel J-P, Weber T, Bonavita V, Zeidler M, Alpérovitch A, Poser S, Granieri E, Heye N, Hensen S, Müller N. Creutzfeldt-Jakob disease and blood transfusion (letter). Lancet 1994; 343:298–299.

57. Brown P, Rohwer RG, Dunstan BC, Macauley C, Gajdusek DC, Drohan WN. The distribution of infectivity in blood components and plasma derivatives in experimental models of transmissible spongiform encephalopathy. Transfusion 1998; 38:810–816.

58. Sullivan MT, Schonberger LB, Kessler D, et al. Creutzfeldt-Jakob disease (CJD) investigational lookback study. Transfusion 1997; 37(suppl):2S.

59. Operaskalski EA, Mosley JW. Pooled plasma derivatives and Creutzfeldt-Jakob disease (letter). Lancet 1995; 346:1224–1224.

60. Evatt BL. Prions and hemophilia: assessment of risk. Haemophilia 1998; 4:628–633.

61. Rahman A, Bullman TA, Kang HK, Muniz A, Kizer KW, Roselle GA, Booss J. A search for Creutzfeldt-Jakob disease in veterans treated with potentially contaminated blood products. Infect Control Hosp Epidemiol. In press.

62. Créange A, Gray F, Cesaro P, Adle-Biassette H, Duvoux C, Cherqui D, Bell J, Parchi P, Gambetti P, Degos J-D. Creutzfeldt-Jakob disease after liver transplantation. Ann Neurol 1995; 38:269–272.

63. Busch MP, Glynn SA, Schreiber GB. Potential increased risk of virus transmission

due to exclusion of older donors because of concern over Creutzfeldt-Jakob disease. Transfusion 1997; 37:996–1002.

64. Klein MA, Frigg R, Flechsig E, Raeber AJ, Kalinke U, Bluethmann H, Bootz F, Suter M, Zinkernagel RM, Aguzzi A. A crucial role for B cells in neuroinvasive scrapie. Nature 1997; 890:687–690.

65. Dodelet VC, Cashman NR. Prion protein expression in human leukocyte differentiation. Blood 1998; 91:1556–1561.

66. Centers for Disease Control. Adverse ocular reactions following transfusions—United States, 1997-1998, MMWR 1998; 47:49–51.

67. Korth C, Stierli B, Streit P, Moser M, Schaller O, Fischer R, Schulz-Schaeffer W, Kretzschmar H, Raeber A, Braun U, Ehrensperger F, Hornemann S, Glockshuber R, Riek Safar J, Wille H, ltri V, Groth D, Serban H, Torchia M, Cohen FE, Prusiner SB. Eight prion strains have PrPSc molecules with different conformations. Nat Med 1998; 4:1157–1165.

68. Otto M, Wiltfang J, Schuetz E, Zerr I, Otto A, Pfahlberg A, Gefeller O, Uhr M, Giese A, Weber T, Kretzschmar HA, Poser S. Diagnosis of Creutzfeldt-Jakob disease by measurement of S100 protein in serum: prospective case-control study. BMJ 1998; 316:577–582.

69. Dormont D. Evaluation du risque de transmission des agents transmissibles non conventionnels par l'albumine plasmatique humaine. (Evaluation of transmission of unconventional agents by human albumin.) Ann Franc Anesth Reanim 1996; 15:560–568.

70. Lynch TJ, Weinstein MJ, Tankersley DL, Fratantoni JC, Finlayson JS. Considerations of pool size in the manufacture of plasma derivatives. Transfusion 1996; 35:513–529.

71. Hsich G, Kenney K, Gibbs CJ, Lee KH, Harrington MG. The 14-3-3 brain protein in cerebrospinal fluid as a marker for transmissible spongiform encephalopathies. N Engl J Med 1996; 335:924–930.

72. Billeter M, Wuthrich K, Oesch B. Prion (PrPSc)-specific epitope defined by a monoclonal antibody. Nature 1997; 390:74–77.

16
The Protozoan Parasites—
Malaria and Chagas' Disease

Silvano Wendel
Hospital Sirio Libanes, São Paulo, Brazil

I. INTRODUCTION

Protozoan infections affect millions of people in the world, mainly in tropical, developing countries. Malaria and American trypanosomiasis (Chagas' disease) have been linked to blood transfusion transmission for decades. Both parasites have a complex life cycle involving a definitive host (insect or mammal), and humans are usually intermediary hosts, quite often as a result of invasion of wild habitats, where these diseases are in equilibrium as zoonoses. Transfusion-transmitted parasites are usually restricted to tropical areas, and immunocompromised recipients are the most affected; a few cases of Chagas' disease are reported in industrialized, developed countries, whereas transfusion-transmitted malaria (TTM) has been described in hundreds of recipients worldwide. Nevertheless, the ongoing migration processes that have taken place during recent decades have opened new frontiers for these somewhat geographically restricted diseases.

II. MALARIA

A. Historical Aspects and Epidemiology

The first case of TTM was reported in 1911 by Wolsey (1), and more than 3000 cases have been described so far (2), although these numbers may represent less than 50% of the actual cases (3). Although malaria has been eradicated in almost all European countries, the United States, Australia, and Japan, it is still present in 102 countries (4–6), where more than 120 million people are infected annually, with 1 million deaths and nearly 300 million carrying the parasite. Countries in tropical Africa are responsible for 80% of all clinical cases and more than 90% of all parasite carriers in the world. Excluding the African continent, 90% of cases reported to WHO are from 19 different countries, with some 75% of them concentrated in 9 countries: India, Brazil, Afghanistan, Sri Lanka, Thailand, Indonesia, Vietnam, Cambodia, and China (decreasing order of frequency). Malaria is concentrated in certain regions within a single country. For example, though 85% of the Brazilian geographic territory is exposed to malaria, less than 15% of the Brazilian population lives in the affected area, with nearly 99% of all cases detected in the Amazon region. In addition, nearly 40% of the world population, or 1.8 billion people (1992), still remain exposed to varying degrees of risk of malarial infection (4,5).

Transmission by blood components is either a consequence of the sanitary conditions of a country or region, when complete eradication has not yet been achieved (e.g., tropical Africa, India, Sri Lanka, Brazilian Amazon basin, etc.), or a result of imported cases into developed, nonendemic places by immigrants or travelers from endemic areas—mainly described in France, the United Kingdom, the United States, and Spain (3–11).

The annual incidence of TTM ranges from 0.25 cases/million units in the United States (12) to more than 50 cases/million units in endemic regions (7–9). Even in nonendemic countries where complete eradication has been accomplished, the ever-increasing migration flow played a great role in the last three decades, as observed in France in the 1980s when more than 100 cases were described (10). Table 1 shows the prevalence of infected donors from some endemic and nonendemic countries.

B. The Agent and Its Life Cycle

Human malaria is transmitted by four different species: *Plasmodium falciparum, Plasmodium vivax, Plasmodium ovale,* and *Plasmodium malariae,* all of which require two different hosts to complete their life cycle: a mosquito (*Anopheles*), where the sexual stage ensues, and humans, where the asexual stage is observed.

When infected female mosquitoes bite humans, they release, through their salivary glands, small asexual sporozoites—motile, spindle-shaped, 10–15 μm long organisms—into the bloodstream. These circulate for a very short time (<60 min), until hepatocytes invasion (exoerythrocytic stage), followed by a schizogony step (a repeated nucleus division), which lasts from 5 to 31 days, ending with the rupture of mature schizonts and release of merozoites (from 2,000 for *P. malariae* to 40,000 for *P. falciparum*) into the bloodstream. The merozoites in turn invade circulating red blood cells (erythrocytic stage). Another schizogony step occurs in red cells, with generation of schizonts (ring forms) and subsequent release of additional merozoites (4–24 depending on *Plasmodium* species), infect-

Table 1 Prevalence of Malaria-Infected Donors in Some Countries

Author (Ref.)	Country	% Infected donors	Species	Method
Chikwem et al. (42)	Nigeria	4.0	P.f.	Thick and thin blood films
Ibhanesebor et al. (24)	Nigeria	40	P.f.	Thick and thin blood films
Ferreira et al. (19)	Brazil[a]	32	P.f.	IgG antibodies (IFAT)
		24	P.v.	
		37	P.f.+P.v.	
Kiesslich et al. (20)	Brazil[a]	15.7	P.f.+P.v.	IFAT
		0.8		Thick films
		1.6		Acridine orange (QBC®)
Hong et al. (41)	Vietnam	0.2	P.f.	PCR (repetitive genomic DNA)
Chiodini et al. (27)	United Kingdom	1.5[b] 0.45[c]	P.f.	ELISA (antibody)
Tabor (11)	France	10[b]		IFAT

P.f. = *Plasmodium falciparum*; P.v. = *Plasmodium vivax*; IFAT = indirect immunofluorescence assay; PCR = polymerase chain reaction.
[a]Donors only from the Brazilian Amazon, a highly endemic area. Other parts of the country are not considered.
[b]Donors from endemic, tropical countries.
[c]Donors from nonendemic countries, never exposed to malaria. This group most likely represent false-positive results, as none were confirmed by IFAT.

ing other red cells and continuing this asexual stage. This schizogonic process is regular, lasting 48 hours for *P. malariae, P. vivax,* and *P. ovale* (Tertian fever) and 72 hours for *P. falciparum* (Quartan fever).

The merozoites released from liver cells cannot subsequently reinvade other hepatocytes and perpetuate the process. However, some *P. vivax* and *P. ovale* sporozoites give rise to hypnozoites (a very latent exoerythrocytic form), which stay dormant inside the hepatic parenchyma for approximately up to 5 years before starting the exoerythrocytic schizogonic stage, inducing late relapses if proper treatment is not applied.

In parallel, after several divisions, some erythrocytic parasites undergo another cycle step and differentiate into sexual gametocytes. They are released in the bloodstream and, instead of invading red cells, are ingested by another mosquito during a blood meal, beginning a sexual reproduction (fertilization) in the insect stomach. This step leads to the development of oocysts under the basal membrane, which undergo a sporogony (a reduction division), releasing thousands of free sporozoites in the insect's hemocele that migrate towards the mosquito salivary gland, ending their life cycle (6,11,13,14).

In addition to classical, vectorial transmission, malaria can also be transmitted by blood transfusion, organ transplants, sharing of intravenous drugs or needles, accidental laboratory exposure, or congenitally. The life cycle of *Plasmodium* and the different patterns of transmission are shown in Figures 1 and 2, respectively.

C. Transmission by Blood Components

Infected blood donors may harbor parasites for many years, especially those partially immune from endemic regions where such immunity leads to an absence of symptoms, or after chemoprophylaxis. Different periods of infection are seen for each species; it is widely known that *P. falciparum* can be cleared within one year, although longer periods (8–13 years) have been described. *P. vivax* and *P. ovale* usually do not persist for more than 3–4 years, but infections after 6–8 years or even more have also been described. However, longer periods of longevity ranging from 10 to 50 years were seen for *P. malariae*, as reported in the former Soviet Union and the United States (7–9). Because of the shorter infectivity periods for *P. falciparum, P. ovale,* and *P. vivax,* it seems unlikely that a donor will remain infective after 5 years of infection.

TTM is transmitted by asexual forms present in the red blood cells, usually from asymptomatic donors who carry a low level of parasitemia and, rarely, in the period between subclinical parasitemia and the onset of symptoms (usually associated with previous chemoprophylaxis, a suppressive rather than therapeutic regimen). Gametocytes are not infective, and free merozoites are present in the bloodstream for a very short period and do not maintain viability in the stored units. The chances of infection by circulating sporozoites right after the insect biting, though theoretically possible within a 60-minute period (15), has not been associated with transfusion cases. Transmission from symptomatic donors is very unlikely and, when present, usually occurs in endemic regions.

The minimum number of parasites that leads to infection is not known; for *P. vivax,* a total of 10 parasites/mL was successful in inducing experimental transmission (7). In addition, an infection rate of 1–2 parasites/mL will result in nearly half a million parasites in a single whole blood unit, a number far above the minimum necessary to induce an active infection in the recipient (3).

Although transmission occurs mainly by the use of red cell components, other blood components (untreated liquid or frozen plasma, platelets, and granulocyte concentrates) cannot be regarded as cell-free and, therefore, devoid of viable infective parasites (16). Infectivity remains even in deglycerolized post-thaw units stored at –70°C. Red cell preservatives containing adenine seem to enhance the plasmodia viability. No infection has been associated with freeze-dried plasma or industrialized derivatives (albumin, immunoglobulin, etc.), even if derived from potentially infected donors; these donations can be regarded as

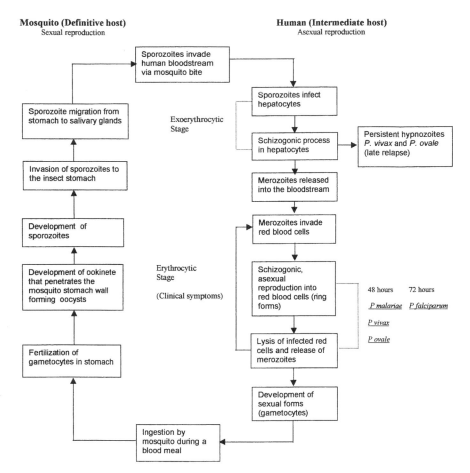

Mosquito (Definitive host)
Sexual reproduction

Human (Intermediate host)
Asexual reproduction

Sporozoites invade
human bloodstream
via mosquito bite

Sporozoite migration from
stomach to salivary glands

Exoerythrocytic
Stage

Sporozoites infect
hepatocytes

Invasion of sporozoites to
the insect stomach

Schizogonic process
in hepatocytes

Persistent hypnozoites
P. vivax and *P. ovale*
(late relapse)

Development of
sporozoites

Merozoites released
into the bloodstream

Development of ookinete
that penetrates the
mosquito stomach wall
forming oocysts

Merozoites invade
red blood cells

Erythrocytic
Stage

(Clinical symptoms)

Schizogonic,
asexual
reproduction into
red blood cells (ring
forms)

48 hours   72 hours

P malariae   *P falciparum*

P vivax

P ovale

Fertilization of
gametocytes in stomach

Lysis of infected red
cells and release of
merozoites

Development of
sexual forms
(gametocytes)

Ingestion by
mosquito during a
blood meal

Figure 1 The life cycle of malaria. Although recently infected donors bearing sporozo-ites in the bloodstream are able to induce infection in experimentally infected volunteers, this is a very unusual situation. TTM has been observed basically from donors in the erythrocytic stage through the transfusion of merozoite-infected red cells.

safe if used exclusively for fractionation. Though viability at 4–6°C storage is less than 5 days for *P. malariae* and up to 10 days for *P. falciparum,* holding units for 7–10 days in order to achieve a relative protection is not justified.

A survey covering the 1973–1980 period showed distribution of 38% for *P. malariae,* 42% for *P. vivax,* 42% for *P. ovale,* and 20% for *P. falciparum* (7). Another survey conducted in the United States (12) covering the 1972–1988 period, when 45 TTM cases were reported, showed that a distribution of 38% for *P. malariae,* 29% for *P. falciparum,* 24% for *P. vivax,* and 9% for *P. ovale.*

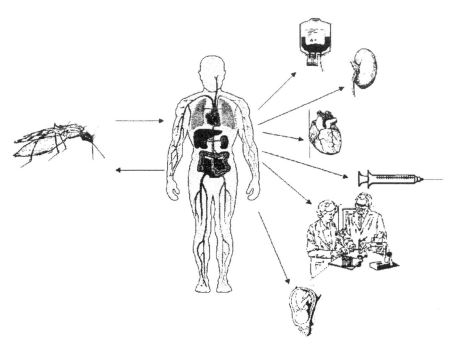

Figure 2 Malaria transmission: The natural, vectorial transmission through *Anopheles* mosquitoes is shown in the left. Malaria can be transmitted through blood transfusion, organ transplants, sharing of intravenous drugs or needles, accidental laboratory exposure, or congenitally.

Conversely, the distribution among different endemic regions also shows a wide variation; in Africa, *P. falciparum* is the most common agent (4,5), while *P. vivax* is the most common in India (17) and Brazil (18–20).

D. Clinical Symptoms

The incubation period depends on several factors: the number of viable transfused parasites, the species and the strain, the host immunity, and the previous use of malarial chemoprophylaxis. On average, TTM has a longer incubation period than that observed in natural transmission, with a 16-day mean period (8–29 days) for *P. falciparum,* a 19.6–day mean period (8–30 days) for *P. vivax* and *P. ovale,* and a 57.2-day mean period (6–106 days) for *P. malariae* (2,7,8).

The first symptoms are usually nonspecific, mainly fever that only reaches its peculiar periodicity in 2 weeks. Since most physicians in nonendemic areas are unaware of this possibility, a period is observed between the onset of the symptoms and diagnosis ranging from 12 to 43 days, but periods of 160 days up to one year have been reported. Even in endemic countries, a long delay may be observed (18). Symptoms are more severe in splenectomized, organ-transplanted, or immunodeficient recipients. In developed countries, TTM is usually associated with previously splenectomized recipients, cardiopulmonary bypass surgery patients, and organ transplant recipients (21–23), whereas in endemic countries, particularly in Africa, neonates who undergo exchange transfusions are one of the most severely affected patient groups (24).

The rate of lethal cases is highly related to late diagnosis (especially in nonimmune recipients) and plays an important role when infection is due to *P. falciparum* (with cerebral, renal, and pulmonary lesions). This was particularly important in the United States after the Vietnam war when a 24-fold higher mortality was seen in patients diagnosed in civilian hospitals compared to those in military hospitals (11). Fatalities are still high, with some reports of up to 20% of cases, much higher than the imported cases (<1%), where the index of suspicion is higher. Thus, one must always bear in mind this possibility whenever fever ensues after a transfusion episode. Since no exoerythrocytic stage is observed in TTM, no relapse is found (irrespective of the causative species) after appropriate treatment.

E. Preventive Measures

A dramatic decrease in TTM should be expected after malaria eradication in the United States. American troops returning from Korea, Vietnam, and, lately, Somalia brought back a remarkable number of infected personnel responsible for TTM, despite preventive measures having been taken. On the other hand, migratory movements, particularly from Africa and India into Europe and from Southeast Asia and South America into North America (3), were also responsible for TTM. Therefore, specific measures have been taken in order to prevent it.

The first strategy is taking an accurate history including place of birth, previous residence locations, immigration status, and a complete account of traveling during the previous 3 years. The use of specific questionnaires aims at excluding three types of infected donors:

1. Nonimmune travelers who acquired malaria abroad, preventing relapses after specific treatment (*P. vivax* and *P. ovale*) or asymptomatic parasitemia following inadequate chemoprophylaxis
2. Military personnel returning from endemic areas
3. Foreign visitors or immigrants from endemic regions who are usually immune and asymptomatic

Although rules in different countries vary (16,25), blood donors are generally not accepted until 6 months after chemoprophylaxis has been finished in the absence of symptoms. As a general policy, those with alleged past infection or who had taken chemoprophylaxis in the presence of symptoms are not accepted during a 3-year period. This measure is highly effective for *P. falciparum, P. vivax,* and *P. ovale* but not for *P. malariae,* for which longer periods of infectivity are recorded. The questions apply only to products where viable red cells are present, but may be disregarded for donations intended exclusively as sources for plasma for fractionation. Since the world malarial zone is so vast, an alphabetical list of countries reporting malaria transmission and a geographical malarial map (provided by WHO) (4,5) should be present in every collection facility. Unfortunately, avoiding infected donors only by using questionnaires brings two additional problems (26):

1. *Low specificity*—A study in the United States (12), where the incidence of TTM is 0.25 cases/million units, claimed that reducing the interval to 6 months after travel, irrespective of prophylaxis, would allow some 70,000–315,000 (mean of 44,000) additional blood units to be collected each year, with an additional calculated risk of 0.03 cases/million units in the annual incidence. The authors stated that the 6-month deferral was accurate for 88% of cases and the 3-year deferral period used for preventing *P. vivax* and *P. ovale* (which accounted for only 33% of cases) would have prevented only one case in 17 years.

2. *Low sensitivity*—After a careful examination of all cases of TTM in the United States, it was stated that at least 50% of them could be avoided if the aforementioned questionnaire was correctly filled out (12); additionally, the interviewer must rely upon the accuracy of the donor's history, which may be in error. This same study reported that a positive history could be ascertained in only 20–30% of the implicated donors, since many of them were infected in childhood or do not remember the episode.

In the light of these problems, some nonendemic countries have introduced specific serological screening (see below), which is applicable only to selected donors at increased risk, such as immigrants from or individuals born in endemic areas or those who had malaria at least 3 years before donation (10,16,27). With this strategy, about 10% of donors in France (10) who were tested by an indirect immunofluorescence assay (IFAT) were confirmed as infective; in the United Kingdom a recent work detecting antibodies by an antiglobulin ELISA (27) with *P. falciparum* antigens reported a 98.5% saving of nonplasma components from donors from tropical areas, which would lead to approximately 40,000 units recovered annually. Other, more radical positions, such as a permanent exclusion of all persons born or having lived in endemic areas, have been proposed, but they should be carefully analyzed, especially in locations with blood shortage (28).

In countries where malaria is endemic, the exclusion for 3 years of donors previously infected may be inappropriate. The use of some screening tests, such as detection of malarial antibodies, may also be inadequate, since most cases denote only a previous infection and not the presence of circulating parasites. In such cases testing for malarial antigens with monoclonal antibodies may be helpful (29).

The use of inactivating agents might be a suitable alternative in the near future. Currently, three agents are under investigation:

1. *Merocyanine 540 (MC 540)*—This photosensitizing dye has been used in preclinical trials for purging leukemia and lymphoma cells (30). In the presence of light irradiation, it has been demonstrated to protect experimental animals challenged with *P. yoelii*–infected cells with no deleterious effect on red cells. Its inactivating action is probably dependent on binding to the parasitophorous vacuole membrane of intracellular parasites. However, its absorption spectrum overlaps that of hemoglobin, requiring that the treatment be performed only at low hematocrits (31), which would carry some inconvenience for a routine red cell malaria inactivation in the blood bank setting.

2. *Pc4*—This silicon phthalocyanin (32), a psoralenic photosensitizing dye, is used for the photodynamic treatment of tumor cells and sterilization of other infectious agents present in blood components (33). A considerable inactivation of *P. falciparum* in infected red blood cells was observed ($\geq$3 $\log_{10}$), in either low (35%) or high (60%) hematocrit levels, after a 40-minute light exposure. In addition, a strong activity was obtained even in the absence of light, rendering this agent a suitable one for malaria inactivation. Although its mechanism is still unknown, it seems very likely that it plays a role through oxidative stress and generation of singlet oxygen, as with crystal violet in the photoinactivation of *Trypanosoma cruzi* (see below). Unfortunately, no further results are available concerning the effect when large volumes (e.g., a full RBC unit) are concerned, including the effect of plasma present in the treated components or their posttransfusional survival.

3. *Crystal violet (gentian violet)*—This agent has been used for *Trypanosoma cruzi* inactivation for over 40 years and has also shown some effect in inactivating *P. berghei*–infected red blood cells (34). However, this issue still deserves further investigation.

1. Screening Based on Detection of Antibodies

Detection of antibodies is achieved mainly by indirect immunofluorescence assay (IFAT), indirect hemagglutination assay (IHA), or ELISA using *P. falciparum*, nonhuman parasites (showing some cross-reactivity with human antibodies), or purified or recombinant antigens. These tests are useful to interpret high-titered or negative sera denoting, respectively, the presence or absence of infection.

However, low-titered sera must, in most cases, be supplemented by a thorough interview with the donor (3). Though IgG antibodies usually correlate with the number of past malarial attacks (19), the presence of antibodies does not necessarily mean the presence of circulating parasites, especially among donors from endemic regions. Antibodies detected by IFAT are present in >95% of infected donors, usually arising 7–14 days after the onset of infection by *P. falciparum* (with longer periods for other species), persisting for several years in those who are subject to continuous exposure (immune donors from endemic countries), especially when infection occurs by *P. malariae*, where a long latency period and high titers are found. After proper treatment, these antibodies tend to persist for 6–12 months. Thus, this method is highly recommended for screening donors in nonendemic countries; a substantial array of experience has been gained in France for over 15 years (10). On the other hand, it seems to be unsuitable in highly endemic regions, where a high number of antibody-positive donors are to be found; in such cases, the adoption of antigen detection is recommended (see below). Although in the window phase the sensitivity of IFAT or ELISA ranges from 50 to 80% (35), it is unlikely that donors in the acute infection period will feel well enough to donate blood, especially in nonendemic countries. A proposed action of combined IFAT and ELISA tests for malarial antibodies screening (27) in blood donors is shown in Table 2. Because of the wide window phase period, detection of antibodies is not recommended as diagnosis of early, acute cases.

2. Screening Based on Detection of Antigens

The most used method of antigen detection is the thick smear test. However, it lacks sensitivity, with a threshold of 10–100 parasites/μL (the lower limit achieved only in the hands of highly qualified technicians), which is by far more than the minimum necessary for the transmission. It is also highly subjective, leads to lapses of concentration by the technical staff because it is a very boring procedure, and cannot be used as a mass screening method, particularly where blood services are not fully established or developed, as in regions where TTM is an important problem. One study in the United States showed prevention by thick smear of only 10% of potential TTM and positivity in 31% (8/26) of donors implicated in TTM (12).

The detection of parasites within erythrocytes has been achieved by IFAT in endemic countries (13,29). Sensitivity reaches 5–30 parasites/μL, but lower levels of parasitemia may reach up to 2.5×10^6 parasites in one unit of blood (7).

PfHRP-2, a water soluble, histidine-rich antigen present in immature *P. falciparum* gametocytes (36), and the production of monoclonal antibodies (mAb) against it have been the basis of two distinct methods for circulating antigen detection. The first is an ELISA test, which achieved a 98% sensitivity in field studies in Thailand (38). The second is a dipstick test, based on mAb

Table 2 Proposed Action as the Result of a Positive Malaria ELISA Screening Test for Donors Donating in Nonendemic Countries

Test results	Action
ELISA screen-reactive or borderline	Repeat ELISA + IFAT; if one is positive, reject donation
ELISA positive IFAT negative	Exclude from further donation No medical follow-up
ELISA positive IFAT positive	Reject donation Clarify history; last possible exposure to malaria (i.e., last visit to malarial area)?
Medical history >2 years	Exclude from further donation No medical follow-up
Medical history 6 months to 2 years	Review in local infectious diseases unit or advise donor: positive antibodies test Will need investigation if febrile in the next year or inform physician of antibody result and suggest options as above

For long-term follow-up all donors should be retested by IFAT. If not exposed to malaria, antibodies will usually disappear within 3 years, and donors may be reintegrated to the donor panel, if not rejected by otherwise cause.
Source: Adapted from Ref. 27.

fixed onto a cellulose strip, which allows detection of circulating *P. falciparum* antigen present in whole blood. This method has an overall sensitivity of 96.5–100% when parasitemia is $\geq 60/\mu L$ (with a lower level in cases with smaller parasitemia) (39) and is particularly useful for screening in urban areas, although comprehensive studies among blood donors are still pending. Unfortunately, both tests dependent on the *PfHRP-2* antigen are species specific and should be regarded with caution in countries where *P. falciparum* is not the most common agent.

Recently, the detection of parasites in the bloodstream using the automatic acridine orange dye test (QBC system®) has gained experience in the Amazon region (20,40), with an overall sensitivity of 73%.

A screening procedure using the polymerase chain reaction (PCR) was published using Vietnamese blood donors, with a sensitivity for *P. falciparum* of 1–4 parasites/50 μL, and for *P. vivax* of 40–130 parasites/50 μL, or roughly 100 times that achieved by blood films. Although this test has been applied in a developing country, its high cost, particularly in regions with limited resources where malaria is of great concern, still renders it unsuitable for routine use.

F. Diagnosis and Treatment

Diagnosis is supported by clinical findings and by the presence of circulating parasites. Thick smears should be done every 8 hours for 2–3 days by an experienced technician, followed by serological tests (which are usually positive when symptoms are present). The current treatment of malaria is quite complex. Chloroquine and several other antimalarial agents are effective against the erythrocytic forms of *P. vivax* and *P. ovale*, while primaquine is used for hepatic forms (which is not necessary for TTM, as only the erythrocytic stage occurs). Quinine is effective against most *P. falciparum* strains, although an increase in resistant forms has been described. Treatment must be rapidly instituted, since outcome correlates with time to treatment. In case of doubt, it is advisable to treat the case as a drug-resistant *P. falciparum* strain until a final diagnosis can be achieved. The subject has been reviewed elsewhere (13,14).

G. Conclusion

A great deal of concern still exists related to the increase in incidence of TTM for several reasons (3): increased travel by asymptomatic individuals from endemic areas to nonendemic regions (e.g., immune donors to a group of nonimmune recipients); the atypical incubation period (6 to >60 days); the lack of awareness of attending physicians in most nonendemic countries, who may additionally be unable to reach an accurate diagnosis when inadequate malarial chemoprophylaxis is performed (which may change TTM natural evolution); the ever-increasing appearance of drug-resistant strains, particularly of *P. falciparum*, which causes the most severe cases; the resurgence of malaria in previously eradicated areas; and, finally, the settlement of individuals in previously unhabitated and virgin areas, mainly in South America, with a dramatic increase of vector-transmitted malaria.

III. AMERICAN TRYPANOSOMIASIS (CHAGAS' DISEASE)

A. Historical Aspects and Epidemiology

American trypanosomiasis, or Chagas' disease, whose agent is the protozoa *Trypanosoma cruzi*, occurs only in the Americas. Chagas' disease was initially described in 1909 in the hinterlands of Brazil, by Carlos Chagas, who demonstrated by a series of several papers the nature of the protozoa, its morphology in the bloodstream, its life cycle in the digestive system of invertebrates (triatomines), cultivation in agar blood, and transmission to vertebrates (43–49).

Transmission by blood transfusion was first suggested by Mazza in Argentina in 1936 (50). Others later supported his original concept in Brazil, Uruguay, and Argentina.

The first donors found to be infected were described in 1949 in Belo Horizonte (Brazil) (51) and confirmed by others in São Paulo in 1951 (52). The first two cases of transfusion-transmitted Chagas' disease were published in 1952 (53) in Brazil, and during the same period the value of chemoprophylaxis with crystal violet (gentian violet) was studied (54). Though regarded as a strictly Latin American problem, Chagas' disease transmission through blood components became recognized in North America in the late 1980s (55–59). Several authors demonstrated the existence of infected donors in this region, although lookback studies have not proved the transmission of *T. cruzi* to any recipient from these infected donors (60–62).

Some 90 million people are at risk in endemic areas and 18–24 million are possibly infected (63,64) in 18 Latin American countries (it has not yet been described in Cuba or the Dominican Republic). It is estimated that 2–3 million people manifest any chronic feature (cardiac or gastrointestinal), with nearly 45,000 annual deaths (65). As a result, Chagas' disease is the main cause of early retirement and years lost from incapacity; when Chagas' disease is measured by disability-adjusted life-years (DALYs), it shows the highest DALY in all Latin America, whereas the remaining infectious diseases (malaria, schistosomiasis, leishmaniasis, leprosy, filariasis, and onchocercosis) with public importance represent altogether less than 25% of infectious disease–related economic burden. On a global scale, Chagas' disease represents the third tropical disease in DALYs, right after malaria and schistosomiasis (66).

B. The Agent

Trypanosoma cruzi is a long and slender protozoa, belonging to the order *Kinetoplastida*, family *Trypanosomatidae*, with a single nucleus, a flagellum, and a kinetoplast, a DNA particle present in the mitochondria. There are three stages in its evolutive life cycle.

1. *Amastigotes*—These are round, intracellular forms, with 1.5–4.0 μm in diameter, found as clusters in infected cells. No flagellum is seen in this form. They are found in vertebrates in macrophages, muscle fibers, testis, ovaries, thyroid and adrenal glands, and in the central nervous system.
2. *Epimastigotes*—These forms have a juxtanuclear kinetoplast and a flagellum. They are rarely found in the bloodstream of vertebrates and are found mainly in the foregut of the insect vector.

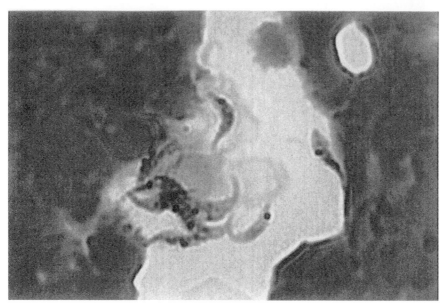

A

Figure 3   (A and B) Trypomastigote forms present in the bloodstream from a patient with acute transfusion-transmitted Chagas' disease. This evolutive form is seen only in the acute phase, where high parasitemia is usually present. In the chronic phase, this form is seldom observed, usually recovered only by enrichment methods.

> 3. *Trypomastigotes*—There are usually C or U shaped, 12–20 μm in diameter, with the flagellum emerging from a postnuclear kinetoplast, allowing great motility (Fig. 3). In vertebrates they are found in the bloodstream, lymph, and cerebrospinal fluid, especially in the acute phase.

There are more than 100 different strains, each with a particular preference for human, domestic, or sylvatic reservoirs (67). In the bloodstream, a polymorphism is also observed where two different "polar" forms are present. One is mainly *macrophagetropic* (slender forms, represented by the Y strain) with preferential parasitism for spleen, liver, and bone marrow cells, with high susceptibility to complement lysis in experimental infected animals, inducing high parasitemia and animal mortality. The *nonmacrophage* form (a broad one, represented by the CL strain) induces a preferential tropism for muscle cells (cardiac and striated), with an almost negligible parasitemia, low acute mortality in infected animals, high resistance to complement-mediated lysis, and a higher susceptibility to chronic persistence. In addition to the morphological differences

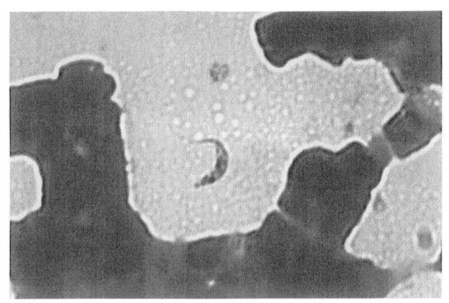

B

among different strains, polymorphism can also be observed according to different isoenzymes patterns (zymodemes) (68,69), kDNA cleavage by RFLP (schyzodemes) (70), or molecular sequencing of several parasite genes (71).

C. The Vector

The invertebrates responsible for transmission of *T. cruzi* are hematophagous bugs belonging to the family *Reduviidae* and subfamily *Triatominae* (Fig. 4), with over 110 different species listed worldwide. Only 40 are adapted to human habitats, and they are a significant vector for *T. cruzi* only in the New World, where they can be detected from latitude 42N (northern California, Utah, Maryland) to latitude 46S (Patagonia). They are known in English as the kissing bug or cone-nose bug, in Spanish as *vinchuca*, and in Portuguese as *barbeiro*. The most important reduviids are shown in the Table 3.

D. Mechanism of Transmission and Life Cycle (Vertebrate-Invertebrate)

In nature, invertebrate triatomines feed basically on monkeys, marmosets, sloths, armadillos, and skunks and live mainly in holes in bark of trees. For peridomestic or intradomiciliary transmission (where cats, dogs, rodents, and humans are the

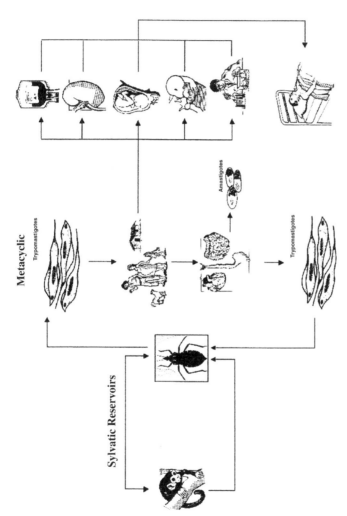

Figure 4 Chagas' disease patterns of transmission. Sylvatic reservoirs (monkeys, marmosets, sloths, armadillos, skunks) perpetuate the zonosis in the wild, while cats, dogs, rodents, and humans are the main domestic reservoirs. In this setting some species have adapted to some very rudimentary huts, where they are prone to feed on humans. If the blood meal derived from an already infected individual, the infective cycle will be closed; additionally, infected persons may transmit Chagas' disease through blood transfusion, organ transplants, congenitally, breast feeding, or by accidental laboratory exposure, leading to new acute cases. Further details about transmission and life cycle can be found in the text.

Table 3 The Most Important Reduviid Species Linked to Chagas' Disease Transmission[a]

Species	Country
Triatoma infestans	Argentina, Bolivia, Brazil, Chile, Uruguay, southern Peru
Rodnius prolixus	Colombia, Mexico, Venezuela, Central America
Triatoma dimidiata	Ecuador, Mexico, Central America
Triatoma sordida	Argentina, Bolivia, Brazil, Paraguay
Triatoma brasiliensis	Brazil
Panstrongylus megistus	Brazil
Triatoma berberi	Mexico
Rodnius pallescens	Panama

[a]*Triatoma infestans*, *Rodnius prolixus*, and *Triatoma dimidiata* are considered as the primary vectors for Chagas' disease transmission, whereas the remaining five species are secondary ones. *T. infestans* is the only one that has mainly an intradomiciliar behavior, being the target of a multicountry effort in South America for its complete eradication (the Southern Cone Ministerial Initiative) (72).

main reservoirs), some species are well adapted to very rudimentary human dwellings made with wattle or bamboo, having unplastered walls with palm-thatched roofs. These huts or shacks are usually found in isolated poor areas of Latin America, grouped into small clusters or scattered around tiny villages. After having a blood meal, the infected bug defecates in the sucking area, leaving infective metacyclic trypomastigotes in feces, entering the host through the feeding puncture or through mucosal membranes or by local scratching. In humans, invasion into the macrophages occurs either via specific cellular receptor or by endocytosis, and after a 20- to 30-hour period, a binary division begins in the cytoplasm, generating 50–500 intracellular amastigotes every 12 hours, with later differentiation to epimastigotes and trypomastigotes, which lyse the infected cells, leading to release into the bloodstream. This, in turn, enables the invasion of other cells, leading to host death or, more frequently, to the development of an immune process that controls parasitemia, although with no parasite eradication. Thus, parasitemia is present only in the acute process, while in the chronic stage of Chagas' disease, subpatent parasitemia is observed, evidenced only by parasite-enrichment methods. There are no spontaneous cures or normal relapses, except when a host immunosuppressive status occurs, such as after organ transplants, oncological treatments, or in AIDS (73).

Chagas' disease is also transmitted congenitally and by breast-feeding, accidental laboratory contamination, organ transplants (74,75), or blood transfusion (Fig. 4) (67).

E. Prevalence Among Blood Donors

Since the Americas comprise more than 20 different countries, a wide array of infected donors is observed in different regions, ranging from as low as 0.01% in the United States to 60% in certain Bolivian cities (63,67,76–80), as shown in Table 4 and Figure 5. In São Paulo, Brazil, a study of over 105,000 blood donations yielded a repeatedly reactive rate of 1.76%, with a final prevalence of 1.03% (95% CI, 0.97–1.09%) using an experimental confirmatory test (Western blot) (81). In California, where 40% of donors are of Latin origin, the estimated prevalence ranged from 0.1 to 1.1% (84). A multicenter study of Hispanic donors (as evidenced by the surname given by the donors) demonstrated a prevalence rate of 0.166% (85). Another U.S. study with donors who responded positively to a broad risk concerning Chagas' disease ($n = 3978$) gave a repeatedly reactive (RR) rate (by ELISA) in 15 (0.38%) donors, 8 (0.201%) confirmed by radio-immunoprecipitation assay (RIPA) (86). As a negative control, donors who during questioning denied risk for Chagas' disease ($n = 3224$) were tested. Four (0.124%) were RR (ELISA); one was (0.031%) confirmed positive on RIPA. Overall 19 (0.264%) of 7,202 donors were RR, with 9 (0.125%) confirmed by RIPA. A study by Winkler et al. (87) of 13,309 donors gave 16 repeatedly reactive samples by ELISA (0.12%), 9 confirmed by RIPA (final rate of 0.07%). Another U.S. (62) study in a low-risk population (Texas and Oklahoma), where 100,089 donors were tested by ELISA found an overall repeat reactivity of 0.15%. Two percent were confirmed by RIPA, giving a final confirmed positivity of 0.003%, or 1 in 33,000 donors. However, all of these infected donors came from a single area in Texas; the final rate in this particular region was 1 of 7700 donors. These data clearly indicate that *T. cruzi*–infected donors are no longer restricted to Latin American countries.

Continuous surveys display a progressive decrease in the prevalence of *T. cruzi* among Latin American blood donors. Three main reasons for this are (a) implementation of efficient sanitary programs, (b) urbanization of the population and (c) replacement of paid donors with volunteer, altruistic donors. Although better transfusion services are in place in Latin America today, many places are devoid of such efficient programs, still rendering blood transfusion as the second most important route for Chagas' disease transmission.

F. Transmission by Blood Components

With the exception of lyophilized plasma (89) and blood derivatives subjected to sterilization procedures (e.g., albumin, gamma globulin and clotting factor concentrates), all blood products are infective. *Trypanosoma cruzi* remains viable at 4°C for at least 18 days (90) or up to 250 days when kept at room temperature (91) (92,93). The viability of the parasite is somewhat lower in frozen compo-

Table 4 Prevalence of *Trypanosoma cruzi* Antibody Among Blood Donors from Several Countries

Country	Samples	Year	Positive results by screening tests (%)	Positive results by supplemental tests (%)
Argentina	194,752	1993	6.7	
	498,380	1994	5,6	
Bolivia	1,298	1990	25.0	
Brazil	105,506	1992	1.97	1.03[a]
	835,764	1993	0.44	
	1,099,601	1994	0.70	
Chile	163,979	1992	1.33	
Colombia	1,716	1994	1.5	
Costa Rica	2,574	1991	1.01	
Ecuador	44,172	1994	0,11	
El Salvador	20,438	1994	1,47	
Guatemala	34,070	1994	1,4	
Honduras	27,885	1994	1.24[b]	
Mexico	3,419	1991–92	1.28	
Paraguay	30,252	1994	5.3	
Peru	1,481	1994	2.9	
Uruguay	57,205	1994	0.8	
Venezuela	961,933	1984–92	1.20[c]	
	584,795	1993	1.14	
United States[d]	988	1991	0.1 to 1.1[e]	
	7,835	1992	0.17[f]	
	3,978	1994	0.38	0.201 (HR)[g]
	3,224	1994	0.12	0.03 (LR)[g]
	13,309	1995	0.12[h]	0.07
	23,978	1997	0.30	0.14 (HR)[i]
	25,487	1997	0.13	0.004 (LR)[i]
	100,089	1997	0.15	0.003 (LR)[j]

Data are mainly derived from screening tests, except when specified in results by supplemental tests.
[a]Western blot.
[b]From Ref. 82.
[c]From Ref. 83
[d]RIPA data from supplemental results in United States: HR = high-risk donors; LR = low-risk donors.
[e]From Ref. 84.
[f]From Ref. 85.
[g]From Ref. 86.
[h]From Ref. 87.
[i]From Ref. 88.
[j]From Ref. 63.
Source: Modified from Refs. 63, 67, 79, 80.

Figure 5 Estimated prevalence of Chagas' disease among blood donors from 16 different countries from the American continent, based on data from Table 4, and considering each country as a whole, although marked regional differences are observed within each country (Adapted from Refs. 63, 67, 80, 104.) Countries depicted in white have unknown data.

nents (up to 24 hours), although several patients with hemophilia treated only with cryoprecipitate have been infected (94,95). In many places, blood transfusion is recognized as the second most important way of transmission of Chagas' disease; on the other hand, it can be recognized as the main important route in industrialized countries (e.g., Canada, the United States, and Spain) (55–58,96).

The true number of reported cases is grossly underestimated, since no more than 300 cases have been recently published in the literature (63,67), clearly representing the "tip of the iceberg." One reason for this is the lack of knowledge or awareness of the disease (especially observed in industrialized, nonedemic areas). In addition, there has been a decrease in observed cases in most developed

Latin American urban services, particularly in Argentina, Brazil, Chile, and Uruguay (97).

Although the number of reported cases in countries of the northern hemisphere is quite low, the recent and intense emigration from these countries is of some concern. Currently, it is estimated that there are at least 7,000,000 legal Latin American immigrants in the United States, 250,000 in Europe, 150,000 in Japan, and 80,000 in Australia (Fig. 6) (63,67,77,98). Although they still do not represent a great percentage of the donor pool, the observed prevalence in some selected donor population in the United States (several times higher than for HIV, HTLV I/II, or HBsAg) clearly confirms what was predicted a few years ago (78). Furthermore, it is expected that 50,000–370,000 immigrants to North America are infected by *T. cruzi* (99–101), nearly 75,000 of whom might bear some cardiac manifestation (102). Chagas' disease is slowly but gradually changing its natural geographical limits, putting other countries at risk unexpected only a decade ago (103).

G. Risk Factors and Probability of Infection

The possibility of infection by blood components depends on several factors, such as the amount of transfused blood, the parasite strain, presence of parasitemia at the time of donation, and the recipient immune status. Additionally, the probability of infection is highly dependent on whether screening tests are performed in blood banks (67,78,104).

1. Unscreened Blood Components

In 1972, Cerisola et al. in Argentina (94) reported that the risk of transfusion-transmitted Chagas' disease could be estimated based on Newton's binomial distribution:

$$P = 1 - (1-f)^n$$

where f = the prevalence of infected donors in the population and n = the number of transfused units. However, no attention was paid to the probability of a patient becoming infected when receiving one unit of infected blood; this is actually not 100%, but rather an average of 12–25% although higher rates (47.6%) were observed in Bolivia, a hyperendemic region (107). Thus, it seems rather prudent to add to the original Cerisola formula the *k* factor for infectivity. It is not known why the infectivity is not very high, but the low parasitemia rate (1 parasite per 20 mL of blood) and the simultaneous presence of inhibitory antibodies in the plasma may be responsible. On the other hand, the survival rate (SR) of recipients 1 or 2 years after the transfusion event, averages 40–50% (108). Therefore, the

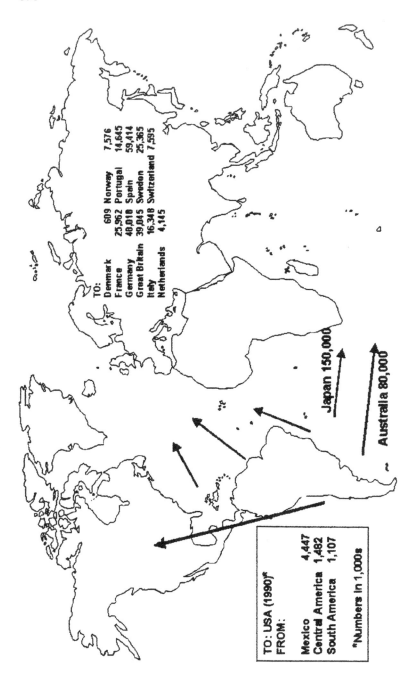

TO:

Denmark	609	Norway	7,576
France	25,962	Portugal	14,645
Germany	48,018	Spain	59,414
Great Britain	39,045	Sweden	25,365
Italy	16,348	Switzerland	7,595
Netherlands	4,145		

Japan 150,000

Australia 80,000

TO: USA (1990)* FROM:

Mexico	4,447
Central America	1,482
South America	1,107

*Numbers in 1,000s

Figure 6 The main pattern of human migration from Latin America to North America, Europe, Australia, and Japan, with the corresponding expected legal immigrants in each region, although the actual number is expected to be more than this. (Based on Refs. 63,67,77.)

final estimated risk formula for transfusion-transmitted Chagas' disease when unscreened units are used should be calculated as:

$$P = 1 - (1-f)^n \times k \times SR$$

In addition, one can speculate that the risk is also proportional to the ratio of components produced (CP) from a single whole blood unit related to the number of individual patients transfused with such units (PtTx), i.e., one whole blood unit is transformed into "x" components that are transfused into "y" recipients. Naturally, this additional index (CP/PtTx) should be included in the formula above; however, it seems to be quite difficult to really estimate it, especially in Latin America.

2. Screened Blood Components

Currently, there are several screening tests for *T. cruzi* antibodies. However, a Brazilian report showed that transmission is still possible despite serological screening. A rate of 0.79% (12 of 1503) false-negative results has been reported, due mainly to the use of a single screening test (IHA, the least sensitive method available). The chances decreased when two different screening procedures are used, a strategy promoted by WHO (110,111), the Pan-American Health Organization (PAHO) (112) and the Brazilian Ministry of Health (113). With the use of two screening methods, Takei reported a sensitivity of at least 99.7% (114).

3. Partially Screened Components

While evaluating data from 12 different Latin American countries (Bolivia, Chile, Colombia, Costa Rica, Ecuador, El Salvador, Guatemala, Honduras, Nicaragua, Paraguay, Peru, and Venezuela) with some 1,200,000 donations in 1993–94, Schmunis et al. (104) reported that only Honduras had a full screening program for *T. cruzi*. Among the other countries, by calculating the number of donations, the coverage of the blood supply, the actual prevalence of infected donors, the sensitivity of the diagnostic kits used for screening, and the fractionation index (i.e., the number of final components produced from the whole blood units donated), these authors reached that the probability of getting a *T. cruzi* transfusion-transmitted infection, P(I), ranged from as low as 2.1:10,000 units in Nicaragua to 219:10,000 units in Bolivia.

A different approach to calculate the residual risk based on screened components would be one linked to the window period, as already calculated for some viral diseases (113,114,115). This method would have limited utility in calculating the residual transfusion risk of Chagas disease, since the likelihood of donors being in the window period is quite remote as infection is usually acquired during childhood. In addition, such studies involve hundreds of thousands of donors, with millions of units tested—a number quite difficult to be fully evaluated in Latin America.

Based on the previous formula and a test sensitivity of 99.7% in a location with a prevalence rate of 1%, one can predict that the risk of an acute transfusion-transmitted Chagas' disease (2–4 months after transfusion) is approximately 1:200,000 units, not accounting for the survival rate. Although these estimates are theoretical and no clear-cut prospective epidemiological studies have confirmed these data, limited studies have reinforced the estimated risk (116).

Data presented at the Brazilian Ministry of Health in 1999, using the assumptions previously reported (104) and a national prevalence of 0.83%, showed that this risk would now be 1:109,000 units (117) in Brazil.

H. Clinical Symptoms in Recipients

The clinical findings observed in recipients of infected units are almost the same as those observed when infection occurs by insect transmission, except that the chagoma of inoculation, a typical swelling of skin, face, or eyelids (representing the entry site of parasites), is not observed. The incubation period varies from 20 to 40 days (range 8–120 days). Fever is by far the most common and sometimes the only manifestation. Lymphadenopathy and hepatosplenomegaly may also be present, and the association of these latter symptoms must always be suspected as Chagas' disease in recipients transfused from untested Latin American donors.

Cardiac arrhythmia, with disturbances of atrioventricular conduction, ECG alterations, or reduction of ejection fraction may occur, leading to pericardial effusion and/or cardiac arrest. Death, although uncommon, may be seen in the most severe cases, usually in immunocompromised recipients.

The central nervous system can also be affected, with somnolence, fatigue, and tremors as the most common symptoms. Myoclonus, seizures, meningitis, or meningoencephalitis, although very rare, is seen in the most severe cases, usually in immunocompromised patients.

The gastrointestinal system is usually spared in acute Chagas' disease. A key feature of transfusion-transmitted Chagas' disease is that approximately 20% of infected recipients are completely asymptomatic, raising no suspicion of diagnosis.

After the acute phase, a spontaneous recovery will ensue after 6–8 weeks, but may extend up to 4 months. Thereafter, the disease follows its natural course to an indeterminate phase (persisting for years or decades), which represents the majority of cases. The chronic phase, with cardiac, gastrointestinal, or neurological symptoms, is observed after several years and usually is not linked to an acute phase.

When the heart is affected, the myocardium becomes thin, with right and left chamber enlargement. Disturbances of atrioventricular conduction and

Adams-Stokes syndrome (due to right bundle branch block) may occur. Apical aneurysm of the left ventricle with attached thrombi to the endocardium is often found, leading to peripheral embolism.

The gastrointestinal system is compromised in 8–10% of patients, with denervation of autonomic parasympathetic ganglia (Auerbach's plexus) with esophageal or colonic hypotonia. Enlargement of internal organs (esophagus or colon) are known as megasyndromes (e.g., megacolon or megaesophagus).

I. Clinical Symptoms in Donors

One of the key issues concerning the clinical findings among blood donors is that they are, in the vast majority, asymptomatic. Nevertheless, they can be subdivided into three main groups.

1. *Serological Chagas' disease*—Only antibodies are found, without any evidence of symptoms, comprising 60–80% of all infected donors.
2. *Latent chronic phase*—Donors show some visceral abnormalities as evidenced by different diagnostic tests (x-ray, CT scan, ECG) but are still asymptomatic, requiring a close monitoring and follow-up, since clinical symptoms may develop in the future.
3. *Symptomatic donors*—Considered the tip of the iceberg; many times the symptoms are not persistent or specific.

As there can be an overlapping between the two latter groups, the true prevalence of each one is difficult to determine, although about 50% of patients with any heart or gastrointestinal abnormalities show clinical symptoms. According to Gontijo (118), a study of 291 chagasic donors revealed that 54% were in the indeterminate phase, 38% had cardiac symptoms, 18% had digestive symptoms, and 10% had both cardiac and digestive symptoms. Among them, 79.5% with chronic cardiopathy and 75% with esophagopathy were in the initial stage of clinical evolution; severe heart disease was found in only 3.1% of cases.

J. Preventive Measures

Prevention of Chagas' disease can be accomplished by three different strategies (119).

1. Anamnesis and Questionnaires to the Donors

Paid blood donors are no longer accepted in Brazil, although they still represent almost 40% of donors in some Latin American regions (most notably in Bolivia). An increased rate of infected donors is associated with a higher age, first-time donation and longer duration of living in endemic areas (120,121). In endemic and nonendemic regions, donors who lived in infested dwellings or acknowledge having been bitten by the bug must be deferred from donation. Specific questionnaires are in use in California to identify high-risk donors; in 70 of 3492 eligible donors who were disqualified due to their answers, 45 samples were tested for *T. cruzi* antibodies, and two had a positive result (122); similar findings were reported in a subsequent North American study (86).

2. Serological Tests

Several method are available for screening, some of which are licensed in the United States. Complement fixation was gradually replaced by IHA, IFA, or ELISA, but none can be considered 100% sensitive. The possibility that serological markers currently in use in blood banks (e.g., HBsAg, anti-HCV, -HIV, -HTLV I/II, -HBc, ALT, or syphilis) could be used as surrogate markers for *T. cruzi* was evaluated in 26,365 Brazilian donors (121). A very slight association was observed only between syphilis in female donors ($p = 0.005$), but the low number of cases ($n = 4$) precluded considering this to be a potential surrogate once the same effect was not found in male donors or when the whole group was considered. Thus, it seems that if *T. cruzi*–infected donors are to be screened, specific serological tests must be performed. Unfortunately, mandatory serological screening is not a current approach in all Latin American countries, except for Argentina, Brazil, Honduras, Paraguay, Uruguay, and Venezuela. Chile only applies it in endemic regions. In Ecuador, although not mandatory, the majority of Blood Services utilize testing.

3. Chemoprophylaxis

Because some countries still have a high prevalence of *T. cruzi*–infected donors, it is almost impossible to find enough noninfected donors to meet blood supply needs. In addition, some of these areas are poor and devoid of a sophisticated blood service. Also, some countries with a very low prevalence of infected donors still do not consider Chagas' disease a transfusion problem. Thus, it seems quite reasonable to develop the sterilization of blood components, a procedure currently under consideration in Bolivia, as advised by WHO (123). The first attempt to promote sterilization of whole blood was by addition of thimerosal in 1952 (124). Subsequently, other drugs were tested. An ideal model for screening drugs has been developed, and more than 1000 drugs have been tested so far; among them, only a few showed some trypanocidal effect. To have some value as a chemoprophylactic agent, a drug must fulfill the following criteria, irrespective of its mode of action (125).

1. The drug must be active at pH 7.4 and at temperatures ranges from –30 to 22°C, at which blood components are stored.

2. The drug must be active in undiluted blood and not adversely affect the main metabolic and energetic pathways of red blood cells, platelets, and plasma proteins throughout their storage period. In addition, no interference must arise with the original antigenic composition of human cells, nor should new antigens be generated.

3. The drug must not only be safe, but must also be used at a concentration that, when transfused into the recipient, should not cause any pharmacological response for which it was originally designed.

Crystal Violet. This phenylmethanic dye totally eradicates *T. cruzi* viability within 24 hours at a concentration of 1:4000 or 200 µg/mL (0.6 mM) (54). It comprises 96% of the composition of gentian violet, the main commercial salt available (the other components are penta- and tetramethylparasaniline, the latter known as brilliant green). The structural formula of crystal violet and its mechanism of action are shown in Figure 7.

Mechanism of action. Crystal violet is reduced in the organism in the presence of NADPH, forming carbon-centered free radicals, which are able to remove hydrogen from other molecules, be added across unsaturated bonds, or combine with themselves to form dimers (126,127). This carbon-centered free radical can also auto-oxidize, producing a superoxide anion ($\bar{O_2}$). This anion, in the presence of superoxide dismutase (SOD), is converted into hydrogen peroxide (H_2O_2). Because *T. cruzi* is deficient in catalase and reduced gluthatione (GSH), which degrades H_2O_2 in H_2O and O_2, whenever there is an increase in H_2O_2, a direct trypanocidal effect is observed; this can also be enhanced by the action of Fe^{2+}. The interaction between $\bar{O_2}$ and H_2O_2 generates the hydroxyl radical (OH·), one of the most toxic radicals, which targets the organism's mitochondria. Since the action of crystal violet is not immediate, an incubation period is necessary for complete parasite kill (24 hours at 4°C). The presence of light enhances this reaction 17-fold (126) additionally, reducing agents such as ascorbate acid will increase H_2O_2 generation (128). A combination of light (130 W/m^2) and ascorbate (10 mM) reduce both the time exposure (20 min) and the dye concentration (1:16,000 or 0.4 mM) with the same efficacy (129,130). Generation of H_2O_2 is not toxic to red or white blood cells because there is a high activity of catalase and GSH in these cells. Furthermore, the dilution effect after transfusion leads to a low concentration of H_2O_2 in the recipient.

Parasite sensitivity. A study of a patient in the acute phase whose blood (treated with crystal violet at a concentration of 1:2000 for 48 hours) was deliberately administered to a volunteer showed no evidences of transmission, seroconversion, or xenodiagnosis in the recipient up to 90 days after the transfusion; an untreated sample was highly infective when injected in experimental mice (131). The effect of crystal violet has been extensively studied in blood from

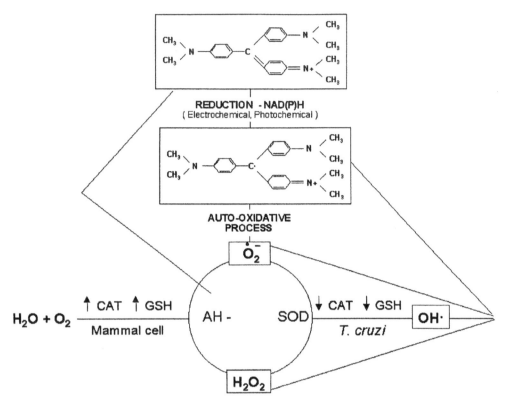

Figure 7 Mechanism of action from crystal violet against *Trypanosoma cruzi*. CAT, Catalase; AH, ascorbate; GSH, reduced gluthatione; SOD, superoxide dismutase. (Adapted from Refs. 126–129.)

donors belonging to the chronic phase. It has been proved to be effective against all parasite stages (amastigotes, epimastigotes, and trypomastigotes) (126,132) and several different strains (e.g., Y, FL, G, J, M, Peru, and Sonya). In an experimental study with 18 recipients transfused with seropositive treated blood, none developed infection (133). Rezende et al. (134) reported that among a group of 774 recipients transfused with unscreened blood components, at least 300 of which could be assumed to derive from infected donors, none developed acute or chronic infection. The Brazilian experience using over 50,000 units has confirmed the efficacy of crystal violet treatment (129).

Side effects.   There are some mild effects on red blood cells (Rouleaux formation), but no changes in hemoglobin, pO_2, pCO_2, pH, Na^+, or K^+ have been observed. ATP and 2,3 DPG levels are slightly decreased, but the results are not statistically different from controls. The major imbalance of crystal violet occurs on platelets, perhaps by a direct action on the mitochondrial calcium metabolism (135). In recipients, a slight purple color is observed that lasts for 24 hours, which must not be considered an obstacle to use in highly endemic and remote areas, particularly when developed blood services are not available. In addition, crystal violet has been shown to be carcinogenic in rodents, but no effect was observed in humans (136). The maximal infusion dosage into recipients is still uncertain, although one report states it as 5–10 mg/kg (easily achieved with 2500 mL of treated whole blood); its effect in massive transfusions is contradictory. Infusion of crystal violet in infants is associated with white blood cell depression. When used for other therapeutic purposes, it leads to gastrointestinal irritation (nausea and vomiting), skin necrosis, thrombophlebitis, and keratoconjunctivitis. The long-germ effect is also unknown, although some patients successfully transfused with over 36,000 mL of treated blood over a 6-month period have been reported (134).

Pc4. This phthalocyanin has also been discussed in Section II. A complete inactivation ($\geq$4–5 log $_{10}$ kill) of *T. cruzi* (Y strain) was observed at 2 μM with 7.5 J/cm^2 for FFP and 15 J/cm^2 for red blood cells after a 5-minute treatment with photoirradiation (137). As with crystal violet, the main target for *T. cruzi* inactivation is the protozoan mitochondria, where a swelling and a shearing effect upon the kinetoplast is observed; in the absence of light irradiation, less extensive damage is observed. Unfortunately, no clinical studies dealing with survival rates of transfused red blood cells have been published so far.

Other Agents. Phenolic antioxidants, amphotericin B, imidazole derivatives, quinolines (WR6202), and gamma irradiation have been tested, but all either failed to prove a superior effect over crystal violet or are still pending further safety studies. Recently, the role of leukocyte filters in *T. cruzi* retention has been studied; preliminary studies achieved a partial protection in mice heavily transfused with the Y strain (a highly pathogenic strain) in doses 500–1000 higher than observed in chronic infected donors (138–140).

K. Laboratory Screening

Several laboratory methods for blood donor screening are available.

1. Detection of Antibodies

Because of the easy application of the procedure and its relative low cost and high sensitivity (though with variable specificity), methods aimed at *T. cruzi* antibody detection are currently in use as a routine clinical diagnosis or as a blood donor screening procedure. Several methods are commercially available in Latin America and the United States. The majority use whole parasites or crude lysates as the antigen source, although some research has been based on the development of synthetic peptides or recombinant antigens. *Trypanosoma cruzi* antibody titer is quite variable in an infected population and usually bears no relationship to clinical symptoms; it also varies in the same individual during his or her lifetime.

The current serological methods are prone to cross-reacting with sera containing antibodies against other infectious agents, such as yeasts, *Leishmania* (Kala-azar and mucocutaneous leishmaniasis), *T. rangeli* (a nonpathogenic agent found in Venezuela, Colombia, Peru, Ecuador, Panama, and Costa Rica), *T. gambiense* (the agent of the sleeping sickness or African trypanosomiasis), *H. muscarum, L. seymoury, C. fasciculata,* and other trypanosomatids. Additionally, nonspecific IgM directed against phosphocoline (145), an antigenic fraction widely present in several mycobacteria and parasites, is also responsible for cross-reactivity, rendering the serological methods for *T. cruzi* antibody detection still open for improvement. One has also to bear in mind that inconclusive results are seen in approximately 3–5% of all blood donors, characterized by a reactive result in only one assay (usually with clear negative or very low titer in a second test). Even when a sample displays a clear reactive pattern, one cannot expect a high positive predictive value. These events usually pose a major problem in counseling of donors. For this reason, supplemental assays are also necessary in order to confirm the screening tests. Finally, it is currently rather difficult to obtain seroconversion panels as a result of the successful eradication of disease in several countries, which makes the standardization of new tests a very difficult task.

The main serological methods used for antibody detection are described in the following sections (114,146).

Complement Fixation. This, the first serological test, was described in 1913. It shows low sensitivity in acute cases (<35%), reaching maximum sensitivity (90–95%) within 4–6 weeks after infection. Although very inexpensive, the difficulties found in standardizing all components of the assay and low sensitivity, render this test unsuitable for routine screening.

Latex Agglutination. This test is based on the principle of aqueous antigen solution fixed onto latex particles, rendering a visual agglutination in the presence of antibodies. It also has a variable sensitivity and specificity and is used only in some remote areas of Latin America.

Direct Agglutination. This test is based on epimastigote forms treated with trypsin and fixed in formaldehyde, which are directly agglutinated in the presence of antibodies. Treatment of sera with 2-mercaptoethanol allows also a distinction between IgG and IgM antibodies. Because of its high sensitivity in the acute phase, it is particularly useful in those rare cases. However, false-positive results are usually found in the presence of heterophil antibodies or nonspecific agglutinins. Because of its relative high cost and the difficulty in finding suitable commercially available reagents, this method is not used currently as blood donor screening.

Indirect Hemagglutination Assay. Aqueous, soluble epimastigote extracts can be easily fixed onto avian, sheep, or human red cells treated with tannic acid, glutaraldehyde, or formaldehyde (147), maintaining satisfactory stability for several months; several commercial kits are available. Although widely used with easy performance, this method shows a lower sensitivity than IFAT or ELISA (148–150).

Indirect Immunofluorescence Assay. This test is based on fixed cultured cells on slides and read by fluorescence microscopy (151,152). This very sensitive test is usually the first to detect seroconversion samples (both IgM and IgG). The practical performance of the test, its commercial availability, the long storage period, relatively low cost, and high sensitivity were responsible for its wide use as a screening test in Latin American countries since the mid-1970s. There are two main problems with IFAT: the first is its nonapplicability to high-volume screening. The second is its relatively high rate of false-positive results, since the antibodies react mainly against intact membrane antigens, which are common to other agents (especially *Leishmania* spp.) or epitopes displaying phosphocholine (145). There is a wide array of autoimmune antibodies that also show considerable cross-reactivity (153).

ELISA. Since the early report by an immunoenzymatic test using crude lysates (154) with some problems in its early phase (155,156) several important improvements have been developed, including more purified antigens that enhanced the sensitivity and specificity of the test (157–159). Recombinant proteins or synthetic peptides show better specific results than parasite extracts (lower cross-reactions) (160,161) but still have variable sensitivities according to the patient and clinical manifestation of the disease, but still have to enhance the sensitivity, an alternative would be to combine several recombinant antigens or synthetic peptides to sensitize microwells. However, some interferences, such as histeric hindrance, leads to poorer results for the mixed antigens than for individual antigens (159,162), still leaving this alternative for the future. The possibility of automation and large use to several samples make this method as the most reliable one for screening blood donors. Several kits are commercially available, including in the United States, all based in epimastigote antigens.

2. Supplemental Tests

As previously discussed, there is still a need for good supplemental assays in order to validate the original antibody screening tests used in the blood bank. Currently, two assays are under evaluation.

Western Blot and Line Immunoassay. Crude or purified antigens are run in polyacrilamide gel electrophoresis and then transferred onto nitrocellulose strips. All reactive bands are detected by an immunoenzymatic reaction. Although this method is widely used for viral tests, there are still several problems when it is applied to *T. cruzi.* The first one is the large number of bands present in the test, according to each antigenic preparation, with some authors reporting up to 15 or 20 different bands ranging from 10 to 300 kDa; in addition, two-dimensional electrophoresis reveals the presence of different proteins with the same molecular weight (163). The second problem is that several antibodies are not quite specific and when eluted from a single band and put again to react against a new nitrocellulose strip, specimens will react against bands other than those originally eluted (164). The sensitivity of Western blot has been reported to range from 86.8 to 100% (116,165,166). Highly purified antigens (natural or recombinant) or synthetic peptides on nitrocellulose strips have been developed either in combination or individually, as single (167) or multiple line assays (168–170).

Radioimmunoprecipitation Assay. Cultured epimastigotes, when placed in a medium containing a radioisotope (^{125}I or ^{35}S), will incorporate radioactivity, which will be demonstrated when lysed forms are reacted against specific antibodies present in the serum. Two major glycoprotein bands are related to a positive result: gp 72 and gp 90 (171). With some slight modifications in the principle, there are three groups in the United States (87, 171,172) currently in the process of validating the method; however, due to its complexity and high cost, it will be restricted to only a few labs.

PCR. Chagas' disease is a model of intense PCR efforts due to the relative low sensitivity and technical difficulties involved with xenodiagnosis of and hemoculture attained from chronic patients; in addition, both methods require as long as 120 days to reach a conclusive result.

The main difficulty faced in applying PCR for the detection of Chagas' disease in chronic patients derives from the low and intermittent parasitemia observed in an important fraction of chronic carriers. In order to obviate that, investigators have focused on DNA sequences largely represented on the *T. cruzi* genome, such as on the kinetoplast (141). Even though no methodology has achieved 100% sensitivity compared to serology of chronic patients, the results of all published comparative studies clearly favor the use of PCR for confirmation of a serology-positive result for Chagas' disease.

One problem still unsolved is the large blood volume that must be sampled and extracted to detect *T. cruzi* DNA by PCR. PCR methods achieve a sensitivity of about one parasite in 20 mL of blood, but chronic carriers may harbor a parasitemia less than that amount.

There has been a report of a PCR method based on DNA extracted from serum that achieved similar results when whole blood DNA was obtained from the same samples, which led investigators to suggest that serum could replace whole blood for PCR detection of *T. cruzi* (142). These results must be interpreted with caution based on the fact that parasites tend to remain on the buffy coat of separated blood, as observed by many groups.

PCR is currently applied for the diagnosis of Chagas' disease in both chronic and acutely infected patients and is under scrutiny as a confirmatory test for blood banks. It is also the method of choice for testing chemotherapeutic agents for *T. cruzi* on experimentally infected animals (143), and a quantitative PCR method has been developed that can be used to monitor patients during treatment (144).

L. Therapy

Treatment of acute cases is done by controlling the symptoms and by the use of nifurtimox or benznidazole (173). These drugs are effective only in the acute phase and should be used immediately after diagnosis; benznidazole might be effective in the chronic phase in infected children (174), though it is not devoid of severe side effects. The clinical management of chronic Chagas' disease is directed toward the control of signs and symptoms, but no permanent cure can be achieved.

M. Conclusion

As in malaria, several problems related to the geographical distribution, pattern of emigration, high number of asymptomatic donors, lack of medical knowledge to correctly diagnose most of the cases, particularly in developed countries, and the still pending technical refinements for laboratory screening result in Chagas' disease remaining a major public health problem in all American countries. In addition, even with complete vectorial elimination, Chagas' disease will remain as a zoonosis. Millions are already infected, requiring medical attention throughout their lifetime. Finally, some asymptomatic patients are women of childbearing age, who will continue to propagate the disease congenitally. Nevertheless, continuous efforts in several countries are yielding positive results; complete elimination of the main vector is expected in fewer than 10 years. Also, one can speculate that, given the association between exposure and age (120,121), it is likely that no further vectorially contaminated donors younger than 30 years of age will be found within 10–20 years in Brazil (175). Thus, it seems that the strategies currently developed to prevent transfusional transmission of Chagas' disease will certainly need a reassessment in a decade. This is a remarkable feat, because only 100 years will have elapsed between the discovery and elimination of Chagas' disease, an unprecedented accomplishment in the history of human infectious diseases.

REFERENCES

1. Woolsey G. Transfusion for pernicious anaemia: two cases. Ann Surg 1911; 53:132–135.
2. Turc JM. Malaria and blood transfusion. In: Westphal RG, Carlson KB, Turc JM, eds. Emerging Global Patterns in Transfusion-Transmitted Infections. Arlington, VA: AABB, 1990:31–43.
3. International Forum: Which are the appropriate modifications of existing regulations designed to prevent the transmission of malaria by blood transfusion, in view of the increasing frequency of travel to endemic areas? Vox Sang 1987; 52:138–148.
4. WHO. World malaria situation in 1990. Weekly Ep Rec 1992; 67:161–168.
5. WHO. World malaria situation in 1990. Weekly Ep Rec 1992; 67:169–176.
6. Gilles HM, Warrell DA. Bruce-Chwatt's Essential Malariology. 3rd ed. London: Edward Arnold, 1993.
7. Bruce-Chwatt LJ. Transfusion malaria revisited. Trop Dis Bull 1982; 79:827–840.
8. Bruce-Chwatt LJ. Transfusion malaria. Bull WHO 1974; 50:337–346.
9. Bruce-Chwatt LJ. Blood transfusion and tropical disease. Trop Dis Bull 1972; 69:825–862.
10. Chataing B. Prevention du paludisme transfusionel. Rev Franc Transf Immuno-hematol 1988; 31:81–88.
11. Tabor E. Infectious Complications of Blood Transfusion. New York: Academic Press, 1982.
12. Nahlen BL, Lobel HO, Cannon SE, Campbell CC. Reassessment of blood donor selection criteria for the United States travellers to malarious areas. Transfusion 1991; 31:798–804.
13. WHO. The biology of malaria parasites. Technical Report Series 743. Geneva: World Health Organization, 1987.
14. López-Antuñano FJ, Schmunis G, eds. Diagnosis of malaria. Scientific Publication No. 512. Washington, DC: Pan American Health Organization, 1990.
15. Fairley NH. Trans R Soc Trop Med Hyg 1947; 40:621–676.
16. Council of Europe. Guide to the preparation, use and quality assurance of blood components. Strasbourg, 1992: 17.
17. Wells L, Ala FA. Malaria and blood transfusion. Lancet 1985; i:1317–1318.
18. Andrade JCR, Wanderley DMV. Malária induzida no Estado de São Paulo, Brasil. Rev Soc Bras Med Trop 1991; 24:157–161.
19. Ferreira MV, Camargo LMA, Carvalho ME, Ninomia RT, Garcia LAV, Santos FR. Prevalence and levels of IgG and IgM antibodies against *Plasmodium falciparum* and *P. vivax* in blood donors from Rondonia, Brazilian Amazon. Mem Inst Oswaldo Cruz 1993; 88(2):263–269.
20. Kiesslich D, Torres KL, Fraiji NA. Métodos de triagem para Malária em Doadores de Sangue de Área Endêmica. Bol Soc Bras hematol Hemot 1997; 19:21–27.
21. Salutari P, Sica S, Chiusolo P, Micciulli G, Plaisant P, Nacci A, Antinori A, Leone G. *Plasmodium vivax* malaria after autologous bone marrow transplantation: an unusual complication. Bone M Transpl 1996; 18:805–806.
22. Talabiska DG, Komar MJ, Wytock DH, Rubin RA. Post-transfusion acquired

malaria complicating orthotopic liver transplantation. Am J Gastroenterol 1996; 91:376–379.

23. Tran VB, Tran VB, Lin KH. Malaria infection after allogeneic bone marrow transplantation in a child with talassemia. Bone M Transpl 1997; 19:1259–1260.

24. Ibhanesebor SE, Otobo ES, Ladipo OA. Prevalence of malaria parasitemia in transfused donor blood in Benin City, Nigeria. Ann Trop Ped 1996; 16:93–95.

25. Standards for Blood Banks and Transfusion Services—AABB, 15th ed. Bethesda, MD: 1993.

26. Sazama K. Prevention of transfusional-transmitted malaria: Is it time to revisit the standards (editorial). Transfusion 1991; 31:786–788.

27. Chiodini PL, Hartley S, Hewitt PE, Barbara JAJ, Lalloo K, Bligh J, Voller A. Evaluation of a malaria antibody ELISA and its value in reducing potential wastage of red cell donations from blood donors exposed to malaria, with a note on a case of transfusion-transmitted malaria. Vox Sang 1997; 73:143–148.

28. BPAC considers malaria deferral, ICL study, plasma source. Blood Bank Week 10(25):1n4.

29. Choudhury N, Jolly JG, Mahajan RC, Dubey ML, Kalra A, Ganguly NK. Selection of blood donors in malaria endemic countries. Lancet 1988; ii:972–973.

30. Smith OM, Traul DL, McOlash L, Sieber F. Evaluation of merocyanine 540-sensitized photoirradiation as a method of purging malarially infected red cells from blood. J Infect Dis 1991; 163:1312–1317.

31. Smith OM, Dolan AS, Dvorak JA. Merocyanine 540-sensitized photoinactivation of human erythocytes parasitized by *Plasmodium falciparum*. Blood 1992; 80:21–24.

32. Lustigman S, Ben-Hur E. Photosensitized inactivation of *Plasmodium falciparum* in human red cells by phthalocyanines. Transfusion 1996; 36:543–546.

33. Ben-Hur E, Horowitz B. Advances in photochemical approaches for blood sterilization. Photochem Photobiol 1995; 62:383–388.

34. Amato Neto V, Sant'Ana EJ, Pinto PLS, Moura AAB, Duarte MFS, Campos R. Estudo experimental sobre a possibilidade de prevençá da malária pós transfusional através do uso de violeta de genciana. Rev Saúde Publ S Paulo 1987; 21(6):497–500.

35. Draper CC, Sirr SS. Serological investigation in retrospective diagnosis of malaria. Br J Med 1980; 2:1575–1576.

36. Parra ME, Evans CB, Taylor DW. Identification of *Plasmodium falciparum* histidine-rich protein 2 in the plasma of humans with malaria. J Clin Microbiol 1991; 29:1629–1634.

37. Taylor DW, Voller A. The development of a simple antigen detection ELISA for *Plasmodium falciparum* malaria. Trans R Soc Trop Med Hyg 1993; 87:29–31.

38. Namsiriponpun V, Wilde H, Pamsandang P, Tiersansern P. Field study of an antigen-detection ELISA specific for *Plasmodium falciparum* malaria. Trans R Soc Trop Med Hyg 1993; 87:32–34.

39. Peyron F, martet G, Vigier JP. Dipstick antigen-capture assay for malaria detection. Lancet 343:1502–1503.

40. Avila SLM, Leandro MC, Carvalho NB, Oliveira MS, Arruk VG, Sanchez MCA, Boulos M, Ferreira AW. Evaluation of different methods for "plasmodia" detection

in well defined population groups in an endemic area of Brazil. Rev Inst Med Trop São Paulo 1994; 36:157–162.

41. Hong VT, VanBe T, Tran PN, Thanh LT, Hien LV, O'Brien E, Morris GE. Screening donor blood for malaria by polymerase chain reaction. Trans R Soc Trop Med Hyg 1995; 89:44–47.
42. Chikwem JO, Mohammed I, Okara GC, Ukwandu NCD, Ola TO. Prevalence of transmissible blood infections among blood donors at the University of Maiducuri teaching hospital, Maiduguri, Nigeria. East Afr Med J 1997; 74:213–216.
43. Chagas C. Nova espécie morbida do homem, produczida por um *Trypanosoma* (*trypanosoma cruzi*): Nota prévia. Brasil Méd 1909; 23:161.
44. Chagas C. Neue Trypanosomen. Arch Schiffs Tropenhyg 1909; 13:120–122.
45. Chagas C. Über eine neue Trypanosomiasis des Menschen. Arch Schiffs Tropenhyg 1909; 13:351–353.
46. Chagas C. Nova tripanozomiase humana. Estudos sobre a morfolojia e o ciclo evolutivo do *Schizotrypanum cruzi* n.g., n.s.p., ajente etiolójico de nova entidade mórbida no homem. Mem Inst Oswaldo Cruz 1909; 1:159–218.
47. Chagas C. Nova entidade mórbida do homem. Resumo geral de estudos etiolójicos e clínicos. Mem Inst Oswaldo Cruz 1911; 3:219–275.
48. Chagas C. The discovery of *Trypanosoma cruzi* and of American trypanosomiasis. Mem Inst Oswaldo Cruz 1922; 15:1–11.
49. Chagas Filho C. Carlos Chagas–Ofícina Gráfica da Universidade do Brazil, 1959.
50. Mazza S, Montana A, Benitez C, Juzin E. Transmisión de "*Schizotrypanum cruzi*" al niño por leche de la madre con enfermedad de Chagas. Publ MEPRA 28:41–46.
51. Pellegrino J. Transmissão da doença de Chagas pela transfusão de sangue. Primeiras comprovações sorológicas em doadores e candidatos a doadores de sangue. Rev Bras Med 1949; 6:297–301.
52. Faria P. Sifilis, Maleita, Doença de Chagas e Transfusão. Folia Clin Biol 1951; 17:113–117.
53. Freitas, JLP, Amato V, Sonntag R, Biancalana A, Nussenszweig V, Barreto JG. Primeiras verfícacões de transmissão acidental da moléstia de Chagas ao homem por transfusão de sangue. Rev Paul Med 1952; 40:36–40.
54. Nussenzweig V, Sonntag R, Biancalana A, Freitas JLP, Amato Neto V, et al. Ação de corantes tri-fenil-metanicos sobre o *Trypanosoma cruzi* "in vitro." Emprego da Violeta de Genciana na profílaxia da transmissão da Moléstia de Chagas por transfusão de sangue. O Hospital 1953; 44:731–744.
55. Geiseler PJ, Ito JI, Tegtemeier BR, Kerndt PR, Krance R. Fulminant Chagas' disease in bone marrow transplantation. 27th Intersc. Conf. on Antimicro Agents and Chemoter. Washington: Am Soc for Microbiol 1987:418.
56. Grant I, Gold JWH, Wittnee M, et al. Transfusion associated acute Chagas' disease acquired in the United States. Ann Intern Med 1989; 111:849–851.
57. Nickerson P, Orr P, Schoeder MC, Sekla L, Johnson J. Transfusion associated *Trypanosoma cruzi* infection in a non endemic area. Ann Intern Med 1989; 111:851–853.
58. Cimo PL, Luper WE, Scouros MA. Transfusion-associated Chagas' disease in Texas: report of a case. Tex Med 1993; 89:48–50.
59. Lenes BA, Leiby DA, Tibbals MA, Olmedo M. A prospectively identified case of

transfusion transmitted *Trypanosoma cruzi*: a defining window period. Transfusion 1998; 10 (suppl):390.

60. Leiby DA, Yund J, Read EJ, Lenes BS, Dodd RY. Risk factors for *Trypanosoma cruzi* infection in seropositive blood donors. Transfusion 1996; 36(suppl):228.

61. Galel S, Wolles S, Stumpf R. Evaluation of a selective donor testing strategy. Transfusion 1997; 37(suppl):296.

62. Leiby DA, Jensen NC, Fucci MC, Stumpf RJ. Prevalence of *Trypanosoma cruzi* antibodies in a blood donor population at low risk. Transfusion 1997; 37(suppl):297.

63. Schmunis GA. American trypanosomiasis as a Public Health Problem, in PAHO: Chagas' disease and the nervous system. Scientific Publication No. 547, Washington DC: 1994:3–29.

64. Hayes RJ, Schofield CJ. Estimación de las tasas de incidencia de infecciones y parasitosis crónicas a partir de la prevalencia: la enfermedad de Chagas en America Latina. Bol Of Sanit Panam 1990; 108:308–316.

65. Moncayo A. Chagas' disease. Tropical Disease Research. Progress 1991–92. Eleventh Programme Report of the UNDP/World Bank/WHO Special Programme for Research and Training in Tropical Diseases (TDR). Geneva: World Health Organization, 1993:67–75.

66. World Bank. The World Bank Development Report 1993. Investing in Health. World development indicators. Washington: University Press, 1993.

67. Wendel S, Brener Z, Camargo M, Rassi A, eds. Chagas disease (American trypanosomiasis): its impact on transfusion and clinical medicine. ISBT, Brasil '92, SBHH, 1992.

68. Miles MA. Further enzymic characters of *Trypanosoma cruzi* and their evaluation for strain identification. Trans Roy Sci Trop Med Hyg 1980; 74:221–237.

69. Miles MA. The epidemiology of South American trypanosomiasis—biochemical and immunological approaches and their relevance to control. Trans Roy Soc Trop Med Hyg 1983; 77:5–23.

70. Morel C, Chiari E, Plessman-Camargo E, Mattei D, Romanha AJ, Simpson L. Strains and clones of *Trypanosoma cruzi* can be characterized by pattern of restriction endonuclease products of kinetoplast DNA minicircles. Proc Natl Acad Sci USA 1980; 77:6810–6814.

71. Avila H, Gonçalves AM, Nehme NC, Morel CM, Simpson L. Schizodeme analysis of *Trypanosoma cruzi* stocks from South and Central America by analysis of PCR-amplified minicircle variable region sequences. Mol Biochem Parasitol 1990; 42:175–188.

72. PAHO-OPS. III Reunión de la Comisión Intergubernamental para la Eliminación del Triatoma infestans y la interrupción de la tripanosomiais Americana Transfusional. OPS/HPC/HCT/94—37:1–21, Montevideo, Uruguay.

73. Nishioka AS, Ferreira MS, Rocha A, Burgarelli MKN, Silva AM, Duarte MIS, Schmitt FC. Reactivation of Chagas' disease successfully treated with benznidazole in a patient with acquired immunodeficiency syndrome. Mem Inst Oswaldo Cruz 1993; 88:493–496.

74. Chocair PR, Sabbaga E, Amato Net V, Shiroma M, Goes GM. Transplante de rim: nova modadlidade de transmissão da doença de Chagas. Rev Med Trop S Paulo 1981; 23:282–282.

75. Ferraz AS, Figueiredo JFC. Transmission of Chagas' disease through transplanted kidney: occurrence of the acute form of the disease in two recipients from the same donor. Rev Inst Med Trop S Paulo 1993; 35:461–463.
76. Dias JCP, Brener Z. Chagas' disease and blood transfusion. Mem Inst Oswaldo Cruz 1984; 79:139–147.
77. Schmuñis GA. *Trypanosoma cruzi*, the etiologic agent of Chagas' disease: status in the blood supply in endemic and non endemic countries. Transfusion 1991; 31:547–557.
78. Wendel S, Gonzaga AL. Chagas disease and blood transfusion: a new world problem? Vox Sang 1993; 64:1–12.
79. Schmunis GA. Tripanosomíase Americana: seu impacto nas Américas e perspectivas de eliminacão. In: Dias JCP, Coura JR, eds. Clinica e terapêutica da Doença de Chagas. Rio de Janeiro: Edotora Fiocruz, 1997:411–427.
80. Wendel S. Doença de Chagas Transfusional. In: Dias JCP, Coura JR, eds. Clinica e terapêutica da Doença de Chagas. Rio de Janeiro: Edotora Fiocruz, 1997:411–427.
81. Wendel S, Neitzert E, Lopes VHG, Batemarchi MV. Evaluation of different screening tests for *T. cruzi* antibodies and correlation with immunoblotting technique. Rev Paul Med 1992; 110: Abstract TTD17.
82. Trujillo FC, Kasten FL, Gutiérrez MMS, Gutiérrez RH. Prevalencia de infección a *Trypanosoma cruzi* en donadores de sangre en el estado de Jalisco, Mexico. Rev Soc Bras Med Trop 1993; 26:89–92.
83. Ache A. Prevalencia de infección humana por *Trypanosoma cruzi* en Bancos de Sangre en Venezuela. Rev Inst Med Trop S Paulo 1993; 35:443–448.
84. Kerndt PR, Waskin HA, Kirhhoff LV, Steurer F, Waterman SH, Nelson JM, Gellert GA, Shulman IA. Prevalence of antibody to *Trypanosoma cruzi* among blood donors in Los Angeles, California. Transfusion 1991; 31:814–818.
85. Pan AA, Brashear J, Schur JD, Winkler MA, Hall H, Shih J, Decker R. Prevalence study and confirmation of seropositive antibodies to *Trypanosoma cruzi* (Chagas' disease) in Hispanic and Non-Hispanic blood donors in the United States. Rev Paul Med 1992; 110(5) (suppl.): Abstract TTD-18.
86. Read EJ, Leiby DA, Dodd RY. Seroprevalence of *Trypanosoma cruzi* (*T. cruzi*) in blood donors with and without risk infection. Blood 1994; 84 (suppl 1): Abstract 1853.
87. Winkler MA, Brashear RJ, Hall HJ, Schur JD, Pan AA. Detection of antibodies to *Trypanosoma cruzi* among blood donors in the southwestern and western United States. II—Evaluation of a supplemental enzyme immunoassay and radio-immuneprecipitation assay for confirmation of seroreactivity. Transfusion 1995; 35:219–225.
88. Leiby DA, Read EJ, Lenes BA, Yund AJ, Stumpf RJ, Kirchhoff LV, Dodd RY. Seroepidemiology of *Trypanosoma cruzi*, etiologic agent of Chagas' disease, in US blood donors. J Infect Dis 1997; 176:1047–1052.
89. Amato Neto V, Leonhardt H, Souza HBWT. Liofilização do plasma: Medida capaz de evitar a transmissão da Doença de Chagas em Bancos de Sangue. Rev Inst Med trop São Paulo 1966; 8:122–124.
90. Sullivan TS. Viability of *Trypanosoma cruzi* in citrated blood stored at room temperature. J Parasitol 1944; 30:200.
91. Weinman D, MacAlister J. Prolonged storage of human pathogenic protozoa with conservation of virulence. Am J Hyg 1947; 45:102–121.

92. Filardi LS, Brener Z. Cryopreservation of *Trypanosoma cruzi* bloodstream forms. J Protozool 1975; 22:398–401.

93. Schlemper BR Jr. Estudos experimentais de quimioprofílaxia de transmissão da doença de Chagas por transfusão sangüínea. Rev Patol Trop 1978; 7:55–111.

94. Cerisola JA, Rabinovich A, Alvarez M, Di Corleho CA, Pruneda J. Enfermedad de Chagas y la transfusion de sangre. Bol Of Sanit Panam 1972; 63:203–221.

95. Lorca M, Lorca J, Child R, Atias A, Conales M, et al. Prevalencia de la infección por *Trypanosoma cruzi* en pacientes politransfundidos. Rev Med Chile 1988; 116:112–116.

96. Villalba R, Fornés G, Alvarez MA, Román J, Rubio V, Fernandez M, Garcia JM, Viñals M, Torres A. Acute Chagas' disease in a recipient of a bone marrow transplant in Spain: case report. Clin Infect Dis 1992; 14:594–595.

97. World Health Organization. TDR News 1999; 59:10.

98. Wendel S. Transfusion-transmitted Chagas' disease. Curr Opin Hematol 1998; 5:406–411.

99. Kirchhoff LV, Neva FA. Chagas' disease in Latin American immigrants. JAMA 1985; 254:3058–3060.

100. Kirchhoff LV. *Trypanosoma cruzi*: a new threat to our blood transfusion supply (editorial). Ann Intern Med 1989; 111:773–775.

101. Kirchhoff LV. American trypanosomiasis (Chagas disease)—a tropical disease now in the United States. N Engl J Med 1993; 329:639–644.

102. Milei J, Mautner B, Storino R, Sanchez JÁ, Ferrans VS. Does Chagas' disease exist as an undiagnosed form of cardiomyopathy in the United States? (editorial). Am Heart J 1992; 123:1732–1735.

103. Wendel S. Chagas disease: an old entity in new places (editorial). Int J Art Organs 1993; 16:117–119.

104. Schmunis GA, Zicker F, Pinheiro F, Brandling-Bennett D. Risk for transfusion-transmitted infectious diseases in Central and South America. Emerg Inf Dis 1998; 4:5–11.

105. Coura JR, Nogueira ES, Silva JR. Indices de transmissão da doença de Chagas por transfusão de sangue de doadores na fase crônica da doença. O Hospital 1966; 69:115–122.

106. Rohwedder RW. Infección chagásica en doadores de sangre y las probabilidades de transmitirla por medio de la transfusion. Bol Chile Parasitol 1969; 24:88–93.

107. Zuna H, Recacoechea M, Bermudez H, Romero A, Castedo J. Transmissión de la enfermedad de Chagas por via transfusional en Santa Cruz de la Sierra, Bolivia. Bol Inf CENENTROP 1979; 5:49–56.

108. Vamvakas EC, Taswell HF. Long-term survival after blood transfusion. Transfusion 1994; 34:471–477.

109. Andrade ALLS, Martelli CMT, Loquetti AO, Oliveira OS, Silva AS, Zicker F. Triagem sorológica para o *Trypanosmoa cruzi* entre doadores de sangue do Brasil central. Bol Of Sanit Panam 1992; 113:19–27.

110. World Health Organization. Parasite antigens. Bull WHO 1975; 52:237–249.

111. World Health Organization. (WHO) report—Newsletter 1982; 18:7.

112. Cura E, Wendel S, eds. Manual de Procedimientos de Control de Calidad para los

Laboratorios de Serologia de los Bancos de Sangre. PAHO/HPC/HPT/94.21, Washington DC, 1994.

113. Brazilian Ministery of Health, Portaria No. 1376, 1993.

114. Takei K. Estudo da eficiência relativa dos diferentes testes serológicos utilizados no diagnóstico da doença de Chagas. Resultados observados na análise de 10.181 soros; doctoral thesis. São Paulo Departamento de Microbiologia e Immunologia do Instituto de Ciências Biomédicas da Universidade de São Paulo, 1982.

115. Lackritz, EM, Satten GA, Aberle-Grasse J et al. Estimated risk of transmission of the human immunodeficiency virus by screened blood in the United States. N Engl J Med 1005; 333:1721–1725.

116. Wendel S, Siqueira RV, Lopes VHG, Batemarchi MV, Neitzert E, Antunes MF, Mejias S. Assessing the performance of *Trypanosoma cruzi* antibody detection currently in use in Brazilian blood centres: a few answers from a large prevalence study. Rev Paul Med 1992; 110(5):16.

117. Souza HM. Chagas Infection Transmission Control: Situation of Transfusional Transmission in Brazil and Other Countries of Latin America. Simósio Internacional Sobre Avanços do Conhecimento da Doença de Chagas 90 Anos após sua Descoberta. Rio de Janeiro, April 1999.

118. Gontijo ECD. Doença de Chagas Transfusional na Região Metropolitana de Belo Horizonte: aspectos clínico-epidemiológicos e a questão institucional. Thesis. Belo Horizonte, Universidade Federal de Minas Gerais, 1989.

119. Wendel S. Blood banking preventive approaches for Chagas disease. Mem Inst Oswaldo Cruz 1993; 88(suppl):59–60.

120. Zicker F, Martelli CMT, Andrade ALLS, Silva SA. Trends of *T. cruzi* infection based on data from blood bank screening. Rev Inst Med Trop S Paulo 1990; 39:132–137.

121. Wendel S, Biagini S. Absence of serological surrogate markers for *Trypanosoma cruzi* infected blood donors. Vox Sang 1995; 69:44–49.

122. Appleman MD, Shulman IA, Saxena S, Kirchhoff LV. Use of a questionnaire to identify potential blood doors at risk for infection with *Trypanosoma cruzi*. Transfusion 1993; 33:61–64.

123. World Health Organization/Panamerican Health Organization. Iniciativa del Cono Sur. VI Reunión Intergubernamental para la eliminación de Triatoma infestans y la interrupcón del la tripanosomiasis americana por transfusión. Documento OPS/HPC/HCT 98/102, 1997.

124. Freitas JLP, Biancalana A, Amato Neto, Nussenzweig V, Barreto JG. Moléstia de Chagas em Bancos de Sangue na capital de S Paulo. O Hospital 1952; 41:99–106.

125. Cover B, Gutteridge WE. A primary screen for drugs to prevent transmission of Chagas' disease during blood transfusion. Trans Roy Soc Trop Med Hyg 1982; 76:633–635.

126. Docampo R, Moreno SNJ, Muniz RP, Cruz FS, Mason RP. Light-enhanced free radical formation and trypanocidal action of gentian violet (crystal violet). Science 1983; 220:1292–1295.

127. Docampo R, Moreno SNJ. Free radicals metabolites in the mode of action of chemotherapeutic agents and phagocytic cells on *Trypanosoma cruzi*. Ver Inf Dis 1984; 6:223–238.

128. Docampo R, Moreno SNJ, Cruz F. Enhancement of the cytotoxicity of crystal violet

against *Trypanosoma cruzi* in the blood by ascorbate. Mol Biochem parasitol 1988; 27:241–248.

129. Souza HM. The present state of chemoprophylaxis in transfusional Chagas' disease (editorial). Rev Soc Bras Med Trop 1989; 22:1–3.

130. Ramirez LE, Lages-Silva E, Painetti GM, Rabello RMC, Bordin JO, Souza HM. Prevention of transfusion-associated Chagas' disease by sterilization of *Trypanosoma cruzi*-infected blood with gentian violet, ascorbic acid, and light. Transfusion 1995; 35:226–230.

131. Amato Neto V, Mellone O. Estudo sobre a efícácia da Violeta de Genciana na profílaxia da transmissão da doença de Chagas em bancos de sangue: investigação em voluntário, receptor de sangue de caso agudo, ao qual foi adicionado o corante. O Hospital 1959; 55:343–346.

132. Schlemper BR Jr. Estudos experimentais de Quimio-profílaxia de transmissão da doença de Chagas por transfusão sangüínea. Rev Pat Trop 1978; 7:55–111.

133. Amato Neto V. Contribuição ao conhecimento da forma aguda da Doença de Chagas—Tese: Faculdade de Medicina da Universidade de São Paulo, 1958.

134. Rezende JM, Zupelli W, Bafutto M. O problema da transmissão da doença de Chagas por transfusão de sangue. Emprego da Violeta de Genciana como medida profílática. Ver Goiana Med 1965; 11:35–47.

136. Docampo R, Moreno SNJ. The metabolism and mode of action of gentian violet. Drug Met Rev 1990; 22:161–178.

137. Gottlieb P, Shen LG, Chimezie E, Bahng S, Keeney ME, Horowitz B, Bem-Hur E. Inactivation of *Trypanosoma cruzi* trypomastigote forms in blood component by photodynamic treatment with phthalocyanines. Photochem Photobiol 1995; 62:869–874.

138. Wendel S, Takaoka DT, Jancsó MM, Mariano M, Fragata Filho AA, Pereira-Chioccola Lourenco AM. A possible role of leukocyte filters to prevent transfusion-transmitted *Trypanosoma cruzi*. Vox Sang 1994; 67(suppl 2):22.

139. Souza HM, Bordin JO, Bordossy L, MacPhereson DW, Blajchman MA. Prevention of transfusion-associated Chagas' disease: efficacy of white cell-reduction filters in removing *Trypanosoma cruzi* from infected blood. Transfusion 1995; 35:723–726.

140. Wendel S, Takaoka DT, Jancsó MM, Mariano M, Leite KM, Chioccola VLP, Lorenço AM, Fragata Filho AA. Is there a role for leukocyte depletion filters to remove *Trypanosoma cruzi* infection from donor blood? Bol Soc Bras Hematol Hemot 1995; 17:25–31.

141. Moser DR, Kirchhoff LV, Donelson JE. Detection of *Trypanosoma cruzi* by DNA amplification using the polymerase chain reaction. J Clin Microbiol 1989; 27:1477–1482.

142. Russomando G, Figueredo A, Almirón M, Sakamoto M, Morita K. Polymerase chain reaction-based detection of *Trypanosoma cruzi* DNA in serum. J Clin Microbiol 1992; 30:2864–2868.

143. Urbina J, Payares G, et al. Cure of short and long-term experimental Chagas' disease using D0870. Science 1996; 273:969–971.

144. Centurion-Lara A, Barrett L, van Voohis WC. Quantitation of parasitemia by competitive polymerase chain reaction amplification of parasite kDNA minicircles

during chronic infection with *Trypanosoma cruzi*. J Infect Dis 1994; 170:1334–1338.

145. Lal RB, Ottesen EA. Phosphocoline epitopes on helminth and protozoal parasites and their presence in the circulation of infected human patients. Trans Roy Soc Trop Med Hug 1989; 83:652–655.

146. Ferreira AW. Serological diagnosis—tests for Chagas disease serodiagnosis: a review. In: Wendel S, Brener Z, Camaro ME, Rassi A, eds. Chagas Disease (American Trypanosomiasis): Its Impact on Transfusion and Clinical Medicine. São Paulo: ISBT, 1992: 179–193.

147. Sasaki AT, Hoshino-Shimizu S, Nakamura PM, Vaz AJ, Camargo ED, Silva MD. Sorodiagnóstico da doença de Chagas: novo reagente para o teste de Hemaglutinação indireta (THAI^{IAL}). Rev Soc Bras Med Trop 1996; 29:137–144.

148. Luquetti AO. Use of *Trypanosoma cruzi* defined proteins for diagnosis—multicentre trial, serological and technical aspects. Mem Inst Oswaldo Cruz 1990; 85:497–505.

149. Zicker F, Smith PG, Luquetti AO, Oliveira OS. Mass screening for *Trypanosoma cruzi* infections using the immunofluorescence, ELISA and hemagglutination tests on serum samples and on blood eluates from filter paper. Bull WHO 1990; 68:465–471.

150. Andrade ALSS, Martelli CMT, Luquetti AO, Oliveira OS, Silva SA, Zicker F. Serologic screening for *Trypanosoma cruzi* among blood donors in central Brazil. Bull Pan Am Health Organ 1992; 26:157–164.

151. Fife EH Jr, Mushel LH. Fluorescent antibody technique for serodiagnosis of *Trypanosoma cruzi* infection. Proc Soc Exp Biol NY 1959; 101:540–543.

152. Camargo ME, Souza SL. The use of filter paper blood smears in a practical fluorescent test for American trypanosomiasis serodiagnosis. Rev Inst Med Trop S Paulo 1966; 8:255–258.

153. Velasquez L, Reyes L, Thors C, Miettinen A, Chinchella M, Linder E. Autoantibodies give false positive reactions in the serodiagnosis of *Trypanosoma cruzi*. Trans Roy Soc Trop Med Hyg 1993; 87:35.

154. Voller A, Draper C, Bidwell DE, Bartlett A. A micro-plate enzyme-linked immunosorbent assay (ELISA) for Chagas disease. Lancet 1975; 1:426–429.

155. Wendel S, Lopes VHG, Batemarchi MV, Takaoka DT, Neitzert E. High levels of false positive reaction for *Trypanosoma cruzi* antibodies tests used for blood donors screening. Transfusion 1993; 33(suppl):41S.

156. Carvalho MR, Krieger MA, Almeida E, Oelemann W, Shikanai-Yasuda MA, Ferreira AW, Pereira JB, Sáez-Alquézar A, Dorlhiac-Llacer PE, Chamone DF, Goldenberg S. Chagas' disease diagnosis: evaluation of several tests in blood bank screening. Transfusion 1993; 33;830–834.

157. Ferreira AW, Belem ZR, Moura MEG, Camargo ME. Aspectos da padronização de testes sorológicos para a Doença de Chagas: Um teste imunoenzimático para a triagem de doadores de sangue. Rev Inst Med Trop S Paulo 1991; 33:123–128.

158. Brashear RJ, Winkler MA, Schur JD, Lee H, Burczak JD, Hall HJ, Pan AA. Detection of antibodies to *Trypanosoma cruzi* among blood donors in the southwestern and western United States. I. Evaluation of the sensitivity and specificity of an enzyme immunoassay for detecting antibodies to *T. cruzi*. Transfusion 1995; 35:213–218.

159. Oelemann WMR, Teixeira MGM, Costa GCV et al. Evaluation of three commercial enzyme-linked imunosorbent assays for diagnosis of Chagas' disease. J Clin Microbiol 1998; 36:2423–2427.

160. Houghton RL, Benson D, Skeiky Y, Sleath P, Lodes M, Badaró R, Krettli A, Reed SG. Multi-epitope peptide elisa for detection of serum antibodies to *Trypanosoma cruzi* in patients with treated and untreated Chagas' disease. Transfusion 1996; 36(suppl):137.

161. Hoffman A, Jaczko B, Jones J, Tursi N, Lee SR. Evaluation of a prototype screening ELISA and supplemental analysis for the serological identification of Chagas disease. Transfusion 1997; 37(suppl):181.

162. Umezawa ES, Bastos SF, Camargo ME, Yamauchi LM, Santos MR, Gonzales A, Zingales B, Levin MJ, Souza O, Rangel-Adão R, Franco da Silveira J. Evaluation of recombinant antigens for serodiagnosis of Chagas' disease in South and Central America. J Clin Microbiol 1999; 37:1554–1560.

163. Lanar DE, Manning JE. Major surface proteins and antigens on the different in vivo and in vitro forms of *Trypanosoma cruzi*. Mol Biochem Paras 1984; 11:119–131.

164. Rosfjord EC, Mikhael KS, Rowland EC, Powell MR. Analysis of antibody cross-reactivity in experimental american trypanosomiasis. J Parasitol 1990; 76:698–702.

165. Reiche EMV, Cavazzane M Jr., Okamura H, Tagata EC, Jankevicius SI, Jankevicius JV. Evaluation of the Western blot in the confirmatory serologic diagnosis of Chagas' disease. Am J Trop Med Hyg 1998; 59:750–756.

166. Teixeira MGM, Borges-Pereira J, Neitzert E, Souza MLNX, Peralta JM. Development and evaluation of an enzyme linked immunotransfer blot technique for serodiagnosis of Chagas' disease. Trop Med Parasitolo 1994; 45:308–312.

167. Pastini AC, Iglesias SR, Carricate VC, Guerin ME, Sanchez DO, Frasch AC. Immunoassay with recombinant *Trapanosoma cruzi* antigens potentially useful for screening donated blood and diagnosing Chagas disease. Clin Chem 1994; 40:1893–1897.

168. Sabino EC, Salles N, Stoops E, Santos ML, Saez-Alquezar A. Evaluation of Chagas Innolia assay as a confirmatory test for Chagas disease. Mem Inst Oswaldo Cruz 1997; 92(suppl 1):266.

169. Costa GCV, Teixeira MGM, Borges-Pereira J, Castro JAF, Coura JR, Vanderborght BOM, Stroops E, Zrein M, Peralta JM, Oelemann WMR. A recombinant antigen and peptide line immunoassay (LIA) as an alternative diagnostic test for Chagas' disease. Mem Inst Oswaldo Cruz 1997; 92(suppl 2):267.

170. Oelemann WMR, Vanderborght BOM, Veríssimo da Costa GC, Teixeira MGM, Borges-Pereira J, Castro JAF, Coura JR, Stoops E, Hulstaert F, Zrein M, Peralta JM. A recombinant peptide antigen line immunoassay optimized for the confirmation of Chagas' disease. Transfusion 1999; 39:711–717.

171. Kirchhoff LV, Gam AA, Gusmão RA, Goldsmith RS, Rezende JM, Rassi A. Increased specificity of serodiagnosis of Chagas' disease by detection of antibody to the 72- and 90-kilodalton glycoproteins of *Trypanosoma cruzi*. J Infect Dis 1987; 155:561–564.

172. Leiby DA, Wendel S, Takaoka DT, Fachini R, Oliveira LC, Tibbals MA. Confirmatory testing for *Trypanosoma cruzi* antibodies: validation of radioimmuneprecipitation (RIPA) testing. Transfusion 1997; 37(suppl 95):5301.

173. Rassi A, Luquetti AO. Therapy of Chagas disease. In: Wendel S, Breuer Z, Camargo ME, Rassi A, eds. Chagas Disease (American Trypanosomiasis): Its Impact on Transfusion and Clinical Medicine. São Paulo: ISBT, 1992:237–247.

174. Andrade ALLS, Zicker F, Oliveira RM, Silva AS, Luquetti AO, Travassos LR, Almeida IC, Andrad SS, Andrade JG, Martelli CMT. Randomised trial of efficacy of benznidazole in treatment of early *Trypanosoma cruzi* infection. Lancet 1996; 348:1407–1412.

175. Dias JCP, Schofield CJ. Controle da transmissão transfusional da doença de Chagas na *Iniciativa do Cone Sul.* Rev Soc Bras Med Trop 1998; 31:373–383.

17
Tickborne Infections

Ritchard G. Cable
*American Red Cross Blood Services—Connecticut Region,
Farmington, Connecticut*

Jonathan Trouern-Trend
*Epidemiology and Surveillance Program, American Red Cross
ARCNET, Farmington, Connecticut*

I. INTRODUCTION

Tickborne diseases are achieving increased recognition in the United States as a public health problem. Lyme disease has been identified to have occurred in 45 states and has attracted increased public interest. Babesiosis, transmitted by the same tick, has important transfusion implications. Newly identified diseases such as ehrlichiosis raise new questions about the role of the tick in human disease. Much of this interest has been accelerated by increases in animal populations (deer in particular), as well as increased movement of the human population into outdoor environments, which are conducive to tick bites.

Simultaneously, heightened public scrutiny of blood safety in the wake of the AIDS epidemic has resulted in a "raising of the bar" regarding potential threats. Thus, new regulatory and public pressures are likely to focus on tickborne diseases and their relationship to blood safety. The most striking example of this is the recall of nearly 700 units of blood donated by Army reservists who trained at Fort Chaffee, Arkansas, during the summer of 1997. The measure was initiated at the request of the U.S. Food and Drug Administration (FDA) because the exposure of the trainees to tick bites on maneuvers was high and a large number of exposed troops reported illnesses following the exposure. At least some of the illnesses were due to tickborne diseases such as Rocky Mountain spotted fever. More than one type of tickborne disease was reported, none of which is classically thought of as transfusion transmitted (1,1a). Previously, this kind of event would not have been considered a threat to the blood supply. It is clear that an increased understanding of tickborne disease and the possibility of transfusion transmission will be required by transfusion medicine experts and blood banking organizations.

Initially this chapter will discuss important ticks, their geographic distribution, and life cycles. Then an overview of tickborne human diseases will be presented, with emphasis on the diseases likely to be (or to become) of interest in transfusion medicine. Finally, we will discuss babesiosis, the most important transfusion-transmitted tickborne disease, as well as the possibility that several other tickborne diseases may be transfusion transmitted.

II. BIOLOGY OF TICKS

Ticks are small parasitic arachnids in the order Acari, which they share with the mites. Of approximately 850 species described, all are epidermal parasites throughout their life cycle and feed on the blood of reptiles, birds, or mammals. The ticks are divided taxonomically into two main families, the Ixodidae, or hard, ticks and the Argasidae, or soft, ticks. The Ixodidae is represented by 13 genera including the medically important genus *Ixodes* (2,3).

III. LIFE CYCLE OF TICKS

The life cycle of a tick includes four stages: egg, larvae, nymph, and adult. Copulation usually occurs on the host. A blood meal is normally required for egg production. After feeding, the engorged female drops from the host and lays between 100 and 20,000 eggs, depending on species and environmental conditions (4). Larval ticks hatch from the eggs, then begin to search for a host. Four alternate life cycles can be found among ticks. First is the one-host tick. The cycle of feeding and molting until maturity is reached on one host. This reduces the vector potential. The second type of life cycle is the two-host tick. In this situation, a larval tick hatches on the ground and finds a host, usually a small mammal or bird. The larva feeds on the host, then molts and becomes a nymph. After the nymph feeds, it drops to the ground and molts into the adult stage. A three-host tick feeds on a separate host for each stage. Finally, a many-host tick feeds intermittently and on multiple hosts during its life cycle (2,4).

IV. TICK- AND MITEBORNE DISEASE

Ticks are important to human and veterinary medicine. They cause disease and act as vectors and reservoirs for many serious pathogens. Several factors make these organisms efficient vectors of disease. First, the ingestion of host blood allows collection of pathogens in the body of the tick. If the tick subsequently moves to another host, transmission may occur. The long period of attachment on a host increases the likelihood of transmission. High reproductive potential ensures high populations of ticks and increases possibility of disease transmission. Pathogens are transmitted between life stages in some ticks (e.g., between the larva and the nymph), a phenomenon known as transstadial transmission. Pathogens may also be passed to the next generation by transovarial transmission. Both types of transmission are important in the maintenance of pathogens in tick populations (2).

Mites belong to the same order as ticks and share many of the same characteristics and parasitic lifestyles. Ticks are really giants in the mite family, most mites being much smaller than the smallest ticks (5). Scrub typhus, which is miteborne, is discussed here since it may be transfusion-transmitted.

A great many tickborne diseases have been described. A number of these have the potential for transfusion transmission. The more important tickborne diseases of interest in transfusion medicine are summarized in Table 1. The remainder of the chapter will expand upon these diseases.

V. VIRAL TICKBORNE DISEASES

A large number of viral agents related to human diseases have been identified as being transmitted by ticks. Since some of these pathogens pass transovarially, even one-host ticks are capable of transmitting disease via the next generation. However, because many tickborne viruses have short incubation periods, the likelihood of transmission by a blood donor is small. Donors are deferred for fever, which should prevent collection of viremic blood in many cases. Some tickborne viruses (especially those with longer incubation periods or with many asymptomatic infections) have been transmitted by transfusion or have that potential. The current deferral for blood donors who have traveled to malaria-endemic areas reduces the risk of transmitting many of these tickborne viruses in North America and Europe, since the ranges of the involved tick vectors overlap those of malaria (6).

A. Flaviviruses

These enveloped single-stranded RNA viruses replicate in the cytoplasm. The Flavivirus family contains nonarborviruses such as hepatitis C and hepatitis G (7,8). Only one of the tickborne flaviviruses, the central European subtype of tickborne encephalitis, has been documented as causing transfusion-transmitted disease (9). Theoretically, others could do so. Two cases of tickborne viral en-

Table 1 Tickborne Diseases of Interest in Transfusion Medicine

Agent	Disease	Transfusion-transmitted?	Country	Ref.
Viruses				
Tickborne encepha-litis virus	Kumlinge disease, tickborne encephalitis	Yes	Finland	8,9
Deer tick virus	None known	Possible	United States	11
Colorado tick fever virus	Colorado tick fever	Yes	United States	12,13
Bacteria				
Borrelia burgdorferii	Lyme disease	Possible	United States	17–19
Borrelia recurrentis	Relapsing fever	Possible	Africa, China	24–27
Rickettsia				
Rickettsia rickettsi	Rocky Mountain spotted fever	Yes	United States	28
Orienta tsutsugamushi	Scrub typhus	Possible	Asia, Australia	30
Ehrlichia chaffiensis	Human monocytic ehrlichiosis	Possible	United States	31
Ehrlichia spp.	Human granulo-cytic ehrlichiosis	Possible	United States	31,32
Protozoa				
Babesia microti	Babesiosis	Yes	United States	33–36, 63–68
WA1	Babesiosis-like	Yes	United States	37,38
MO1	Babesiosis-like	Possible	United States	39
TW1	None known	Possible	Taiwan	40

cephalitis (Kumlinge disease) were reported from a single donor from Kumlinge, Finland. The disease, endemic on this isolated island, was reportedly transmitted by a blood donation a few hours before the donor became ill. The transfusion illness was indistinguishable from the tickborne illness. No details on the blood component's storage or transfusion were published, and it is not clear how the disease was recognized. The recipients recovered.

Another flavivirus, deer tick virus, was described in 1997. It has been found in *Ixodes scapularis*, a vector of several human diseases, including Lyme disease and babesiosis (10,11). This virus has not been demonstrated to cause disease in humans. However, its close relationship to other viruses in the tickborne encephalitis complex warrants some concern. In a serosurvey of ticks from New England, a small percentage was found to be harboring this virus

(11). Further studies will be needed to determine whether this virus is a public health problem.

B. Retroviruses

This family contains enveloped double-stranded RNA viruses that replicate in the cytoplasm. Ticks spread several of these viruses to humans. Most are responsible for only a few cases of disease, although Colorado tick fever virus causes several hundred cases a year in North America.

Only Colorado tick fever virus has been demonstrated to cause transfusion-transmitted disease. Cases of Colorado tick fever occur in the Rocky Mountains and Pacific slope of the western United States and Canada. The vector is the wood tick, *Dermacentor andersoni*. Up to 15% of humans at high risk (forest rangers, loggers, back-country hikers) have antibodies to the virus. Most cases occur between April and July, mirroring tick activity. Several hundred cases are reported each year. Since reporting requirements vary by region, cases are thought to be significantly underestimated. Cases have been imported to other parts of the United States by people traveling in the endemic areas. Incubation is usually 3–5 days after a tick bite, sometimes up to 14 days. No prodromal manifestations occur. Onset of symptoms is rapid. Fever, headache, and myalgia are the most common symptoms. Encephalitis, thrombocytopenia, disseminated intravascular coagulation (DIC), and a hemorrhagic state resembling Dengue hemorrhagic fever have occurred. Many individuals, especially adults over 30 years, experience a prolonged convalescence (12).

Colorado tick fever was transmitted in Montana from a healthy blood donor who developed fever 18 hours after blood donation and 4 days after removing a tick (13). The blood was transfused during surgery to an 82-year-old with bowel obstruction, who developed a prolonged febrile illness lasting 23 days. Both donor and recipient blood were demonstrated to have Colorado tick fever virus by mouse inoculation, confirming the diagnosis. This case illustrates again the importance of reporting postdonation illness in order to recognize these rare disease transmissions.

The virus can be isolated from plasma for up to 7 days after the onset of symptoms and up to 20 weeks in the red cell fraction. An infection usually confers immunity; however, rare cases of reinfection have been reported.

VI. BACTERIAL TICKBORNE DISEASES

A. Lyme Disease (*Borrelia burgdorferi* and Others)

Lyme disease is an important tickborne disease, with worldwide distribution caused by a number of spirochetes in the genus *Borrelia*. Most cases are found in the United States and western Europe. This disease accounts for more than 90% of arthropodborne diseases reported in North America each year. In the United States, endemic foci exist along the Atlantic seaboard from Massachusetts to Maryland, in the upper Midwest (Wisconsin and Minnesota), and in the West (California and Oregon). Cases have been reported from 45 states as well as the Canadian provinces of British Columbia and Ontario (14). Elsewhere, cases have been seen in the former Soviet Union, China, Japan, and Australia. The main vectors are four host Ixodid ticks: *I. scapularis* (also called *I. dammini*) in the Eastern and midwestern United States, *I. pacificus* in the western United States, *I. ricinus* in Europe, and *I. persulcatus* in Asia.

In North America, the spirochete responsible for Lyme disease circulates between the white-footed mouse (*Peromyscus leucopus*) and the white-tailed deer (*Odocoileus virginianus*) via *I. scapularis*. The transmission cycle of the spirochete starts with an infected mouse. Larval ticks hatch in the spring or early summer and search out their first host, usually a mouse. After feeding for about 2 days, the tick drops off. The tick does not feed again until the next spring, after it has molted to the nymphal stage. Usually the nymph feeds once, again usually on a mouse, then molts to an adult. If the preferred host cannot be found, the nymph will feed on other mammals, including humans. Nymphal ticks, infected from their first blood meal, transmit the spirochete to humans. The spirochete enters the host's body at the site of the tick bite, then travels via the blood and lymphatics to other organs of the body, where pathogenesis occurs. Adult ticks feed on deer, then lay eggs. This association between Lyme disease and deer is responsible for the dramatic increase in cases in this century. The abundance of the vector correlates with the number of deer in the area.

Lyme disease can be divided into three stages. In the first stage there is a localized skin lesion at the bite site called erythema migrans (EM). This lesion can progress to a bull's-eye–type lesion with the inner part clear and the edges red. About 60% of cases have this sign. Other symptoms of the disease can be fever, malaise, fatigue, myalgia, and migratory arthralgias. A wide range of neurological symptoms have been reported, including facial palsy, aseptic meningitis, chorea, myelitis, and encephalitis. Cardiac symptoms may occur a few weeks to months after EM, including atrioventricular block. Rarely acute myopericarditis or cardiomegaly have been reported. A chronic infection may lead to arthritis in the large joints, polyneuropathy, or leukoencephalitis.

When *Borrelia burgdorferi* was first described, it was thought to be the only agent of Lyme disease (15). Research in the last decade has indicated that at least eight species of *Borrelia* have been found in the *Ixodes* vectors, four of which have been demonstrated to cause human disease. All four species are known to cause EM. *B. burgdorferi* is present in North America and Europe but is absent from Russia and Asia. This species is most often associated with polyarthritis. In Eurasia, *Borrelia garinii* is associated with neurological symptoms; it has been isolated from Japan to western Europe. *Borrelia afzelii*, another Eurasian *Borrelia*, found from Japan and China to western Europe, is associated with the chronic skin condition acrodermatitis chronica atrophicans. VS116 occurs in Europe and has only been associated with EM (15a).

Though antibodies to *B. burgdorferi* are present in a significant fraction of blood donors in endemic areas, no case of transfusion-transmitted Lyme disease has been reported. *B. burgdorferi* has been cultured from the blood of patients with early Lyme disease (16), which has led to the concern that Lyme disease may be transmissible by transfusion (17). We have shown (18) that *B. burgdorferi* can survive in stored blood products under frozen, refrigerated, or 20–24°C storage conditions for the duration of the storage period of fresh frozen plasma (FFP), red cells, and platelets, respectively. Because the characteristic EM rash is thought to be caused by skin growth of spirochetes at the site of the tick bite, it is likely that intravenously injected *B. burgdorferi* would not cause EM. Since the remainder of the symptoms of Lyme disease are nonspecific, it is likely that, if transfusion-transmitted Lyme disease exists, it would not be easily recognized.

Despite active surveillance for transfusion-transmitted Lyme disease, no cases have been identified. However, we reported a case in which *B. burgdorferi* DNA was detected in red cells and plasma from a donor who discovered EM the day after blood donation and notified the blood center (19). He was confirmed serologically to have Lyme disease. The involved blood products were cultured but were negative for *B. burgdorferi*. Had this donor not called the blood center, and had his blood products been transfused, it is not clear whether the recipients would have been infected. It is also not clear whether the PCR-positive blood units contained viable organisms.

In a case that illustrates the difficulty of transfusion transmission of Lyme disease, we identified an implicated donor in a case of posttransfusion babesiosis. Upon interview, the donor gave a history of having developed EM several days following his blood donation and had been diagnosed and treated for Lyme disease with a characteristic serial serological pattern for *B. burgdorferi*. The recipient, who had a renal transplant and was on an immunosuppressive agent, developed a typical serological response to babesiosis but did not seroconvert for *B. burgdorferi* or become ill with Lyme disease (20). This was the case despite the likelihood that both agents were transmitted to the donor by the bite of a single, doubly infected, tick (21) 1–3 weeks before the blood donation. This case suggests that the spirochetemic phase of *B. burgdorferi* after an infected tick bite must be very short.

In an effort to estimate the risk of Lyme disease from transfusion, we conducted serological follow-up on 155 open heart surgery patients who received a total of 601 red cells and 371 platelet concentrates. None of the recipients seroconverted for *B. burgdorferi* (95% CI, 0–0.5% for red cells and 0–0.8% for platelet concentrates) (22). At the same time, the study detected one case of seroconversion for babesiosis and placed the per unit risk of exposure to babesiosis from a red cell transfusion in Connecticut at 0.17% (95% CI, 0.004–0.9%).

B. Relapsing Fever (*Borrelia recurrentis* and Others)

This disease, caused by a spirochete, is characterized by periods of fever lasting 2–9 days followed by afebrile periods lasting 2–4 days. The number of relapses ranges from 1 to 10 or more. The initial febrile period may be accompanied by transitory petechial rashes. Mortality ranges from 2 to 5% in untreated cases. Antibiotics provide effective treatment.

A number of species of *Borrelia* are responsible for endemic or tickborne relapsing fever (23). This disease is present in small endemic foci on every continent except Australia. Rodents are thought to be the natural reservoir for this disease. Argasid ticks in the genus *Ornithodoros* are the vector. Since the spirochete can be transmitted transovarially, ticks can serve as long-term reservoirs, passing infection from generation to generation. Epidemics have occurred in western Canada and the United States. Epidemics are usually associated with sleeping in cabins infested with rodents and the Argasid tick vector. In 1973, an outbreak in Arizona associated with cabins near the Grand Canyon resulted in 62 cases (24,25).

The spirochete is present in the blood only during the febrile stage, particularly the first one. Cases of transfusion-transmitted relapsing fever have been reported from both Africa and China (26,27). However, current practices of excluding febrile donors and the low incidence of this disease should make this a negligible transfusion risk.

VII. RICKETTSIAE

The rickettsia are aerobic gram-negative bacilli that are obligate intracellular parasites. Several genera (*Rickettsia, Ehrlichia, Coxiella,* and *Orientia*) are associated with human disease. Humans are most often accidental hosts. Infection usually circulates in nature between animal hosts and arthropod vectors (ticks, mites, fleas, lice). In some infections an asymptomatic rickettsemic stage may precede symptoms. It is most likely during this period that rickettsial disease may be transmitted by donated blood.

A. Rocky Mountain Spotted Fever (*Rickettsia rickettsii*)

This infection is found throughout the United States. Infections have also been reported from Central and South America. The illness is characterized by a fever of sudden onset, persisting for 2–3 weeks in untreated individuals. Fever is accompanied by myalgia, fatigue, severe headache, chills, and conjunctival injection. In about half the cases a maculopapular rash appears about the third day. Hemorrhage is a common complication. Case fatality rates in untreated cases are 13–25%. In recent years, with treatment, case fatality rates in the United States have been 3–5%. The disease is maintained in ticks by transovarian and transstadial passage. In the eastern United States *Ixodes variabilis* is the primary vector; in the western United States it is *Dermacentor andersoni*; in the southwestern United States it is *Amblyomma americanum*. In Central and South America the primary vector is *Amblyomma cajennense*. The incubation period is 2–14 days.

Rocky Mountain spotted fever was transmitted in 1977 from a healthy blood donor in Baltimore (28). Three days after his blood donation he developed chills, headache, and a typical rash, and 7 days after donation he died. The infected red cell was refrigerated for 9 days before transfusion. The recipient developed fever 6 days after transfusion and was treated with antibiotics not indicated for Rocky Mountain spotted fever. Four days later, after the donor's diagnosis was reported to the recipient's physician, the recipient was treated with chloramphenicol for Rocky Mountain spotted fever and eventually recovered. Diagnosis in both donor and recipient was confirmed serologically and bacteriologically. The report comments on the importance of postdonation disease reporting by the donor to the blood center and then to the recipient hospital to allow appropriate and timely treatment. This case of rickettsial transmission also reinforces the possibility of transfusion transmission of other rickettsial diseases, such as ehrlichiosis.

B. Scrub Typhus (*Orientia tsutsugamushi*)

This miteborne disease, also known as tsutsugamushi disease, is characterized by a primary lesion, that develops at the site of a mite bite. Symptoms appear after an incubation period of 6–21 days. Symptoms include headache, malaise, fever, regional lymphadenitis, and a macular or maculopapular rash on the trunk and the extremities. The case fatality rate varies between 1 and 60%. The reservoir and the vector for this disease are mites in the family Trombiculidae. The disease is endemic in southern and southeastern Asia from India to Indonesia, Japan, Korea, parts of China, New Guinea, and northern Australia (29).

This rickettsia has recently been shown to persist in packed red cells, so it appears there is potential for transmission (30). Large areas where the disease is endemic are also in the malarial deferral zone, so travelers to these areas would be deferred from donating blood in North America or Europe.

C. Human Monocytic Ehrlichiosis (*Ehrlichia chafeensis*)

This is an acute febrile illness found in the United States, primarily in the southeastern and south central regions. Infections have been confirmed from 30 states. The pathogen infects mononuclear lymphocytes causing leukopenia and thrombocytopenia. Sometimes referred to as "Rocky Mountain spotted fever without the spots," the disease usually presents as a fever with headache and malaise. Nausea, vomiting, and myalgia are often present. Hepatitis and elevation of serum hepatic aminotransferases are often noted. The case fatality rate is 2–5%, with death resulting from renal failure or respiratory insufficiency. The vector for this disease is the Lone Star tick, *Amblyomma americanum*. White-tailed deer are thought to be a major reservoir for the disease. Since subclinical infections have been reported, there is some possibility of transfusion transmission, although no cases have been reported (31).

D. Human Granulocytic Ehrlichiosis (*Ehrlichia* spp.)

This disease has a clinical picture similar to human monocytic ehrlichiosis, with a higher case fatality rate (7–10%). The vector of this disease is *Ixodes scapularis*, the same vector as in Lyme disease and babesiosis. Ticks harboring multiple pathogens have been recorded and antibodies to multiple tickborne diseases reported (32). Most cases have come from the eastern and upper midwestern United States. Other cases have been seen in Arkansas, California, and Florida. White-tailed deer and rodents are suspected to be the reservoirs.

A single case of probable transfusion transmission of human granulocytic ehrlichiosis (HGE) has been reported from Wisconsin in 1998 (32a). The recipient was transfused with 2 units of red cells. Nine days later, the recipient was hospitalized with fever, rigors, nausea, and vomiting. A pretransfusion blood sample was negative for HGE by PCR. Testing 2 days posthospitalization was positive for HGE by PCR and antibody. In addition, neutrophilic morulae could be visualized by microscopy. The implicated donor had a history of Lyme Disease and reported tick bites two months prior to blood donation. The donor tested positive for HGE antibodies, however a test on the implicated unit was PCR negative. The implicated unit had been stored for 30 days prior to transfusion. This case illustrates the potential for asymptomatic donor transmission of HGE.

VIII. PROTOZOAL TICKBORNE DISEASES

A. Babesiosis

Babesia are intracellular sporozoan parasites that can resemble malarial parasites both morphologically and clinically. More than 70 species have been described, and some are serious veterinary pathogens. At least five species of *Babesia* or *Babesia*-like organisms have been shown to infect humans, four with demonstrable disease.

1. *Babesia microti*

Primarily a parasite of small rodents, particularly the white-footed deer mouse (33), this species has caused several hundred infections in the United States, primarily in the Northeast and upper Midwest (34). A significant number of these cases have been asymptomatic. The vector *Ixodes scapularis* (*Ixodes damini*) ranges from New Hampshire to Maryland, west to Wisconsin and Minnesota (14). The ecology of *B. microti* infections in humans closely mirrors that of Lyme disease and human granulocytic ehrlichiosis (HGE). Nymphs of the vector *I. scapularis* bite humans and transmit the parasite. The ticks are infected as larvae and acquire the infection from parasitic mice or voles. Deer, important to the life cycle of *I. scapularis* and transmission of Lyme disease, are not infected with *B. microti* and are not reservoirs for the parasite.

Infection follows a bite of an infected nymphal tick. This stage feeds from May through September. The *Babesia* organism penetrates an erythrocyte. The trophozoite multiplies by binary fission and forms tetrads. Lysis of the erythrocyte releases the merozoites into the blood where they can reinfect other cells, maintaining the infection or infecting a feeding tick. Transovarial passage occurs in ticks allowing maintenance of the infection without a host (35).

Posttransfusion babesiosis is discussed below.

2. *Babesia divergens* and *Babesia bovis*

These two bovine Babesia species cause babesiosis in Europe and are more often associated with fatal outcome than North American species of *Babesia*. *Babesia divergens* is the most common *Babesia* found in European cattle. The vector is *Ixodes ricinus*, the European vector of Lyme disease. Most patients were splenectomized, a major risk factor for all forms of babesiosis. The mortality rate is higher than 50%. Reported cases presented with fulminant, febrile, hemolytic disease (34,36). No transfusion-associated cases have been reported for this species.

3. WA1 (WAshington Case 1)

This *Babesia*-like organism has been isolated from human cases in northern California, Oregon, and Washington. This organism is more closely related to *Babesia gibsoni*, a parasite of dogs and coyotes, than *B. microti*. This species has been implicated in transfusion transmission (see below). Seroprevalence rates up to 16% have been reported from northern California. Infections have occurred in both splenectomized persons and those with intact spleens (37,38).

4.   MO1 (MissOuri Case 1)

This *Babesia*-like parasite, found to cause disease in a patient from Missouri, is most closely related to the bovine parasite *B. divergens* (39). No transfusion cases have been reported yet, although it is likely cases will appear.

5.   TW1 (TaiWan Case 1)

A recently reported *Babesia* species similar to *B. microti* was isolated from an asymptomatic Taiwanese patient (40). Local rodents also harbored the parasite. This species has not yet been reported to cause any human disease.

B.   Clinical Babesiosis (*B. microti*) (Table 2)

The incubation period is usually 1–3 weeks after a tick bite, sometimes up to 6 weeks (41). Transfusion-associated infections appear to have a longer incubation period, from 2 to 8 weeks (see Table 3). Symptoms begin gradually and are nonspecific. Common symptoms include malaise, fatigue, anorexia, arthralgias, nausea, vomiting, abdominal pain, and dark urine. Also common are malaria-like symptoms of fever, chills, myalgia, and sweating. The fever can be either sustained or intermittent, reaching temperatures of 40°C. Hemolytic anemia can produce jaundice and renal failure. Disseminated intravascular coagulation can be a serious complication.

　　B. microti infection differs from European *Babesia* infection in several ways. First, European babesiosis is a much more serious, fulminant disease. It is more often associated with asplenic patients and with fatal outcomes. Most clinical *B. microti* infections, though serious, are not fatal. Only 30% of affected patients in the United States have been asplenic. Of the spleen-intact patients with clinical disease, most were over 50 years old, indicating that age is a factor in the severity of disease (42).

　　The percentages of erythrocytes parasitized in clinical cases range from 10 to 85%. Antibiotic therapy (currently clindamycin and quinine) (43) is usually curative: in more severe cases exchange transfusion has been utilized to reduce the level of parasitemia (44).

　　Asymptomatic infections appear to be common and have been implicated in some transfusion cases. Seroprevalence rates for *B. microti* have been recorded as high as 6.9% in individuals with high risk of tick exposure on Shelter Island, New York (45). Concurrent infection with *B. burgdorferi* has been reported. In one study, 54% of patients with babesiosis had antibodies for *B. burgdorferi* (46).

Table 2 Known Cases of Transfusion Babesiosis (*B. microti*) as of July 1999

Case	Age, gender, year	Evidence[a]	Blood component	Patient factors	Donor infection	Ref.
1	70 yo M, 1979	Probable	Platelets	ITP; splenectomy after transfusion	Nantucket, MA	44
2	23 yo F, 1980	Probable	Frozen RBC	Splenectomy; thalassemia	Fire Island, NY	63
3	8 Weeks F, 1980	Definite	RBC	Premature birth	Fire Island, NY	51
4	79 yo F, 1982	Definite	RBC	Perforated diverticulum; colon resection	Cape Cod, MA	64,65
5	72 yo M, 1985	Probable	RBC	Myelodysplasia	Martha's Vineyard, MA	66
6	46 yo M, 1989	Definite	RBC	Splenectomy	Old Lyme, CT	67
7	57 yo M, 1989	Possible	RBC	Esophagectomy for adenocarcinoma	Unknown	68
8	65 yo M, 1990	Probable	RBC	Splenectomy	Cape Cod, MA	Unpublished
9	56 yo F, 1992	Definite	RBC	Kidney transplant	Southeast CT	69
10	73 yo M, 1992	Probable	RBC	CABG	Southeast CT	70
11	64 yo M, 1993	Possible	RBC	CABG	No donor id	Unpublished
12	44 yo M, 1993	Possible	RBC	Splenic vein thrombosis	Wisconsin	Unpublished
13	73 yo F, 1994	Definite	Platelets	Aortic valve replacement	Southeast CT	Unpublished
14	51 yo M, 1996	Possible	Pheresis platelets	Lymphoma	Southeast CT	Unpublished
15	72 yo F, 1996	Definite	RBC	CHF, renal failure	Southeast CT	Unpublished
16	67 yo M, 1997	Probable	Platelets	Lung cancer	Southeast CT	Unpublished
17	Newborn, 1997	Definite	Red cells	Prematurity	Suffolk County, NY Long Island	56
	Newborn, 1997		Red cells	Newborn		
	70 yo F, 1997		Red cells	None		

[a]Definite—a donor has been identified with a positive smear, hamster inoculation, or PCR or with a clear-cut serological progression. Patient meets criteria below. Probable—a donor has been identified who is seropositive at some time after the implicated donation. Patient meets criteria below. Possible—no donor has been identified, but the recipient has a clear-cut history of babesiosis with no other source.

Table 3 Transfusion-Transmitted Babesiosis—Patient
Factors (N = 19)

Sex	
Male	10
Female	7
Newborn—unknown	2
Age	
Newborn	3
1–20 years	0
21–40 years	1
41–60 years	5
Over 60 years	10
Risk factors	
Splenectomy	4
Splenic vein thrombosis	1
Prematurity	2
Renal failure	2
Cancer/Hematological malignancy	4
None identified	6
Incubation period, (excluding case 14)	17 days–8 weeks
Clinical outcome	
Death associated with babesiosis	1
Death unrelated to babesiosis	2
Recovered with treatment	9
No information	7

IX. POSTTRANSFUSION BABESIOSIS

Babesia species, particularly *B. microti*, meet the requirements to be transfusion transmitted. First, there is documented evidence for subclinical parasitemia in healthy individuals (36) and for persistent parasitemia after acute babesiosis (47). Donors with a history of babesiosis are deferred permanently from blood donation. Second, the *Babesia* parasite survives well under blood bank storage conditions (48). *B. microti* survive well at refrigerated temperatures for up to 21 days, while they did not survive well at 25°C for more than 3 days. Finally, intraerythrocytic *B. microti* are infectious to hamsters when inoculated intravenously or intraperitoneally (the basis for the classic bioassay of infectivity). From the evidence of human transfusion cases, *Babesia* are also infectious to humans by the intravenous route.

This discussion will focus on cases reported in the United States. Although there have been human cases of babesiosis in Europe due to species other than *B. microti*, no cases of transfusion-transmitted babesiosis have been reported outside of the United States (34).

Until recently, all reported cases of transfusion babesiosis have been caused by *B. microti*, which is endemic in New England, on Long Island, and in the upper Midwest. Other recently reported species of *Babesia* and *Babesia*-like piroplasms are discussed below.

The first case of transfusion babesiosis was reported in 1980 (44) (Table 2, Case 1). The patient was a 70-year-old man who was on prednisone and transfused in 1979 with 20 units of platelet concentrates for neutropenia, anemia, and thrombocytopenia, diagnosed as ITP, then splenectomized 4 weeks later. Four weeks after the splenectomy (8 weeks after the transfusion), he developed a fever and was noted to have *Babesia* on a peripheral smear. He was resistant to treatment with chloroquine and pentamidine and was treated successfully with two exchange transfusions 6 weeks apart. This case is typical in that the patient had had a splenectomy and was elderly and immunosuppressed. It was atypical in that the only blood components received were platelet concentrates. However, platelet concentrates can contain up to 0.5 mL of red cells.

By today's standards, the case for transfusion transmission in this first report was not particularly compelling, since the only evidence for the alleged infected donor, a summer resident of Nantucket, was an elevated *Babesia* serological titer 3 months after donation. Hamster bioassay of a new sample from the donor 3 months after the donation was negative. In addition, the incubation period was 8 weeks, on the long side. A follow-up letter (49) correctly suggested that the patient may have been already infected with unrecognized babesiosis and that the splenectomy and/or prednisone, not the transfusion, may have been responsible for the clinical observations. Although the patient had no history of a visit to hyperendemic areas such as Nantucket or the New England off-shore islands, much of coastal New England may have had *Babesia*-infected ticks. (Most babesiosis patients do not report a specific tick bite.) However, the patient seroconverted for *Babesia* antibody during the course of his illness, making transfusion transmission more likely.

Confirmation of transfusion babesiosis requires the following evidence (50):

1. The patient must display clear-cut evidence of babesiosis with no other source identified. Ideally the serologic and clinical evidence excludes long standing subclinical infection.
2. In addition, a donor must be identified in the typical incubation period of transfusion babesiosis who, at a minimum, has a history of travel or residence in an endemic area and a positive *Babesia* antibody.
3. The donor should demonstrate recent infectivity by hamster inoculation, PCR, or (less definitively) typical acute serologic progression.

For the purpose of analysis of case reports, we have used "Possible" to describe cases in which only criteria 1 are met, "Probable" for cases in which criteria 1 and 2 are met, and "Definite" for cases in which all three criteria are met.

The first definite case of transfusion babesiosis was reported in 1982 (51) from a transfusion in 1980 (Table 2, Case 3). The recipient was a premature infant. The donor was a healthy summer resident of Fire Island (Long Island, NY), who was demonstrated to be parasitemic by hamster inoculation a year after the original exposure to infected ticks.

In 1994, stimulated by an increase of tickborne babesiosis in Connecticut (52) and by three transfusion case reports to the Connecticut Red Cross Blood Center, the authors initiated a registry of posttransfusion babesiosis cases. Blood centers and *Babesia* researchers in New England, New York City, Long Island, and Minnesota were contacted and asked to provide case reports. The reports were tabulated in a standardized format and returned to the reporter for verification. An update to this survey was conducted in 1996.

The data that follow are a summary of the data retained in this registry as of July 1999. In total, 17 cases of transfusion-transmitted babesiosis have been reported: 10 published and 7 unpublished. Table 2 is a summary of those cases, along with references to the published cases.

Table 3 is a summary of patient factors revealed by these case reports. Transfusion babesiosis occurs in all age groups and both sexes. There appears to be a preponderance of older recipients, but this observation may merely reflect the transfused population. Splenectomy, which is a risk factor for tickborne disease, also appears to be a risk factor for transfusion transmission. Other possible risk factors—prematurity, cancer and immunosuppressive chemotherapy, and renal failure—may or may not be real, since these are also prevalent in transfused patients. In any event, a significant proportion of cases appear to have no complicating medical illness, with transfusion occurring in the context of surgery or trauma.

The transfusion incubation period appears to be 2–8 weeks, with case 14 being an outlier. Case 14 illustrates the difficulty of identifying an implicated donor. The case involved 49 donors, many of whom could not be contacted. However, 22 were tested for *Babesia* antibody. Since the seroprevalence of babesiosis in Connecticut is reported to be 1.0–2.6% (53), there is a high likelihood of falsely implicating a donor not responsible for transmission. The apparently implicated donor was seropositive and had a clear risk history. However, he donated platelets by apheresis, which are relatively free of red cells, and the apparent incubation period was 4.5 months, much longer than previously reported in the other cases.

Transfusion babesiosis is a treatable disease, with the current recommended therapy being clindamycin and quinine (43). Case 17 illustrates drug resistance to clindamycin and quinine in a newborn, who subsequently responded to atovoquone. Exchange transfusion to remove infected erythrocytes has also been used successfully in the past (44). Outcome in general is favorable, with only one death attributed to the infection among 19 patients.

Early detection and a high index of suspicion are important in the management of transfusion babesiosis. The disease is often missed, particularly in areas not endemic for the disease. It is also confused with transfusion malaria, although a skilled hematology technologist should be able to differentiate the intra-erythrocytic parasites. Any patient who develops fever and a hemolytic anemia after transfusion (otherwise not explained) should be suspected to have transfusion babesiosis or malaria. They should be evaluated with review of a thick blood smear by a hematology technologist experienced in such diagnoses.

Table 4 illustrates the geographic origin of implicated donors. Most were from New England or Long Island, NY. The two cases from the Midwest reflect the known endemic focus of infected ticks in this area. The predominance of cases from Connecticut may, in fact, reflect the relatively high degree of exposure of Connecticut blood donors. But it may also reflect an effort on the part of the blood center and Connecticut health officials to educate physicians about babesiosis (54). It is likely that a large number of cases are subclinical throughout the endemic areas for babesiosis.

Implicated donors, in general, are asymptomatic and, typical of subclinical babesiosis, often appear to have been infected for months to years. Some donors have evidence for systemic disease, which may also reflect Lyme disease and other tickborne illnesses (55).

Table 5 considers the blood components involved in the 17 reported cases. Not surprisingly, most cases are transmitted by red cells. Platelets have been

Table 4 Transfusion-Transmitted Babesiosis—
Geographic and Donor Factors (N = 17)

Donor origin	
Southeast CT	8
Cape Cod, MA	2
Offshore islands, MA	2
Long Island, NY	3
Wisconsin	1
Minnesota	1
Period of donor infection	
<1 month	3
1–12 months	3
>12 months	1
Donor symptoms	
Chronic fatigue, hot flashes, night sweats	1
Lyme disease	1
None reported	15

Table 5   Transfusion-Transmitted Babesiosis—Blood Product Implicated (N = 19)

Blood component	
Red cells	14
Frozen red cells	1
Platelets/Platelet pheresis	4
Red cell storage	
1–7 days	0
8–21 days	7
>21 days	2
No data	5
Platelet storage	
1–3 days	2
4–5 days	1
No data	1
Infectivity—co-components	
Platelets from implicated RBC donor	One case evaluated (Case 17)—platelet recipient not infected
Red cells from implicated platelet donor	No data available
Red cells (from Case 17)	2/4 co-RBC components were infectious

implicated in only four of the reported cases, and in only one of these cases is there definite implication of the involved donor.

In only one case (Case 17) has it been possible to evaluate co-components. This interesting case illustrates the variable reactivity of red cells, since four other patients besides the index case were transfused with other aliquots of the red cells and only two were infected. The two uninfected red cell recipients were new-borns, who received smaller doses of infected red cells (56) compared with the three infected patients. A platelet concentrate made from the same donation did not transmit *Babesia* to the recipient.

These cases also provide information on the survival of the *Babesia* parasite under blood bank storage conditions. Definite cases of transfusion babesiosis have been reported with red cells as old as 35 days and platelets as old as 4 days. This is considerably longer than predicted from laboratory storage conditions (48). However, in the laboratory, storage was in EDTA whole blood in glass tubes. It is likely that blood bank storage conditions favoring red cell and/or platelet survival would also be more favorable for the survival and infectivity of the *Babesia* parasite.

The transfusion-transmission of *Babesia* species other than *B. microti* that affect humans is to be expected. However, there has been no report of transfusion transmission of *B. divergens*, the clinical babesiosis in Europe. Recently, two or three different human species in the United States have been described—in Washington State (WA-1) (37,57), in Missouri (MO1) (39), and in northern California (38). The reports of WA-1 infection have now been supplemented with a report of a transfusion-transmitted case caused by a WA-1–like organism (58), the first transfusion babesiosis not caused by *B. microti*.

This case occurred in a multiply transfused, 76-year-old, spleen-intact man with myelodysplasia and post–coronary artery bypass graft and aortic valve replacement. Originally thought to have malaria, he was treated with chloroquine and primaquine with initial resolution of symptoms. Later review at the Centers for Disease Control and Prevention (CDC) identified the unusual piroplasm in his red cells. The species was identified as very close to WA-1 serologically and non–cross-reactive with *B. microti*. His symptoms of fever and persistent parasitemia recurred, and he was treated with clindamycin and quinine; he appeared to clear his parasitemia. Fifty-seven blood donors were investigated—2 units of whole blood, 15 red cells, 36 platelets, and 4 FFP. The implicated donor was a 34-year-old red cell donor with a titer against the recipient's organism of 1:4096. He lived in rural Washington State and was frequently exposed to deer. He was parasitemic by hamster inoculation 7 months after his implicated donation. No co-component or lookback donations could be evaluated because the recipients had died or were unavailable.

This case report is strikingly similar to many *B. microti* case reports: misdiagnosis early (in this case, as malaria), chronic infection in both donor and recipient, and a mild clinical course in the recipient. It cannot be determined from the available case reports of tickborne illnesses and this transfusion case whether any of the newly reported piroplasms will represent a significant public health threat, either from tick transmission or blood transfusion. It is clear that apparent transfusion babesiosis should be suspected outside of the endemic areas for *B. microti*. The characteristic intraerythrocytic forms are the most reliable diagnostic tool. Serology to *B. microti* is likely to be negative or only weakly positive in infections with these new organisms.

X. PREVENTION STRATEGIES AND FUTURE PROSPECTS

Of all the tickborne diseases, only babesiosis currently represents a substantial risk for transfusion transmission. The disease is probably more common than is currently appreciated, but many cases are subclinical. Further work is required to establish the frequency of transmission, the possibility of other, unrecognized, clinical syndromes in infected donors and recipients, and appropriate prevention strategies.

A history of tick bite is not an effective strategy to prevent babesiosis or any other tickborne disease from entering the blood supply. More than 20% of

Connecticut blood donors who were residents of *Babesia*-endemic areas reported a tick bite during a 5-month summer season (59), as did 0.7–9.0% of donors in a postcard survey of geographically dispersed U.S. blood donors (60). Deferring such a number of donors is not feasible. Furthermore, many patients with Lyme disease and/or babesiosis do not report a tick bite.

The current indirect fluorescent antibody (IFA) screening test for babesiosis is inadequate, even for large-scale blood donor population surveys, much less as a potential donor-screening method. The test requires maintaining an infected hamster population to serve as a source of infected red cells. It also is quite subjective. This test has not been standardized for use in clinical laboratories, although it is a useful research method (61). Development of an automated microplate format test that could be applied to donor specimens is badly needed. Unlinked studies would be needed to characterize the assay and establish confirmatory methods, followed by linked testing and lookback, similar to studies currently being carried out using linked Chagas' disease screening of blood donors (62). Other *Babesia*-like organisms need further investigation, since it appears that tests for *B. microti* will not detect these organisms.

Enhanced clinical suspicion of *Babesia* is warranted, particularly in endemic areas, but also in nonendemic areas, since early clinical suspicion, laboratory recognition, and appropriate treatment appear to be important to good clinical outcome. Hematologists and blood bank professionals need to consider babesiosis in any transfused patient with fever and hemolysis. Not all hemolytic episodes after transfusion are the result of red cell antibodies! Similar recommendations exist for transfusion malaria for the same reasons.

Although Lyme disease may be transmissible by blood transfusion, it is unlikely this will represent an important means of transmission. It is likely to be overlooked if transmission occurs in areas with limited Lyme awareness or if the manifestations of transfusion transmission are found to be highly atypical for tickborne disease. In these cases, the rare case may go undetected and untreated, resulting in substantial and unnecessary morbidity. Thus, it is appropriate that transfusion medicine consultants maintain a high index of suspicion that Lyme disease could be transfusion transmissible.

Other tickborne diseases will need continued monitoring for their importance to the blood supply, but it does not appear today that they will represent important threats.

Public health methods to reduce tickborne disease should certainly help lessen exposure to infected ticks. As new exposure-prevention methods are implemented, the resultant public awareness is likely to increase their expectation that blood banks will increase their understanding of tickborne diseases and respond appropriately to their potential threat to the blood supply.

REFERENCES

1. AABB. FDA issues statement on blood donors possibly exposed to tick-borne pathogens. AABB FAXNET 1997; No. 341.

1a. Arguin PM, Singleton J, Rotz LD, Marston E, Treadwell TA, Slater K, Chamberland M, Schwartz A, Tengelsen L, Olson JG, Childs JE. An investigation into the possibility of transmission of tick-borne pathogens via blood transfusion. Transfusion 1999; 39·828–833.

2. Harwood RF, James MT. Entomology In Human and Animal Health. New York: Macmillan Publishing Company, 1979:371–378.

3. Krantz GW. A Manual of Acarology. 2nd ed. Corvalis: Oregon State University, 1878:211–215.

4. Schmidt GD, Roberts LS. In: Foundations of Parasitology. 4th ed. St. Louis: Times Mirror/Mosby College Publishing, 1989:660–663.

5. Schmidt GD, Roberts LS. In: Foundations of Parasitology. 4th ed. St. Louis: Times Mirror/Mosby College Publishing, 1989:671–679.

6. Shulman IA, Appleman MD. An overview of unusual diseases transmitted by blood transfusion within the United States. In: Westphal RG, Carlson KB, Turc JM, eds. Emerging Global Patterns in Transfusion-Transmitted Infections. Arlington, VA: American Association of Blood Banks, 1990:1–11.

7. Murray PR, Drew WL, Kobayashi GS, Thompson JH. Medical Microbiology. C.V. St. Louis: Mosby, 1990:628–632.

8. Monath TP, Tsai TF. Flaviviruses. In: Richman DD, Whitley RJ, Hayden FG, eds. Clinical Virology. New York: Churchill Livingston, 1997:1133–1134.

9. Wahlberg P, Saikku P, Brummer-Korvenkontio M. Tick-borne viral encephalitis in Finland. The clinical features of Kumlinge disease during 1959–1987. J Intern Med 1989; 225(3):173–177.

10. Costero A, Grayson MA. Experimental transmission of Powassan virus (Flaviviridae) by *Ixodes scapularis* ticks (Acari:Ixodadae). Am J Trop Med Hyg 1996; 55(5):536–546.

11. Telford SR 3rd, Armstrong PM, Katavolos P, Foppa I, Garcia AS, Wilson ML, Spielman A. A new tick-borne encephalitis-like virus infecting New England deer ticks, *Ixodes dammini*. Emerg Infect Dis 1997; 3(2):165–170.

12. Wong JK. Colorado tick fever virus and other arthropod-borne Reoviridae. In: Richman DD, Whitley RJ, Hayden FG, eds. Clinical Virology. New York: Churchill Livingston, 1997:755–764.

13. Transmission of Colorado tick fever virus by blood transfusion. MMWR 1975; 24:425–427.

14. CDC. Lyme disease—United States, 1996. MMWR 1997; 46(23):531–535.

15. Johnson RC, Schmid GP, Hyde FW, Steigerwalt AG, Brenner DJ. *Borrelia burgdorferi* sp. nov.: etiological agent of Lyme disease. Int J System Bacteriol 1984; 34:496–497.

15a. Baranton G, Postic D, Saint Girons I, Boerlin P, Piffaretti JC, Assous M, Grimont PA. Delineation of *Borrelia burgdorferi* sensu stricto, *Borrelia garinii* sp. nov. and group VS461 associated with Lyme borreliosis. Int J System Bacteriol 1992; 42:378–383.

16. Benach JL, Bosler EM, Hanrahan JP. Spirochetes isolated from the blood of two patients with Lyme disease. N Engl J Med 1983; 308:740–742.

17. Aoki SK, Holland PV. Lyme disease—another transfusion risk? Transfusion 1989; 29:646–650.

18. Badon SJ, Fister RD, Cable RG. Survival of *Borrelia burgdorferi* in blood products. Transfusion 1989; 29:581–583.

19. Badon SJ, Cable RG, Morse EE, Aslanzadeh J, Malawista SE. Evidence of *Borrelia burgdorferi* in a blood donation. Blood 1995; 86(suppl 1):355a.

20. Cable RG, Krause P, Badon S, Silver H, Ryan R. Acute blood donor co-infection with *Babesia microti* (Bm) and *Borrelia burgdorferi* (Bb) (abstr). Transfusion 1993; 33(suppl):50s.

21. Piesman J, Hicks TC, Sinsky RJ, Obiri G. Simultaneous transmission of *Borrelia burgdorferi* and *Babesia microti* by individual nymphal *Ixodes dammini* ticks. J Clin Microbiol 1987; 25:2012–2013.

22. Gerber MA, Shapiro ED, Krause PJ, Cable RG, Badon SJ, Ryan RW. The risk of acquiring Lyme disease or babesiosis from a blood transfusion. J Infect Dis 1994; 170:231–234.

23. Harwood RF, James MT. Entomology in Human and Animal Health. New York: Macmillan Publishing Company, 1979:400–403.

24. Boyer KM, Munford RS, Maupin GO, et al. Tick-borne relapsing fever: an interstate outbreak originating at Grand Canyon National Park. Am J Epidemiol 1977; 105(5): 469–479.

25. Pratt HD, Darsie RF. Highlights in medical entomology in 1974. Bull Entomol Soc Am 1975; 21:173–176.

26. Hira PR, Husein SF. Some transfusion-induced parasitic infections in Zambia. J Hyg Epidemiol Microbiol Immunol 1979; 23(4):436–444.

27. Wang CW, Lee CU. Malaria and relapsing fever following blood transfusion. Chin Med J 1936; 50:241.

28. Wells GM, Woodward TE, Fiset P, Hornick RB. Rocky Mountain spotted fever caused by blood transfusion. JAMA 1978; 239(26):2763–2765.

29. Benenson AS, ed. Control of Communicable Diseases Manual. 16th ed. Washington, DC: American Public Health Association, 1995:392–395.

30. Casleton BG, Salata K, Dasch GA, Strickman D, Kelly DJ. Recovery and viability of *Orientia* tsutsugamushi from packed red cells and the danger of acquiring scrub typhus from blood transfusion. Transfusion 1998; 38:680–689.

31. Walker DH, Dumler JS. Emergence of the ehrlichioses as human health problems. Emerg Infect Dis 1996; 2(1):18–29.

32. Magnarelli LA, Dumler JS, Anderson JF, Johnson RC, Fikrig E. Coexistence of antibodies to tick-borne pathogens of babesiosis, ehrlichiosis and Lyme borreliosis in human sera. J Clin Microbiol 1995; 33:3054–3057.

32a. Eastlund T, Persing D, Mathiesen D. Human granulocytic ehrlichiosis after red cell transfusion. Transfusion 1999; 39(suppl):117s.

33. Spielman A, Etkind P, Piesman J. Reservoir hosts of human babesiosis on Nantucket Island. Am J Trop Med Hyg 1981; 30:560–565.

34. Dammin GJ, Spielman A, Benach JL. The rising incidence of clinical *Babesia microti* infection. Hum Pathol 1981; 12:398–400.

35. Murray PR, Drew WL, Kobayashi GS, Thompson JH. Medical Microbiology. St. Louis: Mosbey, 1990:375–377.

36. Gelfand JA. *Babesia*. In: Mandell GL, Bennett JE, Dolin RA, eds. Principles and Practice of Infectious Diseases. 4th ed. New York: Churchill Livingston, 1995:2497–2500.

37. Quick RE, Herwaldt BL, Thomford JW, Garnett ME, Eberhard ML, Wilson M, Spach DH, Dickerson JW, Telford SR 3d, Steingart KR. Babesiosis in Washington State: a new species of *Babesia*? Ann Intern Med 1993; 119(4):284–290.

38. Persing DH, Herwaldt BL, Glaser C, Lane RS, Thomford JW, Mathiesen D, Krause PJ, Phillip DF, Conrad PA. Infection with a *Babesia*-like organism in northern California. N Engl J Med 1995; 332(5):298–303.

39. Herwaldt B, Persing DH, Précigout EA, Goff WL, Mathiesen DA, Taylor PW, Eberhard ML, Gorenflot AF. A fatal case of babesiosis in Missouri: identification of another piroplasm that infects humans. Ann Intern Med 1996; 124(7):643–650.

40. Shih CM, Liu LP, Chung WC, Ong SJ, Wang CC. Human babesiosis in Taiwan: asymptomatic infection with a *Babesia microti*-like organism in a Taiwanese woman. J Clin Microbiol 1997; 35(2):450–454.

41. Ruebush TK II, Juranek DD, Spielman A. Epidemiology of human babesiosis on Nantucket Island. Am J Trop Med Hyg 1981; 30:937–941.

42. Benach JL, Habicht GS. Clinical characteristics of human babesiosis. J Infect Dis 1981; 144:481.

43. Clindamycin and quinine treatment for *Babesia microti* infections. MMWR 1983; 32:65–72.

44. Jacoby GA, Hunt JV, Kosinski KS, Demirjian ZN, Huggins C, Etkind P, Marcus LC, Spielman A. Treatment of transfusion-transmitted babesiosis by exchange transfusion. N Engl J Med 1980; 303:1098–1100.

45. Popovsky MA, Lindberg LE, Syrek AL, Page, PL. Prevalence of *Babesia* antibody in a selected blood donor population. Transfusion 1988; 28:29–61.

46. Benach JL, Coleman JL, Habicht GS. Serological evidence for simultaneous occurences of Lyme disease and babesiosis. J Infect Dis 1985; 152:473–477.

47. Krause PJ, Spielman A, Telford SR III, Sikand VK, McKay K, Christianson D, Pollack RJ, Brassard P, Magera J, Ryan R, Persing EH. Persistent parasitemia after acute babesiosis. N Engl J Med 1998; 339:160–165.

48. Eberhard ML, Walker EM, Steurer F. Survival and infectivity of *Babesia* in blood maintained at 25C and 2-4C. J Parasitol 1995; 81:790–792.

49. Przyjemski CJ. Was babesiosis transmitted by transfusion? N Engl J Med 1981; 304:733.

50. Badon SJ, Cable RG. Investigation of suspected cases of post-transfusion babesiosis (abstr). Transfusion 1997; 37(suppl):56S.

51. Wittner M, Rowin KS, Tanowitz HB, Hobbs JF, Saltzman S, Wenz B, Hirsch R, Chisholm E, Healy GR. Successful chemotherapy of transfusion babesiosis. Ann Intern Med 1982; 96:601–604.

52. State of Connecticut Department of Health Services. Babesiosis—Connecticut 1990–1996. Conn Epidemiol 1997; 17:18–19.

53. Krause PJ, Telford SR, Ryan R. Geographic and temporal distribution of Babesial infection in Connecticut. J Clin Microbiol 1991; 29:1–4.

54. State of Connecticut Department of Health Services. Babesiosis update. Conn Epidemiol 1992; 12:15–16.

55. Meldrum SC, Birkhead GS, White DJ, Benach JL, Morse DL. Human babesiosis in New York State: an epidemiologic description of 136 cases. Clin Infect Dis 1992; 15:1019–1023.

56. Dobroszycki J, Herwaldt BL, Boctor F, Miller JR, Linden J, Eberhard ML, Yoon JJ, Ali NM, Tanowitz HB, Graham F, Weiss LM, Wittner M. A cluster of transfusion-associated babesiosis cases traced to a single asymptomatic donor. JAMA 1999; 281:927–930.

57. Thomford JW, Conrad PA, Telford SR III. Cultivation and phylogenetic characterization of a newly recognized human pathogenic protozoan. J Infect Dis 1994; 169:1050–1056.

58. Herwaldt BL, Kjemtrup AM, Conrad PA, Barnes RC. Transfusion-transmitted babesiosis in Washington State: first reported case caused by a WA-1 parasite. J Infect Dis 1997; 1275:1259–1262.

59. Trouern-Trend JJ, Leiby DA, Cable RG, Badon SJ. Self-reported tick exposure in a *Babesia*-endemic area. (abstr) Transfusion 1997; 37(suppl):48S.

60. Chung APS, Leiby DA, Persing DH, Cable RG, Trouern-Trend JJ, McCullough J. Seroprevalence of *Babesia microti* and *Ehrlichia* sp in US blood donors (abstr). Transfusion 1998; 38(suppl):S392.

61. Krause P, Telford S, Ryan R, Conrad P. Antibody testing for babesiosis: standardization of a serologic test for the diagnosis of human *Babesia microti* infection. J Infect Dis 1994; 923–926.

62. Leiby DA, Jensen NC, Fucci M-C, Stumpf RJ. Prevalence of *Trypanosoma cruzi* antibodies in a blood donor population at low risk (abstr.) Transfusion 1997; 37(suppl):S297.

63. Grabowski EF, Giardina PJ, Goldberg D, Masur H, Read SE, Hirsch RL, Benach JL. Babesiosis transmitted by a transfusion of frozen-thawed blood. Ann Int Med 1982; 96:466–467.

64. Marcus LC, Valigorsky JM, Fanning W. A case of transfusion-induced babesiosis. JAMA 1982; 248:465–467.

65. Gordon S, Cordon RA, Mazdzer EJ, Valigorsky JM, Blagg NA, Barnes SJ. Adult respiratory distress syndrome in babesiosis. Chest 1984; 86:633–634.

66. Smith RP, Evans AT, Popovsky M. Transfusion-acquired babesiosis and failure of antibiotic treatment. JAMA 1986; 256:2726–2727.

67. Mintz ED, Anderson JF, Cable RG, Hadler JL. Transfusion-transmitted babesiosis: a case report from a new endemic area. Transfusion 1991; 31:365–368.

68. Reddy RL, Dalmasso AP. Transfusion acquired babesiosis in Minnesota (abstr). In: ISBT and AABB 1990 Joint Congress Abstract Book. Arlington, VA: American Association of Blood Banks, 1990:11.

69. Cable RG, Krause P, Badon S, Silver H, Ryan R (abstr) Acute blood donor co-infection with *Babesia microti* (Bm) and *Borrelia burgdorferi* (Bb). Transfusion 1993; 33(suppl.):50s.

70. Gerber MA, Shapiro ED, Krause PJ, Cable RG, Badon SJ, Ryan RW. The risk of acquiring Lyme disease or babesiosis from a blood transfusion. J Infect Dis 1994; 170:231–234.

18

Surveillance for Transfusion-Transmitted Infectious Diseases

Mary E. Chamberland and Rima F. Khabbaz
Centers for Disease Control and Prevention, Atlanta, Georgia

I. INTRODUCTION

The U.S. blood supply is among the safest in the world. The risk of transfusion-transmitted infections has been markedly reduced as a result of improvements in donor screening and serological testing, the development and implementation of viral inactivation procedures for plasma-derived products, and changes in transfusion practices. Nevertheless, since blood is a human tissue, it is a natural vehicle for transmission of infectious agents. The transmission of human immunodeficiency virus (HIV) through the blood supply in the early 1980s and the more recent experiences with hepatitis C virus (HCV) transmission from intravenous immune globulin (IVIG) (1) and bacterial sepsis from contaminated albumin (2) point to the need for continued vigilance regarding both known and unrecognized or uncharacterized threats to the blood supply.

An important component of the multifaceted approach to help ensure the safety of the blood supply is surveillance. As part of its retrospective review of the events of the early 1980s that led to the transmission of HIV through blood and blood products, the Institute of Medicine developed a series of recommendations to help thwart future threats to the blood supply. One of these was a recommendation to establish "a surveillance system . . . [to] detect, monitor, and warn of adverse effects in recipients of blood and blood products" (3).

Surveillance is defined as "the ongoing systematic collection, analysis, and interpretation of health data, closely integrated with the timely dissemination of these data both to those providing the data and to those who can apply the data to control and prevention programs" (4). While surveillance is distinct from epidemiological research, the two are often complementary (5). Epidemiological research studies usually start with a specific hypothesis to be tested, are conducted in a well-defined population, and are often time-limited; in addition, the data are complete. In contrast, surveillance data are often used to identify or describe a problem, identify cases for epidemiological research, monitor temporal trends, or estimate the magnitude of a problem. Surveillance usually encompasses many more individuals than might be enrolled in a research study. As a consequence, data collected by surveillance, which can either be active or passive, are usually less complete, less detailed, and more open-ended than research data. Importantly, surveillance programs provide an infrastructure or network, such that in the event of an unusual case report or an acute problem, even if not related to the surveillance program, an established methodology is in place for communicating information directly to public health authorities.

This chapter will review the Centers for Disease Control and Prevention's (CDC) major systems of surveillance for transfusion-transmitted infectious diseases in the United States. CDC has several different programs of surveillance for current or potential risks related to transfusion of blood and blood products. Some programs are disease-based, while others monitor donors and recipients of blood and blood products. In addition, applied research conducted by CDC and others to assess the risk of transmission of infections through transfusion will be presented.

II. HUMAN IMMUNODEFICIENCY VIRUSES

A. National Surveillance for Acquired Immunodeficiency Syndrome

National surveillance and reporting of acquired immunodeficiency syndrome (AIDS) has been in place for nearly 15 years. All states and U.S. territories require reporting of AIDS cases to local health authorities. State and local health departments, in turn, transmit cases electronically to CDC (6). Health department staff actively survey case reports submitted from physicians, hospitals, laboratories, and other medical care facilities and from record systems, such as death certificates and tumor registries. Although completeness of reporting of diagnosed AIDS cases varies by geographic region and patient population, reporting of AIDS cases in most areas of the United States is more than 85% complete (7,8). Overall, about 50% of all AIDS cases are reported to CDC within 3 months of diagnosis (6).

AIDS surveillance captures data on cases resulting from transfusion of blood and blood products and among persons with hemophilia. Such cases increased dramatically during the mid-1980s and then stabilized or declined slightly until 1993 (Figs. 1 and 2). AIDS case reports received after January 1993 were influenced by an expanded AIDS surveillance case definition and chiefly represent reporting of persons who had $CD4^+$ cell counts below 200/uL with or without illness. This change greatly altered the pattern of case reports, and was most pronounced in the first 3 months of 1993. Since that time, the number of case reports each year among transfusion recipients and persons with hemophilia has returned to pre-1993 levels. Most cases reported since 1985 reflect infections that occurred before serological screening of donors and heat and chemical inactivation of clotting factor concentrates were initiated and the long period between infection with HIV and progression to AIDS. Since the institution of these practices, AIDS surveillance has identified persons who report receipt of blood and blood products screened negative for HIV antibody. Such reports trigger epidemiological and laboratory investigations of case-patients and of donors. Through December 1996, 36 adults and adolescents and 3 children had developed AIDS after receiving blood screened negative for HIV antibody (i.e., during the "window period" before the development of detectable HIV antibodies) (6). To assist in the identification of AIDS cases related to transfusion of blood products, algorithms have been developed for follow-up of persons with hemophilia and AIDS who report no other risk factors (P. Sullivan, personal communication). In particular, AIDS cases are examined and investigated for persons born after 1985 who should have received only screened blood products and for persons who have evidence of a recent seroconversion. In addition, as part of CDC's and state and local health departments' investigation of AIDS cases with no identified risk, information is sought about possible exposure to blood products. These investigations employ systematic and standardized procedures, including review of pertinent records and interview of the patient and others (6).

B. Serosurveillance of Blood Donors for HIV

The national HIV serosurveillance program, which includes seroprevalence surveys conducted in selected sentinel sites throughout the country, also contributes to monitoring the safety of the blood supply. CDC has collaborated with the American National Red Cross since 1985 to establish donor-based systems of surveillance, using data from the routine testing of blood donors (9). HIV prevalence data are available from nearly 50 American National Red Cross blood centers, which account for approximately half of the blood collected in the United States. Since monitoring began, the overall HIV prevalence rate has decreased nearly fourfold, from one positive for every 4,500 persons tested in late 1985 to less than one positive for every 15,000 persons tested (Fig. 3) (10). This decline

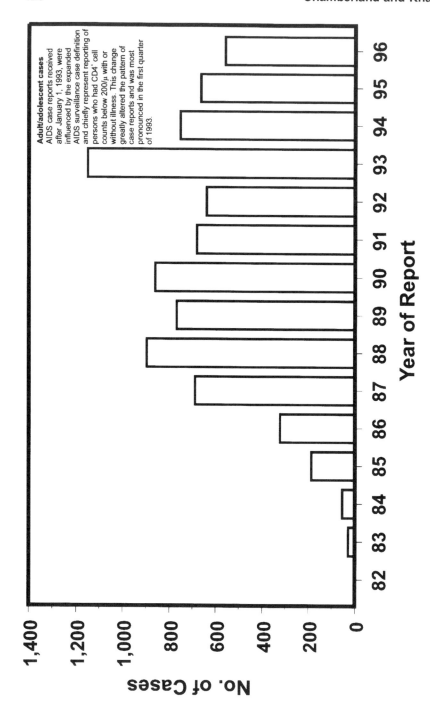

Figure 1 Adult and pediatric cases of acquired immunodeficiency syndrome in the United States attributed to receipt of blood transfusion, blood components, or tissue, by year of report, 1982–1996.

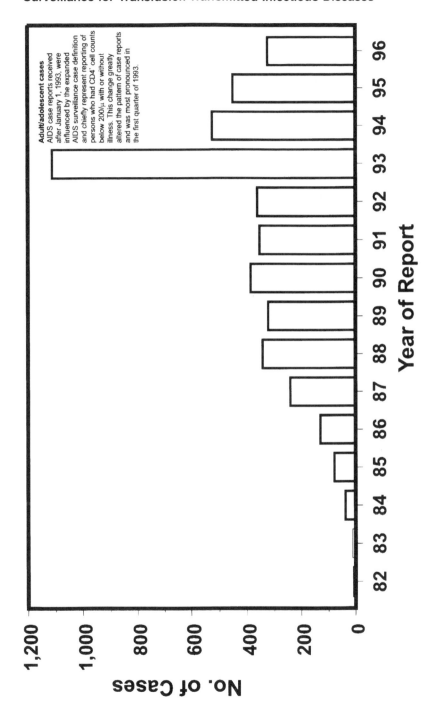

Adult/adolescent cases
AIDS case reports received after January 1, 1993, were influenced by the expanded AIDS surveillance case definition and chiefly represent reporting of persons who had CD4⁺ cell counts below 200/μ with or without illness. This change greatly altered the pattern of case reports and was most pronounced in the first quarter of 1993.

Figure 2 Adult and pediatric cases of acquired immunodeficiency syndrome in the United States among persons with hemophilia or other coagulation disorders, by year of report, 1982–1996.

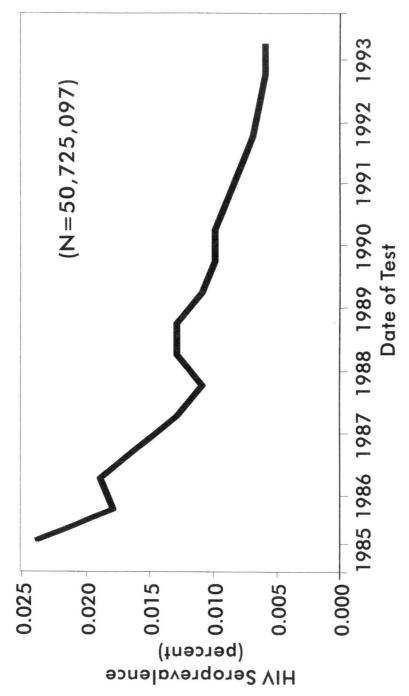

Figure 3 HIV seroprevalence in blood donors in the United States, by date of donation, November 1985–December 1993. (From Ref. 10.)

likely reflects aggressive donor education programs, improved donor selection and screening through interview and serological testing, the progressive elimination of HIV-infected donors among repeat donors (repeat donors comprise approximately 80% of all donations), and increased awareness among potential donors of their HIV infection status due to the widespread availability of HIV testing and counseling (11–13).

Incidence data from a subset of blood centers in this surveillance system have been used to derive estimates of the residual risk of transmission of HIV by screened blood; current risk estimates are one case of HIV transmission for every 450,000–660,000 donations of screened blood in the United States (13). In addition, the National Institutes of Health coordinates a multidisciplinary epidemiological research program, the Retrovirus Epidemiology Donor Study (REDS), to study the incidence of various infectious agents among volunteer blood donors in five blood centers (14). REDS found a similar estimate (one HIV transmission per 493,000 donations) for HIV transmitted by transfusion of screened blood (15). To further reduce the risk of transfusion-transmitted HIV-1 infection, p24 antigen screening of all blood and plasma donations was instituted in March 1996. HIV-1 p24 antigen detects HIV infection an average of 6 days before antibody tests are positive (16). Initial projections estimated that four to six infectious donations, not captured by other screening tests, would be detected among the 12 million blood donations collected annually. However, in the first 9 months, only one antigen-positive/antibody-negative donation was detected among 6.1 million blood donations evaluated (17).

Another important outgrowth of CDC and the American National Red Cross' serosurveillance of blood donors is evaluation of HIV-infected blood donors. Since 1988, CDC, in collaboration with the American National Red Cross and other major blood collection agencies, has conducted follow-up interviews and serological testing of HIV-seropositive donors. Information from these studies has been used to develop epidemiological and behavioral profiles of HIV-seropositive donors, learn more about their reasons and motivations for donation, and help blood centers improve strategies for encouraging appropriate self-deferral (18). Despite these efforts, some donors with risk behaviors that may put them at increased risk for HIV and other infectious diseases continue to donate. REDS used an anonymous mail survey of a sample of persons who had donated blood in 1993 and found that 1.9% of respondents reported a deferrable risk that was present at the time of their past donation (19).

C. Surveillance for Divergent Strains of HIV-1

The overwhelming majority of HIV infections throughout the world are caused by HIV-1 viruses belonging to group M. HIV-1 viruses in group O (i.e., "outlier" group) have been recently identified and characterized. The number of group O infections reported worldwide is small, and most have occurred among persons in West and Central Africa countries (20). However, because these infections are inconsistently detected by current enzyme immunoassays (EIAs) for antibodies to HIV-1, there are important implications for blood safety (21). CDC has an ongoing program to evaluate HIV-seropositive blood donors for unusual variants; previous studies that evaluated blood donors and other populations have not found any evidence of infection with HIV-1 group O (22). In addition, CDC has established active international and domestic surveillance for divergent HIV strains to monitor their prevalence, evaluate the sensitivity of licensed HIV serological tests for detecting these variants, and assist in the modification of screening tests to improve their sensitivity. As part of this surveillance program, CDC, in collaboration with state health departments, is undertaking epidemiological and laboratory investigations of persons who were reported with HIV/AIDS and who were born in a country where HIV-1 group O has been documented (i.e., West and Central Africa). Two HIV-1 group O infections among persons in the United States have been reported through this sentinel surveillance; both persons were originally from Africa, and neither was a blood donor (23,24). Efforts are underway to modify existing HIV-EIAs to improve detection of group O strains, without compromising sensitivity for the group M viruses. As an interim measure, the U.S. Food and Drug Administration (FDA) has recommended that donors at increased risk for HIV-1 group O infection (e.g., resident in areas where group O strains are endemic) be deferred from donating blood or plasma.

D. HIV-2

HIV-2, another retrovirus that causes AIDS and is endemic in many countries in West Africa, has been transmitted by transfusion of blood and blood products in Europe (25). Epidemiological and donor testing data indicate that the prevalence of HIV-2 among blood donors in the United States is very low. Nevertheless, because of the potential for transmission by blood and blood products and the availability of licensed combination HIV-1/HIV-2 EIAs, FDA recommended in June 1992 that blood and plasma donors be screened for antibodies to HIV-2. No cases of transfusion-acquired HIV-2 infection have been reported in the United States, and only three HIV-2 seropositive units have been found among whole blood and plasma donors (26).

III. HEPATITIS B AND HEPATITIS C VIRUSES

The Viral Hepatitis Surveillance Program (VHSP) provides nationwide information about hepatitis (27). VHSP receives reports of hepatitis from state and local health departments using a standardized case record that is either mailed or transmitted electronically to CDC. The form collects clinical, laboratory, and epidemiological data. Since VHSP is a passive system for surveillance, interpretation of data is complicated by underreporting and incomplete reporting of serologic and epidemiological data.

Consequently, beginning in 1979, CDC began a complementary, more intensive program of surveillance for acute viral hepatitis in several sentinel counties, which are representative of the United States as a whole (28). In the Sentinel Counties Study of Acute Viral Hepatitis, attempts are made to stimulate reporting by writing to physicians, making on-site visits to hospital infection-control and laboratory personnel, and through publicity in local medical newsletters (29). Patients are interviewed to identify risk factors for hepatitis, and blood for serological testing is obtained from all patients and contacts whenever possible. The sentinel counties study has facilitated the identification of new or emerging types of hepatitis viruses (e.g., hepatitis G virus), because it incorporates state-of-the-art serological and nucleic acid-based testing. Both the VHSP and sentinel counties systems collect data on transfusion of blood and blood products.

The data collected in these systems have been useful in monitoring epidemiological trends for the various types of hepatitis. For example, the VHSP and the sentinel counties study have documented declines in transfusion-associated hepatitis B virus (HBV) and HCV infection (Fig. 4) (27,28,30). The population-based sentinel counties study found that most non-A, non-B hepatitis in the United States is not transfusion-associated and that the number of cases of transfusion-associated hepatitis C declined significantly after 1985 (31). Most of this decline occurred before surrogate testing of blood donors began and was temporally associated with changes in the donor population resulting from exclusion of persons at high risk for HIV infection and HIV antibody–positive donors, as well as with changes in transfusion practices.

No direct measures of transfusion-transmitted viral hepatitis are available. The current incidence of transfusion-associated hepatitis infections is so low in the sentinel counties study that the small sample size precludes further identification of transfusion-associated cases. Current estimates for HBV infection range from one infection in 500,000 units transfused (32), derived from the frequency of HBV infection among donors and the sensitivity of serological assays for identifying hepatitis B surface antigen (HBsAg) and antibody to hepatitis B core antigen (anti-HBc), to one in 63,000, derived from a study of incident infections among repeat blood donors, which estimated the infectious window period for HBV prior to HBsAg seroconversion (15). The residual risk for transfusion-acquired HCV infection is estimated to range from one in 10,000 (32) to one in 103,000 donations (15). This risk is higher than that for HBV and HIV infections because of the lower sensitivity (90–95%) of contemporary tests (i.e., second-version EIAs) used to screen blood donors; a longer window period (average 82

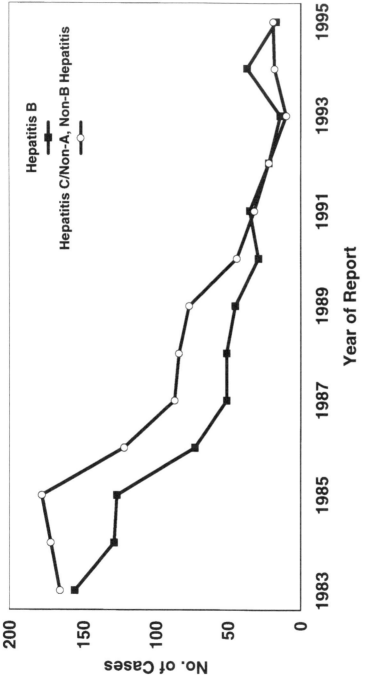

Figure 4 Cases of hepatitis B and hepatitis C/non-A, non-B hepatitis attributed to blood transfusion from selected states, by year of report, 1983–1995. (From Ref. 27.)

days; range 54–192 days) during which antibodies cannot be detected; and an inability to reliably detect chronic infection (15,32). A third-version anti-HCV test, recently approved for screening blood donors, may further improve the ability to detect anti-HCV antibodies in a low-prevalence population, such as blood donors (33).

Although viral inactivation procedures have virtually eliminated the risk of HCV infection from plasma-derived products, the first outbreak of hepatitis C associated with contaminated IVIG was reported in the United States in 1994 (1). Infection was associated with lots of Gammagard™ (Baxter Healthcare Corporation, Deerfield, IL) produced from plasma screened by second-version anti-HCV assays that were positive for HCV RNA. It has been hypothesized that the second-version tests removed most of the complexing antibodies from plasma used to make IGIV, ultimately resulting in more HCV in the IG fraction than in the non-IG fraction. In addition, manufacture of this particular product did not include a viral inactivation step as a further measure for product safety.

IV. HUMAN T-LYMPHOTROPIC VIRUSES TYPE I AND TYPE II

Currently, there is no national program of surveillance for infections caused by human T-lymphotropic viruses type I and type II (HTLV-I and HTLV-II). Epidemiological studies conducted in the United States have found that HTLV-I infection is concentrated largely among blacks in the southeastern states and among immigrants from countries where HTLV-I is highly endemic (e.g., Japan, countries in the Caribbean basin) (34). In contrast, HTLV-II is very prevalent among injecting drug users and several American Indian populations in the United States. Modes of transmission include sexual contact, sharing contaminated needles, from mother to child (primarily through breast-feeding), and blood transfusion (34).

Both viruses are cell-associated and have been transmitted by transfusion of cellular blood products (e.g., whole blood, red blood cells, and platelets); noncellular blood components derived from plasma, such as cryoprecipitate, have not been associated with transmission (34). A screening EIA to test blood donors for HTLV-I was introduced in late 1988; however, because the two viruses are quite homologous, significant cross-reactivity with HTLV-II occurs with both screening and confirmatory tests. Among the more than 8.5 million donations tested during 1989, 0.015% were confirmed as seropositive; based on polymerase chain reaction (PCR) testing of a sample of the seropositive donations, approximately half were infected with HTLV-I and half with HTLV-II (35).

Estimates of the residual risk of transfusion-transmitted HTLV range from one in 50,000 screened donated units (based on seroprevalence rates among donors and screening test sensitivity) (36) to one in 641,000 (based on a study of incident infections among repeat blood donors in the infectious window period) (15). The former estimate is similar to that observed in a prospective study by Nelson and coworkers of patients who received transfusions during cardiac surgery between 1985 and 1991 (37). They found that the combined rate of transfusion-transmitted HTLV-I and -II fell from about one in 8,500 units transfused before donor screening to one in 69,272 units after institution of screening. The relative insensitivity of combined tests, particularly in detecting HTLV-II (the more common retrovirus of the two in the United States), has been a concern. Although as many as 43% of HTLV-II–infected donations may have gone undetected when earlier EIAs were used (38), more recent assays have reduced this proportion to about 3–4% (39).

V.   CREUTZFELDT-JAKOB DISEASE

Creutzfeldt-Jakob disease (CJD) is a rare, invariably fatal neurodegenerative disease believed to be caused by an unconventional, disinfection-resistant infectious agent (40). The likely causative agent is a prion protein, which is a confirmationally altered form of a normal plasma membrane protein. Iatrogenic cases of CJD in recipients of human pituitary-derived growth hormone and dura mater grafts have had incubation periods of as long as 20 years. The CJD agent has been reported occasionally in the blood of CJD patients at low titer, and inoculation of peripheral blood mononuclear cells and some derivatives of plasma from CJD patients into rodent brains has resulted in CJD-like lesions (40–43). In contrast to these experimental data, there has been to date no confirmed reports of CJD resulting from receipt of blood transfusion. Epidemiological case-control studies show no increase in the frequency of transfusions among CJD patients compared with controls (44–47).

CDC has several systems of surveillance in place to help assess the risk, if any, of transmission of CJD by transfusion of blood and blood products. CDC conducts routine surveillance for CJD through ongoing review of national mortality data. Results from 1979 through 1994 indicate that annual rates of CJD have remained stable (at about one case per million population) (48). Thus, despite regular blood donation by persons who subsequently develop CJD, blood transfusions do not appear to be amplifying CJD infections in the U.S. population. None of the 3642 reported cases of CJD was also reported to have hemophilia, thalassemia, or sickle cell disease—diseases associated with increased exposure to blood or blood products, such as clotting factor concentrates and/or cryoprecipitate or red blood cells (49). Two studies suggest that routine mortality surveillance has good sensitivity to detect CJD cases. The first study, conducted in 11 states, found that 80% of all neuropathologically confirmed cases of CJD during 1986–1988 could be ascertained by review of death certificates (50). The second study was conducted in April 1996 in four Emerging Infections Program sites in three states and two metropolitan areas as part of active surveillance for the newly reported variant of CJD and physician-diagnosed cases of CJD (51). In these surveillance areas, greater than 90% of all pathologists, neurologists, and neuropathologists were contacted. Of the 94 CJD deaths identified during 1991–1995, 81 (86%) were found from death certificate review.

In 1995, CDC began to supplement this routine surveillance for CJD by actively soliciting more than 140 hemophilia treatment centers in the United States for any case reports of CJD. This effort also included arranging for neuropathological examinations of brain tissue from deceased hemophilic patients with neurological disorders to look for signs of CJD and the presence of the agent thought to cause the disease. Despite active solicitation of treatment centers, as well as efforts to increase providers' awareness about CJD through educational symposia at national hemophilia meetings, no center has reported a patient with clinical CJD (B. Evatt, personal communication). Neuropathological examination has been completed for 26 deceased persons with hemophilia; none had evidence of CJD (B. Evatt, personal communication).

Finally, to further enhance the evidence derived from routine surveillance, CDC is assisting in coordinating a long-term, follow-up study of recipients who received blood components from donors who were subsequently reported to have been diagnosed with CJD (52). The vital status of 179 recipients of transfusable blood components from 14 donors who subsequently developed CJD has been determined by using primarily the national death index through 1995; none of these recipients were reported to have died of CJD. Among these recipients, 41 persons lived 5 or more years after their transfusion, including 9 who lived as long as 13–24 years. At least one additional follow-up study of recipients of blood from donors who subsequently developed CJD has not detected CJD in recipients (53).

VI. BACTERIAL CONTAMINATION

The incidence and range of adverse clinical outcomes from bacterial contamination of blood have been poorly characterized (54,55). From 1986 through 1991, FDA received reports of 182 transfusion-associated fatalities, of which 29 (16%) were caused by bacterial contamination of blood products (56,57). However, the incidence of both fatal and nonfatal bacteria-associated transfusion-related complications is likely underestimated (55,56). Recently, the U.S. General Accounting Office estimated that the rate of bacteria-associated adverse reactions from random donor platelet pools was 0.6 per 1000 pooled units (58). Transfusion of red blood cells has been associated with bacterial sepsis, most often due to

Yersinia enterocolitica, which grows readily in refrigerated blood. From November 1985 through November 1996, CDC received 21 reports of sepsis, including 12 deaths, associated with transfusion of red blood cells contaminated with *Y. enterocolitica* (56). Similar to what has been reported for platelet-related bacteremia, the risk for sepsis increases with duration of storage of red blood cells, and most episodes are associated with erythrocytes stored for ≥25 days (54,55). The risk for red blood cell–associated sepsis has been estimated to be one per 500,000 units transfused (59); similarly, AuBuchon has estimated that one of every 1,000,000 units may be associated with endotoxin-induced septic shock caused by gram-negative bacteria (60).

Because rates of bacteria-associated transfusion reactions in the United States are unknown, CDC, in collaboration with national blood-collection organizations, is initiating a prospective study to determine the rates of bacteria-associated transfusion reactions from whole blood, red blood cells, and platelets (56). This study will establish standardized definitions and systematic procedures for the recognition, reporting, and clinical, epidemiological, and laboratory evaluation of adverse transfusion reactions in recipients of contaminated blood or blood components.

VII. TRANSFUSION-INDUCED PARASITIC DISEASES

A. Babesiosis

Babesia are intraerythrocytic parasites that can cause chronic asymptomatic infection and hence pose a transfusion risk. Although there is no national surveillance program for cases of babesiosis, hundreds of cases of babesiosis have been reported in the United States, mostly in the Northeast. Of these, fewer than 25 cases of transfusion-associated babesiosis from asymptomatic infected blood donors, mostly caused by *Babesia microti* but also by the more recently recognized WA1-type *Babesia* parasite, have been reported (61–63). The parasite survives blood banking conditions and is transmissible by transfusion of red blood cells and platelet concentrates (64). With the expansion of deer populations in the northeastern United States, concerns exist that the incidence of transfusion-transmitted babesiosis may increase (65). The tick vector and animal reservoir of the *Babesia* more recently found in the northwestern United States remain to be identified. Current strategies for prevention of transfusion-transmitted *Babesia* rely on questioning donors for history of babesiosis and on performing a hematocrit determination at the time of donation. Babesiosis classically manifests as a febrile illness with hemolytic anemia, but infection can also cause chronic asymptomatic or mildly symptomatic parasitemia. The risk for severe disease is higher in the elderly, asplenic, and immunocompromised patients.

B. Chagas' Disease

Chagas' disease, a vectorborne disease caused by the parasite *Trypanosoma cruzi*, is endemic in parts of Central and South America and Mexico. Transmission in nature occurs by cutaneous or mucosal contact with the feces of reduvid bugs. If untreated, Chagas' disease can result in lifelong, asymptomatic parasitemia; infected individuals can in turn transmit *T. cruzi* through transfusion. Receipt of blood transfusions is the most common means of transmission in some disease-endemic areas (66).

The immigration of thousands of persons from *T. cruzi*–endemic areas and increased international travel have raised concerns about the increased potential for transfusion-transmitted Chagas' disease in North America (54). It has been estimated that at least 100,000 persons with chronic *T. cruzi* infection reside in the United States (66). To date, there have been three reported cases of Chagas' disease from transfusions in the United States and one in Canada; all four patients were immunocompromised and developed acute, symptomatic disease, which facilitated their recognition (54,66). The American National Red Cross has conducted limited lookback studies of recipients of blood and blood products that were seropositive for antibodies to *T. cruzi* and found no evidence of transmission, suggesting that the transmission rate in the United States may be no higher than 10% (58,67). Until recently, reliable seroprevalence estimates among blood donors have been hampered by the lack of serological tests with adequate sensitivity and specificity. More recent studies using screening and confirmatory testing schemas and conducted among selected blood donors who were more likely to be at increased risk for *T. cruzi* infection because of birth in or travel to disease-endemic countries have found approximately 0.1% of such donors to be seropositive for antibodies to *T. cruzi* (58,67–69). Extrapolating from these and other studies, Dodd estimated that the overall risk for *T. cruzi* contamination is one in 42,000 per unit of donated blood in the United States (58). Although there is no national surveillance system in place to monitor transfusion-associated Chagas' disease, the drug (nifurtimox) that is used to treat acute infection in the United States is available only through CDC's Drug Service. Hence, CDC would likely learn of diagnosed, symptomatic cases of acute infection.

C. Leishmaniasis

Leishmaniasis is a parasitic disease, primarily found in the tropics and subtropics, that is transmitted in nature by the bite of infected sand flies. Leishmaniasis can cause skin lesions (cutaneous leishmaniasis) or mucosal lesions (mucosal leishmaniasis) or invade internal organs (e.g., liver, spleen, bone marrow) of the body (visceral leishmaniasis) and cause anemia, weakness, and sometimes death, if untreated. Visceral leishmaniasis, caused by organisms in the *Leishmania donovani* species complex, can be associated with parasitemia and therefore with the potential for transmission by blood transfusion. Transmission of leish-maniasis by blood transfusion has been reported only in rare instances (fewer than 15 cases worldwide), and no case of any type of leishmaniasis acquired by blood transfusion has been reported in the United States (B. Herwaldt, personal communication).

Concern about the potential for transmission of leishmania through blood transfusion occurred when a previously undescribed type of visceral leishmania-sis was found to affect a small number of persons who had been deployed to the Persian Gulf as part of Operation Desert Storm (70). To date, the Department of Defense has parasitologically confirmed 12 cases of this unusual type of visceral leishmaniasis, called viscerotropic leishmaniasis, among the almost 700,000 deployed personnel (A. Magill, personal communication) (70,71). Viscerotropic leishmaniasis is unusual in that it is caused by a parasite (*Leishmania tropica*) that typically causes cutaneous leishmaniasis, but in this instance the parasite invades the internal organs of the body. All but one of the 12 detected cases of viscerotropic leishmaniasis were in symptomatic persons; however, the clinical manifestations were nonspecific. Parasitological confirmation of an active case of viscerotropic leishmaniasis is difficult because it requires an invasive proce-dure (e.g., a bone marrow or lymph node aspiration), and infected persons generally have low levels of the parasite.

In November 1991, the U.S. Department of Defense and the American Association of Blood Banks recommended that all persons who had traveled to the Persian Gulf after August 1, 1990, be deferred as blood donors. This was a precautionary measure because the prevalence of viscerotropic leismaniasis was not known. In addition, *L. tropica* is known to survive in refrigerated components and retain its infectivity (72). In January 1993, the American Association of Blood Banks and the Department of Defense lifted the ban; no additional cases of viscerotropic leishmaniasis had been identified during the nearly 14 months of the ban (73).

D. Malaria

Malaria is a reportable disease in the United States, and cases confirmed by blood smear are reported to local and/or state health departments by health care providers and/or laboratories (74). CDC also directly obtains reports of other cases from health care providers who request assistance in the diagnosis or treatment of malaria. All reported cases of malaria that are acquired in the United States are fully investigated to collect detained clinical and epidemiological data. For cases in persons who report no history of international travel but who received a blood transfusion, the blood bank is contacted to identify and collect blood specimens from potentially implicated donors. Donors are serologically tested, and any seropositive donors are investigated. Implicated donors are more likely to be identified by indirect fluorescent-antibody detection than by blood smear examination alone; most have subpatent parasitemia, and a positive blood smear is found only in approximately 30% of donors (75).

On average, approximately three cases per year of transfusion-induced malaria are reported in the United States (75). The overall incidence of transfusion-transmitted malaria in the United States is about one case per every 4 million units of blood collected (75). The infecting *Plasmodium* species for the 99 cases of transfusion-induced malaria reported in 1958–1994 were: *P. malariae*, 32 (32%); *P. falciparum*, 31 (31%); *P. vivax*, 28 (28%); *P. ovale*, 7 (7%); and *P. falciparum* and *P. malariae*, 1 (1%) (M. Parise, personal communication). Of the 70 implicated donors, 39 (56%) were foreign nationals (M. Parise, personal communication). At present, the optimal means of preventing transmission of malaria by blood transfusion is through deferral of donors with a history of malaria or a relevant travel history. CDC's investigations of transfusion-acquired malaria cases indicate that most commonly implicated donors incorrectly answer questions regarding travel to a malaria-endemic area.

VIII. HEMOPHILIA SURVEILLANCE ACTIVITIES

Another approach to monitoring the virological safety of blood products relies on surveillance programs that focus on recipients of blood and plasma products. CDC has two such systems of surveillance: the Hemophilia Surveillance System (HSS) and the Universal Data Collection System (J. M. Soucie, personal communication). The HSS is a population-based program designed to identify all persons with hemophilia in six states (Colorado, Georgia, Louisiana, Massachusetts, New York, and Oklahoma). Cases are identified from various sources, including hemophilia treatment centers, practicing hematologists, and others. To date, approximately 4000 patients (or 25% of the estimated U.S. hemophilia population) have been identified. Data are collected through retrospective chart abstraction and include available serological testing data for hepatitis A, B, and C viruses and HIV. In addition, information about any infectious diseases diagnosed during hospitalizations is collected. Data abstraction began in 1995 for the years 1993 and 1994 and is planned to continue through 1999. Analyses that are planned include determination of prevalence and incidence rates of hepatitis and HIV infection and examination of any unusual clinical illnesses.

To complement the HSS, CDC, in cooperation with health care providers in comprehensive hemophilia treatment centers, has developed a new national, prospective system called the Universal Data Collection System, which will be fully implemented in 1998 (J. M. Soucie, personal communication). This system gathers a uniform set of data about the health outcomes of an estimated 17,000–

20,000 persons with hemophilia and related congenital blood clotting disorders in the United States. Data about the nature and extent of joint and infectious disease complications are collected in all 144 federally sponsored, specialized hemophilia treatment centers throughout the country. In addition, a serum specimen is sent to CDC for serological testing for hepatitis and HIV infection and for storage in a national serum bank for use in future investigations related to blood safety issues. The system also has an acute illness–reporting system that facilitates identification and investigation of potential infection sources and outbreaks and the development of intervention strategies to prevent further disease occurrence.

IX. CONCLUSION

Since blood is a biological product, it is unlikely that the risk of transfusion-transmitted infections will ever be reduced to zero. Nonetheless, the blood supply in the United States in the 1990s is among the safest in the world and is safer now than it has ever been. Factors contributing to the reduced risk of transfusion-transmitted infections include improvements in donor selection, donor screening by serological tests and other markers of infection, and viral inactivation procedures for plasma-derived products. These approaches, coupled with surveillance to monitor for trends in infection, are the mainstay of public health strategies to protect the blood supply from known pathogens and to monitor for the emergence of new infectious agents. CDC views surveillance as a critical component of its overall mission. One of the four goals of CDC's strategic plan to help address emerging infectious threats is the improvement and expansion of surveillance capabilities for infectious diseases in the United States and internationally (76). Enhanced surveillance can play an important role in helping to ensure the safety of blood and plasma products.

REFERENCES

1. Bresee JS, Mast EE, Coleman PJ, Baron MJ, Schonberger LB, Alter MJ, Jonas MM, Yu MW, Renzi PM, Schneider LC. Hepatitis C virus infection associated with administration of intravenous immune globulin. A cohort study. JAMA 1996; 276:1563–1567.
2. Centers for Disease Control and Prevention. Bacterial sepsis associated with receipt of albumin. MMWR 1996; 45:866–867.
3. Committee to Study HIV Transmission Through Blood and Blood Products, Division of Health Promotion and Disease Prevention, Institute of Medicine. Leveton LB, Sox HC Jr, Stoto MA, eds. HIV and the Blood Supply. An analysis of crisis decisionmaking. Washington, DC: National Academy Press, 1995.
4. Thacker SB, Berkelman RL, Stroup DF. The science of public health surveillance. J Public Health Policy 1989; 10:187–203.

5. Thacker SB, Berkelman RL. Public health surveillance in the United States. Epidemiol Rev 1988; 10:164–190.

6. Centers for Disease Control and Prevention. HIV/AIDS Surveillance Report 1996; 8(no. 2):1–39.

7. Buehler JW, Berkelman RL, Stehr-Green JK. The completeness of AIDS surveillance. J AIDS 1992; 5:257–264.

8. Rosenblum L, Buehler JW, Morgan MW, Costa S, Hidalgo J, Holmes R, Lieb L, Shields A, Whyte BM. The completeness of AIDS case reporting, 1988: A multistate collaborative surveillance project. Am J Public Health 1992; 82:1495–1499.

9. Petersen LR, Dodd R, Dondero TJ Jr. Methodologic approaches to surveillance of HIV infection among blood donors. Pub Health Rep 1990; 105:153–157.

10. Centers for Disease Control and Prevention. National HIV Serosurveillance Summary: Update—1993. Vol 3. Atlanta: U.S. Department of Health and Human Services, 1995.

11. Centers for Disease Control and Prevention. National HIV Serosurveillance Summary: Results through 1992. Vol 3. Atlanta: U.S. Department of Health and Human Services, 1993.

12. Johnson ES, Doll LS, Satten GA, Lenes B, Shafer AW, Kamel H, Casanova RJ, Petersen LR. Direct oral questions to blood donors: the impact on screening for human immunodeficiency virus. Transfusion 1994; 34:769–774.

13. Lackritz EM, Satten GA, Aberle-Grasse J, Dodd RY, Raimondi VP, Janssen RS, Lewis WF, Notari EP, Petersen LR. Estimated risk of transmission of the human immunodeficiency virus by screened blood in the United States. N Engl J Med 1995; 333:1721–1725.

14. Zuck TF, Thomson RA, Schreiber GB, Gilcher RO, Kleinman SH, Murphy EL, Ownby HE, Williams AE, Busch MP, Smith JW, Nass CC, Hollingsworth CG, Nemo GJ for the REDS Group. The Retrovirus Epidemiology Donor Study (REDS); rationale and methods. Transfusion 1995; 35:944–951.

15. Schreiber GB, Busch MP, Kleinman SH, Korelitz JJ, for the Retrovirus Epidemiology Donor Study. The risk of transfusion-transmitted viral infections. N Engl J Med 1996; 334:1685–1690.

16. Busch MP, Lee LLL, Satten GA, Henrard DR, Farzadegan H, Nelson KE, Read S, Dodd RY, Petersen LR. Time course of detection of viral and serologic markers preceding human immunodeficiency virus type 1 seroconversion: implications for screening of blood and tissue donors. Transfusion 1995; 35:91–97.

17. Lackritz EM, Stramer SL, Jacobs TA, Strauss D, Busch MP, Schable CA. Results of national testing of U.S. blood donations for HIV-1 p24 antigen [Abstract 751]. In: Program and Abstracts of the 4th Conference on Retroviruses and Opportunistic Infections, Washington DC, January 22–26, 1997.

18. Doll LS, Petersen LR, White CR, Ward JW, HIV Blood Donor Study Group. Human immunodeficiency virus type 1-infected blood donors: behavioral characteristics and reasons for donation. Transfusion 1991; 31:704–709.

19. Williams AE, Thomson RA, Schreiber GB, Watanabe K, Bethel J, Lo A, Kleinman SH, Hollingsworth CG, Nemo GJ, for the Retrovirus Epidemiology Donor Study. Estimates of infectious disease risk factors in US blood donors. JAMA 1997; 277:967–972.

20. Hu DJ, Dondero TJ, Rayfield MA, George JR, Schochetman G, Jaffe HW, Luo C-C, Kalish ML, Weniger BG, Pau C-P, Schable CA, Curran JW. The emerging genetic diversity of HIV. The importance of global surveillance for diagnostics, research and prevention. JAMA 1996; 275:210–216.

21. Schable C, Zekeng L, Pau C-P, Hu D, Kaptue L, Gurtler L, Dondero T, Tsague J-M, Schochetman G, Jaffe H, George JR. Sensitivity of United States HIV antibody tests for detection of HIV-1 group O infections. Lancet 1994; 344:1333–1334.

22. Pau CP, Hu DJ, Spruill C, Schable C, Lackritz E, Kai M, George JR, Rayfield MA, Dondero TJ, Williams AE, Busch MP, Brown AE, McCutchan FE, Schochetman G. Surveillance for human immunodeficiency virus type 1 group O infections in the United States. Transfusion 1996; 36:398–400.

23. Sullivan PS, Jones J, Schable CA, Schochetman G, Pau C, Rayfield M, Do A, Tetteh C, Ward JW. National surveillance for HIV-1 group O infections: Preliminary results [Abstract 159]. In: Program and Abstracts of the 4th Conference on Retroviruses and Opportunistic Infections, Washington, DC, January 22–26, 1997.

24. Sullivan PS, Do AN, Robbins K, Kalish M, Subbarao S, Pieniazek D, Schable C, Afaq G, Markowitz J, Myers R, Joseph JM, Benjamin G. Surveillance for variant strains of HIV: subtype G and group O HIV-1 [letter]. JAMA 1997; 278:292.

25. O'Brien TR, George JR, Holmberg SD. Human immunodeficiency virus type 2 infection in the United States: epidemiology, diagnosis, and public health importance. JAMA 1992; 267:2775–2779.

26. Sullivan M, Williams A, Guido E, Metler R, Schable C, Stramer S. Detection and characterization of an HIV type 2 antibody positive blood donor in the U.S. [abst S229]. Transfusion 1997; 37(suppl):58S.

27. Centers for Disease Control and Prevention. Hepatitis Surveillance Report No. 56. Atlanta: U.S. Department of Health and Human Services, 1995.

28. Alter MJ, Hadler SC, Margolis HS, Alexander WJ, Hu PY, Judson FN, Mares A, Miller JK, Moyer LA. The changing epidemiology of hepatitis B in the United States. Need for alternative vaccination strategies. JAMA 1990; 263:1218–1222.

29. Alter MJ, Mares A, Hadler SC, Maynard JE. The effect of underreporting on the apparent incidence and epidemiology of acute viral hepatitis. Am J Epidemiol 1987; 125:133–139.

30. Centers for Disease Control. Public Health Service inter-agency guidelines for screening donors of blood, plasma, organs, tissues, and semen for evidence of hepatitis B and hepatitis C. MMWR 1991; 40 (RR-4):1–17.

31. Alter MJ, Hadler SC, Judson FJ, Mares A, Alexander WJ, Hu PY, Miller JK, Moyer LA, Fields HA, Bradley DW, Margolis HS. Risk factors for acute non-A, non-B hepatitis in the United States and association with hepatitis C virus infection. JAMA 1990; 264:2231–2235.

32. Alter MJ. Residual Risk of Transfusion-Associated Hepatitis. NIH Consensus Development Conference on Infectious Disease Testing for Blood Transfusions. Bethesda, National Institutes of Health, 1995.

33. Gretch D. Diagnostic tests for hepatitis C. In Program and Abstracts of NIH Consensus Development Conference on Management of Hepatitis C. Bethesda, National Institutes of Health, 1997.

34. Khabbaz RF, Heneine W, Kaplan JE. Testing for other human retroviruses: HTLV-I

and HTLV-II. In: Schochetman G, George JR, eds. AIDS Testing. 2d ed. New York: Springer-Verlag, 1994:206–223.

35. Centers for Disease Control. Human T-lymphotropic virus type I screening in volunteer blood donors—United States, 1989. MMWR 1990; 39:915, 921–924.

36. Dodd RY. The risk of transfusion-transmitted infection [editorial]. N Engl J Med 1992; 327:419–421.

37. Nelson KE, Donahue JG, Munoz A, Cohen ND, Ness PM, Teague A, Stambolis VA, Yawn DH, Callicott B, McAllister H, Reitz BA, Lee H, Farzadegan H, Hollingsworth CG. Transmission of retroviruses from seronegative donors by transfusion during cardiac surgery: a multicenter study of HIV-1 and HTLV-I/II infections. Ann Intern Med 1992; 117:554–559.

38. Hjelle B, Wilson C, Cyrus S, Bradshaw P, Lo J, Schammel C, Wiltbank T, Alexander S. Human T-cell leukemia virus type II infection frequently goes undetected in contemporary U.S. blood donors. Blood 1993; 81:1641–1644.

39. Gallo D, Yeh ET, Moore ES, Hanson CV. Comparison of four enzyme immunoassays for detection of human T-cell lymphotropic virus type 2 antibodies. J Clin Microbiol 1996; 34:213–215.

40. DeArmond SJ, Prusiner SP. Etiology and pathogenesis of prion diseases. Am J Pathol 1995; 146:785–811.

41. Manuelidis EE, Kim JH, Mericangas JR, Maneulidis L. Transmission to animals of Creutzfeld-Jakob disease from human blood [letter]. Lancet 1985; II:896–897.

42. Tamai Y, Kojima H, Kitajima R, Taguchi F, Ohtani Y, Kawaguchi T, Miura S, Sata M, Ishihara Y. Demonstration of the transmissible agent in tissue from a pregnant woman with Creutzfeldt-Jakob disease [letter]. N Engl J Med 1992; 327:649.

43. Tateishi J. Transmission of Creutzfeldt-Jakob disease from human blood and urine into mice [letter]. Lancet 1985; II:1074.

44. Davanipour Z, Alter M, Sobel E, Asher DM, Gajdusek DC. A case-control study of Creutzfeldt-Jakob disease. Dietary risk factors. Am J Epidemiol 1985; 122:443–451.

45. Esmonde TFG, Will RG, Slattery JM, Knight R, Harries-Jones R, DeSilva R, Matthews WB. Creutzfeldt-Jakob disease and blood transfusion. Lancet 1993; 341:205–207.

46. Kondo K, Kuroiwa Y. A case control study of Creutzfeldt-Jakob disease: association with physical injuries. Ann Neurol 1982; 11:377–381.

47. Little BW, Mastrianni J, DeHaven AL, Brown P, Goldfarb L, Gajdusek DC. The epidemiology of Creutzfeldt-Jakob disease in eastern Pennsylvania [Abstract 614P]. Neurology 1993; 43:A316.

48. Holman RC, Khan AS, Belay ED, Schonberger LB. Creutzfeldt-Jakob disease in the United States, 1979–1994: using national mortality data to assess the possible occurrence of variant cases. Emerg Infect Dis 1996; 2:333–337.

49. Schonberger LB, Sullivan M, Holman RC, Austin H, Dodd R, Khan A. Creutzfeldt-Jakob Disease (CJD) and blood safety [Abstract PW 40-4]. In: Abstracts of Xth International Congress of Virology, Jerusalem, Israel, August 11–16, 1996.

50. Davanipour Z, Smoak C, Bohr T, Sobel E, Liwnicz B, Chang S. Death certificates: an efficient source for ascertainment of Creutzfeldt-Jakob disease cases. Neuroepidemiology 1995; 14:1–6.

51. Centers for Disease Control and Prevention. Surveillance for Creutzfeldt-Jakob disease—United States. MMWR 1996; 45:665–668.

52. Sullivan MT, Schonberger LB, Kessler D, Williams AE, Dodd RY. Creutzfeldt-Jakob disease (CJD) investigational lookback study [Abstract S6]. Transfusion 1997; 37(suppl):2S.

53. Heye N, Hensen S, Muller N. Creutzfeldt-Jakob disease and blood transfusion [letter]. Lancet 1994; 343:298–299.

54. Sloand EM, Pitt E, Klein HG. Safety of the blood supply. JAMA 1995; 274:1368–1373.

55. Wagner SJ, Friedman LI, Dodd RY. Transfusion-associated bacterial sepsis. Clin Micro Rev 1994; 7:290–302.

56. Centers for Disease Control and Prevention. Red blood cell transfusions contaminated with Yersinia enterocolitica—United States, 1991–1996, and initiation of a national study to detect bacteria-associated transfusion reactions. MMWR 1997; 46:553–555.

57. Hoppe PA. Interim measures for detection of bacterially contaminated red cell components [editorial]. Transfusion 1992; 32:199–201.

58. U.S. General Accounting Office. Blood Supply. Transfusion-Associated Risks. GAO/PEMD-97-2. Washington, DC: Government Printing Office, 1997.

59. Dodd RY. Adverse consequences of blood transfusion: quantitative risk estimates. In: Nance ST, ed. Blood Supply Risks, Perceptions and Prospects for the Future. Bethesda, MD: American Association of Blood Banks, 1994:1–24.

60. AuBuchon JP. Blood transfusion options. Improving outcomes and reducing costs. Arch Pathol Lab Med 1997; 121:40–47.

61. Gerber MA, Shapiro ED, Krause PJ, Cable RG, Badon SJ, Ryan RW. The risk of acquiring Lyme disease or babesiosis from a blood transfusion. J Infect Dis 1994; 170:231–234.

62. Herwaldt BL, Kjemtrup AM, Conrad PA, Barnes RC, Wilson M, McCarthy MG, Sayers MH, Eberhard ML. Transfusion-transmitted babesiosis in Washington State: first reported case caused by a WA1-type parasite. J Infect Dis 1997; 175:1259–1262.

63. Mintz ED, Anderson JF, Cable RG, Hadler JL. Transfusion-transmitted bebesiosis: a case report from a new endemic area. Transfusion 1991; 31:365–368.

64. Eberhard ML, Walker EM, Steurer FJ. Survival and infectivity of *Babesia* in blood maintained at 25°C and 2–4°C. J Parasitol 1995; 81:790–792.

65. Popovsky MA. Transfusion-transmitted babesiosis [editorial]. Transfusion 1991; 31:296–298.

66. Schmunis GA. Trypanosoma cruzi, the etiologic agent of Chagas' disease: status in the blood supply in endemic and nonendemic countries. Transfusion 1991; 31:547–557.

67. Leiby DA, Read EJ, Lenes BA, Yund AJ, Stumpf RJ, Kirchoff LV, Dodd RY. Seroepidemiology of *Trypanosoma cruzi*, etiologic agent of Chagas' disease, in US blood donors. J Infect Dis 1997; 176:1047–1052.

68. Brashear RJ, Winkler MA, Schur JD, Lee H, Burczak JD, Hall HJ, Pan AA. Detection of antibodies to *Trypanosoma cruzi* among blood donors in the southwestern and western United States. I. Evaluation of the sensitivity and specificity of an enzyme immunoassay for detecting antibodies to *T cruzi*. Transfusion 1995; 35:213–218.

69. Schulman IA, Appleman MD, Saxena S, Hiti AL, Kirchhoff LV. Specific antibodies to *Trypanosoma cruzi* among blood donors in Los Angeles, California. Transfusion 1997; 37:727–731.

70. Magill AJ, Grogl M, Gasser RA Jr, Sun W, Oster CN. Visceral infection caused by *Leishmania tropica* in veterans of Operation Desert Storm. N Engl J Med 1993; 328:1383–1387.

71. Magill AJ, Grogl M, Johnson SC, Gasser RA. Visceral infection due to *Leishmania tropica* in a veteran of Operation Desert Storm who presented 2 years after leaving Saudi Arabia. Clin Infect Dis 1994; 19:805–806.

72. Grogl M, Daugirda JL, Hoover DL, Magill AJ, Berman JD. Survivability and infectivity of viscerotropic *Leishmania tropica* from Operation Desert Storm participants in human blood products maintained under blood bank conditions. Am J Trop Med Hyg 1993; 49:308–315.

73. Gunby P. Desert Storm veterans now may donate blood; others called for discussion of donor tests. JAMA 1993; 269:451–452.

74. Centers for Disease Control and Prevention. Malaria surveillance—United States, 1994. MMWR 1997; 46(SS-5):1–18.

75. Nahlen BL, Lobel HO, Cannon SE, Campbell CC. Reassessment of blood donor selection criteria for United States travelers to malarious areas. Transfusion 1991; 31:798–804.

76. Centers for Disease Control and Prevention. Addressing Emerging Infectious Disease Threats. A Prevention Strategy for the United States. Atlanta: U.S. Department of Health and Human Services, 1994.

19

Alternatives to Allogeneic Blood and Strategies to Avoid Transfusion

Lawrence T. Goodnough

Washington University School of Medicine, St. Louis, Missouri

I. INTRODUCTION

Approximately 12 million red blood cell (RBC) units are transfused to nearly 4 million patients annually in the United States (1). The conservation of blood has historically arisen from awareness that the inventory of this resource is limited (2) as well as the knowledge that blood transfusion carries a risk (3). In addition, emphasis on the costs of health care has raised issues related to the costs of blood transfusion (4–6). Recent guidelines have emphasized that in the elective transfusion setting, "no blood transfusion" is a desirable outcome (7). Furthermore, consensus conference recommendations (8) have emphasized that if blood is to be transfused, autologous (the patient's own) blood is preferable to allogeneic (from an anonymous, volunteer donor) blood. Thus the costs of blood conservation, for which an increasing array of technological procedures and products have become available, have also become an issue. The purpose of this review is to provide an overview of emerging trends in blood transfusion and blood conservation interventions in order to help identify areas important for future investigation.

II. STRATEGIES TO AVOID BLOOD TRANSFUSION

Indications for blood transfusion have been impaired by the lack of data quantitating the benefits of blood for reducing the morbidity or mortality of anemia in otherwise untransfused patients (9). A randomized trial to determine at what level of anemia blood transfusion can reduce morbidity or mortality cannot be done for ethical reasons. Attempts to reach conclusions from the considerable experience obtained in managing Jehovah's Witnesses, who refuse blood on the basis of religious beliefs, have been problematic (10). This is illustrated by the randomized prospective study of the synthetic oxygen carrier Fluosol-DA compared to placebo in such a population, in which patients generally did well if their lowest hematocrit (HCT) level exceeded 12% but did not do well at a HCT level of less than 12%, irrespective of treatment group (11). One cannot reach conclusions from these data regarding the "transfusion trigger" appropriate for populations who would accept blood. Moreover, it is recognized that patients are heterogeneous, so that patients with medical (chronic, due to underproduction) anemias are transfused differently from patients with surgical (acute, due to blood loss) anemias (9). A more recent study (12) of surgical mortality in Jehovah's Witness patients was able to show that preoperative hemoglobin levels and subsequent blood loss were related to mortality, especially in patients known to have cardiovascular disease. Attempts to link transfusions with outcomes such as length of stay (13,14) have been unsuccessful. Two studies have found that females are more likely to be transfused than are their male counterparts in the elective surgical setting (15,16). The latter study found, even when using "generous" criteria to define excessive transfusions in which transfusion to replace losses of less than 15% of the initial RBC volume was deemed inappropriate, that 21% of patients undergoing joint replacement surgery received blood unnecessarily.

III. UTILIZATION REVIEW: IS IT EFFECTIVE?

A recent review concluded that transfusion audits can improve transfusion practices if they are performed in a timely manner and are combined with education of the individual ordering physician (17). Plasma and platelet products are particularly amenable to this approach. Two studies using concurrent education or consultation reduced plasma usage by 46% and 77%, respectively (18,19). Another study using a retrospective audit was able to reduce inappropriate plasma use from 53 to 22% of units transfused (20). Similarly, use of platelet transfusions were reduced by 56% and 14% in two studies that used consultation (21) and audit (22), respectively. Another study followed all requests for transfusions with a nonrequested consultation. The authors report a reduction in transfusion of platelets by 44%, and plasma and cryoprecipitate by 57%, but a reduction in red blood cells (RBC) of only 19% over a 4-year period (23). Other studies cast doubt on whether utilization review is really an effective process. Hoeltge et al. (24) used a combination of indicators to evaluate transfusions on medical and surgical services and concluded that only 4% of transfusions were unjustified. Renner et al. (25) found the percentage of unjustified transfusions to be 1.4% before and

0% after an educational intervention; while this could be interpreted to be a triumph for the educational intervention, a more reasonable conclusion is that the identification of unjustified transfusions, before and after the intervention, was flawed (26). At our own institution in 1994, during which 23,002 RBC units were transfused, 48 transfusion events underwent peer review by the transfusion committee, and, of these, only 2 cases were felt to be unjustified.

These extraordinary low rates of "inappropriate" transfusions may be a consequence of several factors. First, RBC transfusion audits in circumstances of hemorrhage are difficult, if not impossible, to perform accurately. These settings would include the emergency room/trauma unit, operating rooms, and intensive care units. For this reason, our institutional process of utilization review does not include transfusions administered intraoperatively. Yet, studies of transfusions practices in orthopedic surgery indicate that at least 25% of RBC transfusions in this setting can, in retrospect, be identified as inappropriate (16). Second, the clinical indicators that define "appropriate" transfusion practice may be too generous. In the study that concluded that 96% of transfusions were "appropriate," a posttransfusion hemoglobin (Hgb) concentration of 11 g/dL was used as a threshold to distinguish "appropriate" from "inappropriate" (24). Third, the medical chart audit has substantial limitations. Clearly documented information as to why the transfusion was administered is commonly unobtainable. We found that in orthopedic surgical patients, only 68% of postoperative transfusion events on the day of surgery had chart documentation of blood loss and/or change in vital signs (27). Nevertheless, these patients can be inferred to have been transfused during periods of substantial blood loss, since recorded hematocrits were $33.5 \pm 0.9\%$ before transfusion and $31.3 \pm 0.5\%$ after transfusion. Furthermore, the rationale for transfusion was recorded in only 16% of day-of-surgery transfusions and in only 27% of transfusions administered on postoperative days.

A recent multiinstitution study concluded that retrospective utilization review was not effective at altering transfusion practice (28). One alternative approach to retrospective chart audit is the prospective use of transfusion algorithms, in which the transfusion decision process is coupled with information that can serve as clinical indicators for transfusion.

IV. TRANSFUSION ALGORITHMS

Studies have evaluated the impact of point-of-care testing (29,30), in which intraoperative assays (whole blood prothrombin time, activated partial thromboplastin time and platelet count results available within 4 minutes) were linked with a transfusion algorithm (Fig. 1) for plasma and platelet products in cardiac surgical patients with a diagnosis of microvascular bleeding (MVB). Patients were randomized to either standard therapy, in which blood products were

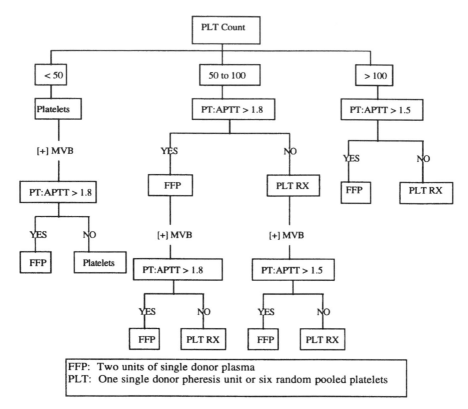

Figure 1   An algorithm approach for hemostatic therapy in cardiac patients determined to have microvascular bleeding after heparin neutralization. Platelets = Platelet transfusion (6 units of random-donor or apheresis unit equivalent); PLT RX = platelet therapy (platelet transfusion and/or DDAVP therapy at physician's discretion); FFP = plasma therapy (2 units of fresh-frozen plasma); [+] MVB = continued MVB; PT:APTT = whole blood prothrombin time and activated partial thromboplastin time control values (values/mean values from a normal reference population); PLT count = platelet count ($\times 10^3$/mm^3). (From Ref. 30.)

transfused at the discretion of the physician according to any laboratory-based tests requested, or to an algorithm group, in which platelet and plasma therapy were given according to an algorithm based initially on platelet count, followed by branch pathways determined by PT and aPTT results. Both intraoperative and initial postoperative chest tube drainage were less in the algorithm group. One patient in the algorithm group required later surgical reexploration, compared to five patients in the standard group. The more effective therapy in the algorithm group was reflected in the lower RBC transfusion needs in the algorithm group compared with the standard therapy group (5.9 ± 3.8 vs. 9.8 ± 9.4 units, respectively). The improved patient care, along with reduced blood transfusions, resulted in substantial economic savings. This approach has been described as a "powerful engine of change" (31).

Approaches to red cell transfusion therapy in the surgical patient need to acknowledge that patients are heterogeneous for risks related to anemia. In one such approach to risk stratification for cardiac surgical patients has been published (32), clinical variables determine whether a patient is considered at "standard" or at "increased" risk for morbidity associated with cardiac surgery. While complications related to anemia represent only one aspect of morbidity/mortality in this setting, the physiological changes known to accompany acute anemia (33) and the potential for myocardial tissue injury (34) suggest that risk stratification for RBC transfusion decisions would be prudent. A recent analysis of over 2000 cardiac bypass patients led to a model that calculated a transfusion risk score, which was then validated prospectively in over 400 additional patients (35). Now that cardiac surgery can be prospectively stratified, not only for surgical risk but also for transfusion likelihood, the role of algorithms may be especially productive in the standardization of blood transfusion and blood conservation practices.

If transfusion outcomes can be predicted from patient-related factors, then blood transfusion and blood conservation algorithms can be utilized to minimize the variability of transfusion outcomes related to institutional (procedural) and physician (transfusion practices) factors. Algorithms could take into account patient heterogeneity by using the Higgins et al. (32) and McGovern et al. (35) stratification of "standard" and "increased" risk patients. Blood transfusions and blood-conservation strategies could be administered according to algorithms that are incorporated into the daily practice of coronary revascularization (36). Such an algorithm is illustrated in Figure 2. This approach can then enable physicians to analyze transfusion outcomes, and the relationship of these outcomes, to transfusion triggers, autologous blood procurement, pharmacological interventions, and even emerging blood substitutes. The knowledge that we learn from the standardization of these practices, and the comparison of transfusion outcomes of different institutions or different therapeutic approaches, would form an important database that could serve as a reference for the continuous improvement of care in the surgical setting (37).

V. ALTERNATIVES TO ALLOGENEIC BLOOD

A. Autologous Blood Donation

For transfusion settings such as elective surgery, preoperative autologous blood donation (PAD) represents an attractive alternative to allogeneic blood transfu-

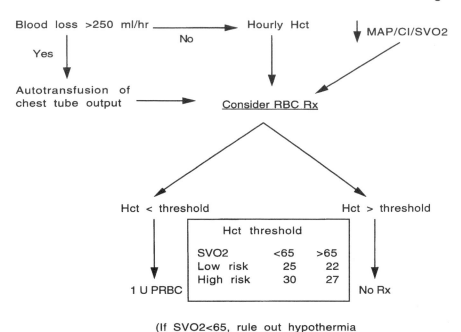

Figure 2 An algorithm approach for red cell transfusion in cardiac surgical patients postoperatively. After establishing that the patient's volume status is adequate, decisions to transfuse would be based on hemoglobin/hematorcrit level, rate of blood loss, and hemodynamic parameters [mean arterial pressure (MAP) and cardiac index (CI)]. Thresholds for transfusion would differ for patients determined to be a "low" risk and "high" risk for perisurgical complications. Mixed venous oxygen percent saturation (SVO_2) could serve as a physiological indicator of the balance between oxygen supply and demand for transfusion decision making. (From Ref. 36.)

sion. This previously underutilized practice (38) has now become a standard of care in elective surgical procedures such as orthopedic and urological surgery (39,40). Guidelines on the criteria for utilization of this intervention, along with selection of patients suitable for the technique, have been published (42,42). Potential candidates for PAD prior to surgery include any patient scheduled for a procedure for whom blood type and crossmatch is requested. Using this approach, studies have found that, overall, 9% of autologous donors undergoing elective surgery receive allogeneic blood (43). Under conditions of "standard" collection (i.e., one unit weekly) the likelihood of exposure to allogeneic blood for autologous blood donors has ranged from 10% for radical prostatectomy (39) to 17% for elective orthopedic surgery (44) to 56% for patients undergoing coronary revascularization (45).

The efficacy of PAD is dependent on the degree to which the patient's bone marrow is stimulated to increase the production of red blood cells in order to replace blood donated. Several studies have shown that the endogenous erythropoietin response is suboptimal at the level of mild anemia achieved during collection of autologous blood (46,47). Under "standard" conditions of one autologous unit donated weekly, a computer model demonstrated that if the erythropoietic response to autologous blood phlebotomy is not able to maintain hematocrit level during the donation interval, the predeposit of autologous blood may actually be harmful (48).

In contrast to autologous blood donation under "standard" conditions, studies of "aggressive" autologous blood phlebotomy (twice weekly for 3 weeks, beginning 25–35 days before surgery) have demonstrated that endogenous erythropoietin levels do rise when orthopedic surgical patients undergo a blood donation (blood "loss") of up to 1000 mL weekly during PAD. In a controlled clinical trial of aggressive phlebotomy (49), serial erythropoietin levels showed a logarithmic rise even in the Hgb concentration range of 110–114 g/dL. This was accompanied by significant erythropoiesis, in which a RBC volume equivalent to three allogeneic blood units [at 200 mL each (50)] was generated over a preoperative interval of 28 days (51). The erythropoietin response to blood loss and the subsequent erythropoietic response have been shown to be independent of patient gender or age (52). The ability of recombinant human erythropoietin (EPO) to further accelerate the erythropoietic recovery from blood loss during PAD has been demonstrated in several controlled trials (51,53,54). When aggressive autologous phlebotomy was accompanied by simultaneous EPO administration, the equivalent of an additional two blood units (nearly five total) was generated for subsequent blood conservation. Subsequent clinical trials have demonstrated that EPO therapy during autologous blood donation can reduce the need for allogeneic blood in patients undergoing elective orthopedic surgery (55,56), even in patients with anemia of chronic inflammatory disease such as rheumatoid arthritis (57).

Guidelines for autologous blood transfusion are controversial. Some published guidelines recommend that the same criteria be used for utilization review for autologous as are used for allogeneic blood units (57). This view is supported by the risks of an immediate transfusion reaction, in which administrative error and bacterial contamination account for nearly 50% of fatalities from transfusions (58). These risks can occur for autologous blood units as well as for allogeneic blood units. The alternative view holds that the risk/benefit relationship is lower for autologous blood than for allogeneic blood, since the risk for disease transmissible by autologous blood has been reduced; this viewpoint argues for different standards for transfusion of autologous than for allogeneic blood. While transfusion services may choose to establish different guidelines for transfusion of autologous and allogeneic blood (59), physicians should not retransfuse autologous blood simply because it is available (60).

B. Acute Preoperative Hemodilution

Acute isovolemic hemodilution is the removal of blood from a patient shortly before surgery and replacement with crystalloid and colloid solutions. Blood is collected in standard blood bags containing anticoagulant, stored at room temperature to preserve platelet function, and reinfused after major blood loss has ceased or sooner, if indicated. The rationale for the use of hemodilution is that if intraoperative blood loss is relatively constant with or without preoperative normovolemic hemodilution, it is better to lose blood at a lower hematocrit.

With moderate hemodilution, blood is withdrawn until the hematocrit level is a certain value, e.g., 27–30% (61). Recently, the efficacy of moderate hemodilution has been questioned (62,63). For example, the removal of three blood units in a 100 kg man with a reduction in preoperative hematocrit level from 44% to 32% and who subsequently undergoes radical prostatectomy with an estimated blood loss of 2600 mL, results in "savings" in surgical RBC volume lost of only 215 mL, or the equivalent of one blood unit (62). The safety and efficacy of more extensive hemodilution remains unproven (64).

The procurement of autologous blood by acute hemodilution has substantial cost advantages over autologous blood predeposit; costs of inventory and testing are not incurred for autologous blood procured by hemodilution, since this blood does not leave the operating suite. A recent study demonstrated that moderate hemodilution is a cost-effective alternative to preoperative autologous blood donation in patients undergoing radical prostatectomy (65). If hemodilution is coupled with emerging but still experimental artificial oxygen carriers or hemoglobin solutions (66), in which these blood substitutes are used to replace blood removed by hemodilution, the conservation benefit of this technique may be greatly enhanced.

C. Intraoperative Blood Recovery

The term intraoperative blood recovery describes the technique of salvaging and reinfusing blood lost by a patient during surgery. The oxygen-transport properties of recovered red blood cells are equal to or better than stored allogeneic red cells, and the survival of recovered red blood cells appears to be at least comparable to that of transfused allogeneic red cells (67). The incidence of adverse events resulting from reinfusion of recovered blood is not known but is thought to be an infrequent (<1:15,000) occurrence. Fatal air embolism has been reported with recovered blood infused under pressure (68). Hemolysis of recovered blood can occur during suctioning from the surface instead of deep pools of shed blood, particularly when blood is aspirated at vacuum settings greater than 100 torr. The clinical importance of free hemoglobin in the concentrations usually seen has not been established, although excess free hemoglobin may indicate inadequate washing. Dilutional coagulopathy may occur if large volumes of salvaged blood are administered (69).

As with preoperative autologous blood donation and acute preoperative hemodilution, intraoperative autologous blood recovery should undergo scrutiny concerning both safety and cost-effectiveness. A controlled study recently demonstrated a lack of efficacy for intraoperative blood recovery when transfusion requirements and clinical outcome were followed (70). A second study found that only a minority of patients undergoing major orthopedic and cardiac surgery achieved cost equivalence with intraoperative recovery using semi-automated instruments compared with banked blood (71). While the recovery of a minimum of one blood unit equivalent is possible for less expensive methods (with unwashed blood), it is generally agreed that at least two blood unit equivalents would need to be recovered using an automated recovery device (with washed blood) in order to achieve cost-effectiveness (72). A recent study of this approach in patients undergoing aortic aneurism repair concluded that this strategy is particularly valuable in patients with at least 1000 mL surgical blood loss (73).

D. Postoperative Autologous Blood Recovery

In the postoperative orthopedic surgical setting, a number of reports have described the successful recovery and reinfusion of washed (74,75) and unwashed (76–78) wound drainage from patients undergoing arthroplasty or spinal procedures. The volume of reinfused drainage blood has been reported to be as much as 3000 mL, with an average of more than 1100 mL in patients undergoing cementless knee replacement (77). The corresponding red cell volume can be substantial, ranging from 174 to 704 mL red cell volume or 0.75 to 3.5 units of blood (79). Perioperative blood loss has been shown to be greater in patients undergoing modern cementless total joint replacement when compared with cases using cemented fixation technique (74,80), making postoperative red cell recovery especially attractive for cementless procedures.

The safety of reinfused unwashed orthopedic wound drainage has been controversial. Theoretical concerns have been expressed regarding infusion of potentially harmful materials in salvaged blood, including free hemoglobin, red cell stroma, marrow fat, toxic irritants, tissue or methacrylate debris, fibrin degradation products, and activated coagulation factors and complement (81). Two small series have reported complications (82,83); the etiology of the complications is not clearly identified. Several larger studies have reported no serious adverse effects when drainage was passed through a standard 40 µm blood filter (76,84).

E. Designated (Directed) Blood Transfusions

This transfusion practice (in which the blood donor is known to the transfusion recipient) is commonly requested by patients as an alternative to allogeneic volunteer blood transfusion. This transfusion practice, unlike autologous blood transfusion, is controversial; no evidence to date indicates that designated blood is safer than allogeneic blood (85). Reports of fatal graft-versus-host disease (GVHD) in surgical patients who received blood from blood relatives serve to emphasize the potential risks of this practice; directed donations from blood relatives must be irradiated in order to prevent GVHD (86). While all allogeneic blood and blood components, including designated donations, undergo testing before transfusion, an additional mechanism to ensure blood safety is the confidential donor screening process (87). Here the allogeneic blood donor is given information identifying high-risk behaviors indicating that people should not donate blood; high-risk donors can withdraw from blood donation or identify themselves as high risk, confidentially, by checking a box indicating that the blood donated by them should not be transfused. This screening mechanism is compromised in designated blood donation, since the blood donor is known to the transfusion recipient and is therefore arguably nonvoluntary. Furthermore, directed blood donation has a potentially adverse effect on blood donor recruitment, since individuals who "save" themselves for the unexpected transfusion needs of family and friends might be less inclined to become allogeneic volunteer blood donors (88). Finally, procurement of designated blood does not provide additional protection against allogeneic blood exposure in patients who qualify for autologous blood donation (89), reinforcing that the superior transfusion practice of autologous blood donation should not be replaced by a controversial transfusion practice.

An analysis of our own directed donor program illustrates how this practice can create problems for patients and physicians (90). In 220 consecutive requests for directed donors, 29 (29%) of the 101 patients were in nonelective transfusion settings, such as hospitalized patients on medical services or surgical patients within 24 hours of surgery. These requests potentially delayed transfusion therapy because of the time (8–24 h) required for donor screening, phlebotomy, and unit testing. Only 40% (46) of 115 units ultimately collected were of "benefit" to the designated recipient. Directed donor programs need to better reflect their purpose of providing an alternative to allogeneic volunteer blood in the elective, rather than nonelective, transfusion setting.

VI. CONCLUSION

The procurement of autologous blood has become a standard of care for elective surgery in the United States. However, the costs and potential complications, as well as the potential benefits, of autologous blood-procurement strategies need to be considered. Autologous blood donation under "routine" conditions of one blood unit donation weekly is not accompanied by any significant erythropoietic response and therefore results simply in "chronic" hemodilution. Interventions that stimulate preoperative erythropoiesis, via either "aggressive" phlebotomy or EPO therapy, represent more effective approaches to blood conservation than conventional autologous blood predeposit. Second, point-of-care autologous blood procurement strategies such as intraoperative blood recovery and acute normovolemic hemodilution represent more cost-effective approaches. Acute hemodilution will be utilized as a building block for emerging pharmacological strategies such as EPO therapy, blood substitutes, and artificial oxygen transport solutions.

REFERENCES

1. Wallace EL, et al. Collection and transfusion of blood in the United States, 1992. Transfusion 1995; 35:802–812.
2. Roche JK, Stengle JM. Open heart surgery and the demand for blood. JAMA 1973; 225:1516–1521.
3. Goodnough LT, Shuck JM. Review of risks, options, and informed consent for blood transfusion in elective surgery. Am J Surg 1990; 159:602–609.
4. Schwartz WB, Mendelson DN, Hospital cost containment in the 1980s. N Engl J Med 1991; 324:1037–1042.
5. Forbes JM, Anderson MD, Anderson GF, et al. Blood transfusion costs: a multicenter study. Transfusion 1991; 31:319–323.
6. Goodnough LT, Bodner MS, Martin JW. Blood transfusion and blood conservation: cost and utilization issues. Amer J Med Qual 1994; 9:172–183.
7. American College of Physicians. Strategies for elective red cell transfusion. Ann Intern Med 1992; 116:403–406.
8. National Institute of Health Consensus Conference. Perioperative red cell transfusion. JAMA 1988; 260:2700–2703.
9. Welch GH, Meehan K, Goodnough LT. Prudent strategies for elective red cell transfusion. Ann Intern Med 1992; 116:393–403.
10. Mann MC, Votto J, Kambe J, McNamee MJ. Management of the severely anemic patients who refuses transfusion: lessons learned during the care of a Jehovah's witness. Ann Int Med 1992; 117:1042–1048.
11. Gould SA, Rosen AL, Sehgal LR, et al. Fluosol-DA As a red cell substitute in acute anemia. N Engl J Med 1986; 314:1953–1956.
12. Carson JL, Duff A, Poses RM, et al. Effect of anamia and cardiovascular disease on surgical mortality and morbidity. Lancet 1996; 348:1055–1060.
13. Kim DM, Brecher ME, Estes TJ, Morrey BF. Relationship of hemoglobin and duration of hospitalization after total hip arthroplasty: implications for the transfusion target. Mayo Clin Proc 1993; 68:37–41.
14. Goodnough LT, Vizmig K, Riddell J IV, Soegiarso RW. Discharge haematocrit as

clinical indicator for blood transfusion audit in surgery patients. Transfusion Med 1994; 4:35–44.

15. Friedman BA, Burns TL, Schork MA. An analysis of blood transfusion of surgical patients by sex: a quest for the transfusion trigger. Transfusion 1980; 20:179–188.

16. Goodnough LT, Verbrugge D, Vizmrg K, Riddell J. Identifying elective orthopaedic surgical patients with amounts of blood in excess of need; the transfusion trigger revisited. Transfusion 1992; 32:648–653.

17. Toy PTCY. Effectiveness of transfusion audits and practice guidelines. Arch Pathol Lab 1994; 118:435–437.

18. Ayoub MM, Clark JA. Reduction of fresh frozen plasma use with a simple education program. Am Surg 1989; 55:563–565.

19. Shanberge JN. Reduction of fresh-frozen plasma use through a daily survey and education program. Transfusion 1987; 27:226–227.

20. Barnette RE, Fish DJ, Eisenstaedt RS. Modification of fresh-frozen transfusion practices through educational intervention. Transfusion 1990; 30:253–257.

21. McCullough J, Steeper TA, Connelly DP, Jackson B, Huntington S, Scott EP. Platelet utilization in a university hospital. JAMA 1988; 259:2414–2418.

22. Simpson MB. Prospective-concurrent audits and medical consultation for platelet transfusions. Transfusion 1987; 27:192–195.

23. Lichtiger B, Fisher HE, Huh YO. Screening of transfusion service requests by the blood bank pathologist: impact on cost containment. Lab Med 1988; 19:228–230.

24. Hoeltge GA, Brown JC, Herzig RH, et al. Computer-assisted audits of blood component transfusion. Cleve Clin J Med 1989; 56:267–269.

25. Renner SW, Howanitz JH, Fishkin BG. Toward meaningful blood usage review: comprehensive monitoring of physician practice. QRB Qual Rev Bull 1987; 13:76–80.

26. Goodnough LT. Retrospective utilization review—Are we just going through the motions? Arch Pathol Lab Med 1996; 120:802.

27. Audet AM, Goodnough LT, Parvin CA. Evaluating the appropriateness of red blood cell transfusions: the limitations of retrospective medical record reviews. Int J Qual Health Care 1996; 8:41–49.

28. Lam HT, Schweitzer SO, Petz L, et al. Are retrospective peer-review transfusion monitoring systems effective in reducing red blood cell utilization. Arch Pathol Lab Med 1996; 120:810–816.

29. Despotis GJ, Grishaber JE, Goodnough LT. The effect of an intraoperative treatment algorithm on physician transfusion behavior in cardiac surgery. Transfusion 1994; 34:290–296.

30. Despotis GJ, Santoro SA, Spitznagel E, Kater KM, Cox JL, Barnes P, Lappas DL. Prospective evaluation and clinical utility of on-site coagulation monitoring in cardiac surgical patients. J Thorac Cardiovasc Surg 1994; 107:271–279.

31. Reinersten JL. Algorithms, guidelines, and protocols: can they really improve what we do? Transfusion 1994; 34:281–228.

32. Higgins TL, Estafanous FG, Loop FD, Beck GJ, Blum JM, Paranand L. Stratification of morbidity and mortality outcome by preoperative risk factors in coronary artery bypass patients. JAMA 1992; 267:2344–2348.

33. Rao TLK, Montoya A. Cardiovascular, electrocardiographic and respiratory changes following acute anemia with volume replacement in patients with coronary artery disease. Anesth Dev 1985; 12:49–54.

34. Parksloe MRJ, Wuld R, Fox M, Reilly CS. Silent myocardial ischemia in a patient with anaemia before operation. Br J Anaesth 1990; 64:634–637.

35. Magovern JA, Sakert T, Benckart DH, et al. A model for predicting transfusion after coronary artery surgery. Ann Thorac Surg 1996; 61:27–35.

36. Goodnough LT, Despotis GJ, Hogue CW, Ferguson TB. On the need for improved transfusion indicators in cardiac surgery. Ann Thorac Surg 1995; 60;473–480.

37. Hannan EL, Kilburn H, Racz M, Shields E, Chassin MR. Improving the outcomes of coronary artery bypass surgery in New York State. JAMA 1994; 271:761–766.

38. Toy PTCY, Strauss R, Stehling L, et al. Predeposit autologous blood for elective surgery: a multicenter study. NEJM 1987; 316:517–520.

39. Goodnough LT, Shafron D, Marcus RE. The impact of preoperative autologous blood donation on orthopaedic surgical practice. Vox Sang 1990; 59:65–69.

40. Goodnough LT, Grishaber JE, Birkmeyer JD, Monk TG, Catalona WJ. Efficacy and cost-effectiveness of autologous blood predeposit in patients undergoing radical prostatectomy procedures. Urology 1994; 44:226–231.

41. British Committee for Standards in Haematology Blood Transfusion Task Force. Guidelines for autologous donation: preoperative autologous donation. Transfusion Med 1993; 3:307–316.

42. NHLBI.Transfusion alert: use of autologous blood. Transfusion 1995; 35:703–711.

43. Renner SW, Howanitz PJ, Bachner P. Preoperative autologous blood donation in 612 hospitals. Arch Pathol Lab Med 1992; 116:613–619.

44. Goodnough LT. The implications of cost-effectiveness for autologous blood procurement. Arch Pathol Lab Med 1994; 118:471–472.

45. Surgenor DM, Churchill WH, Wallace EL, et al. Determinants of red cell, platelet, plasma, and cryoprecipate transfusions during coronary artery bypass graft surgery. Transfusion 1996; 36:521–532.

46. Kickler TS, Spivack JL. Effect of repeated whole blood donations on serum immunoreactive erythropoietin levels in autologous donors. JAMA 1988; 260:65–67.

47. Goodnough LT, Brittenham G. Limitations of the erythropoietic response to serial phlebotomy: implications for autologous blood donor programs. Lab Clin Med 1990; 115:28–35.

48. Cohen JA, Brecher ME. Preoperative autologous blood donation: benefit or detriment? A mathematical analysis. Transfusion 1995; 35:640–644.

49. Goodnough LT, Price TH, Parvin CA, et al. Erythropoietin response to anemeia is not altered by surgical or recombinant human erythropoietin therapy. Br J Haematol 1994; 87:695–699.

50. Goodnough LT, Bravo J, Hsenh Y, Keating L, Brittenham GM. Red blood cell volume in autologous and homologous blood units: implications for risk/benefit assessment for autologous blood "crossover" and directed blood transfusions. Transfusion 1989; 29:821–822.

51. Goodnough LT, Price TH, Rudnick S, Soegiarso RW. Preoperative red blood cell

production in patients undergoing aggressive autologous blood phlebotomy with and without erythropoietin therapy. Transfusion 1992; 32:441–445.

52. Goodnough LT, Price TH, Parvin CA. The endogeneous erythropoietin response and the erythropoietic response in blood loss anaemia: the effects of gender and age. J Lab Clin Med 1995; 126:57–64.

53. Goodnough LT, Rudnick S, Price TH, et al. Increased collection of autologous blood preoperatively with recombinant human erythropoietin therapy. N Engl J Med 1989; 321:1163–1167.

54. Goodnough LT, Price TH, Friedman KD, et al. A phase III trial of recombinant human erythropoietin therapy in non-anemic orthopaedic patients subjected to aggressive autologous blood phlebotomy: dose, response, toxicity and efficacy. Transfusion 1994; 34:66–71.

55. Price TH, Goodnough LT, Vogler W, et al. The effect of recombinant erythropoietin on the efficacy of autologous blood donation in patients with low hematocrits. Transfusion 1996; 36:29–36.

56. Mercuriali F, Zanella A, Barosi G, et al. Use of erythropoietin to increase the volume of autologous blood donated by orthopedic patients. Transfusion 1993; 33;55–60.

57. Silberstein LE, Kruskall MS, Stehling LC, et al. Strategies for the review of transfusion practices. JAMA 1989; 262:1993–1997.

58. Sazama K. Report of 355 transfusion associated deaths: 1976 through 1985. Transfusion 1990; 30:583–590.

59. Stehling L, Luban NLC, Anderson KC, et al. Guidelines for blood utilization review. Transfusion 1994; 34:438–448.

60. Welch GH, Meehan K, Goodnough LT. Prudent strategies for elective red cell transfusion. Ann Intern Med 1992; 116:393–403.

61. Messmer K, Kreimeier M, Intagliett A. Present state of intentional hemodilution. Eur Surg Res 1986; 18:254–263.

62. Goodnough LT, Grishaber J, Monk TG, Catalona WJ. Acute preoperative hemodilution in patients undergoing radical prostatectomy: a case study analysis of efficacy. Anesth Analg 1994; 78:932–937.

63. Brecher ME, Rosenfled. Mathematical and computer modeling of acute normovolemic hemodilution. Transfusion 1994; 34:176–179.

64. Weiskopt RB. Mathematical analysis of isovolemic hemodilution indicates that it can decrease the need for allogeneic blood transfusion. Transfusion 1995; 35:37–41.

65. Monk TG, Goodnough LT, Birkmeyer JD, Brecher ME, Catalona WJ. Acute normovolemic hemodilution is a cost-effective alternative to preoperative autologous donation in patients undergoing radical retropubic prostatectomy. Transfusion 1995; 35:559–565.

66. Winslow RM. Blood substitutes. Curr Status Transfusion 1989; 29:753–754.

67. Ray JM, Flynn JC, Bierman AH. Erythrocyte survival following intraoperative autotransfusion in spinal surgery: an in vivo comparative study and 5-year update. Spine 1986; 11:879–882.

68. Linden JV, Kaplan HS, Murphy MT. Fatal air embolism due to perioperative blood recovery. Anesth Analg 1997; 84:422-6.

69. Horst HM, Dlugos S, Fath JJ, et al. Coagulopathy and intraoperative blood salvage. J Trauma 1992; 32(5):646–653.
70. Bell K, Stott K, Sinclair CJ, Walker WS, Gillon J. A controlled trial of intraoperative autologous transfusion in cardiothoracic surgery measuring effect on transfusion requirements and clinical outcome. Transfusion Med 1992; 2:295–300.
71. Solomon MD, Rutledge ML, Kane LE, Yawn HD: Cost comparison of intraoperative autologous versus homologous transfusion. Transfusion 1988; 28:379–382.
72. Bovill DF, Moulton CW, Jackson WS, Jensen JK, Barcellos RW. The efficacy of intraoperative autologous transfusion in major orthopaedic surgery: a regression analysis. Orthopedics 1986; 9:1403–1407.
73. Goodnough LT, Monk TG, Sicard G, et al. Intraoperative salvage in patients undergoing elective abdominal aortic aneurism repair: an analysis of costs and benefit. J Vasc Surg 1996; 24:213–218.
74. Semkiew LB, Schurman OJ, Goodman SB, Woolson ST. Postoperative blood salvage using the cell saver after total joint arthroplasty. J Bone J Surg 1989; 71A:823–827.
75. Flynn JC, Price CT, Zink WP. The third step of total autologous blood transfusion in scoliosis surgery. Spine 1991; 16:S328–329.
76. Faris PM, Ritter MA, Keating EM, Varleri CR: Unwashed filtered shed blood collected after knee and hip arthroplasties. J Bone J Surg 1991; 73A:1169–1177.
77. Martin JW, Whiteside LA, Milliano MT, Reedy ME. Postoperative blood retrieval and transfusion in cementless total knee arthroplasty. J Arthroplasty 1992; 7:205–210.
78. Ayers DC, Murray DG, Duerr DM. Blood salvage after total hip arthroplasty. J Bone Oint Surg 1995; 77A:1347–1351.
79. Goodnough LT, Verbrugge D, Marcus RE. The relationship between hematocrit, blood lost, and blood transfused in total knee replacement: implications for post-operative blood salvage and reinfusion. Am J Knee Surg 1995; 8:83–87.
80. Mylod AG, France MP, Muser DE, Parsons JR. Perioperative blood loss associated with total knee arthroplasty: a comparison of procedures performed with and without cementing. J Bone J Surg 1990; 72A:110–112.
81. McCarthy JC, Turner RH, Reuten JJ, Valeri CR, Ragno GM, Korten KW. The effect of cell washing on the quality of shed blood in major reconstructive surgery. Orthop Trans 1992; 16:484.
82. Clements DH, Sculco TP, Burke SW, Mayer K, Levine DB. Salvage and reinfusion of postoperative sanguineous wound drainage. J Bone J Surg 1992; 74A:646–651.
83. Woda R, Tetzlaff JE. Upper airway oedema following autologous blood transfusion from a wound drainage system. Can J Anesth 1992; 39:290–292.
84. Blevins FT, Shaw B, Valeri RC, Kasser J, Hall J. Reinfusion of shed blood after orthopaedic procedures in children and adolescents. J Bone J Surg 1993; 75A:363–371.
85. Kruskall MS, Umlas J. Acquired immunodeficiency syndrome and directed blood donations: a dilemma for American medicine. Arch Surg 1988; 123:23–25.
86. Thaler M, Shamiss A, Orgad S, et al. The role of blood from HLA-homozygous donors in fatal transfusion-associated graft-vs-host disease. N Engl J Med 1989; 321:25–28.

87. Perkins HA, Samson S, Busch MP. How well has self-exclusion worked? Transfusion 1988; 28:601–602.
88. Chambers LA, Kruskall MS, Leonard SS, Ellis AM. Directed donor programs may adversely affect autologous donor participation. Transfusion 1988; 28:645.
89. Goodnough LT. Predeposit of designated blood does not protect against homologous blood exposure in patients who predeposit autologous blood for elective surgery. Am J Clin Pathol 1989; 92:484–487.
90. Ali S, Goodnough LT. An analysis of a directed donor program in 1995. Blood 1995; 86:852A.

20
Leukoreduction

Anne B. McDonald
Beth Israel Deaconess Hospital, Boston, Massachusetts

Walter H. Dzik
Beth Israel Deaconess Hospital and Harvard Medical School, Boston, Massachusetts

I. INTRODUCTION

Transfusion of allogeneic donor leukocytes present in cellular blood components results in a number of both proven and perceived adverse effects in recipients. Over the last decade, a greater understanding of these possible adverse effects has been the impetus for improving methods of leukoreduction. Advances in technology have allowed more widespread use of leukoreduced components and have prompted active investigation into the potential benefits of these products. This chapter will describe the methods, indications for, and efficacy of leukoreduction.

Cellular blood components contain a large number of residual donor leukocytes (Table 1). The point at which a component can be considered adequately leukoreduced has varied in the past, with the level of 5×10^6 white blood cells (WBCs) per unit of red blood cells (RBCs) being established by the American Association of Blood Banks in 1991 and extension of the standard to leukoreduced platelets in 1996.

II. METHODS OF LEUKOREDUCTION

A. Centrifugation

The use of centrifugal force to separate blood components by density has been used for many years. The removal of the buffy coat from whole blood is widely

Table 1 Approximate Number of Leukocytes
in Blood Components

Fresh whole blood	10^9
Red cell concentrate	10^8–10^9
Buffy coat depleted red cells	10^8
Washed red cell concentrate	10^7
Frozen deglycerolized red cells	10^6–10^7
Platelet concentrate	10^7–10^8
Apheresis platelets	10^5–10^8
Fresh frozen plasma	$<10^4$

practiced. The process of centrifugation separates the least dense leukocytes from the packed red cells, with more efficient removal of lymphocytes and monocytes than granulocytes (1). In a variation of this process—the "top and bottom" method—whole blood is centrifuged at relatively high centrifugal force to compress both platelets and leukocytes into the buffy coat. The supernatant plasma is then expressed out of the top of the primary bag into one satellite bag, while the red cells are removed via the bottom into another. The buffy coat, composed of donor white cells and platelets, is then pooled with further buffy coats and centrifuged again at a lower centrifugal force. This allows separation of the platelet-rich plasma from the white cell component, which is then discarded. This method removes 70–80% of leukocytes, a reduction sufficient to prevent many febrile nonhemolytic transfusion reactions, but not other complications whose prevention requires a higher degree of leukoreduction.

A variation of this method involves manipulation of the temperature of whole blood prior to centrifugation. It was found that if the whole blood was first cooled and then warmed prior to centrifugation, the removal of leukocytes could be increased to 90%, with no apparent evidence of damage to red cells or coagulation factors (2).

Other methods used in the past include washing and use of frozen/thawed red cells. Washing is not the most efficient way to remove leukocytes because of the wide variation in the number removed (3). Significant red cell loss may occur. Because preparation takes place in an open system, washed red cells must be used within 24 hours. Frozen deglycerolized red cells reduce the risk of cytomegalovirus (CMV) transmission (4), but, because of the presence of viable lymphocytes (5), they are inadequate to prevent graft-versus-host disease in immunodeficient recipients.

B. Filtration

Advances in filtration technology have made consistent production of leuko-reduced components a viable option. Table 2 summarizes the changes in filtration over recent years.

1. Mechanism of Filtration

Removal of leukocytes by filtration results primarily from retention by a barrier. The interior of most modern leukocyte removal filters consists of layers of synthetic mesh made of nonwoven fibers. The design is such that the blood entering the filter encounters a large surface area of the medium. Optimally, the blood cannot bypass the filtration medium and the amount of blood retained in the filter is minimal.

Adsorption of leukocytes to the synthetic fibers also contributes to leuko-reduction. Modification of synthetic surfaces, by increasing "wettability" to decrease the surface tension or by alteration in surface charge of the fibers (6), has improved the performance of filters.

Biological mechanisms also influence leukoreduction. Electron micro-scopic analysis of filters demonstrates that platelets undergo activation and spreading on the surface of filter fibers during filtration of red blood cells. Leukocytes, especially polymorphonuclear leukocytes, adhere to the activated platelets and are removed (7). Platelets may also contribute by forming micro-aggregates that trap cells (8).

2. Factors Affecting Filtration Performance

As leukoreduction methods have evolved, the factors that influence the residual number of leukocytes have become increasingly important as variables that can

Table 2 History of Filters for Blood Transfusion

Generation	Removal target	Filter material
First	Clots	Screen filter; pore size: 170–240 µm
Second	Micro-aggregates	Screen/depth woven filter; pore size: 40 µm
Third	Leukocytes	Nonwoven web of microfibers; fiber diam: 2–20 µm

be controlled to improve the quality of the end product. These factors are summarized in Table 3.

The capacity of the filter used is of prime importance in the degree of leukoreduction achieved. Current high-performance filters can reduce the residual WBC content by 3–4 logs. The input load of the WBCs to be filtered has a direct relation to the postfiltration WBC content. Manufacturers' guidelines provide filter capacity, or number of units of RBCs or platelets, for the average WBC load. The cellular composition of the input product will affect the filtration process in other ways, too. For example, elevated hematocrit in red cell concentrate may result in slightly decreased leukocyte removal performance because of inhibited leukocyte approach to adsorption points (9). The nature of the erythrocyte may also affect filter performance. Filtration of hemoglobin AS (sickle cell trait) blood results in poorer WBC removal than does filtration of hemoglobin AA blood (10,11). It is thought that sickling of the red cells within the filter results in obstruction of flow, preventing adequate contact of the leukocytes with the filtration medium. Platelets in red cell concentrates also influence filtration. Filters have decreased retention for fresh RBCs in the presence of platelets; this has been attributed to biological interaction between platelets and WBCs that promotes retention of the latter (8).

The flow rate through the filter is also a factor in leukoreduction; accelerated blood flow (100 mL/min) is associated with decreased reduction (9). This may result from partial detachment of adsorbed leukocytes due to accelerated shear stress or from decreased contact time with the filtration medium. Alternatively, slow filtration rate may result in insufficient pressure to ensure adequate contact of leukocytes with the filtering medium or may allow an increase in temperature resulting in increased leukocyte deformability (12). Studies have shown that the efficiency of filtration is improved at refrigerated temperatures (13). The reason for this may relate to decreased plasticity of leukocytes at lower temperatures. The medium in which cells are suspended also influences the efficiency of leukoreduction. The addition of small volumes of plasma to RBCs

Table 3   Factors Affecting Filter Performance

Capacity of the filter
Input number of leukocytes
Flow rate, pressure, priming, rinsing
Temperature, viscosity
Number and function of platelets
Holding time between blood collection and filtration
Erythrocyte and leukocyte deformability
Plasma content of cell suspension media

suspended in SAGMAN (saline/adenine/glucose/manitol)-additive solution resulted in a marked improvement in filtration efficiency (14). This may result from adhesive proteins present in plasma contributing to leukocyte retention.

3. Timing of Filtration

Leukocyte reduction can be performed before storage, before issuance from the blood bank, or at the bedside (Table 4) (15). Prestorage leukoreduction is gaining acceptance as the use of leukoreduced components becomes more routine. In-line

Table 4 Timing of Filtration

Prestorage	In blood bank	At bedside
Advantages		
May prevent accumulation of cytokines of donor origin during storage.	Red cell units filtered in short time span—?improved leukoreduction.	Convenience—filter added to intravenous line at time of filtration.
May decrease risk of bacterial contamination.	Smaller no. of staff performing procedure—less variability.	
Leukoreduced units readily available on request.	Easier to control quality compared with bedside filtration.	
Easier to control quality compared with bedside filtration.	Record of special needs of particular patients.	
Disadvantages		
Transfusion of leukoreduced components to patients with no defined clinical indication.	Additional labor cost in blood bank.	Filtration occurs slowly (2–4 h)—red cell unit warms—may lead to less efficient filtration.
	May not remove leukocyte fragments that accumulate during storage.	More difficult to institute quality control measures.
	Does not remove cytokines that may accumulate during platelet storage.	Units which fail quality control have already been transfused.
	Cost of filter.	More staff involved in process—more difficult to institute standard procedures.
		Cost of filter.

filtration (a blood bag system with integrated filter) allows for separation of components and filtration without the need for opening the system, thereby avoiding contamination and bacterial overgrowth during subsequent storage. Prestorage leukoreduction has theoretical advantages of standardization and easy availability of filtered units. Prestorage leukoreduction may decrease the incidence of febrile nonhemolytic transfusion reactions (FNHTRs) from platelet transfusion that results from passive transfer of cytokines. In an animal model (16), the incidence of platelet refractoriness was decreased by prestorage leukoreduction. This may have resulted from removal of leukocyte fragments that may not be removed during poststorage filtration. The issue of the importance of leukocyte fragments has not been resolved. Some studies in an animal model indicate a greater degree of platelet refractoriness following transfusion of plasma supernatant of blood leukoreduced after storage when compared with that leukoreduced before storage (17). However, it has also been demonstrated that leukoreduction had no effect on soluble class I human leukocyte antigen (HLA) substance, and that deliberately prepared leukocyte fragments bearing HLA antigens did not seem to stimulate an alloimmune response in vitro (18).

There have not yet been any clinical trials in humans to determine the effect of prestorage versus poststorage leukoreduction on prevention of alloimmunization. Therefore, the issue remains unresolved.

The choice of filtration in the laboratory prior to issuance by the blood bank versus filtration at the bedside would appear to many to be a minor issue in leukoreduction. However, recent investigations have confirmed that bedside filtration may be less than optimal in many cases for a variety of reasons. Bedside filtration carries the advantage that expensive filters are restricted to units transfused to patients for whom leukoreduction is indicated. However, concerns have arisen regarding the quality of leukoreduction during bedside filtration. Ledent and Berlin (12) found a 78% failure rate ($>5 \times 10^6$ WBC/unit) when leukoreduction was performed under conditions mimicking those of bedside filtration. The failure rate when performed as in a blood bank setting was less than 1%. The major difference in conditions was flow rate, with the rate at the bedside very much slower than that in the laboratory. Slow filtration allows time for warming of the unit, perhaps allowing increased leukocyte deformability and thus less efficient removal of leukocytes. Deliberate warming of blood to 27°C resulted in a 20-fold increase in the number of leukocytes passing through the filter (19), adding further weight to the importance of temperature control. Therefore, the ideal time span in which to filter a unit of red cells would appear to be slow enough so as not to generate excess shearing forces on the white cells trapped in the filter, yet fast enough to minimize any potential warming of the unit. Filtration at a relatively fast flow rate (by gravity over 10–15 minutes), rather than the slow flow at the bedside (over 2–3 hours), would appear to be the most appropriate.

Familiarity with the process of leukoreduction and adequate staff training may be further variables in the process of leukoreduction. Sirchia et al. (20) initially found that, in a hematology outpatient setting with staff trained in the use of bedside filters, the quality of leukoreduced product was not significantly different from that filtered in the laboratory setting. However, subsequent studies at the same center (19) found that, even under ideal conditions for bedside filtration, there was a 5% filtration failure rate. Again, the issue of rise in temperature during filtration was felt to be important, with improved results if transfusion was completed within 100 minutes of removal of the blood from the refrigerator.

In addition to the important issue of quality control, other considerations may influence the decision concerning when to leukoreduce blood. One issue investigated recently is the effect of leukoreduction on the likelihood of bacterial overgrowth of blood products. Investigation of the potential role of leukoreduction has involved experiments using deliberate inoculation of units. Units of blood are "spiked" with varying concentrations of bacteria and then split into pairs, one of which is then filtered. Comparison of bacterial growth is then made at variable times. Most RBC experiments have focused on *Yersinia enterocolitica*, the most commonly encountered serious bacterial contaminant in RBCs. A significant reduction in bacterial concentration occurs during the time between inoculation and filtration (7 hours at room temperature)—an effect attributed to the natural antibacterial properties of blood (21). In addition, it was found that if the initial inoculation was of low concentration, filtration was successful in preventing bacterial overgrowth at 42 days. However, overgrowth during storage was not prevented when higher initial concentrations (greater than 3 colony-forming units/mL) were used. Whether or not routine prestorage filtration of white cells may be of benefit in reducing bacterial overgrowth in the clinical setting is not known. The optimal time to filter is not clear, but it appears there may be a benefit in an early delay to allow bacteriocidal activity of polymorphonuclear phagocytes in the first few hours after collection (22). However, the application of chemical sterilants may, in the future, make discussion of leukoreduction for this reason unnecessary.

Prevention of the storage lesion has also been proposed as an argument in favor of widespread use of prestorage leukoreduction. It was initially felt that leukocyte degeneration during storage would result in release of lysosomal enzymes that could damage the red cell or platelet. However, comparison studies have shown little difference in the degree of hemolysis of red cells stored with or without prestorage leukoreduction, and in vivo survival studies failed to show any advantage to prestorage filtration. Prestorage filtration of platelet concentrates also failed to have any major impact on either in vitro measures of effects of storage or posttransfusion survival of radiolabeled platelets.

C. Low Leukocyte Apheresis Platelets

In recent years, improvements in apheresis technology have led to increased collection of platelets with decreased concentration of residual donor leukocytes in the final product (Table 5). Further reduction has been achieved by some manufacturers through the use of in-line filters in the disposable tubing used in the process. One large study evaluated the performance of the MCS+ system (Haemanetics Corporation, Braintree, MA). With the use of an in-line filter, it was found that 98.3% of 432 collections contained less than 5×10^6 leukocytes. Collection variables, such as use of donors with platelet count less than 200,000 per μL, lipemic samples, anticoagulant citrate dextrose solution (ACD) reactions, or red cell contamination, were found to predict those collections in which leukoreduction was not adequate (23).

Manipulation of the path of the blood flow during apheresis has also been used by manufacturers to improve separation of cellular elements. In the COBE

Table 5 Methods of Leukoreduction: Advantages and Disadvantages

Method of leukoreduction	% removal	Advantages	Disadvantages
Centrifugation	70–80	Simple inexpensive method Adequate for prevention of FNH transfusion reactions	Variable degree of leuko-reduction Inadequate for many of clinical indications for leukoreduction
Freeze/thaw/wash	90–95	Relatively simple method Adequate for most clinical indications for leukoreduction[a]	Time-consuming Significant red cell loss may occur Red cells must be transfused within 24 h because of risk of contamination
Filtration	99.9	Simple method Highly efficient Adequate for most clinical indications for leukoreduction[a]	Expense Potential red cell/platelet loss
Low-WBC apheresis platelets	99.9	Leukoreduced at source Adequate for most clinical indications for leukoreduction[a]	Expense

[a]Inadequate for prevention of transfusion-associated graft-versus-host disease.

BCT Spectra system (Lakewood, CO), a platelet-rich interface is separated from the denser red cells by centrifugation, the interface then being drawn towards a separation "dam." Platelets, being more buoyant, rise over the dam and continue to flow in the same direction to the outlet line and platelet collection bag. Leukocytes, being less buoyant, are drawn in the opposite direction toward the red cell return line. This counterdirectional flow of platelets improves separation of these cellular components. In recent times, further modifications have been made by the same company with the introduction of the Spectra Leukocyte Reduction System (Spectra LRS) based upon the principle of fluidized particle bed separation. A cone-shaped chamber is added to the disposable set at the platelet collection line. The platelet concentrate enters at the narrow base of the conical chamber. Flow patterns that develop in the widening portion of the chamber result in slowing of particle velocity. The deceleration is greatest for heavy particles, such as leukocytes, while lighter particles, such as platelets, advance to the higher chamber level and subsequently escape to the collection bag. The width of the conical chamber increases in stepwise gradations. The design is such that any white cells that advance to a higher level are directed back into the center of the chamber and away from the outlet by the spinning forces. The conical chamber narrows at the top, resulting in acceleration of the platelets prior to entering the outlet tubing. Preliminary results indicate that this method achieves leukoreduced products without the need for secondary filtration (24).

An alternative method used in the CS3000 series of Baxter Biotech (Round Lake, IL) involves the initial separation of platelet-rich plasma from the leukocytes and red cells in a separation chamber. The leukocytes and red cells are returned to the patient, while the platelet-rich plasma enters a second chamber and is centrifuged with return of the plasma to the patient. The manufacturers have again used the geometry of the separation chamber to minimize the number of leukocytes remaining in the platelet-rich plasma. In addition, a system of optics monitors the density of the platelet-rich plasma and can be adjusted to achieve consistently leukoreduced platelet collections.

III. COUNTING METHODS FOR LOW LEUKOCYTE NUMBERS

It is important in terms of the clinical, financial, and technical aspects of leukoreduced components to verify that the end product meets expectations for leukocyte content. The low concentration of white cells now achieved in many products is below the threshold of routine methods of counting cells. In some circumstances it may be adequate to ensure that a product has "passed" or "failed" in terms of the accepted standard of leukoreduction. However, the lower limit of leukoreduction at which all the various adverse effects of transfused white cells can be seen has not yet been determined. As such, development of improved counting methods has paralleled the development of improved leukoreduction. This is important in order to evaluate new technology critically and to gain a better understanding of clinical trials involving leukoreduced components.

Methods to count residual leukocytes have used light or fluorescent microscopy, radioimmunoassays, flow cytometry, volumetric capillary cytometry, and the polymerase chain reaction (PCR) (25). The most widely used method involves a large volume (50 μL) hemocytometer (Nageotte chamber). The sample to be counted is mixed with a red cell or platelet lysing agent and a nuclear stain, allowed to settle undisturbed in the counting chamber, and then examined under 200× magnification. When viewed by a trained observer, the method is simple and has been shown to be accurate to approximately 1 WBC per μL (26). By concentrating a larger volume prior to sampling, the lower limit of detection of Nageotte-based methods may be reduced even further (27).

Flow cytometry, by which a larger volume of sample can be analyzed, achieves a lower limit of accurate detection of 0.1 WBC per μL. Most flow cytometric methods stain leukocytes with a fluorescent nuclear stain and analyze the emission of light. The major disadvantage of this method is the need for expensive instrumentation.

Other methods that have not yet achieved widespread use include volumetric capillary cytometry and PCR-based counting methods. PCR-based methods have an acceptable lower limit of detection, but have disadvantages of labor intensity, equipment cost, and sample contamination.

IV. CLINICAL INDICATIONS FOR LEUKOREDUCTION

A. Prevention of Febrile Nonhemolytic Transfusion Reactions

Febrile nonhemolytic transfusion reactions (FNHTRs) can be a troublesome and often frightening aspect of transfusion to both patient and clinician. Modest reduction in the WBC count was found to be effective in reducing this complication with RBC transfusion, and prevention of FNHTRs is an established indication for transfusion of leukoreduced components.

The cause of FNHTRs may be multifactorial, with the final common pathway being elaboration of inflammatory cytokines that react with receptors in the thermoregulatory centers of the brain. Proposed mechanisms for FNHTRs (Table 6) include recipient antibodies reacting with donor leukocytes, release of inflammatory cytokines by recipient cells in response to antigen-antibody complexes between recipient antibody and donor antigenic material (28), and the passive transfer of inflammatory cytokines that may accumulate in platelets during storage (29). Filtration of RBCs has been found to be effective in

Table 6 Mechanism of FNH Transfusion Reactions

Mechanism	Source of cytokine	Clinical situation
Classic	Donor WBCs	Recipient with leukocyte antibody attacks donor WBCs. Donor cells release cytokine. Prevented by leukoreduction.
Passive cytokine	Donor WBCs	Cytokines released in components stored at room temperature and passively infused into recipient. Prevented by leukoreduction prior to storage.
Immune complex	Recipient WBCs	Recipient with antibody to cells (or proteins) in donor unit attacks donor material after transfusion. Resulting immune complex triggers recipient immune system to release cytokines. Leukoreduction confers incomplete protection.

prevention of FNHTRs in multitransfused patients. Conversely, prevention of FNHTRs with platelet concentrate transfusion has been found to be more difficult (30), favoring the hypothesis that passive transfer of cytokines accumulating during storage is a causative factor. Prestorage leukoreduction of platelet concentrates has been found to moderate the increase in cytokine concentration that occurs with storage (31). Further studies have shown a lower incidence of reactions to plasma-reduced concentrates compared with poststorage leukoreduced units (32).

B. Prevention of HLA Alloimmunization

Formation of HLA alloantibodies has been recognized as one of the causes of refractoriness to platelet transfusions. Prevention of this immunization has been attempted with the use of leukoreduced components. It has been shown that the use of leukoreduced components has decreased the overall incidence of HLA sensitization among multiply transfused patients (33). Analyses of particular subgroups of patients have demonstrated in some studies that, for patients previously exposed to HLA antigens, such as females with history of pregnancy, the use of leukoreduced components did not as effectively prevent immunization or delay time to development of refractoriness (34). The National Institutes of Health Trial to Reduce Alloimmunization to Platelets found that transfusion support with leukoreduced pooled platelets, leukoreduced apheresis platelets, or ultraviolet B–treated platelets resulted in significantly less HLA alloimmunization and platelet refractoriness compared with unmodified pooled platelets. This trial provides the best clinical evidence to date that leukoreduction prevents HLA alloimmunization in patients undergoing cytoreductive chemotherapy.

A major issue for consideration is that HLA alloimmunization may be only a poor surrogate marker for bleeding complications due to platelet refractoriness. Because HLA alloimmunization is only one cause of refractoriness to platelet transfusions, its elimination may not necessarily prevent this problem. Furthermore, serious bleeding complications are infrequent even when unmodified components are used, and it may be difficult to justify the widespread use of a costly procedure, such as leukoreduction, for a potentially small gain. Analysis of this issue continues.

C. Prevention of Transmission of Cytomegalovirus and Other Leukotropic Viruses

The human leukotropic viruses—cytomegalovirus (CMV), Epstein-Barr virus (EBV), and human T-cell lymphotropic virus (HTLV-I/II)—reside within leukocytes of infected individuals. In terms of pathogenicity, CMV is the most important and is capable of causing significant complications in immunocompromised patients. HTLV-I/II is potentially a serious problem, but screening measures have minimized the risk of transmission by transfusion. EBV has high prevalence in the community, but transfusion-transmitted disease has not been a significant problem.

Early studies demonstrated that leukoreduction could prevent transfusion-transmitted CMV (35). In one large study, Bowden et al. (36) randomized 502 CMV seronegative patients undergoing bone marrow transplantation to receive either CMV-seronegative blood components or leukoreduced components from CMV-unscreened donors. Infection occurring more than 21 days after the day of transplant was considered related to transfusion. Infections occurring prior to day 21 were considered to be due to infection prior to enrollment in the study. There was no significant difference between the two study arms in either probability of infection or survival. However, the occurrence of a small number of infections in the filtered arm when compared to the complete absence of cases in the seronegative arm is of concern (Table 7).

Problems identified with this study include the fact that filtration was done at the bedside with no assessment of the adequacy of leukoreduction and that the platelet filters used in the early phase (PL_{50}) had a lower performance rating than filters currently in use. Therefore, it may be that a proportion of the patients received inadequately filtered units. A further smaller study by van Prooijen et al. (37) using blood center leukoreduced units showed no evidence of CMV transmission with filtered units, supporting the current recommendation that adequately leukoreduced components can be regarded as equivalent to

Table 7 Filtered Versus Seronegative Study Arms

	Filtered	Seronegative	p-value
Probability CMV disease (d1-100)	2.4%	0%	0.03
Probability CMV disease (>d21)	1.2%	0%	0.25
Deaths attributed to CMV	5	0	0.56

CMV-seronegative, and can be used to prevent CMV transmission to a seronegative recipient.

It has been suggested that exposure of seropositive recipients to allogeneic donor leukocytes may promote activation of latent recipient virus. In vitro studies have suggested that this effect is not seen with exposure to other allogeneic cellular elements (38). There has also been analysis of the possibility that there may be transmission through transfusion of a second strain of CMV to a seropositive recipient. This phenomenon has been seen with solid organ transplantation (39) but not yet with blood transfusion.

V. CONCLUSION

Leukoreduction has become an important consideration for choosing appropriate blood components for transfusion. The major disadvantages of leukoreduction are additional cost and loss of cellular components intended for transfusion. The potential advantages of adequately leukoreduced components have been outlined. Emphasis on quality control is essential to ensure that leukoreduced components confer maximal benefit.

REFERENCES

1. Nakajo S, Chiba S, Takahashi TA, Sekiguchi S. Comparison of a 'top and bottom' system with a conventional quadruple-bag system for blood component preparation and storage. In: Sekiguchi S, ed. Clinical Applications of Leukocyte Depletion. Oxford: Blackwell Scientific Publications, 1982:18–30.
2. Takahashi TA, Nakajo S, Chiba S, Hoseda M, Sekiguchi S. Cooling and warming method for preparation of 1-log leukocyte-removed red cell concentrates using the top and bottom method. In: Hogman CF, ed. Leukocyte Depletion of Blood Components—Present Trends and the Future. Amsterdam: VU University Press, 1994:145–148.
3. Wenz B. Clinical and laboratory precautions that reduce the adverse reactions, allo-immunization, infectivity and possible immunomodulation associated with homologous transfusions. Trans Med Rev 1990; 4(suppl 1):3–7.

4. Tolkoff-Rubin NE, Rubin RH, Keller EE, et al. Cytomegalovirus infection in dialysis patients and personnel. Ann Intern Med 1978; 89:625–628.

5. Kurtz SR, Van Deinse WH, Valeri CR. The immunocompetence of residual leukocytes at various stages of red cell cryopreservation with 40% w/v glycerol in an ionic medium at –80°C. Transfusion 1978; 18:441–447.

6. Nishimura T, Kuroda T, Mizoguchi Y, et al. Advanced methods for leukocyte removal by blood filtration. In: Brozovic B, ed. The Role of Leukocyte Depletion in Blood Transfusion Practice. Oxford: Blackwell Scientific, 1989:35–40.

7. Steneker I, van Luyn MJA, van Wachen PB, et al. Electron microscope examination of white cell depletion on four leukocyte depletion filters. Transfusion 1992; 32:450–457.

8. Steneker I, Prins HK, Florie M, Loos JA, Biewenga J. Mechanism of leukocyte depletion of red cell concentrates by filtration. The effect of the cellular composition of the red cell concentrate. Transfusion 1993; 33:42–50.

9. Nishimura T, Oka S, Yamawaki N. Technical aspects of leukocyte depletion. In: Hogman CF, ed. Leucocyte Depletion of Blood Components—Present Trends and the Future. Amsterdam: VU University Press, 1994:51–58.

10. Mijovic V, Kruse A. Filtration of blood from donors with HbAS: an unexpected problem. In: Brozovic B, ed. The Role of Leucocyte Depletion in Blood Transfusion Practice. Oxford: Blackwell Scientific, 1989:48–50.

11. Bodensteiner D. White cell reduction in blood from donors with sickle cell trait (letter). Transfusion 1994; 34:84.

12. Ledent E, Berlin G. Inadequate white cell reduction by bedside filtration of red cell concentrates. Transfusion 1994; 34:765–768.

13. Steneker I, Pieterz RNI, Reesink HW. Leukocyte depletion capacity in relation to filtration temperature (abstr). Vox Sang 1994; 67(suppl 2):71.

14. Ledent E, Berlin G. Does plasma influence the efficiency of leukocyte filtration (abstr)? Vox Sang 1994; 67(suppl 2):20.

15. Dzik WH. Leukoreduced components: you can filter now or you can filter later. Transfus Sci 1992; 13:207–210.

16. Engelfreit CP, Diepenhorst P, Gissen MVD, von Riesz E. Removal of leukocytes from whole blood and erythrocyte suspensions by filtration through cotton wool. Vox Sang 1975; 28:81–89.

17. Blajchman MA, Bardossy L, Carmen RA, Goldman M, Heddle NM, Singal DP. An animal model of allogeneic donor platelet refractoriness: the effect of time of leukoreduction. Blood 1992; 79:1371–1375.

18. Dzik S, Szulflad P, Eaves S. HLA antigens on leukocyte fragments and plasma proteins: prestorage leukoreduction by filtration. Vox Sang 1994; 66:104–111.

19. Sirchia G, Rebulla P, Sabbioneda L, Garcea F, Greppi N. Optimal conditions for white cell reduction in red cells by filtration at the patient's bedside. Transfusion 1996; 36:322–327.

20. Sirchia G, Rebulla P, Parravicini A, Marangoni F, Cortelezzi A, Stefania A. Quality control of red cell filtration at the patient's bedside. Transfusion 1994; 34:26–30.

21. Buchholz DH, AuBouchon JP, Snyder EL, et al. Removal of *Yersinia enterocolitica* from AS-1 red cells. Transfusion 1992; 32:667–672.
22. Hogman CF, Gong J, Eriksson L, Hambraeus A, Johansson CS. White cells protect donor blood against bacterial contamination. Transfusion 1991; 31:612–626.
23. Fitzpatrick JE, Orsini F, Pantano J. Residual leukocyte content of plateletpheresis concentrates produced on the Haemonetics MCS+: evaluation of a method to predict high post filter white cell counts (abstr). Transfusion 1995; 35(suppl 1):2S.
24. Riggert J, Zingsem J, Fourmel JJ, et al. European multicenter evaluation of the COBE Spectra LRS leukoreduction system (abstr). Vox Sang 1996; 70(S2):11.
25. Dzik S. Principles of counting low numbers of leukocytes in leukoreduced blood components. Trans Med Rev 1996;
26. Rebulla P, Dzik WH. Multicenter evaluation of methods for counting residual white cells in leukocyte depleted red blood cells. Vox Sang 1994; 66:25–32.
27. Sadoff BJ, Dooley DC, Kapoor V, Law P, Friedman LI, Stromberg RR. Methods for counting a 6 log 10 white cell depletion in red cells. Transfusion 1991; 31:150–156.
28. Dzik WH. Is the febrile response to transfusion due to donor or recipient cytokine (letter)? Transfusion 1992; 32:594.
29. Heddle NM, Klama L, Singer J, et al. The role of plasma from platelet concentrates in transfusion reactions. N Engl J Med 1994; 331:625–628.
30. Goodnough LT, Riddell JV, Lazarus H, et al. Prevalence of platelet transfusion reactions before and after implementation of leukocyte-depleted platelet concentrates by filtration. Vox Sang 1993; 65:103–107.
31. Aye MT, Palmer DS, Giulivi A, Hashemi S. Effect of filtration of platelet concentrates on the accumulation of cytokines and platelet release factors during storage. Transfusion 1995; 35:117–124.
32. Heddle NM, Klama L, Kelton JG, Walker I, Meyer R, Levine M. Investigations of two interventions to prevent acute reactions to platelets (abstr). Proceedings of the 24th congress of the ISBT, Mukuhari, Japan, 1996, p. 27.
33. Heddle NM. The efficiency of leukodepletion to improve platelet transfusion response: a critical appraisal of clinical studies. Transfus Med Rev 1994; 8:15–28.
34. Sintnicolaas K, van Marwijk KM, van Prooijen HC, et al. Leukocyte depletion of random single-donor platelet transfusions does not prevent secondary human leukocyte antigen-alloimmunization and refractoriness: a randomized prospective study. Blood 1995; 85:824–828.
35. Brady MT, Milam JD, Anderson DC, et al. Use of deglycerolized red blood cells to prevent posttransfusion infection with cytomegalovirus in neonates. J Infect Dis 1984; 150:334–339.
36. Bowden RA, Slichter SJ, Sayers M, Weisdorf D, Cays M, Schoch G, Banaji M, Haake R, Welk K, Fisher L, McCullough J, Miller W. A comparison of filtered leukocyte-reduced and cytomegalovirus (CMV) seronegative blood products for the prevention of transfusion-associated CMV infection after marrow transplant. Blood 1995; 86:3599–3603.
37. van Prooijen HC, Visser JJ, van Oostendorp WR, de Gast GC, Verdonck LF. Prevention of primary transfusion-associated cytomegalovirus infection in bone

marrow transplant recipients by the removal of white cells from blood components with high-affinity filters. Br J Haematol 1994; 84:144–147.

38. Busch MP, Lee TH, Heitman J. Allogeneic leukocytes but not therapeutic blood elements induce reactivation and dissemination of latent human immunodeficiency virus type 1 infection: implications for transfusion support of infected patients. Blood 1992; 80:2128–2135.

39. Dzik S, Blajchman MA, Blumberg N, Kirkley SA, Heal JM, Wood K. Current research on the immunomodulatory effect of allogeneic blood transfusion. Vox Sang 1996; 70:187–194.

21

Viral Inactivation

Bernard Horowitz
VITEX (V.I. Technologies, Inc.), New York, New York

Ehud Ben-Hur
Consultant in Photomedicine, New York, New York

I. INTRODUCTION

The emergence of human immunodeficiency virus (HIV) as a transfusion-transmitted virus in the early 1980s caused great concern about the safety of the blood supply. Since that time the introduction of improved donor screening and testing has reduced the risk of developing a transfusion-associated HIV infection in the United States to a very low level. The risk of transmission of hepatitis B virus (HBV) and hepatitis C virus (HCV) is similarly very low today, although it is 5- to 10-fold higher than the risk of HIV (1).

For pooled blood products the risk of viral transmission is increased proportionately to the number of pooled donations: probability of infection = $1-[(1-\text{risk per donor})^{\text{no.donors}}]$. As a result, between 1979 and 1985, 70% of patients with severe hemophilia in the United States were infected with HIV, which contaminated the coagulation factor concentrates used in their treatment (2), and most adult hemophiliacs are infected with HBV, HCV, or both (3,4). This situation was the driving force behind the efforts to develop methods for virus inactivation in blood products. These efforts were successful, and the emphasis is now on developing methods that will be applicable to blood components. The established methods and those still under development will be reviewed in this chapter.

II. HISTORICAL BACKGROUND

During World War II there was an unprecedented need for large quantities of plasma derived from pooled sources. Sterilization efforts to prevent the increase of hepatitis were focused on the use of short wavelength ultraviolet light (UVC, 254 nm), with initially promising results (5). However, this approach was abandoned when it became clear that adequate inactivation of viruses in plasma could be achieved only by UVC doses that inactivated plasma components (6). Serum albumin, a relatively heat-stable protein that could be stabilized further by addition of fatty acids, was the only blood product available in a virally sterile form for a long time. It was heated at 60°C for 10 hours, a process that remains in use today.

The concerns about the spread of hepatitis viruses, and subsequently HIV, through blood transfusion stimulated development of other virus-inactivation methods with remarkable success (7). However, these methods have certain limitations. They are applicable only to plasma and its fractions but not to the cellular components of blood. In addition, these methods can inactivate effectively lipid-enveloped viruses such as HIV, HBV, and HCV, but some nonenveloped viruses [hepatitis A virus (HAV) and parvovirus B19)] are not completely inactivated. The last two viruses are of minor concern and remain a challenge for the future.

In addition to reducing or eliminating the risk of virus transmission, adopting viral inactivation procedures presents numerous advantages. The window period will no longer be of concern, and efforts to reduce it by direct detection of viral nucleic acid will no longer be needed. Errors in testing or the inadvertent release of blood that tests positive will not result in viral transmission. Viruses that are not tested for, including new ones, will be eliminated, obviating the need to introduce new tests. Of course, the virus-inactivation procedure should not affect the blood component in a way that reduces its therapeutic activity. In addition, the approach should not pose a health risk from, for example, new immunogenic structures or toxic residues. The process should also be efficient with respect to yield and ease of implementation and thus be economical. In this age of managed care, costs are not a minor consideration.

III. ESTABLISHED METHODS

A. Wet Heat (Pasteurization)

The use of heat in the liquid state (60°C, 10 h) is the oldest method of sterilization and is termed after its inventor, Pasteur. It is based on the sensitivity of most proteins to heat. Heat-labile proteins in the product to be treated have to be stabilized prior to pasteurization by addition of low molecular weight solutes, such as sugars, amino acids, and salts (7,8). These additives prevent unwanted protein denaturation and loss of biological activity. The stabilization of the virus by the added solute is much lower than that of the clotting factors (Table 1). Treatment that achieves a sufficiently high level of virus elimination (over 6 $\log_{10}$) results in 60–80% recovery of clotting factors. Nonenveloped viruses, however, which tend to be heat-stable, are killed to a lesser extent by this process. Other advantages of pasteurization are its ease of implementation in a factory setting, avoidance of potentially toxic chemicals, and homogeneity of the treatment (i.e., virus is inactivated at the same rate throughout the treated product).

B. Dry Heat

Virus inactivation by heating of lyophilized blood proteins occurs at higher temperatures and takes a longer time than pasteurization because proteins are stabilized in the absence of water. HIV can be eliminated from lyophilized Factor VIII by heating at 68°C for 96 hours (10). Recovery of Factor VIII activity can be high under these conditions (11). However, because of heterogeneity of lyophilized cakes with respect to solute and moisture content, heating has to be conducted at 80°C for 72 hours to achieve reproducible viral safety (12). Recovery of Factor VIII activity exceeds 90%. As with pasteurization, nonenveloped viruses are more resistant to dry heat than are enveloped viruses, and their titer (e.g., that of parvovirus) is reduced but not eliminated (13). A particular advantage of dry heating is that it can be performed in the final container, eliminating the possibility of posttreatment recontamination.

C. Solvent-Detergent

The use of the solvent tri(n-butyl)phosphate (TNBP), typically with Tween 80 or other detergents, disrupts the viral lipid envelope with concomitant inactivation of lipid-enveloped viruses (14). The treatment is rapid (4–6 h at 24–30°C), plasma

Table 1 Inactivation Velocity, K, of Lipid-Enveloped Viruses at 60°C With or Without Stabilization

| Virus | K (ln/hr) | | |
	A. Stabilized AHF	B. Buffer	B/A
VSV	1.61	≥175	≥109
Sindbis	0.30	≥230	≥769
Sendai	0.74	≥276	≥375

Source: Adapted from Ref. 9.

proteins are not affected, and recovery of clotting factors can reach 100%. The added solvent and detergent are removed after treatment, either simply in the course of purifying the protein or with hydrophobic chromatography using a C18 resin. The safety of solvent-detergent (SD)–treated blood products with respect to HBV, HCV, and HIV is supported by studies in chimpanzees, 14 independent clinical trials, and the preparation of HIVIG, a hyperimmune gamma globulin to HIV prepared from HIV-infected donors (15–17). A summary of viral safety from clinical trials conducted with products treated by these methods is given in Table 2. Advantages of SD treatment include its ease of implementation in a factory setting and its very high level of virucidal action under conditions where virtually all proteins are unaffected.

The excellent safety record of coagulation factors treated with solvent-detergent encouraged the development of SD-treated plasma as a substitute for fresh frozen plasma (FFP) (18). The procedure involves pooling of up to 2500 units of FFP, treatment with 1% TNBP and 1% Triton X-100 at 30°C for 4 hours, and removal of the reagents by hydrophobic chromatography. The final product is sterile-filtered and frozen. Under these conditions, the rate of inactivation of the model lipid-enveloped viruses, vesicular stomatitis virus (VSV) and Sindbis virus, exceed those observed with Factor VIII concentrates. In addition, more than 10^6 infectious doses (ID_{50}) of HBV, more than 10^5 ID_{50} of HCV, and more than $10^{7.2}$ ID_{50} of HIV are killed. Approximately 15% of donor units contain anti-HAV antibody. We have shown that more than $10^{4.5}$ ID_{50} of HAV are neutralized in the process (19). Because of pooling, SD-treated plasma has 30-fold more anti-HAV antibody than intramuscular immune globulin, which is known to prevent HAV spread, and has approximately the same quantity of antiparvovirus antibody as intravenous immune globulin, a preparation used therapeutically to treat parvo-

Table 2 Safety of Virally Sterilized Coagulation Factor Concentrates

Method	Quantity tested ($U \times 10^6$)	No. of patients infected/No. treated		
		HBV	HCV	HIV
Wet heat (60°C, 10 h)	18.8	2/?	2/95	0/237
Dry heat (80°C, 72 h)	0.1	0/16	0/32	0/32
Dry heat and vapor (60°C, 10 h)	1.1	4/46	0/70	0/110
Solvent-detergent	17.6	0/55	0/449	0/524

[a]Results from patients with hemophilia who received standard therapy with coagulation factor concentrates virally sterilized by the indicated method. Following infusion, patients were monitored for 6–12 months using standard serological assays.
Source: Data from Refs. 15, 17.

virus infections in immunocompromised patients. The coagulation factor content is similar to that of the start pool (20,21) and is more consistent than that found in individual donor units. There is no activation of coagulation factors during treatment, and the level of other proteins is normal. Toxicological studies indicate that the tiny amounts of solvent and detergent that remain (below 3 ppm) are safe.

SD-treated plasma has been extensively evaluated in the United States and Europe (22–24) and has been approved for use in most European countries, the United States, and Canada. In the United States, more than 20 clinical study sites took part in the clinical trials that preceded licensure. The principal efficacy endpoints were the correction of coagulation factor deficiencies and the treatment of thrombotic thrombocytopenic purpura. SD-treated plasma behaved like FFP in all cases. Enveloped viruses have not been transmitted in studies cited above or in more than 4 million units of SD-treated plasma infused to date. Studies being conducted in the United States indicated that parvovirus, a nonenveloped virus found in approximately one of 1000 blood donors, could be transmitted by SD plasma despite the presence of antiparvovirus antibody in the unit being transfused. Consequently, in the United States, SD plasma is now tested for parvovirus by polymerase chain reaction (PCR).

IV. NEW APPROACHES

A. Plasma and Blood Proteins

Additional techniques for virus inactivation are being studied because the established methods do not eliminate completely the nonenveloped and heat-resistant HAV and parvovirus B19. Given the extensive history of safety achieved by currently employed methods and the limitations of laboratory and preclinical virus validation studies, it is likely that any new procedure will be added to rather than replace existing processes. Combining methods that act by independent mechanisms has the advantage of inactivating a broader spectrum as well as a higher quantity of viruses.

1. Antibody Affinity Purification

During purification of Factor VIII with immunoaffinity column chromatography, HIV infectivity is reduced 10^4-fold. This approach has been combined with either SD (24) or heat treatment (25) for enhanced safety.

2. Nanofiltration

Viruses can be removed by newly developed filters. The term nanofiltration comes from the ability of the process to remove viruses as small as 15 nm (26,27). The use of nanofiltration has the advantage of easy addition to existing processes.

However, 35 nm filters do not remove HAV or parvoviruses. Although 15 nm filters are effective for this purpose (28), recovery of high molecular weight proteins is unacceptably low. In addition, the question of manufacturing consistency of each filter needs to be addressed. As a result, nanofiltration would be limited to sterilization of only some blood-derived proteins.

3. UVC Light Irradiation

UVC light targets the viral nucleic acid, producing photochemical modifications of the pyrimidines (29). As a result, a wide variety of viruses are inactivated irrespective of the nature of their envelope. Viruses containing single-stranded nucleic acids are more sensitive. In addition, sensitivity is correlated with the size of the nucleic acid (30). The former is due to the inability to repair damage in the absence of a complementary strand, while the latter reflects the fact that a larger target is hit more often.

Photochemical modification of nucleic acids by UVC proceeds via direct reactions of the excited pyrimidines, whereas damage to proteins involves free radical reactions. This difference in mechanism has been used to enhance the specificity of virus inactivation by UVC in protein solutions by adding scavengers of free radicals. The most effective scavenger found so far is the plant flavonoid rutin, an efficient quencher of reactive oxygen species (ROS). Rutin has no effect on the inactivation kinetics of various viruses but protects several coagulation factors against UVC-induced damage (31). Rutin also protects fibrinogen, albumin, and IVIG against UVC irradiation of fibrin sealant for viral inactivation (32,33). Fibrin sealant sterilized with SD and UVC is now in clinical trials evaluating its role in hemostasis and wound healing during surgery. It has been concluded that addition of UVC treatment to existing processes used in the manufacture of blood derivatives will provide an added margin of safety. This is especially true with respect to nonenveloped viruses.

4. Starch-Bound Iodine

Iodine is a strong oxidizing agent and, as a result, is a powerful microbicide. However, in its free form iodine is not sufficiently selective. When bound to polymers such as polyvinylpyrrolidone (34) and in particular crosslinked starch (35), the virucidal action of iodine is more controlled. Thus, starch-bound iodine at a concentration of 1.05 mg/mL resulted in more than 7 $\log_{10}$ inactivation of model lipid enveloped and nonenveloped viruses, while more than 70% of clotting factors activity in plasma was retained (35). Additional research is needed to determine the efficacy of crosslinked starch-iodine on human pathogenic viruses, as well as the effect on plasma proteins.

5. Methylene Blue and Visible Light

Methylene blue (MB) is a photosensitizer, i.e., in conjunction with light it can inactivate biological systems. Because the presence of oxygen is required, MB is a photodynamic agent. The virucidal action of MB is well known (36), but the mechanism of action is not entirely clear. Nucleic acid damage is usually produced as a result of MB photosensitization but was ruled out as the cause of virus kill in one case (37) but not in others (38). Recently, a procedure has been developed in which individual plasma units are treated with 1 µM MB and white fluorescent light for one hour at 60,000 lux (39). The individual units are refrozen and stored for later use. Model enveloped viruses and cell-free HIV are inactivated effectively; cell-associated HIV and nonenveloped viruses are less affected (40,41). Complete virus studies, including hepatitis viruses and a demonstration that infectious units can be rendered noninfectious, have yet to be reported. The advantage of this approach compared with SD treatment is that pooling is not required (i.e., recipients would received plasma from individual donations, rather than from a plasma pool made from hundreds or thousands of donations). On the other hand, treatment of individual units does not allow for careful monitoring and control of procedures as can be achieved with plasma pools processed in a factory setting.

MB photodynamic treatment of plasma resulted in no adverse reactions in a controlled clinical study (42), and neoantigens were not produced in the treated plasma (43). The in vitro coagulation capacity of MB-treated plasma is reduced mainly because of reduced fibrinogen and Factor VIII activity (44). It was therefore recommended that such plasma not be used for patients with severely reduced ability for synthesizing clotting factors (44). Recently it has been reported that MB is mutagenic in a cultured mammalian cell system (45). Considerable investigation will be required, therefore, to assess the genotoxic potential of MB-treated plasma prior to its clinical use in the United States. This may be the reason that MB-treated plasma has been withdrawn from the market in Germany.

B. Platelet Concentrates

The cellular components of blood are more difficult to sterilize than protein solutions, because cell structure and function are disrupted more easily than protein structure and function. In addition, infectious virus or its nucleic acid can be harbored intracellularly. The challenge is eased somewhat because red blood cells (RBCs) and platelets lack a nucleus and are nonreplicating. A decontaminating process must leave cellular function intact during both the treatment period and subsequent storage. The storage period for platelets is 5 days, and the critical functions require adhesion to subendothelial matrix proteins, aggregation, and secretion of intracellular organelles. After transfusion, sufficient numbers of platelets should persist in the circulation. In vitro measures of platelet function, such as aggregation response to agonists, are most commonly used to assess platelet concentrate quality. However, in vitro assays do not adequately predict posttransfusion platelet recovery and survival in vivo (46).

The use of psoralens and UVA light (PUVA) is a promising approach for inactivation of pathogenic organisms in platelet concentrates and is now in clinical trials. The ability of PUVA to target nucleic acids is an obvious advantage for sterilizing platelets, which lack a nucleus. Psoralens preferentially bind to nucleic acids in the dark and upon exposure to UVA light form adducts with the pyrimidines, which effectively inhibit nucleic acid replication, transcription, and translation (47). As a result, PUVA inactivates not only pathogens but also leukocytes. The inactivation of the latter is beneficial, since transfused leuko- cytes may lead to alloimmunization (48), nonhemolytic febrile transfusion reac- tions (49), and graft-versus-host disease (50). In addition to covalent binding to nucleic acids upon exposure to UVA light, psoralens can also produce reac- tive oxygen species (ROS), such as singlet oxygen, and induce photodamage in lipids and proteins. Platelet damage can, therefore, occur under treatment conditions that result in greater than 6 $\log_{10}$ virus inactivation. This problem has been dealt with by adding the plant flavonoid rutin as a quencher of ROS to eliminate photodynamic damage during treatment with 4'-aminomethyl-4,5',8- trimethylpsoralen (AMT) and UVA (51). Others use psoralens with reduced photodynamic activity (52).

The advantages of AMT over other psoralens as an agent for virus inacti- vation are that (a) it is water soluble and (2) because it is cationic, it binds more tightly to nucleic acids and is highly effective for photoinactivation of single- stranded RNA viruses. The disadvantage of AMT is that it is mutagenic in the dark after metabolic activation with some of the Ames tester strains (53). To circumvent this potential problem with the clinical use of AMT, we developed a procedure to remove it after light exposure. The method employs a hydrophobic resin (C18), which adsorbs >99% of AMT and is effective in reducing mutagen- icity below detection level without affecting platelets' aggregation response (53). In addition to quenchers, the exclusion of the shorter UVA wavelengths ($\lambda < 340$ nm) is also helpful in enhancing the specificity of platelet decontamination by PUVA (54).

In addition to viruses, PUVA can inactivate bloodborne parasites (55) and bacteria (56) in platelet concentrates. Because the risk of bacterial contamination is currently the reason for limiting the storage of platelet concentrates to 5 days, inactivation of bacteria may extend the allowable storage time to 7 days. It should be noted that the genomes of parasites and bacteria are usually inactivated at lower doses of PUVA. It is also important to stress that treatment of platelet concentrates with AMT-UVA appears to result in fully functional platelets in vivo under conditions resulting in inactivation of free and cell-associated HIV (57,58).

Other psoralens being studied for use in decontamination of platelet concentrates include brominated psoralens, which were claimed to possess improved efficiency and selectivity for viral inactivation (59). Psoralens with undisclosed structure are reported to be highly virucidal, nonmutagenic, and lacking photodynamic activity (52). In the absence of published data, the latter claims are difficult to evaluate, but one of these psoralens, termed S59, is in clinical trials.

C. Red Blood Cell Concentrates

The use of PUVA is not applicable for the sterilization of RBCs because of the strong absorption of UVA light by hemoglobin. Only red light ($\lambda > 600$ nm) can effectively penetrate RBCs, and for this reason sensitizers that absorb maximally in the red are being studied. These compounds do not target the viral nucleic acid and are therefore less specific than PUVA. Their virucidal action requires oxygen; they are thus defined as photodynamic agents. Many classes of photosensitizers have been tested over the years for their virucidal activity; however, only a few are being seriously studied for RBC sterilization.

1. Methylene Blue

The absorption maximum of methylene blue (MB), 665 nm, is favorable for sterilization of RBCs, and there is some clinical experience with its use for sterilizing FFP (see above). However, there are problems associated with the use of MB in RBCs. The main problem is the lack of inactivation by MB of cell-associated HIV (40). Moreover, MB can photosensitize induction of HIV in latently infected cells (60), and at a dose range in which sufficient virus elimination is achieved, the treatment causes RBC membrane damage (61). Other MB derivatives are being studied that may circumvent these problems (62).

2. Benzoporphyrin Derivative

Benzoporphyrin derivative (BPD) is a photosensitizer undergoing clinical trials for photodynamic treatment of skin cancer and other indications. BPD has an absorption band at 692 nm and at concentrations of 2–4 µg/mL plus 57 J/cm^2 was able to inactivate both cell-free and cell-associated HIV in whole blood (63). There was only minimal hemolysis during 2 days of storage. Interestingly, ziduvidine-resistant and -sensitive strains of HIV appear to be equally sensitive to BPD photoinactivation. More work is required to evaluate RBC quality following this virucidal treatment.

3. Hypericin

Initial work with hypericin suggested that this plant pigment may be an anti-HIV agent (64). However, later studies indicate that most of the antiretroviral activity of hypericin is light-dependent (65). This is in agreement with a large body of literature on hypericin as a photodynamic agent. Maximal absorption of hypericin occurs at 590 nm, and it is therefore not ideal for sterilization of RBCs. Even so, there are efforts to optimize its virucidal potential by studies of structure-activity relationships of several hypericin derivatives (66).

4. Phthalocyanines

Arguably, these are the most promising photosensitizers for sterilization of RBCs. Phthalocyanines are porphyrin-like synthetic dyes. Because of their expanded macrocycle, they absorb intensely at 660–700 nm. Aluminum phthalocyanine (AlPc) and its sulfonated derivatives are effective in photosensitizing inactivation of lipid-enveloped viruses, including HIV (67). Other phthalocyanines were shown to inactivate nonenveloped viruses (68). While tetrasulfonate AlPc caused the least RBC damage under virucidal conditions, there was a need to eliminate residual damage to erythrocytes, evidenced by reduced circulatory survival (69). This was achieved by adding quenchers of ROS such as mannitol, glutathione, and trolox (69–71) prior to light exposure. While protecting RBCs, these quenchers had no effect on virus inactivation.

Other ways to reduce RBC damage while maintaining the virucidal potency of phthalocyanines are the use of an appropriate light source to achieve high irradiance (72) at a selective wavelength (73) and a special delivery vehicle (74). These additional procedures to increase the specificity of the treatment were required following the observation that inactivation of HIV in all its forms, as well as inactivation of bloodborne parasites, was achieved only with the silicon phthalocyanine Pc 4 (75–77). Pc 4, however, caused more RBC damages in the absence of these special precautions.

When RBCs are treated with Pc 4 and red light, taking into consideration all of the above, virus sterilization can be achieved with little or no hemolysis during storage (78). In vivo circulatory survival of rabbit RBCs is also close to normal. Toxicological studies of Pc 4 are underway prior to evaluation of this procedure in clinical trials.

5. Inactine

Inactine has recently been reported to inactivate both enveloped and nonenveloped viruses. RBCs were reported to store well following treatment (79). The structure of inactine has not bee disclosed, but it is said to covalently modify DNA and to be mutagenic prior to but not following neutralization.

V. CONCLUSIONS

The inactivation of viruses in blood proteins and plasma has made the transfusion of these products absolutely safe with respect to transmission of HBV, HCV, and HIV. The addition of nanofiltration, where applicable, or UVC irradiation to the currently established methods (heat and SD treatment) should make these products safe also with respect to HAV and parvovirus B-19, the two nonenveloped viruses reported to be transmitted by plasma derivatives. The remaining challenge is the sterilization of red cell and platelet concentrates. The use of photosensitizers for this purpose appears to be promising. PUVA is in clinical trials for platelets, and Pc 4 is about to enter clinical trials for red cells. Table 3 summarizes the

Table 3 Comparison of the Approaches for Virus Inactivation in Blood

Approach	Blood component	Advantages	Disadvantages
Wet heat	Purified proteins Plasma	Convenient—all viruses are susceptible	Protein activity recovery is medium Nonenveloped virused killed to a lesser extent Plasma must be pooled
Dry heat	Purified proteins	Can be performed in the final container High protein recovery	Nonenveloped viruses not completely killed
Solvent-detergent	Purified proteins Plasma	Enveloped viruses very sensitive Recovery of protein activity is close to 100%	Nonenveloped viruses not inactivated Plasma must be pooled
Nanofiltration	Purified proteins	Easy to add to existing process	Limited to proteins of lower molecular weight
UVC light	Purified proteins Plasma	Inactivates all virus types	Rutin must be added to protect protein activity Specialized equipment required
Photosensitization	Plasma	Compatible with the sterilization of cellular components	Not yet commercially available, except for methylene blue for plasma in Germany and Switzerland
	Platelets	Plasma does not have to be pooled	Efficacy for viruses yet to be proven
	Red cells		

relative merits of these methods. Since none of them is perfect, currently employed screening methods are unlikely to be discontinued. On the other hand, adoption of virus inactivation procedures may make the addition of new screening tests unnecessary.

ACKNOWLEDGMENT

This work was supported in part by grant No. 2 RO1-HL 412221 from the National Heart, Lung and Blood Institute.

REFERENCES

1. Schreiber GB, Busch MP, Kleinman SH, Korelitz JJ. The risk of transfusion-transmitted viral infections. N Engl J Med 1996; 334:1685–1690.
2. Goedert JJ, Kessler CM, Aldort LM, Biggar RJ, Andes WA, White GC, Drummond JE, Vaidya K, Mann DL, Eyster ME, Ragni MV, Lederman MM, Cohen AR, Bray GL, Rosenberg PS, Friedman RM, Hilgartner MW, Blattner WA, Kroner B, Gail MH. A prospective study of human immunodeficiency infection and the development of AIDS in subjects with hemophilia. N Engl J Med 1989; 321:1141–1148.
3. Brettler DB, Alter HJ, Dienstag JL, Frosberg AD, Levine PH. The prevalence of antibody to hepatitis C in a cohort of hemophilic patients. Blood 1990; 76:254.
4. Troisi CL, Hollinger FB, Hoots WK, Contant C, Gill J, Ragni M, Parmley R, Sexauer C, Gomperts E, Buchanan G, Schwartz B, Adair S, Fields H. A multi-center study of viral hepatitis in a United States hemophilic population. Blood 1993; 81:412–428.
5. Oliphant JW, Hollander A. Homologous serum jaundice: experimental inactivation of etiologic agent in serum by ultraviolet irradiation. Public Health Rep 1946; 61:598–600.
6. Murray R, Oliphant JW, Tripp JT, Hampi B, Ratner F, Diefenbach WCL. Effect of ultraviolet irradiation on the infectivity of ictrogenic plasma. J Am Med Assoc 1955; 157:8–14.
7. Hilfenhaus J, Herrman A, Mauler R, Prince AM. Inactivation of the AIDS-causing retrovirus and other human viruses in antihemophilic plasma protein preparations by pasteurization. Vox Sang 1986; 50:208–211.
8. Hilfenhaus J, Weidmann E. Pasteurization as an efficient method to inactivate blood borne viruses in factor VIII concentrates. Arzneimittelforschung 1986; 36:621–625.
9. Horowitz B, Weibe ME, Lippin A, Vandersand J, Stryker MH. Inactivation of viruses in labile blood derivatives. II. Physical methods. Transfusion 1985; 25:523–527.
10. Levy JA, Mitra GA, Wong MF, Mozen MM. Inactivation by wet and dry heat of AIDS-associated retroviruses during factor VIII purification from plasma. Lancet 1985; 1:1456–1457.
11. Hollinger B, Dolana G, Thomas W, Gyorkey F. Reduction in risk of hepatitis transmission by heat treatment of a factor VIII concentrate. J Infect Dis 1984; 150:250–262.

12. Winkelman L, Owen NE, Evans DR, Evans H, Haddan ME, Smith JK, Prince PJ, Williams JD, Lane RS. Severely heated therapeutic factor VIII concentrate of high specific activity. Vox Sang 1989; 57:97–103.

13. Mannucci PM. Clinical evaluation of viral safety of coagulation factor VIII and IX concentrates. Vox Sang 1993; 64:197–203.

14. Horowitz B, Wiebe ME, Lippin A, Stryker MII. Inactivation of viruses in labile blood derivatives. I. Disruption of lipid-enveloped viruses by tri(n-butyl) phosphate detergent combinations. Transfusion 1985; 25:516–522.

15. Horowitz B, Prince AM, Hamman J, Watklevicz C. Viral safety of solvent/detergent-treated blood products. Blood Coagul Fibrinol 1994; 5(suppl):S21–S28.

16. Prince AM, Horowitz B, Baker L, Shulman RW, Ralph H, Valinsky J, Cundell A, Brotman B, Boehle W, Rey F, Piet M, Reesink H, Lelie N, Tersmette M, Miedema F, Barbosa L, Nemo G, Nastala CL, Allan JS, Lee DR, Eichberg JW. Failure of human immunodeficiency virus (HIV) immune globulin to protect against experimental challenge with HIV. Proc Natl Acad Sci USA 1988; 85:6944–6948.

17. Horowitz B. Inactivation of viruses found with plasma proteins: In: Goldstein J, ed. Biotechnology of Blood. Stoneham: Butterworth-Heinemann, 1991:417–430.

18. Horowitz B, Bonomo R, Prince AM, Chin SN, Brotman B, Shulman RW. Solvent/detergent-treated plasma: a virus inactivated substitute for fresh frozen plasma. Blood 1992; 79:826–831.

19. Lemon SM, Murphy PC, Smith A, Zou J, Hamman J, Horowitz B. Removal/neutralization of hepatitis A virus during manufacture of high purity, solvent/detergent treated plasma. Blood 1992; 79:826–831.

20. Piquet Y, Janvier G, Selosse P, Doutremepuich C, Journeau J, Nicolle G, Platel D, Vezon G. Virus inactivation of fresh frozen plasma by a solvent-detergent procedure: biological results. Vox Sang 1992; 63:251–256.

21. Hellstern P, Sachse H, Schwinn H, Overfrank K. Manufacture and in vitro characterization of solvent/detergent-treated human plasma. Vox Sang 1992; 63:178–185.

22. Solheim BG, Svennevig JL, Mohr B, et al. The use of Octasplas in patients undergoing open heart surgery. In: Muller-Berghanns G, et al., eds. DIS: Pathogenesis, Diagnosis and Therapy of Disseminated Intravascular Fibrin Formation. Amsterdam: Elsevier Science Publishers, 1993:253–262.

23. Moake J, Chintagumpala M, Turner J, McPherson P, Nolasco L, Steuber C, Santiago-Borrero P, Horowitz M, Pehta J. Solvent/detergent-treated plasma suppresses shear-induced platelet aggregation and prevents episodes of thrombotic thrombocytopenic purpura. Blood 1994; 84:490–497.

24. Pehta JC. Clinical studies with solvent-detergent-treated products. Transfusion Med Rev 1996; 10:303–311.

25. Piszkeiwicz D, Sun CS, Tondreau SC. Inactivation and removal of human immunodeficiency virus in monoclonal purified antihemophilic factor (human) (Hemophil M). Thromb Res 1989; 55:627–634.

26. Hamamoto Y, Harada S, Kobayashi S, Yamaguchi K, Iijima H, Manabe S, Tsurumi T, Aizawa H, Yamamoto N. A novel method for removal of human immunodeficiency virus: filtration with porous polymeric membranes. Vox Sang 1989; 56:230–236.

27. Burnouf-Radosevich M, Appourchaux P, Huart JJ, Burnouf T. Nanofiltration, a new

specific virus elimination method applied to high purity factor IV and factor XI concentrates. Vox Sang 1994; 67:132–138.

28. Horowitz B, Zou J, Hamman J, Gottlieb P, Chin S, Marx G, Golyakhovsky V. Elimination of small, heat and solvent/detergent (S/D)-resistant viruses in factor VIII concentrate and fibrin sealant. Throm Haemost 1995; 73:1460.

29. Patrick MH, Rahn RO. Photochemistry of DNA and polynucleotides: photoproducts. In: Wang SY, ed. Photochemistry and Photobiology of Nucleic Acids, Vol. 2. New York: Academic Press, 1976:35–95.

30. Rauth AM. The physical state of viral nucleic acid and the sensitivity of viruses to ultraviolet light. Biophys J 1965; 5:257–273.

31. Chin S, Williams B, Gottlieb P, Margolis-Nunno H, Ben-Hur E, Hamman J, Jin R, Dubovi E, Horowitz B. Virucidal UVC treatment of plasma and factor VIII concentrate: protection of proteins by antioxidants. Blood 1995; 86:4331–4336.

32. Marx G, Mou X, Freed R, Ben-Hur E, Yang C, Horowitz B. Protecting fibrinogen with rutin during UVC irradiation for viral inactivation. Photochem Photobiol 1996; 63:541–546.

33. Chin S, Jin R, Wang XL, Hamman J, Marx G, Mou X, Andersson I, Lindquist LO, Horowitz B. Virucidal treatment of blood protein products with UVC. Photochem Photobiol 1997; 65:432–435.

34. Highsmith FA, Caple M, Walthall B, Shanbron E, Drohan WN. Viral inactivation of vesicular stomatitis virus in normal human serum by crosslinked polyvinyl-pyrrolidone. J Infect Dis 1993; 167:1027–1033.

35. Highsmith FA, Xue H, Caple M, Walthall B, Drohan WN, Shanbrom E. Inactivation of lipid-enveloped and non-lipid-enveloped model viruses in normal human plasma by crosslinked starch-iodine. Transfusion 1994; 34:322–327.

36. Wallis C, Melnick JL. Photodynamic inactivation of animal viruses: a review. Photochem Photobiol 1965; 4:159–170.

37. Specht K. The role of DNA damage in PM2 viral inactivation by methylene blue photosensitization. Photochem Photobiol 1994; 59:506–514.

38. Abe H, Wagner SJ. Analysis of viral DNA, protein and envelope damage after methylene blue, phthalocyanine derivative or merocyanine 540 photosensitization. Photochem Photobiol 1995; 61:402–409.

39. Lambrecht B, Mohr H, Knuver-Hopf J, Schmitt H. Photoinactivation of viruses in human fresh plasma by phenothiazine dyes in combination with visible light. Vox Sang 1991; 60:207–213.

40. Wagner SJ, Robinette D, Storry J, Chen XY, Shumaker J, Benade L. Differential sensitivities of viruses in red cells suspensions to methylene blue photosensitization. Transfusion 1994; 34:521–526.

41. Mohr H, Lambrecht B, Selz A. Photodynamic virus inactivation of blood components. Immunol Invest 1995; 24:73–85.

42. Wieding JU, Neumeyer H. Erste Erfahrungen mit Methylenblau-virus inaktiviertem Fresh-frozen-plasma: Ergebnisse einer klinischen und einer in vitro Studie. Infusion Ther 1992; 19:84–90.

43. Mohr H, Knuver-Hopf J, Lambrecht B, Scheidecker H, Schmitt H. No evidence for neoantigens in human plasma after photochemical virus inactivation. Ann Hematol 1992; 65:224–228.

44. Zeiler T, Riess H, Wittman G, Hintz G, Zimmerman R, Muller C, Geuft HG, Huhn D. The effect of methylene blue phototreatment on plasma proteins and in vitro coagulation capability of single-donor fresh-frozen plasma. Transfusion 1994; 34:685–689.

45. Wagner SJ, Cifone MA, Murli H, Dodd RY, Myhr B. Mammalian genotoxicity assessment of methylene blue in plasma: implications for virus inactivation. Transfusion 1995; 35:407–413.

46. Murphy S, Rebulla P, Bertolini F, Holme S, Moroff G, Snyder E, Stromberg R. In vitro assessment of the quality of stored platelet concentrates. Transfusion Med Rev 1994; 8:29–36.

47. Ben-Hur E, Song PS. Photochemistry and photobiology of furocoumarins (psoralens). Adv Radiat Biol 1984; 11:131–171.

48. Kao KJ. Effects of leukocyte depletion and UVB irradiation on allogenicity of major histocompatibility antigens in platelet concentrates: a comparative study. Blood 1992; 80:2931–2937.

49. Heddle NM, Klama L, Singer J, Richards C, Fedak P, Walker I, Kelton JG. The role of plasma from platelet concentrates in transfusion reactions. N Engl J Med 1994; 331:625–628.

50. Lehmann PV, Shumm G, Moon D, Hurtenbach U, Falcioni F, Muller S, Zagy ZA. Acute lethal graft-versus-host reaction induced by major histocompatibility complex class II reactive T helper cell clone. J Exp Med 1990; 171:1485–1496.

51. Margolis-Nunno H, Robinson R, Ben-Hur E, Horowitz B. Quencher enhanced specificity of psoralens photosensitized viral inactivation in platelet concentrates. Transfusion 1994; 34:802–810.

52. Lin L, Cook DN, Wiesehahn GP, Alfonso R, Behrman B, Cimino GD, Corten L, Damonte PB, Dikeman R, Dupuis K, Fang YM, Hanson CV, Hearst JE, Lin CY, Londe HF, Metchette K, Nerio AT, Pu JT, Reames AA, Rheinschmidt M, Tessman J, Isaacs ST, Wollowitz S, Corash L. Photochemical inactivation of viruses and bacteria in platelet concentrates by use of a novel psoralen and long wavelength ultraviolet light. Transfusion 1997; 37:423–435.

53. Margolis-Nunno H, Robinson R, Ben-Hur E, Chin S, Orme T, Horowitz B. Elimination of potential mutagenicity in platelet concentrates that are virally inactivated with psoralens and ultraviolet A light. Transfusion 1995; 35:855–862.

54. Margolis-Nunno H, Robinson R, Horowitz B, Geacintov NE and Ben-Hur E. Psoralen-mediated virus photoinactivation in platelet concentrates: enhanced specificity of virus kill in the absence of shorter UVA wavelengths. Photochem Photobiol 1995; 62:917–922.

55. Gottlieb P, Marolis-Nunno H, Robinson R, Shen LG, Chimezie E, Horowitz B, Ben-Hur E. Inactivation of *Trypanosoma cruzi* trypomastigote forms in blood components with a psoralen and ultraviolet A light. Photochem Photobiol 1996; 63:562–565.

56. Lin L, Londe H, Janda JM, Hanson CV, Corash L. Photochemical inactivation of pathogenic bacteria in human platelet concentrates. Blood 1994; 83:2698–2706.

57. Benade L, Shumaker J, Xu Y, Shen X, Dodd RY. Inactivation of free and cell-associated human immunodeficiency virus in platelet suspensions by aminomethyl psoralen and ultraviolet light. Transfusion 1994; 34:680–684.

58. Margolis-Nunno H, Bardossy L, Robinson R, Ben-Hur E, Horowitz B, Blajchman MA. Psoralen-mediated photodecontamination of platelet concentrates: inactivation of cell-free and cell associated forms of human immunodeficiency virus and assessment of platelet function in vivo. Transfusion 1997;

59. Goodrich RP, Yerram NR, Tay-Goodrich BH, Forster P, Platz MS, Kasturi C, Park SC, Aebischer JN, Rai S, Kulaga L. Selective inactivation of viruses in the presence of human platelets: UV sensitization with psoralen derivatives. Proc Natl Acad Sci USA 1994; 91:5552–5556.

60. Piet B, Legrand-Poels S, Sappety C, Piette J. NF-κB transcription factor and human immunodeficiency virus type 1 (HIV-1) activation by methylene blue photosensitization. Eur J Biochem. 1995; 228:447–455.

61. Wagner SJ, Storry JR, Mallory DA, Stromber RR, Benade LE, Friedman LI. Red cell alterations associated with virucidal methylene blue phototreatment. Transfusion 1993; 33:30–36.

62. Skripchenko A, Robinette D, Wagner SJ. Comparison of methylene blue and methylene violet for photoinactivation of intracellular and extracellular virus in red cell suspension. Photochem Photobiol 1997;

63. North J, Coombs R, Levy J. Photodynamic inactivation of free and cell-associated HIV-1 using the photosensitizer benzoporphyrin derivative. J AIDS 1994; 7:891–898.

64. Meruelo D, Lavie G, Lavie D. Therapeutic agents with dramatic antiretroviral activity at effective doses: aromatic polycyclic diones hypericin and pseudohypericin. Proc Natl Acad Sci USA 1988; 85:5230–5234.

65. Carpenter S, Kraus GA. Photosensitization is required for inactivation of equine infectious anemia virus by hypericin. Photochem Photobiol 1991; 53:169–174.

66. Lavie G, Mazur Y, Lavie D, Prince AM, Pascual D, Liebes L, Levin B, Meruelo D. Hypericin as an inactivator of infectious virus in blood products. Transfusion 1995; 35:392–400.

67. Horowitz B, Williams B, Rywkin S, Prince AM, Pascual D, Geacintov N, Valinsky J. Inactivation of viruses in blood with aluminum phthalocyanine derivatives. Transfusion 1991; 31:102–108.

68. Gaspard S, Tempete C, Werner GH. Studies on photoinactivation by various phthalocyanines of a free or replicating non-enveloped viruses. J Photochem Photobiol B:Biol 1995; 31:159–162.

69. Rywkin S, Lenny L, Goldstein J, Geacintov NE, Margolis-Nunno H, Horowitz B. Importance of type I and type II mechanisms in the photodynamic inactivation of viruses in blood with aluminum phthalocyanine derivatives. Photochem Photobiol 1995; 56:463–469.

70. Rywkin S, Ben-Hur E, Reid ME, Oyen R, Ralph H, Horowitz B. Selective protection against IgG binding to red cells treated with phthalocyanines and red light for virus inactivation. Transfusion 1995; 35:414–420.

71. Ben-Hur E, Rywkin S, Rosenthal I, Geacintov NE, Horowitz B. Virus inactivation in red cell concentrates by photosensitization with phthalocyanines: protection of red cells but not of vesicular stomatitis virus with a water-soluble analog of vitamin E. Transfusion 1995; 35:401–406.

72. Ben-Hur E, Geacintov NE, Studamire B, Kenney ME, Horowitz B. The effect of

irradiance on virus sterilization and photodynamic damage in red blood cells sensitized by phthalocyanines. Photochem Photobiol 1995; 61:190–195.

73. Ben-Hur E, Zuk MM, Kenney ME, Oleinick NL, Mulvihill J, Horowitz B. Action spectra (660-700 nm) for virus inactivation and red cell damage photosensitized by the silicon phthalocyanine Pc 4. Lasers Med Sci 1996; 11:221–225.

74. Ben-Hur E, Zuk MM, Chin S, Banerjee D, Kenney ME, Horowitz B. Biodistribution and virus inactivation efficacy of the silicon phthalocyanine Pc 4 in red blood cell concentrates as a function of delivery vehicle. Photochem Photobiol 1995; 62:575–579.

75. Margolis-Nunno H, Ben-Hur E, Gottlieb P, Robinson R, Oetjen J, Horowitz B. Inactivation of multiple forms of human immunodeficiency virus in red cell concentrates by phthalocyanine photosensitization. Transfusion 1996; 36:743–750.

76. Gottlieb P, Shen LG, Chimezie E, Bhang S, Kenney ME, Horowitz B, Ben-Hur E. Inactivation of *Trypanosoma cruzi* trypomastigote forms in blood components by photodynamic treatment with phthalocyanines. Photochem Photobiol 1995; 62:869–874.

77. Lustigman S, Ben-Hur E. Photosensitized inactivation of *Plasmodium falciparum* in human erythrocytes by phthalocyanines. Transfusion 1995; 36:562–565.

78. Ben-Hur E, Oetjen J, Zuk MM, Chan WS, Horowitz B. Photochemical decontamination of red cell concentrates with silicon phthalocyanine (Pc 4) and red light. Transfusion 1996; 36(suppl):64S.

79. Zhang Q-X, Edson C, Budowsky E, Purmal A. Inactine: a method for viral inactivation in red blood cell concentrate. Transfusion 1998; 38(suppl):75S.

22
The Role of Quality in Blood Safety

Lucia M. Berte
Quality Systems Consultant, Elmhurst, Illinois

David E. Nevalainen
Quality Consultant, Health Care, Bailey's Harbor, Wisconsin

Assuring blood transfusion safety means having error-free processes that begin with donor selection and continue through blood component administration. High-quality blood products and safe patient outcomes are best assured when errors are prevented along the entire range of blood banking activity. Two goals are desirable: (a) reduce to zero the number of blood components made from unsuitable donations that result in any finished, labeled blood product that could be distributed for clinical use, and (b) get the right blood products in the right quantity to the right patient in the right place at the right time (1). These two broad collections of processes and subprocesses involve different groups of people in different locations at different times. However, a logical approach to apply error-prevention initiatives across the entire range of activities can have the desired end results.

I. BLOOD COMPONENT MANUFACTURING

The objective of the blood manufacturing process—as it is regarded by the U.S. Food and Drug Administration (FDA)—is to put safe, finished, labeled blood products into stock at the point of distribution for future clinical use (1). The major steps of this process include obtaining the whole blood (raw material) from qualified blood donors, testing the blood for infectious diseases, preparing blood components, and distributing the components to entities who prepare them for transfusion. To underscore the importance of this objective, FDA has chosen to aggressively treat blood bank facilities as manufacturers of pharmaceutical products and thus applies strict pharmaceutical manufacturing regulations to blood collection and testing activities—an environment distinctly different from the hospital clinical laboratory in which many technical blood banking personnel had their training. The transition from a service-oriented culture, as blood banks have always perceived themselves, to a manufacturing culture, as FDA perceives them, occurred slowly but steadily during the 1990s.

To achieve their respective manufacturing objectives, highly regulated pharmaceutical and medical device manufacturers must operate within the boundaries of current good manufacturing practice (cGMP) described in the Code of Federal Regulations (CFR). Meeting CFR requirements fosters an environmental culture known as "total process control" (TPC). By practicing TPC, blood banks can safely operate within the applicable CFR regulations found in 21 CFR Parts 210, 211, 606, 640, and 820 (2–4), as shown in Table 1.

II. CLINICAL TRANSFUSION PROCESS

The major steps of the clinical transfusion process include obtaining and labeling a patient sample, submitting it to the transfusion service with an indication of requirements including the degree of emergency, testing for compatibility, delivering the correct blood component to the correct location within the required time, correctly transfusing the component to the patient for whom it was originally intended, and monitoring the outcome (1). Transfusion services are also under the ultimate purview of FDA, but because of a memorandum of understanding between FDA and the Health Care Financing Administration (HCFA) to reduce duplicative inspections, most transfusion services are routinely inspected by laboratory accreditation agencies authorized to inspect by HCFA. This has resulted in a misconception that CFR requirements do not apply; they do apply and can be found in CFR Part 606 (3). The principles of TPC are equally appropriate to assuring a safe transfusion process, particularly because there are so many interdepartmental interactions involved.

III. PRINCIPLES OF TPC

Total process control satisfies CFR requirements because it reduces the variability in process performance and outcome that leads to errors. In blood banking terms, this translates to reducing errors that allow unsuitable blood donors being drawn, positive disease marker test results being overlooked, untested or test-positive components in the blood supply, mislabeled specimens for compatibility testing, transfusion of the wrong patient, or lack of patient monitoring. TPC methods take variation out of the process, thus ensuring a more predictable outcome. From this

Table 1 Contents of Applicable Parts of the Code of Federal Regulations (CFR) for Blood Banks

Part 210 / Part 211 Subparts:	Part 606 Subparts:	Part 640 Subparts:	Part 820 Subparts:
210.1 Status of cGMP	A: General provisions	A: Whole blood	A: General provisions
210.2 Applicability of cGMP	B: Organization and personnel	B: Red blood cells	B: Quality system requirements
210.3 Definitions	C: Plant and facilities	C: Platelets	C: Design controls
A: General provisions	D: Equipment	D: Plasma	D: Document and record controls
B: Organization and personnel	E: (Reserved)	E: (Reserved)	E: Purchasing controls
C: Buildings and facilities	F: Production and process controls	F: Cryoprecipitate	F: Identification and traceability
D: Equipment	G: Finished product control	G: Source plasma	G: Productions and process controls
E: Control of components . . .	H: Laboratory controls	H: Albumin	H: Acceptance activities
F: Production and process controls	I: Records and reports	I: Plasma protein fraction	I: Nonconforming product
G: Packaging and labeling control		J: Immune globulin	J: Corrective and preventive action
H: Holding and distribution		K: Alternative procedures	K: Handling, storage, distribution and installation
I: Laboratory controls			L: Packaging and label control
J: Records and reports			M: Records
K: Returned and salvaged drugs . . .			N: Servicing
			O: Statistical techniques

Source: Refs 2–4.

perspective, blood banks cannot afford not to practice TPC if we are true to our objective of providing safe, efficacious blood transfusions.

The essential principles of TPC are summarized in these statements from an FDA guidance document (5):

> Quality, safety, and effectiveness are built into a product.
> Quality cannot be inspected or tested into a product.
> Each step in the process must be controlled to meet quality standards.

These three statements provide facilities with a roadmap for *what* to do to assure quality blood products and patient outcomes but do not describe *how* to do it. Facilities determine for themselves what resources and methods they need to apply to accomplish the intent of GMP. The important features of TPC are shown in Figure 1.

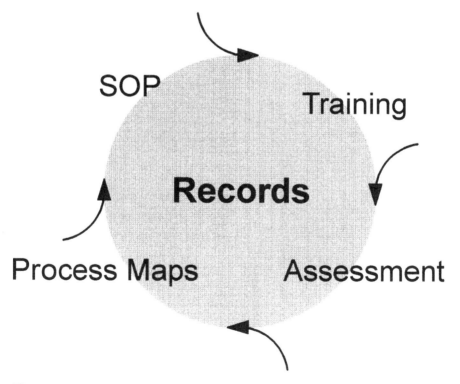

Figure 1   The elements of Total Process Control (TPC) form a circular flow of process analysis, SOP development, training, and assessment for which records document all necessary activities. (From Ref. 14.)

To best explain how the elements of TPC work, examples will be used. An example for blood processing is a new screening test for a transfusion-transmitted disease to be performed on each unit of donated blood. The example for clinical transfusion is the implementation of a new armband system to specifically identify transfusion recipients and link them with their compatibility testing specimens. The following sections briefly describe the elements of TPC in relation to these two examples and provide references for readers to access important "how-to" details.

A. Validation

Before a new test, a new computer system or a new process is implemented, or if there has been a significant change in an existing test method, instrument, software, or process, an activity known as validation must take place. Process validation is a requirement of cGMP Parts 211 (2) and 820 (4) for manufactured pharmaceuticals and medical devices. It establishes documented evidence that a specific process will consistently produce a product meeting its predetermined specifications and quality characteristics. The facility must prepare a written validation protocol that specifies what procedures and tests are to be conducted and the data to be collected during practice runs of the new process. Only when the data demonstrate that the process functions reliably and invariably can standard operating procedures (SOPs) be finalized, remaining personnel trained, and actual operations begun.

Table 2 outlines the activities of the major phases of a validation protocol that are briefly described in the following paragraphs. Some details may vary between processes to be validated, but the major concepts remain unchanged. Validation examples specific to blood banking have been published (6).

1. Installation Qualification

In the example of a new blood donation screening test, all equipment used must undergo installation qualification—activities that demonstrate and document that the equipment is suitable for its intended purpose, has been installed properly, and is functioning as intended. For an enzyme immunoassay screening test, equipment to be qualified would include specimen pipettors and dilutors, incubators, tray washers, and spectrophotometric readers. Draft procedures for equipment calibration, maintenance, quality control, and troubleshooting are first derived from the directions included in the manufacturer's equipment manuals, to which are then added facility-specific details. Respective forms are designed to capture measurements, data, and observations for the ongoing quality control program. The new armband in our clinical transfusion example does not require installation

Table 2 Validation Activities

Installation qualification (IQ)	Operational qualification (OQ)	Performance qualification (PQ)	Revalidation
Identification of items requiring calibration	Evaluation of process capabilities	Development of testing plan	Development of protocol
Determination of calibration method and schedule for each item	Coordination of multiple processes and operations	Predetermination of process/product specifications	Reaffirmation of IQ
Identification of items requiring maintenance	Consideration of process variables	Performance of process by operations personnel	Reaffirmation of OQ
Determination of maintenance methods and schedules for each item	Quantification of process variables	Comparison of process outcomes to specifications for acceptability	Review of performance history, OR
Development of operating procedures, including adjustments	Determination of acceptable operating limits and variations	Training and documentation	Performance of a process run
Development of troubleshooting procedures	Development of process procedures	Implementation of process	Comparison of outcomes to specifications for acceptability
Development of monitoring and control procedures			Retraining, if needed
Listing of equipment parts			Recommendation for improvements
Training and documentation			

Source: Ref. 7.

qualification unless barcode readers and/or electronic label printers are part of the new armband-generation process.

2. Operational Qualification

This second phase of a validation protocol consists of evaluating the capability of the process—in this case, that the new blood screening test performs acceptably according to the manufacturer's procedure using the newly qualified equipment. The effectiveness and reproducibility of the new test is vigorously challenged with conditions simulating those expected to be encountered during actual production. In our testing example, challenges would include both strongly and weakly reactive test samples, borderline reactive samples, and previous proficiency testing material. In our armbanding example, the process would be tested to see that barcodes and labels are readable and that the identification linkages are traceable throughout specimen collection, compatibility testing, and transfusion. The challenges should be repeated often enough to assure that the results are consistent and meaningful. The draft testing procedures and related forms are then readied for the validation runs.

3. Process Qualification

This phase of the validation protocol requires that selected operations personnel (a) perform the new process as it would be done during actual operations, (b) capture data about how the process worked, and (c) compare data to predetermined acceptance criteria. For the donor blood test, this final phase should not proceed until operations and quality assurance personnel are confident that the validation will be successful because of the high cost of performing full test runs. In the testing example, a preset number of test runs would be performed by staff members according to procedures derived from the manufacturer's package insert and facility-specific activities that were qualified in the preceding operational qualification phase. In the armband example, all patients in a specified location only would receive the new armband for a predetermined time. Any problems in the new processes are documented and followed up. Results of the validations are reviewed by quality assurance personnel who reach a formal conclusion as to the acceptability of the new process. Acceptance includes all appropriate reviews and signatures and the finalization of, training in, and activation of all related calibration, maintenance, quality control, troubleshooting, and operating procedures.

4. Revalidation

Revalidation of manufacturing processes should be performed periodically and whenever there are changes in raw materials, equipment, or processes that could affect the quality of the process outcome. Revalidation should also be considered when there are significant changes in the process's quality performance history as determined by statistical process control measurements. Revalidation consists of reaffirming installation qualification and operational qualifications and either performance of a validation run or comprehensive review of the process's quality history records. In our testing example, revalidation would be required if the manufacturer should change any test equipment, the test methodology, significant reagents, or other variables of the blood screening test that could potentially affect the quality of the test results. In our armband example, revalidation would be required if there were changes to barcoding software or symbology or to label-printing equipment.

B. Calibration and Maintenance

Initial calibration and maintenance procedures and schedules were established as part of installation qualification in the validation process. Recalibration is required periodically and after repairs or adjustments (3). Routine and preventive maintenance procedures prolong the operating life of equipment, which minimizes equipment problems and changes that lead to a requirement for revalidations. In our testing example, all calibrations and maintenance are performed according to the established procedures and schedules and the results documented and periodically reviewed to assure continued acceptable function. TPC requires an identification mechanism, tracking process, and cumulative file of all records generated for each piece of equipment used in the new donor test process.

C. Standard Operating Procedures

Standard operating procedures (SOPs) are the key feature of TPC. Properly written, controlled SOPs used by trained personnel are a blood bank facility's best assurance of quality and safety in the blood supply. In the donor screening test example, SOPs are drafted from instructions provided in the manufacturer's equipment manuals and package inserts for the specific test. In the armband example, existing SOPs for specimen collection, compatibility testing, and blood administration are modified to include the new identification steps. After the successful validation, draft SOPs are finalized. When validated SOPs are used to train employees, processes become less variable, errors are reduced, and the desired quality is more consistently achieved. Document control is an additional process that promotes consistent coordinated handling of a facility's many procedures (7). In our examples, procedures would be developed using a pre-established format for completeness and consistency that featured an SOP identification mechanism essential to the timely review, revision, removal, and archiving of all the process's SOPs and related forms. SOP management includes the use of an SOP for how to write SOPs and another for how to change them.

Many external inspection deficiency citations involve lack of, outdated, or incomplete SOPs or personnel found not to be following existing SOPs. These problems lead to personal variations that can and have been shown to cause errors that reduce blood safety and compromise the benefit of transfusion.

D. Training and Competence Assessment

When TPC is not the basic operating philosophy, personal deviations can significantly contribute to the numbers and types of errors that occur. Establishing current, validated SOPs is one aspect of an approach to minimize variation. The complementing aspect is to train personnel in the contents, exclusive use of, and unwavering adherence to approved SOPs.

To minimize the effect of personnel being the most variable entity, approved SOPs are used as the basis for developing task-specific training guides. Qualified trainers use the guides to train personnel and assess demonstrated competence in the specific SOPs for the new process. All training and competence outcomes are documented. In the donor testing example, training activities and schedules can be more easily controlled because personnel work in the testing department. In the armband example, trainees would include personnel who collect compatibility testing specimens, perform compatibility testing, or administer blood transfusions and would include laboratory phlebotomists, nonlaboratory specimen collection personnel, medical technologists and technicians, nurses, and physicians. Only a comprehensive, coordinated training process with well-written SOPs will assure that all involved personnel understand and follow the procedures for blood transfusion identification traceability. At this level of complexity, it is easy to see how variations can be made that lead to mistransfusions.

E. Monitoring

After the new procedures are validated, personnel trained, and a start-up date selected, TPC requires ongoing monitoring of process variables to assure that the process remains in control. A number of monitoring activities should be ongoing.

1. Quality Control

Laboratories have a long history of using quality control (QC) methods to assure the accuracy of test results. For every test method or piece of equipment, there are general and specific regulations and accreditation requirements for laboratories for QC monitoring and requirements for follow-up action when the results are out of acceptable range. The types of QC commonly performed in blood banks are shown in Table 3. QC schedules are to be established and all results documented and reviewed for trends and patterns that could suggest out-of-control performance. In the donor testing example, QC monitoring would include positive and negative controls with every test run, blank, and background controls for spectrophotometric measuring accuracy, monitoring of all temperature-regulated equipment, and periodic recalibrations of pipettors and dilutors, among other activities. The armband system needs no QC.

Table 3 Blood Bank Quality Control

Equipment	
Item	Testing
Blood drawing scales	Check with standard weight
Hemoglobinometers	Calibration to standards
Shipping containers	Ability to hold temperature
Centrifuges	Functional calibration, RPM, timer
Serologic	
Cell-washer	
Refrigerated	
Microhematocrit	
Cell-washer centrifuge	Tube fill and decant
Refrigerated centrifuge	Internal temperature
	Temperature of component after
	centrifugation
Refrigerators:	Internal temperature
Blood storage	
Reagent storage	
Refrigerator:	Continuous temperature recording;
Blood storage	comparison of graph to thermometer;
Freezer: (mechanical/liquid nitrogen)	alarm activation; nitrogen level
Component storage	(freezer)
Platelet incubator	
Platelets—open storage area	Temperature every 4 hours
pH meter	Calibration to standard
Thermometers	Compare against NIST standard
Water baths	Single point temperature check
Dry baths	Several point temperature check
Incubators	
View boxes	

Table 3 Continued

Equipment	
Item	Testing
Component thawing devices	Temperature, Cleanliness
Blood Irradiators	Decay of source
	Radiation leaks
	Dosage delivery
Blood warmers	Plate/bath temperature
	Effluent temperature
	Alarm activation

Components	
Item	Testing
Red blood cells	Hematocrit
Cryoprecipitate	Factor VIII level
Granulocytes	Granulocyte count
Platelets, random	Platelet count, pH, volume
Platelets, apheresis	
Fresh frozen plasma	Volume
Leukocyte-reduced red blood cells	Removal of leukocytes
	Red blood cell recovery
Intraoperatively recovered red blood cells	Contamination
	Free hemoglobin
Frozen-deglycerolized red blood cells	Osmolality
	Free hemoglobin
	Red cell recovery
	Red cell viability

Reagents	
Item	Testing
Reagent antisera (anti-A, anti-B, anti-D, etc)	Positive control
Reagent red blood cells (A_1 & B cells, Screening Cells, Coombs Control Cells)	Positive control
Antiglobulin serum	Reactivity
Tests for syphilis, HIV-1-Ag, anti-HIV-1, anti-HIV-2, anti-HCV, anti-HTLV-I, anti-HTLV-II, anti-HBc, HBsAg	Control testing of each lot, each test run

Source: Ref. 3 and Ziebell L, Kavemeier K, eds. Quality Control: A Component of Process Control in Blood Banking and Transfusion Medicine. Bethesda, MD: American Association of Blood Banks, 1999.

2.   Statistical Process Control

Using statistical process control (SPC) tools such as control charts, histograms, bar charts, and other tools, QC and other collected data are analyzed and converted into valuable information about the status of the facility's processes. The information provided by these tools helps identify if there are process problems and where they may be occurring. When the causes of system problems are removed, both quality and productivity are improved. Use of the graphical tools shown in Table 4 would inform where the facility is currently, where the variations are, the relative importance of the identified problems, and whether the changes made had the desired impact (8). These tools facilitate the use of a structured problem-solving process to achieve better solutions. In our testing example, a Pareto chart could show the number, time of day, and operator for failed test runs. A bar graph would depict the number of repeat tests by shift or by operator or by analyzer used. In the armband example, the number and source of specimens without armband-traceable identification could be visualized on a bar chart. Direct observation of specimen collection and blood administration personnel would provide information on whether SOPs were understood and followed. The information obtained from using SPC tools helps the facility visualize the data and prioritize the types and sources of problems so that improvement efforts can be better organized.

3.   Occurrence Reporting and Follow-Up

One of the best methods to identify problems is to have the staff who perform the daily work report occurrences whenever an expected outcome is not realized. Whatever names are given to occurrences—incidents, errors, deviations, accidents, nonconformances, events, complaints etc.—the most important issue is to encourage the reporting and make it nonpunitive to employees. The objective is to identify wherever something is not working as it should and take action to eliminate the cause of the problem. Process-improvement methods are then applied, and follow-up is performed by monitoring selected indicators and continuing analysis of occurrence reports. Occurrence analysis should lead to identification of problems as either system (process), knowledge (training), or behavior (discipline), each of which requires a different form of corrective action. In the donor-testing example, operators would complete an occurrence report form for each failed test run. In the armband example, each instance when a patient to be transfused was not wearing the proper blood bank armband would result in an occurrence report. The reports are analyzed to determine whether (a) the root cause was in the process, (b) involved personnel were insufficiently trained, or (c) personnel merely did not follow directions.

Table 4 Statistical Process Control Tools and Uses

Tool	Use	Manifestation
Flowchart	To identify the actual path that a product or service follows to identify problems that lead to deviations and errors	Symbols to depict process steps and decisions
Check sheet	To gather data based on sample observations to begin to detect patterns	Plot of defects vs. dates or times
Pareto chart	To display relative importance of all problems or conditions to a) identify basic cause of a problem, b) prioritize problem solving, c) monitor success	Vertical bar graph with bars in descending order
Cause and effect diagram	To identify, explore, and display the possible causes of a problem or condition	"Fishbone"
Run chart	To display trends with observation points over a specified time period	Plot of measurement vs. time
Histogram	To discover and display the distribution of data by bar graphing the number of amounts in each category	Bar graph in frequency of distribution curve
Scatter diagram	To display what happens with one variable when another variable changes to test a theory that the two variables are related	Plot of one variable on the x axis and the other variable on the y axis
Control chart	To discover how much variability in a process is due to random variation and how much is due to unique events to determine whether a process is in statistical control	Run chart with statistically determined upper and lower control limit lines on either side of the process average
Process capability chart	To determine whether the process, given its natural variation, is capable of meeting established specifications	Distribution curve showing allowable spread of specification limits and measure of actual process variation

Source: Ref. 8.

4. Internal Quality Audit

Another assessment tool is the quality system audit. The facility's quality system consists of its policies and procedures for the critical quality processes in TPC such as those already described above and others. The audit compares the facility's stated quality policies, processes, and procedures to a predetermined reference standard such as cGMP, the American Association of Blood Banks (AABB) *Standards for Blood Banks and Transfusion Services* (9), the Clinical Laboratory Improvement Amendments of 1988 (CLIA '88) (10), and other regulations and accreditation requirements for laboratories. The auditor determines the conformity of the facility's actual operations with the documented system. To avoid any conflicts of interest, quality system audits should be conducted by personnel who do not have responsibility for the areas being audited. The audit results are reported to the facility's top management for corrective action. In the examples, the facility's quality auditors compare the policies, processes, and procedures of the involved departments with both the reference standards for blood donation testing and specimen/patient identification and their actual observations of documents and personnel performing testing, specimen collection, and blood administration. Any discrepancies—known in auditing language as "nonconformances"— are reported to the facility's management for corrective action. Follow-up audits may be conducted to determine if the necessary corrective action took place and was successful.

F. Corrective Action

The monitoring activities of QC, SPC, occurrence reporting, and quality audit all provide an overview of where the facility's problems lie. The root cause of each problem must be identified using a tool such as a cause-and-effect diagram (8) and the problems categorized as system, knowledge, or behavior prior to taking any corrective action. The chosen long-term corrective action must be appropriate for the type of problem or the fix will not work. For example, training solutions are often applied to system problems because it is easier to schedule a retraining session than to dismantle a multistep process and rebuild it with error-prevention steps to eliminate the problem's root cause. In this scenario, follow-up monitoring would, unfortunately, demonstrate that personnel have been further trained in a process that still does not work.

G. Process Improvement

The time and resources expended in correcting quality problems are best utilized when following a systematic approach for solving problems and improving processes. The facility should adopt one of the common specialized problem solving models, such as those shown in Table 5, train personnel in its use, and use the model for each performance improvement effort it undertakes. Most of the improvement methods use multidisciplinary teams to work through the successive steps.

Process improvements should not only be generated for problem areas. When facilities truly practice continuous quality improvement, they will periodically reassess current processes to determine whether there may be a way to perform them faster, better, or more cost-effectively. At any given time, there may be several process-improvement efforts simultaneously underway as the facility works through its prioritized list of problems and scheduled routine reviews.

IV. CONNECTION OF TPC TO A QUALITY SYSTEM

As more blood donor screening questions and tests were added in the years after anti-HIV testing was first implemented in 1985, the complexity of managing testing information, donor deferrals, and computer software increased dramatically. Because rising numbers of untested and unsuitable blood components were entering the blood supply, FDA began actively to apply the quality and process control provisions of CFR Parts 210-211 (2) for pharmaceutical manufacturing to blood banking facilities. The various TPC activities must be coordinated to truly

Table 5 Process Improvement Models

Source	Model name
Shewhart[a]	Plan - Do - Check - Act (PDCA)
JCAHO[b]	Plan - Design - Measure - Assess - Improve
Juran[c]	Diagnostic and Remedial Journeys
HCA[d]	FOCUS - PDCA
Scholtes[e]	Team Process
ODI[f]	Focus - Analyze - Develop - Execute (FADE)

[a]From Shewhart WA. Economic Quality Control of Manufactured Product. New York: Van Nostrand, 1931.
[b]From Comprehensive Accreditation Manual for Hospitals. Oakbrook Terrace, IL: Joint Commission on Accreditation of Healthcare Organizations, 1999.
[c]From Juran JM. Juran on Leadership for Quality. New York: The Free Press, 1989.
[d]From Hospital Corporation of America, Nashville, TN.
[e]From Scholtes PR. The Team Handbook: How to Use Teams to Improve Quality. 2d ed. Madison, WI: Joiner Associates, Inc., 1996.
[f]From Quality Action Teams. Burlington, MA: Organizational Dynamics, Inc., 1991.

build quality into all processes and monitor the outcomes; current CFR cGMP and laboratory regulations alone do not facilitate this coordination. To assist blood banks in this effort, FDA introduced the *Guideline for Quality Assurance in Blood Establishments* (11) as a draft in 1993; the document was finalized in 1995 after considerable public input.

Concurrently with revision of the FDA draft guideline, the AABB produced *The Quality Program* (12), a detailed expansion of the FDA guideline combining the elements of TPC with the operational functions of blood banking from donor selection through blood administration. Both FDA and AABB require blood banks and transfusion services to have a quality program in place, though not necessarily theirs. The AABB program, however, has the comprehension and simplicity necessary for facilities of any size.

The framework of the AABB quality program is shown in Figure 2. The elements of TPC are organized onto the left side of the quality program frame and are collectively called the "quality system." AABB refers to the TPC elements as quality system essentials (QSEs). The important feature of the QSEs is that they are to be uniformly applied to the operational functions shown across the top of the frame. For example, training is to be given to all personnel in each operational function and should minimally include organizational, safety, quality, computer, and job-specific training. Likewise, the process for changing an SOP should be the same in all the facility's operational functions.

Whatever the size or scope of a blood bank facility (i.e., however many or few activities or personnel in the operational functions at the top of the frame), the QSEs remain unchanged because they are so fundamental to the facility's ability to build quality and safety into blood banking products and services. To emphasize the importance of this concept, the AABB requires its institutional members to have written quality policies that state what the facility intends to do to implement the QSEs (TPC elements) in its operational functions. The quality policies are supported by quality processes and procedures that describe how the facility implements its stated intentions.

V. QUALITY SYSTEM DOCUMENTATION

A model exists for how a facility can organize the documentation for its quality system and operational functions. The model comes from the ISO 9000 quality standards compendium, which is a collection of definitions, guidelines, standards, and requirements for quality management (13). The section of the compendium that describes how to develop a quality manual (ISO 10013) provides a document hierarchy for a quality system in three levels: quality policy, quality procedures, and work instructions.

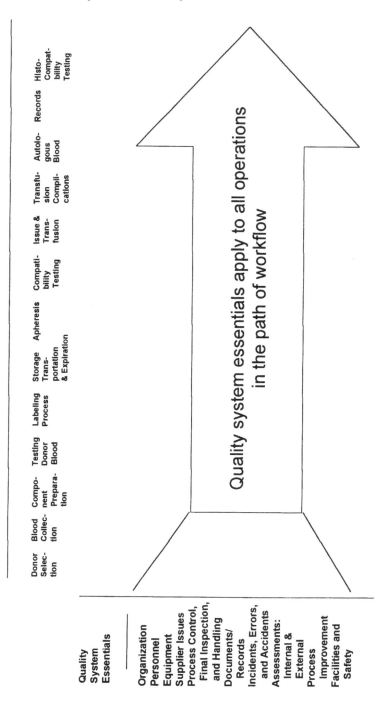

Figure 2 The AABB Quality Program grid showing cross-functional total process control elements (quality system essentials) applied to all blood bank operational functions. (From Ref. 15.)

A. Level A Documentation

As mentioned previously, the AABB requires that institutional members have a written quality plan that states the facility's quality objectives and policy. The quality plan describes in a narrative or outline format what the facility's policy is with regard to each QSE (TPC element). The plan need not be lengthy, as other documents will provide more detail for how the facility implements its quality objectives. Sample quality plans are available to help facilities draft their own (13–15).

B. Level B Documents

Quality system processes describe the "what, when, where, who" of the TPC elements/QSEs on the left side of the quality program frame. These documents describe the processes for generating an SOP, training personnel, reporting an occurrence, developing a validation protocol, and other tasks as shown in Table 6. Quality system processes are cross-functional—that is, they are applied across all facility operating functions. For example, a person reporting an occurrence in the component-processing area would follow the same procedure and use the same reporting form as a person reporting an occurrence in the donor-testing area. Important to note is that quality system processes often cross departmental lines as to actions taken, responsibilities, and documentation to be generated and thus have broad applicability. They are not written with the outline and detail of the technical operating procedures used for the task specifics of employees' jobs. Flowcharts and tables are often used to describe processes.

C. Level C Documents

Level C documents are the technical operating procedures and related forms used by employees in the facility's operational functions. They are the work instructions that provide the detail necessary for personnel to perform their specific job tasks. Using the donor testing example, a Level B quality process for SOP development would be used to draft the Level C operating procedures for calibration and maintenance of the spectrophotometric equipment, performance of the immunoassay tests, reporting test results in the computer, and documenting daily quality control. In the patient-identification example, the format described in the same Level B "SOP for SOPs" would be used to write all the operating procedures for patient specimen collection, compatibility testing, and blood administration. Each Level C procedure may have one or more associated forms that must be linked to it in some prescribed fashion as described in the Level B process for the facility's document control. All Level C procedures in one facility

Table 6 Sample Contents of a Quality Manual

Level A: Quality Policies	Level B: Quality Processes
Quality Plan Overview	
Quality Program Organization Policy	Review of the Quality Program
Personnel Policy	Training Process
	Staff Competence Assessment
	Continuing Education
Validation Policy	Validation Protocol Preparation
Calibration and Preventive Maintenance Policies	Laboratory Equipment Calibration
	Laboratory Equipment Maintenance
Proficiency Testing Policy	Proficiency Testing Process
Vendor Qualification Policy	Vendor Qualification Process
	Contract Review Process
	Receipt/Inspection of Incoming Reagents and Supplies
Process Control Policy	Change Control Process
	Quality Control Program
Documents, Records, Reviews	Writing Standard Operating Procedures
	Writing Training Documents
	Controlling Documents
Incidents, Errors, Accidents Policy	Occurrence Reporting and Follow-Up
Internal Assessment Policy	Internal Assessment Process
Process Improvement Policy	Corrective Action Process
	Process Improvement Using CQI Tools

Source: Ref. 15.

would be written in prescribed formats. A Level B document describing the process for change control would be used to request any Level C procedure changes in any operational function.

Figure 3 depicts the levels of the quality documentation pyramid showing the written quality plan at Level A, the TPC/QSE cross-functional elements at Level B, and the operational functions at Level C. In any operational function, one is guided by the facility's Level A quality policy, applies the appropriate Level B cross-functional quality processes, such as validation, training, and document control, and performs the resulting Level C operating procedures without personal deviations. The quality system approach provides the means to build quality, safety, and effectiveness into blood products and services, monitor the outcomes, and make improvements where needed.

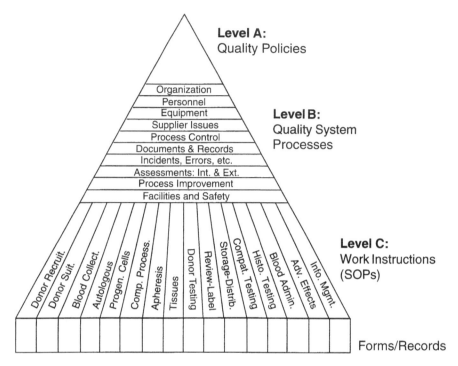

Figure 3 A modification of the quality system documentation pyramid showing the quality policies, blood bank cross-functional quality processes, and operational functions. (Courtesy of Abbott Quality Institute®, Abbott Park, IL.)

VI. QUALITY SYSTEM ASSESSMENTS

As previously stated, quality cannot be inspected or tested into a product or service. Experience in manufacturing has shown this philosophy to be sound. Therefore, the historical approach of external inspections to detect a facility's deficiencies, such as those conducted by laboratory regulatory and accreditation agencies, must change into a process that more effectively evaluates the facility's ability to detect its own weaknesses and take action to prevent errors.

In well-designed quality systems, total process control is the corporate culture. Continuous process improvement is fervently practiced to reduce errors and satisfy customers, which, by definition, increases productivity and decreases cost. Self-assessment is the means for blood banks and transfusion services to determine their current state of performance so that they can prioritize and target their improvement efforts.

A. Self-Assessment

What should be assessed? The AABB has divided the scope of blood banking activity into the operational functions shown across the top of the frame in Figure 2. For each operational function, processes and subprocesses have been identified. For each process, one or more quality indicators have been identified that can be used by facilities to monitor their performance over time (7). Operations personnel collect data and compare actual performance to preset expectations. Areas needing improvement are prioritized, and the chosen continuous process improvement model is applied. Follow-up monitoring of the quality indicators informs the facility of its progress. Periodic reporting provides information for executive management to make important decisions about resource allocations.

Self-assessment is an ongoing activity for which data should be collected as part of the work process wherever possible. As an example from processing, the log of unsuitable components should be updated as the components are identified and quarantined. Occurrence reports should be generated as soon as problems are discovered. Computers can be used to update blood donation, deferral, and incomplete unit statistics as donor records are entered. As a transfusion service example, persons performing compatibility testing can add to the log of unacceptable specimens on specimen receipt in the laboratory. Computers can be used to capture specimen receipt-to-result turnaround times for emergent compatibility testing. Incomplete or incorrect transfusion report forms can be logged on return to the transfusion service.

B. Quality Audits

Internal audits assess the conformance of the facility's written quality system to the standard and compare the actual activities to the written system. First-party audits are performed by the facility's own auditors as part of TPC monitoring. Second-party audits are performed by facilities on their suppliers and take place external to the facility. For example, a hospital blood bank may choose to perform a second-party audit on the supplier of the blood components it procures for transfusion. Third-party external quality audits are conducted by contracted auditors to assess the facility's quality system with respect to national or international quality system standards and to provide registration or certification of acceptable quality systems. The most common type of third-party audit is an ISO 9000 registration audit.

Table 7 is a comparison of the AABB QSEs to the ISO 9001 quality system conformance model that demonstrates their compatibility. Some U.S. blood banks have totally embraced the TPC and quality system philosophies and are preparing for ISO 9000 registration audits. Two U.S. blood bank quality systems (16,17) and several in other countries (18) have already become registered. Both the

Table 7 Comparison of the AABB Quality System Essentials to the ISO 9001 Quality System Conformance Model

AABB Quality System Essentials	ISO 9001 Quality System Conformance Model
Organization	4.1 Management responsibility
	4.2 Quality system
Personnel	4.18 Training
Equipment	4.11 Control of inspection, measuring and test equipment
Supplier issues	4.3 Contract review
	4.6 Purchasing
Process control	4.4 Design control (N/A for 9002)
	4.7 Control of customer supplied product
	4.8 Product identification and traceability
	4.9 Process control
	4.10 Inspection and testing
	4.12 Inspection and test status
	4.15 Handling, storage, packaging, preservation and delivery
	4.19 Servicing (if applicable)
Documents and records	4.5 Document and data control
	4.16 Control of quality records
Incidents, errors, accidents	4.13 Control of nonconforming product
Internal and external assessment	4.17 Internal quality audits
Process improvement	4.14 Corrective and preventive action
	4.20 Statistical techniques
Facilities and safety	[4.9(b) Process control]

Source: Courtesy of Abbott Quality Institute®, Abbott Park, IL.

AABB and FDA have redesigned their inspection programs to better evaluate whether the facility's quality system conforms to regulations and accreditation requirements and whether the facility has demonstrated compliance with and effective implementation of its own quality policies, processes, and procedures.

VII. SUMMARY

The desirable and necessary patient outcome of safe, efficacious blood transfusion requires a paradigm shift to the fervent belief that quality, safety, and effectiveness must be built into all of a facility's blood banking activities. In manufacturing facilities, personnel are usually working in a single management structure, which affords much more control in cooperation and coordination for process development, validation, monitoring, and improvement. In contrast, the clinical transfusion process involves the interaction of individuals who work in numerous management settings for which the provision of safe blood transfusion is just one of many priorities that may not be recognized as an important responsibility. The challenges to building TPC in each environment are many, but the rewards outweigh the efforts.

Total process control fosters processes and procedures that prevent errors, thereby building safety into the blood supply and blood transfusion. To manage TPC throughout the various activities of blood donation, component processing, testing, and transfusion, a quality system is needed. Quality models for transfusion medicine combine the elements of the ISO 9000 quality standards with the elements of blood bank and laboratory technical standards to accomplish a truly comprehensive quality system.

REFERENCES

1. McClelland DBL, McMenamin JJ, Moores HM, Barbara JAJ. Reducing risks in blood transfusion: process and outcome. Transfusion Med 1996; 6:1–10.
2. Food and Drug Administration, Department of Health and Human Services. 21 CFR Parts 200-299. Washington, DC: U.S. Government Printing Office, revised annually.
3. Food and Drug Administration, Department of Health and Human Services. 21 CFR Parts 600-799. Washington, DC: U.S. Government Printing Office, revised annually.
4. Food and Drug Administration, Department of Health and Human Services. 21 CFR Part 820. Washington, DC: U.S. Government Printing Office, revised annually.
5. Food and Drug Administration, Department of Health and Human Services. Guideline on general principles of process validation. Washington, DC: U.S. Government Printing Office, 1987.
6. Holliman S, ed. Validation in blood establishments and transfusion services. Bethesda, MD: American Association of Blood Banks, 1996.
7. Nevalainen DE, Berte LM, Callery MF. Quality systems in the blood bank environment, 2d ed. Bethesda, MD: American Association of Blood Banks, 1998.
8. Brassard M, Ritter D. The memory jogger™ II. Methuen, MA: GOAL/QPC, 1994.
9. Standards for Blood Banks and Transfusion Services, 19th ed. Bethesda, MD: American Association of Blood Banks, 1999.
10. Department of Health and Human Services. 42 CFR Parts 430 to end. Washington, DC: U.S. Government Printing Office, revised annually.
11. Guideline on quality assurance in blood establishments; FDA Docket #91N-0450. Bethesda, MD: U.S. Food and Drug Administration, 1995.
12. The quality program. Bethesda, MD: American Association of Blood Banks, 1994.
13. ISO Standards Compendium: ISO 9000 Quality Management, 6th ed. Geneva: International Organization for Standardization, 1996.
14. Nevalainen DE, Callery MF. Module VIII: Quality system documentation. In: Quality systems in the blood bank and laboratory environment. Bethesda, MD: American Association of Blood Banks, 1994.

15. AABB Transfusion Service Quality Assurance Committee. A model quality system for the transfusion service. Bethesda, MD: American Association of Blood Banks, 1997.
16. South Texas Blood and Tissue receives ISO accreditation. AABB Weekly Report 1996; 2(44):4.
17. Denver blood center granted ISO 9000 certification. AABB Weekly Report 1998; 4(26):1.
18. Nevalainen DE, Lloyd HL. ISO 9000 quality standards: a model for blood banking? Transfusion 1995; 35(6):521–524.

23
Cost-Effectiveness Analysis of Risk-Reduction Strategies

James P. AuBuchon
Dartmouth-Hitchcock Medical Center, Lebanon, New Hampshire

I. INTRODUCTION

From the time of Hippocrates, the intention of doing no harm to one's patient has been codified as a physician's duty. Viral transmission through transfusion clearly represents an untoward outcome that both physician and patient would like to avoid, and both parties would certainly prefer to minimize the risks of a transfusion. Laudable and effective efforts have been directed at reducing transfusion risks through donor screening, infectious disease marker testing, and viral-inactivation efforts, but the risks of transfusion can only be lowered or replaced, not eliminated. In addition to an ongoing balancing of risks and benefits, the medical community is now also asked by society to achieve more with fewer resources. The desire to reduce transfusion risk must be accomplished in an era of finite resources. This situation is an appropriate one for application of decision analysis tools—not only to determine the relative return on investments in new approaches to this health care problem, but also to illustrate where blood safety efforts are most likely to yield substantial payoffs.

II. A PRIMER IN DECISION ANALYSIS

Cost-effectiveness analyses (CEAs) have been used widely in medicine to quantitate the benefits and costs of interventions. Their construction and reporting follow some general rules, and further standardization should improve their applicability and comparisons. A brief introduction is offered here for those unfamiliar with the techniques of CEAs.

There are several basic assumptions on which cost-effectiveness analyses are predicated. The first is that there is a desire to maximize the health of the population. This outcome is usually measured in terms of longevity, such as additional years of life saved for a group of patients to which an intervention has been applied. This measure is often modified by a quality-of-life factor. This factor is meant to represent the perceived quality of life in the presence of residual disease symptoms, morbidity from treatment side effects, or other factors that prevent the patient from enjoying perfect health. The exact quality adjustment factor assigned to various states of morbidity can be determined by an analysis of patients' preferences conducted in one of a variety of manners, such as determining how much time they would be willing to trade from their lifespan for amelioration of symptomatology or what risk of death they would accept in a therapeutic maneuver to be free of symptoms (1–4). Multiplying the quality-of-life factor for an outcome state (perfect health = 1.0; death = 0) by the longevity yields a commonly used outcome measure, the quality-adjusted life-year (QALY). This measurement of outcome is particularly useful because it is not linked to a specific disease or treatment, and outcomes expressed in a generally applicable term such as this can be readily compared.

A second precept of CEAs is that a choice must be made between interventions that are competing for a finite pool of resources. Therefore quantitating the difference in benefits obtained between two interventions and contrasting those with the difference in the costs of their use should define the relative cost-effectiveness of the approach under study. Thus the two interventions, such as medical vs. surgical treatment of angina, are seen as competing for the limited resources available to care for patients with this condition.

Practically, the construction of a CEA begins with a decision tree. In laying out all the possibilities that may develop following selection of a particular course of action, the tree represents all the various courses that a patient may follow after an intervention is begun and the various outcomes that are possible. The tree would include representations of all side effects of treatments and their outcomes, partial or complete cures of a condition, etc. Once all the possibilities have been embodied in the tree, the probabilities that each might occur need to be determined, either through a review of the literature, consultation with experts, or performance of experiments. Similarly, the costs of each individual step must be determined and the total expenditures for a patient reaching each outcome state be summed. Also, the longevity of a patient in each outcome state and the quality of life in those states must be quantified. Finally, mathematically "rolling back the tree" allows calculation of the total outcome achieved with each intervention; similarly, the costs associated with the intervention are tallied and compared between interventions. The "marginal cost-effectiveness" is then calculated as:

$$\text{Cost–effectiveness}_{(A \text{ vs. } B)} = (\Sigma \text{costs}_A - \Sigma \text{costs}_B)/(\Sigma \text{outcomes}_A - \Sigma \text{outcomes}_B)$$

There are, of course, many nuances and pitfalls in the construction and evaluation of these decision trees and a variety of mathematical tools and statistical models that can be applied. For example, the preference for spending money later rather than in the present is usually captured by application of a discount rate to distant costs of an intervention; similarly, future benefits are also discounted, and the rate(s) applied must be reasonable representations of society's time preferences (5). Models can also include tools [e.g., a Markov model (6)] that represent conditions involving a variety of health states emerging over time. The perspective chosen for the analysis can also be critical for its results. Usually, a "societal" perspective is selected to capture globally the expenses and benefits of an intervention. However, in some circumstances, the decision maker or the party most directly affected by a decision can be identified more precisely, and this may lead to inclusion of a different set of costs (7).

Properly constructed, a cost-effectiveness analysis can yield a concise estimation of relative costs and benefits expressed in a common measure, dollars per QALY, that can readily be compared between interventions. The reader is referred to standard texts and consensus statements to gain additional information on the construction and interpretation of these analyses (7–12).

III. SAMPLES OF COST-EFFECTIVENESS ANALYSIS APPLICATIONS IN TRANSFUSION MEDICINE

A. Autologous Transfusion Strategies

A number of options in transfusion medicine have been evaluated for their cost-effectiveness. These analyses are valuable from two points of view: determination of the cost-effectiveness of a technique and identification of factors having an effect on the cost-effectiveness estimation (13,14). While the former application may be of most interest to health economists and those charged with health-planning decisions for society, it is the latter application that is most meaningful and useful to those actually practicing transfusion medicine. Furthermore, application of CEA techniques to blood safety decisions has helped to identify the importance of avoiding new complications as attempts are made to decrease the likelihood of those that are already diminishing.

1. Preoperative Autologous Donation

Preoperative autologous donation (PAD) is an excellent example of how an analysis can be used to highlight several aspects of an intervention's use. Although the benefits of PAD are self-evident, growing concern has been expressed about the costs associated with this form of hemotherapy and the wastage that is inevitable since the need for transfusion is so difficult to predict. Through CEA, the magnitude of the benefits and costs have been quantitated for specific situations and for general application (Table 1). The fact that PAD has much poorer cost-effectiveness than most medical interventions (19–21) in many applications is not surprising given the relatively high level of safety of allogeneic transfusion at present (15,22,23) and the need to collect many more units than are necessary for transfusion in order to have autologous units available to cover the potential need.

Through these analyses, however, those charged with delivering this option to patients can gain valuable insights into how best to apply the technique. For example, while it may be intuitive that collecting blood for a surgical procedure that rarely results in transfusion is likely to be wasteful, the magnitude of the impact of such use of PAD is clearly evident in the calculations of Etchason et al., who documented that cost-effectiveness varied exponentially with the likelihood

Table 1 Cost-Effectiveness of Transfusion Risk Reduction Strategies

Intervention	Cost-effectiveness (cost/year of life extended)
Preoperative autologous donation	
Coronary artery bypass surgery (2 units) (19)	$500,000
Primary unilateral hip arthroplasty (20)	$557,000
Primary unilateral knee arthroplasty (20)	$1.3 million
Bilateral or revision arthroplasty (20)	$140,000
Hysterectomy (20)	$1.4 million
Transurethral resection of prostate (20)	$23.6 million
Alanine aminotransferase testing (for NANB hepatitis detection) (15)	
Before anti-HCV test availability	(cost-saving)
In addition to anti-HCV testing	$7.9 million
HIV antibody testing (vs. no testing) (16)	$3,600
Additions to HIV antibody testing	
p24 antigen (16)	$2.2 million
PCR for HIV genome (16)	$2.0 million
Hepatitis B core antibody (17)	$2.3 million
Solvent-Detergent Treatment of Plasma (62,63)	
Overall (based on conservative plasma usage)	$2–10 million

Published estimates of cost-effectiveness of a variety of interventions designed to improve transfusion safety. In comparison, most medical/surgical interventions have a cost-effectiveness of <$50,000/year of life extended.
NANB = Non-A, non-B; TTP = thrombotic thrombocytopenic purpura; anti-HCV = hepatitis C antibody test; PCP = polymerase chain reaction testing.

of discard (21) (Fig. 1). Examining factors related to cost-effectiveness in particular situations in more detail, Birkmeyer et al. (19,20) showed that not only was collection of units without anticipated need likely to result in poor cost-effectiveness, but transfusion of autologous units in situations where there was less likelihood of clinical benefit also contributed to poor cost-effectiveness (Table 2). Also, both of these groups have defined the importance of applying the technique in those patients having greater expectations of longevity: the longer a patient is expected to survive after surgery, the greater the time period in which the patient could enjoy the benefits of having avoided viral infection through allogeneic transfusion. Thus, pursuing PAD more aggressively in younger patients may offer more benefit than when PAD is applied in older patients.

These analyses have also highlighted the costs of certain decisions that have been made. For example, testing autologous units for infectious disease markers provides no benefit to the donor/recipient but adds cost to the system. This testing has been explained as necessary (24) because of the potential for mistransfusion of autologous units, i.e., transfusion to the wrong patient. While mistransfusion remains a large problem in transfusion medicine, placing some of the burden for it on autologous units distorts their true cost. Placing suitable, unused autologous units in the allogeneic inventory would reduce some of the economic burden of "overcollection" inherent in a PAD program and justify some of the testing costs. However, "crossover" is not widely practiced for a variety of ethical and practical reasons (23). CEAs can help identify the costs and implications associated with policy decisions such as these and may prompt reconsideration of choices or additional documentation of the rationale for their having been made in the first place.

On reflection, the poor cost-effectiveness of PAD in many situations was predictable. These calculations did provide useful assistance, however, in that their quantitations assisted in providing imperatives for improvement in ordering practices, for example (26), and they also yielded other, unexpected insights that could help redefine the provision of PAD services. For example, the PAD analyses mentioned above all included the assumption that the donation process was risk-free. However, this is certainly not the case. Approximately 1 in 17,000 autologous donations is followed by reactions so severe that hospitalization is required (27). The frequency of a serious postdonation reaction is even higher in patients/donors not meeting usual allogeneic donation criteria; about 1 in 220 may develop a serious reaction, and the identification of those at greatest risk is problematic (28). These statistics are alarming when applied to patients scheduled for CABG: removal of the assumption of safety of donation for these patients demonstrated that only 1 in 101,000 donations by CABG patients would need to result in a fatal peri-donation reaction before all the health benefits of having autologous blood available were entirely negated (19). This poses the obvious question: Can (this many) units be collected safely from a group of patients with

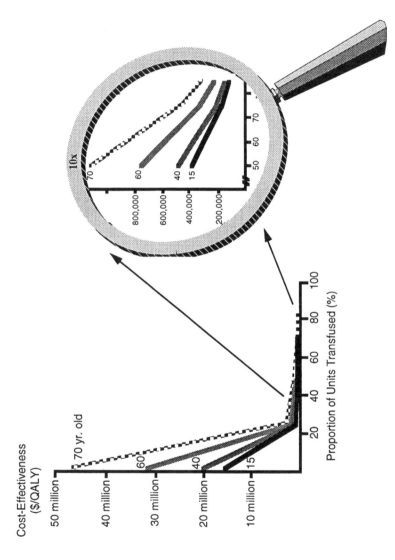

Figure 1 Effects of patients age (15, 40, 60, or 70 years) and likelihood of the use of autologous units on the cost-effectiveness of PAD. Note the exponential relationship between cost-effectiveness and proportion of PAD units actually transfused. Patient age (i.e., projected longevity) also has a large impact on cost-effectiveness calculations for PAD. Except in cases of long postoperative lifespan and high likelihood of use, PAD cost-effectiveness is far poorer than that of most medical and surgical interventions (which usually have cost-effectiveness estimates better than $50,000/QALY). (Data adapted from Ref. 20.)

Table 2 Factors Affecting the Cost-Effectiveness of PAD Applications

Patient variables	Practice variables
Reaction risk	Proportion of units discarded
Reaction consequences	Transfusion threshold with autologous vs. allogeneic units
Longevity expectation	

coronary artery disease so severe that surgery is necessary? While no study has been of sufficient size to answer the question directly, a prospective donor also needs to take into account that just delaying coronary revascularization in order to allow for the collection of several units may have substantial mortality risk—approximately 0.5–2% per month (29). These concerns call into question whether PAD is the safest course of action for all patients.

Safety and efficacy questions extend to patients in more healthy states as well. For example, 10% of patients donating for themselves before hysterectomy ultimately needed to be transfused in a recent study, a transfusion rate 12 times higher than that of patients who did not donate for themselves; the subset of patients who donated preoperatively had lower admission hemoglobin values, and autologous donation was an independent risk factor for transfusion (30). Obviously no benefit (at some cost and some, albeit small, risk) is achieved through PAD when there is only a small likelihood of significant blood loss. Furthermore, judicious use of erythropoetin to stimulate regeneration or expansion of red cell mass and application of iron-replacement therapy may minimize complications of repetitive phlebotomies (31–33); however, any universal application of a pharmacological adjunct or, indeed, any single PAD strategy cannot be supported. Rather, judicious, patient-specific decisions must be made to identify the most appropriate course of action based on the patient's condition and the likelihood of transfusion need, among other factors.

The cost-effectiveness analyses of PAD detailed above focused on prevention of viral transmission as the primary benefit of using one's own blood for surgery. Concerns have arisen over the last several years about the potential immunosuppressive effect of allogeneic blood exposure and the possibility of decreased tumor cell surveillance and increased risk of postoperative infection following allogeneic transfusion (34–37). Understanding the clinical significance of these studies has been difficult because of the many confounding factors embedded in the analyses and because of frankly contradictory results from similarly designed studies. One group of researchers did include an estimate of substantially increased risk of postoperative infection as a consequence of allogeneic transfusion in a CEA model of PAD before orthopedic surgery (38). Inclusion of this complication led to the conclusion that PAD would be cost-effective or even cost-saving. On the other hand, a study performed for the Canadian health care system concluded that even if the immunosuppressive effects of allogeneic exposure were clinically significant, these would have a relatively small impact on health care costs (39). Once the immunomodulatory effects of allogeneic transfusion are well characterized and their clinical consequences defined, any immunosuppressive effects of allogeneic transfusion could be included in recalculation of a PAD model previously focused on viral transmission. However, indications that leukoreduction may provide an alternative that avoids this complication of allogeneic transfusion (40) raises another approach to be considered: since a leukoreduction filter for a red cell unit generally costs about half of the additional amount that a hospital must pay for an autologous unit (41), leukoreduction may be a less costly and simpler approach to avoiding this complication than PAD (42). For example, use of leukoreduced red cell units in colorectal surgery resulted in a postoperative infection rate and length of hospital stay similar to that of patients not requiring a transfusion and significantly better than those receiving leukocyte-replete units. Additional studies to define more precisely the relative costs and benefits of options to avoid complications such as this are necessary to clarify their cost-effectiveness.

2. Acute Normovolemic Hemodilution

Acute normovolemic hemodilution (ANH) is another technique that makes autologous blood available. As the units remain with the patient and are not tested, a simple, low-cost system is often envisioned that should be cost-effective. However, as several mathematical models have demonstrated (43,44), the volume of red cells "saved" by the procedure is quite small, often less than one unit's worth, unless multiple units (four to six) can be collected from the patient and significant blood loss actually occurs. In circumstances such as these, ANH can supply at least as much autologous hemotherapy support as PAD and may do so at approximately half the cost (45). As preoperative administration of erythropoietin may increase a patient's red cell mass and allow more extensive hemodilution, or since use of a "blood substitute" may allow a lower hematocrit to be tolerated during ANH, greater application of ANH may be seen in the future. Again, there are insufficient data today to conduct a formal CEA, but additional work toward reduction of the dose (and cost) of erythropoietin used in this approach would improve cost-effectiveness estimates (46). Similarly, addition of an oxygen-carrying solution to the hemotherapy protocol would allow for greater reduction in a patient's hematocrit, the collection of a larger number of units, and, potentially, avoidance of a larger number of allogeneic units. As with other autologous hemotherapy options, selection of patients who are most likely to need transfusion and from whom adequate quantities of blood can be collected will be central to determining the yield (and thus the cost-effectiveness) of the approach (47).

3. Intra- and Postoperative Red Cell Recovery

Intraoperative and postoperative recovery of red cells are also widely practiced means of avoiding or reducing allogeneic transfusion. For surgical procedures in which large volumes of blood are shed, "recycling" the red cells can dramatically reduce the volume of allogeneic red cells required (48,49). The devices are often used in cardiac surgery, although blood loss may be minimal in a "simple" primary operation performed by a careful operator. In such cases, the devices are used more as hemoconcentrators for blood left in the extracorporeal circuit at the end of the procedure than as a tool to salvage red cells that would otherwise have been discarded. Applications in vascular surgery and in orthopedic procedures where several liters of blood may be lost have resulted in reductions in allogeneic blood usage by over half. As the cost of disposables, amortization of the capital equipment expense, and support of the operator can total $250–500 per case, the most commonly quoted wisdom is that a transfusion need of at least two to three units of red blood cells must be anticipated before intraoperative recovery is less expensive than allogeneic transfusion (50,51). [The distributed costs of infectious disease transmission through transfusion are approximately $1/unit, and the summed cost of all complications of allogeneic transfusion has been estimated at less than $10/unit (46). Therefore, there is little room for providing an alternative approach to allogeneic transfusion that reduces overall cost!]

Care must be taken in using intraoperative red cell recovery techniques that complications of their use do not develop that outweigh the potential benefits. For example, aspiration of tumor cells or bacteria may lead to an inadvertent intravenous bolus of the cells since neither are completely removed by even washing techniques (52,53). Operators must remain aware that only red cells are being returned and that other components of blood may be needed by the patient undergoing a massive transfusion. Finally, the potential for activating a disseminated intravascular coagulation-like scenario when unwashed red cells are reinfused must be considered, although this is a rare phenomenon.

Of more questionable benefit is the application of technology to recover red cells shed postoperatively. As with preoperative collection, a primary difficulty is predicting who will bleed and who will need transfusion. In orthopedic surgery, for example, the usual volume collected after arthroplastic surgery is approximately that of one unit of whole blood (300–500 mL), but the hematocrit is much lower (15–25%) (54). As a result, only about 5% of patients receive a unit's worth of red cells when postarthroplasty recovery is practiced. Therefore, the cost-effectiveness of postoperative recovery of red cells usually provides little real benefit to most patients at an extraordinarily poor cost-effectiveness estimate (55,56). However, reducing the cost of postoperative salvage by piggybacking the collection on disposables already used for intraoperative collection and reinfusion may make salvage of red cells lost postoperatively not only feasible but also cost-effective.

B. Infectious Disease Marker Testing

As the risk of viral transmission through allogeneic transfusion continues to fall, additional measures to reduce this risk further become increasingly less cost-effective. Implementation of human immunodeficiency virus (HIV) antibody testing in 1985 almost paid for itself, since it culled so many potentially infective units from the allogeneic supply (16) (Table 1). On the other hand, starting from a base of infrequent transmission (approximately 1/453,000 units with the most current form of HIV antibody testing), addition of HIV p24 antigen testing reduces the risk only a small amount (to approximately 1/676,000); this decreased the projected number of annual HIV transmissions through transfusion in the United States from 32 to 24. In consequence of this relatively small yield, its cost-effectiveness was very poor (16). Recalculation of the cost-effectiveness of HIV p24 antigen testing based on updated estimates of its yield suggest that its true cost-effectiveness is more in the range of $20 million/QALY. Addition of nucleic acid testing (NAT) techniques to "close the window" for HIV infection would have even poorer cost-effectiveness. (The higher residual risk of HCV even with version 3.0 HCV EIA testing would suggest that it would be a more cost-effective target for NAT.) Similarly, use of alanine aminotransferase testing as a surrogate marker for non-A, non-B hepatitis in the mid-1980s actually saved the health care system money despite low sensitivity and specificity because of the relatively high rate of hepatitis transmission. Implementation of a specific test (anti-HCV) was also cost-saving since neither of the surrogate tests in place were highly effective. However, once a very sensitive anti-HCV test was implemented, the yield from surrogate testing plummeted, resulting in poor cost-effectiveness estimates (15) and recommendations to drop this approach to avoiding non-A, non-B hepatitis (57).

However, despite the advances in allogeneic transfusion safety that have occurred in the last decade, the public, through the media and through their congressional representatives, still clamors for increased levels of safety. While regulatory agencies may be forced for political reasons to require additional screening and testing measures, it is clear that these will have limited yields and will result in increasingly astronomical cost-effectiveness estimations (58).

Beyond the economic perspective, there are potential safety drawbacks to implementing new blood-testing efforts. A significant proportion (15–25%) of blood donors found to be HIV antibody positive admit on interview that they had been aware of their exposure risks and donated, at least in part, to have HIV testing performed in a free and socially acceptable venue (59). Media publicity about introduction of a "new and improved" HIV test could attract more persons to donate for the purposes of discerning their HIV status rather than altruism. Because no test is 100% sensitive (and some window period of negativity will always exist following infection and infectivity), implementation of a new test to make the blood supply safer could have its impact negated or ever reversed (60). The greatest risk of this "magnet effect" is in situations where the incremental sensitivity gained from implementation is small and the probability of infection is relatively high. This combination (plus a high proportion of false positives that would have erroneously been interpreted by donors as indicative of AIDS) led blood bankers generally to avoid use of hepatitis B core antibody testing as a surrogate marker for HIV infection prior to availability of HIV antibody testing (61). The potential for the magnet effect to yield an unexpected, unfortunate, and unintended result must be kept in mind when new interventions to improve blood safety are being considered.

C. Microbial Inactivation

Additional increments in blood safety may be more readily achievable, however, through microbial inactivation of blood components. These techniques would have to be applied to all units, the vast majority of which were already free from infectious agents, and thus cost-effectiveness would be expected to be relatively poor unless the invervention were quite inexpensive. [For example, if solvent-detergent (SD) treatment of frozen plasma (FP) cost $20 per unit, the cost-effectiveness of this intervention would be close to $300,000/QALY (18). Updating the cost-effectiveness to current infectious risks and prevailing costs brings the cost-effectiveness of SD FP to approximately $2–10 million/QALY (62,63).]

Beyond the obvious economic concern, the potential "side effects" of a microbial inactivation treatment must also be considered. Any of the treatments under consideration at present have the potential for leaving a small chemical residual in the unit or generating a reactive intermediate molecule. This raises the potential for chemical toxicity or mutagenicity following transfusion. Undoubtedly, toxicological tests will be performed prior to licensure documenting that such untoward effects are exceedingly unlikely and/or small. However, when the risk of transmission of a viral agent is also extremely small, just a minute toxicological risk could outweigh all the benefit obtained from viral inactivation. Manufacturers are clearly searching for ways to minimize residual agent following inactivation, such as through adsorption filtration to remove methylene blue from plasma (64), but this concern will have to be evaluated individually for each proposed inactivation method.

The SD treatment process raises another issue of unintended negative effects. For manufacturing logistics and economic reasons, this technique is performed on pools of plasma rather than on individual units. If the technique inactivated all microbes, the pooling would be of no concern. However, the SD technique does not inactivate nonenveloped viruses, and the pooling might provide access for a nonenveloped microbe from a single donor to be distributed to a large number of recipients. While the nonenveloped viruses known to be capable of parenteral spread, including hepatitis A and parvovirus B19, are of limited concern for most transfusion recipients, a nonenveloped virus could certainly arise with clinical consequences analogous to those of HIV infection. Were such a virus to evolve, estimates from a CEA have suggested that such a virus would have to be present at only an undetectably low frequency in the donor population (1/71,000,000) before all the benefits of avoiding HIV, HBV, and HCV through SD treatment of FP were negated (18). Concerns such as this have prompted suggestions that the pool size for SD treatment should be made smaller, but in most circumstances reducing pool sizes will have only a minimal impact on avoidance of contamination (65).

Avoiding disease agents that are not readily inactivated, such as in Creutzfeld-Jakob disease (CJD), would also seem prudent. While transmission of CJD via transfusion has never been documented, even the remote possibility of this event still generates fear. Because of a lack of a simple test for the disease and the stability of CJD prions in a wide variety sterilizing solutions, some have suggested deferring donors over the age of 50 or 60 to reduce the possibility of donation by a person in the presymptomatic phase of CJD. Deferral of long-time donors with a history of travel to the United Kingdom is another mechanism designed to reduce the risk of transmissible spongiform encephalopathy. However, because these segments of the donating population are the least likely to be recently infected with a blood-transmissible agent, their units represent a smaller risk of transfusion-transmitted viral disease. Replacing these multiply tested donors with first-time donors, who are also younger, may actually decrease the safety of the donor pool (66). This is another situation where an unintended side effect of a "safety" measure may actually produce new risk of a magnitude greater than the original risk to be avoided.

D. Mistransfusion

Successful reduction of infectious disease risks through allogeneic transfusion might have been predicted to lead to a redirection of attention to other transfusion safety issues. Rather than this, however, additional effort has been directed toward reducing these risks even further, ignoring estimates of low yield and concerns about availability of financial support to match the desires for safer blood. As a result, larger risks remain that might be addressed through interventions that are more cost-effective than yet another infectious disease screening test.

An obvious example is mistransfusion and the risk of an ABO-related fatality. The importance of ABO compatibility and the potentially catastrophic consequences of an error have been appreciated for a century. However, the frequency of fatal ABO errors has remained relatively constant (67–69). The majority of these are due to "systems problems." The safety of the process depends on human adherence to a protocol that is imperfect, and "human error" can result in the transfusion of a unit of blood to someone other than the intended recipient (67,70–72). The magnitude of this problem is not trivial. European studies have shown that errors surrounding transfusions occur with surprising frequency. Misidentification occurred with 0.74% of patients and 0.2% of units, and other major errors occurred with 0.5% of patients (73). A thorough, recent study of transfusions in New York State documented that the same kinds of problems that have been reported before are still occurring at the same frequency despite safeguards such as unit labeling, double-checking of information, and so forth (69). Extrapolating the frequency of mistransfusion (1/12,000 units) and ABO-related fatalities (1/600,000 unit) to the country as a whole, approximately two dozen patients die each year as a result of a fatal mistransfusion. This fatality rate exceeds the number of HIV transmissions annually (22). However, the public remains extremely fearful of HIV transmission through transfusion and ignorant of the greater risks of mistransfusion; as a consequence, additional efforts are directed toward viral safety and few are targeted at reducing mistransfusions.

This apparent contradiction is reflected in cost-effectiveness analyses as well. A barrier system capable of preventing >99.99% of mistransfusions due to labeling and patient identification errors is commercially available (74). When its cost-effectiveness was evaluated from a societal perspective, it was somewhat less cost-effective than most medical interventions (approximately \$200,000/QALY)—although more cost-effective than most blood safety initiatives; however, when evaluated from a hospital's perspective (where the costs of legal ramifications are logically included), use of the device was found to reduce a hospital's overall costs (75). Thus society has directed the blood banking system to focus resources toward reducing the risk of HIV transmission, although the same resources directed at preventing mistransfusion would yield 10 times the benefit. The reasons for this apparent inconsistency are explored in a later section.

E. Bacterial Contamination

The reappearance of concern regarding bacterial contamination (at least among transfusion medicine professionals) highlights another dilemma faced by those charged with providing a safe blood supply. While the risk of septic or endotoxic shock after a red cell transfusion is on the order of 1 in 1–9,000,000 units, the result is frequently fatal; far more platelet transfusions (perhaps 1/1,000–113,000 platelet units) may harbor significant concentrations of bacteria, but because they are more likely "skin contaminants," their potential for inducing morbidity or mortality is less (76). The source of these contaminants has been well described—

asymptomatic bacteremia of skin flora escaping surface decontamination—but no practical, generally feasible technological solutions have as yet been identified. Gram staining and/or culture prior to unit release from the transfusion service has been discussed most frequently, but the poor sensitivity of the former and the time required for and expense of the latter have precluded widespread implementation of these techniques. Genetic probe assays are under development that could provide improved sensitivity (77), but the time and reagents involved may well result in this bacterial detection system having a significant cost attached to its use. Should such a system be used routinely when it is available? Given the relatively short longevity of most transfusion recipients [due to their underlying illness (78)] and the rarity of significant red cell contamination, even a detection system of modest cost will probably be associated with astronomical cost-effectiveness estimates when applied to red blood cells. Because of the higher probability of bacterial contamination of platelets, such a system would provide a higher "safety yield" when applied to this component. However, the mortality associated with contamination of platelet units appear lower than for red cells, and the even shorter longevity of the average recipient of platelets might still yield a very poor cost-effectiveness estimate. If documentation of sterility allowed a lengthened storage period, however, cost savings might result.

The previous paragraph outlines some of the major features of a CEA for a bacterial detection system; once the details of such a practical system were available, including its sensitivity, specificity, and cost, a formal CEA could be readily constructed. Would such an analysis determine whether such an intervention were warranted? Would the results help shape policy regarding its implementation?

IV. DECISIONS, DECISION MAKERS, AND CEAs

The increasing constraints on health care expenditures in the United States have made all in the health care field keenly aware of the importance of spending resources wisely. Nevertheless, those charged with the direct care of patients have not relinquished their duty to act as a patient's advocate, seeking the best possible treatment and outcome for a patient, regardless of its cost. At the same time, those who administer health care plans and institutions—some of whom also have patient care responsibilities in other roles—must make difficult decisions about what treatments to offer to whom under what circumstances in order to maximize the benefit provided to the population served.

Judgments of decision makers in modern health care frequently employ some type of formal or informal decision analysis tool. The questions "Does it work?" or "Is it better?" always come first to a physician. These are followed by "What does it cost?" and at least a quick mental check on the presumed return for the investment. These questions may be followed by a formal CEA, but other factors also need to be considered.

Avoidance of HIV is a good example. Why is the public "scared to death" of HIV transmission through transfusion yet apparently complacent about the risks of mistransfusion?

A key factor may be the inevitability of premature death associated with HIV infection. Surety of death as an outcome will prompt extreme measures of avoidance (79,80). Although an intervention such as PAD will provide actual benefit to only a tiny minority of those using this transfusion option, all patients donating blood for themselves—even those ultimately not needing a transfusion—receive the psychological benefit of having taken steps to avoid a dreaded outcome. Not only is the intensity of this drive significant, but it is poorly captured in CEAs. As only tangible benefits are readily counted in the outcomes (unless lingering psychic stress would alter quality of life or require medical intervention), the importance of avoiding HIV for many people would not be fully captured in an enumeration of the years of life extended by prevention of a certain number of HIV transmissions.

Another facet of fear leads to a parallel problem. Activities in which the untoward outcome is obvious and predictable are associated with less dread than risks that occur in an unseen fashion and that occur "indiscriminately," that is, are not abetted by the actions of the victim. A transfusion-transmitted infection would thus fall into the quadrant of highest dread since it occurs without warning to an unsuspecting and "undeserving" victim and manifests only after a period of latency (81). This situation, coupled with inordinate fear of HIV in particular, as detailed above, may help explain the public's "irrational" fear of HIV transmission via transfusion and the continued push for further reductions in that risk.

Finally, the "rule of rescue" may apply to transfusion safety decisions (82). In considering various therapeutic interventions, there is a human tendency to favor implementation of approaches that result in preventing an imminent death over those that would prolong the life of a patient beginning at some time in the future. Although most blood safety initiatives are "preventive" rather than "therapeutic" in nature, the concept of the "rule of rescue" may still be applicable since the outcome of a blood safety initiative is often seen as preventing a premature death. In addition, although measures taken to improve the safety of the blood supply ultimately benefit only a small number of recipients, this group of patients is readily identifiable and highly visible. In most situations, both lay and professional people will opt for the intervention that benefits a small, clearly identifiable group of recipients over one that provides a similar or even greater aggregate benefit spread in small increments over a large number of people (83,84). Thus, the benefit of a blood safety initiative may have more psychological value than as measured in QALYs.

Therefore, there are several psychological factors driving decisions to increase the safety of the blood supply that are not readily embodied in a decision tree or in the calculations of a CEA. What is the role, then, of decision analysis techniques in transfusion safety decisions? Are they helpful at all? If properly constructed and carefully reported, they can offer important information even if they are not the primary decision-making tool.

In situations lacking high emotional content, CEAs might be expected to provide immediately applicable guidance. For example, should leukocyte reduction or seronegativity be used to avoid transfusion-transmitted cytomegalovirus (CMV) infection? If the two techniques have equivalent capabilities of interdicting infectious units (85) but different associated costs, a simple comparative cost analysis may direct future decisions. If additional studies reveal some difference in their capabilities, then a CEA would reveal which approach provided the best use of resources. In the current climate where there is competition for fixed-fee contracts for marrow transplant patients and there is a strong focus on outcomes (including length of hospital stay as well as mortality), a well-constructed CEA could provide useful guidance for a CMV hemotherapy strategy.

In other situations, the conclusion of a CEA may not be congruent with the final course of action selected. FDA's decision to recommend HIV p24 antigen testing of donated blood was made with the knowledge of its very poor cost-effectiveness but after congressional input that clearly indicated that blood supply safety—and not cost—needed to be the driving motivation. Nevertheless, CEA can play a useful role even in these situations. To begin, their quantification of costs and benefits afford a clearer understanding of the implications of the final decision. Because a CEA must include a determination of costs, these data should highlight what resources will be consumed if the intervention is implemented. In a situation of finite resources, this information can be translated to changes in the outcomes of other aspects of medical care since the resources available for their use will necessarily be decreased. Alternatively, it might be hoped that those persons or institutions requiring the intervention's use would be in analogous position of power to ensure that the required resources would be supplied.

For the individual health care provider, the economic output from a CEA is probably only of academic interest. Physicians should continue to apply all the resources available to their disposal to provide the best care possible consonant with their patients' wishes. However, these same CEAs can help guide physicians' decisions to provide information and insight so that they can indeed provide the best care possible. The quantification of risks and the likelihood of various outcomes may be key information for a patient faced with a difficult decision without clear choices. Recognition that a particular intervention may be more cost-effective in certain situations may prompt the health care provider to investigate this aspect of the model's implications carefully and lead him or her to be more aggressive in applying the technique in situations where the benefits are greatest and the risks minimized.

V. FUTURE BLOOD SAFETY DECISIONS

Many CEAs have already been completed addressing key questions in blood safety. The successes of a variety of blood safety initiatives of the past decade—improved donor selection, expanded blood testing, availability of hemotherapy alternatives—have left little room for improvement to be accomplished by future interventions. Inevitably, as we progress on the "safety curve" to increasingly flatter portions, smaller and smaller returns can be expected for the investment of limited health care resources. Those having decision-making authority in these situations must be made aware of the implications of their choices.

At the same time, those charged with implementing these options or directly caring for patients will have to deal with tighter budgets and an increasing list of options. CEAs can be helpful in highlighting trade-offs that must occur or options that might be pursued in order to provide the greatest service to patients.

The tools of CEA cannot be expected always to identify the path that should be taken, but they help illuminate the way that has been chosen.

REFERENCES

1. McNeil BJ, Pauker SG, Sox HC, Jr, Tversky A. On the elicitation of preferences for alternative therapies. N Engl J Med 1982; 306:1259–1262.
2. Nease RF, Jr. Risk attitudes in gambles involving length of life: aspirations, variations and ruminations. Med Decis Making 1994; 14:201–203.
3. Llewellyn-Thomas HA. Patients' health-care decision making: a framework for descriptive and experimental investigations. Med Decis Making 1995; 15:101–105.
4. Sutherland HJ. Assessing patients' preferences (editorial). Med Decis Making 1995; 15;286–287.
5. Chapman GB, Elstein AS. Valuing the future: temporal discounting of health and money. Med Decis Making 1995; 15:373–386.
6. Beck JR, Pauker SG. The Markov process in medical prognosis. Med Decis Making 1983; 3:419–458.
7. Russell LB, Gold MR, Siegel JE, Daniels N, Weinstein MC, for the Panel on Cost-Effectiveness in Health and Medicine. The role of cost-effectiveness analysis in health and medicine. JAMA 1996; 276:1172–1177.
8. Weinstein MC. Clinical Decision Analysis. Philadelphia: Saunders, 1980.
9. Eisenberg JM. Clinical economics. A guide to the economic analysis of clinical practices. JAMA 1989; 262:2879–2886.
10. Weinstein MC, Stason WB. Foundation of cost-effectiveness analysis for health and medical practices. NEJM 1977; 276:716–721.

11. Weinstein MC, Siegel JE, Gold MR, Kamlet MS, Russell LB, for the Panel on Cost-Effectiveness in Health and Medicine. Recommendations of the Panel on Cost-Effectiveness in Health and Medicine. JAMA 1996; 276:1253–1258.

12. Siegel JE, Weinstein MC, Russell LB, Gold MR, for the Panel on Cost-Effectiveness in Health and Medicine. Recommendations for reporting cost-effectiveness analyses. JAMA 1996; 276:1339–1341.

13. AuBuchon JP. Lessons learned from decision analysis. Transfusion 1996; 36:755–760.

14. AuBuchon JP. The role of decision analysis in transfusion medicine. Vox Sang 1996; 71:1–5.

15. Busch MP, Korelitz JJ, Kleinman SH, Lee SR, AuBuchon JP, Schreiber GB. Declining value of alanine aminotransferase in screening of blood donors to prevent posttransfusion hepatitis B and C virus infection. The Retrovirus Epidemiology Donor Stuedy. Transfusion 1995; 35:903–910.

16. AuBuchon JP, Birkmeyer JD, Busch MP. Cost-effectiveness of expanded HIV test protocols for donated blood. Transfusion 1997; 37:45–51.

17. AuBuchon JP, Birkmeyer JD, Busch MP, Dodd RY, Lackritz EM, Petersen LR and HIV Blood Donor Study Group. Cost-effectiveness of anti-HBc testing to reduce HIV transmission risk (abstr). Transfusion 1996; 36:43S.

18. AuBuchon JP, Birkmeyer JD. Safety and cost-effectiveness of solvent-detergent treated plasma. In search of a zero-risk blood supply. JAMA 1994; 272:1210–1214.

19. Birkmeyer JD, AuBuchon JP, Littenberg B, O'Connor GT, Nease RF, Nugent WC, Goodnough LT. The cost-effectiveness of preoperative autologous donation in coronary bypass surgery. Ann Thoracic Surg 1994; 57:161–169.

20. Birkmeyer JD, Goodnough LT, AuBuchon JP, Noordsij PG, Littenberg B. The cost-effectiveness of preoperative autologous blood donation in total hip and knee replacement. Transfusion 1993; 33:544–551.

21. Etchason J, Petz L, Keeler E, Calhoun L, Kleinman S, Snider C, Fink A, Brook R. The cost effectiveness of preoperative autologous blood donations. N Engl J Med 1995; 332:719–724.

22. Lackritz EM, Satten GA, Aberle-Grasse J, Dodd RY, Raimondi VP, Janssen RS, Lewis WF, Notari EP, IV, Petersen LR. Estimated risk of HIV transmission by screened blood in the United States. N Engl J Med 1995; 333;1721–1725.

23. Schreiber GB, Busch MP, Kleinman SH, Korelitz JJ. The risk of transfusion-transmitted viral infections. N Engl J Med 1996; 334:1685–1690.

24. Silvergleid AJ. All blood collected should be tested for infectious disease markers. In: Maffei LM, Thurer RL, eds. Autologous blood transfusion: current issues. Arlington, VA: American Association of Blood Banks, 1988:177–182.

25. AuBuchon JP, Dodd RY. Analysis of the relative safety of autologous blood units available for transfusion to homologous recipients. Transfusion 1988; 28:403–405.

26. AuBuchon JP, Gettinger A, Littenberg B. Determinants of physician ordering of preoperative autologous donations. Vox Sang 1994; 66:176–181.

27. Popovsky MA, Whitaker B, Arnold NL. Severe outcomes of allogeneic and autologous blood donation: frequency and characterization. Transfusion 1995; 35:734–737.

28. AuBuchon JP, Popovsky MA. The safety of preoperative autologous blood donation in the non-hospital setting. Transfusion 1991; 31:513–517.

29. Rankin JS, Hennein HA, Keith FM. The heart: I. Acquired diseases. In: Way LW, ed. Current Surgical Diagnosis and Therapy. 10th ed. Norwalk, CT: Appleton & Lange, 1994:358–382.

30. Kanter MH, van Maanen D, Anders KH, Castro F, Mya WW, Clark K. Preoperative autologous blood donations before elective hysterectomy. JAMA 1996; 276:798–801.

31. Brugnara C, Chambers LA, Malynn E, Goldberg MA, Kruskall MS. Red blood cell regeneration induced by subcutaneous recombinant erythropoietin: iron-deficient erythropoiesis in iron-replete subjects. Blood 1993; 81:956–964.

32. Canadian Orthopedic Perioperative Erythropoietin Study Group. Effectiveness of perioperative recombinant human erythropoietin in elective hip replacement. Lancet 1993; 341:1227–1232.

33. de Andrade JR, Jove M, Landon G, Frei D, Guilfoyle M, Young DC. Baseline hemoglobin as a predictor of risk of transfusion and response to epoetin alfa in othopedic surgery patients. Am J Orthop 1996; 25:533–542.

34. Vamvakas EC, Taswell HF. Blood transfusion as a predictor of long-term mortality (abstr). Transfusion 1993; 33:28S.

35. Vamvakas EC, Moore SB. Blood transfusion and postoperative septic complications. Transfusion 1994; 34:714–727.

36. Vamvakas E, Moore SB. Perioperative blood transfusion and colorectal cancer recurrence: a qualitative statistical overview and meta-analysis. Transfusion 1993; 33:754–765.

37. Vamvakas EC, Moore SB. Confounding and the effect of allogeneic transfusion on survival (letter). Vox Sang 1995; 69:142–143.

38. Healy HC, Frankforter SA, Graves BK, Reddy RL, Beck JR. Preoperative autologous blood donation in total-hip arthroplasty. A cost-effectiveness analysis. Arch Pathol Lab Med 1994; 118:465–470.

39. Canadian Coordinating Office for Health Technology Assessment. Leukoreduction: the techniques used, their effectiveness and costs. Ottawa: Canadian Coordinating Office for Health Technology Assessment (CCOHTA), 1998.

40. Jensen LS, Kissmeyer-Nielsen P, Wolff B, Qvist N. Randomised comparison of leucocyte-depleted versus buffy-coat-poor blood transfusion and complications after colorectal surgery. Lancet 1996; 348:841–845.

41. Forbes JM, Anderson MD, Anderson GF, Breecker GC, Rossi EC, Moss GS. Blood transfusion costs: a multicenter study. Transfusion 1991; 31:318–323.

42. Jensen LS, Grunnet N, Hanberg-Sorensen F, Jorgensen J. Cost-effectiveness of blood transfusion and white cell reduction in elective colorectal surgery. Transfusion 1995; 35:719–722.

43. Cohen JA, Brecher ME. Preoperative autologous blood donation: benefit or detriment? A mathematical analysis. Transfusion 1995; 35:640–644.

44. Goodnough LT, Monk TG, Brecher ME. Autologous blood procurement in the surgical setting: Lessons learned in the last 10 years. Vox Sang 1996; 71:133–141.

45. Monk TG, Goodnough LT, Birkmeyer JD, Brecher ME, Catalona WJ. Acute normovolemic hemodlution is a cost-effective alternative to preoperative autologous donation in patients undergoing radical retropubic prostatectomy. Transfusion 1995; 35:559–565.

46. AuBuchon JP. Blood transfusion options: improving outcomes and reducing costs. Arch Pathol Lab Med 1997; 121:40–47.

47. Brecher ME, Goodnough LT, Monk T. The value of oxygen-carrying solutions in the operative setting, as determined by mathematical modeling. Transfusion 1999; 39:396–402.

48. Solomon MD, Rutledge ML, Kane LE, Yawn DH. Cost comparison of intraoperative autologous versus homologous transfusion. Transfusion 1988; 28:379–382.

49. Popovsky MA, Devine PA, Taswell HF. Intraoperative autologous transfusion. Mayo Clin Proc 1985; 60:125–134.

50. AuBuchon JP. Autologous transfusion and directed donations: current controversies and future directions. Transf Med Rev 1989; 3:290–306.

51. Solomon MD, Rutledge MI, Kane LE, Yawn DH. Cost comparison of intraoperative autologous versus homologous transfusion. Transfusion 1988; 28:379–382.

52. Rumisek JD, Weddle RL. Autotransfusion in penetrating abdominal trauma. In: Hauer JM, Thurer RL, Dawson RB, eds. Autotransfusion. New York: Elsevier/North Holland, 1981:105–113.

53. Karczewski DM, Lema MJ, Glaves D. The efficiency of an autotransfusion system for tumor cell removal from blood salvaged during cancer surgery. Anesth Analg 1994; 78:1131–1135.

54. Umlas J, Foster RR, Dalal SA, O'Leary SM, Garcia L, Kruskall MS. Red cell loss following orthopedic surgery: the case against postoperative blood salvage. Transfusion 1994; 34:402–406.

55. Umlas J, Sager A. Cost-effectiveness of recovering blood post-arthroplasty (abstr.) Transfusion 1994; 34:27S.

56. Jackson BR, Umlas J, AuBuchon JP. The cost-effectiveness of postoperative red cell recovery for preventing transfusion-associated viral transmission following orthopedic surgery. Transfusion (in press).

57. Infectious disease testing for blood transfusions. NIH Consensus Development Panel on Infectious Disease Testing for Blood Transfusions. JAMA 1995; 274:1374–1379.

58. AuBuchon JP, Birkmeyer JD, Busch MP. Blood Safety: Challenges and opportunities. Ann Int Med 1997; 127:904–909.

59. Leitman SF, Klein HG, Melpolder JJ, Read EJ, Estaban JI, Leonard EM, Harvath L, Shih W-K, Nealon R, Foy R, Darr F, Alter HJ. Clinical implications of positive tests for antibodies to human immunodeficiency virus type 1 in asymptomatic blood donors. N Engl J Med 1989; 321:917–924.

60. Korelitz JJ, Busch MP, Williams AE for the Retrovirus Epidemiology Donor Study. Antigen testing for human immunodeficiency virus (HIV) and the magnet effect: Will the benefit of a new HIV test be offset by the numbers of higher-risk, test-seeking donors attracted to blood centers. Transfusion 1996; 36:203–208.

61. Zuck TF, Eyster ME. Blood safety decisions, 1982-1986: perceptions and misconceptions. Transfusion 1986; 36:928–931.

62. Pereira A. Cost-effectiveness of transfusing virus-inactivated plasma instead of standard plasma. Transfusion 1999; 39:479–487.

63. Jackson BR, AuBuchon JP, Birkmeyer JD. Update of cost-effectiveness analysis for solvent-detergent treated plasma. JAMA 1999; 282:329.

64. AuBuchon JP, Pickard C, Herschel L, O'Connor JL, Williams S. Preparation of methylene blue (MB) plasma with reduction in residual MB content by adsorption filtration (abstr). Transfusion 1996; 36:65S.

65. Lynch TJ, Weinstein MJ, Tankersley DL, Fratantoni JC, Finalyson JS. Considerations of pool size in the manufacture of plasma derivatives. Transfusion 1996; 36:770–775.

66. Busch M, Glynn S, Schreiber G for the Retrovirus Epidemiology Donor Study. Increased risk of viral transmission due to exclusion of older donors because of Creutzfeld-Jakob disease (CJD) (abstr). Transfusion 1996; 36:59S.

67. Sazama K. Reports of 355 transfusion-associated deaths: 1976 through 1985. Transfusion 1990; 30:583–590.

68. Honig CL, Bove JR. Transfusion-associated fatalities: review of Bureau of Biologics reports. Transfusion 1980; 20:653–661.

69. Linden JV, Paul B, Dressler KP. A report of 104 transfusion errors in New York State. Transfusion 1992; 32:601–606.

70. Renner SW, Howanitz PJ, Bachner P. Wristband identification error reporting in 712 hospitals. A College of American Pathologists' Q-Probes study of quality issues in transfusion practice. Arch Pathol Lab Med 1993; 117:571–577.

71. Reason J. Human Error. Cambridge: Cambridge University Press, 1990.

72. Voelker R. "Treat systems, not errors," experts say. JAMA 1996; 276:1537–1538.

73. Baele PL, De Bruyere M, Deneys V, Dupont E, Flament J, Lambermont M, D, Steensens L, van Camp B, Waterloos H. Bedside transfusion errors. A prospective study by the Belgium SAnGUIS group. Vox Sang 1994; 66:117–121.

74. Wenz B, Burns ER. Improvement in transfusion safety using a new blood unit and patient identification system as part of safe transfusion practice. Transfusion 1991; 31:401–403.

75. AuBuchon JP, Littenberg B. A cost-effectiveness analysis of using a mechanical barrier system to reduce the risk of mistransfusion. Transfusion 1996; 36:222–226.

76. Wagner SJ, Friedman LI, Dodd RY. Transfusion-associated bacterial sepsis. Clin Microbiol Rev 1994; 7:290–302.

77. Brecher ME, Hogan JJ, Boothe E, Kerr A, McClannan L, Jacobs MR, Yomtovian R, Chongokolwatana V, Tegtmeier G, Henderson S, Pineda A, Halling V, Kemper M, Kuramato K, Holland PV, Longiaru. Platelet bacterial contamination and the use of a chemiluminescence-linked universal bacterial ribosomal RNA gene probe. Transfusion 1994; 34:750–755.

78. Vamvakas EC, Taswell HF. Long-term survival after blood transfusion. Transfusion 1994; 34:471–477.

79. Fowler FJ, Jr, Cleary PD, Massagli MP, Weissman J, Epstein A. The role of reluctance to give up life in the measurement of the values of health states. Med Decis Making 1995; 15:195–200.

80. Schneiderman LJ, Kaplan RM. Fear of dying and HIV infection vs hepatitis B infection. Am J Publ Health 1992; 82:584–586.

81. Morgan MG. Risk analysis and management. Sci Am 1993; 269:32–35, 38–41.

82. Hadorn DC. Setting health care priorities in Oregon. Cost-effectiveness meets the rule of rescue. JAMA 1991; 265:2218–2225.

83. Hux JE, Leviton CM, Naylor CD. Prescribing propensity: influence of life-expectancy gains and drug costs. J Gen Intern Med 1994; 9:195–201.

84. Rose G. Sick individuals and sick populations. Int J Epidemiol 1985; 14:32–38.

85. Bowden RA, Slichter SJ, Sayers M, Weisdorf D, Cays M, Schoch G, Banaji M, Haake R, Welk K, Fisher L, McCullough J, Miller W. A comparison of filtered leukocyte-reduced and cytomegalovirus (CMV) seronegative blood products for the prevention of transfusion-associated CMV infection after marrow transplant. Blood 1995; 86:3599–3603.

24
Red Blood Cell Substitutes

Zbigniew M. Szczepiorkowski and Christopher P. Stowell
Harvard Medical School and Massachusetts General Hospital, Boston, Massachusetts

I. INTRODUCTION

A. Background

During the last 15 years there has been a rapid development in the number of materials with the ability to transport and deliver oxygen and other gases. While many of them were conceived as substitutes for red blood cells (RBC),* it is becoming apparent that their unique characteristics suit them for new applications beyond the scope of RBC. In this chapter, the different approaches that are being taken to develop non-RBC oxygen carriers will be discussed and the status of the clinical trials in progress as of June 2000 will be reviewed.

B. Desirable Characteristics for a RBC Substitute

The major factors driving the development of RBC substitutes have been concerns about the adequacy of the blood supply and the infectious complications of transfusion. Although the elimination of infectious risks has been a primary goal,

---

*The terms "blood substitute" and "RBC substitute" are used commonly, including in medical literature databases. The term "RBC substitute" will be used in this chapter recognizing that these oxygen-carrying materials are not intended to replicate all of the functions of the many elements of whole blood and that they have characteristics that suit them for clinical roles beyond those possible for the erythrocyte.

a number of other favorable characteristics are highly desirable in a RBC substitute, some of which are listed in Table 1.

A fundamental property for any RBC substitute, of course, is the ability to carry physiologically useful amounts of oxygen and carbon dioxide in a volume small enough to minimize the occurrence of volume overload or excessive dilution of other elements of the blood. Not only must the substitute carry an adequate amount of oxygen, it must also be able to load and unload gases under the appropriate conditions. Since the capacity and oxygen-loading characteristics of some RBC substitutes can be manipulated, the possibility of designing substitutes for specific applications exists. For example, a high-affinity substitute may be desirable to enhance oxygen loading in patients with impaired pulmonary function, whereas a lower-affinity substitute may improve oxygen delivery to tissue in shock.

In addition, the substitute must have a useful intravascular half-life. Most of the RBC substitutes in development have half-lives in the range of 12–24 hours as compared to 40–60 days for an erythrocyte. These half-lives may suffice in the setting of acute bleeding but would obviously be inadequate for the support of patients with chronic anemia.

At least initially, it was implicitly assumed that the oncotic pressure and osmolarity of a blood substitute should be as close as possible to that of blood in order to preserve biocompatibility and that low viscosity would be an asset by reducing resistance to flow. More recent work with various oxygen carriers indicates that the effect of these properties is more complex than was initially appreciated. For example, the vascular endothelium is sensitive to changes in

Table 1 Desirable Characteristics for RBC Substitutes

Characteristics	Requirement
Efficacy	High capacity for O_2 and CO_2
	Physiological gas exchange
	Suitable intravascular half-life
	Approximately isoncotic and isosmotic
	Favorable rheological properties
Safety	Minimal infectious risk
	Minimal immunogenicity (e.g., neoantigens, xenoantigens)
	Lack of toxicity
	Limited extraneous physiological effects
Logistics	Stability under a wide range of conditions
	Immediate availability
	Abundance
	Low cost

shear stress, a property of a flowing fluid directly proportional to viscosity. Decreased viscosity, uncompensated for by increased flow velocity, lowers the shear stress, in response to which the vascular endothelium decreases the output of various endothelium-derived relaxing factors such as endothelin and prostacyclin (1,2). The resulting vasoconstriction paradoxically limits blood flow, despite the "improved" hemodynamic characteristics of the RBC substitute.

Since a major driving force for the development of RBC substitutes has been safety, a material intended for this purpose must essentially eliminate the transmission of enveloped and nonenveloped viruses and pose a risk of bacterial contamination no greater than the intravenous solutions in current use. It is presumed that such materials would pose less of a risk, if one exists, of parenteral transmission of prion-associated diseases.

Ideally, the substitute would be immunologically inert. Hypersensitivity reactions or the development of a humoral or cellular response to the substitute would obviously limit its utility. These concerns are particularly pertinent to substitutes based on animal hemoglobin or chemically modified human hemoglobins that may bear neoantigens. Preferably, the substitute would lack alloantigens altogether.

As with any therapeutic agent, the ideal RBC substitute must also have minimal toxicity and lack biological effects other than those desired. Certainly the untoward effects of the substitute must pose no greater hazard than the transfusion of conventional blood components.

There are several practical considerations that have influenced the development of RBC substitutes as well. The RBC substitute must be stable under reasonable storage conditions, preferably at room temperature, and for prolonged periods of time. Immediate availability without prolonged or complicated preparation is also an asset, particularly for use out of the hospital, such as at a trauma site or on the battlefield. If it is to be clinically useful, the substitute must also be available in large quantities and at a reasonable cost.

The potential advantages of RBC substitutes lie in the areas of safety and convenience. The developmental goal has been to maximize these features while retaining as much of the functional efficacy of the erythrocyte as possible.

C. The Major Approaches

Three quite different approaches have been taken in the development of RBC substitutes. One line of investigation has pursued the use of the perfluorocarbons, compounds in which gases, including oxygen, are highly soluble. The second major approach has been to modify hemoglobin to minimize the problems created when this molecule is free in the plasma while taking advantage of its favorable and well-understood abilities to acquire and deliver oxygen. Progress towards clinical application has been much greater with these two approaches than with the development of liposome-encapsulated hemoglobin (LEH), or neo-hematocytes, the third avenue of investigation.

Some key features of these three types of RBC substitutes are represented in Figure 1 and compared to the native erythrocyte, whose characteristics are diagrammed in the panels to the right. As each of the main types of RBC substitutes is discussed, a comparison of its characteristics to those of the erythrocyte will be made by referring to this figure.

II. PERFLUOROCARBON RBC SUBSTITUTES

A. Physiology and Background

The perfluorocarbons were first developed as part of the Manhattan Project in the course of a search for an inert fluid in which highly reactive uranium species could be handled. These cyclic or linear molecules consist of a carbon backbone extensively substituted with fluorine atoms (Fig. 1). They are chemically and biologically inert and do not support the growth of any known microorganism. The characteristic that initially attracted interest to the perfluorocarbons is their high solubility for gases. Volume for volume, perfluorocarbons can dissolve at least 20 times more gas than can water. The oxygen content of perfluorocarbon emulsion is linearly proportional to the oxygen tension in its environment, as shown by the solid line in Figure 1. Oxygen "loading" and "unloading" is driven by mass action, diffusing from areas of high oxygen tension to areas where it is low, e.g, in vivo from the lungs to the perfluorocarbon and from the per-fluorocarbon to the tissue. The dashed line in Figure 1 represents the oxygen saturation curve for blood and demonstrates the important point that, at physio-logical oxygen tensions, blood is much more readily saturated with oxygen and has a greater oxygen-carrying capacity. The oxygen-carrying capacity of per-fluorocarbons only approaches that of blood at very high oxygen tensions, levels reached in vivo only when supplemental oxygen is provided. Nonetheless, the oxygen capacity of the perfluorocarbons is substantially greater than that of plasma or other intravenous replacement fluids.

The perfluorocarbons are not miscible in water, but they can be induced to form stable emulsions with the addition of surfactants and stabilizers, such as lecithin. Following intravenous injection into mammals, the droplets of the emulsion are removed from the circulation by the reticuloendothelial system (RES), usually in a matter of hours, as illustrated in Figure 1, in which the intravascular clearance of a perfluorocarbon emulsion (solid line) is compared to that of the erythrocyte (dotted line). The perfluorocarbons are eventually exhaled via the lungs, but they may remain in the RES for prolonged periods before excretion. Some of the earlier perfluorocarbons studied remained in the RES for months; the newer formulations are excreted within several days.

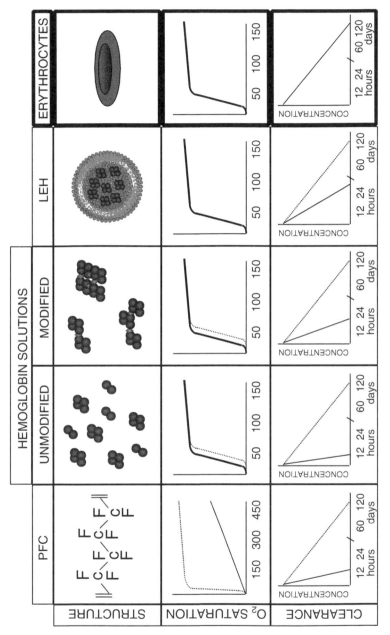

Figure 1 Comparison of several characteristics of three types of RBC substitutes to one another and to erythrocytes: structure, oxygen binding, and intravascular clearance. The dotted lines in the panels for the RBC substitutes represent the behavior of the erythrocyte and are shown for comparison. The RBC substitutes are perfluorocarbon (PFC), unmodified and modified (polymerized/cross-linked) hemoglobin, and liposome-encapsulated hemoglobin (LEH).

Some of the potential advantages and disadvantages of perfluorocarbons as RBC substitutes are listed in Table 2. Because of their synthetic source, the composition of these materials can be strictly controlled and could be modified to meet specific needs. Most of the perfluorocarbon emulsions have extended shelf lives, and production of huge quantities at relatively low cost is possible. Infectious and immunological complications are virtually nonexistent, although the same might not be true for other components of the preparation such as the surfactant or the stabilizer, particularly if they are of biological origin. The viscosity of perfluorocarbon emulsions is low, which might favor its use of oxygenating low flow or obstructed areas not accessible to erythrocytes.

One of the drawbacks of using perfluorocarbons in biological systems is the requirement for preparing them as emulsions. While this technology is reasonably well established, reproducibly obtaining emulsions with uniform characteristics and guaranteed stability is a challenge. The sizes of the emulsion particles may be quite heterogeneous with unknown biological effects. Clearance of the different perfluorocarbons is highly variable and the consequences of their extended half-lives in the RES are unknown. The need for elevated oxygen tensions in order to load these preparations with useful amounts of oxygen also imposes limitations.

The first perfluorocarbon to reach clinical trials was Fluosol-DA, a mixture of two perfluorocarbons, a surfactant, and an emulsion stabilizer that required storage as a frozen emulsion (Table 3). In early clinical trials, Fluosol-DA proved to be relatively well tolerated. Although 5–10% of people receiving this perfluorocarbon emulsion experienced rash and blood pressure lability, these effects were eventually attributed to the emulsion stabilizer. Hepatosplenomegaly was also observed accompanied by mild, transient changes in liver function tests, presumably reflecting the uptake of perfluorocarbons by the RES. Mild elevations in serum creatinine and blood urea nitrogen (BUN) were noted in some patients as well. Phase II clinical trials were conducted administering Fluosol-DA to

Table 2   Potential Advantages and Disadvantages of Perfluorocarbon RBC Substitutes

Advantages	Disadvantages
1. Control of composition	1. Requirement for emulsification/stabilization
2. Possibility of specific modification	2. Heterogeneous particle size
3. Large-scale production	3. Variable (long) RES clearance
4. Low production costs	4. High FiO_2 required
5. Prolonged shelf life	5. Low O_2 capacity at physiological PO_2
6. Minimal infectious risk	6. Rapid plasma clearance
7. Minimal immunogenicity	
8. Low viscosity (?)	

Table 3 Perfluorocarbon RBC Substitutes Studied[a]

Product (manufacturer)	Perfluorocarbon	Trial level	Application
Fluosol-DA (Green Cross/ Alpha)	Perfluorodecalin Perfluoropropylamine	Phase II (discontinued)	Acute blood loss
		Approved (withdrawn)	PTCA
Oxygent (Alliance)	Perflubron	Phase II	CABG—ANH, surgery—acute blood loss
		Phase III	Surgery—ANH
Imagent GI (Alliance)	Perflubron	Approved	GI imaging
Liquivent (Alliance)	Perflubron (neat)	Phase Ib/II Phase II/III (discontinued)	Liquid ventilation— IRDS Liquid ventilation— pedi and adult ARDS
Oxyfluor (HemaGen/PFC)	Perfluorodichlorooctane	Phase II (discontinued)	Surgery, Neuro-protectant/bypass

[a]Information current to 6/00.
PCTA, Percutaneous, transluminal coronary angioplasty; CABG, coronary artery bypass graft; ANH, acute normovolemic hemodilution; GI, gastrointestinal; IRDS, infant respiratory distress syndrome; ARDS, adult respiratory distress syndrome.

patients with acute, life-threatening bleeding; however, other than a temporary improvement in hemodynamics, the performance of the preparation was disappointing (3). The poor results were due, at least in part, to the low dose of perfluorocarbon administered, the low oxygen capacity of this particular preparation, and the dire condition of the patients receiving it. After this experience, interest in Fluosol-DA as a RBC substitute waned rapidly and clinical trials for this application ceased. Fluosol-DA was eventually licensed by the U.S. Food and Drug Administration (FDA) for oxygenation of the distal vascular bed in percutaneous transluminal coronary angioplasty (PTCA) (4), but it was removed from the market because of poor sales and improvements in angioplasty catheter design. However, the shortcomings of Fluosol-DA were instrumental in highlighting where improvements were necessary and guiding the development of new perfluorocarbons.

B. The Next Generation of Perfluorocarbon Oxygen Carriers

1. Perflubron

Two manufacturers have conducted clinical trials of new perfluorocarbon oxygen carriers (see Table 3). Alliance Pharmaceutical Corporation has developed an emulsion of perfluorooctyl bromide (Perflubron) stabilized with lecithin that has a much higher oxygen capacity than earlier perfluorocarbon preparations and can be stored as an emulsion at room temperature (5). Physiological studies of Perflubron emulsion in animal model systems showed that it was capable of delivering oxygen to several target tissues with improvement in their metabolic condition and function (6–8). In human safety studies, it was well tolerated with the principal side effects being a mild thrombocytopenia (nadir in the range of $100–150 \times 10^9/L$) that resolves within a few days and a transient, flu-like syndrome, which begins within a few hours of the infusion. The latter has been attributed to the release of cytokines and arachidonic acid metabolites from the cells of the RES as the perfluorocarbon is phagocytosed (9).

One formulation of perflubron, named Oxygent, is being developed as a means of facilitating oxygen delivery during acute normovolemic hemodilution (ANH). Instead of replacing the withdrawn blood with crystalloid solution, an oxygen carrier such as Oxygent is used, thereby minimizing any potential problems created by the iatrogenically produced anemia. Oxygent has been tested as a replacement fluid in ANH in general surgery patients and in patients undergoing cardiopulmonary bypass in phase II and III clinical trials.

Although the use of Oxygent as an "extender" in ANH is being pursued vigorously, other applications have been studied and illustrate the potential versatility of the perfluorocarbons. The ability of the perfluorocarbon emulsions to deliver oxygen is being exploited to sensitize solid tumors to radiation. Oxygen potentiates the effects of radiation and chemotherapy on malignant cells, and its absence in hypoperfused and hypoxic areas of a tumor limits the effectiveness of these therapies (10). In animal studies (11) and phase II studies in patients with solid tumors, Oxygent augmented the effect of radiation therapy, presumably by improving oxygen delivery to the tumor.

Perflubron, unlike most of the perflurocarbons, contains a bromine substituent that renders it radiopaque. A Perflubron preparation named Imagent has been studied as a contrast medium for several imaging applications and was approved (as Imagent GI) for use in gastrointestinal radiography, although it is not being actively promoted. Imagent US is a Perflubron formulation that has reached phase II trials for use as an ultrasound contrast medium (5) for the detection of tumors and metastases as well as for cardiac applications. However, Alliance is presently not pursuing these imaging applications.

One of the most novel applications of the perfluorocarbons is in partial liquid ventilation. In this application, perfluorocarbon is instilled, neat, into a patient's lungs, partially filling the alveoli. The instilled perfluorocarbon serves as a source of readily available oxygen and as a surfactant as well, helping to expand the alveoli and improve gas diffusion. In preliminary studies, Perflubron (Liquivent) was instilled into the lungs of infants with severe infant respiratory distress syndrome (12). Based on the improvement in the clinical condition of many of the patients, phase II and subsequently phase III studies were conducted in infants, children, and adults with respiratory distress syndrome. However, patient accrual in the phase III trials was discontinued because of unexpectedly high mortality rates in the treatment arm.

2. Oxyfluor

HemaGen/PFC formulated a perfluorocarbon emulsion named Oxyfluor consisting of perfluorodichlorooctane stabilized with lecithin and safflower oil, which may be stored for a year at room temperature. Animal studies showed that Oxyfluor was capable of delivering oxygen in models of shock resuscitation and surgical bleeding and was well tolerated. Lung hyperinflation was noted in the treated animals, as has been observed with many of the perflurocarbons, although it has not emerged as a significant problem in humans. Safety studies in humans have demonstrated that thrombocytopenia and a flu-like syndrome occur with this perfluorocarbon preparation, as was the case with Oxygent.

Although Oxyfluor underwent phase II trials in surgery patients, HemaGen/PFC chose to exploit the ability of perfluorocarbons to dissolve gases by using Oxyfluor to remove the microbubbles that form in the circulation of patients undergoing cardiopulmonary bypass. These microbubbles are thought to embolize to the microvasculature of the brain, where they produce the neurological and neuropsychiatric changes seen in some patients following bypass (13,14). In animal cardiopulmonary bypass model systems, Oxyfluor was effective in scavenging microbubbles and reducing the formation of these microemboli (15). HemaGen/PFC ceased operations for financial reasons. Hence, Oxyfluor is no longer in development.

III. HEMOGLOBIN-BASED RBC SUBSTITUTES

A. Physiology and Background

The concept of using cell-free hemoglobin solutions to replace RBC has an obvious rationale and was first demonstrated to be feasible by Mulder, who in 1934 showed that cats could survive and function normally for a brief period of time after their blood was replaced with stroma-free hemoglobin. Some of the advantages of using hemoglobin as an RBC substitute are listed in Table 4, among them good oxygen-carrying capacity and the ability to function at physiological oxygen levels. The potential advantages and disadvantages of low viscosity were discussed previously. The oncotic pressure of hemoglobin solutions is high, which may be particularly desirable in the treatment of acute bleeding where volume resuscitation is, if anything, more important than the restoration of RBC mass. The absence of erythrocyte antigens eliminates the need for compatibility testing, and the stability of hemoglobin solutions, even at room temperature, reduces many of the logistic problems entailed in red cell transfusion. In addition to the processes for isolating and purifying the source hemoglobin, the technology for inactivating and removing viruses from protein solutions has the potential of reducing the infectious risks to the levels associated with plasma derivatives such as albumin and intravenous immunoglobulin.

There are, however, a number of problems that can arise when cell-free hemoglobin is present in the plasma (Table 4). As a result, considerable effort has been expended to modify cell-free hemoglobin so as to minimize these potential problems. The extent to which these strategies have been successful is in the process of being evaluated in clinical trials.

The first of the problems with cell-free hemoglobin is that the tetramer rapidly dissociates to dimer in the circulation and is filtered out by the kidney, producing hemoglobinuria and having toxic effects on the proximal tubular cells. The other consequence, of course, is that the infused hemoglobin disappears within a matter of a few hours (see Fig. 1) via glomerular filtration and haptoglobin-mediated clearance.

The loss of hemoglobin from the plasma and its toxic effect on the kidneys can be avoided if dissociation to the dimer is reduced. One of the strategies that has been effective in minimizing dissociation is to crosslink the dimers forming stable tetramers or higher order oligomers. The reagents used to form stable, higher molecular weight hemoglobin species include bis(3,5-dibromosalicyl)

Table 4 Advantages and Disadvantages of Unmodified Hemoglobin

Advantages	Disadvantages
1. High capacity for O_2 and CO_2	1. Rapid clearance
2. Functions at physiological PO_2 level	2. Renal toxicity
3. Low viscosity (?)	3. Vasoactivity
4. High oncotic pressure	4. Increased oxygen affinity
5. Absence of RBC antigens	5. Autoxidation
6. Prolonged shelf life	6. Immunogenicity (modified or nonhuman)
7. Purification/viral inactivation possible	7. Potentiation of sepsis (?)

fumarate, glutaraldehyde, and open-chain raffinose. Another approach to minimize rapid clearance of hemoglobin is to increase its molecular weight by attaching oligomers of polyoxyethylene (POE) or polyethylene glycol (PEG).

A second potential problem with hemoglobin in solution is that it is vasoactive, a property that manifests as a hypertensive effect in both animals and humans. Hemoglobin binds nitric oxide (NO), thereby releasing the constitutive relaxing effect it exerts on the smooth muscle in the vascular wall and producing vasoconstriction (16–18). In general, the hemoglobin-based RBC substitutes with the smallest proportions of dimers and tetramers also exhibit the least vasoactivity. Other mechanisms undoubtedly also influence the vasoactivity of hemoglobin-based RBC substitutes, among them the autoregulatory response to oxygen delivery (19,20) and the effect of viscosity and shear stress on endothelin-regulated vascular tone (21).

A third potential problem with hemoglobin in solution is the tendency for its oxygen affinity to increase, primarily in response to the loss of 2,3-diphosphoglycerate (2,3-DPG). As oxygen affinity increases and the oxyhemoglobin dissociation curve shifts to the left, as shown in Figure 1, a greater degree of tissue hypoxia is required to induce oxygen unloading. Although there may be situations in which a high-affinity oxygen carrier would be useful, the general assumption has been that hemoglobin-based oxygen carriers should replicate the characteristics of intraerythrocytic hemoglobin. Hence, restoration of the native oxyhemoglobin dissociation curve has been achieved by several methods, among them chemical modification. For example, pyridoxylation and di-aspirin crosslink formation also have the salutary effect of shifting the dissociation curve to the right. Another way to avoid the left shift is through the use of bovine hemoglobin, whose activity is modulated by chloride ion in a manner analogous to the allosteric response of human hemoglobin to 2,3-DPG. When released into a solution with a physiological chloride ion concentration, bovine hemoglobin does not exhibit the left shift seen with human hemoglobin. Other chemical modifications, as well as the use of site-directed mutagenesis to introduce chloride-binding sites into recombinant human hemoglobin, are possible strategies to minimize this change.

In solution, extraerythrocytic hemoglobin tends to autoxidize to methemoglobin and eventually to irreversibly altered metabolites (22). In the erythrocyte, methemoglobin reductase operates to reclaim methemoglobin, but it is obviously not available to cell-free hemoglobin. Autoxidation might result in the loss of functional hemoglobin and, even more concerning, lead to the formation of free radicals. Although methemoglobin does form during the storage of hemoglobin in solution, it represents only a small proportion (<10%) of most of the hemoglobin-based oxygen carriers that have been studied.

The possibility that animal hemoglobin, or even human hemoglobin that has been chemically altered, might stimulate an immune response must also be considered as a potential drawback to the use of these materials. The tendency to stimulate immune reactions must be established for each of the hemoglobin preparations, particularly if repeat use is anticipated. The coupling of PEG to hemoglobin may have the effect of reducing its antigenicity.

The concern that cell-free hemoglobin might exacerbate sepsis was raised by the results of the experiments in a murine model system where the infusion of autologous hemoglobin was associated with increased mortality following bacterial challenge (23). This potentiating effect might be related to the ability of hemoglobin to promote the growth of microorganisms or to impair RES clearance of bacteria. Cell-free hemoglobin may also have a direct effect on sepsis, since it has been shown to bind bacterial endotoxin and enhance its activity in vitro (24). In vivo, exogenous hemoglobin seems to potentiate the lethal effect of endotoxin administered to mice (25), although there is also a report of the failure of polymerized hemoglobin to increase mortality in another murine infection model system (26). Until the basis for these observations of in vitro and animal systems is better understood, potentiation of sepsis must be regarded as a possible hazard of infusion of hemoglobin-based RBC substitutes.

Some of the potential problems with cell-free hemoglobin, and the approaches that have been taken to minimize them, are summarized in Table 5.

B. Human Hemoglobin-Based RBC Substitutes

Seven hemoglobin-based RBC substitutes have reached various stages of development in the past decade, although only five are still being actively pursued. Four of these use human hemoglobin; two are based on bovine hemoglobin; and

Table 5 Approaches Used to Solve Problems Associated with Cell-Free Hemoglobin

Problem	Possible modifications
Rapid clearance	Polymerization
	Increase molecular weight
	Stabilization of tetramer (di-α recombinant)
Vasoactivity	Polymerization
	Increase molecular weight
High oxygen affinity	Bovine hemoglobin
	Chemical modification
	Site-directed mutagenesis
Autoxidation	Site-directed mutagenesis
	Chemically linked methemoglobin reductase
Immunogenicity	Attach polyethylene glycol

one takes advantage of recombinant technology to produce a modified human hemoglobin in vitro. Some of the features of each of these RBC substitutes, which are summarized in Table 6, are as follows:

Table 6 Modified Hemoglobin-Based RBC Substitutes[a]

Product (manufacturer)	Hemoglobin source	Trial level	Application
PolyHeme (Northfield)	Human	Phase III	Trauma, surgery
Hemolink (Hemosol)	Human	Phase II	Cardiopulmonary bypass—ANH, orthopedic surgery—acute blood loss, dialysis
		Phase III	Cardiac surgery
HemAssist (Baxter)	Human	Phase II	Septic shock, hemodialysis, hemorrhagic shock, cardiopulmonary bypass
		Phase III (all trials terminated)	Acute blood loss—surgery, trauma
PHP (Ajinomoto/Apex)	Human	Phase Ib/II	NO-induced shock
PEG Hemoglobin (Enzon)	Bovine	Phase Ib	Radiosensitizer solid tumors
Hemopure (Biopure)	Bovine	Preclinical	Erythropoiesis
		Phase II	Sickle cell crisis, oncology, surgery—orthopedic, urological, vascular, cardiac surgery
		Phase III	Surgery—cardiac, orthopedic
Oxyglobin (Biopure)	Bovine	Approved	Veterinary—anemia, acute blood loss
Optro (Somatogen Baxter)	Recombinant	Phase I	Erythropoiesis—ESRD, refractory anemia
		Phase II	ANH, Acute blood loss—surgery
		(all trials terminated)	

[a]Information current to 6/00.
ESRD; End-stage renal disease.

1. PolyHeme is a preparation of hemoglobin from outdated human blood that has been polymerized with glutaraldehyde in a process developed by Northfield Laboratories. In human safety studies, it was well tolerated with a notable lack of the pressor effect seen with many hemoglobin-based RBC substitutes (27). Northfield's goal for this product is to develop it as an RBC substitute i.e., as a true equivalent to units of donor blood that may be used in similar circumstances. PolyHeme has been used successfully to maintain adequate total hemoglobin levels (intraerythrocytic plus cell-free hemoglobin) in trauma patients, where it supplanted conventional RBC transfusions (28). Phase III testing in trauma patients and patients undergoing surgery is in progress.
2. Hemolink is the primary hemoglobin derivative being developed by Hemosol, Ltd. and is prepared by polymerizing human hemoglobin using open-chain raffinose. The products subsequently undergo extensive purification and viral-inactivation procedures and are stable for at least 60 days at room temperature. This material has undergone phase I and phase II testing and has initiated phase III trials for acute blood loss in surgery. The eventual goal is to develop this material as an extender in acute normovolemic hemodilution as well as in acute surgical or traumatic blood loss.
3. HemAssist, also known as di-aspirin crosslinked hemoglobin (DCLHb), is a product of Baxter Healthcare, which was produced by crosslinking the two α chains of human hemoglobin using the reagent bis(3,5-dibromosalicyl) fumarate. The cross-linked hemoglobin was purified, heat inactivated, and stored frozen. During early animal experiments, it was noted that this material had a modest hypertensive effect, which was originally attributed to binding of NO, although endothelin release from vascular endothelial cells (29) and adrenergic effects probably also contribute to the pressor activity. It was particularly noteworthy that the vasoactivity of HemAssist countered the effects of hemorrhagic shock in an animal model system (30). Baxter sought to exploit this property in phase II trials, where HemAssist was administered to patients with septic shock, a condition associated with elevated NO levels. Baxter also pursued the use of HemAssist in hemodialysis to reduce the frequency of hypotensive episodes and in patients with hemorrhagic, hypovolemic shock. However, phase III studies in surgery and trauma patients were terminated voluntarily in 1998 because of safety considerations (30a). Baxter, which had acquired Somatogen in 1998, also terminated trials with its recombinant hemoglobin-based RBC substitute, Optro. They have announced plans to develop a second-generation substitute based on recombinant hemoglobin.

4. Pyridoxylated hemoglobin polyoxyethylene (PHP) is produced by a Japanese company, Ajinomoto, but it is being developed in this country by Apex Bioscience. This material is prepared by pyridoxylating human hemoglobin to adjust the oxyhemoglobin dissociation curve back to the right, followed by coupling it to polyoxyethylene to reduce renal clearance. Phase I and II testing did not reveal any clinically important side effects but did demonstrate that this preparation is vasoactive. The clinical role for this substitute, which is being targeted by Apex, is septic shock, based on the supposition that PHP will bind excess NO and exert a pressor effect.

C. Bovine Hemoglobin-Based RBC Substitutes

Two RBC substitutes based on bovine hemoglobin are presently in clinical trials. Bovine hemoglobin, which shares 90% amino acid sequence homology with human hemoglobin, has a few advantages over its human counterpart, the first being its allosteric response to chloride ion and its independence from 2,3-DPG. Bovine hemoglobin is potentially available in large quantities and can be obtained from closed herds with well-documented and regulated health histories, unlike human source hemoglobin. The relative scarcity of human hemoglobin, which must be obtained from outdated donor RBC, may result in higher production costs for human hemoglobin–based substitutes compared to those based on bovine hemoglobin.

Another advantage of bovine hemoglobin is that there is obviously no risk of transmission of human pathogens. On the other hand, public concern about the possibility that viruses or prions might "cross over" from one species to another, even when they are distantly related, may slow acceptance. The attention attracted to the possible relationship between human new variant Jakob-Creutzfeldt disease and bovine spongiform encephalitis certainly attests to the public wariness about possible new pathogens.

Given the high degree of amino acid sequence homology between human and bovine hemoglobins, immunogenicity would be expected to be low. Whether or not it would exceed the immunogenicity of modified human hemoglobin will have to be determined during clinical trials.

1. PEG hemoglobin is prepared by Enzon by coupling multiple molecules of PEG to bovine hemoglobin followed by purification. The coupled PEG increases the molecular weight so that renal clearance is reduced as well as immunogenicity. PEG hemoglobin persists in the circulation for about 48 hours, which is longer than for most of the hemoglobin-based RBC substitutes, which are generally cleared within 24–36 hours. The oncotic pressure and viscosity of PEG hemoglobin are

higher than for many of the hemoglobin-based RBC substitutes. Its volume-expanding properties may make it particularly suitable for use in acute blood loss, ANH, and hypovolemic shock.

PEG hemoglobin was found to be safe and effective in an animal exchange transfusion model (31,32) but is being developed primarily as a sensitizing agent for radiotherapy. Phase I safety studies have been completed and a multicenter, dose-escalation, phase II trial is planned to evaluate PEG hemoglobin as a sensitizer in patients receiving palliative radiation therapy for solid tumors.

2. Hemopure is a bovine hemoglobin preparation polymerized with glutaraldehyde and purified to remove tetramers and dimers. Hemopure can be stored for two years at room temperature. The first formulation, which contained albumin and less highly polymerized hemoglobin, was found in early safety studies to produce gastrointestinal dysmotility and pain, presumably as a result of smooth muscle spasm induced by NO binding (15,16). These experiences led Biopure, the company developing this product, to more thoroughly eliminate the unpolymerized dimers and tetramers. The present formulation has a much lower incidence of gastrointestinal symptoms, primarily mild dysphagia, which is similar to several of the other hemoglobin-based RBC substitutes.

In phase I studies in volunteers and three different groups of patients (sickle cell crisis, orthopedic surgery, prostatectomy), the product was well tolerated (33). Improved exercise tolerance was noted in the sickle cell patients (34). Phase II trials, using Hemopure for perioperative transfusion in patients undergoing cardiac and vascular surgery, as well as in sickle cell crisis, have been carried out. Phase III trials in which patients undergoing noncardiac surgery may receive up to 10 units of Hemopure are in progress. A veterinary formulation, Oxyglobin, was licensed by FDA in 1997.

An interesting and novel property of Hemopure is its apparent ability to stimulate erythropoiesis. This property may be due in part to a hematinic effect, since elevations in serum iron, ferritin, and erythropoietin levels were seen after infusion of this hemoglobin preparation (35).

D. Recombinant Hemoglobin-Based RBC Substitutes

One company, Somatogen, harnessed recombinant technology to produce a modified human hemoglobin, which was expressed in *Escherichia coli* (36). The recombinant was designed to produce a single, di-α chain and conventional β chains that combine to form a crosslinked "tetramer." In addition, a mutation was introduced to correct the leftward shift that occurs when hemoglobin is removed from the influence of 2,3-DPG.

Some of the advantages and disadvantages of the recombinant hemoglobins are summarized in Table 7. While the opportunity for engineering recombinant hemoglobin and the potential of tailoring it for different applications are exciting, Somatogen has faced unprecedented challenges in scaling up the production and purification processes. They have, however, reported success in operating a 50,000 L production-level fermenter.

A series of phase I and II trials were completed with this recombinant hemoglobin preparation, Optro, which was generally well tolerated. Mild gastrointestinal symptoms were reported with this hemoglobin preparation as with others (37).

One of the more novel properties of this product is an erythropoietic effect, which is similar to that observed with Hemopure. In studies of human and murine bone marrow, Optro stimulated the proliferation of burst-forming units—erythroid (BFU-E), and was able to overcome zidovudine suppression (38). Since erythropoietin stimulates a later stage of RBC development, the colony-forming unit—erythroid (CFU-E), their effects should potentiate one another.

Early trials of Optro in end-stage renal disease, surgical blood loss, and ANH were conducted, and a larger-scale trial of the use of this product as an RBC substitute for intraoperative blood loss was mounted. All clinical trials with this product were halted when the parent company, Baxter, terminated their trials with HemAssist.

IV. LIPOSOME-ENCAPSULATED HEMOGLOBIN

The third approach that has been taken to develop RBC substitutes has been the use of liposomes composed chiefly of egg, vegetable, or synthetic phosphatidylcholine, to which other molecules, such as cholesterol and gangliosides, may be added (39). Liposomes may also be formed from other bipolar lipids, which have the virtue of being less expensive, but development of these nonphospholipid liposomes is not as advanced. Liposomes may have a variety of structures,

Table 7 Potential Advantages and Disadvantages of Recombinant Hemoglobins Compared to Modified Hemoglobins

Advantages	Disadvantages
1. Identity to native human hemoglobin	1. Production scale-up
2. Ability to "engineer"	2. Requirement for high level of purification
	3. Production expense

but for this application, a spherical structure delimited by a bilamellar lipid membrane, as shown in Figure 2, serves as a Trojan horse for transporting exogenously supplied hemoglobin through the circulation. Liposome-encapsulated hemoglobin (LEH) offers a number of potential advantages over perfluorocarbon- and hemoglobin-based RBC substitutes, which are listed in Table 8. Many of the problems created by the presence of cell-free hemoglobin in the plasma can be averted, among them the need for crosslinking or other means of protecting hemoglobin from clearance. The native oxyhemoglobin dissociation curve could easily be preserved by encapsulating 2,3-DPG along with hemoglobin in the liposome, and methemoglobin reductase could be added to limit autoxidation. Encapsulated hemoglobin would presumably have minimal vasoactive effects.

The primary disadvantage of this approach lies in the complexity of the technology for making liposomes and the difficulty of producing uniform preparations, which might also have the effect of driving up the cost of production. In addition, the delivery of large volumes of LEH raises the question of the safety and particularly the impact of loading the RES with exogenous phospholipids. In animal systems, several transient effects have been noted following

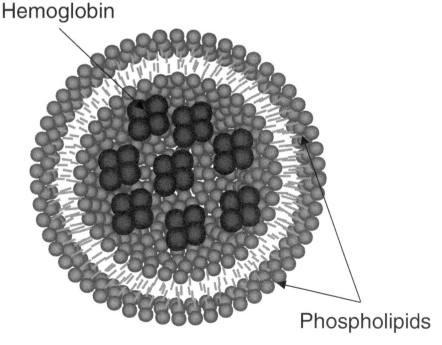

Hemoglobin

Phospholipids

Figure 2 Liposome-encapsulated hemoglobin (LEH).

Table 8 Potential Advantages and Disadvantages of
Liposome-Encapsulated Hemoglobin

Advantages	Disadvantages
1. Hemoglobin modification not required	1. Complex technology
2. Native oxygen affinity (2,3-DPG)	2. Cost (?)
3. Oxidation protection (methemoglobin reductase)	
4. No vasoactivity	

administration of LEH, including liver function test abnormalities, thrombocytopenia, leukocytosis, and complement activation (40). Nonetheless, a considerable body of experimental data from animal studies attests to the interest in
liposomes as a means of delivering not only oxygen, but a variety of other
therapeutic agents as well.

V. IMPACT OF RBC SUBSTITUTES ON TRANSFUSION
SERVICES AND BLOOD BANKS

The impact of the availability of RBC substitutes for clinical use will depend on
several factors, the foremost being which substitutes are licensed and for which
applications. Many of the RBC substitutes and oxygen carriers are being developed for applications where RBC have not had a role (e.g., liquid breathing) and
will clearly have little effect on conventional transfusion practice. The availability
of an RBC substitute licensed for use in the acute transfusion setting obviously
does have the potential of affecting RBC utilization. At least initially, use of these
products may be limited to patients with religious objections to conventional
blood transfusion, military applications, and trauma, particularly in the field, and
would have only a small impact on most transfusion services. However, the
potential for use in the emergency ward and the operating room is extensive and
could substantially decrease the volumes of RBC transfused. If RBC substitutes
with evenly modestly prolonged half-lives could be developed, they would make
even further inroads into the transfusion of RBCs, particularly in the perioperative
setting. While the transfusion service could manage the inventory of RBC
substitutes, it is also quite possible that the permissive storage conditions and
universal compatibility may suit them to be handled by the pharmacy. The
transfusion service would still be required to manage inventories of platelets,
fresh frozen plasma, and cryoprecipitate.

Several factors, particularly safety and cost, may mitigate this progression,
however. As the risk of infectious disease transmission by the conventional blood
supply decreases, the safety margin offered by RBC substitutes narrows and the

tolerance for their side effects diminishes. In addition, cost becomes an increasingly important factor as the safety advantage shrinks. For the products based on human hemoglobin, another possible limiting factor may be the availability of source material. The supply of outdated RBC originating from volunteer donors is presently only great enough to provide hemoglobin sufficient to supplant the RBC supply by about 5%. Other sources of human hemoglobin would have to be sought. The development of the technology to collect multiple units of RBCs at one time may enhance collections, but probably not enough to significantly augment the supply. One possible solution would be to permit collection of red cells for further manufacture from donors who might not otherwise meet the usual criteria or who might be paid. Blood donor centers, finding the demand for their RBC units decreasing, may begin to develop a second category of "source hemoglobin" donors, as well as emphasizing apheresis collections of platelets and plasma. Obtaining source material may not present the same difficulties for substitutes based on perfluorocarbons, animal hemoglobin, or recombinant hemoglobin, assuming, for the latter, that adequate production scale-up can be achieved.

RBC substitutes may also find a niche in the developing world where the majority of transfusions are for acute anemia. In countries where bloodborne pathogens are endemic, substitutes may represent a substantially safer alternative to donor RBC. In some situations, a substitute may be less expensive to supply than developing and maintaining the infrastructure required for a volunteer donor blood system.

VI. CONCLUSION

In addition to the approaches taken to developing clinically useful RBC substitutes described above, a number of other means of enhancing oxygen delivery, listed in Table 9, are being explored. Most of these are much farther from clinical

Table 9 Other Alternatives to Transfusion of Donor RBC in Development

In vitro RBC culture
Persistent oxygen bubbles[a]
Protein (hemoglobin) "bubbles"[b]
Intravenous allosteric modifiers
Hemoglobin from transgenic swine[c]

[a]From Ref. 41.
[b]From Ref. 42.
[c]From Ref. 43.

studies than the products already mentioned, and one promising approach, obtaining human hemoglobin from transgenic pigs, is not being actively pursued by its developer.

The animal and human studies of the materials originally conceived of as RBC substitutes have led to an appreciation for the unique and sometimes unexpected properties of these products and has suggested applications well beyond the role of donor red cells. Some of these potential applications are listed in Table 10.

The search for a RBC substitute is reaching a critical juncture; the final demonstration of safety and efficacy in broad-based phase III clinical trials. Demonstrating the efficacy of an RBC substitute is not entirely straightforward, since there is no uniform or generally accepted method for assessing the efficacy of a RBC transfusion (44). Replacement of allogeneic red cell transfusions and reduction of mortality are likely to be the criteria used to judge the effectiveness of the RBC substitute for transfusion applications.

The demonstration of safety also faces some challenges. The risks of the transfusion-transmitted infections, which gave such impetus to the development of RBC substitutes, have become extremely low. The aggregate risk for the transmission of human immunodeficiency virus (HIV), hepatitis B virus (HBV), hepatitis C virus (HCV), and human T-lymphotropic virus type I (HTLV-I) was estimated to be 1:34,000 units in 1996 (45) and may be even lower at present. Fatal transfusion events are even more rare (46). The RBC substitutes will have to exhibit exemplary side effect profiles to provide this degree of safety. They will, however, have the advantage of being less susceptible to the emergence of new infectious agents in the blood supply. This fear of unknown but dreaded

Table 10 Applications for "RBC Substitutes"

Acute blood loss—trauma, surgery
Acute blood loss—Jehovah's Witnesses, multiple red cell alloantibodies/rare blood type, endemic infection in donor blood supply
Extender in acute normovolemic hemodilution
Septic shock
Anti-ischemic–sickle cell crisis, PTCA, MI, cardiopulmonary bypass, vaso-occlusive stroke
Ex vivo organ/tissue preservation
Neuroprotectant—cardiopulmonary bypass
Sensitizer for chemo- and radiotherapy
Imaging
Partial liquid ventilation—IRDS, ARDS, near-drowning, smoke inhalation, infection
Erythropoiesis

outcomes, which tends to exaggerate the apparent risks of donor blood, may also add to the perceived relative safety of a substitute.

Despite some difficulties, it is likely that one or more of these oxygen-carrying materials will be licensed for clinical use within the next few years, either as an RBC substitute or for some other application. At that point, it will have taken a century from the time that the discovery of the ABO blood groups made red cell transfusion feasible to the time when a RBC substitute becomes a clinical reality.

REFERENCES

1. Intaglietta M, Johnson PC, Winslow RM. Microvascular and tissue oxygen distribution. Cardiovasc Res 1996; 32:632–643.
2. Karmaker N, Dhar P. Effect of steady shear stress on fluid filtration through the rabbit arterial wall in the presence of macromolecules. Clin Exp Pharmacol Physiol 1996; 23:299–304.
3. Gould SA, Rosen AL, Sehgal LR, Sehgal HL, Langdale LA, Krause LM, Rice CL, Chamberlin WH, Moss GS. Fluosol-DA as a red cell substitute in acute anemia. N Engl J Med 1986; 314:1653–1656.
4. Kerins DM. Role of perfluorocarbon Fluosol-DA in coronary angioplasty. Am J Med Sci 1994; 307:218–221.
5. Andre M, Nelson T, Mattrey R. Physical and acoustical properties of perfluorooctyl-bromide, an ultrasound contrast agent. Invest Radiol 1990 25:983–987.
6. Braun RD, Linsenmeier RA, Goldstick TK. New perfluorocarbon emulsion improves tissue oxygenation in cat retina. J Appl Physiol 1992; 72:1960–1968.
7. Hogan MC, Kurdak SS, Richardson RS, Wagner PD. Partial substitution of red blood cells with free hemoglobin solution does not improve maximal O_2 uptake of working in situ dog muscle. Adv Exp Med Biol 1994; 361:375–378.
8. Keipert PE, Faithfull NS, Roth DJ, Bradley JD, Batra S, Jochelson P, Flaim KE. Supporting tissue oxygenation during acute surgical bleeding using a perfluorochemical-based oxygen carrier. Adv Exp Med Biol 1996; 388:603–609.
9. Flaim SF, Hazard DR, Hogan J, Peters RM. Characterization and mechanism of side-effects of Imagent BP (highly concentrated fluorocarbon emulsion) in swine. Invest Radiol 1991; 26(suppl):S122–S128.
10. Suit H. Tumor oxygenation and radiosensitivity. In: Winslow RM, Vandegriff KD, Intaglietta M, eds. Blood Substitutes: Physiological Basis of Efficacy. Boston: Birkhäuser, 1995:187–199.
11. Rockwell S, Kelley M, Irvin CG, Hughes CS, Yabuki H, Porter E, Fischer JJ. Preclinical evaluation of Oxygent (TM) as an adjunct to radiotherapy. Biomater Artif Cells Immobil Biotechnol 1992; 20:883–893.
12. Leach CL, Greenspan JS, Rubenstein DS, Shaffer TH, Wolfson MR, Jackson JC, DeLemos R, Fuhrman BP. Partial liquid ventilation with perflubron in premature infants with severe respiratory distress syndrome. N Engl J Med 1996; 335:761–767.
13. Blauth CI, Arnold JV, Schulenberg WE, McCartney AC, Taylor KM. Cerebral

microembolism during cardiopulmonary bypass. Retinal microvascular studies in vivo with fluorescein angiography. J Thorac Cardiovasc Surg 1988; 95:668–676.

14. Blauth CI, Smith P, Newman S, Arnold J, Siddens F, Harrison MJ, Treasure T, Klinger L, Taylor KM. Retinal microembolism and neuropsychological deficit following clinical cardiopulmonary bypass: comparison of a membrane and a bubble oxygenator. A preliminary communication. Eur J Cardiothorac Surg 1989; 3:135–139.

15. Spiess BD, Braverman B, Woronowicz AW, Ivankovich AD. Protection from cerebral air emboli with perfluorocarbons in rabbits. Stroke 1986; 17:1146–1149.

16. Alayash AI, Cashon RE. Reactions of nitric oxide and hydrogen peroxide with hemoglobin-based blood substitutes. Ann NY Acad Sci 1994; 738:378–381.

17. Rioux F, Petitclerc E, Audet R, Drapeau G, Fielding RM, Marceau F. Recombinant human hemoglobin inhibits both constitutive and cytokine-induced nitric oxide-mediated relaxation of rabbit isolated aortic rings. J Cardiovasc Pharmacol 1994; 24:229–237.

18. Rioux F, Drapeau G, Marceau F. Recombinant human hemoglobin (rHb1.1) selectively inhibits vasorelaxation elicited by nitric oxide donors in rabbit isolated aortic rings. J Cardiovasc Pharmacol 1995; 25:587–594.

19. Gulati A, Sharma AC, Burhop KE. Effect of stroma-free hemoglobin and diaspirin cross-linked hemoglobin on the regional circulation and systemic hemodynamics. Life Sci 1994; 55;827–837.

20. Ulatowski JA, Nishikawa T, Matheson-Urbaitis B, Bucci E, Traystman RJ, Koehler RC. Regional blood flow alterations after bovine fumaryl ββ-crosslinked hemoglobin transfusion and nitric oxide synthase inhibition. Crit Care Med 1996; 24:558–565.

21. Garcia-Sepulcre ME, Carnicer F, Mauri M, Prieto A, Perez-Mateo M. Increased plasma endothelin in liver cirrhosis and response to plasma volume expansion (letter). Am J Gastroenterol 1996; 91:2452–2453.

22. Vandegriff KD. Stability and toxicity of hemoglobin solutions. In: Winslow RM, Vandegriff KD, Intaglietta M, eds. Blood Substitutes: Physiological Basis of Efficacy. Boston: Birkhäuser, 1995:105–131.

23. Griffiths E, Cortes A, Gilbert N, Stevenson P, MacDonald S, Pepper D. Hemoglobin-based blood substitutes and sepsis. Lancet 1995; 345:158–160.

24. Kaca W, Roth RI, Levin J. Hemoglobin, a newly recognized lipopolysaccharide (LPS)-binding protein that enhances LPS biological activity. J Biol Chem 1994; 269(40):25078–25084.

25. Su D, Roth RI, Yoshida M, Levin J. Hemoglobin increases mortality from bacterial endotoxin. Infect Immun 1997; 65:1258–1266.

26. Langermans JA, van Vuren-van der Hulst M, Bleeker WK. Safety evaluation of a polymerized hemoglobin solution in a murine infection model. J Lab Clin Med 1996; 127:428–434.

27. Gould SA, Sehgal LR, Sehgal HL, Moss GS. The development of hemoglobin solutions as red cell substitutes: hemoglobin solutions. Transfus Sci 1995; 16:517.

28. Gould SA, Moore EE, Hoyt DB, Burch JM, Haenel JB, Garcia J, DeWoskin R, Moss GS. The first randomized trial of human polymerized hemoglobin as a blood substitute in acute trauma and emergent surgery. J Am Coll Surg 1998; 187:113–120.

29. Gulati A, Sharma AC, Singh G. Role of endothelin in the cardiovascular effects

of diaspirin crosslinked and stroma reduced hemoglobin. Crit Care Med 1996; 24:137–147.

30. Schultz SC, Powell CC, Burris DG, Nguyen H, Jaffin J, Malcolm DS. The efficacy of diaspirin crosslinked hemoglobin solution resuscitation in a model of uncontrolled haemorrhage. J Trauma 1994; 37:408–412.

30a. Sloan EP, Koenigsberg M, Gens D, Cipolle M, Runge J, Mallory MNRG Jr. Diaspirin cross-linked hemoglobin (DCLHb) in the treatment of severe traumatic hemorrhagic shock. A randomized controlled efficacy trial. JAMA 1999; 282:1857–1864.

31. Conover CD, Malatesta P, Lejeune L, Chang CL, Shorr RG. The effects of hemodilution with polyethylene glycol bovine hemoglobin (PEG-Hb) in a conscious porcine model. J Investig Med 1996; 44:238–246.

32. Nho K, Linberg R, Johnson M, Gilbert C, Shorr R. PEG-hemoglobin: an efficient oxygen delivery system in the rat exchange transfusion and hypovolemic shock models. Art Cells, Blood Subs Immob Biotech 1996; 22:795–803.

33. Hughes GS, Francom SF, Antal EJ, Adams WJ, Locker PK, Yancey EP, Jacobs EE Jr. Effects of a novel hemoglobin-based oxygen carrier on percent oxygen saturation as determined with arterial blood gas analysis and pulse oximetry. Ann Emerg Med 1996; 27:164–169.

34. Hughes GS, Yancey EP, Albrecht R, Locker PK, Francom SF, Orringer EP, Antal EJ, Jacobs EE Jr. Hemoglobin-based oxygen carrier preserves submaximal exercise capacity in humans. Clin Pharmacol Ther 1995; 58:434–443.

35. Hughes GS, Francom SF, Antal EJ, Adams WJ, Locker PK, Yancey EP, Jacobs EE Jr. Hematologic effects of a novel hemoglobin-based oxygen carrier in normal male and female subjects. J Lab Clin Med 1995; 126:444–451.

36. Looker D, Abbott-Brown D, Cozart P, Durfee S, Hoffman S, Mathews A, Miller-Roehrich J, Shoemaker S, Trimble S, Fermi G, Komiyama N, Nagai K, Stetler GL. A human recombinant hemoglobin designed for use as a blood substitute. Nature 1992; 356:258–260.

37. Murray JA, Ledlow A, Launspach J, Evans D, Loveday M, Conklin JL. The effects of recombinant human hemoglobin on esophageal motor functions in humans. Gastroenterology 1995; 109:1241–1248.

38. Schick MR, Rosenthal GJ. A comparative evaluation of hemin and recombinant hemoglobin in the stimulation of erythropoietic precursors (abstr). Blood 1996; 88(suppl 1):104b.

39. Rudolph AS. Encapsulation of hemoglobin in liposomes. In: Winslow RM, Vandegriff KD, Intaglietta M, eds. Blood Substitutes: Physiological Basis of Efficacy. Boston: Birkhäuser, 1995:90–104.

40. Szebeni J, Wassef NM, Rudolph AS, Alving CR. Complement activation in human serum by liposome-encapsulated hemoglobin: the role of natural anti-phospholipid antibodies. Biochem Biophys Acta 1996; 1285:127–130.

41. Burkard ME, Van Liew HD. Oxygen transport to tissue by persistent bubbles: theory and simulations. J Appl Physiol 1994; 77(6):2874–2878.

42. Sakai H, Hamada K, Takeoka S, Nishide H, Tsuchida E. Physical properties of hemoglobin vesicles as red cell substitutes. Biotechnol Prog 1996; 12:119–125.

43. O'Donnell JK, Martin MJ, Logan JS, Kumar R. Production of human hemoglobin in transgenic swine: an approach to a blood substitute. Cancer Detect Prev 1993; 17:307–312.
44. Fratantoni J. Demonstration of efficacy of a therapeutic agent. In: Winslow RM, Vandegriff KD, Intaglietta M, eds. Blood Substitutes: Physiological Basis of Efficacy. Boston: Birkhäuser, 1995:20–24.
45. Schreiber GB, Busch MP, Kleinman SH, Korelitz JJ, for the Retrovirus Epidemiology Donor Study. The risk of transfusion-transmitted viral infections. NEJM 1996; 334:1685–1690.
46. Linden JV, Tourdalt MA, Scribner CL. Decrease in frequency of transfusion fatalities (letter). Transfusion 1997; 37:243–244.

25
Professional Standards and Voluntary Accreditation

Jay E. Menitove
Community Blood Center of Greater Kansas City, Kansas City, Missouri

Hillary V. Schaeffler
American Association of Blood Banks, Bethesda, Maryland

The American Association of Blood Banks (AABB) is the professional society for almost 8500 individuals involved in blood banking and transfusion medicine. It also represents more than 2000 institutional members, including community and Red Cross blood collection centers, hospital-based blood banks, and transfusion services that collect, process, distribute, and transfuse blood and blood components. Members are responsible for virtually all of the blood collected and more than 80% of the blood transfused in the United States. Throughout its 50-year history, the AABB's highest priority has been to maintain and enhance the safety of the nation's blood supply. To ensure the safety and adequacy of the nation's blood supply, the AABB sets voluntary standards and accredits institutions that implement the standards.

To ensure harmonization and consistency in all of AABB's standards and accreditation activities, in 1998 the Board of Directors created an umbrella committee, the Standards Program Committee. This committee, whose primary role is to oversee the development and/or revision of all AABB standards, comprises a chairperson, chairs of two subcommittees (Quality Management Subcommittee and Communications Subcommittee), and chairs of five specialty program units (Blood Banks/Transfusion Services, Hematopoietic Progenitor Cell Services, Immunohematology Reference Laboratories, Parentage Testing Laboratories, and Perioperative Collection and Transfusion Services). The Quality Management Subcommittee develops/revises quality standards and ensures that all Standards quality concepts are consistent, and the Communications Subcommittee disseminates guidance related to the standards. The program units are responsible for creating or revising the technical/scientific standards, which are specific for each standard-setting activity (Fig. 1).

In 1997, an Accreditation Program Committee was created to oversee all accreditation activities. This committee comprises a chairperson, chairs of two subcommittees (Quality Systems Subcommittee and Education Advisory Subcommittee), and chairs of seven specialty program units (Donor Centers, Transfusion Services, Hematopoietic Progenitor Cell Services, Immunohematology Reference Laboratories, Parentage Testing Laboratories, Perioperative Collection and Transfusion, and SBB Schools). The Quality Systems Subcommittee works with the Accreditation Program Committee to fully implement quality principles into AABB's Accreditation Program and to provide quality assessment tools for AABB's institutional members. The Education Advisory Subcommittee serves as the educational advisory group and coordinator for the Accreditation Program's educational and training activities. Each program unit oversees and coordinates the specific program unit activities, including coordinating and reviewing the program assessment tools and assessor guidance (Fig. 2).

I. STANDARDS PROGRAM

The AABB entered the voluntary standard-setting arena in 1958 when it published the first edition of *Standards for a Blood Transfusion Service*, the purpose of which was to improve the quality and safety of human blood transfusions. In 1990, the first edition of the *Standards for Parentage Testing Laboratories* was published. In 1991, the first hematopoietic progenitor cell standards were added to the *Standards for Blood Banks and Transfusion Services*, and 5 years later the first edition of the *Standards for Hematopoietic Progenitor Cells* was published. In 1999 the first edition of the *Standards for Immunohematology Reference Laboratories* was published, and currently the first edition of *Standards for Perioperative Collection and Transfusion* is being developed (Table 1).

Voluntary standards provide a benchmark for judging performance in a specific field. For many years professionals in the legal, accounting, and engineering fields have set minimum voluntary standards to determine a baseline for compliance. Although higher standards of practice may be targeted, defining the minimum provides a basis for measurement. When voluntary standards are implemented, the public and current and potential customers may judge an organization's compliance. Further, as international trade and communication increase, voluntary standards form the basis for an objective method of distinguishing between those who implement the standards and those who do not.

The first edition of the blood bank Standards focused on technical specifications and followed a "path of workflow" approach for the blood bank and

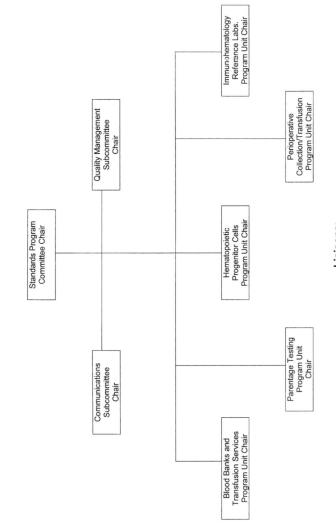

STANDARDS PROGRAM COMMITTEE

Standards Program Committee Chair

Communications Subcommittee Chair

Quality Management Subcommittee Chair

Blood Banks and Transfusion Services Program Unit Chair

Parentage Testing Program Unit Chair

Hematopoietic Progenitor Cells Program Unit Chair

Perioperative Collection/Transfusion Program Unit Chair

Immunohematology Reference Labs. Program Unit Chair

Liaisons:

FDA
Accreditation Program Committee
Technical Manual
ASBPO

Figure 1 Standards Program Committee.

ACCREDITATION PROGRAM COMMITTEE

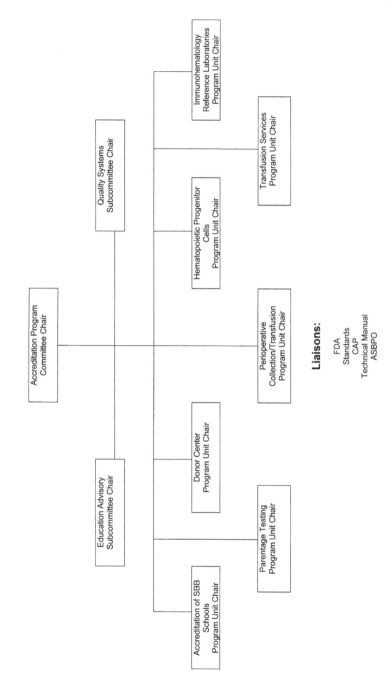

Figure 2 Accreditation Program Committee.

Table 1 AABB Standards, Editions, and Their Effective Dates

Standards	Edition	Effective date	Revision cycle
Standards for Blood Banks and Transfusion Services	19th	June 1999	18 months
Standards for Hematopoietic Progenitor Cell Services	2nd	March 2000	18 months
Standards for Immunohematology Reference Laboratories	1st	July 1999	2 years
Standards for Parentage Testing Laboratories	4th	July 1999	2 years
Standards for Perioperative Collection and Transfusion	1st	July 2001	2 years

transfusion service, i.e., beginning with donor selection and ending with blood administration. Over the last 40 years, 19 editions of blood bank/transfusion service Standards have been published, each edition building on the technical specifications from the prior edition.

Over the last decade, the AABB leadership and Standards committees have recognized the importance of quality systems to ensure consistency in the provision of appropriate components and services. In 1991, the requirement for a "program of quality assurance" was incorporated into the 14th edition of *Standards for Blood Banks and Transfusion Services*. In 1996, a written quality plan was required. The next year, in response to questions about what items should be included in a quality plan, an association policy (Association Bulletin #97-4) identified 10 Quality System Essentials (QSEs) as minimum requirements of a quality system. The premise of the QSEs is that a quality management system ensures that operations are controlled to produce consistent products and services. To achieve and maintain this control, it is required that policies, processes, and procedures are documented and implemented appropriately, and, when appropriate, records of the activities must be created and maintained. Internal assessments are conducted at regular, scheduled intervals, and if problems are identified, corrective action plans must be developed.

In 1999, the 10 QSEs were fully incorporated into the 19th edition of Standards (Table 2). In a further evolution, the framework of the 20th edition of the *Standards for Blood Banks and Transfusion Services*, published in the fall of 2000, is the 10 QSEs. The Standards publication is now organized into 10 sections, each section corresponding with a QSE. The first chapter is Management, the second Resources, the third Equipment, etc. The technical requirements appear in the appropriate chapter, creating a matrix of technical and quality requirements. For example, instead of repeating that equipment must be maintained throughout the standards, the requirement is stated once in Section 3,

Table 2 Quality System Essentials

Organization
Resources
Equipment
Supplier and customer issues
Process control
Documents and records
Incidents, errors, accidents; nonconforming products and services; complications
Assessments: internal and external
Process improvement through corrective and preventive action
Facilities and safety

Equipment. Then the specific requirements for equipment (e.g., blood warmers, alarms) are placed in that section. With this model, the technical standards are as important as the quality requirements, but this system incorporates them into a quality management system.

II. DEVELOPING AABB STANDARDS

Since the first issue of standards was developed, there have been extensive changes to the standard setting process. These changes include modifying the scope of expertise of standards program unit members, modifying the process for reviewing and revising existing standards, standardizing the interval between editions, providing the opportunity for member and public comment, and establishing criteria for new standards.

The AABB Board of Directors appoints the chair and members of the program unit. Criteria for selection and appointment of the chair include a broad knowledge of the program unit topic, a scholarly publication record, and appropriate interpersonal skills. Program unit selection reflects particular expertise in the relevant field and experience in developing applicable policies. Program unit members may serve for two editions of standards. Members are appointed so that half of the members of the latest edition remain to provide a link from one program unit to the next. One or more public members may also be appointed to a program unit. This person represents the interests of the general public.

Liaisons from other organizations, including federal agencies, are also included in the standard setting process. Liaison invitations are based on the standard setting activity. Liaisons participate fully in committee discussions and work assignments, but they do not vote.

Each new standards program unit reviews the prior edition and with consensus deletes, adds, clarifies, or proposes new standards. In order to provide confidence in the standards setting process, the AABB Standards Committee base their decisions on scientific evidence, when available, good medical practice, technological changes, public policy issues, and government regulations and guidelines. When there are differences of opinion, committee decisions are made by a majority vote of the members present.

Once the revision phase of the process is completed, the Standards are presented to the Standards Program Committee and the Board of Directors for approval to publish as proposed Standards. Once approved, the proposed changes are published for comment on the public section of the AABB web site for 60 days. Notice of the proposed Standards is printed in a nationally circulated newspaper and AABB newsletters. Following the comment period, the program unit reviews each comment, and final wording is determined. The final draft undergoes a thorough legal, regulatory, and technical review and is submitted to the Standards Program Committee and Board for final approval. Once the final Standards are issued, institutional members have 60 days to implement them.

If it is determined that a new standard must be set or a current standard must be revised before the next edition is published, a program unit may add or revise a standard if there is scientific evidence for doing so. In this instance, a proposed interim standard is posted for an abbreviated comment period. After consideration of the comments and with Standards Program Committee and Board approval, an interim standard is set and must be implemented by accredited members. In rare circumstances, when an accelerated review and approval process is required, an emergent standard is set with Board approval but without a comment period.

If an institution has data to prove that it can meet the intent of a standard through another mechanism, it may apply to the relevant program unit for a variance or an exemption. In this case, the program unit considers the request, and if the variance is approved the Communications Subcommittee communicates the decision. If an institution disagrees with a variance decision, it may appeal the decision to a Standards Review Committee. Variances apply for one edition of Standards, although institutions may reapply for variances.

III. GUIDANCE DOCUMENTS

Separate guidance documents have been created for each set of standards. Because the standards contain requirements, a need was identified for the explanation of a rationale or intent of specific standards, examples of implementation, and approved variances to standards. Accordingly, the guidance for *Standards for Blood Banks and Transfusion Services* and *Standards for Hematopoietic Progenitor Cell Services* is contained in *Standards Source*, a subscription that consists of six quarterly issues. Separate guidance documents are published for *Standards for Parentage Testing Laboratories* and *Standards for Immunohemato-*

logy Reference Laboratories. It is anticipated that a guidance document will also be developed for the *Standards for Perioperative Collection and Transfusion.*

IV. REGIONAL AND COUNTRY-SPECIFIC STANDARDS

Since 1997, upon request the AABB has been working with regional organizations outside of the United States to develop regional or country-specific voluntary blood banking standards that incorporate specific technical requirements that are appropriate for the region. Regional requirements may differ as a result of federal regulations, standard of care, resources, or regional infectious disease markers. To be consistent with the ISO 9000 standards, which is an internationally recognized set of standards, the AABB expanded the 10 QSEs to 20 quality essentials. The result is a set of standards that is compatible with QSEs and ISO 9000 concepts and merges quality standards with technical requirements.

V. ACCREDITATION PROGRAM

Following publication of the first edition of standards in 1958, AABB's Inspection and Accreditation program was developed to identify whether inspected organizations met the requirements of the standards (a detection-oriented model). Inspectors used a checklist during on-site inspections to determine whether the specific requirements in the standards had been met. Following a review of the inspector's completed checklist, summary reports of the inspections were written by area chairs.

In 1997 a new process was developed to incorporate a systems approach (a prevention-oriented model). Checklists transitioned to assessment tools, and the terminology of "inspectors" transitioned to "assessors." With this new model, summary reports are left on-site at the conclusion of the assessment and assessors identify nonconformances that may be an isolated incident or a systems-related problem. Assessors evaluate both the quality and operational activities performed within an institution. The quality system evaluation is based on the same criteria for every facility; the operational systems are identified by the activities performed by the institution. The result is that each assessment is customized for the facility.

At the core of the accreditation program are hundreds of volunteer assessors. Assessors must have appropriate expertise, participate in assessor continuing education, and perform a minimum number of assessments each year. Assessors and their organizations benefit from free training in quality concepts and auditing techniques, networking with other individuals in their profession, and learning about best practices used in other facilities. In 1999 the AABB also hired three lead assessors who have expertise in the field and are well trained in quality and quality assessments.

As the Food and Drug Administration, Health Care Financing Administration, and Joint Commission on Accreditation of Healthcare Organizations focus on the importance of quality assurance and systems evaluation, the AABB is confident that its standards and accreditation program is preparing AABB-accredited institutions for the changing environment. Institutions that are accredited by the AABB send a signal to their customers and the public that they implement voluntary industry standards, which require control of operations through a quality management system and implementation of the blood banking community's agreed-upon technical standards. After more than 40 years in the standard-setting arena, the AABB's standards and accreditation program has played a significant role in improving patient safety, and institutions with AABB accreditation are respected around the world.

26

The Role of Federal Regulation in Blood Safety

Jay S. Epstein and Mary Gustafson
U.S. Food and Drug Administration, Rockville, Maryland

I. STATUTORY HISTORY

The modern blood industry dates back more than 50 years. Establishments known as blood banks began to appear in the 1930s, and widespread use of blood and its derivatives began during World War II. Federal regulatory control was exerted over blood and blood products almost from their inception based on the preexisting Biologics Control Act of 1902 (also known as the Virus-Toxin Act). This law requiring licensing of biologics was consolidated with other public health laws in 1944 to become the Public Health Service (PHS) Act. The first blood product, Normal Human Plasma, was licensed for medical use in 1940. The first blood bank was licensed for the manufacture of whole blood in 1946. The first blood grouping reagent for serological testing of red blood cells was licensed in 1949. The PHS Act was implemented by the National Institutes of Health (NIH) during the time the first blood licenses were issued. Blood was also considered to be a drug subject to the Federal Food, Drug and Cosmetic (FDC) Act; however, the full scope of regulatory controls available under the FDC Act was not implemented until regulatory control for biologics was transferred from the NIH to the U.S. Food and Drug Administration (FDA) in 1972 (1). Today, blood, blood components, blood-derived and analogous products, and in vitro diagnostic blood screening tests and other medical devices used in the manufacture of blood and blood components are regulated under federal statutes implemented by FDA.

The primary statutes covering blood regulation are the PHS Act (42 USC 202 et. seq.) and the FDC Act (21 USC 302 et. seq.). Both laws have predecessors that date to the early 1900s. Both were enacted following tragic events that motivated the U.S. Congress to insist that medicines and other medical use products be controlled. The impetus for the enactment of the first biologics statute was the death of several children in the fall of 1901. Those children had been given a diphtheria antitoxin contaminated with tetanus toxin. The source of the antitoxin was a horse that later developed tetanus. The event was deemed preventable had controls been in place throughout the procurement and processing of the antitoxin. Congress therefore enacted the Biologics Control Act, which required the licensing of manufacturing establishments as well as the biological products they manufactured. Thus, the Act, which later was incorporated into Section 351 of the PHS Act, serves as the legal basis of licensing biologics (2). The original PHS Act did not specifically address blood and blood derivative products, but these products were regulated as being analogous to a "therapeutic serum," a category specifically included in the language of the statute. This interpretation was challenged in 1968 in *Blank v. United States* (3). Mrs. Maxine Blank had been convicted of misdemeanor charges under the PHS Act for violations incurred in operating a commercial blood bank located in Dallas, Texas. She was found guilty but appealed her conviction. The grounds for appeal were based upon the absence of any reference to blood or blood products in the statute. The court agreed with Mrs. Blank and reversed the conviction. However, it was not the intention of Congress to omit the regulation of blood and blood-derived products from the authority of the PHS Act, and in 1970 Congress amended the Act specifically to include, "blood, blood components and derivatives" (4).

The FDC Act was preceded by the Pure Food and Drug Act of 1906. This early law was passed following disclosure of unsanitary and uncontrolled practices in the meat-packing industry in the popular book *The Asphalt Jungle* by Upton Sinclair. The early law addressed the purity of foods and drugs and was silent with respect to their safety and efficacy. The drug act was strengthened in 1938, however, after more than 100 people died after ingesting elixir of sulfanilamide in which the drug was dissolved in diethylene glycol, an extremely toxic substance, rather than alcohol or water. The recodified 1938 law was the forerunner of the modern FDC Act and included the requirement for safety as well as purity (5). The law was further amended in 1962, after the thalidomide tragedy, to include efficacy as well as safety, and again in 1976, to encompass the regulation of medical devices. Until the Food and Drug Administration Modernization Act of 1997, the only other major change to the FDC Act was strengthening of device regulation and clarification of the regulation of combination drug and device products by the Safe Medical Device Act of 1990 (6,7).

Key provisions of the PHS Act and the FDC Act are outlined in Table 1. Besides differing in structure, the two statutes differ in objective, scope, focus, and enforcement mechanism. The PHS Act was enacted to promote public health and disease prevention by assuring safe and effective vaccines and other biolog-

Table 1 Key Provisions of Statutes Enforced by FDA

Section	Provision
	PHS Act
§351(a)	Requires licenses for biological products
§351(b)	Prohibits false labeling
§351(c)	Authorizes inspections
§351(a)	Authorizes suspension/revocation of licenses
§361	Provides authority to control spread of communicable disease
	FDC Act
§301, et seq	Outlines prohibited acts and penalties
§501	Prohibits adulteration
§502	Prohibits misbranding
§510	Requires registration of producers of drugs and devices
§704	Authorizes inspections

ical products intended to treat and prevent diseases of humans. The FDC Act was intended to guard the consumer against adulterated and misbranded foods, drugs, devices, and cosmetics. The PHS Act provides for administrative actions of license suspension and revocation as the primary remedies for violating the statute. In contrast, the FDC Act is far more enforcement-oriented in that it outlines prohibited acts and describes remedies that are judicial, e.g., product seizure, prosecution, and injunction. However, since biological products under the PHS Act concurrently are drugs or devices under the FDC Act, the enforcement provisions of the FDC Act can be applied.

II. REGULATION AND GUIDANCE

The past decade and a half have brought sweeping changes to practices within the blood industry and to the regulation of that industry. The AIDS epidemic in particular brought a new focus of public concern to blood and blood-derived products. The industry and the regulators of the industry have been faulted for their response to the AIDS crisis (8). Partly in response, activities once thought of as medical services are now considered as pharmaceutical manufacturing by FDA. This change in outlook itself has caused major reorganization of the blood industry.

The blood industry encompasses a broad range of types of product. The industry includes blood donations from individuals processed by physical means only and transfused as single donor blood components or small pools (usually fewer than 10 units); blood-derived products consisting of large pools of donations (thousands) that are extensively manufactured by physical and chemical means to result in specialized products with consistent dosage and intended uses distinct from simple components; blood-related products manufactured by biotechnology to be analogous to a naturally derived blood product; medical devices to test the safety and stability of blood products; medical devices used in the processing of blood components; and drugs used to anticoagulate, provide nutrients during storage, and extend the shelf life of blood components. Each area has different regulatory issues and involves different regulatory approaches. All facets of the blood industry are within the regulatory purview of FDA, except that FDA does not set or enforce medical practice standards.

Agencies tasked with implementing and enforcing laws are given the power to promulgate regulations that more fully interpret the laws from a practical standpoint. These regulations have the force of law. Promulgation of regulations follows a strict procedural path that usually includes public notification of a proposed rule and a period of comment before the rule is issued as final. Regulations affecting blood, blood derivatives, and medical devices used in blood banking are found in Title 21, *Code of Federal Regulations* (21 CFR), Parts 200 (drugs); 300 (investigational drugs); 600 (biologics, including blood); and 800 (medical devices). Table 2 lists provisions of each Part of 21 CFR referenced. Biological products, including blood, are subject to Part 600 and, depending on the intended use of the biological product, are subject to additional provisions included in Parts 200 and 300 for biological drugs and Part 800 for biological devices.

In addition to regulations, which have the force of law, agencies also generate guidance documents. These documents, which include guidelines, points to consider, memoranda, and reviewer's guidances, represent the agency's policy on a particular topic. They are intended to supplement or interpret existing regulations. Guidance documents do not have the force of law, as do regulations. They are not binding on the industry or the agency and are not enforceable, as are regulations. Generally, however, the guidance documents provide the agency's view of how to fulfill the requirements of a regulation. There may be other equivalent ways to fulfill a regulatory requirement. But if a firm adopts the recommendation addressed in a guidance document and makes it part of its standard operating procedures (SOPs), the firm is obliged as a matter of current good manufacturing practices (cGMP) to follow its own procedures.

Guidances, in the form of memoranda addressed to registered blood establishments, have been issued frequently since the mid-1980s. Many of the guidances have been issued upon approval of new test kits to screen the blood supply. The guidances have advised the industry how to use the tests in determining the suitability of donor units and have further clarified such issues as blood component labeling, blood quarantine and disposition, donor deferral, procedures for reinstating deferred donors based on supplemental testing, and lookback

Table 2 Relevant Provisions of Title 21 Code of Federal Regulations

Cite	Addresses
	21 CFR, Part 200—Drugs
201	Drug labeling
202	Prescription drug advertising
207	Drug registration
210, 211	Current good manufacturing practice
	21 CFR, Part 300—Drugs
312	Investigational new drug applications
	21 CFR, Part 600—Biologics
601	Licensing
606	Current good manufacturing practice for blood and components
606.120-122	Blood and component labeling
607	Blood registration
610	General product standards, including labeling and testing
640–680	Additional standards
	21 CFR, Part 800—Medical Devices
801	Device labeling
803	Medical device reporting
807	Device registration
809	In vitro diagnostics, including labeling
810	Device recall
812	Investigational device exemptions
814	Premarket approval
820	Quality system regulation
860	Medical device classification

(i.e., product retrieval or recipient notification related to previous donations). Other guidances have discussed manufacture and use of autologous blood components; standards for donor suitability; licensing criteria for specific product processing steps, e.g., irradiation and leukoreduction; and error/accident reporting. A particular subject may be addressed in more than one guidance document. Blood memoranda and other guidance documents are published and available in hard copy from the Division of Communication and Public Affairs (HFM-43), Center for Biologics Evaluation and Research, Food and Drug Administration, 1401 Rockville Pike, Rockville, MD 20852-1448. These guidance documents are also available in a variety of electronic forms, including on the Internet (www.fda.gov.cber.guidelines.htm), as noted in the listing in Appendix A.

Although not directly enforceable, guidance documents, once promulgated, carry weight in court. Once a guidance is issued, industry, particularly the blood industry, believes it is compelled to follow the guidance whether or not it is thought to be in its best interest. Because of concerns about the way in which guidance documents are established and issued, the agency has prepared an internal procedure for the promulgation of guidance documents, entitled "Good Guidance Practices" (GGP) (9). This procedure stratifies guidance into two levels depending on the nature, significance, and controversiality of the guidance. The GGP requires the agency to publish for public comment any guidance falling into the level one category (significant interpretation of statute or regulation), and unless the guidance addresses an urgent public health issue the guidance will not be effective until it is reissued for implementation after a comment period. Level 2 guidances are deemed to be less significant and less controversial and are effective upon publication, although they remain open for comment. It is important to note that the public may comment on any guidance at any time during its existence.

III. LICENSING AND PRODUCT APPROVAL

Products and manufacturers of products regulated under the purview of FDA are subject to several reporting and approval requirements. First is the requirement for all manufacturers of drugs and medical devices to register with the agency and list their products. This requirement is part of the FDC Act in Section 510. Regulations covering registration and product listing are found in 21 CFR, Part 207, for drugs; Part 607 for blood and blood components; and Part 807 for medical devices. Registration fulfills a manufacturer's obligation to advise the agency of its existence, location, and scope of manufacturing. Information obtained during the registration process is used primarily to assure inspectional oversight.

Products also are subject to premarket approval or clearance prior to being introduced into interstate commerce. Prior to receiving marketing approval, a product can be distributed for the purpose of generating and collecting clinical information to support its intended marketing claim. Generally, distribution of the product requires an exemption from the requirements that only approved products be distributed in interstate commerce. Such an exemption is approved by FDA following a sponsor's filing a request for an exemption. Requests for exemption from the requirements for licensure to permit distribution of biological drugs and devices are filed subject to the provisions for investigational new drugs (IND) in 21 CFR, Part 312. Although legally medical devices, biological devices subject to license are procedurally covered under the IND regulations. Other medical devices regulated by CBER are subject to investigational device exemptions

(IDE) regulations in 21 CFR, Part 812. Just as the preapproval processes differ depending on whether the product is a drug, device, or biological drug or device, the approval processes differ as well. Products that are deemed to be biologics are regulated under the licensing provisions of Section 351 of the PHS Act. Products regulated in this manner include blood and blood components, blood-derived and related products, and in vitro tests required or recommended for testing the blood supply. Other medical devices used to process, test, store, or administer blood are regulated under the medical device amendments to the FDC Act. Depending upon the classification of the device, permission to market it is granted by approval of a premarket approval application (PMA) or clearance of a premarket notification (510k). Blood anticoagulants, additive and rejuvenation solutions, and colloidal plasma volume expanders are subject to the drug-approval mechanisms under Section 505 of the FDC Act. In accordance with intercenter agreements between the Center for Biologics Evaluation and Research (CBER), the Center for Drug Evaluation and Research, and the Center for Devices and Radiological Health, CBER has jurisdiction for the regulation of blood as well as drugs and devices used in the processing of blood regardless of the regulatory mechanism (10,11).

The majority of blood and blood-related products are licensed as biologics under the PHS Act. Therefore, the remainder of this chapter's discussion will focus on licensing and the related regulatory requirements. Prior to the implementation of the Food and Drug Administration Modernization Act of 1997, licensing of blood products required that the product and the establishment responsible for the manufacture of the product each be licensed. That is, separate licenses were issued for the biological product (product license) and the facility manufacturing the product (establishment license). Since February 1998, a single biologics license has been issued. On July 30, 1998, FDA published a proposed rule to amend the biologics regulations to eliminate the filing of a separate establishment license application and a product license application in order to market a biological product in interstate commerce. The separate license applications are being replaced by a single biologics license application (12). The impact of this change is discussed later in this chapter.

IV. POSTLICENSURE REQUIREMENTS

After licensure, a manufacturer of a licensed biological product is responsible for certain postapproval requirements. These include annual updates to registration and listing, compliance with current good manufacturing practices in the manufacture of the product, lot release requirements for some products, and certain reporting requirements. The reporting requirements include reporting changes to the approved application in accordance with 21 CFR, Part 601.12. This regulation was revised in 1997 to reduce reporting requirements and is discussed in greater detail later in this chapter (13).

Adverse experiences associated with use of biological products are reportable under 21 CFR 600.81. Manufacturers of licensed biologics, with the exception of blood and blood components and in vitro diagnostics, are required to report serious, unexpected adverse events as outlined in the regulation. Manufacturers of in vitro diagnostics are subject to medical device reporting requirements in 21 CFR, Part 803. Both types of reports may be filed using FDA's MedWatch reporting program. MedWatch reports are facilitated by using Form 3500A (Appendix B, accessible from the FDA home page www.fda.gov/medwatch/report/hcp.htm). Error and accident (biological product deviation) reporting (21 CFR 600.14) is required for licensed manufacturers and is recommended but is voluntary for manufacturers of unlicensed (intrastate) blood and blood components. FDA has published a proposed rule that would require error and accident reporting for all manufacturers of blood and blood components whether or not the products are in interstate commerce (14). All manufacturers of blood and blood components, whether licensed or not, are required to report fatalities associated with the collection or transfusion of such products (21 CFR 606.170). Fatal events should be reported by telephone (301-827-6220) within 24 hours with a full report submitted within 7 days. An electronic mail account is also available to facilitate preliminary reporting. The e-mail address is <fatalities2@cber.fda.gov>. Additional requirements for reporting of serious adverse reactions to blood and blood components are being considered by FDA.

V. INSPECTION AND ENFORCEMENT

Inspection has been a focus of biologics regulation since the earliest biologics law. Inspections of biologics firms have been accomplished by officers responsible for the review of biological products applications. In recent years, the field investigations force has played greater role in inspections of biological products, including blood. Routine (biennial) surveillance inspections for most blood and blood components have been conducted by FDA field personnel since the late 1970s. As part of an initiative termed Team Biologics, lead responsibility for periodic inspections has been transferred to the FDA field force for all biological products, including licensed fractionated blood products and in vitro diagnostic blood screening reagents (15). As with blood and blood components, Compliance Program Guidance Manuals have been developed to provide guidance for uniform inspections and consistent application of regulatory requirements applicable to plasma derivatives (16).

Inspectional observations are communicated to firms being inspected on FDA Form 483. Observations that are judged by the investigator to be potentially violative of regulations are listed on the form. Further compliance action, such as issuance of a warning letter, follows only after the results of the inspection, including the Form 483 observations, are reviewed by compliance officers at the district level and sometimes at the Center level. Administrative and legal actions such as license suspension or revocation, injunction, seizure, and prosecution are infrequent occurrences. Voluntary compliance is the usual outcome and a goal of FDA.

Except in situations of imminent threat to health, if an establishment is found violating any of the laws that FDA enforces, it usually is given a chance to correct the problem voluntarily before FDA pursues an enforcement action. When an establishment cannot or will not correct a violative situation, FDA can invoke administrative or legal sanctions. If a firm is licensed and deficiencies present are grounds for revocation (21 CFR 601.5), the firm can be advised that the agency will proceed to revoke the firm's license. Further, if a danger to health exists, the firm's license can be summarily suspended. Legal actions against a firm include injunction and prosecution. Mandatory injunction (specifying corrective action), as opposed to prohibitory injunction or license revocation (causing cessation of operations), is the remedy most frequently sought when there is a need to maintain the blood supplied by a firm operating out of compliance. Violative products can be removed from the market by voluntary removal or correction of labeling by the manufacturer. These actions are classified as recalls when FDA otherwise would take action against the violative product, i.e., by seizure (17). See appendix C for a summary of enforcement actions in recent years.

VI. CURRENT TRENDS IN BLOOD SAFETY

A. Role of DHHS

Federal public health agencies, i.e., FDA, NIH, and the Centers for Disease Control and Prevention (CDC) are components of the Department of Health and Human Services (DHHS). These PHS agencies report to the Assistant Secretary for Health within DHHS. Each has a unique role in the nation's public health. The July 1995 Institute of Medicine (IOM) Report recommended that the department's role in blood safety be strengthened and formalized (8). Following a review of decisions made from 1982 to 1986, the IOM panel recommended that the Secretary of Health and Human Services designate a Blood Safety Director at a high level to be responsible for the federal government's efforts to maintain the safety of the nation's blood supply. Additionally, the report recommended that the PHS should establish a Blood Safety Council to assess current and potential future threats to the blood supply, to propose strategies for overcoming these threats, to evaluate the response of the Public Health Service to these proposals, and to monitor the implementation of these strategies.

DHHS responded by establishing the Assistant Secretary for Health as the Blood Safety Director. In addition, a Blood Safety Committee was formed consisting of PHS agency heads, their deputies, and certain other members of DHHS. The role of the Blood Safety Committee is to bring to the Blood Safety Director issues that require department attention and coordination. The PHS Advisory Committee on Blood Safety and Availability (ACBSA) also was formed to advise the Blood Safety Director on matters relating to public health and to provide public communication about blood risks. The advisory committee has met periodically since April 1997 and has addressed safety and availability issues such as hepatitis C lookback, transfusion risk from Creutzfeldt-Jacob disease (CJD), and the availability of blood products such as immune globulins and components for transfusion.

Lines of responsibility necessarily were drawn between the long-standing Blood Products Advisory Committee (BPAC), an FDA scientific advisory committee, and the newly created PHS ACBSA. The BPAC's role is to provide scientific input and advice to FDA regarding regulatory matters such as determinations of product safety and efficacy. The ACBSA has a broader composition and advises the Blood Safety Director on global aspects of public health issues, taking into account social, legal, economic, and ethical concerns as well as current science. For example, while the BPAC may recommend to FDA that a newly developed donor screening test be approved based on the performance characteristics of the test and its demonstrated efficacy in clinical trials, the PHS ACBSA may consider additional factors relevant to its implementation as a blood donor screen, such as the risk/benefit ratio and the overall societal impact of national testing.

B. Changes in Licensing

Section 351 of the PHS Act requires that a biological license be in effect for commercial interstate distribution of a biological product. Regulations (21 CFR, Section 601) implementing the PHS Act in the past required that licensing be accomplished by the application for and issuance of separate licenses for the establishment preparing the biological product and the product itself. The requirement for separate licensing of an establishment and each product manufactured has been changed. The agency has eliminated the establishment license filing for all biological products, including blood, blood components, and derivatives (12). The current establishment license application and multiple product license applications have been replaced with a single form. Applications for product approval (i.e., new drug and biologics licenses) are accomplished by the submission of one harmonized application form for all drugs and biological products, and one biologics license approval will issue covering the biological product and its manufacturing facilities and processes. The harmonized application (FDA Form

356h, see Appendix D or http://forms.psc.gov/forms/FDA/fda.html) should be included with all application submissions. Guidance documents have been prepared to provide instructions on filing information required in the chemistry, manufacturing, and controls (CMC) section and the establishment section of the application. Conversion to the biologics license application (BLA) is voluntary at present but will be required after October 20, 2000 (12).

The requirements and procedures for reporting changes to an approved license application were revised in 1997 (13). Previously, the regulation affecting reporting of changes to an approved application (21 CFR 601.12) required that every "important, proposed" change be reported and that every change in manufacturing and labeling be approved by the Director of the CBER prior to implementation of the change. In an effort to reduce the reporting burden of industry and to more effectively manage limited government resources, the regulation was revised to stratify reporting responsibilities based on a risk assessment according to defined criteria. Changes judged to pose a significant risk, to adversely affect the product must be reported in a license application supplement and reviewed and approved prior to distribution of product prepared with the change. Changes judged to have a moderate risk of adversely affecting the product must be reported at least 30 days prior to distribution of product produced with the change and remain subject to approval even after implementation. Changes with a minimal risk to the product may be implemented and reported to the agency in an annual report. Changes in labeling are reported in a similar fashion.

In addition to the two changes in blood and blood product licensing noted above, work is progressing towards reinventing the mechanism for oversight of blood products. These efforts may modify licensing requirements further, particularly for blood and blood components. FDA intends to pilot development of monograph-type standards for conventional blood components as an alternative to review SOPs and other supporting information in license applications. In this regulatory scheme, license applicants would certify their compliance with the published standards as a basis for licensure. Inspections would assess the validity of applicants' certifications and their adherence to published component standards.

C. Changes in the FDA Inspection Program

Inspections of licensed biologics establishments have been the responsibility of agencies tasked with implementing the PHS Act since the beginning of this century. When the NIH's Division of Biologics Standards joined FDA in 1972 as the Bureau of Biologics (BoB), it retained its independent responsibility for inspections, even though FDA had an established inspection program for other products regulated under the FDC Act. However, in the late 1970s the BoB (now CBER) transferred routine surveillance inspections of blood and plasma establishments to FDA's inspection force located within FDA's Office of Regulatory Affairs (ORA) because of the increased inspection inventory resulting from the registration of a large number of intrastate blood establishments and the promulgation of cGMP regulations for blood (21 CFR 606 et. seq.) that applied to intrastate as well as interstate blood establishments. Experience over the past two decades has proved this strategy to be practical and successful. However, recent criticisms from industry also reflected in a General Accounting Office (GAO) audit have focused on inconsistency among investigators and among FDA regions; inadequate technical and policy training of investigators; and lack of a centralized monitoring program to oversee investigator performance, identify industry trends, and determine areas needing policy development (18). FDA has taken steps to remedy these problems by creation of a specialized cadre of investigators who inspect blood and plasma collection establishments.

With the exception of blood and plasma establishment inspections, both prelicensing and routine surveillance inspections of all other biologics, including plasma derivatives, until recently were the responsibility of FDA's CBER. However, reviews by oversight organizations, such as GAO, IOM, the DHHS Inspector General and Congress, indicated a need for change. Key criticisms were that CBER inspections, although science based and product oriented, lacked stringency in assessment of compliance cGMP, evidence development, and follow-up enforcement actions. To address these concerns and as part of FDA's continuing review of its practices under the National Performance Review (NPR), CBER transferred the lead responsibility for periodic inspections of biologics to ORA. This was accomplished within a partnership between FDA's ORA and CBER called Team Biologics (15). The goal of Team Biologics is to improve the compliance of biologics firms by combining the different strengths of ORA and CBER in the inspection process. Part of this initiative involves creation of a dedicated group of biologics investigators in ORA and the formation of ORA/CBER teams to direct, conduct, and monitor inspections and compliance actions for biologics firms. Most inspections now routinely are conducted by teams consisting of both ORA investigators and CBER product specialist inspectors. The transfer to ORA of the lead role for blood fractionator inspections was accomplished in the fall of 1997, and the transfer of CBER-regulated in vitro diagnostic products occurred in the spring of 1998.

The Team Biologics inspectional approach is being evaluated periodically by a steering committee charged with oversight of the program.

D. Gene-Based Testing

In September 1994, FDA sponsored a workshop entitled "Conference on the Feasibility of Genetic Technology to Close the HIV Window in Donor Screening." The purpose of the workshop was to gather data on ways to close the window of infectivity (i.e., the period in which infectious virus is present in donated units of blood but not detected by current test methodology) for HIV. Information presented at this workshop and in later publications showed that nucleic acid testing, if applied to individual units of donated blood, could significantly reduce the number of infectious donations in the blood supply. It also was recognized that screening donors for the HIV-1 p24 antigen could be beneficial as an interim measure. Such testing later was recommended by FDA in August 1995 (19). This policy is controversial, however, because of its high cost and limited benefits (low rate of detections and remaining risk). Recently, estimates have indicated that nucleic acid testing of individual units of blood could prevent approximately 12 HIV infectious donations per year, 84 HCV infectious donations per year, and 81 HBV infectious donations per year (20). Unfortunately, the technology available at present makes it impractical to test individual units of blood; however, concurrent testing of small pools of donor samples (minipools) is being studied as an interim measure.

Initially, manufacturers of fractionated blood products approached FDA with proposals to utilize various nucleic acid (NAT) technologies to detect nucleic acid sequences of HIV, HCV, and HBV viruses in preproduction pools of donated plasma. While supportive of this initiative as a safety measure in the manufacture of plasma derivatives, FDA took the view that testing of pooled plasma samples de facto also was donor screening. FDA therefore requested that the proposals under study contain algorithms for testing pools in a manner that allows identification of the individual positive unit(s) within the pool. Test sponsors further were advised to trace donors and notify them about test information that could affect their health and their status for future donations. More recent studies of NAT include not only plasma intended for fractionation, but also testing of transfusible blood and blood components.

This area of testing is the first time that FDA has permitted use of pooled sample testing for determining individual donor suitability, and the concept has presented some novel challenges in addressing regulatory concerns. Among those concerns are: test sample issues (sample quality and impact of pool size on the sensitivity of the screen as a whole); test issues per se (sensitivity and specificity of the test, manufacturing consistency, and test reproducibility); the test environment (operator training and proficiency, adherence to cGMPs, and control of contamination); and logistics (retrieving or removing the infected units, time required for test performance, product retrieval, effect on short-dated transfusible products, ability to trace positive results back to the donor, and notification of recipients later found to have been transfused with investigational NAT-positive blood).

FDA foresees the possibility that gene-based tests could replace some current test methodologies. The first such replacement may be substitution of HIV

NAT testing for the currently approved HIV-1 p24 antigen test if pool testing is shown to be sufficiently sensitive.

E. Precautions Related to Creutzfeld-Jakob Disease

Between 1983 and 1992, the FDA received four reports of persons who had donated blood and, subsequently, were diagnosed with CJD. Implicated products were managed ad hoc. However, subsequent to publication in 1993 of an FDA guidance document on reporting of postdonation information, increasing numbers of such cases became known. As a result, CJD and its safety implications for blood and blood products were discussed at meetings of the BPAC in December 1994 and then again in June 1995 before a special advisory committee chartered as the Transmissible Spongiform Encephalopathies Advisory Committee (TSEAC). Based on advice of the TSEAC, FDA issued recommendations on August 8, 1995, and again on December 11, 1996, regarding donor deferral criteria for CJD and risk of CJD, and the quarantine and destruction of in-date source plasma and plasma derivatives and in-date transfusible blood and blood components from such donors (21,22). These recommendations identified several categories of donors at increased risk of developing CJD based on iatrogenic and familial risk. Iatrogenic risk applies to persons who have had injections with human pituitary-derived growth hormone or have had dura mater transplants. Familial risk applies to persons with one or more genetically related family members with CJD who were told that their families have increased risk for CJD. The FDA recommended permanent deferral of donors with CJD or CJD risks unless, for cases of genetic risk, the donor underwent genetic testing that did not reveal a familial CJD-associated abnormality of the prion protein gene.

While beneficial as a precautionary measure to reduce the theoretical risk of transmission of CJD from blood products, FDA's policy on withdrawal of plasma derivatives affected by a CJD-implicated donor has unintended consequences in exacerbating shortages of plasma derivatives. The shortage situation became a serious problem in the fall of 1997, leading to extensive reexamination of the policy. Additionally, the emergence of a novel variant of CJD necessitated further scientific assessment of the policy.

In 1996, a previously unrecognized variant of CJD was described in the United Kingdom. The disease is referred to as new variant CJD (nvCJD) (23). Laboratory and epidemiological studies have linked nvCJD to an outbreak of bovine spongiform encephalopathy (BSE) in the United Kingdom. BSE infection in cattle in the United Kingdom appeared in 1980, peaked in 1992, and fell to low levels by 1996. To date, no cases of nvCJD or BSE have been identified in the United States. The risk for transmission of nvCJD by blood and blood products is unknown. However, theoretical considerations suggest that the risk may be greater than for classical CJD.

Laboratory and epidemiological studies have been conducted to assess the risk of transmission of classical CJD through blood and blood products, and accumulating information indicates that the transmission of the CJD infectious agent is highly unlikely (24,25). In contrast, epidemiological studies of nvCJD are too small to provide useful risk assessments, and laboratory studies are only starting to be conducted.

On January 19, 1998, the PHS ACBSA reviewed available information concerning CJD transmissibility by blood as well as the impact of CJD-related withdrawals upon the supply of medically necessary plasma derivatives. Based upon this review, the committee recommended that FDA consider revising its guidance to the extent necessary to relieve shortages of medically necessary plasma derivatives. The recommendation subsequently was considered by the PHS ACBSA. At its July 23, 1998, meeting, Assistant Secretary for Health and Surgeon General David Satcher, M.D., Ph.D., announced that plasma derivatives should be withdrawn and intermediates quarantined only if a blood donor developed nvCJD and that previously recommended withdrawals and quarantines be discontinued for classical CJD and CJD risk factors. FDA made a consistent recommendation available on the internet on September 8, 1998 (26).

It is recognized that residents of the United Kingdom have an increased risk of developing nvCJD; however, the extent of the risk is not yet known. Prompted by a February 1998 decision in the United Kingdom to import all plasma for fractionation, the TSEAC met on December 18, 1998, and June 2, 1999, to consider whether donors who have traveled to or resided in the United Kingdom should be deferred. At these meetings, the TSEAC recommended that such donors be deferred until more is known about the scope of the epidemic of nvCJD and the risk of transmission of nvCJD by blood. A policy decision by the PHS that donors should be deferred indefinitely if they have spent 6 months or more cumulatively in the United Kingdom between January 1, 1980, and December 31, 1996, was announced at the June 1999 meeting of the BPAC, and a guidance document recommending this deferral was published by FDA in November 1999 (27).

F. Hepatitis C Virus Lookback

Non-A, non-B hepatitis, now known to be caused predominantly by HCV, was first identified in studies of posttransfusion hepatitis in the 1970s (28). Once thought to be a benign form of hepatitis, HCV is now known to be a major cause of chronic liver disease with significant risk of progression to cirrhosis, liver failure, and hepatocellular carcinoma decades after the initial infection. Donor testing for HCV infection was not possible until May 1990, following FDA's approval of an antibody-detection test with sensitivity between 50 and 80% based on a single recombinant antigen, FDA recommended at that time that units of blood from donors testing reactive on screening not be used for transfusion. On

April 23, 1992, the recommendation was revised to extend testing to both products for transfusion and for further manufacturing into injectable products. This decision coincided with FDA approval of the first multiantigen test for antibodies to HCV, a test with sensitivity greater than 90%. A supplemental, more specific test was licensed (available previously only as an investigational test) in mid-1993.

Tracing of recipients who received blood components from donors later found reactive for antibodies to HCV has been termed "targeted lookback." Although targeted lookback for HCV had been discussed in public meetings since October 1989, it was not recommended for a variety of reasons. Most importantly, in the absence of supplemental testing, the positive predictive value of the first HCV screening test was low and the significance of a reactive test in terms of infectivity was not known. Additionally, few HCV-infected individuals were eligible for investigational treatment of their liver disease, and the long-term effect of treatment was unknown.

Over time, it became known that individuals reactive for anti-HCV in a supplemental assay are likely to be chronically infected with HCV. More specifically, in studies of blood donors, 73–95% of supplemental test–positive and 14–21% of supplemental test–indeterminate blood donors had detectable HCV RNA by PCR (29–31). It also is now recognized that negative or unscreened units from donors later found reactive for anti-HCV may have been contaminated with HCV. In parallel with these improved understandings, there have been improvements in the management and treatment of HCV infections that were recognized by publication of treatment guidelines developed at a NIH Consensus Conference in March 1997. Driven in large measure by congressional concerns over the emerging epidemic of liver disease from chronic HCV infections, the issue of targeted lookback for HCV was brought before the PHS ACBSA. The Committee discussed the topic at its April 24–25, 1997, meeting and its August 11–12, 1997, meeting. After careful consideration, the Committee recommended that the PHS initiate a targeted lookback program extending back 10 years to identify recipients of previously donated units from donors who have tested positive for antibody to HCV following screening by a multiantigen screening test [enzyme immunoassay (EIA)] since 1992.

In March 1998 and September 1998, FDA issued guidance consistent with this recommendation. At public meetings on November 24, 1998, and January 28, 1999, the PHS ACBSA reconsidered the issue of recipient notification related to repeatedly reactive results on the EIA 1.0 test. Following acceptance by the committee, FDA issued guidance on June 22, 1999, to replace earlier guidances (32). This current guidance provides for lookback to EIA 1.0 testing and also recommends that the search of records of prior donations from donors with repeatedly reactive screening tests for HCV extend back indefinitely to the extent that electronic or other readily retrievable records exist.

G. Donor Recruitment and Quality Issues

Recruitment and selection of quality donors are critical steps in ensuring the safety and availability of the nation's blood supply. Existing regulations address suitability of the donor (21 CFR 640.3 and 640.63) and labeling of products based on donor source, either from a paid or volunteer donor [21 CFR 606.121(c)(5)]. In recent years, there have been renewed concerns about donor quality. The issue of donor incentives and their impact on blood donor motivation was highlighted at a workshop co-sponsored by FDA and the NIH's National Heart, Lung, and Blood Institute (NHLBI) in September 1996. Since then, data from the Retrovirus Epidemiology Donor Study (REDS) has indicated that approximately 2% of blood donors in the sample reported at least one or more risk behaviors that should have resulted in their deferral at the time of the screening interview. Within this group approximately 0.4% reported a deferrable risk behavior within 3 months before the donation, i.e., within the "window" period of many bloodborne infections (33). The need to study donor behavior and motivation issues and validate donor history questions was discussed at the March 25–26, 1999, BPAC meeting. Information was presented to the PHS Advisory Committee on Blood Safety and Availability at its April 29–30, 1999, meeting suggesting that the demand for blood is increasing faster than the supply. Strategies to address donor motivation and quality issues with respect to increasing a safe blood supply are under study. This is particularly important at this time since it is anticipated that the deferral of donors who have traveled to or resided in the United Kingdom for 6 months or more cumulatively from January 1980 through December 1996 will reduce the donor population by 2.2% nationally.

The federal role in ensuring blood safety continues to evolve under public pressure and scrutiny. Likewise, the blood industry is being held to higher standards for adherence to cGMP by FDA. The goal of many current efforts is to prevent the possibility for another bloodborne epidemic similar to AIDS. The American public expects and deserves the safest blood supply that is achievable. This goal lies at the heart of federal regulation of blood safety.

REFERENCES

1. Solomon JM. The evolution of the current blood banking regulatory climate. Transfusion 1994; 34:272–277.
2. Noguchi PD. From Jim to Gene and beyond: an odyssey of biologics regulation. Food Drug Law 1996; 51:367–373.
3. *Blank* v. *United States*. Federal Reporter, 2d Series 1968; 400:302–306.
4. Public Law No. 91-515, 58 Stat. 702 (1970).
5. Beatrice MG. Regulation, licensing and inspection of biological products. Pharmaceut Eng 1991; 10:29–35.

6. The Food and Drug Administration Modernization Act of 1997. Public Law No. 105-115, 1997.
7. Compilation of Laws Enforced by the U.S. Food and Drug Administration and Related Statutes. Vol 1. Washington, DC: U.S. Government Printing Office, 1996.
8. Leveton LB, Sox HC Jr., Stoto MA, eds. HIV and the Blood Supply: An Analysis of Crisis Decision Making. Washington, DC: National Academy Press, 1995.
9. The Food and Drug Administration's Development, Issuance, and Use of Guidance Documents. Fed Reg 1997; 62:8961–8972.
10. Intercenter Agreement Between the Center for Drug Evaluation and Research and the Center for Biologics Evaluation and Research. Rockville, MD: Food and Drug Administration, 1991.
11. Intercenter Agreement Between the Center for Drug Evaluation and Research and the Center for Devices and Radiological Health. Rockville, MD: Food and Drug Administration, 1991.
12. Biological Products Regulated under Section 351 of the Public Health Service Act: Implementation of Biologics License Elimination of Establishment License and Product License. Fed Reg 1999; 64:S6441–S6454.
13. Changes to an approved application. Fed Reg 1997; 62:39890–39906.
14. Biological products; reporting of errors and accidents in manufacturing: proposed rule. Fed Reg 1997; 62:49642–49648.
15. Team Biologics: A Plan for Reinventing FDA's Ability to Optimize Compliance of Regulated Biologics Industry. Rockville, MD: Food and Drug Administration, 1997.
16. Compliance Program Guide for Plasma Fractionation Facilities. Rockville, MD: Food and Drug Administration, 1997.
17. Tourault MA. Modern principles of blood banking compliance with Food and Drug Administration regulations, In: Harmening DM, eds. Modern Blood Banking and Transfusion Practices. 3rd ed. Philadelphia: F.A. Davis Company 1994:288–302.
18. Blood Supply: FDA Oversight and Remaining Issues of Safety. Washington, DC: General Accounting Office, 1997; PEMD-97-1.
19. Recommendations for Donor Screening with a Licensed Test for HIV-1 Antigen. Food and Drug Administration, 1995.
20. Schreiber GB, Busch MP, Kleinman SH, Korelitz JJ. The risk of transfusion-transmitted viral infections. N Engl J Med 1996; 334:1685–1690.
21. Precautionary Measures to Further Reduce the Possible Risk of Transmission of Creutzfeldt-Jakob Disease by Blood and Blood Products. Rockville, MD: Food and Drug Administration, 1995.
22. Revised Precautionary Measures to Reduce the Possible Risk of Transmission of Creutzfeldt-Jakob Disease (CJD) by Blood and Blood Products. Fed Reg 1997; 62:49694–49695.
23. Will RG, Ironside JW, Zeidler M. A new variant of Creutzfeldt-Jakob disease in the U.K. Lancet 1996; 347:921–925.
24. Sullivan MT, Schonberger LB, Kessler D, Williams A, Dodd R. Creutzfeldt-Jakob disease (CJD) investigational lookback study. Transfusion 1997; 37(suppl):2S.
25. Heye N, Hensen S, Muller N. Creutzfeldt-Jakob disease and blood transfusion. Lancet 1994; 343:298–299.
26. Change to the Guidance Entitled "Revised Precautionary Measures to Reduce the

Possible Risk of Transmission of Creutzfeldt-Jakob Disease (CJD) by Blood and Blood Products,"—Information Sheet. Rockville, MD: Food and Drug Administration, 1998.

27. Guidance for Industry: Revised Precautionary Measures to Reduce the Possible Risk of Transmission of Creutzfeldt-Jakob Disease (CJD) and New Variant Creutzfeldt-Jakob Disease (NVCJD) by Blood and Blood Products; Availability. Fed Reg 1999; 64:65715–65716.

28. Public Health Service Interagency Guidelines for Screening Donors of Blood, Plasma, Organs, Tissues, and Semen for Evidence of Hepatitis B and Hepatitis C. MMWR 1991; 40:1–17.

29. Sayers MH, Gretch DR. Recombinant immunoblot and polymerase chain reaction testing in volunteer whole blood donors screened by a multi-antigen assay for hepatitis C virus antibodies. Transfusion 1993; 33:809–813.

30. Kleinman SH, Alter H, Busch M, Holland P, Tegtmeier G, Nelles M, Lee S, Page E, Wilber J, Polito A. Increased detection of hepatitis C virus (HCV)-infected blood donors by a multiple-antigen HCV enzyme immunoassay. Transfusion 1992; 32:805–813.

31. Yun Z, Lindh G, Weiland O, Johansson B, Sonnerborg A. Detection of hepatitis C virus (HCV) RNA by PCR related to HCV antibodies in serum and liver histology in Swedish blood donors. J Med Virol 1993; 39:57–61.

32. Draft guidance for industry: Current Good Manufacturing Practice for blood and blood components: (1) quarantine and disposition of prior collections from donors with repeatedly reactive screening tests for hepatitis C virus (HCV); (2) supplemental testing, and the notification of consignees and transfusion recipients of donor test results for antibody to HCV (anti-HCV). Notice of availability. Fed Reg 1999; 64:33309–33313.

33. Williams AE, Thomson RA, Schreiber GB, Watanabe K, Bethel J, Lo A, Kleinman SH, Hollingsworth CG, Nemo G. Estimates of infectious disease risk factors in U.S. blood donors. J Am Med Assoc 1997; 277:967–972.

APPENDIX A: U.S. FOOD AND DRUG ADMINISTRATION CENTER FOR BIOLOGICS EVALUATION AND RESEARCH INFORMATION SOURCES

As a service to the public, FDA's Center for Biologics Evaluation and Research (CBER) provides information in a variety of ways.

Internet

CBER's Internet site is located at: **http://www.fda.gov/cber/**
The site contains a myriad of information including:

- Product information, e.g., recall/withdrawal/safety issues, product approvals, information sheets, adverse event reporting information (**www.fda.gov/cber/products.htm**);
- On line documents, e.g., guidelines/guidances, product approval documents, establishment and product files, Federal Register notices, information sheets, letters to industry and healthcare providers, memoranda to blood establishments, points to consider, and general and administrative information about CBER (**www.fda.gov/cber/publications.htm**);
- Documents available electronically under the Freedom of Information Act (FOI) and how to submit an FOI request (**www.fda.gov/cber/efoi.htm**);
- Information on FDA Modernization Act (**www.fda.gov/cber/fdama.htm**) and Prescription Drug User Fee Act (**www.fda.gov/cber/pdufa.htm**)

Additional Internet Sources

- Office of Regulatory Affairs (ORA) Web Site (**www.fda.gov/ora**) This site has direct links to a variety of information including **ORA Field Contacts**
- FDA downloadable forms, e.g., Biologics License Application, registration and label submittal forms (**http://forms.psc.dhhs.gov/fdaforms.htm**)

Fax Information System

- Direct toll free access in the U.S.: **1-888-CBER-FAX or 1-888-223-7329**
- Outside the U.S. & local to Rockville, MD: **301-827-3844**

Updated August 23, 1999

Callers outside the U.S. must call this system from a FAX machine with a touch-tone telephone attached or built in.

When prompted to enter your FAX number, please enter the entire 10 digit number, including the 3 digit area code, even if you are local to Rockville, MD. Do not include a 1 for long distance dialing.

- To obtain a complete list of documents available from this system, select document **9999**
- To obtain a list of documents added to the system in the last 30 days, select document **9998**
- To obtain a list of Recall/Withdrawal/Safety notifications, select document **9997**

Up to 5 documents can be ordered at a time. Please enter the document number(s) listed on the index.

E-Mail

- Consumer questions about biological products can be sent by e-mail to: **OCTMA@CBER.FDA.GOV**
- Manufacturers assistance questions can be sent by e-mail to: **MATT @CBER.FDA.GOV**
- Documents can be requested by e-mail from: **CBER_INFO@CBER. FDA.GOV**

Telephone

- **Voice Information System**
  Direct access to Consumer Safety Officers or Public Affairs Specialists:
  1-800-835-4709 or 301-827-1800
- **Blood and Plasma Products Information**
  Recall and market withdrawal notices for fractionated plasma products:
  1-888-CBER-BPI or 301-827-4604
- **Division of Blood Applications** 301-827-3543 (for questions about your application)
  Blood and Plasma Branch (fax: 301-827-2857)
  Regulatory Project Management Branch (fax: 301-827-3534)
  Devices Review Branch (fax: 301-827-3535)

Automated E-Mail List

- CBER has established three automated e-mail lists to distribute information within CBER and to the public.

FPRECALL
Members of this list will receive notices of recalls and market withdrawals of fractionated products.

BLOODINFO
Members of this list will receive all FPRECALL notices and other blood-related documents.

CBERINFO
Members of this list will receive FPRECALL and BLOODINFO documents, and notification of ALL new documents, including guidelines, points to consider, What's New on CBER's web site, and other CBER information.

Subscribing to multiple lists will result in receiving multiple copies.
To subscribe, send an e-mail message to **FDALISTS@ARCHIE.FDA.GOV**

THE FIRST LINE OF THE MESSAGE MUST CONTAIN:
subscribe <listname> <e-mail address>
Example: *If Joan Smith, at company.com, wanted to subscribe to the* CBERINFO *list, the first line of her message would look like this*:
subscribe CBERINFO JSmith@company.com

Printed Copy

Single copies of documents are available. Requests may be sent in writing to:

Office of Communication, Training and Manufacturers Assistance (HFM-40),
Center for Biologics Evaluation and Research (CBER),
Food and Drug Administration
1401 Rockville Pike
Rockville, MD 20852-1448

Documents may also be obtained by calling **CBER's Voice Information System** at:
1-800-835-4709 or **301-827-1800**

For a complete list of guidelines, guidance, points to consider and other documents available in hard copy, request document **D9001** (hard copy ID number) or document **9001** from the FAX Information System.

For a complete list of memoranda and related documents pertaining to blood and blood products available in hard copy, request document **D9002** (hard copy ID number) or document **9002** from the FAX Information System.

APPENDIX B

Form Approved: OMB No. 0910-0291 Expires: 8/31/00
See OMB statement on reverse

MED**W**ATCH
THE FDA MEDICAL PRODUCTS REPORTING PROGRAM

For use by user-facilities,
distributors and manufacturers for
MANDATORY reporting

Mfr report #

UF/Dist report #

Page _____ of _____

FDA Use Only

A. Patient information

1. Patient identifier	2. Age at time of event:		3. Sex	4. Weight
	or		☐ female	_____ lbs
	Date			or
In confidence	of birth:		☐ male	_____ kgs

B. Adverse event or product problem

1. ☐ Adverse event and/or ☐ Product problem (e.g., defects/malfunctions)

2. Outcomes attributed to adverse event
(check all that apply)

☐ death _____
  (mo/day/yr)
☐ life-threatening
☐ hospitalization – initial or prolonged

☐ disability
☐ congenital anomaly
☐ required intervention to prevent
  permanent impairment/damage
☐ other: _____

3. Date of event (mo/day/yr)	4. Date of this report (mo/day/yr)

5. Describe event or problem

6. Relevant tests/laboratory data, including dates

7. Other relevant history, including preexisting medical conditions (e.g., allergies, race, pregnancy, smoking and alcohol use, hepatic/renal dysfunction, etc.)

C. Suspect medication(s)

1. Name (give labeled strength & mfr/labeler, if known)
#1
#2

2. Dose, frequency & route used	3. Therapy dates (if unknown, give duration) from/to (or best estimate)
#1	#1
#2	#2

4. Diagnosis for use (indication)	5. Event abated after use stopped or dose reduced
#1	#1 ☐ yes ☐ no ☐ doesn't apply
#2	#2 ☐ yes ☐ no ☐ doesn't apply

6. Lot # (if known)	7. Exp. date (if known)	8. Event reappeared after reintroduction
#1	#1	#1 ☐ yes ☐ no ☐ doesn't apply
#2	#2	#2 ☐ yes ☐ no ☐ doesn't apply

9. NDC # – for product problems only (if known)
_____ – _____ – _____

10. Concomitant medical products and therapy dates (exclude treatment of event)

D. Suspect medical device

1. Brand name

2. Type of device

3. Manufacturer name & address	4. Operator of device
	☐ health professional
	☐ lay user/patient
	☐ other: _____
	5. Expiration date (mo/day/yr)

6.
model # _____
catalog # _____
serial # _____
lot # _____
other # _____

7. If implanted, give date (mo/day/yr)

8. If explanted, give date (mo/day/yr)

9. Device available for evaluation? (Do not send to FDA)
☐ yes ☐ no ☐ returned to manufacturer on _____ (mo/day/yr)

10. Concomitant medical products and therapy dates (exclude treatment of event)

E. Initial reporter

1. Name & address	phone #

2. Health professional?	3. Occupation	4. Initial reporter also sent report to FDA
☐ yes ☐ no		☐ yes ☐ no ☐ unk

FDA
FDA Form 3500A

Submission of a report does not constitute an admission that medical personnel, user facility, distributor, manufacturer or product caused or contributed to the event.

Medication and Device Experience Report
(continued)

Refer to guidelines for specific instructions

Submission of a report does not constitute an admission that medical personnel, user facility, distributor, manufacturer or product caused or contributed to the event.

U.S. DEPARTMENT OF HEALTH AND HUMAN SERVICES
Public Health Service • Food and Drug Administration

Page ____ of ____

FDA Use Only

F. For use by user facility/distributor–devices only

1. Check one
☐ user facility ☐ distributor

2. UF/Dist report number

3. User facility or distributor name/address

4. Contact person

5. Phone Number

6. Date user facility or distributor became aware of event (mo/day/yr)

7. Type of report
☐ initial
☐ follow-up #

8. Date of this report (mo/day/yr)

9. Approximate age of device

10. Event problem codes (refer to coding manual)

patient code ☐ – ☐ – ☐
device code ☐ – ☐ – ☐

11. Report sent to FDA?
☐ yes _____ (mo/day/yr)
☐ no

12. Location where event occurred
☐ hospital ☐ outpatient diagnostic facility
☐ home ☐ ambulatory surgical facility
☐ nursing home
☐ outpatient treatment facility
☐ other: _____
specify

13. Report sent to manufacturer?
☐ yes _____ (mo/day/yr)
☐ no

14. Manufacturer name/address

G. All manufacturers

1. Contact office – name/address (& mfring site for devices)

2. Phone number

3. Report source
(check all that apply)
☐ foreign
☐ study
☐ literature
☐ consumer
☐ health professional
☐ user facility
☐ company representative
☐ distributor
☐ other:

4. Date received by manufacturer (mo/day/yr)

5.
(A)NDA # _____
IND # _____
PLA # _____
pre-1938 ☐ yes
OTC product ☐ yes _____

6. If IND, protocol #

7. Type of report
(check all that apply)
☐ 5-day ☐ 15-day
☐ 10-day ☐ periodic
☐ Initial ☐ follow-up # _____

8. Adverse event term(s)

9. Mfr. report number

H. Device manufacturers only

1. Type of reportable event
☐ death
☐ serious injury
☐ malfunction (see guidelines)
☐ other: _____

2. If follow-up, what type?
☐ correction
☐ additional information
☐ response to FDA request
☐ device evaluation

3. Device evaluated by mfr?
☐ not returned to mfr.
☐ yes ☐ evaluation summary attached
☐ no (attach page to explain why not) or provide code:

4. Device manufacture date (mo/yr)

5. Labeled for single use?
☐ yes ☐ no

6. Evaluation codes (refer to coding manual)

method ☐ – ☐ – ☐
results ☐ – ☐ – ☐
conclusions ☐ – ☐ – ☐

7. If remedial action initiated, check type
☐ recall ☐ notification
☐ repair ☐ inspection
☐ replace ☐ patient monitoring
☐ relabeling ☐ modification/ adjustment
☐ other: _____

8. Usage of device
☐ initial use of device
☐ reuse
☐ unknown

9. If action reported to FDA under 21 USC 360i(f), list correction/removal reporting number:

10. ☐ **Additional manufacturer narrative** and/or **11.** ☐ **Corrected data**

FDA Form 3500A - back

APPENDIX C

CBER Enforcement Actions

Action	FY95	FY96	FY97	FY98	FY99
Revocations[a]	5	0	3	5	5
Suspensions	3	1	3	3	0
Injunctions	0	1	3	1	0
Seizures	0	0	3	0	1
Warning letters	19	21	46	31	27

[a]Includes Notices of Intent to Revoke.

Recalls Classified

Type of product	FY95	FY96	FY97	FY98	FY99
Blood	592	669	1423	1524	1199
Source plasma	19	23	27	38	36
Device[a]	29	7	30	23	12
Vaccine[b]	0	1	8	4	14
Therapeutic[c]	3	4	29	4	15
Tissue	5	3	2	5	19
Total	648	707	1519	1598	1295

[a]Includes in vitro diagnostic test kits and blood bank software.
[b]Includes allergenic products.
[c]Includes blood and plasma derivatives.

APPENDIX D

DEPARTMENT OF HEALTH AND HUMAN SERVICES FOOD AND DRUG ADMINISTRATION **APPLICATION TO MARKET A NEW DRUG, BIOLOGIC, OR AN ANTIBIOTIC DRUG FOR HUMAN USE** *(Title 21, Code of Federal Regulations, Parts 314 & 601)*	Form Approved: OMB No. 0910-0338 Expiration Date: March 31, 2003 See OMB Statement on page 2.
	FOR FDA USE ONLY
	APPLICATION NUMBER

APPLICANT INFORMATION

NAME OF APPLICANT	DATE OF SUBMISSION
TELEPHONE NO. *(Include Area Code)*	FACSIMILE (FAX) Number *(Include Area Code)*
APPLICANT ADDRESS *(Number, Street, City, State, Country, ZIP Code or Mail Code, and U.S. License number if previously issued):*	AUTHORIZED U.S. AGENT NAME & ADDRESS *(Number, Street, City, State, ZIP Code, telephone & FAX number)* IF APPLICABLE

PRODUCT DESCRIPTION

NEW DRUG OR ANTIBIOTIC APPLICATION NUMBER, OR BIOLOGICS LICENSE APPLICATION NUMBER *(If previously issued)*

ESTABLISHED NAME *(e.g., Proper name, USP/USAN name)*	PROPRIETARY NAME *(trade name)* IF ANY
CHEMICAL/BIOCHEMICAL/BLOOD PRODUCT NAME *(If any)*	CODE NAME *(If any)*

DOSAGE FORM:	STRENGTHS:	ROUTE OF ADMINISTRATION:

(PROPOSED) INDICATION(S) FOR USE:

APPLICATION INFORMATION

APPLICATION TYPE
(check one) ☐ NEW DRUG APPLICATION (21 CFR 314.50)   ☐ ABBREVIATED NEW DRUG APPLICATION (ANDA, 21 CFR 314.94)
☐ BIOLOGICS LICENSE APPLICATION (21 CFR Part 601)

IF AN NDA, IDENTIFY THE APPROPRIATE TYPE   ☐ 505 (b)(1)   ☐ 505 (b)(2)

IF AN ANDA, OR 505(b)(2), IDENTIFY THE REFERENCE LISTED DRUG PRODUCT THAT IS THE BASIS FOR THE SUBMISSION
Name of Drug   Holder of Approved Application

TYPE OF SUBMISSION *(check one)*   ☐ ORIGINAL APPLICATION   ☐ AMENDMENT TO A PENDING APPLICATION   ☐ RESUBMISSION
☐ PRESUBMISSION   ☐ ANNUAL REPORT   ☐ ESTABLISHMENT DESCRIPTION SUPPLEMENT   ☐ EFFICACY SUPPLEMENT
☐ LABELING SUPPLEMENT   ☐ CHEMISTRY MANUFACTURING AND CONTROLS SUPPLEMENT   ☐ OTHER

IF A SUBMISSION OF PARTIAL APPLICATION, PROVIDE LETTER DATE OF AGREEMENT TO PARTIAL SUBMISSION: _____

IF A SUPPLEMENT, IDENTIFY THE APPROPRIATE CATEGORY   ☐ CBE   ☐ CBE-30   ☐ Prior Approval (PA)

REASON FOR SUBMISSION

PROPOSED MARKETING STATUS *(check one)*   ☐ PRESCRIPTION PRODUCT (Rx)   ☐ OVER THE COUNTER PRODUCT (OTC)

NUMBER OF VOLUMES SUBMITTED_____   THIS APPLICATION IS   ☐ PAPER   ☐ PAPER AND ELECTRONIC   ☐ ELECTRONIC

ESTABLISHMENT INFORMATION (Full establishment information should be provided in the body of the Application.)
Provide locations of all manufacturing, packaging and control sites for drug substance and drug product (continuation sheets may be used if necessary). Include name, address, contact, telephone number, registration number (CFN), DMF number, and manufacturing steps and/or type of testing (e.g. Final dosage form, Stability testing) conducted at the site. Please indicate whether the site is ready for inspection or, if not, when it will be ready.

Cross References (list related License Applications, INDs, NDAs, PMAs, 510(k)s, IDEs, BMFs, and DMFs referenced in the current application)

FORM FDA 356h (4/00)   Created by Media Arts/USDHHS (301) 443-2454 EF

PAGE 1

	This application contains the following items: *(Check all that apply)*
	1. Index
	2. Labeling *(check one)* ☐ Draft Labeling ☐ Final Printed Labeling
	3. Summary (21 CFR 314.50 (c))
	4. Chemistry section
	A. Chemistry, manufacturing, and controls information (e.g., 21 CFR 314.50(d)(1); 21 CFR 601.2)
	B. Samples (21 CFR 314.50 (e)(1); 21 CFR 601.2 (a)) (Submit only upon FDA's request)
	C. Methods validation package (e.g., 21 CFR 314.50(e)(2)(i); 21 CFR 601.2)
	5. Nonclinical pharmacology and toxicology section (e.g., 21 CFR 314.50(d)(2); 21 CFR 601.2)
	6. Human pharmacokinetics and bioavailability section (e.g., 21 CFR 314.50(d)(3); 21 CFR 601.2)
	7. Clinical Microbiology (e.g., 21 CFR 314.50(d)(4))
	8. Clinical data section (e.g., 21 CFR 314.50(d)(5); 21 CFR 601.2)
	9. Safety update report (e.g., 21 CFR 314.50(d)(5)(vi)(b); 21 CFR 601.2)
	10. Statistical section (e.g., 21 CFR 314.50(d)(6); 21 CFR 601.2)
	11. Case report tabulations (e.g., 21 CFR 314.50(f)(1); 21 CFR 601.2)
	12. Case report forms (e.g., 21 CFR 314.50 (f)(2); 21 CFR 601.2)
	13. Patent information on any patent which claims the drug (21 U.S.C. 355(b) or (c))
	14. A patent certification with respect to any patent which claims the drug (21 U.S.C. 355 (b)(2) or (j)(2)(A))
	15. Establishment description (21 CFR Part 600, if applicable)
	16. Debarment certification (FD&C Act 306 (k)(1))
	17. Field copy certification (21 CFR 314.50 (k)(3))
	18. User Fee Cover Sheet (Form FDA 3397)
	19. Financial Information (21 CFR Part 54)
	20. OTHER *(Specify)*

CERTIFICATION

I agree to update this application with new safety information about the product that may reasonably affect the statement of contraindications, warnings, precautions, or adverse reactions in the draft labeling. I agree to submit safety update reports as provided for by regulation or as requested by FDA. If this application is approved, I agree to comply with all applicable laws and regulations that apply to approved applications, including, but not limited to the following:

1. Good manufacturing practice regulations in 21 CFR Parts 210, 211 or applicable regulations, Parts 606, and/or 820.
2. Biological establishment standards in 21 CFR Part 600.
3. Labeling regulations in 21 CFR Parts 201, 606, 610, 660, and/or 809.
4. In the case of a prescription drug or biological product, prescription drug advertising regulations in 21 CFR Part 202.
5. Regulations on making changes in application in FD&C Act Section 506A, 21 CFR 314.71, 314.72, 314.97, 314.99, and 601.12.
6. Regulations on Reports in 21 CFR 314.80, 314.81, 600.80, and 600.81.
7. Local, state and Federal environmental impact laws.

If this application applies to a drug product that FDA has proposed for scheduling under the Controlled Substances Act, I agree not to market the product until the Drug Enforcement Administration makes a final scheduling decision.

The data and information in this submission have been reviewed and, to the best of my knowledge are certified to be true and accurate.

Warning: A willfully false statement is a criminal offense, U.S. Code, title 18, section 1001.

SIGNATURE OF RESPONSIBLE OFFICIAL OR AGENT	TYPED NAME AND TITLE	DATE
ADDRESS *(Street, City, State, and ZIP Code)*		Telephone Number ( )

Public reporting burden for this collection of information is estimated to average 24 hours per response, including the time for reviewing instructions, searching existing data sources, gathering and maintaining the data needed, and completing and reviewing the collection of information. Send comments regarding this burden estimate or any other aspect of this collection of information, including suggestions for reducing this burden to:

Department of Health and Human Services   Food and Drug Administration
Food and Drug Administration   CDER, HFD-94
CBER, HFM-99   12420 Parklawn Dr., Room 3046
1401 Rockville Pike   Rockville, MD 20852
Rockville, MD 20852-1448

An agency may not conduct or sponsor, and a person is not required to respond to, a collection of information unless it displays a currently valid OMB control number.

FORM FDA 356h (4/00)

Index

Page numbers in italic indicate figures or tables.

T - #0988 - 101024 - C0 - 229/152/34 [36] - CB - 9780824702632 - Gloss Lamination